K. R. (Karl Rudolf) Hagenbach

A history of Christian doctrines

K. R. (Karl Rudolf) Hagenbach

A history of Christian doctrines

ISBN/EAN: 9783742895448

Hergestellt in Europa, USA, Kanada, Australien, Japan

Cover: Foto ©ninafisch / pixelio.de

Manufactured and distributed by brebook publishing software (www.brebook.com)

K. R. (Karl Rudolf) Hagenbach

A history of Christian doctrines

CONTENTS.

SECOND PERIOD.

FROM THE DEATH OF ORIGEN TO JOHN DAMASCENE, FROM THE YEAR 254–730.

THE AGE OF POLEMICS.

B. SPECIAL HISTORY OF DOCTRINES DURING THE SECOND PERIOD (CONTINUED).

SECOND CLASS.

CHURCH DOCTRINES EITHER NOT CONNECTED, OR BUT REMOTELY, WITH THE HERESIES OF THE AGE.

(DIDACTIC PART.)

§		PAGE
115.	Introduction,	1

1. *Apologetic and Normal Doctrines (Prolegomena).*

116.	The Idea of Religion and Revelation,	2
117.	Writings in Defence of Christianity,	4
118.	Miracles and Prophecy,	5
119.	Sources of Religious Knowledge—Bible and Tradition,	8
120.	The Canon,	10
121.	Inspiration and Interpretation,	14
122.	Tradition and the Continuance of Inspiration,	20

2. *The Doctrine concerning God.*

123.	The Being of God,	22
124.	The Nature of God,	26

		PAGE
125.	The Unity of God,	30
126.	The Attributes of God,	31
127.	Creation,	34
128.	The Relation of the Doctrine of Creation to the Doctrine of the Trinity,	36
129.	Object of Creation—Providence—Preservation and Government of the World,	37
130.	Theodicy,	40
131.	Angelology and Angelolatry,	41
132.	The same subject continued,	46
133.	Devil and Demons,	47

3. *Soteriology.*

134.	Redemption through Christ—The Death of Jesus,	52

4. *The Church and the Sacraments.*

135.	The Church,	62
136.	The Sacraments,	67
137.	Baptism,	69
138.	The Lord's Supper,	77

5. *The Doctrine of the Last Things.*

139.	Millenarianism—The Kingdom of Christ,	87
140.	The Resurrection of the Body,	89
141.	General Judgment—Conflagration of the World—Purgatory,	94
142.	The State of the Blessed and the Damned,	98

THIRD PERIOD.

FROM JOHN DAMASCENE TO THE PERIOD OF THE REFORMATION, A.D. 730–1517.

THE AGE OF SYSTEMATIC THEOLOGY.

(SCHOLASTICISM IN THE WIDEST SENSE OF THE WORD.)

A. GENERAL HISTORY OF DOCTRINES DURING THE THIRD PERIOD.

143.	Character of this Period,	106
144.	The Relation of the Systematic Tendency to the Apologetic,	108

		PAGE
145.	The Polemics of this Period—Controversies with Heretics,	109
146.	The Greek Church,	111
147.	The Western Church,	113
148.	The Carolingian Period (with the Phenomena immediately preceding and following),	114
149.	Scholasticism in general,	118
150.	The Principal Scholastic Systems,—	
	(a) First Period of Scholasticism—to the time of Peter Lombard,	121
151.	(b) Second Period—to the end of Thirteenth Century,	126
152.	(c) Third Period—the Fall of Scholasticism in the Fourteenth and Fifteenth Centuries,	131
153.	Mysticism,	134
154.	Scientific Opposition to Scholasticism,	141
155.	Practical Opposition—Forerunners of the Reformation,	144
156.	The Connection of the History of Doctrines with the History of the Church and the World in the present Period,	147

B. SPECIAL HISTORY OF DOCTRINES DURING THE THIRD PERIOD.

FIRST DIVISION.

APOLOGETICO-DOGMATIC PROLEGOMENA.

TRUTH OF CHRISTIANITY—RELATION OF REASON TO REVELATION—SOURCES OF REVELATION—SCRIPTURE AND TRADITION.

157.	Truth and Divinity of Christianity,	151
158.	Reason and Revelation—Faith and Knowledge,	153
159.	Sources of Knowledge—Bible and Tradition,	161
160.	The Canon of the Bible and Biblical Criticism,	165
161.	Inspiration,	166
162.	Interpretation of Scripture—The Reading of the Bible,	170

SECOND DIVISION.

THEOLOGY.

(INCLUDING COSMOLOGY, ANGELOLOGY, DEMONOLOGY, ETC.)

163.	The Existence of God,	175
164.	The Comprehensibility of God,	183
165.	The Nature of God in general,	188
166.	The Attributes of God,—	
	(a) God in relation to Time, Space, and Number (the Omnipresence, Eternity, and Unity of God),	192
167.	(b) God in relation to Things—Omnipresence and Omniscience,	197
168.	(c) Moral Attributes,	203

CONTENTS.

§		PAGE
169.	Doctrine of the Trinity—Doctrine of the Procession of the Holy Ghost,	204
170.	The Doctrine of the Trinity,	209
171.	The Doctrine of Creation, Providence, and the Government of the World—Theodicy,	226
172.	The Angels and the Devil,	233

THIRD DIVISION.

ANTHROPOLOGY.

173.	General Definitions,	239
174.	The Immortality of the Soul,	242
175.	Man in the State of Innocence before the Fall,	245
176.	The Fall of Man, and Sin in general,	251
177.	Consequences of the First Sin—Original Sin—Freedom of the Will,	256
178.	Exceptions from Original Sin—The Immaculate Conception of Mary,	260

FOURTH DIVISION.

CHRISTOLOGY AND SOTERIOLOGY.

179.	Christology in the Greek Church—The Adoptianist Controversy in the West—Nihilianism,	267
180.	Redemption and Atonement,	275
181.	Further Development of the Doctrine,	282
182.	Connection of Soteriology with Christology,	290

FIFTH DIVISION.

THE ORDO SALUTIS.

183.	Predestination (the Gottschalk Controversy),	293
184.	Further Development of the Doctrine of Predestination,	299
185.	Appropriation of Grace,	302
186.	Faith and Works—The Meritoriousness of the latter,	308

SIXTH DIVISION.

THE DOCTRINE OF THE CHURCH AND THE SACRAMENTS.

187.	The Church,	312
188.	The Worship of Saints,	317
189.	The Sacraments,	319

§		PAGE
190.	The same subject continued,	325
191.	Baptism,	330
192.	Confirmation,	334
193.	The Lord's Supper,	337
	(1) *The Controversy on the Eucharist previous to the Rise of Scholasticism. Paschasius Radbertus and Ratramnus. Berengarius*,	337
194.	(2) *Scholastic Development of the Doctrine. Transubstantiation. The Sacrifice of the Mass*,	345
195.	The Withholding of the Cup from the Laity—Concomitance,	355
196.	Dissenting Opinions,	358
197.	The Greek Church,	362
198.	The Sacrament of Penance,	365
199.	Extreme Unction,	368
200.	The Sacrament of Orders,	371
201.	The Sacrament of Matrimony,	374

SEVENTH DIVISION.

ESCHATOLOGY.

202.	Millenarianism (Chiliasm)—The approaching End of the World—Antichrist,	378
203.	Influence of Mediæval Tendencies and of Christian Art upon Eschatology,	381
204.	The Resurrection of the Body,	382
205.	The Last Judgment,	385
206.	Purgatory,	388
207.	The Sleep of the Soul,	392
208.	The Localities of the Future World—(Heaven, Hell, and Intermediate State),	393
209.	Future State of the Blessed and the Damned,	396
210.	Eternity of the Punishments of Hell—Restitution of all Things,	401

FOURTH PERIOD.

FROM THE REFORMATION TO THE RISE OF THE PHILOSOPHY OF LEIBNITZ AND WOLF IN GERMANY (1517 TO ABOUT 1720).

THE AGE OF POLEMICO-ECCLESIASTICAL SYMBOLISM.

(THE CONFLICT OF CONFESSIONS OF FAITH.)

A. GENERAL HISTORY OF DOCTRINES DURING THE FOURTH PERIOD.

211.	Introduction,	406
212.	The Principles of Protestantism,	407
213.	Relation of the History of Doctrines of the present Period to that of the former Period (Symbolism),	419

1. *The Lutheran Church.*

§		PAGE
214.	Luther and Melanchthon,	411
215.	The Symbolical Books of the Lutheran Church,	415
216.	The Systematic Theology of the Lutheran Church,	421
217.	Lutheran Mysticism, Theosophy, and Asceticism,	426
218.	Reforming Tendencies—John Valentin Andreä, Calixt, Spener, Thomasius,	429

2. *The Reformed Church.*

219.	Zwingli and Calvin,	431
220.	The Symbolical Books of the Reformed Church,	436
221.	(*a*) Symbolical Writings prior to the Time of Calvin,	437
222.	(*b*) Symbolical Writings under the Influence of Calvin,	439
223.	The Systematic Theology of the Reformed Church,	445
224.	Mysticism in the Reformed Church,	452
225.	Influence of the Cartesian Philosophy—More Liberal Tendencies,	453
225*a*.	[The French School of Saumur],	455
225*b*.	[Theology in England and Scotland],	456

B. SPECIAL HISTORY OF DOCTRINES DURING THE SECOND PERIOD.

SECOND CLASS.

CHURCH DOCTRINES EITHER NOT CONNECTED, OR BUT REMOTELY, WITH THE HERESIES OF THE AGE.

(DIDACTIC PART.)

§ 115.

Introduction.

THE doctrinal views on fundamental points, which had been matured by controversy, exerted more or less influence upon the development of other dogmas. Thus, the further theological definitions respecting the nature and attributes of God, creation, etc., depended upon the views held on the Trinity; those which relate to the atonement of Christ, and the significance of the Lord's Supper, were closely connected with the opinions held concerning the person of Christ; those respecting the Church, baptism, and the sacraments as means of grace, with the view taken of anthropology; and, lastly, eschatology was influenced by all the other doctrines together. Even the more general definitions concerning the nature of Christianity, the canon and its relation to tradition, etc., are in some way or other connected with one or another of the fundamental dogmas.

Nevertheless, we are justified in treating of these doctrines separately, inasmuch as, in some respects at least, they were not affected by the contests, and present themselves rather as a development of earlier opinions.

1. APOLOGETIC AND NORMAL DOCTRINES (PROLEGOMENA).

§ 116.

The Idea of Religion and Revelation.

Though the theologians of the present period had not the conception of a merely abstract religion, without a positive historical basis and form, yet we meet in the writings of *Lactantius* with a more precise definition of the word *religion*, which was borrowed from the Latin. He applies the term in question not only to the external forms of worship (as *Tertullian* had done before him), but—though with an incorrect etymology—to the union and fellowship of men with God, which he also regards as something purely human (1). Faith in revelation was required as a necessary condition (2).

(1) *Lactant.* Inst. iv. 28 : Hac enim conditione gignimur, ut generanti nos Deo justa et debita obsequi præbeamus, hunc solum noverimus, hunc sequamur. *Hoc vinculo pietatis obstricti Deo et religati sumus, unde ipsa religio nomen accepit, non, ut Cicero interpretatus est, a relegendo.* Comp. iii. 10 : Summum igitur bonum hominis in sola religione est; nam cætera, etiam quæ putantur esse homini propria, in cæteris quoque animalibus reperiuntur. 11 : Constat igitur totius humani generis consensu, religionem suscipi oportere. He compared it with *sapientia* (iv. 4), from which it is not to be separated. By sapientia he understands the knowledge, by religio the worship, of God. God is the source of both. The one without the other leads to such errors as paganism represents, on the one hand, in the unbelieving philosophers (the apostate and disinherited sons); and, on the other, in the superstitious multitudes (the runaway slaves).—*Augustine* follows the terminology of *Tertullian* ; he contrasts religio with fides or pietas ; De Pecc. Mer. et Rem. ii. 2, see *Baumgarten-*

Crusius, ii. s. 751, and comp. *Nitzsch*, über den Religionsbegriff der Alten, Theologische Studien und Kritiken, i. 3, 4.

Concerning the *nature* of religion, and the questions whether it principally consists in *knowledge*, or in the *form of worship*, or whether it consists in inner, living fellowship with God, see the controversy between Eunomius and his opponents in § 125, and *Neander*, Kg. ii. 2, s. 857. [Comp. *M. Müller*, Hibbert Lectures, Lond. 1879.]

(2) On the necessity of *faith* in revelation in general, see *Rufini* Expos. Fidei (in *Fell's* edition of Cypr.), p. 18 : Ut ergo intelligentiæ tibi aditus patescat, recte primo omnium te credere profiteris; quia nec navem quis ingreditur et liquido ac profundo vitam committit elemento, nisi se prius credat posse salvari, nec agricola semina sulcis obruit et fruges spargit in terram, nisi credideret venturos imbres, affuturum quoque solis teporem, quibus terra confota segetem multiplicata fruge producat ac ventis spirantibus nutriat. Nihil denique est, quod in vita geri possit, si non credulitas ante præcesserit. Quid ergo mirum si accedentes ad Deum credere nos primo omnium profitemur, cum sine hoc nec ipsa exigi possit vita communis? Hoc autem idcirco in principiis præmisimus, quia pagani nobis objicere solent, quod religio nostra, quia quasi rationibus deficit, in sola credendi persuasione consistat. Comp. *Augustine*, De Utilitate Credendi, c. 13 : Recte igitur catholicæ disciplinæ majestate institutum est, ut accedentibus ad religionem fides persuadeatur ante omnia. *He*, too, shows that without faith there can be no friendship even among men (c. 10), no filial love and piety (c. 12). Augustine knows of no other religion than positive Christianity, and insists that reason should submit to it; for *faith* precedes the knowledge of reason, l.c. c. 14 : Deinde fateor, me jam Christo credidisse et in animum induxisse, id esse verum, quod ille dixerit, etiamsi nulla ratione fulciatur. Reason would never have saved man from darkness and misery, nisi summus Deus *populari quadam clementia* divini intellectus auctoritatem usque ad ipsum corpus humanum declinaret atque submitteret, cujus non solum *præceptis*, sed etiam *factis* excitatæ animæ redire in semetipsas et respicere patriam etiam sine disputationum concertatione potuissent. . . . Mihi autem certum est, nusquam prorsus a Christi

auctoritate discedere, non enim reperio valentiorem (Contra Academ. l. iii. c. 19, 20). Comp. De Vera Rel. c. 5; De Moribus Eccles. Cath. c. 7: Quare deinceps nemo ex me quaerat sententiam meam, sed potius audiamus oracula, nostrasque ratiunculas divinis submittamus afflatibus. Comp. *Bindemann's* Augustinus, ii. s. 113 ff.

§ 117.

Writings in Defence of Christianity.

Baur, Dogmengeschichte (Vorlesungen), i. 2, s. 66 ff.

In proportion as the polemical tendency of the present period prevailed over the apologetic, the proofs of the truth and divinity of Christianity lost originality, and most writers were satisfied with the mere repetition of former statements (1). The attacks of *Porphyry, Julian the Apostate*, and others, however, called forth new efforts in defence of Christiantiy (2); the accusations of the heathen, when Christianity was established as the religion of the world upon the ruins of the Western Empire, induced *Augustine* to compose his apologetical treatise, "De Civitate Dei."

(1) Among the apologists *previous* to the apostasy of Julian, *Arnobius* (Adversus Gentes) deserves to be noticed. His argument *a tuto*, ii. 4, is as follows: ... nonne purior ratio est, ex duobus incertis et in ambigua exspectatione pendentibus id potius credere, quod aliquas spes ferat, quam omnino quod nullas? In illo enim periculi nihil est, si quod dicitur imminere cassum fiat et vacuum: in hoc damnum est maximum, i.e. salutis amissio, si cum tempus advenerit aperiatur non fuisse mendacium ... *Eusebius* of Caesarea likewise defended Christianity in his Praepar. and Demonstr. Evang. (§ 82, note 1); *Athanasius* in his λόγος κατὰ Ἑλλήνων, etc.; *Julius Formicus Maternus*, De Errore Profanarum Religionum (between 340 and 350), and others.

(2) *Eusebius*, l.c., *Theodoret, Augustine,* and others combated *Porphyry*; *Eusebius* also opposed Hierocles in a separate

treatise. *Cyril* of Alexandria wrote ten books against the Emperor Julian, who charged Christianity with contradictions. —The dialogue entitled Philopatris, formerly ascribed to Lucian, may have been composed under the same emperor, see *Neander*, Kg. ii. 1, s. 191. On the apologetic writings of this period, see *Gieseler*, Dg. 274 ff. [The Spanish presbyter, *Irosius*, Historiæ adv. Paganos. The last important work in the Greek Church against the heathen was *Theodoret*, Ἑλληνικῶν θεραπευτικὴ παθημάτων, about 440. Against the Jews, *Eusebius*, Demonstr. Evang.; *Chrysostom*, Adv. Jud. Orat. viii.; *Augustine*, Tract. adv. Judaeos.]

[*Baur*, Dg. 156, says that Athanasius, Eusebius of Cæsarea, and Augustine elevated apologetics, by representing Christianity as the perfect religion in comparison with all others—viewing it in the light of the philosophy of religion and of the general religious history of mankind. *Augustine's* work, De Civitate Dei, is the grandest attempt to consider Christianity as realizing the idea of a divine plan and order for the world—as containing the immanent idea of the world and its history; even the greatness of the Roman Empire is fully seen only in its relation to Christianity.]

§ 118.

Miracles and Prophecy.

F. *Nitzsch*, Augustin's Lehre vom Wunder, Berlin 1865. [*Isaac Taylor*, Ancient Christianity, 4th ed. 1844, ii. 233–336, The Nicene Miracles. *Newman's* Preface to Fleury, in Collected Writings.]

Since the Christians were constantly accustomed to appeal to miracles and prophecies in support of the truth of their religion, it became important to define more precisely the idea of a miracle. *Augustine* did this by defining miracles as events which deviate not so much from the order of nature in general, as from that particular order of nature which is known to us (1). With regard to prophecies, many passages of the Old Testament were still applied to the Messiah which had no reference to Him, and the truly Messianic passages were taken in a narrower sense than historical interpretation required (2). The apologists also appealed to Christ's prophecy respecting the destruction of Jerusalem, which had long since received its accomplishment, to the fate of the Jewish nation (3), and the similar judgment with which God had visited the old Roman world, and compared those events with the triumphant spread of the gospel (4). And, lastly, even *Augustine* takes notice of the Sibylline oracles, mentioned by *Lactantius* (5).

(1) *Augustine*, De Utilitate Cred. c. 16: Miraculum voco, quidquid arduum aut insolitum supra spem vel facultatem mirantis apparet. De Civ. Dei, lib. xxi. c. 8: Omnia portenta *contra* naturam dicimus esse, sed non sunt. Quomodo est enim contra naturam quod Dei fit voluntate, quum voluntas tanti utique conditoris conditæ rei cujusque natura sit? Portentum ergo fit non contra naturam, sed *contra quam est nota natura* ... quamvis et ipsa quæ in rerum natura omnibus nota sunt, non minus mira sint, essentque stupenda considerantibus cunctis, si solerent homines mirari nisi rara.—On the significance and application of these expressions, see *Baur*, l.c. ii. 1, s. 83 f., and particularly *Nitzsch*, l.c. s. 10: "*What Augustine calls the known rule of nature* (nota natura), *is the same that we mean by the laws of nature. That which he sets in opposition to this, nature in and by itself, is the totality of that which the divine government of the world brings with itself, in which the laws of nature form merely a part, and which, on the other side, contains in itself the necessity for miracles.*" From the miracle of creation *Augustine* argues in favour of all other miracles, De Civ. Dei, x. 12: Quidquid mirabile fit in hoc mundo, profecto minus est, quam totus hic mundus, i.e. cœlum et terra et omnia quæ in eis sunt, quæ certe Deus fecit. And even when miracles are wrought by men, man himself remains the greatest miracle. Nam et omni miraculo, quod fit per hominem, majus miraculum est homo.—That *Augustine*, however, did not base religion upon the evidence of miracles, and thought less of these than of the intelligent contemplation of the works of God, is shown by the expression used in Ep. 120 (ad Consentium), c. 5: Multi sunt, qui plus tenentur admiratione

rerum quam cognitione causarum, and the striking comparison between those who are astonished at the performances of a rope-dancer, and those who are charmed with the harmony of music. Apart from the view taken of miracles in general, it now became a matter of importance (since the canon of the New Testament was closed) to make a distinction between the miracles related in Scripture, as historically authenticated facts, and those miracles which were generally believed still to occur in the Church. Respecting faith in miracles in general, *Augustine* employed a free criticism; De Civit. Dei, xxi. c. 6, 7 (in reference to wonderful natural phenomena, but his language is also applicable to other miraculous stories of the age): Nec ergo volo temere credi cuncta, quæ posui, exceptis his, quæ ipse sum expertus. Cetera vero sic habeo, ut neque ut affirmanda, neque neganda decreverim. Comp. De Util. Cred. l.c.; De Vera Rel. 25 (Retract. i. c. 13). With regard to the miracles related in Scripture, it was of importance to distinguish the miracles performed by Jesus from those wrought by Apollonius of Tyana, and similar wonder-workers, to which Hierocles and others appealed. *Augustine* therefore directed attention to the benevolent design of Christ's miracles, by which they are distinguished from those which are performed merely from ostentation (*e.g.* the attempt to fly in the presence of an assembled multitude), De Util. Cred. l.c. Cf. *Nitzsch*, l.c. App. *Cyril Alex.* Contra Jul. i. 1: Ἐγὼ δὲ, ὅτι μὲν τῶν Ἑλλήνων ἀπηλλάγμεθα ἐμβροντησίας καὶ πολὺς ἀποτειχίζει λόγος τῶν ἐκείνων τερθρείας τὰ χριστιανῶν, φαίην ἄν· κοινωνία γὰρ οὐδεμία φωτὶ πρὸς σκότος, ἀλλ' οὐδὲ μερὶς πιστῷ μετὰ ἀπίστου.—On *Gregory the Great's* view of miracles, see *Neander*, Kg. iii. s. 294, 295.

(2) *Augustine* gives a canon on this point, De Civit. Dei, xvii. c. 16 ss.; comp. xviii. 20 ss., and below, § 122, note 4.

(3) *Aug.* De Civ. Dei, iv. 34: . . . Et nunc quod (Judæi) per omnes fere terras gentesque dispersi sunt, illius unius veri Dei providentia est. Comp. xviii. c. 46.

(4) *Arnob.* ii. p. 44, 45: Nonne vel hæc saltem fidem vobis faciunt argumenta credendi, quod jam per omnes terras in tam brevi temporis spatio immensi nominis hujus sacramenta diffusa sunt? quod nulla jam natio est tam barbari moris et mansuetudinem nesciens, quæ non ejus amore versa

molliverit asperitatem suam et in placidos sensus adsumta tranquillitate migraverit? *Aug.* De Civ. Dei, v. 25, 26, xviii. 50: ... inter horrendas persecutiones et varios cruciatus ac funera Martyrum prædicatum est toto orbe evangelium, contestante Deo signis et ostentis et variis virtutibus, et Spiritus Sancti muneribus: ut populi gentium credentes in eum, qui pro eorum redemtione crucifixus est, Christiano amore venerarentur sanguinem Martyrum, quem diabolico furore fuderunt, ipsique reges, quorum legibus vastabatur Ecclesia, ei nomini salubriter subderentur, quod de terra crudeliter auferre conati sunt, et falsos deos inciperent persequi, quorum causa cultores Dei veri fuerant antea persecuti.

(5) *Lactantius*, iv. 15 s. *August.* De Civ. Dei, xviii. 23. *Cyril Alex.* Contra Jul. i. 1. But the enemies of Christianity maintained, even in the times of *Lactantius*, non esse illa carmina Sibyllina, sed a Christianis conficta atque composita.

§ 119.

Sources of Religious Knowledge—Bible and Tradition.

During the present period both the *Bible* and *Tradition* were already regarded as the sources of Christian knowledge (1). The statement of *Augustine*, that he was induced by the authority of the Church alone to believe in the gospel, only proves that he considered the believer (subjectively), but not the Bible (objectively), to be dependent on that authority (2). It was rather the case, that in ecclesiastical controversies and elsewhere, the Bible was appealed to as the highest authority (2), and was also in practice most urgently recommended to the people. It was constantly held in reverence as the purest source of truth, the book of books (4).

(1) Nihil aliud præcipi volumus, quam quod Evangelistarum et Apostolorum fides et traditio incorrupta servat; *Gratian* in Cod. Theod. lib. xvi. tit. vi. 1, 2.

(2) Adv. Man. 5: Evangelio non crederem, nisi me eccle-

siæ catholicæ commoveret auctoritas. This passage is to be compared in its whole connection: see *Lücke*, Zeitschrift für evangel. Christen. i. 1, 4. *Lücke* justly rejects, ibid. s. 71, the expedients adopted by older Protestant theologians, *e.g.* *Bucer* and *S. Baumgarten* (Untersuchung theologischer Streitigkeiten, Bd. iii. s. 48), viz. to assign to the imperfect tense the signification of the pluperfect *"according to the African dialect."* Comp. also *Neander*, Dg. s. 288 f. [Protestant theologians have been disposed to explain it as meaning, " I was first led to the Bible by the tradition of the Church ;" but without doubt it rather means, " The authority of the Church is the witness for the divinity of the Scriptures ; for how could I convince unbelievers if I were not permitted to appeal to the authority of the Church ? I must depend upon this to know what the canon of Holy Writ is, and its right interpretation." Yet, in arguing against the Donatists, he proves the authority of the Church from the Scriptures, allowing no argument to be valid which was not derived from this source ; and in arguing against Pelagius, he refuses to be satisfied by the statement that the Church has tolerated the views of his opponent, and appeals to the teaching of the New Testament.] On a similar declaration of *Gregory the Great*, that he reverenced the four General Councils as much as the four Gospels (lib. i. Ep. 25, and lib. iii. Ep. 10), see *Lau*, ubi supra, s. 330.

(3) *Athanasius*, Contra Gent. i. p. 1 B: Αὐτάρκεις μὲν γάρ εἰσιν αἱ ἁγίαι καὶ θεόπνευστοι γραφαὶ πρὸς τὴν τῆς ἀληθείας ἀπαγγελίαν. *Cyrillus Hierosol.* Cat. 4 et 5. *Chrys.* Contra Anomæos, xi. (Opp. i. p. 542). *Augustine*, Doct. Christ. i. 37 : Titubabit fides, si scripturarum sacrarum vacillet auctoritas. Ibid. ii. 9 ; De Baptismo contra Donatistas, ii. 3, and many other passages, especially Ep. 19 ad Hieron. (comp. § 122, 2).

(4) *Aug.* Ep. 137 (Opp. ii. p. 310): [Scriptura Sacra] omnibus [est] accessibilis, quamvis paucissimis penetrabilis. Ea, quæ aperte continet, quasi amicus familiaris sine fuco ad cor loquitur indoctorum atque doctorum.—De Doct. Christ. ii. 63 : Quantum autem minor est auri, argenti, vestisque copia, quam de Ægypto secum ille populus abstulit in comparatione divitiarum, quas postea Hierosolymæ consecutus est,

quæ maxime in Salomone ostenduntur, tanta fit cuncta scientia, quæ quidem est utilis, collecta de libris gentium, si divinarum scripturarum scientiæ comparetur. Nam quicquid homo extra didicerit, si noxium est, ibi damnatur, si utile est, ibi invenitur, Et cum ibi quisque invenerit omnia, quæ utiliter alibi didicit, multo abundantius ibi inveniet ea, quæ nusquam omnino alibi, sed in illarum tantummodo Scripturarum mirabili altitudine et mirabili humilitate discuntur. Comp. *Theodoret*, Protheoria in Psalm. (Opp. t. i. p. 602); *Basilii M.* Hom. in Ps. i. (Opp. i. p. 90); *Rudelbach*, l.c. s. 38; and *Neander*, Gewichtvolle Aussprüche alter Kirchenlehrer über den allgemeinen und rechten Gebrauch der heil. Schrift, in his Kleine Gelegenheitsschriften (Berlin 1839), s. 155 ff. *Chrysostom*, too, is far from making salvation dependent on the letter of Scripture. In his opinion, it would be much better if we needed no Scripture at all, provided the grace of God were as distinctly written upon our hearts as the letters of ink are upon the book. (Introduct. to the Homilies on Matth. Opp. t. vii. p. 1.) In the same manner *Augustine* says, De Doctr. Christ. i. 39: Homo itaque fide, spe, et caritate subnixus, eaque inconcusse retinens, non indiget Scripturis nisi ad alios instruendos. Itaque multi per hæc tria etiam in solitudine sine codicibus vivunt. Unde in illis arbitrare jam impletum esse quod dictum est (1 Cor. xiii. 8): Sive prophetiæ evacuabuntur, sive linguæ cessabunt, sive scientia evacuabitur, etc.

§ 120.

The Canon.

* *Lucke*, über den neutestamentlichen Kanon des Eusebius von Cäsarea, Berlin 1816. *L. T. Spittler*, Kritische Untersuchung des 60sten Laodicäischen Kanons, Bremen 1777.—On the other side: *Bickel* in the Theologische Studien und Kritiken, 1830, Heft 3, s. 591 ff. [*Stuart*, Critical History and Defence of the Old Test. Canon, p. 438 ff., 447 ff. *Westcott*, Hist. Canon N. Test., Lond. 1855, etc. *C. Wordsworth*, Inspiration and Canon. *Credner*, Gesch. d. N. Test. Kanons, ed. Volkmar, Berlin 1860. *Ewald*, Gesch. d. Volkes Israel, Bd. vii. 1859. *H. J. Holtzmann*, Kanon und Tradition, Tübing. 1859. *Hilgenfeld*, Historisch-Krit. Einleitung in das N. T., Leipz. 1875. *Martin*, Origin and Hist. of N. T., London 1877. Supernatural Religion, London 1874, etc. *Lightfoot* on S. R. in Contemporary Review, 1875, ff.]

The more firmly the doctrine of the Church was established, the nearer the canon of the Sacred Scriptures, the principal parts of which had been determined in the time of *Eusebius* (1), was brought to its completion. The Synods of Laodicea (2), of Hippo, and (the third) of Carthage (3), contributed to this result. The theologians of the Eastern Church distinctly separated the later productions of the Graeco-Judaic literature (*i.e.* the apocryphal books, Libri Ecclesiastici) from the canon of the Old Testament Hebrew national literature (4). But although *Rufinus* (5) and *Jerome* endeavoured to maintain the same distinction in the Latin Church, it became the general custom to follow the Africans and *Augustine* in doing away with the distinction between the canonical and apocryphal books of the Old Testament, and in considering both as one (6).—The canon of the Manichaeans differed considerably from that of the Catholic Church (7).

(1) *Eusebius*, Hist. Eccl. iii. 25, adopts three classes, viz. ὁμολογούμενα, ἀντιλεγόμενα, νόθα (whether and in how far the last two classes differed, see *Lücke*, l.c.; also *Hilgenfeld*, l.c.; *Baur*, ii. 1, s. 86).—To the first class belong the four Gospels, the Acts of the Apostles, the Epistles of Paul (including the Epistle to the Hebrews), the first Epistle of John, and the first Epistle of Peter; to the Antilegomena belong the Epistles of James, Jude, the second of Peter, and lastly, the second and third Epistles of John. With regard to the Book of Revelation, opinions differ. The following are reckoned among the νόθα: Acta Pauli, the Shepherd of Hermas, the Apocalypse of Peter, the Epistle of Barnabas, and the Apostolical Constitutions. The ἄτοπα καὶ δυσσεβῆ ranked below the νόθα. On the canon of *Athanasius* (according to the Epistola festalis), see *Voigt*, l.c. s. 6 ff.

(2) The Synod of Laodicea was held about the middle of the fourth century (between the years 360 and 364). In the 59th canon it was enacted, that no uncanonical books should be used in the churches, and in the 60th a list was given of the canonical books (*Mansi*, ii. 574). The doubts of *Spittler*, *Bickel* has endeavoured to refute in his dissertation (referred

to above) in the Theol. Stud. und Kritiken for 1830. In this list all the Hebrew writings of the Old Testament are received, and the apocryphal books excluded (with the exception of the Book of Baruch and the Epistle of Jeremiah). The catalogue of New Testament writings is the same as ours, except the Book of Revelation, which, however, was considered genuine in Egypt (by *Athanasius* and *Cyril*). But mention is made of seven Catholic Epistles, and the Epistle to the Hebrews is ascribed to Paul (especially on the authority of *Jerome*).—For further particulars, see the Introductions to the New Testament, and *Giesler*, Dogmengesch. s. 287.

(3) A.D. 393 and A.D. 397. These synods number the Apocrypha of the Old Testament among the canonical books. Comp. the 36th canon Conc. Hippon. in *Mansi*, iii. 921, and Concil. Carth. 11, c. 47, *Mansi*, iii. 891. Innocent I. (A.D. 405) and Gelasius I. (A.D. 494 ?) confirmed their decisions.

(4) On the view of *Athanasius*, who clearly distinguishes the κανονιζόμενα and the ἀναγινωσκόμενα (only Baruch and the Epistle of Jeremiah fall, according to him, into the former class), cf. *Voigt*, l.c. The heretical writings he consistently designates as ἀπόκρυφα.

(5) *Rufinus*, Expos. Symb. (l.c.) p. 26 : Sciendum tamen est, quod et alii libri sunt, qui non catholici, sed ecclesiastici a majoribus appellati sunt, ut est Sapientia Salomonis et alia Sapientia, quae dicitur filii Syrach, qui liber apud Latinos hoc ipso generali vocabulo Ecclesiasticus appellatur . . . Ejusdem ordinis est libellus Tobiae et Judith et Maccabaeorum libri. He places the Shepherd of Hermas on the same footing with the Apocrypha of the Old Testament, and maintains that they might be read, but not quoted as authorities, " ad auctoritatem ex his fidei confirmandam." Comp. *Hier.* in Prologo Galeato, quoted by *De Wette*, Einleitung, i. s. 45. *Giesler*, Dogmengesch. 284 ff., is very instructive upon the Apocrypha, and the way it was treated in this period. [*Origen*, in his Hexapla, had carried out the distinction between the old Hebrew books and those extant only in Greek ; and all the Greek Fathers of this period followed his example. *Athanasius* distinguishes the κανονιζόμενα, the ἀναγινωσκόμενα (not canonical, but useful), and the ἀπόκρυφα (fictitious works by heretics). In the Old Testament he received only twenty-two Hebrew works ;

what is now called the Apocrypha he reckoned in the second class, and in the third class he put the so-called pseudepigrapha. The Greek Church to the present day follows this order. The fact that they (and *Origen*) put Baruch and the Epistle of Jeremiah in the canon, was a consequence of these works being appended to the genuine writings of Jeremiah in the MSS. of the Septuagint.—In the Latin Church, *Hilary*, *Rufinus*, and *Jerome* also followed *Origen*. *Jerome* enumerates the twenty-two books of the Old Testament, and adds: quidquid extra hos est, est inter apocrypha ponendum. But the Latin Church generally followed *Ambrose*, *Augustine*, and the above-named councils. — As to the New Testament, it was generally received, in the course of the fourth and fifth centuries, in the form in which we now have it. As the Church became more united, those who had doubted as to some of the books, accepted the general tradition. In the fourth century all of the seven general Epistles were received as a part of the canon. *Jerome*, in his Epist. ad Dardanum, says the only differences were that the Latin Churches did not receive the Epistle to the Hebrews, nor the Greek Church the Apocalypse, though he himself held both to be genuine. In Africa the Hebrews was in the canon of *Augustine* and of the Councils of Hippo and Carthage. *Innocent I.*, in his Epist. ad Exsuperium, A.D. 405, puts the Hebrews in the canon. In the East the Apocalypse was received by *Athanasius* and *Cyril* of Alex., and also by *Ephraem* the Syrian and *Epiphanius*; but *Cyril* of Jerusalem, *Gregory* of Nazianzus, *Chrysostom*, and *Theodoret*, did not recognize it. Since the sixth century, however, it has been in the Greek canon. *Athanasius* applies the same distinctions to the books of the New Testament, etc., as (above) to the Old; he receives as canonical those which we now have; as ἀναγινωσκόμενα, the so-called Doctrine of the Apostles and the Shepherd of Hermas; as ἀπόκρυφα, the works falsely ascribed to apostles. So *Rufinus* makes three classes, reckoning the Shepherd of Hermas and the Judgment of Peter among the Libri Ecclesiastici.]

(6) *Aug.* De Doct. Chr. ii. 8, and other passages quoted by *De Wette*, l.c. Comp. *Münscher*, Handb. iii. s. 64 ff. *Gregory the Great*, Mor. lib. xix. c. 21: Non inordinate agimus, si ex libris, licet non canonicis, sed tamen ad aedificationem ecclesiae

editis testimonium proferamus. He makes only a relative distinction between the Old and New Testament, lib. i. Hom. 6, in Ezech.: Divina eloquia, etsi temporibus distincta, sunt tamen sensibus unita. Comp. *Lau*, s. 331.

(7) *Münscher*, l.c. s. 91 ff. *Trechsel*, über den Kanon, die Kritik und Exegese der Manichäer, Bern, 1832. The authenticity of the Old Testament, and the connection between the Old and the New Testaments, were defended in opposition to the Manichaeans, especially by *Augustine*, De Mor. Eccles. Cath. i. c. 27, De Utilitate Credendi, and elsewhere.

§ 121.

Inspiration and Interpretation.

On the literature, comp. § 32.

The idea of inspiration, in this as in the previous period, was understood by some in a dynamic and spiritual sense, by others in a mechanical and external sense. Not only were the contents of Holy Writ considered as divinely inspired (1), but it was also esteemed an offence to suppose the possibility of chronological errors and historical contradictions in the compositions of the sacred writers (2). And yet, in other instances, their different peculiarities as men were not overlooked, but made use of, to explain the diversities of their mode of thought and style (3). — The Origenistic allegorical system of interpretation gave way in the East to the sober grammatical method of the Antiochene school (4). In the West, on the contrary, some intimations of *Augustine* led to the adoption of a fourfold sense of Scripture, which was afterwards confirmed by the scholastic divines of the next period (5).

(1) This may be seen from certain general phrases which, having originated in the preceding period, had now come into general use, such as θεία γραφή, κυριακαὶ γραφαί, θεόπνευστοι γραφαί, coelestes litterae (*Lact.* Inst. iv. c. 22), as well as the

simile of the lyre (comp. § 32, note 4), which was applied in a somewhat different sense by *Chrys.* Hom. de Ignat. (Opp. ii. p. 594).

(2) *Eusebius* of Cæsarea says that it is θρασὺ καὶ προπετές to assert that the sacred writers could have substituted one name for another, *e.g.* Abimelech for Achish (Ἀγχοῦς); Comment. in Ps. xxxiii. in *Montfaucon,* Coll. Nov. t. i. p. 129. That *Chrysostom* designates the words of the apostle not as his, but as words of the Holy Spirit, or of God (in Ev. Joh. Hom. i. Opp. t. viii. p. 6, de Lazaro Conc. 4, Opp. i. p. 755, and elsewhere), may partly be ascribed to his practical and rhetorical tendency. *Jerome,* too, expresses the same opinions in various parts of his commentaries and his letters (see *Zöckler,* s. 429, 431); and to the same effect Augustine. As *Chrysostom* calls the mouth of the prophets the mouth of God (in Act. App. Hom. xix. Op. t. ix. p. 159), so *Augustine* (De Consensu Evv. i. 35) compares the apostles with the hands which noted down that which Christ, the Head, dictated. [Comp. *Trench,* Augustine as an Interpreter.] He also calls (in Conf. vii. 21) the Sacred Scriptures venerabilem stilum Spir. S. He communicates to Jerome his theory of inspiration in the following manner (Ep. 82, Opp. ii. p. 143): Ego enim fateor caritati tuæ, solis eis Scripturarum libris, qui jam canonici appellantur, didici hunc timorem honoremque deferre, ut nullum eorum auctorem scribendo aliquid errasse firmissime credam. Ac si aliquid in eis offendero litteris, quod videatur contrarium veritati, nihil aliud, quam vel mendosum esse codicem,[1] vel interpretrem non assecutum esse, quod dictum est, vel me minime intellexisse non ambigam. Alios autem ita lego, ut quantalibet sanctitate doctrinaque præpolleant, non ideo verum putem, quia ipsi ita senserunt, sed quia mihi vel per illos auctores canonicos, vel probabili ratione, quod a vero non abhorreat, persuadere potuerunt. Nevertheless, he admits (ibid. p. 150, § 24) that the canonical authority may be restricted, inasmuch as in reference to the dispute between Paul and Peter he concedes to the former an undoubted superiority. Comp. De Civ. Dei, xviii.

---

[1] A challenge to textual criticism! [So, too, De Consensu Evangelistarum, comparing the accounts of Mark and Luke of the words from heaven at Christ's baptism.]

41 : Denique auctores nostri, in quibus non frustra sacrarum litterarum figitur et terminatur canon, absit ut inter se aliqua ratione dissentiant. Unde non immerito, cum illa scriberent, eis Deum vel per eos locutum, non pauci in scholis atque gymnasiis litigiosis disputationibus garruli, sed in agris atque in urbibus cum doctis atque indoctis tot tantique populi crediderunt. — His opinion respecting the miraculous origin of the Septuagint version accords with that of the earlier Fathers, ibid. c. 42–44, where he attributes (as many ultra-Lutherans afterwards did in reference to the Lutheran translation) the defects of that translation to a kind of inspiration which had regard to the circumstances of the times.[1] But behind this fantastic notion lies the grand idea of a revelation, which continues to manifest itself in a living way—an idea which is above the narrow adherence to the letter, and is expressed in the belief in tradition. — Similar views probably induced *Gregory the Great* to say, in reference to the researches of learned men respecting the authorship of the Book of Job, that it was not necessary to know the pen with which the great King had written His royal letter; it sufficed to have a full conviction of its divine contents. Thus he assigns, on the one hand, the authorship of this book to the Holy Spirit; while, on the other, he leaves open all discussions concerning the human instruments—discussions which were chiefly dreaded in later times. *Gregory the Great*, Moral. in Job. præf. c. 1, § 2 ; the other views of *Gregory*, see in *Lau*, ubi supra.

(3) Thus *Theodore* of Mopsuestia, who in this respect went perhaps farther than any other writer, assumed different degrees of inspiration. He ascribed to Solomon not the gift of prophecy, but only that of wisdom, and judged of the Book of Job and the Song of Solomon from a purely human point of view. Hence the fifth Œcumenical Council found fault with him on this very account (*Mansi*, ix. 223). [Comp. *Lee*, ubi supra, p. 443–448.] But *Chrysostom*, and also *Jerome*, admitted human peculiarities, the one in reference to the Gospels (Hom. i. in Matt.), the other with respect to the Apostle Paul (on Gal. v. 12). *Chrysostom* even finds a proof of their credibility

---

[1] The prejudices of the time, with reference to the Septuagint, are shown by the excitement evoked by Jerome's corrected translation. On this see *Zöckler*, l.c. § 355 ff.

in the minor disagreements of the Gospels; for, he says, if all agreed in everything, the enemies would suspect collusion (in Matt. Hom. 1, § 2). *Jerome* finds in Paul solecisms, hyperbata (transpositions of words and clauses), and abrupt periods (on Eph. iii. and Gal. v. 12). *Basil the Great* says respecting the prophets (in the commentary on Isaiah commonly ascribed to him, Opp. t. i. p. 379, ed. Ben.): "As it is not every substance which is fitted to reflect images, but only such as possess a certain smoothness and transparency; so the effective power of the Spirit is not visible in all souls, but only in such as are neither perverse nor distorted" (*Rudelbach*, s. 28). *Augustine* (De Consensu Evang. ii. 12) asserts that the evangelists had written, ut quisque meminerat, ut cuique cordi erat, vel brevius vel prolixius; but he is careful not to be misunderstood, lib. i. c. 2: Quamvis singuli suum quendam narrandi ordinem tenuisse videantur, non tamen unusquisque eorum velut alterius ignarus voluisse scribere reperitur, vel ignorata praetermisisse, quae scripsisse alius invenitur: sed sicut unicuique inspiratum est, non superfluam co-operationem sui laboris adjunxit. — *Arnobius* calls the style of the biblical writers sermo trivialis et sordidus (Adv. Gent. i. 58), but he also sees in this an evidence of their truthfulness: Nunquam enim veritas sectata est fucum, nec quod exploratum et certum est, circumduci se patitur orationis per ambitum longiorem. The barbarisms and solecisms he compares (c. 59) to thorns on fruit. Etenim vero dissoluti est pectoris in rebus seriis quaerere voluptatem, et cum tibi sit ratio cum male se habentibus atque aegris, sonos auribus infundere dulciores, non medicinam vulneribus admovere. Moreover, even the language of the schools has its abnormities: Quaenam est enim ratio naturalis aut in mundi constitutionibus lex scripta, ut *hic paries* dicatur et *haec sella*? etc. — Concerning *Gregory* of Nazianzus, comp. Orat. ii. 105, p. 60 s. See *Ullmann*, s. 305, note. — *Epiphanius* opposed very decidedly the notions derived from the old μαντική (comp. § 32), according to which the inspired writers were entirely passive, and supposed that the prophets enjoyed a clear perception of the divine, a calm disposition of mind, etc. Comp. Hær. 48, c. 3, and *Jerome*, Procem. in Nahum, in Habacuc et in Jesaiam: Neque vero, ut Montanus cum insanis feminis somniat, Prophetae in exstasi sunt locuti, ut nescirent, quid loquerentur, et quum alios erudirent, ipsi ignorarent, quod dicerent. Though *Jerome* allows that human (*e.g.* grammatical) faults might have occurred, yet he guards himself against any dangerous inferences which might be drawn from his premises (Comment. in Ep. ad Ephes. lib. ii. ad cap. iii. 1): Nos, quotiescunque solœcismos aut tale quid annotamus, non Apostolum pulsamus, ut malevoli criminantur, sed magis Apostoli assertores sumus, etc. According to him, the divine power of the word itself destroyed these apparent blemishes, or caused believers to overlook them. " *The opinion of these theologians manifestly was, that the external phenomena do not preclude the reality of the highest influences of divine grace,*" *Rudelbach,* s. 42.[1]

(4) *Theodoret*, who may be considered as the representative of this tendency, rejects both the false allegorical and the bare historical systems of interpretation, Protheoria in Psalmos (ed. *Schulze*), t. i. p. 603 (in *Rudelbach*, s. 36). He calls the latter a Jewish rather than a Christian interpretation. Comp. *Münter*, über die antiochen. Schule, l.c., and *Neander*, Kg. ii. 2, s. 748 ff. The hermeneutical principles of *Theodore* of Mopsuestia are here of special weight. [*Neander*, judging from *Theodore's* general position, conjectured the value of his commentaries in this matter, " if more of them had come down to us." The conjecture has been confirmed by the discovery of the commentaries.] See the extracts, as given by *Jacobi*, in the notes to *Neander*, Dg. s. 296. *Athanasius*, on the contrary, makes use, particularly in practical exposition, of the allegorical method. See *Voigt*, l.c. s. 11.

(5) It is remarkable that *Augustine*, on the one hand, understands all biblical narratives in their strictly historical, literal sense; and, on the other, leaves ample scope for allegorical interpretation. Thus he takes much pains, De Civ.

---

[1] Thus *Jerome* and *Chrysostom* answered those who would exclude the Epistle to Philemon from the canon, because it contained only human matters, who took umbrage at the φαιλόνη which the apostle ordered (2 Tim. iv. 13), that employment in human affairs did no damage to divine things. See *Neander*, Dg. s. 295 f. A complete reduction of the truths of Scripture to the universal truths of reason, particularly moral truths (in the sense of Rationalism), is found in the writings of the Pelagian *Julian* (qu. by *Augustine*, opus imperfectum, ii.): "Sanctas quidem esse Apostoli paginas confitemur, non ob aliud nisi quia rationi, fidei, pietati, congruentes erudiunt nos."

Dei, xv. 27, to defend the account of the ark of Noah against mathematical and physical objections (he even supposes a miracle by which carnivorous animals were changed into herbivorous); nevertheless, he thinks that all this had happened only ad præfigurandam ecclesiam, and represents the clean and unclean animals as types of Judaism and paganism, etc. [Comp. also *Davidson*, l.c. p. 138, where another specimen is given.] The passage De Genes. ad Litter. ab init.: In libris autem omnibus sanctis intueri oportet, quæ ibi æterna intimentur, quæ facta narrentur, quæ futura prænuntientur, quæ agenda præcipiantur, has given rise to the doctrine of a fourfold sense of Scripture; comp. with it De Util. Cred. 3: omnis igitur scriptura, quæ testamentum vetus vocatur, diligenter eam nosse cupientibus quadrifariam traditur, secundum historiam, secundum ætiologiam, secundum analogiam, secundum allegoriam; the further exposition of his views is given ibid. [*Davidson*, l.c. p. 137]. According to *Augustine*, seven things are necessary to the right interpretation of Scripture, Doctr. Christ. ii. 7: *timor, pietas, scientia, fortitudo, consilium, purgatio cordis, sapientia*. But he who will perfectly interpret an author, must be animated by love to him, De Util. Cred. 6: Agendum enim tecum prius est, ut auctores ipsos non oderis, deinde ut ames, et hoc agendum quovis alio modo potius, quam exponendis eorum sententiis et literis. Propterea quia, si Virgilium odissemus, imo si non eum, priusquam intellectus esset, majorum nostrorum commendatione diligeremus, nunquam nobis satisfieret de illis ejus quæstionibus innumerabilibus, quibus grammatici agitari et perturbari solent, nec audiremus libenter, qui cum ejus laude illas expediret, sed ei faveremus, qui per eas illum erasse ac delirasse conaretur ostendere. Nunc vero cum eas multi ac varie pro suo quisque captu aperire conentur, his potissimum plauditur, per quorum expositionem melior invenitur poëta, qui non solum nihil peccasse, sed nihil non laudabiliter cecinisse ab eis etiam, qui illum non intelligunt, creditur . . . Quantum erat, ut similem benevolentiam præberemus eis, per quos locutum esse Spiritum Sanctum tam diuturna vetustate firmatum est? Even *misunderstanding* of the Scriptures (according to *Augustine*) is not corrupting, so long as the regula caritatis is observed; one may err about a text without becoming a liar. He who, with good intent, though with wrong exegesis, is steering loosely towards the one end of edification (the love of God), is like him who runs to the goal across the fields instead of in the beaten road. Yet we must always try to set such an one right, lest he get into the way of wandering from the true road, and so in the end run to perdition; De Doct. Christ. i. 36.

§ 122.

Tradition and the Continuance of Inspiration.

The belief in the inspiration of the Scriptures excluded faith neither in an existing tradition nor in a continuance of the inspirations of the Spirit. Not only transient visions, in which pious individuals received divine instructions and disclosures (1), were compared to the revelations recorded in Scripture, but still more the continued illumination which the Fathers enjoyed when assembled in council (2). But as the Scriptures were formed into a canon, so, too, in course of time it became necessary to lay down a canon, to which the ecclesiastical tradition, developing itself on its own historical foundation, might be made subject, so that every spirit need not be believed. Such an one was more definitely sketched by *Vincent* of Lérins, who laid down the three criteria of *antiquitas* (vetustas), *universitas*, and *consensio*, as marks of true ecclesiastical tradition; and thus the *quod ubique, quod semper, quod ab omnibus* was fixed as the canon of what had authority in the Church (3).

(1) Comp. *Münscher*, Handbuch, iii. s. 100 : "*Such exalted views on inspiration cannot appear strange to us, since they existed in an age when Christians believed and recorded numerous divine revelations and inspirations still granted to holy men, and especially to monks.*"—Such revelations, of course, were supposed not to be contradictory either to Scripture or to the tradition of the Church. Thus the voice from heaven, which said to *Augustine*, "*Ego sum, qui sum,*"

and "*tolle lege*," directed him to the Scriptures; Confessions, viii. 12.

(2) The utterances of the councils were represented as utterances of the Holy Spirit (placuit Spiritui Sancto et nobis). Comp. the letter of *Constantine* to the Church of Alexandria, Socrat. i. 9: Ὁ γὰρ τοῖς τριακοσίοις ἤρεσεν ἐπισκόποις, οὐδέν ἐστιν ἕτερον, ἢ τοῦ θεοῦ γνώμη, μάλιστά γε ὅπου τὸ ἅγιον πνεῦμα τοιούτων καὶ τηλικούτων ἀνδρῶν διανοίαις ἐγκείμενον τὴν θείαν βούλησιν ἐξεφώτισεν. The emperor, indeed, spoke thus as a layman. But Pope *Leo the Great* expressed himself in the same way, and claimed inspiration not only for councils (Ep. 114, 2; 145, 1), but also for emperors and imperial decretals (Ep. 162, 3; Ep. 148, 84, 1), even for himself (Ep. 16, and Serm. 25). Comp. *Griesbach*, Opusc. i. p. 21. *Gregory the Great*, too, declares that he ascribes to the first four Œcumenical Councils equal authority with the four Gospels (Ep. i. 24). Concerning the somewhat inconsistent opinions of *Gregory* of Nazianzus (Ep. ad Procop. 55) on the one hand, and *Augustine* (De Bapt. contra Don. ii. c. 3) and *Facundus* of Hermiane (Defensio Trium. Capitul. c. 7) on the other, see *Neander*, Kg. ii. 1, s. 374–379, and Dg. s. 291. In accordance with his views on the relation of the Septuagint to the original Hebrew (§ 121), *Augustine* supposes that the decisions of earlier councils were completed by those of later ones, without denying the inspiration of the former, since "*the decision of councils only gives public sanction to that result which the development of the Church had reached;*" and this entirely falls in with the view of the relation of the LXX. to the original given in the previous section. Inspiration accommodates itself to the wants of the time. Respecting this "economy" and its abuses, see *Münscher*, l.c. s. 156 ff. But not only the formal *utterances* of councils, but also the *silent* development of the Church and its ceremonies and institutions, was regarded as standing under the guidance of the Holy Spirit, and hence the validity of a doctrine (like that of the Holy Ghost, see above § 93), in support of which no complete Scripture proof can be adduced. Thus *Basil the Great* asks (De Spir. S. c. 27) where it is written that we are to sign ourselves with the sign of the cross, or turn to the east

in prayer, etc. This is connected with the distinction, already noticed, between δόγμα and κήρυγμα. Comp. *Baur*, Dg. ii. 1, s. 92.

(3) Commonitorium, or Tractatus pro Catholicæ Fidei Antiquitate et Universitate (composed in the year 433). *Vincentius* sets forth a twofold source of knowledge: (1) Divinæ legis auctoritas. (2) Ecclesiæ catholicæ traditio. The latter is necessary on account of the different interpretations given to Scripture. The sensus ecclesiasticus is the only right one. *Vincentius*, like *Augustine*, also supposes that tradition may in a certain sense *advance*, so that an opinion, respecting which the Church has not as yet pronounced a decision, is not to be considered heretical; but it may afterwards be condemned as such, if it be found contrary to the more fully developed faith of the Church. Thus many of the opinions of the earlier Fathers might be vindicated as archaisms. [*Baur*, Dogmengesch. 159 ff., says that the notion of tradition was already more methodically and definitely fixed than any other doctrine of the Church. The canon of Vincent, he states, was brought forward in relation to the Augustinian predestination —the latter could not stand this test. This canon was mechanical, allowing no room for progress, and it also contradicted the principle of the sufficiency of the Scriptures.]

2. THE DOCTRINE CONCERNING GOD.

§ 123.

The Being of God.

The prevailing tendency to dialectic demonstration led to the attempt to prove, in a logical way, the existence of God, which Christian faith had received as an uncontested axiom (1). In the writings of some of the Fathers, both of the preceding and present periods, *e.g. Athanasius* and *Gregory* of Nazianzus, we meet with what may be called the *physico-theological argument*, if we understand by it an argument drawn from the beauty and wisdom displayed in nature, which is always calculated to promote practical piety. But both these writers mistrusted a merely objective proof, and showed that a pure and pious mind would best find and know God (2). The *cosmological* proof propounded by *Diodorus* of Tarsus (3), and the *ontological* argument of *Augustine* and *Boethius* (4), lay claim to a higher degree of logical precision and objective certainty. The former argument was based upon the principle that there must be a sufficient ground for everything. *Augustine* and *Boethius* inferred the existence of God from the existence of general ideas: a proof which was more fully developed in the next period by *Anselm*.

(1) Even *Arnobius* considered this belief to be an *axiom*, and thought it quite as dangerous to attempt to *prove* the existence of God as to deny it; Adv. Gent. i. c. 33: Quisquamne est hominum, qui non cum principis notione diem nativitatis intraverit? cui non sit ingenitum, non affixum, imo ipsis pæne in genitalibus matris non impressum, non insitum, esse regem ac dominum cunctorum quaecunque sunt moderatorem?

(2) *Athanasius*, Adv. Gent. i. p. 3 ss. (like *Theophilus* of Antioch, comp. § 35, note 7), starts with the idea that none but a pure and sinless soul can see God (Matt. v. 8). *He*, too, compares the heart of man to a mirror. But as it became sullied by sin, God revealed Himself by means of His *creation*, and when this proved no longer sufficient, by the prophets, and, lastly, by the Logos. Comp. further in *Voigt*, s. 20 ff. *Gregory* of Nazianzus argues in a similar way; he infers the existence of the Creator from His works, as the sight of a lyre reminds us both of him who made it and of him who plays it, Orat. xxviii. 6, p. 499; comp. Orat. xxviii. 16, p. 507, 508; Orat. xiv. 33, p. 281. *He*, too, appeals to Matt. v. 8. "Rise from thy low condition by thy conversation, by purity of heart unite thyself to the pure. Wilt thou become a theologian, and worthy of the Godhead? Then keep the commandments of God, and walk according to His precepts, *for the act is the first step to knowledge,*" *Ullmann*, s. 317.—*Augustine* also propounds in an eloquent manner, and in the form of a prayer, what is commonly called the physico-theological argument (Conf. x. 6): Sed et cœlum et

terra et omnia, quæ in eis sunt, ecce undique mihi dicunt, ut te amem, nec cessant dicere omnibus, ut sint inexcusabiles, etc. *Ambrose, Basil the Great, Chrysostom*, and others, express themselves in much the same manner.

(3) *Diodorus*, κατὰ εἱμαρμένης, in *Phot.* Bibl. Cod. 223, p. 209 B. The world is subject to change. But this change presupposes something constant at its foundation; the variety of the creatures points to a creative unity; for change itself is a condition which has had a commencement: Εἰ δέ τις ἀγένητον λέγει αὐτῶν τὴν τροπὴν, τὸ πάντων ἀδυνατώτερον εἰσάγει· τροπὴ γὰρ πάθος ἐστὶν ἀρχόμενον, καὶ οὐκ ἄν τις εἴποι τροπὴν ἄναρχον· καὶ συντόμως εἰπεῖν, τῶν στοιχείων καὶ τῶν ἐξ αὐτῶν ζώων τε καὶ σωμάτων ἡ πάνσοφος τροπὴ, καὶ τῶν σχημάτων καὶ χρωμάτων καὶ τῶν ἄλλων ποιοτήτων ἡ ποικίλη διαφορὰ μονονουχὶ φωνὴν ἀφίησι μήτε ἀγέννητον μήτε αὐτόματον νομίζειν τὸν κόσμον, μήτ' αὖ ἀπρονόητον, Θεὸν δὲ αὐτοῖς καὶ τὸ εὖ εἶναι παρασχόμενον σαφῶς εἰδέναι καὶ ἀδιστάκτως ἐπίστασθαι.

(4) *August.* De Lib. Arbitr. lib. ii. c. 3-15. There are general ideas, which have for every one the same objective validity, and are not (like the perceptions of sense) different and conditioned by the subjective apprehension. Among these are the mathematical truths, as $3 + 7 = 10$; to this class belongs the higher metaphysical truth—truth in itself, *i.e.* wisdom (veritas, sapientia). This absolute truth, however, which is necessarily demanded by the human mind, is God Himself. He asserts that man is composed of existence, life, and thinking, and shows that the last is the most excellent; hence he infers that that by which thinking is regulated, and which, therefore, must be superior to thinking itself, is the summum bonum. He finds this summum bonum in those general laws which every thinking person must acknowledge, and according to which he must form his opinion respecting thinking itself. The sum total of these laws or rules is called *truth* or *wisdom* (veritas, sapientia). The absolute is therefore equal to truth itself. God is truth. [Illa veritatis et sapientiæ pulcritudo, tantum adsit perseverans voluntas fruendi, nec multitudine audientium constipata secludit venientes, nec peragitur tempore, nec migrat locis, nec nocte intercipitur, nec umbrâ intercluditur, nec sensibus

corporis subjacet. De toto mundo ad se conversis qui diligunt eam omnibus proxima est, omnibus sempiterna; nullo loco est, nusquam deest; foris admonet, inter docet; cernentes se commutat omnes in melius, a nullo in deterius commutatur; nullus de illa judicat, nullus sine illa judicat bene. Ac per hoc eam manifestum est mentibus nostris, quæ ab ipsa una fiunt singulæ sapientes, et non de ipsa, sed per ipsam de ceteris judices, sine dubitatione esse potiorem. Tu autem concesseras, si quid supra mentes nostras esse monstrarem, Deum te esse confessurum, *si adhuc nihil esset superius*. Si enim aliquid est excellentius, ille potius Deus est: *si autem non est, jam ipsa veritas Deus est. Sive ergo illud sit, sive non sit, Deum tamen esse negare non poteris*, lib. ii. c. 14, 15. (*Ritter*, Christl. Phil. i. 407 ff.)]—*Boëthius* expresses himself still more definitely, De Consol. Phil. iii. Prosa 10; he shows that empirical observation and the perception of the imperfect lead necessarily to the idea of perfection and its reality in God: Omne enim, quod imperfectum esse dicitur, id diminutione perfecti imperfectum esse perhibetur. Quo fit, ut si in quolibet genere imperfectum quid esse videatur, in eo perfectum quoque aliquid esse necesse sit. Etenim perfectione sublata, unde illud quod imperfectum perhibetur extiterit, ne fingi quidem potest. Neque enim a diminutis inconsummatisque natura rerum cepit exordium, sed ab integris absolutisque procedens, in hæc extrema atque effeta dilabitur. Quod si . . . est quædam boni fragilis imperfecta felicitas, esse aliquam solidam perfectamque non potest dubitari . . . Deum rerum omnium principum *bonum* esse, communis humanorum conceptio probat animorum. Nam cum nihil Deo melius excogitari queat, id quo melius nihil est, bonum esse quis dubitet? ita vero bonum esse Deum ratio demonstrat, ut perfectum quoque in eo bonum esse convincat. Nam ni tale sit, rerum omnium princeps esse non poterit. . . . Quare ne in infinitum ratio procedat, confitendum est summum Deum summi perfectique boni esse plenissimum. Compare *Schleiermacher*, Geschichte der Philosophie, s. 166: "*Augustine is said to have given the first proof of the existence of God. But we are not to understand this in an objectionable manner, as though he would demonstrate this in an objective way; he only desires to show that the idea of God is at the foundation of all human* thought."—*Gregory the Great* also reasons in a similar manner; Moral. xv. c. 46 ; comp. *Lau*, s. 347.

[*Baur*, Dogmengesch. s. 162: *Augustine* went into the most profound speculation respecting the nature of God. On the one hand, he viewed God in such an abstract and negative way, that He must appear to be wholly indefinable, and we could only say what He is not (De Trin. v. 2); on the other hand, he held fast to the two most essential ideas of God, viz. that He is the *essentia* (De Trin. v. 3), the immanent being of all being, and the bonum incommunicabile. To remove all finite conceptions, he defines the knowledge of God as an absolute identity with itself, as the immediate vision of that which is eternally present (De Civ. Dei, xi. 10, 21, xii. 17).—The peculiarity of the Augustinian proof of the being of God consists in this, that he starts from thinking (thought) itself, not from thought with any definite contents, and not from the idea of God, but from thought as such. All subjective thought presupposes objective truth. Thought itself involves the idea of God. His argument is an analysis of thought itself, and not an inference from the imperfect to the perfect.]

§ 124.

The Nature of God.

The definitions of orthodox theologians respecting the Trinity had this peculiarity, that, on the one hand, they were based on the supposition that God may be known by means of revelation ; and, on the other, implied that the contents of that same revelation, as unfolded by the Church in definite conceptions, are a *mystery*. These theologians, therefore, took no offence at the contradiction involved in such definitions, but found it quite natural that the understanding should here come short (1). The *Arians*, on the contrary, in accordance with their more rationalistic system, particularly as carried out to all its logical consequences by *Eunomius*, demanded the possibility of a complete knowledge of God (2).—Although the ideas concerning the divine being and the doctrinal definitions of the Church were still mixed up with much that savoured of anthropomorphism (3), yet the speculative tendency of the most eminent theologians of the present period kept them on an elevation where they avoided all gross representations of the Godhead. Thus *Athanasius* taught that God is incomprehensible and above all essence; *Augustine* doubted whether it would be proper to call God a *substance* (4). *Gregory* of Nazianzus, on the other hand, showed that it is not sufficient merely to deny the sensuous (5). The gross and carnal notions of the *Audians* concerning God met with little approval (6); while the *Monophysites*, by blending the divine and the human, promoted anthropomorphism under the mask of Christian orthodoxy (7).

(1) On this apparent contradiction, see *Baur*, Dg. ii. 1, s. 100, who criticises it from his purely speculative point of view, and draws particular attention to the connection between the teaching of the Fathers concerning the nature of God, and that which is contained in the writings of the pseudo-Dionysius.

(2) According to *Socrat.* iv. 7, *Eunomius* maintained that God knows no more about His nature than we do. It does not follow (he further maintained) that, because the minds of some are impaired by sin, the same is true in reference to all. The natural man, indeed, does not possess the knowledge in question; but what is the use of a revelation which reveals nothing? Christ has opened to us the way to the perfect knowledge of God. He is the door, viz. to this knowledge. *Eunomius* attached the greatest importance to the theoretical, didactic part of Christianity, and supposed its very essence to consist in the ἀκρίβεια τῶν δογμάτων. *Gregory* of Nazianzus, *Gregory* of Nyssa, and *Basil*, attempted to refute him. *Basil* reminds him (Ep. 16) of the impossibility of explaining the nature of God, since he cannot explain the nature even of an ant! Accused on the orthodox side of transforming theology into technology, the Arian *Philostorgius*, on the contrary, thought it praiseworthy that *Eunomius* had abandoned the doctrine of the incomprehensibility of God, which *Arius* himself defended. Hist. Eccles. x. 2, 3. This last statement also favours the conclusion, that the accusations of his opponents were something

more than their own inferences from his doctrines, as *Gieseler*, Dogmengesch. s. 303, seems to assert. Comp. *Neander*, Dogm. 324, and his Chrysostom, i. 355. *Klose*, Gesch. d. Lehre des Eunomius, Kiel 1833, s. 36 ff. *Ullmann's* Greg. s. 318 ff. *Baur*, Dg. ii. 1, s. 104.

(3) Examples are given by *Münscher, von Cölln*, i. s. 136. [*Athanas.* De Decret. Syn. Nic. 11. *Cyril*, Catech. iv. 5. *August.* Ep. 178. 14, 18, De Divers. Quæst. 20.] Comp. also *Lact.* Inst. vii. 21, where he calls the Holy Spirit purus ac liquidus, and in aquæ modum fluidus.

(4) *Athan.* Ep. ad Monachos, 2: Καὶ εἰ μὴ δυνατὸν καταλαβέσθαι, τί ἐστι θεός, ἀλλὰ δυνατὸν εἰπεῖν, τί οὔκ ἐστιν. In this sense he calls Him (Contra Gent. p. 3): Ἐπέκεινα τῆς οὐσίας, ὑπερούσιος. *Aug.* De Trin. v. 2, demands ut sic intelligamus Deum, si possumus, sine qualitate bonum, sine quantitate magnum, sine intelligentia creatorem, sine situ præsentem, sine habitu omnia continentem, sine loco ubique totum, sine tempore sempiternum, sine ulla sua mutatione mutabilia facientem nihilque patientem. Comp. vii. 5. He prefers the use of the word *essentia* to *substantia*, comp. De Civ. Dei, xii. 2, though he himself (Ep. 177, 4) speaks of God as *substantialiter ubique diffusus*.[1] Comp. (*Pseudo-*)*Boëthius*, De Trin. c. 4: Nam quum dicimus: Deus, substantiam quidem significare *videmur*, sed eam, quæ sit *ultra substantiam*. *Augustine's* writings, however, contain many profound thoughts relative to the knowledge of God. But everything he says shows how much he felt the insufficiency of language to express the nature of God; De Doctr. Christ. i. c. 6: Imo vero me nihil aliud quam dicere voluisse sentio. Si autem dixi, non est quod dicere volui. Hoc unde scio, nisi quia Deus ineffabilis est: quod autem a me dictum est, si ineffabile esset, dictum non esset. Ac per hoc ne ineffabilis quidem dicendus est Deus, quia et hoc cum dicitur, aliquid dicitur. Et fit nescio quæ pugna verborum, quoniam si illud est ineffabile, quod dici non potest, non est ineffabile quod vel ineffabile dici potest. Quæ pugna verborum silentio cavenda potius quam voce pacanda est. Et tamen Deus, cum de illo nihil digne

---

[1] The (*Pseudo-*)*Dionysius* the Areopagite (De Divinis Nominibus) goes still further, having no hesitation in saying that God, because elevated above all being, is τὸ μὴ ὄν. [Comp. *Baur*, Dogmengesch. 161.]

dici possit, admisit humanae vocis obsequium et verbis nostris in laude sua gaudere nos voluit. Nam inde est quod et dicitur Deus. On this account he, as well as *Tertullian* (§ 38, note 3), assigns to anthropomorphism its proper position, De Vera Rel. 50 : Habet enim omnis lingua sua quaedam propria genera locutionum, quae cum in aliam linguam transferuntur, videntur absurda; and the subsequent part of the passage; De Genesi, c. 17 : Omnes, qui spiritaliter intelligunt scripturas, non membra corporea per ista nomina, sed *spiritales potentias* accipere didicerunt, sicut galeas et scutum et gladium et alia multa.—But he prefers this anthropomorphism, which forms an idea of God from corporeal and spiritual analogies, though it may be erroneous, to the purely imaginary speculations of a self-satisfied idealism, De Trin. lib. i. ab init. It is not *we* that know God, but God who makes Himself known to *us*, De Vera Rel. c. 48 : Omnia, quae de hac luce mentis a me dicta sunt, nulla quam eadem luce manifesta sunt. Per hanc enim intelligo vera esse quae dicta sunt, et haec me intelligere per hanc rursus intelligo.—The same spirit is expressed in the beautiful passage from the (spurious) Soliloq. Animae, c. 31 : Qualiter cognovi te ? Cognovi te in te ; cognovi te non sicut tibi es, sed certe sicut mihi es, et non sine te, sed in te, quia tu es lux, quae illuminasti me. Sicut enim tibi es, soli tibi cognitus es ; sicut mihi es, secundum gratiam tuam et mihi cognitus es. . . . Cognovi enim te, quoniam Deus meus es tu (comp. *Cyril* of Jerusalem below, § 127, note 1).—According to *Gregory the Great*, Mor. xx. c. 32, our knowledge of God does not correspond to His nature. But it is not on that account false ; we see Him reflected. Thus none can look stedfastly at the sun when it rises; but from the mountains it shines upon, we perceive that it is rising, comp. *Lau*, s. 348.

(5) Orat. xxviii. 7–10, p. 500 ss., in *Ullmann*, s. 530. The negative knowledge of God is of no more use than to be told that twice five are neither 2, nor 3, nor 4, nor 5, nor 20, nor 40, without being told that it is 10.—*Gregory* thinks that the words ὁ ὤν and θεός are, comparatively speaking, the best expressions to denote the divine being ; but gives the preference to the name ὁ ὤν, partly because God applied it to Himself (Ex. iii. 14), partly because it is more significant. For

the term θεός is a derivative, and to be understood relatively (like the name *Lord*); but the application ὁ ὤν is in every respect independent, and belongs to none but God. Orat. xxx. 17 and 18, p. 552, 553. *Ullmann*, s. 324, note.

(6) Comp. above, § 106, note 7.

(7) Comp. what is said respecting Theopaschitism, § 102, note 3.

§ 125.

The Unity of God.

Polytheism and Gnosticism having been defeated, it was of less importance in the present period than in the preceding to defend the *unity* of God. The dualism of the Manichæans alone called for a defence of Monotheism against those outside the Church (1). The definitions respecting the Trinity, moreover, made it necessary that the Church should distinctly declare that the doctrine of the Trinity does not exclude that of the *unity* of God (2). In treating of this subject, theologians used much the same language as those of the former period (3).

(1) *Athanasius*, Contra Gent. p. 6, combated the dualism of the Gnostics. In opposition to the Manichæans, *Titus* of Bostra (Contra Manich. lib. i. in *Basnagii* Mon. t. 1, p. 63 ss.),[1] *Didymus* of Alexandria (ibid. p. 204, 205), *Gregory* of Nyssa (Contra Manich. Syllogismi, x. Opp. iii. p. 180), *Cyril* of Jerusalem (Cat. vi. 20, p. 92 [94]), and *Augustine* in his polemical writings, defended the doctrine of one divine being. See *Baur*, Dg. i. 2, s. 115. These objections, however, did not make the desired impression upon the Manichæans, since they held that only the good being, the ground of all, was really God; comp. *Gieseler*, Dogmengesch. s. 302.

(2) Comp. *e.g.* the Symbolum Athanasianum, § 97: Et tamen non sunt tres Dii, etc. On the controversy with the Tritheites and Tetratheites, see § 96.

[1] [*Titi Bostr.* quæ ex Opere contra Manich. edito in codice Hamburgensi servata sunt græce, ed. *P. Ant. de Lagarde*, Berol. 1854.—The same work, libri quatuor syriace, also edited by *Lagarde*, Berol. 1859.]

(3) *E.g. Lact.* i. 3. *Arnob.* lib. iii. *Rufin.* Expos. p. 18: Quod autem dicimus, Orientis ecclesias tradere unum Deum, patrem omnipotentem et unum Dominum, hoc modo intelligendum est, unum non numero dici, sed universitate. Verbi gratia: si quis enim dicit unum hominem, aut unum equum, hic unum pro numero posuit; potest enim et alius homo esse et tertius, vel equus. Ubi autem secundus vel tertius non potest jungi, unus si dicatur, non numeri, sed universitatis est nomen. Ut si e. c. dicamus unum solem, hic unus ita dicitur, ut alius vel tertius addi non possit; unus est enim sol. Multo magis ergo Deus cum unus dicitur, unus non numeri, sed universitatis vocabulo notatur, i.e. quia propterea unus dicatur, quod alius non sit.

§ 126.

The Attributes of God.

Several theologians, *e.g. Gregory* of Nazianzus, *Cyril* of Jerusalem, and others, maintained that what we call the attributes of God are only expressions by which we designate His relation to the world, and that these predicates are either negative or figurative (1). But *Augustine* proved, in a very acute manner, that the attributes of God cannot be separated from His nature as contingent phenomena (2). Other theologians of the present period were equally cautious in defining particular attributes, *e.g.* those of omniscience and omnipresence (3). Some endeavoured to refine the idea of the retributive justice of God, and to defend it against the charge of arbitrariness (4); while others, again, sought to reconcile the omniscience of God, and consequently His foreknowledge, with human liberty (5).

(1) *Gregory* says, Orat. vi. 12, p. 187: "There can be no *antagonism* in the Godhead, because it would *destroy* its very nature; the Godhead, on the contrary, is in such perfect harmony not only with itself, but also with other beings, that some of the *names* of God have a particular reference to this agreement. Thus He is called *peace* and *love*." Among the

attributes of God he assigns (next to His eternity and infinity) the first place to love, see *Ullmann*, s. 333.—*Cyril* of Jerusalem maintains that our ideas of God, and the attributes which we ascribe to Him, are not adequate to His nature, Cat. vi. 2, p. 87 (Oxon. 78): Λέγομεν γὰρ οὐχ ὅσα δεῖ περὶ θεόν (μόνῳ γὰρ αὐτῷ ταῦτα γνώριμα), ἀλλ' ὅσα ἡμετέρα ἀσθένεια βαστάσαι δύναται. Οὐ γὰρ τὸ, τί ἐστι θεὸς, ἐξηγούμεθα· ἀλλ' ὅτι τὸ ἀκριβὲς περὶ αὐτοῦ οὐκ οἴδαμεν, μετ' εὐγνωμοσύνης ὁμολογοῦμεν· ἐν τοῖς γὰρ περὶ θεοῦ μεγάλη γνῶσις, τὸ τὴν ἀγνωσίαν ὁμολογεῖν (comp. also the subsequent part of the passage). *Arnobius*, Adv. Gentes, iii. 19, protests very strongly against all predicating of attributes: Quis enim Deum dixerit fortem, constantem, frugi, sapientem? quis probum? quis sobrium? quis immo aliquid nosse? quis intelligere? quis providere? quis ad fines officiorum certos actionum suarum decreta dirigentem? Humana sunt hæc bona, et ex oppositione vitiorum existimationem meruerunt habere laudabilem. Quis est autem tam obtusi pectoris, tam bruti, qui humanis bonis Deum esse dicat magnum? aut ideo nominis majestate præcellere, quod vitiorum careat fœditate? Quidquid de Deo dixeris, quidquid tacitæ mentis cogitatione conceperis, in humanum transiit et corrumpitur sensum; nec habet propriæ significationis notam, quod nostris dicitur verbis, atque ad negotia humana compositis. Unus est hominis intellectus de Dei natura certissimus, si scias et sentias, nihil de illo posse mortali oratione depromi.

(2) De Civ. Dei, xi. 10: Propter hoc itaque natura dicitur simplex, cui non sit aliquid habere, quod vel possit amittere; vel aliud sit habens, aliud quod habet; sicut vas aliquem liquorem, aut corpus colorem, aut aër lucem sive fervorem, aut anima sapientiam. Nihil enim horum est id quod habet: nam neque vas liquor est, nec corpus color, nec aër lux sive fervor, neque anima sapientia est. Hinc est, quod etiam privari possunt rebus quas habent, et in alios habitus vel qualitates verti atque mutari, ut et vas evacuetur humore quo plenum est, et corpus decoloretur, et aër tenebrescat, et anima desipiat, etc. (This reasoning is identical with the proposition of *Schleiermacher*, that in the absolute the subject and the predicate are one and the same thing; see his work, Geschichte der Philosophie, s. 166.) Comp. (*Pseudo-*)*Boëthius*,

De Trin. 4: Deus vero hoc ipsum, quod est, Deus est; nihil enim aliud est, nisi quod est, ac per hoc ipsum Deus est. *Gregory the Great* treats of the attributes of God in the same manner, comp. *Lau*, s. 350 ff.

(3) The omnipotence of God is, according to *Augustine*, conditioned by His wisdom and His very nature. Thus, God cannot die, or lose His perfection, or sin (Ep. 162, § 8); neither can He make that not to be which has happened, nor that which is true to be false (C. Faustum, i. 26; comp. *Nitzsch*, l.c. s. 63 f.). Similarly he judges of the divine omniscience. God does not *know* things because they are, but things are because He *knows* them, *Aug.* De Civ. Dei, l.c.: Ex quo occurrit animo quiddam mirum, sed tamen verum, quod iste mundus nobis notus esse non posset, nisi esset: Deo autem nisi notus esset, esse non posset. With reference to the divine *omnipresence*, *Athanasius* taught that God is to be thought of as (potentially) in His works, but also as (substantially) external to them: ὁ δὲ θεὸς ... ἐν πᾶσι μέν ἐστι κατὰ τὴν ἑαυτοῦ ἀγαθότητα καὶ δύναμιν, ἔξω δὲ τῶν πάντων πάλιν ἐστὶ κατὰ τὴν ἰδίαν φύσιν (De Decret. 11). Of the Latin Fathers, *Arnobius* had already taught (i. 31) that God is cause, place, and space (prima causa, locus, et spatium rerum). So, too, *Augustine* says, l.c. qu. 20: Deus non alicubi est; quid enim alicubi est, continetur loco, quid loco continetur, corpus est. Non igitur alicubi est, te tamen quia est et in loco non est, in illo sunt potius omnia, quam ipse alicubi. He also excluded not only the idea of place, but (in reference to the *eternity* of God) that of succession of time, Conf. ix. 10, 2: Fuisse et futurum esse non est in vita divina, sed esse solum quoniam aeterna est. Nam fuisse et futurum esse non est aeternum. Comp. De Civ. Dei, xi. 5.—He also rejected the notion of *Origen* (condemned by *Justinian*), that God had created only as many beings as He could see to; De Civ. Dei, xii. 18.

(4) *Lactantius* wrote a separate treatise, De Ira Dei (Inst. lib. v.), on this subject. His principal argument is the following: If God could not hate, He could not love; since He loves good, He must hate evil, and bestow good upon those whom He loves, evil upon those whom He hates. Comp. *Augustine*, De Vera Rel. c. 15: Justa vindicta peccati plus

tamen clementiæ Domini quam severitatis ostendit. Ita enim nobis suadetur a corporis voluptatibus ad æternam essentiam veritatis amorem nostrum oportere converti. Et est justitiæ pulchritudo cum benignitatis gratia concordans, ut, quoniam bonorum inferiorum dulcedine decepti sumus, amaritudine pœnarum crudiamur. De Civ. Dei, i. 9, and elsewhere.

(5) *Chrys.* in Ep. ad Eph. Hom. i. (on ch. i. 5), distinguishes in this respect between an *antecedent* (θέλημα προηγούμενον) and a *subsequent* will (θέλημα δεύτερον). According to the former (τὸ σφοδρὸν θέλημα, θέλημα εὐδοκίας), all are to be saved; according to the latter, sinners must be punished. Comp. the section on predestination. [*August.* De Civ. Dei, v. c. 9; De Lib. Arbitr. iii. c. 4. *Boëthius,* De Cons. Phil. v.]

§ 127.

Creation.

After the idea of generation from the essence of the Father was applied to the Son of God alone, and employed to denote the difference between Him and the other persons of the Godhead on the one hand, and between Him and all created beings on the other, the idea of *creation* was limited by a more precise definition. The views of *Origen* were combated by *Methodius* (1), and rejected by the chief supporters of orthodoxy, viz. *Athanasius* and *Augustine* (2). The figurative interpretation of the history of creation fell into disrepute along with the allegorical sytem of interpretation. It became the more necessary to abide by the historical view of the Mosaic account, inasmuch as it forms the basis of the history of the fall, and its objective historical reality was the foundation of the Augustinian theology. But *Augustine* endeavoured, even *here*, to spiritualize the literal as much as possible, and to blend it with the allegorical (3). The dualistic theory of emanation held by the Manichæans and Priscillianists was still in conflict with the doctrine of a creation out of nothing (4).

(1) In his work περὶ γενητῶν. Extracts from it are given by *Photius*, Bibl. Cod. 235, p. 301. [Transl. in Ante-Nicene Library.]

(2) *Athan.* Contra Arian. Orat. ii. (Opp. t. i. p. 336). Cf. *Voigt*, s. 101 ff. *Augustine* endeavoured to remove the idea of time from the idea of God, and to save the doctrine that the creation had a beginning in time, by representing God as the Creator of time. Conf. xi. 10 s., c. 13: . . . Quae tempora fuissent, quae abs te condita non essent? Aut quomodo praeterirent, si nunquam fuissent? Cum ergo sis operator omnium temporum, si fuit aliquod tempus, antequam feceras coelum et terram, cur dicitur, quod ab opere cessabas? Id ipsum enim tempus tu feceras, nec praeterire potuerunt tempora, antequam faceres tempora. Si autem ante coelum et terram nullum erat tempus, cur quaeritur, quid tunc faciebas? Non enim erat tunc, ubi non erat tempus. *Nec tu tempore tempora praecedis;* alioquin non omnia tempora praecederes. *Sed praecedis omnia praeterita celsitudine semper praesentis aeternitatis,* et superas omnia futura, quia illa futura sunt, et cum venerint, praeterita erunt; tu autem idem ipse es, et anni tui non deficiunt.[1]—Cf. De Civ. Dei, vii. 30, xi. 4–6 (non est mundus factus *in* tempore, sed *cum* tempore), xii. 15–17.

(3) Thus he said, in reference to the six days: Qui dies cujusmodi sint, aut perdifficile nobis, aut etiam impossibile est cogitare, quanto magis dicere, De Civ. Dei, xi. 6. Concerning the seventh day (ibid. 8), his views are very nearly those of Origen: Cum vero in die septimo requievit Deus ab omnibus operibus suis et sanctificavit eum, nequaquam est accipiendum *pueriliter*, tanquam Deus laboraverit operando, qui *dixit* et *facta sunt*, verbo intelligibili et sempiterno, non sonabili et temporali. Sed requies Dei requiem significat eorum, qui requiescunt in Deo, sicut laetitia domus laetitiam significat eorum, qui laetantur in domo, etiamsi non eos domus ipsa, sed alia res aliqua laetos facit, etc. On the system of chronology,

---

[1] "*A confounding of the antagonism of the ideal and the real with that of the universal and particular, is the reason why in the above we neither have creation in time clearly enounced, nor yet the difference from (contrast with) the emanation theory distinctly brought out. . . . To make Augustine consistent, we must distinguish the eternal being of ideas in the divine intelligence, from that act of God by which they become productive. The former is then their ideal, the latter their real side,*" etc. *Schleiermacher*, Gesch. der Phil. i. s. 167.

comp. xii. 10. On the whole, see *Bindemann's* Augustin, ii. 425 ff.

(4) *Baur*, Manichæisches Religionssystem, s. 42 ff.: "*The Manichæan system acknowledges no creation, properly speaking, but only a mixture, by means of which the two opposite principles so pervade each other, that their product is the existing system of the world, which partakes of the nature of both.*" Comp. the statements of the Manichæan Felix, which are there given. On the Priscillianists, see *Orosii* Commonitor. ad August. *Neander*, Kg. ii. 3, s. 1488 ff. *Baumgarten-Crusius*, Compend. i. s. 111. [*Gieseler*, i. § 86. *J. M. Mandernach*, Gesch. des Priscillianismus, Trier. 1851.] *Lübkert*, l.c.

§ 128.

The Relation of the Doctrine of Creation to the Doctrine of the Trinity.

After the distinguishing characteristics of each of the persons of the Trinity had been more precisely defined (§ 95), the question arose among theologians, to which of the persons the work of creation was to be assigned? While, in the so-called Apostles' Creed, God the Father was simply and solely declared to be Creator of the world, in the Nicene Creed the Son was said to have part in the creation, and the Council of Constantinople asserted the same with regard to the Holy Ghost (1). *Gregory* of Nazianzus maintained, in accordance with *Athanasius* (2) and other theologians of this period, that the work of creation had been brought about by the Son, and completed by the Holy Ghost (3). Following Augustine, the western divines regarded creation as an act of the Triune God (4).

(1) Symb. Ap.: Credo in Deum Patrem omnipotentem, creatorem coeli et terrae. Comp. what *Rufinus* says on this passage; he shows that all things are created *through* the Son. The Nicene Creed calls the Father παντοκράτορα πάντων ὁρατῶν τε καὶ ἀοράτων ποιητήν, but says in reference to the Son: δἰ οὗ τὰ πάντα ἐγένετο, τά τε ἐν τῷ οὐρανῷ καὶ τὰ ἐν

τῇ γῇ. The symbol of Constantinople calls the Holy Spirit τὸ ζωοποιοῦν.

(2) According to *Athanas.* it is the Logos (ἐκ πηγῆς ἀγαθῆς ἀγαθὸς προελθών) who came down to the creatures, and made them after His image, and who guides them by His direction and His power (νεύματι καὶ δυνάμεσι). Comp. Cont. Gent. 41-44, and Cont. Arian. 2. See further in *Voigt*, l.c.

(3) Orat. xxxviii. 9, p. 668: . . . καὶ τὸ ἐννόημα ἔργον ἦν, λόγῳ συμπληρούμενον καὶ πνεύματι τελειούμενον. He calls the Son also τεχνίτης λόγος. Comp. *Ullmann*, s. 490.

(4) Thus *Fulgentius* of Ruspe, De Trin. c. 8, and others.

§ 129.

Object of Creation—Providence—Preservation and Government of the World.

That creation was not for the sake of God (1), but of man, was asserted doctrinally, and rhetorically set forth (2). In opposition to a mechanical view of the universe, the profound *Augustine* directed attention to the connection subsisting between creation and preservation (3). Special care was bestowed during the present period upon the doctrine of providence, on which *Chrysostom* and *Theodoret* in the East, and *Salvian* in the West, composed separate treatises (4). They took special pains to show, in accordance with the spirit of Christianity, that the providence of God extends to particulars (5). *Jerome*, however, did not agree with them, and, thinking it derogatory to the Divine Being to exercise such special care respecting the lower creation, maintained that God concerns Himself only about the species, but not about the individual (6). He thus prepared the way for the distinction made by the African bishop *Junilius* (who lived about the middle of the sixth century) between gubernatio generalis and gubernatio specialis (7), which, though justifiable from the theological standpoint, yet, when mechanically understood, was prejudicial to the idea of God as a living God.

(1) Thus *Augustine* maintained, De Vera Rel. 15, that the angels in serving God do not profit Him, but themselves. Deus enim bono alterius non indiget, quoniam a se ipso est.

(2) *Nemesius*, De Nat. Hom. i. p. 30 s. (ed. Oxon. 1671): Ἀπέδειξεν οὖν ὁ Λόγος τὴν τῶν φυτῶν γένεσιν μὴ δι᾽ ἑαυτὴν, ἀλλ᾽ εἰς τροφὴν καὶ σύστασιν τῶν ἀνθρώπων καὶ τῶν ἄλλων ζώων γεγενημένην· and in reference to the animal she says, p. 34: κοινῇ δὲ πάντα πρὸς θεραπείαν ἀνθρώπων συντελεῖν πέφυκε, καὶ τὰ μὴ ταῖς ἄλλαις χρείαις χρήσιμα. In support of his views he adduces the example of useful domestic animals, and observes with regard to noxious animals, that they were not so prior to the fall, and that man possesses even now means sufficient to subdue them.—Comp. *Chrys.* Hom., πρὸς τοὺς καταλείψαντας τὴν ἐκκλησίαν (Opp. t. vi. p. 272, ed. *Bauermeister*, p. 8): Ἥλιος ἀνέτειλε διὰ σὲ, καὶ σελήνη τὴν νύκτα ἐφώτισε, καὶ ποικίλος ἀστέρων ἀνέλαμψε χορός· ἔπνευσαν ἄνεμοι διὰ σὲ, ἔδραμον ποταμοί· σπέρματα ἐβλάστησαν διὰ σὲ, καὶ φῶτα ἀνεδόθη, καὶ τῆς φύσεως ὁ δρόμος τὴν οἰκείαν ἐτήρησε τάξιν, καὶ ἡμέρα ἐφάνη καὶ νὺξ παρῆλθε, καὶ ταῦτα πάντα γέγονε διὰ σέ. But *Chrysostom* also teaches that God created the world δι᾽ ἀγαθότητα μόνην, De Prov. i. t. iv. p. 142. Comp. *Aug.* De Div. Quæst. 28 (Opp. t. vi.). *Gregor. Nyss.* Or. Catech. c. 5; De Hominis Opificio, c. 2; *Lact.* Inst. vii. 4.

(3) His general views on the subject may be seen in De Morib. Eccles. Cath. c. 6: Nullum enim arbitror aliquo religionis nomine teneri, qui non saltem animis nostris divina providentia consuli existimet.—He then objects particularly to the popular notion of a master-builder whose work continues to exist, though he himself withdraws. The world would at once cease to exist, if God were to deprive it of His presence; De Genesi ad Litt. iv. c. 12; Enchirid. ad Laurent. c. 27. He defends himself against the charge of pantheism, De Civ. Dei, vii. 30: Sic itaque administrat omnia, quæ creavit, ut etiam ipsa proprios exercere et agere motus sinat. Quamvis enim nihil esse possint sine ipso, non sunt quod ipse. "*The world exists not apart from God, everything is in God; this, however, is not to be understood as if God were space itself, but in a manner purely dynamic,*" *Schleiermacher*, Geschichte

der Philosophie, s. 168. *Gregory* of Nazianzus uses similar language, Orat. xvi. 5, p. 302 ; see *Ullmann*, s. 491.

(4) *Chrys.* 3 books, de Fato et Providentia.—*Theodoret*, 10 orations περὶ τῆς θείας προνοίας.—*Salvianus*, De Gubernatione Dei sive de Prov. Comp. also *Nemesius*, De Natura Hominis (περὶ φύσεως ἀνθρώπου), c. 42 ss.

(5) This is indirectly proved by *Arnob*. Adv. Gent. iv. 10, p. 142 (in opposition to polytheism): Cur enim Deus praesit melli uni tantummodo, non praesit cucurbitis, rapis, non cunilae, nasturtio, non ficis, betaceis, caulibus? Cur sola meruerint ossa tutelam, non meruerint ungues, pili, cæteraque alia, quae locis posita in obscuris et verecundioribus partibus, et sunt casibus obnoxia plurimis, et curam magis deorum, diligentiamque desiderant? A direct proof is given by *Nemesius*, l.c. c. 44, p. 333 : Πάντα γὰρ ἤρτηται τοῦ θεοῦ θελήματος· καὶ ἐντεῦθεν ἀρύεται τὴν διαμονὴν καὶ σωτηρίαν. Ὅτι δὲ καὶ ἡ τῶν ἀτόμων καὶ πεπληθυσμένων ὑπόστασις προνοίας ἐστὶ δεκτικὴ, δῆλον ἐκ τῶν ζώων τῶν ἀρχαῖς τισι καὶ ἡγεμονίαις διοικουμένων, ὧν πολλὰ εἴδη· καὶ γὰρ μέλισσαι καὶ μύρμηκες καὶ τὰ πλεῖστα τῶν συναγελαζομένων ὑπό τισιν ἡγεμόσι τέτακται, οἷς ἀκολουθεῖ πειθόμενα. *Nemesius*, however, makes a distinction between *creation* and *providence*, and gives a definition of the latter, c. 42, p. 308 : Οὐ γὰρ ταυτό ἐστι πρόνοια καὶ κτίσις· κτίσεως μὲν γὰρ τὸ καλῶς ποιῆσαι τὰ γινόμενα· προνοίας δὲ τὸ καλῶς ἐπιμεληθῆναι τῶν γενομένων; and c. 43, p. 315 : Πρόνοια τοίνυν ἐστὶν ἐκ Θεοῦ εἰς τὰ ὄντα γινομένη ἐπιμέλεια· ὁρίζονται δὲ καὶ οὕτως αὐτήν· πρόνοιά ἐστι βούλησις Θεοῦ, δι' ἣν πάντα τὰ ὄντα τὴν πρόσφορον διεξαγωγὴν λαμβάνει κ.τ.λ. Generally speaking, we find here a complete system of teleology.

(6) *Hier.* Comment. in Abacuc, c. 1 (Opp. t. vi. p. 148): Sicut in hominibus etiam per singulos currit Dei providentia, sic in ceteris animalibus generalem quidem dispositionem et ordinem cursumque rerum intelligere possumus; verbi gratia: quomodo nascatur piscium multitudo et vivat in aquis, quomodo reptilia et quadrupedia oriantur in terra et quibus alantur cibis. Ceterum absurdum est ad hoc Dei deducere majestatem, ut sciat per momenta singula, quot nascantur culices, quotve moriantur (comp. on the other hand, Matt. x. 29, 30), quae cimicum et pulicum et muscarum sit multi-

tudo in terra, quanti pisces in mari natent, et qui de minoribus majorum praedæ cedere debeant. Non simus tam fatui adulatores Dei, ut, dum potentiam ejus etiam ad ima detrahimus, *in nos ipsi injuriosi simus* (?), eandem rationabilium quam irrationabilium providentiam esse dicentes.—A similar notion had been already advanced by *Arnobius*, who does not even grant that God created the lower animals (Adv. Gent. ii. 47), from which indeed it must follow that there was a special providence for them (iv. 10).

(7) *Junil.* de Partibus Legis Divinæ, l. ii. c. 3 ss. (Bibl. Max. PP. t. x. p. 345). *Münscher, von Cölln*, i. s. 154. General providence manifests itself in the preservation of the species, and the circumstances in which it is placed; special providence is displayed—(1) in the care of God for angels and men; (2) in that of the angels for men; and (3) in that of men for themselves.

§ 130.

Theodicy.

The controversy with the Manichæans, whose notions were to some extent adopted by *Lactantius* (1), required a more precise definition of the nature of the evil which is in the world, and such a distinction between physical evil and moral evil (sin) as would represent the latter as the true root of the former. Hence the evils existing in the world were regarded either (objectively) as the necessary consequence and punishment of sin, or (subjectively) as phenomena which, though good in themselves, assumed the appearance of evil only in consequence of our limited knowledge, or the corruption of our hearts, or the perverse use of our moral freedom. But the wise and pious, looking forward to that better time which is to come, use those evils as means of advancing in knowledge, and of practising patience (2).

(1) Inst. Div. ii. c. 8. Here he advances the unsatisfactory notion, which even *Augustine* seems to have entertained

(Enchir. ad Laur. c. 27), that evil would exist, though it were merely for the sake of *contrast;* as if good were good only by the contrast which it forms with bad, and would cease to be so if there were no contrast.

(2) *Athan.* Contra Gent. c. 7. *Basil* in Hexaëm. Hom. ii. 4. Hom. quod Deus non est auctor malorum (the passage should be read in its connection), Opp. t. ii. p. 78 (al. i. p. 361). *Klose,* s. 54–59. *Greg. Nyss.* Orat. Catech. c. 6. *Greg. Naz.* Orat. xiv. 30, 31, xvi. 5 (quoted by *Ullmann,* s. 493). *Chrys.* in 2 Tim. Hom. viii. (Opp. xii. 518 E). *Arnob.* i. 8, 9. *Aug.* De Civ. Dei, xi. 9: Mali enim nulla natura est, sed amissio boni mali nomen accepit. Comp. c. 22. Fire, frost, wild beasts, poisons, etc., may all be useful in their proper place, and in connection with the whole; it is only necessary to make such a use of them as accords with their design. Thus poisons cause the death of some, but heal others; food and drink injure only the immoderate. . . . Unde nos admonet divina providentia, non res insipienter vituperare, sed utilitatem rerum diligenter inquirere, et ubi nostrum ingenium vel firmitas deficit, ita credere occultam, sicut erant quaedam, quae vix potuimus invenire; quia et ipsa utilitatis occultatio, aut humilitatis exercitatio est aut elationis attritio; cum omnino natura nulla sit malum, nomenque hoc non sit nisi privationis boni. Sed a terrenis usque ad coelestia et a visibilibus usque ad invisibilia sunt aliis alia bona meliora; ad hoc inaequalia, ut essent omnia, etc. Comp. De Vera Rel. c. 12. Evils are beneficial as punishments, ibid. c. 15: . . . amaritudine poenarum erudiamur. On the question why the righteous have to suffer as well as the unrighteous, see De Civ. Dei, i. 8–10. Christians rise above all trials only by love to God: *Toto mundo est omnino sublimior mens inhaerens Deo,* De Morib. Eccles. Cath. c. 11. This seems to be the turning-point of all theodicy (Rom. viii. 28).

§ 131.

Angelology and Angelolatry.

J. B. Carpzovii Varia Historia Angelicorum ex Epiphanio et aliorum veterum Monumentis eruta, Helmst. 1772, 4to. *Keil,* Opuscula Academica, ii. p. 548 ss.

When the ideas of generation and procession from the Father came to be exclusively applied to the Son and the Holy Ghost, it also began to be stated more and more sharply that the angels are creatures, and not æons emanating from the essence of God (1). Nevertheless, they were still regarded as highly endowed beings, far superior to mankind (2). Reverence was paid to them; but *Ambrose* was the only Father during this period—and he did it merely in a passing remark—who recommended the invocation of angels (3). But both the prohibition of the worship of angels (angelolatry) by the Synod of Laodicea (about the middle of the fourth century), and the testimony of *Theodoret*, prove that such a worship must have been practised in some parts of the East (perhaps coming from earlier ages) (4). *Theodoret*, as well as *Augustine*, opposed the adoration, or at least the invocation of angels, which was disapproved of even by *Gregory I.*, who would have it that it was confined to the Old Testament dispensation (5). But the practice of dedicating churches to angels (6), which was favoured by emperors and bishops, would necessarily confirm the people in their belief, that angels heard and answered prayer, notwithstanding all dogmatic explanations. As to other dogmatic definitions concerning the nature of angels, *Gregory* of Nazianzus asserted that they were created prior to the rest of the world; others, as *Augustine*, dated their existence from the first day of creation (7). In the work of *Pseudo-Dionysius* (De Hierarchia Cœlesti), which, though composed during the present period, did not come into general use till the next, the angels were divided, almost in the systematic style of natural history, into three classes and nine orders (8).

(1) *Lact.* Inst. iv. c. 8 : Magna inter Dei filium et *cæteros* [sic] *angelos* differentia est. Illi enim ex Deo taciti spiritus exierunt. . . . Ille vero cum voce ac sono ex Dei ore processit.

(2) *Basil*, De Spir. S. c. 16, calls the angels ἀέριον πνεῦμα, πῦρ ὕλον, according to Ps. civ. 4, and hence ascribes to them

a certain corporeity. *Gregory* of Nazianzus says, Orat. vi. 12, p. 187: ... φῶς εἰσι καὶ τελείου φωτὸς ἀπαυγάσματα. According to Orat. xxviii. 31, p. 521 ss., the angels are servants of the divine will, powerful partly by original and partly by derived strength, moving from place to place, everywhere present, and ready to assist all, not only by reason of their zeal to serve, but also on account of the lightness of their bodies; different parts of the world are assigned to different angels, or placed under their dominion (Orat. xlii. 9, p. 755, and 27, p. 768), as *He* knows who has ordained and arranged all things. They have all one object in view (Orat. vi. 12, p. 187), and all act according to the one will of the Creator of the universe. They praise the divine greatness, and ever behold the eternal glory; not that God may thus be glorified, but that unceasing blessings may flow even upon those beings who stand nearest to God. Comp. *Ullmann*, s. 494, 495. *Augustine* calls the angels *sancti angeli*, De Civ. Dei, xi. 9. In another passage, in a more rhetorical strain (Sermo 46), they are called domestici Dei, cœli cives, principes Paradisi, scientiæ magistri, doctores sapientiæ, illuminatores animarum, custodes earum corporum, zelatores et defensores bonorum. God performs His miracles by angels, De Civ. Dei, xxii. 9. *Fulgentius* of Ruspe, De Trin. c. 8 (on the authority of great and learned men), distinguishes in the angels definitely body and spirit; they know God by the latter, and appear to men by means of the former. According to *Gregory the Great*, the angels are limited (circumscripti) spirits, without bodies, while God alone is incircumscriptus; Dial. lib. iv. c. 29; Moral. ii. c. 3. He also terms them rationalia animalia, see *Lau*, l.c. s. 357 ff. On the views of *Athan.*, see *Voigt*, s. 109.

(3) *Ambrose*, De Viduis, cap. ix. § 55: Videtis enim quod magno peccato obnoxia minus idonea sit quae pro se precetur, certe quae pro se impetret. Adhibeat igitur ad medicum alios precatores. Ægri enim, nisi ad eos aliorum precibus medicus fuerit invitatus, pro se rogare non possunt. Infirma est caro, mens ægra est, et peccatorum vinculis impedita, ad medici illius sedem debite non potest explicare vestigium. *Obsecrandi sunt angeli pro nobis, qui nobis ad præsidium dati sunt*: martyres obsecrandi, quorum videmur nobis quodam corporis pignore patrocinium vindicare. Possunt pro peccatis rogare nostris,

qui proprio sanguine, etiam si quæ habuerunt peccata, laverunt.
... Non erubescamus *eos intercessores nostræ infirmitatis* adhibere, quia et ipsi infirmitates corporis, etiam cum vincerent, cognoverunt. Though he thus mentions angels and martyrs as mediating persons, yet soon after he counsels men to the direct invocation of the divine Physician Himself.

(4) *Theodoret*, ad Col. ii. 18 and iii. 17 (quoted by *Münscher, von Cölln*, i. 86).—Conc. Laod. (A.D. 320–372 ?) in Can. 35 (*Mansi*, ii. p. 570; see *Fuchs*, ii. s. 330 ff., *Bruns*, Bibl. Eccles. i. p. 77. *Gieseler*, Kg. i. s. 517 ff., new ed. s. 594): Ὅτι οὐ δεῖ χριστιανοὺς ἐγκαταλείπειν τὴν ἐκκλησίαν τοῦ θεοῦ καὶ ἀπιέναι καὶ ἀγγέλους ὀνομάζειν καὶ συνάξεις ποιεῖν· ἅπερ ἀπηγόρευται (on which follows an anathema). It is worthy of notice that Dionysius translates *angulos* instead of *angelos*.

(5) *Theodoret*, l.c. *Eusebius* (Præp. Evang. vii. 15) already makes a distinction between τιμᾶν and σέβειν. Only the first is to be rendered to the angels. *Aug*. De Vera Rel. c. 55: Neque enim et nos videndo *angelos* beati sumus, sed videndo *veritatem*, qua etiam ipsos diligimus angelos et his congratulamur. . . . Quare honoramus eos caritate, non servitute. Nec eis templa construimus; nolunt enim, se sic honorari a nobis, quia nos ipsos, cum boni sumus, templa summi Dei esse noverunt. Recte itaque scribitur (Rev. xxii.) hominem ab angelo prohibitum, ne se adoraret, sed unum Deum, sub quo ei esset et ille conservus. Comp. Contra Faust. xx. 21, Conf. x. 42, and other passages quoted by *Keil*, l.c. p. 552. Yet in his sermons he insists upon the duty of loving the angels and of honouring them. He also believes in tutelary angels. *Gregory M.* in Cant. Cant. c. 8 (Opp. t. ii. p. 454).

(6) Constantine the Great had built a church at Constantinople (Μιχαήλιον) to St. Michael,[1] *Sozom*. Hist. Eccl. ii. 3; and *Theodoret* (l.c.) says in reference to the Phrygians and Pisidians: Μέχρι δὲ τοῦ νῦν εὐκτήρια τοῦ ἁγίου Μιχαὴλ παρ' ἐκείνοις καὶ τοῖς ὁμόροις ἐκείνων ἔστιν ἰδεῖν. The Emperor Justinian, and Avitus, Bishop of Vienne († 523), also formally dedicated to angels churches built in honour of them.

(7) *Greg. Naz.* xxxviii. 9, p. 668. All the angels together

---

[1] It was so called, not because it was *consecrated* to the archangel Michael, but because it was believed that he appeared there (*Sozomen*, ii. 3); comp. Gieseler, Dogmengesch. s. 352.

form, in his opinion, the κόσμος νοητός, as distinct from the κόσμος αἰσθητός, ὑλικὸς καὶ ὁρώμενος. Comp. *Ullmann*, s. 497. *Augustine* expresses himself differently, De Civ. Dei, xi. 9. In his opinion they are the light which was created in the beginning before all other creatures; at the same time, he so explains the dies unus (instead of primus, יוֹם אֶחָד), that this one day of light included the other days of creation, and then continues: Cum enim dixit Deus: *fiat lux, et facta est lux*, si recte in hac luce creatio intelligitur angelorum, profecto facti sunt participes lucis æternæ, quod [quæ] est ipsa incommutabilis sapientia Dei, per quam facta sunt omnia, quem dicimus unigenitum Dei filium, ut ea luce illuminati, qua creati, fierent lux, et vocarentur dies participatione incommutabilis lucis et diei, quod est verbum Dei, per quod et ipsi et omnia facta sunt. Lumen quippe verum, quod illuminat omnem hominem in hunc mundum venientem, hoc illuminat et omnem angelum mundum, ut sit lux non in se ipso, sed in Deo: a quo si avertitur angelus, fit immundus.

(8) Some of the earlier theologians, *e.g. Basil the Great* and *Gregory* of Nazianzus, held that there were different orders of angels on the basis of different names given to them in Scripture. *Basil*, De Spir. S. c. 16. *Gregory*, Orat. xxviii. 31, p. 521, mentions ἀγγέλους τινὰς καὶ ἀρχαγγέλους, θρόνους, κυριότητας, ἀρχὰς, ἐξουσίας, λαμπρότητας, ἀναβάσεις, νοερὰς δυνάμεις ἢ νόας. He does not, however, distinctly state by what these different classes are distinguished, since he thinks these internal relations of the world of spirits beyond the reach of human apprehension; *Ullmann*, s. 494. Comp. *Augustine*, Enchirid. ad Laur. 58 : Quomodo autem se habeat beatissima illa et superna societas, quæ ibi sint differentiæ personarum, ut cum omnes tamquam generali nomine angeli nuncupentur . . . ego me ista ignorare confiteor. Sed nec illud quidem certum habeo, utrum ad eandem societatem pertineant sol et luna et cuncta sidera, etc.[1] But *Pseudo-Dionysius*, hardly a century after Augustine, seems to have understood the subject much better; in his Hierarchia Cœlestis (ed. *Lansselii*, Par. 1615, fol.), c. 6, he divided the whole number of angels

---

[1] There are, however, thoughts occurring in *Augustine* on the subject of the angels which were worked out subsequently by the Schoolmen (such as the distinction between a *cognitio matutina* and *vespertina*), De Civ. Dei, xi. 9.

into three classes (hierarchies), and subdivided each class into three orders (τάγματα):—I. (1) Θρόνοι, (2) Χερουβίμ, (3) Σεραφίμ; II. (4) κυριότητες, (5) ἐξουσίαι, (6) δυνάμεις; III. (7) ἀρχαί, (8) ἀρχάγγελοι, (9) ἄγγελοι. He nevertheless observed that the last term, as well as δυνάμεις οὐράνιαι, was common to all (c. 11).[1] *Gregory the Great* followed him (Hom. in Ezek. xxxiv. 7, Opp. t. i. p. 1603, al. ii. p. 477), and knows the following nine classes:—Angeli, Archangeli, Virtutes, Potestates, Principatus, Dominationes, Throni, Cherubim atque Seraphim, which he brought into connection with the nine precious stones spoken of in Ezek. xxviii. 13. At the same time he holds that the angels, through love, have all in common; see *Lau*, s. 359.

§ 132.

The same subject continued.

Metaphysical definitions of the nature of angels were of less interest in the religious and moral, and consequently in the dogmatic point of view, than the question, whether angels, like men, possessed a free will, and were capable of sinning. It was generally admitted that this had been the case *before* the fall of the evil angels. But theologians did not agree in their opinions respecting another point, viz. whether the good angels who at first resisted temptation will always remain superior to it, or whether it is possible that they too may fall into sin. *Gregory* of Nazianzus, and still more decidedly *Cyril* of Jerusalem, pronounced in favour of the latter view (1); *Augustine* and *Gregory the Great* adopted the former (2).

---

[1] *Pseudo-Dionysius*, however (cap. 1 and 2), endeavoured to remove the gross and sensuous ideas respecting the forms of the angels, and designated the common terminology as ἀτίτομον τῶν ἀγγελικῶν ὀνομάτων σκηνήν (durum angelicorum nominum apparatum); comp. his mystical interpretation of the symbols of angels in cap. 15. [*Baur*, Dogmengesch. s. 172, says that in this hierarchy, where all is measured by quantitative distinctions, the difference between the Platonic and Christian view becomes evident—the Christian view being that there is a direct union of God and man; and that *Augustine* (De Civ. Dei, 9, 16) well expressed this difference, by directly denying the Platonic thesis—*nullus Deus miscetur homini.*]

(1) *Gregory* thought that the angels were not ἀκίνητοι, but δυσκίνητοι to evil (Orat. xxviii. 31, p. 521), and supposed that this necessarily follows from the fact that Lucifer once fell, Orat. xxxviii. 9, p. 668, xlv. 5, p. 849; *Ullmann*, s. 496. Comp. also *Basil the Great* (De Spir. S. c. 16).—But *Cyril* of Jerusalem (Cat. ii. 10) insisted that the predicate "sinless" should be applied to none but Christ, and maintained that the angels too stood in need of pardon.—Comp. *Lactantius*, Inst. vii. 20 : Angeli Deum metuunt, quia *castigari* ab eo possunt inenarrabili quodam modo.

(2) *Augustine*, De Ver. Rel. i. 13 : Fatendum est enim, et angelos natura esse mutabiles, si solus Deus est incommutabilis ; sed ea voluntate, qua magis Deum quam se diligunt, *firmi et stabiles manent in illo* et fruuntur majestate ipsius, ei uni libentissime subditi. According to the Enchiridion, c. 28, the good angels received, after the fall of the evil ones, what they had not had before, viz. certam scientiam, qua essent de sua sempiterna et nunquam casura stabilitate securi ; this idea is evidently in accordance with his anthropological views of the donum perseverantiae, and is distinctly brought forward in De Civ. Dei, xi. 13 : Quis enim catholicus christianus ignorat nullum novum diabolum ex bonis angelis ulterius futurum : sicut nec istum in societatem bonorum angelorum ulterius rediturum ? Veritas quippe in Evangelio sanctis fidelibusque promittit, quod erunt aequales angelis Dei ; quibus etiam promittitur, quod ibunt in vitam aeternam. Porro autem si nos certi sumus nunquam nos ex illa immortali felicitate casuros, illi vero certi non sunt : jam potiores, non aequales eis erimus ; sed quia nequaquam Veritas fallit et aequales eis erimus, profecto etiam ipsi certi sunt suae felicitatis aeternae. Comp. *Pseudo-Dionys.* c. 7. *Gregory the Great* also asserted that the good angels obtained the confirmatio in bono as a gift of God ; Ezech. lib. i. Hom. 7, Mor. v. c. 38, and xxxvi. c. 7, *Lau*, s. 362.

§ 133.

Devil and Demons.

[*Isaac Taylor*, Ancient Christianity, 4th ed. 1844, vol. ii. 167–222, on the Ancient Demonolatry.]

According to the prevailing opinion of the age, *pride* was the immediate and real cause of the fall of the evil spirits (1). Almost all the theologians of this period, with the exception of *Lactantius*, whose notions resembled those of the dualistic Manichæans (2), regarded the devil as a being of limited power (3), whose seductions the Christian believer was able to resist (4). *Didymus* of Alexandria and *Gregory* of Nyssa ventured—though with great caution—to revive the notion of Origen, that there was still hope of the final conversion of the devil (5). *Cyril* of Jerusalem, *Jerome*, and *Augustine*, combated this opinion, which was condemned in the sixth century by the Emperor Justinian, together with the other errors of Origen (6). It was, moreover, supposed that demoniacal powers were still in operation (7), and were most effectually resisted not only by the moral, but also by the physical and magical efficacy of the name of Christ, and the sign of the cross (8).

(1) *Eusebius*, Demonst. Evang. iv. 9. *Augustine*, De Vera Rel. i. 13 : Ille autem angelus magis se ipsum, quam Deum diligendo subditus ei esse noluit et *intumuit per superbiam*, et a summa essentia defecit et lapsus est, et ob hoc minus est quam fuit, quia eo quod minus erat frui voluit, quum magis voluit sua potentia frui, quam Dei. De Catechiz. Rudibus, § 30 : *Superbiendo* deseruit obedientiam Dei et Diabolus factus est. De Civ. Dei, xii. c. 6 : Cum vero causa miseriæ malorum angelorum quæritur, ea merito occurrit, quod ab illo qui summe est aversi ad se ipsos conversi sunt, qui non summe sunt : et hoc vitium quid aliud quam superbia nuncupatur? *Initium* quippe *omnis peccati superbia*. Comp. Enchirid. ad Laurent. c. 28. *Envy* was joined with *pride* ; comp. *Gregory Nazianz*. Orat. xxxvi. 5, p. 637, and vi. 13, p. 187. *Ullmann*, s. 499. *Gregory Nyss*. Orat. Catech. c. 6 : Ταῦτα δὲ [viz. the excellence of the first man] τῷ ἀντικειμένῳ τοῦ κατὰ τὸν φθόνον πάθους ὑπεκκαύματα ἦν. *Cassian*, Collat. viii. 10, makes mention of both superbia and invidia. *Gregory the Great* also emphasizes pride ; by this the devil was seduced to strive after a privata celsitudo ; Moral. xxi. c. 2, xxiv. c. 21 ;

Lau, s. 365.—The idea of lasciviousness was put more and more into the background. *Chrysostom*, *Theodoret*, *Cyril* of Alexandria, *Augustine*, and *Cassian* gave also a more correct interpretation of the passage in Gen. vi. 2, which was understood by earlier theologians; although *Eusebius* (Praep. Ev. v. 4), *Ambrose* (De Noë et Arca, c. 4), and *Sulpicius Severus* (Hist. Sacra, i. 3) explained it in a sense similar to that which was formerly attached to it (§ 52, note 3). Comp. *Chrys.* Hom. in Gen. xxii. (Opp. t. ii. p. 216). [*S. R. Maitland* in Brit. Mag. xxi. p. 389 ff., and in his Essays (on False Worship, p. 19 ff.), 1856. *C. F. Keil* in Zeitschrift f. d. luth. Theol. 1855 and 1859; *Engelhardt*, ibid. 1856. *Delitzsch*, review of Kurtz in Reuter's Repertorium, 1857.] *Theodoret* in Gen. Quaest. 47 (Opp. t. i. p. 58): Ἐμβρόντητοι ὄντες καὶ ἄγαν ἠλίθιοι, ἀγγέλους τούτους ἀπέλαβον; and Fab. Haer. Ep. v. 7 (Opp. iv. p. 402): Παραπληξίας γὰρ ἐσχάτης τὸ τοῖς ἀγγέλοις προσάψαι τὴν τῶν ἀνθρώπων ἀκολασίαν. *Cyril. Alex.* Contra Anthropomorphitas, c. 17 (Opp. t. vi. p. 384); Contra Julian. lib. ix. p. 296, 297. *Augustine*, De Civ. Dei, xv. 23; quaest. 3 in Gen.; *Cassian*, Coll. viii. c. 20, 21. [Comp. *Münscher*, *von Cölln*, i. s. 90-92.] *Hilary* (in Ps. cxxxii. p. 403) mentions the earlier interpretation, but without approval. *Philastrius*, on the contrary, numbers it among the heresies, Haer. 107 (De Gigantibus tempore Noë).

(2) Inst. ii. 8. Previous to the creation of the world God created a spirit like unto Himself (the Logos), who possessed the attributes of the Father; but after that He created another spirit, in whom the divine seed did not remain (in quo indoles divinae stirpis non permansit). Moved by *envy* he apostatized, and changed his name (contrarium sibi nomen ascivit). The Greek writers call him διάβολος, the Latin criminator, quod crimina, in quae ipse illicit, ad Deum deferat (hence the appellation obtrectator). He envies especially his predecessor (the first-born), because He continued to enjoy the favour of God.—*Lactantius* thus agrees with the other theologians in supposing that envy was the cause of the fall. But his peculiar manner of representing Satan, as a later-born Son of God, and of drawing a parallel between him and the first-born, reminds us of Gnostic and Manichaean notions. In another passage (now wanting in many MSS., but probably

omitted at an early period to save the reputation of *Lactantius*) he calls the Logos the right, and Satan the left hand of God. If the passage in question were genuine, it would go to prove very clearly that the views of *Lactantius* on this subject were essentially Manichæan, though the unity of the Father would be still preserved above the antagonism of Logos and Satan; but this notion would justly expose its author to the charge of Arianism. This seems to have been felt by those critics who omitted the above passage. Comp. the note of *Cellarius* in the edition of *Bünemann*, i. p. 218. Comp. cap. ix., where the term *Antitheus* occurs (*Arnob.* Contra Gent. iv. 12, and *Orelli* on that passage). *Augustine* opposed the Manichæan notion, Contra Faust. 21, 1 and 2.[1]

(3) *Gregory the Great* calls him outright a stupid animal, since he entertains hopes of heaven without being able to obtain it, and is caught in his own net, Mor. xxxiii. c. 15. *Lau*, s. 364.

(4) *Gregory Nazianz.* Orat. xl. 10, p. 697, makes special mention of the *water of baptism* and the *Spirit* as the means by which to quench the arrows of the evil one. Satan had no power over Christ; deceived by His human appearance, he took Him for a mere man. But the Christian who is united to Christ by faith, can likewise resist Him, Orat. xxiv. 10, p. 443 : Παχύτεραι γὰρ αἱ καθαραὶ ψυχαὶ καὶ θεοειδεῖς πρὸς θήραν τοῦ ἐνεργοῦντος, κἂν ὅτι μάλιστα σοφιστικὸς ᾖ καὶ ποικίλος τὴν ἐπιχείρησιν. The assertion of *Hilary* on Ps. cxli. p. 541, quidquid inquinatum homines gerunt, a Diabolo suggeritur, met with opposition on the part of *Gennadius*, De Eccles. Dogm. c. 48 : Non omnes malæ cogitationes nostræ semper Diaboli instinctu excitantur, sed aliquoties ex nostri arbitrii motu emergunt. *Jerome* also, although he designates the devil as the old serpent, by whom our first parents were led astray, yet does not regard him as the original cause of sin (Contra Rufin. ii. 7). Comp. also *Chrys.* De Prov. c. 5 (Opp. iv. 150). *Augustine*, De Advers. Leg. ii. 12, and elsewhere.

(5) *Didym.* Enarr. Epp. Cathol. e vers. lat. (Bibl. PP. Max. t. iv. p. 325 C), in commenting on 1 Pet. iii. 22, says merely

---

[1] The very appropriate passage adduced by *Baumgarten-Crusius*, s. 987 : Diabolus non simpliciter Deus est, sed illis Deus existit, qui illum Christo anteponunt (according to 2 Cor. iv. 4), is the same in sense, though the identical words are not found here.

that Christ accomplished the work of redemption for all rational beings (cuncta rationalia). *Gregory Nyss.* expresses himself more explicitly, Orat. Catech. c. 26 (see in *Münscher, von Colln,* i. s. 97), but *Germanus* contested the genuineness of the passage in *Photius,* Cod. 233. *Orosius,* too, complained, in a letter to *Augustine* (Opp. Aug. t. viii.), that some men revived the erroneous views of *Origen* on this point.

(6) *Cyril* of Jerusalem, Cat. iv. p. 51, ascribed to the devil an obdurate heart and an incorrigible will; comp. *August.* Ad Orosium Contra Priscillian. et Orig. c. 5 ss. (Opp. t. viii. p. 433 ss.); De Civ. Dei, xxi. 17 : ... Qua in re misericordior profecto fuit Origenes, qui et ipsum Diabolum atque angelos ejus post graviora pro meritis et diuturniora supplicia ex illis cruciatibus eruendos atque sociandos sanctis angelis credidit. Sed illum et propter hoc et propter alia nonnulla ... non immerito reprobavit ecclesia. He shows, too, that the final deliverance of the devil necessarily follows from the idea of the remission of the punishments of hell in the case of all condemned men; but that this notion, being opposed to the word of God, is only the more perverse and dangerous, in proportion as it seems gracious and mild in the eyes of men. [*Jerome,* Ep. 84, ad Pammach. et Ocean. p. 528, Ep. 124, ad Avitum, p. 920.]—Concerning the final condemnation of *Origen's* opinion, see *Mansi,* t. ix. p. 399, 518.—According to *Gregory the Great,* the devil still enjoys, even in his condemned estate, a potentia sublimitatis, Mor. xxiv. 20, xxxii. c. 12, 13. He rejoices in scattering evil broadcast, and has great power, which, however, has been broken by Christ. Final punishment will be inflicted upon him after the general judgment. Before this he will appear as Antichrist. *Lau,* s. 365 ff., gives the passages.

(7) *Eusebius,* Praep. Ev. iii. c. 14–16. *Aug.* De Civ. Dei, ii. 24, x. 21 : Moderatis autem praefinitisque temporibus, etiam potestas permissa daemonibus, ut hominibus quos possident excitatis inimicitias adversus Dei civitatem tyrannice exerceant. Comp. de diversis quaestionibus octoginta tribus, qu. 79, and the further passages in *Nitzsch* (Augustin's Lehre vom Wunder), s. 45, 71 (88).—*Posidonius,* a physician, combated (according to *Philostorgius,* Hist. Eccl. viii. c. 10) the current opinion that madness proceeds from demoniacal in-

fluences, asserting that οὐχὶ δαιμόνων ἐπιθέσει τοὺς ἀνθρώπους ἐκβακχεύεσθαι, ὑγρῶν δέ τινων κακοχυμίαν τὸ πάθος ἐργάζεσθαι, μηδὲ γὰρ εἶναι παράπαν ἰσχὺν δαιμόνων, ἀνθρώπων φύσιν ἐπηρεάζουσαν. The popular view, nevertheless, continued to be defended in most theological systems.
(8) *Athanasius,* De Incarn. Verbi Dei, c. 48 (Opp. t. i. p. 89). *Cyril. Hier.* Cat. xiii. 36: [Ὁ σταυρὸς] σημεῖον πιστῶν καὶ φόβος δαιμόνων· ... ὅταν γὰρ ἴδωσι τὸν σταυρὸν, ὑπομιμνήσκονται τοῦ ἐσταυρωμένου, φοβοῦνται τὸν συντρίψοντα τὰς κεφαλὰς τοῦ δράκοντος. *Cassian,* Coll. viii. 19, distinguishes the true power of faith which defeats the demons, from the magical power, which even the ungodly may exert over evil spirits, when these obey them as servants (familiares). The poem of *Severus Sanctus Endelechius,* De Mortibus Boum, contains a lively description of the magical efficacy of the sign of the cross against demoniacal influences, even in the animal kingdom. (Edition of *Piper,* Gött. 1835; a number of other passages on the point in question are quoted from the works of the Fathers in the introduction to this edition, p. 105 ss.)

> Signum, quod perhibent esse crucis Dei,
> Magnis qui colitur solus in urbibus,
> Christus, perpetui gloria numinis,
> Cujus filius uniens:
>   Hoc signum mediis frontibus additum
> Cunctarum pecudum certa salus fuit.
> Sic vero Deus hoc nomine præpotens
> Salvator vocitatus est.
>   Fugit continuo sæva lues greges,
> Morbis nil licuit. Si tamen hunc Deum
> Exorare velis, credere sufficit:
> Votum sola fides juvat.

3. SOTERIOLOGY.

§ 134.

Redemption through Christ.

The Death of Jesus.

Däbrlein, De Redemtione a Potestate Diaboli, insigni Christi Beneficio (Diss. Inaugur. 1774, 1775), in his Opuscula Academica, Jena 1789. *Baur,* Christliche Lehre von der Versöhnung, s. 67-118. [*Thomasius,* Christi Person und Werk, iii. 1, s. 157 ff., 1859, cf. § 68.]

The doctrine of the devil occupied during this period a prominent place in *Soteriology*, inasmuch as *Gregory* of Nyssa and other theologians still maintained the notion previously held, that God defrauded the devil by a dishonest exchange (1). Though the idea in this form was opposed by *Gregory* of Nazianzus (2), yet it prevailed for some time under different modifications (3). Meanwhile the idea of a penalty endured on the part of God gained the preponderance, after its advocacy by *Athanasius* (4). To this was soon added the further notion, that by the giving up of the infinitely precious life of Jesus, more than the debt was paid; though this is found rather in rhetorical amplifications of the theme than in strict dogmatic definitions (5). Generally speaking, the doctrine was not presented in a final and conclusive form. Along, however, with the objective mode of regarding the death of Christ, we also find the subjective; including in the latter not only the ethical (in which the death of Christ is viewed as a pattern for our imitation) (6), but also the typical and symbolical (mystical), reposing upon the idea of an intimate connection of the whole human race with Christ as its head (7). It was, moreover, generally held that the redemptive principle was found not only in the death of the Redeemer, but in His whole divine and human manifestation and life (8). Free scope was still left to investigation respecting the particular *mode* of redemption (9).

(1) *Gregor. Nyss.* Orat. Cat. c. 22–26. The train of his argument is as follows: Men have become slaves of the devil by sin. Jesus offered Himself to the devil as the ransom which should release all others. The crafty devil assented, because he cared more for the one Jesus, so much superior to them, than for all the rest. But, notwithstanding his craft, he was deceived, since he could not retain Jesus in his power. It was, as it were, a deception on the part of God[1] (ἀπάτη τίς ἐστι τρόπον τινά), that Jesus veiled His divine nature,

---

[1] The close affinity between this supposition and Docetism, which ever and anon endeavoured to crop out, is very plain. See *Baur*, l.c. s. 82, 83.

which the devil would have feared, by means of His humanity, and thus deceived the devil by the appearance of flesh. But *Gregory* allows such a deception according to the jus talionis: the devil had first deceived men, for the purpose of seducing them; but the design of God in deceiving the devil was a good one, viz. to redeem mankind. (*Gregory's* argument looks very much like the well-known maxim, that "the end sanctifies the means."—This dramatic representation of the subject includes, however, that other more profound idea, carried out with much ingenuity in many of the wondrous legends of the Middle Ages, that the devil, in spite of all his cunning, is at last outwitted by the wisdom of God, and appears in comparison as a stupid devil.) Comp. *Ambrose* in Ev. Luc. (Opp. iii. Col. x. 1): Oportuit hanc fraudem Diaboli fieri, ut susciperet corpus Dominus Jesus, et corpus hoc corruptibile, corpus infirmum, ut crucifigeretur ex infirmitate. *Rufinus*, Expos. p. 21: Nam sacramentum illud susceptæ carnis hanc habet causam, ut divina filii Dei virtus velut hamus quidam habitu humanæ carnis obtectus ... principem mundi invitare possit ad agonem: cui ipse carnem suam velut escam tradidit, ut hamo eum divinitatis intrinsecus teneret insertum et effusione immaculati sanguinis, qui peccati maculam nescit, omnium peccata deleret, eorum duntaxat, qui cruore ejus postes fidei suæ significassent. Sicuti ergo hamum esca consceptum si piscis rapiat, non solum escam cum hamo non removet, sed ipse de profundo esca aliis futurus educitur: ita et is, qui habebat mortis imperium, rapuit quidem in mortem corpus Jesu, non sentiens in eo hamum divinitatis inclusum; sed ubi devoravit, hæsit ipse continuo, et disruptis inferni claustris, velut de profundo extractus traditur, ut esca ceteris fiat (in allusion to certain passages in Scripture, especially to Job: Adduces draconem in hamo et pones capistrum circa nares ejus), *Leo M.* Sermo xxii. 3, and other passages (see *Perthel*, u. s., s. 171 ff.). *Greg. M.* in Ev. L. i. Hom. 16, 2, and 25, 8, quoted by *Münscher, von Cölln*, i. s. 429 (comp. *Lau*, l.c. s. 446 ff.); and *Isidor. Hispal.* Sent. lib. iii. dist. 19 (illusus est Diabolus morte Domini quasi avis), quoted by *Baur*, s. 79.

[*Baur*, Dogmengesch. 189 ff. The three chief elements of the doctrine were: 1. The idea of justice—the right of the devil, etc., and the satisfaction of it. 2. The deception practised upon the devil, further carried out by *Gregory* of Nyssa, in the idea that the Saviour, in His incarnation, deceived the devil by His very flesh. 3. The necessity of this mode of redemption is not absolute, but relative; divine omnipotence might have chosen another, but this was the most fitting. *Thomasius*, Christi Person u. Werk, iii., gives the result of the discussion in this period thus: The two theories of deliverance from the devil and atonement by sacrifice, gradually pass over into each other—and this by means of the intermediate idea of death. In proportion, however, as the death is referred to the divine causality, and viewed in the light of Gen. ii. 17 and Gal. iii. 10, Christ's death, too, is viewed as punishment for human sin, as the bearing of the curse, and is consequently referred to the divine justice. A theory of satisfaction begins to be developed. The thought of a reconciliation of justice with mercy, though frequently adduced to explain the redemption from the devil, is only seldom, and in the way of allusion, applied to the atonement. But it is already evident to what the main drift of the doctrine is tending.]

(2) Orat. xlv. p. 862 s.: "We were under the dominion of the wicked one, inasmuch as we were sold unto sin, and exchanged pleasure for vileness. If it now be true that a ransom is always paid to him who is in the possession of the thing for which it is due, I would ask, To whom was it paid in this case? and for what reason? Perhaps to the evil one (Satan) himself? But it would be a burning shame to think so (φεῦ τῆς ὕβρεως). For in that case the robber had not only received *from* God, but *God Himself* (in Christ) as a ransom and an exceedingly great recompense of his tyranny. . . . Or is it paid to the Father Himself? But, in the first place, it might be asked, How could that be, since He (God) did not hold us in bondage? And again, how can we satisfactorily explain it, *that the Father delighted in the blood of the only-begotten Son*, since He did not even accept the offer of Isaac, but substituted the sacrifice of a ram in the place of a rational being? Is it not then evident that the Father received the ransom, not because He demanded or needed it, but on account of the divine economy (διὰ τὴν οἰκονομίαν), and

because man had to be sanctified by the incarnation of God; that having subdued the tyrant, He might deliver and reconcile us to Himself by the intercession of His Son?" See *Ullmann*, s. 456, 457. *Gregory* was, nevertheless, disposed to admit some artifice on the part of Christ in the contest in which He conquered Satan. " It consisted in this, that Christ assumed the form of man, in consequence of which the devil thought that he had only to do with a being like ourselves, while the power and glory of the Godhead dwelt in Him." Orat. xxxix. 13, p. 685. *Ullmann*, l.c.

(3) The doctrine received an essential modification in the statement of *Augustine* (De Trin. xiii.), that the devil, who had overstepped his power, was conquered in the struggle. He had overstepped his power in this, that he thought he could treat the sinless Jesus as a slave, like the other sons of Adam, which last, in fact, belonged to him as prisoners, according to the rights of war. Now, too, he lost the right to the latter, so far as they belong to Christ. (Justissime dimittere cogitur quem injustissime occidit.) Comp. *Baur*, Versöhnungslehre, s. 68 ff. *Gieseler*, Dogmengesch. s. 382. [This, too, says *Gieseler*, was the view of *Hilary* of Poitiers, *Leo the Great*, and *Gregory the Great*. Another representation was this —redemption was the result of a conflict in which Jesus conquered the devil. He conquered him so far as this, that the devil could not seduce Him to commit the least sin; by this victory He made amends for the defeat suffered in Adam, and thus broke the dominion which the devil had on the ground of this defeat. This view is found in *Hilary*, *Leo the Great*, *Gregory the Great*, and, among the Greeks, in *Theodoret*.]

(4) De Incarnat. c. 6 ss. God had threatened to punish transgressors with death, and thus could not but fulfil His threatening: Οὐκ ἀληθὴς γὰρ ἦν ὁ θεός, εἰ, εἰπόντος αὐτοῦ ἀποθνήσκειν ἡμᾶς, μὴ ἀπέθνησκεν ὁ ἄνθροπος κ.τ.λ. But, on the other hand, it was not in accordance with the character of God, that rational beings, to whom He had imparted His own Spirit (Logos), should fall from their first state in consequence of an imposition practised upon them by the devil. This was quite as contrary to the goodness of God (οὐκ ἄξιον γὰρ ἦν τῆς ἀγαθότητος τοῦ θεοῦ), as it would have been contrary to His justice and veracity not to punish the

transgressor. (Here the premisses of the later theory of
Anselm?) When the Logos perceived that nothing but death
could save man from ruin, He assumed a human body, because
the Logos Himself, i.e. the immortal Son of God, could not
die. He offered His human nature as a sacrifice for all, and
fulfilled the law by His death. By it He also destroyed the
power of the devil (ἠφάνιζε τὸν θάνατον τῇ προσφορᾷ τοῦ
καταλλήλου, c. 9, p. 54), etc. Comp. *Möhler's* Athanasius, i.
s. 157. *Baur,* s. 94 ff. *Voigt,* s. 146 ff. [*Baur,* Dg. s. 189:
To set aside the devil, *Athanasius* put personified death in his
place, which was deceived in the same way.] Concerning the
similar though more general notions of *Basil the Great* (Hom.
De Gratiar. Actione—Hom. in Ps. xlviii. and xxviii.—De Spir.
Sancto, 15), comp. *Klose,* s. 65. *Cyril* also says, Cat. xiii. 33:
Ἐχθροὶ ἦμεν θεοῦ δι' ἁμαρτίας, καὶ ὥρισεν ὁ θεὸς τὸν ἁμαρ-
τάνοντα ἀποθνήσκειν· ἔδει οὖν ἓν ἐκ τῶν δύο γενέσθαι,
ἢ ἀληθεύοντα θεὸν πάντας ἀνελεῖν ἢ φιλανθρωπευόμενον
παραλῦσαι τὴν ἀπόφασιν. Ἀλλὰ βλέπε θεοῦ σοφίαν· ἐτήρη-
σεν καὶ τῇ ἀποφάσει τὴν ἀλήθειαν, καὶ τῇ φιλανθρωπίᾳ τὴν
ἐνέργειαν κ.τ.λ. *Eus.* Dem. Ev. x. 1. *Cyr. Alex.* De Recta
Fide ad Regin. (Opp. t. v. pt. ii. p. 132); in Ev. Joh. (Opp.
t. iv. p. 114). [Comp. *Hilary* in Ps. liii. 12: Passio suscepta
voluntarie est, officio ipsa satisfactura poenali; *Ambrose,* De
Fuga Sec. c. 7: (Christus) suscepit mortem ut impleretur
sententia, satisfieret indicato per maledictum carnis peccatricis
usque ad mortem. *Gesler,* Dg. 383, finds the basis of the
later satisfaction theory in *Athanasius, Cyril* of Jerusalem, and,
though less fully drawn out, in *Eusebius* of Caesarea, *Gregory*
of Nazianzus, *Cyril* of Alex., and *Chrysostom.* The points are:
God threatened death to man as a penalty for disobedience.
This threat could not be unfulfilled, if God be true. But, on
the other hand, God's love to man forbade the destruction of
all men. And so He adopted the expedient of allowing Jesus to
die instead of man, so that both His truth and His love might
be inviolate. *Thomasius,* Christi Person, iii. s. 191 ff., gives
a full view of the theory of *Athanasius,* as the most important
in the patristic literature—summed up (De Inc. Verbi, 13):
"The Logos assumed a mortal body, in order thus to fulfil the
law for us, to offer the vicarious sacrifice, to destroy death,
to give immortality, and so to restore the divine image in

humanity." His death was "the death of all," "the death of humanity," etc.]

(5) *Cyr. Hier.* l.c.: Οὐ τοσοῦτον ἡμάρτομεν, ὅσον ἐδικαιοπράγησεν ὁ τὴν ψυχὴν ὑπὲρ ἡμῶν τεθεικώς. *Chrys.* in Ep. ad Rom. Hom. x. 17: "Ὥσπερ εἴ τις ὀβολοὺς δέκα ὀφείλοντά τινα εἰς δεσμωτήριον ἐμβάλοι, οὐκ αὐτὸν δὲ μόνον, ἀλλὰ καὶ γυναῖκα καὶ παιδία, καὶ οἰκέτας δι' αὐτόν· ἐλθὼν δὲ ἕτερος μὴ τοὺς δέκα ὀβολοὺς καταβάλοι μόνον, ἀλλὰ μύρια χρυσοῦ τάλαντα χαρίσαιτο, καὶ εἰς βασιλικὰς εἰσαγάγοι τὸν δεσμώτην . . . οὕτω καὶ ἐφ' ἡμῶν γέγονε· πολλῷ γὰρ πλείονα ὧν ὀφείλομεν κατέβαλεν ὁ Χριστός, καὶ τοσούτῳ πλείονα, ὅσῳ πρὸς ῥανίδα μικρὰν πέλαγος ἄπειρον. On similar ideas of *Leo the Great*, as well as concerning his entire theory of redemption, see *Griesbach*, Opuscula, s. 98 ff.

(6) It is worthy of notice, that especially *Augustine*, on practical grounds, brought this ethical import of the death of Christ very prominently forward (to counterbalance, as it were, the theory of redemption so easily misunderstood): Tota itaque vita ejus disciplina morum fuit (De Vera Rel. c. 16). Christ died, that no one might be afraid of death, nor even of the most cruel manner of putting persons to death; De Fide et Symb. c. 6; De divers. Quaest. qu. 25 (Opp. t. vi. p. 7). The love of Christ displayed in His death should constrain us to love Him in return; De Catech. Rud. c. 4: Christus pro nobis mortuus est. Hoc autem ideo, quia finis praecepti et plenitudo legis charitas est, ut et nos invicem diligamus, et quemadmodum ille pro nobis animam suam posuit, sic et nos pro fratribus animam ponamus. . . . Nulla est enim major ad amorem invitatio, quam praevenire amando, et nimis durus est animus, qui dilectionem si nolebat impendere, nolit rependere. See, too, the extracts from his Sermons, in *Bindemann*, ii. s. 222. [Comp., too, Contra Faust. Manich. xiv. 1: Suscepit autem Christus sine reatu supplicium nostrum, ut inde solveret reatum nostrum et finiret supplicium nostrum. Cf. Comm. in Gal. iii. 13, cited in *Thomasius* (u. s.), iii. 211.] Comp. *Lactantius*, Inst. Div. iv. 23 ss. *Basil M.* De Spir. S. c. 15.

(7) *Athanasius* sets forth admirably this grand idea of substitution, De Incar. 9. If a great king comes to a great city, and takes up his abode in *one* of its houses, the *whole* city is thereby honoured. No enemy or robber makes any attempt

upon it; it is protected by the presence of the king in one house. So the King of kings, etc. Comp. *Voigt*, s. 152. The same thought with a different turn is found in *Gregory* of Nazianzus, Orat. xxiv. 4, p. 439 : " He has ascended the cross, and taken me with Him, to nail my sin on it, to triumph over the serpent, to sanctify the tree, to overcome lust, to lead Adam to salvation, and to restore the fallen image of God," ... Orat. xlv. 28, p. 867. " God became man, and died, that we might live: we have died with Him, to be purified; we are raised from the dead with Him, since we have died with Him; we are glorified with Him, because we have risen with Him from the grave." *Ullmann*, s. 450. Comp. Orat. xxxvi. p. 580, quoted by *Münscher*, *von Cölln*, i. s. 435, and the passages cited there from *Hilary*, De Trin. ii. 24, and *Augustine*, De Trinitate, iv. 12. *Athan.* De Incarn. c. 44. *Greg. Nyss.* Orat. Cat. c. 16, 32.

(8) Comp. in its connection the passage quoted from *Athanasius* in note 4. *Gregor. Nyss.* also says (Orat. Catech. c. 27) that not alone the death of Christ effected the redemption of man, but also the circumstance that He preserved an unspotted character in all the moments of His life: ... μολυνθείσης τῇ ἁμαρτίᾳ τῆς ἀνθρωπίνης ζωῆς (τὸν Χριστὸν) ἐν ἀρχῇ τε καὶ τελευτῇ καὶ τοῖς διὰ μέσου πᾶσιν ἔδει διὰ πάντων γενέσθαι τὴν ἐκπλύνουσαν δύναμιν, καὶ μὴ τῷ μέν τι θεραπεῦσαι τῷ καθαρσίῳ τὸ δὲ περιιδεῖν ἀθεράπευτον. And in the same way *Augustine*, De Vera Rel. c. 26, represents Christ as the second Adam, and contrasts Him as the homo justitiæ with the homo peccati; as sin and ruin are the effects of our connection with Adam, so redemption is the effect of a living union with Christ. Comp. De Libero Arbitrio, iii. 10 ; De Consensu Evang. i. c. 35, where he places the real essence of redemption in the manifestation of the God-man. In like manner, the redemption-work is summarily stated by *Gregory the Great*, Mor. xxi. 6 : Ad hoc Dominus apparuit in carne, ut humanam vitam admonendo excitaret, exemplo præbendo accenderet, moriendo redimeret, resurgendo repararet; comp. *Lau*, s. 435. Hence *Baur* says, s. 109, 110 : " *That the reconciliation of man to God, as affected by the incarnation of God in Christ, and the consciousness of the union of the divine with the human resulting from it, constitutes the higher general principle, including*

all particulars, which was adopted by the theologians of that age. . . . Thus was formed a theory of the atonement, which we may term the mystical, inasmuch as it is founded on a general comprehensive view of the subject, rather than on dialectic definitions." [*Baur*, Dogmengesch. s. 190. The chief contrast to this mystic view was found in the Arians and Apollinarians; the former putting the reconciliation in the bare proclamation of the forgiveness of sins (no real mediation between God and man), and the latter in likeness to Christ.—Both the mystic and moral views are united in *Theodore* of Mopsuestia; redemption is the completion of human nature—what in Adam is found only ideally (in idea), is in Christ perfectly realized. It consists not so much in removing sin and guilt, as in a participation in that which Christ, through His resurrection, has become for us, in the possession of immortality and an absolutely unchangeable divine life, through union with Christ. Comp. *Fritzsche*, Theod. Ep. Mops. p. 55 ss.]

(9) Thus *Gregory* of Nazianzus, Orat. xxxiii. p. 536, numbered speculations on the death of Christ among those things on which it is useful to have correct ideas, but not dangerous to be mistaken, and placed them on the same level with questions concerning the creation of the world, the nature of matter and of the soul, the resurrection, general judgment, etc. Comp. *Baur*, s. 109.—*Eusebius* of Cæsarea (Demonstr. Evang. iv. 12) merely enumerates various reasons for the death of Christ, without bringing them into connection. Christ died—1. In order to prove that He is the Lord over both the quick and the dead; 2. To redeem from sin; 3. To atone for sin; 4. To destroy the power of Satan; 5. To give His disciples a visible evidence of a future life (by His resurrection); and 6. To abrogate the sacrifices of the Old Testament dispensation.

The more anxious theologians were to adduce the reasons which led Christ to suffer, the more natural was it to ask, whether God could have accomplished the work of redemption in any other way. *Augustine* rejects such idle questions in the manner of *Irenæus*, De Agone Christi, c. 10 : Sunt autem stulti, qui dicunt : Non poterat aliter sapientia Dei homines liberare, nisi susciperet hominem, et nasceretur ex femina, et a peccatoribus omnia illa pateretur. Quibus dicimus: *poterat omnino sed si aliter faceret, similiter vestra stultitiæ displiceret.* [*Aug*. de Trin. xiii. 10. *Greg. Naz*. Orat. ix.

p. 157. *Greg. Nyss.* Orat. Cat. c. *Basil the Great* (Hom. in Ps. xlviii. § 3) maintained that the death of the God-man was *necessary* in order to the salvation of mankind.] On the other hand, *Gregory the Great* concedes that the death of Christ was not absolutely necessary, since we could have been delivered from suffering in other ways; yet God chose this way, in order at the same time to set before our eyes the highest example of love and self-sacrifice; Moral. xx. c. 36; *Lau*, s. 445. [But compare Moralia, xxii. 40.] Further particulars may be found in *Münscher*, Handbuch, iv. s. 293 ff.; *Baur*, s. 85. *Rufinus* gives a mystical interpretation of the various separate elements of the passion of Christ, Expos. Symb. ap. p. 22 ss.

Concerning *the extent of the atonement*, it may be observed that *Didymus* of Alexandria (on 1 Pet. in *Gallandii* Bibl. PP. t. iv. p. 325: Pacificavit enim Jesus per sanguinem crucis suæ quæ in cœlis et quæ in terra sunt, omne bellum destruens et tumultum) and *Gregory* of Nyssa in some degree (Orat. Catech. c. 25, where he speaks of πᾶσα κτίσις) revived the idea of Origen, that the effects of the death of Jesus were not limited to this world, but extended over the whole universe; Gregory also asserted that the work of redemption would not have been necessary if all men had been as holy as Moses, Paul, Ezekiel, Elijah, and Isaiah (Contra Apollin. iii. p. 263). [*Cyril* of Jerusalem, De Recta Fide: the injustice of the sinner was not so great as the justice of Him who gave His life for us. *Chrysost.* Ep. ad Rom. Hom. x.: Christ paid far more for us than we were indebted, as much more as the sea is more than a drop.] The opposite view was taken by *Augustine*, who, in accordance with his theory, thought that all men stood in need of redemption, but limited the extent of the atonement; comp. the former sections on the doctrine of original sin, and on predestination; and Contra Julian. vi. c. 24. *Leo the Great*, on the contrary, enlarged the extent of the atonement, Ep. 134, c. 14: Effusio sanguinis Christi pro injustis tam fuit dives ad pretium, ut, si universitas captivorum in redemptorem suum crederet, nullum diaboli vincula retinerent.—According to *Gregory the Great*, redemption extends even to heavenly beings; Moral. xxxi. c. 49. *Lau*, s. 431.

A dramatic representation of the *Descensus ad Inferos* (first found in the ecclesiastical confessions, in the third Sirmian Formula, 359), in imitation of the Evang. Nicodemi, is given in the discourse: De Adventu et Annunciatione Joannis (Baptistæ) apud inferos, commonly ascribed to *Eusebius* of Emisa; comp. also *Epiphanius* in Sepulcr. Christi (Opp. ii. p. 270); *Augusti's* edition of Euseb. of Emisa, p. 1 ss. On the question whether the system of *Apollinaris* caused the introduction of the said doctrine into the Apostles' Creed, as well as concerning the relation in which they stood to each other, see *Neander*, Kg. ii. s. 923, and particularly Dg. s. 338. [This assertion involves an anachronism. "It is certainly difficult to perceive how *Apollinaris* could give his assent to it; yet we are not justified in asserting that he did not acknowledge it, although *Athanasius* does not specially refer to it."] It is a striking remark of *Leo the Great* (Serm. lxxi. in *Perthel*, p. 153 note), that for the sake of the disciples the duration of the intermediate state was contracted as much as possible, so that His death rather resembled sleep (sopor) than death.

The statements respecting the *subjective* appropriation of the merits of Christ on the part of the individual Christian were made to conform to the above views, and to the anthropological definitions (§ 107–114). Comp. *Münscher*,

Handbuch, iv. s. 295, 319. This much is certain, that the benefits of the atonement are chiefly referred to the *consequences of original sin*, and that, consequently, they accrued in the fullest measure to the baptized. How far, now, sins committed after baptism are atoned for by the death of Jesus, or whether this satisfaction must be found somewhere else—on this there is no satisfactory answer. Comp. *Lau*, Greg. d. Grosse, s. 430, 458.

Lastly, with respect to the *whole work* of Christ, we find already the *threefold office* of *Prophet*, *High Priest*, and *King*, if not doctrinally worked out, yet indicated, and brought forward in connection with the name of the Anointed, in *Euseb.* Hist. Eccles. i. 3 (*Heinichen*, p. 30).

4. THE CHURCH AND THE SACRAMENTS.

§ 135.

The Church.

Two causes contributed to confirm the idea of the *Church*: 1. The external history of the Church itself, its victory over paganism, and its rising power under the protection of the State. 2. The victory of Augustinianism over the doctrines of the *Pelagians* (1), *Manichæans* (2), and *Donatists* (3), which in different ways threatened to destroy ecclesiastical unity. The last-mentioned puritanic and separatistic system, like that of *Novatian* in the preceding period, maintained that the Church was composed only of saints. In opposition to them, following *Optatus* of Mileve (4), *Augustine* asserted the system of catholicism, that the Church consists of the sum total of all who are baptized, and that the (ideal) sanctity of the Church was not impaired by the impure elements externally connected with it (5). The bishops of Rome then impressed upon this catholicism the stamp of the papal hierarchy, by already claiming for themselves the primacy of Peter (6). But however different the opinions of the men of those times were respecting the seat and nature of the true Church, the proposition laid down by former theologians, that *there is no salvation out of the Church*, was firmly adhered to, and carried out in all its consequences (7).

(1) The Pelagians were in so far unchurchly as, in their abstract mode of looking at things, they considered only the *individual* Christian as such, and overlooked the mysterious connection between the individual and the totality. Their strict ethical ideas led necessarily to Puritanism; hence the Synod of Diospolis (A.D. 415) blamed *Pelagius* for having said: Ecclesiam hic esse sine macula et ruga; *Augustine*, de Gestis Pelagii, c. 12. Before this time some Christians in Sicily, who, generally speaking, agreed with the Pelagians, had asserted: Ecclesiam hanc esse, quae nunc frequentatur populis et sine peccato esse posse; *August.* Ep. clvi.

(2) The Manichæans, by separating the Electi from the rest (Auditores), gave countenance to the principle of an ecclesiola in ecclesia; and, besides, the great body of the Manichæan Church itself formed, as the one elect world of light, a dualistic contrast with the vast material (hylozoist) mass of darkness. "*The Manichæan Church is in relation to the world what the limited circle of the Electi is in relation to the larger assembly of the Auditores; that which is yet variously divided and separated in the latter, has its central point of union in the former.*" *Baur*, Manich. Religionssystem, s. 282.

(3) On the external history of the Donatists, comp. the works on ecclesiastical history, and especially *F. Ribbeck*, Donatus und Augustinus, oder der erste entscheidende Kampf zwischen Separatismus und d. Kirche, Elberfeld 1858. [*A. Rour*, De August. Adversario Don. 1838. *M. Deutsch*, Drei Actenstücke zur Geschichte des Donatismus, Berlin 1875. Comp. also artic. in *Herzog*, *Wetzer*, and *Smith*.] Sources: *Optatus Milevitanus* (about the year 368), De Schismate Donatistarum, together with the Monumenta Vett. ad Donatist. Hist. pertinentia, ed. *L. E. Du Pin*, Par. 1700 ss. (Opp. Aug. t. ix.) *Valesius*, De Schism. Donat., in the Appendix to Eusebius. *Norisius* (edited by *Ballerini* brothers), Ven. 1729, 4 vols. fol. *Walch*, Ketzergeschichte, vol. iv. Concerning the derivation of the name (whether from Donatus a casis nigris, or from Donat M. ?), see *Neander*, Kg. ii. 1, s. 407. The question at issue, viz. whether Cæcilian could be invested with the episcopal office, having been ordained by a Traditor, and

the election of another bishop in the person of Majorinus, led to further doctrinal discussions on the purity of the Church. In the opinion of the Donatists, the Church ought to be *pure* (sine macula et ruga). It must therefore exclude, without exception, unworthy members (1 Cor. v., and especially passages from the Old Testament). When the opponents of the Donatists appealed to the parable of the tares and the wheat (Matt. xiii.), the latter applied it (according to our Lord's own interpretation) to the *world*, and not to the *Church*. *Augustine*, however, asserted, mundum ipsum appellatum esse pro ecclesiæ nomine.

(4) Concerning the opinions of *Optatus* (which are stated in the second book of his treatise: De Schismate Donatistarum) see *Rothe*, Anfänge der christlichen Kirche, s. 677 ff. He developed the views of *Cyprian*. The Church is one. It has five ornamenta or dotes: 1. Cathedra (the unity of episcopacy in the Cathedra Petri); 2. Angelus (the bishop himself); 3. Spiritus Sanctus; 4. Fons (baptism); 5. Sigillum, *i.e.* Symbolum catholicum (according to Sol. Song iv. 12). These dotes are distinguished from the sancta membra ac viscera of the Church, which appear to him of greater importance than the dotes themselves. They consist in the sacramenta et nomina Trinitatis.

(5) *Augustine* composed a separate treatise, entitled De Unitate Ecclesiæ, on this subject. — Comp. contra Ep. Parmeniani, and De Baptismo. He, no less than the Donatists, proceeded on the principle of the purity of the Church, and advocated a rigorous exercise of ecclesiastical discipline; but this should not lead to the depopulation of the Church. Some elements enter into the composition of the house of God which do not form the structure of the house itself; some members of the body may be diseased without its being thought necessary to cut them off at once, though the disease itself belongs no more to the body than the chaff which is mixed up with wheat forms a part of it. *Augustine* makes a distinction between the corpus Domini verum and the corpus Domini permixtum seu simulatum (de Doctr. Christ. iii. 32), which stands in connection with his negative view concerning the nature of evil. Multi sunt in sacramentorum communione cum ecclesia et tamen jam non sunt *in* ecclesia (De Unit.

Eccles. 74).[1] Comp. *Schmidt*, Augustins Lehre von der Kirche (Jahrbuch für deutsche Theol. 1861).

The grammarian *Tichonius* adopted an intermediate view, viz. that there is a corpus Domini bipartitum, one part of which consists of real, the other of seeming Christians; see *Neander*, l.c. ii. s. 445. The necessity of being externally connected with the Church is set forth by *Augustine* in the same manner as by *Tertullian* and *Cyprian;* De Unit. Eccles. c. 49: Habere caput Christum nemo poterit, nisi qui in ejus corpore fuerit, quod est ecclesia. Ep. xli. § 5: Quisquis ab hac catholica ecclesia fuerit separatus, quantumlibet laudabiliter se vivere existimet, hoc solo scelere, quod a Christi unitate disjunctus est, non habebit vitam sed Dei ira manebit super eum. So, too, *Gregory the Great;* see *Lau*, s. 470.

[" Any other than the empirically existing Church *Augustine* could not conceive, despite the concessions he was obliged to make. *Jovinian*, on the other hand, lived in the abstract idea of the internal supersensible Church, to which we belong only through the baptism of the Spirit;" *Baur*, Dogmengesch. s. 196. *Neander* says that the distinction between the *visible* and the *invisible* Church might have led to an agreement between Augustine and the Donatists. Augustine endeavoured to establish the distinction, but he was afraid to follow out the idea to the full extent, and his notions became obscure. He spoke of those (De Bapt. iv. 1–4) who are in the house of God per communionem sacramentorum, and those who are outside of the house—per perversitatem morum. And De Unit. Eccles. 74: Multi sunt in sacramentorum communione cum ecclesia, et tamen jam non sunt in ecclesia. Further, "those who appear to be in the Church, and contradict Christ, and therefore do not belong to that Church which is called the body of Christ." — In *Jovinian* (Cf. *Hieron.* contra Jovinian. *B. Lindner*, De Joviniano et Vigilantio, etc.) a Protestant element is discernible. " In this spirit he carried on a warfare against hypocrisy, the quantitative scale of morals, the *consilia evangelica;* he laid the utmost stress on the prin-

---

[1] In both the miraculous draughts of fishes, the one *before*, and the other *after* the resurrection of Christ (Luke v. and John xxi.), *Augustine* finds types of the Church here and hereafter; Sermo 248–252 (Opera, tom. v.). Comp. *Bindemann*, ii. 187 ff.

ciple of a living faith, and the unity of the principle of Christian life." ... " The Church, he says, is founded on Faith, Hope, and Love; ... in this Church there is nothing impure; every one is taught of God; no one can break into it by violence, or steal into it by artifice." "As Jovinian taught the Pauline doctrine of faith, so he did the Pauline idea of the invisible Church; while Augustine obstructed the development of his similar fundamental idea by a mixture with the catholic idea of the Church."]

(6) *Leo M.* Sermo I. in Natale Apostolorum Petri et Pauli: Ut inenarrabilis gratiæ per totum mundum diffunderetur effectus, Romanum regnum divina providentia præparavit, etc. Comp. Sermo II. (al. iv. 3): Transivit quidem in Apostolos alios vis illius potestatis, sed non frustra uni commendatur, quod omnibus intimetur. Petro enim singulariter hoc creditur, quia cunctis ecclesiæ rectoribus proponitur. Manet ergo Petri privilegium, ubicunque ex ipsius fertur æquitate judicium; nec nimia est vel severitas vel remissio, ubi nihil erit legatum, nihil solutum, nisi quod Petrus aut ligaverit, aut solverit. Comp. *Perthel*, l.c. s. 237, Anm. 4, and the passages quoted by him.

(7) Comp. § 71. *Lactantius* makes the same assertion, though he is not in all respects churchly; Instit. Div. iii. 30; iv. 14, ab init.: Hæc est domus fidelis, hoc immortale templum, in quo si quis non sacrificaverit, immortalitatis præmium non habebit. Of *Jerome*, the faithful son of the Church, nothing else could be expected than subjection to it. Special proof of this is hardly needed; his whole theology bears witness to this sentiment. But see *Zöckler*, s. 437 ff. *Rufinus*, on the other hand, whom *Jerome* regards as a heretic, does not yet demand fides *in* Ecclesiam, and thus most clearly distinguishes faith in the Church from faith in God and Christ, Expos. Fid. 26, 27. *Gregory the Great* regards the Church as the robe of Christ, as individual souls are also the robe of the Church, Moral. xx. c. 9. It is the civitas Domini, quæ regnatura in cœlo adhuc laborat in terra, Ezech. lib. ii. Hom. 1; comp. *Lau*, s. 468 ff. Heretics were said to be beyond the pale of the *Church*, but not beyond that of *Christianity;* they were accused of defective faith (*kakopistia*), and not of all want of faith (*apistia*). *Augustine* calls them quoquomodo

Christiani, De Civ. Dei, xviii. c. 51. Comp. *Marheineke* in Daub's Studien, l.c. s. 186.—*Jerome*, with greater warmth, designates the congregations of heretics as synagogues of Satan (Ep. 123); their communion is to be avoided, like that of vipers and scorpions (Ep. 130). He testifies of himself (Prolog. Dial. adv. Pelagium): Hæreticis nunquam peperci, et omni studio egi, ut hostes ecclesiæ mei quoque hostes fierent; hence his motto in reference to the persecution of heretics: Non est crudelitas pro Deo pietas.[1]

§ 136.

The Sacraments.

G. L. Hahn, Die Lehre von den Sacramenten in ihrer geschichtlichen Entwicklung innerhalb der abendländischen Kirche bis zum Concil von Trident, Berlin 1864.

The idea of the *Holy Sacraments* was more precisely defined and distinguished in this period; they are the organs by which the Church works upon the individual Christian, and transmits the fulness of divine life, which dwells within it, to its members. *Augustine* saw in them the mysterious union of the (transcendent) Word with the external (visible) element (1), but expressed no definite opinion respecting the number of sacraments (2). *Pseudo-Dionysius* (in the fifth century) already spoke of six ecclesiastical mysteries (3); but even during the present period the chief importance was attached to *Baptism* and the *Lord's Supper* (4).

(1) *Augustine*, Serm. 272 (Opp. t. v. 770): Dicuntur *Sacramenta*, quia in eis aliud videtur, aliud intelligitur. Quod videtur, speciem habet corporalem: quod intelligitur fructum habet spiritalem. This gave rise to the definition of the Augustinian school (in Ev. Joh. Tract. 31, c. 15, and De Cataclysmo): *Accedit verbum ad elementum et fit sacramentum*. Grace works through the sacraments, but is not necessarily

---

[1] *Zöckler*, however (in opposition to Gieseler), attempts to show that by such expressions Jerome intended *spiritual* weapons, not bloody persecutions (s. 438).

confined to them (cf. in Levit. lib. iii. quæstio 84). [Quomodo et Moses sanctificat et Dominus ? Non enim Moses pro Domino, sed Moses visibilibus sacramentis per ministerium suum ; Dominus autem invisibili gratia per spiritum sanctum, ubi est totus fructus etiam visibilium sacramentorum.—De Catechiz. Rudibus, 50 : Sacramenta signacula quidem rerum divinarum esse visibilia, sed res ipsas invisibiles in eis honorari.—*Neander* says, that according to *Augustine*, "there was only one Justificatio, which was foreshadowed in the Old Testament. Sensible signs are necessary in a religious community; but yet these can have no effect on the spirit : they cannot impart holiness and *justification*, but merely serve as the signs and vehicles of divine grace, which is the only source of *justification*." *Baur*, Dg. s. 193, says of *Augustine*, that he put the essence of the sacrament in the distinction of a twofold element, a sensible and a supersensible, related as are the sign and the thing signified ; and that which mediates between them is the word. The rationalizing tendency of the Arians showed its antagonism to the prevailing views in the position of *Eunomius*, that the real essential mystery of piety is not found in mystic symbols, but in precise doctrines ; in *Grry. Nyss.* c. Eunomium, 11 vols. ed. Paris 1638, t. ii. p. 704.]

(2) *Augustine* reckoned not only matrimony ("sacramentum nuptiarum," De Nupt. et Concupiscentia, i. 11) and holy orders ("sacramentum dandi baptismum," De Baptism. ad Donatist. i. 2, and Contra Ep. Parmen. ii. 30), but also occasionally other sacred ceremonies, among the sacraments (at least in a wider sense), so far as he understood by sacramentum, omne mysticum sacrumque signum. Thus he applies (De Peccat. Orig. c. 40) the term sacrament to exorcism, the casting out, and the renunciation of the devil at baptism ; and even to the rites of the Old Testament : circumcisio carnis, sabbatum temporale, neomeniæ, sacrificia atque omnes hujusmodi innumeræ observationes ; Expos. Epist. ad Galat. c. iii. 19 (Opp. iii. pt. ii. p. 692). Comp. *Wiggers*, Augustin und Pel. vol. i. s. 9, Anm. That he so constantly adopted the number four, may perhaps be explained from the general preference which he gave to Aristotelianism (c. Ep. Parm. ii. c. 13). *Neander*, Kg. ii. 3, s. 1382 f. *Leo the Great* also employed the term sacramentum in reference to the most

heterogeneous things, comp. *Perthel*, s. 219, Anm.; and *Gregory the Great* used it sometimes in a more comprehensive, sometimes in a more limited sense, comp. *Lau*, s. 480.[1]

(3) De Hier. Eccles. c. 2–7. 1. *Baptism* (μ. φωτίσματος); 2. *The Lord's Supper* (μ. συνάξεως, εἴτ᾽ οὖν κοινωνίας); 3. *Unction (confirmation?* μ. τελετῆς μύρου); 4. *Holy Orders* (μ. τῶν ἱερατικῶν τελειώσεων); 5. *Monachism* (μ. μοναχικῆς τελειώσεως), which afterwards ceased to be reckoned among the sacraments; 6. *The rites performed on the dead* (μ. ἐπὶ τῶν ἱερῶς κεκοιμημένων)—they were not the same with the unctio extrema, as the unction in question was not applied to dying persons, but to the corpse; yet there was some analogy between the one and the other.—Matrimony, on the other hand, which *Augustine* mentioned, is wanting in this list.

(4) This was done, *e.g.*, by *Augustine*, Sermo 218, 14: Quod latus, lancea percussum, in terram sanguinem et aquam manavit, procul dubio sacramenta sunt, quibus formatur ecclesia (De Symb. ad Catech. c. 6); and by *Chrysostom* in Joh. Hom. 85 (Opp. t. viii. p. 545), who attributed the same import to the same occurrence.—On the relation of the sacraments of the New Testament to those of the Old, see *Augustine*, De Vera Rel. c. 17.

§ 137.

Baptism.

The notions developed in the preceding period concerning the high importance and efficacy of baptism were more fully

---

[1] As the laying on of hands and anointing were early connected with baptism, it was very natural that these usages should be separated from the act of baptism, and be recognized themselves as sacramental acts. And so we find the Roman bishop *Melchiades* († 314), in his letter to the Spanish bishops (Decret. Gratiani, pt. iii. de consecratione dist. v. c. 2 and 3), characterizes the laying on of hands as a sacrament, through which the Holy Ghost imparted by baptism is given anew, and in a higher measure. (Sacrament of Confirmation.) In some parts of the Church (North African, Gallican, North Italian of Milan) the *washing of feet* was regarded as sacramental. Comp. *Hahn*, l.c. s. 89, and the passage there adduced from *Ambrose*, De Sacramentis, lib. iii.

carried out in the present, in a rhetorical way, by *Basil the Great*, *Gregory* of Nazianzus, and *Gregory* of Nyssa (1), and defined with more dogmatic precision by *Augustine* (2). Neither the baptism of blood nor that of tears lost its significance (3). The theologians of the Greek Church zealously defended infant baptism (4), while *Augustine* brought it into more intimate connection with the doctrine of original sin (in opposition to the Pelagians), and adduced it as an additional proof of that doctrine (5). Salvation was denied to unbaptized children (6). On the subject of the baptism of heretics, *Basil the Great* and *Gregory* of Nazianzus followed the views of *Cyprian*; though *Gregory* did not make the validity of baptism depend on the worthiness of the person who performs the ceremony (7). But by the influence of *Augustine*, the mode adopted by the Roman Church became, with certain modifications, the prevalent one (8). The Donatists continued to insist upon the necessity of rebaptizing heretics (9). The baptism of the Manichæans consisted in a kind of lustration altogether different from the baptism of the Catholic Church (10). Among the strict Arians, the Eunomians were distinguished from the orthodox Church by baptizing not into the name of the Trinity, but into the death of Christ (11).

(1) All three composed separate discourses on baptism. *Basil*, De Baptismo (Opp. t. ii. p. 117); *Greg. Naz.* Or. 40; *Greg. Nyss.* De Bapt. Christi (Opp. t. iii. p. 371). *Gregory* of Nazianzus gives a number of different names to Christian baptism, which he carefully distinguished from the baptisms of Moses and John: τὸ φώτισμα λαμπρότης ἐστὶ ψυχῶν, βίου μετάθεσις, ἐπερώτημα τῆς εἰς θεὸν συνειδήσεως (1 Pet. iii. 21). τὸ φώτισμα βοήθεια τῆς ἀσθενείας τῆς ἡμετέρας· τὸ φώτισμα σαρκὸς ἀπόθεσις, πνεύματος ἀκολούθησις, λόγου κοινωνία, πλάσματος ἐπανόρθωσις, κατακλυσμὸς ἁμαρτίας, φωτὸς μετουσία, σκότων κατάλυσις· τὸ φώτισμα ὄχημα πρὸς θεόν, συνεκδημία Χριστοῦ, ἔρεισμα πίστεως, νοῦ τελείωσις, κλεὶς οὐρανῶν βασιλείας, ζωῆς ἄμειψις, δουλείας ἀναίρεσις, δεσμῶν

ἔκλυσις, συνθέσεως μεταποίησις· τὸ φώτισμα, τί δεῖ πλείω καταριθμεῖν; τῶν τοῦ θεοῦ δώρων τὸ κάλλιστον καὶ μεγαλοπρεπέστατον, ὥσπερ ἅγια ἁγίων καλεῖται τινα ... οὕτω καὶ αὐτὸ παντὸς ἄλλων τῶν παρ' ἡμῖν φωτισμῶν ὃν ἁγιώτερον· καλεῖται δὲ ὥσπερ Χριστός, ὁ τούτου δοτὴρ, πολλοῖς καὶ διαφόροις ὀνόμασιν, οὕτω δὲ καὶ τὸ δώρημα κ.τ.λ. He also repeated the appellations formerly used, such as λοῦτρον, σφραγίς, etc. " *The following is the principal thought on which this abundance of names is founded: all the blessings of Christianity appear, as it were, concentrated in one point in baptism, and are dispensed all together in one moment; but all these names can only in so far be applied to baptism, as the person to be baptized possesses the right disposition, without which none can enter into the kingdom of heaven, founded by Christ.*" Ullmann, s. 461, where the other passages bearing on this subject are given. In order to prove the necessity of baptism, *Gregory* further speaks of a *threefold birth* of man (Or. 40, 2, ab init.), viz. natural birth (τὴν ἐκ σωμάτων), that through baptism, and that through the resurrection. The first of these is of the night, is slavish, and connected with lusts (νυκτερινή τέ ἐστι καὶ δούλη καὶ ἐμπαθής); the second is as clear as daylight, and free, delivers from lusts, and elevates to a higher spiritual life (ἡ δὲ ἡμερινὴ καὶ ἐλευθέρα καὶ λυτικὴ παθῶν, πᾶν τὸ αὐτὸ γενέσεως κάλυμμα περιτέμνουσα, καὶ πρὸς τὴν ἄνω ζωὴν ἐπανάγουσα).—On *Basil the Great,* comp. *Klose,* s. 67 ff.; on *Greg. Nyss.,* see *Rupp,* s. 232 ff. Comp. also *Cyril. Hier.* Cat. xvii. c. 37, where he ascribes to baptism not only (negatively) the power of pardoning sin, but also (positively) that of a miraculous elevation of the powers of life; Cat. iii. 3, xix. xx. Yet, how little mere water availed in his view, see Catech. iii. 4; *Cyril. Alex.* Comm. in Joh. (Opp. t. iv. p. 147). [*Münscher, von Cölln,* i. s. 462, 463.]

(2) *Augustine,* Ep. 98, 2 : Aqua exhibens forinsecus *sacramentum gratiæ* et spiritus operans intrinsecus *beneficium gratiæ,* solvens vinculum culpæ, reconcilians bonum naturæ, regenerans hominem in uno Christo, ex uno Adam generatum. Concupiscence remains even in those who are baptized, though their guilt is pardoned; De Nupt. et Concup. i. 28 (c. 25) [Enchir. ad Laur. 43 and 64].—No unbaptized person can obtain salvation. As for the thief who was admitted by

Christ into Paradise without baptism, *Augustine* supposed that he was baptized with blood instead of water; or he might have been baptized with the water which flowed from the side of Jesus (?), unless it were assumed that he had received baptism at some former time; De Anima et ejus Origine, i. 11 (c. 9), ii. 14 (c. 10), 16 (c. 12). According to *Leo the Great*, the baptismal water which is filled with the Holy Ghost is, in relation to the regenerate man, what the womb of the Virgin filled with the same Spirit was in relation to the sinless Redeemer, to whom she gave birth, Sermo 24. 3; 25. 5 (in *Griesbach*, p. 153). Comp. *Perthel*, s. 213 ff.

(3) Thus *Gregory* of Nazianzus adds a fourth baptism to the three already mentioned (viz. the baptisms of Moses, John, and Christ), that of martyrdom and of blood with which Christ Himself was baptized; this baptism surpasses the others, since it is so much less stained with sin. Yea (he adds), I know even a *fifth*, viz. that of tears (τὸ τῶν δακρύων), but it is still more difficult, because it is necessary to wet one's couch every night with tears; Orat. xxxix. 17, p. 688. But ... "how many tears have we to shed before they equal the flood of the baptismal bath?" Orat. lx. 9, p. 696. *Ullmann*, s. 459, 465, 480.

(4) *Gregory* of Nazianzus (Orat. lx.) opposed the delay of baptism, which had its ground partly in deference to the sacrament, partly in perverse and immoral tendencies, partly in absurd prejudices.[1] Comp. *Ullmann*, s. 466 ff. Concerning the baptism of infants, he declared (*Ullm.* s. 713) "that it was better that they should be sanctified without their own consciousness, than that they should depart being neither sealed nor consecrated" (ἢ ἀπελθεῖν ἀσφράγιστα καὶ ἀτέλεστα). In support of his view he appeals to the rite of circumcision, which was a type of baptism, and performed on the eighth day (comp. the opinion of Fidus, § 72, note 6); also to the striking of the blood on the door-posts, etc. *Gregory*, nevertheless, thought that healthy children might

---

[1] Comp. e.g. the Confessions of *Augustine*, i. c. 11. *Greg. Nyss.* also opposed the delay in a separate discourse, πρὸς τοὺς βραδύνοντας εἰς τὸ βάπτισμα (Opp. t. ii. p. 215); *Chrysostom* uses similar language. Comp. *Neander*, Chrysostomus, i. s. 6, and 74–77. *A. F. Büsching*, De Procrastinatione Baptismi apud Veteres ejusque Causis, Halæ 1747, 4to.

wait till the third year, or somewhere thereabout, because they would be able then to hear and to utter something of the words (μυστικόν τι) used at the performance of the rite, though they might not perfectly understand them, but have only a general impression respecting them (τυπούμενα). His judgment, however, was mild concerning those children who die before baptism, because he well distinguished between intentional and unintentional delay. Yet he did not grant that they would obtain perfect salvation. Comp. *Ullmann*, l.c.

(5) That *Gregory* did not, like Augustine, make an intimate connection between baptism and original sin, is evident from his assertion (Orat. 40, quoted by *Ullmann*, s. 476), that sins committed by children from ignorance could not be imputed to them on account of their tender age. Comp. what *Chrysostom* said on this subject, according to the quotation of *Julian* given by *Neander*, Kg. ii. 3, s. 1385: Hac de causa etiam infantes baptizamus, cum non sint coinquinati peccato, ut eis addatur sanctitas, justitia, adoptio, hæreditas, fraternitas Christi, ut ejus membra sint; the opinions of *Theodore* of Mopsuestia are also stated there.[1] *Augustine* did not combat the Pelagians because they rejected the baptism of infants, but because they did not draw the same inferences from the rite in question which he drew from it (non ideo baptizari parvulos, ut remissionem accipiant peccatorum, sed ut sanctificentur in Christo, De Pecc. et Remiss. iii. 6). The Pelagians admitted that the design of baptism was the remissio peccatorum, but they understood by it the remission of future sins. *Julian* went so far as to anathematize those who did not acknowledge the necessity of infant baptism; Opus. imp. Contra Jul. iii. 149. "*Though the Pelagians might have been easily induced by their principles to ascribe a merely symbolical significance to baptism as an external rite, yet in this, as well as in many other respects, they could not develope their system in*

---

[1] *Neander* traces the difference of opinion existing between the Eastern and Western Church with regard to baptism to their different mode of viewing the doctrine of redemption; the former regarded rather the positive, the latter the negative aspect. [The positive aspect is the ennobling of human nature; the negative the relation to sin. "Accordingly, in the East, baptism was regarded chiefly as indicating exaltation to a higher stage, for which the original powers of man were not sufficient." *Gregory* of Nazianzus says: "It is a more divine creation, something higher than the original endowments of nature."]

entire independence of the ecclesiastical tradition of their age; they endeavoured, therefore, to reconcile it in the best possible manner with their principles, which owed their origin to quite different causes," *Neander*, Kg. ii. s. 1389. [" Baptism received a higher dogmatic importance from the Augustinian doctrine of original sin. The assertion of its necessity is one of the points of difference between *Augustine* and *Pelagius.*" *Baur*, u. s., s. 193.]

(6) Concerning infants that die without being baptized, *Pelagius* expressed himself in cautious terms (quo non eant, scio, quo eant, nescio). [*Pelagius*, that he might not be compelled to say that unbaptized children were lost, made a distinction between eternal life and the kingdom of heaven, or blessedness in general and the blessedness of Christians (*Aug.* De Pecc. Orig. c. 21; De Pecc. Mer. 1, 18). The Pelagians could not recognize in the case of children a baptism for the forgiveness of sins; they could only refer it to sanctification in Christ (*August.* c. duas Ep. Pelagii). Comp. *Baur*, l.c.] *Ambrose*, De Abrah. ii. 11, had previously taught: Nemo ascendit in regnum cœlorum, nisi per sacramentum baptismatis. . . . Nisi enim quis renatus fuerit ex aqua et spiritu sancto, non potest introire in regnum Dei. Utique nullum excipit, non infantem, non aliqua præventum necessitate. Habeant tamen illam opertam pœnarum immunitatem, nescio an habeant regni honorem. Comp. *Wiggers*, i. s. 422. *Augustine's* views on this point were at first milder, De libero Arb. iii. c. 23; but afterwards he was compelled, by the logical consequences of his own system, to use harsher expressions. His line of argument is as follows: Every man is born in sin, and stands, therefore, in need of pardon. He obtains this by baptism; it cleanses children from *original sin*, and those who are baptized in later years, not only from original sin, but also from their actual transgressions before baptism. (Enchir. ad Laurent. 43.) Since baptism is the only and necessary condition of salvation (comp. note 2), it follows that unbaptized children are condemned (this fully accorded with his views on predestination). He was, nevertheless, disposed to look upon this condemnation as *mitissima* and *tolerabilior* (Ep. 186, 27 [c. 8]; De Pecc. Mer. i. 28 [c. 20]), though he opposed the doctrine condemned by the

Synod of Carthage, in Canon ii. (A.D. 419), of an intermediate state, in which unbaptized infants were said to be; comp. Sermo 249: Hoc novum in ecclesia, prius inauditum est, esse salutem æternam præter regnum cœlorum, esse salutem æternam præter regnum Dei. With regard to *baptized* children, Augustine, as well as the Catholic Church in general, supposed (the former in accordance with his idealistic doctrine of the Church) that the Church represents (by means of the godfathers and godmothers) the faith of the children. Ep. 98, ad Bonifacium, c. 10: Parvulum, etsi nondum fides illa, quæ in credentium voluntate consistit, jam tamen ipsius fidei sacramentum fidelem facit. Nam sicut credere respondetur, ita etiam fidelis vocatur, non rem ipsa mente annuendo, sed ipsius rei sacramentum percipiendo. . . . Parvulus, etiamsi fidem nondum habeat in cogitatione, non ei tamen obicem contrariæ cogitationis opponit, unde sacramentum ejus salubriter percipit. Consequently, a passive faith? "*His view seems to have been somewhat as follows: As the child is nourished by the natural powers of his mother after the flesh, before his bodily, independent existence is fully developed, so is he nourished by the higher powers of his spiritual mother, the Church, before he has attained to independent spiritual development and self-consciousness. This idea would be true to a certain extent, if the visible Church corresponded to its ideal,*" Neander, Kg. ii. s. 1394.

(7) According to *Athanasius* (Contra Ar. 2, 42), the baptizer as well as the subject of baptism must possess the true faith, in order to the validity of baptism. Because baptism is administered in the name of the Holy Trinity, so baptism must be void when administered by one who takes away anything from the Trinity, and baptizes only in the name of the Father or of the Son. In a like sense, *Basil*, Ep. Can. 1, declared the baptism of heretics void, at least when the baptismal formula differed from that of the Catholic Church, or even when a different meaning was attached to it; thus he rejected the baptism of the Montanists, because they understood Montanus to be the Paraclete. But he was disposed to admit schismatics without baptism, and as a general rule (milder than Cyprian) advised compliance with the custom of each particular Church.—*Gregory* of Nazianzus

rejected the baptism of *notorious* heretics (τῶν προδήλως κατεγνωσμένων). Generally speaking, he did not make the efficacy of baptism depend on the external ecclesiastical, nor on the inherent moral worth (ἀξιοπιστία) of the person who administered the baptism.—He illustrated this by the case of two rings, the one made of gold, the other of brass, bearing the same royal stamp; Orat. 40, in *Ullmann*, s. 473–475.

(8) De Baptismo Contra Donatistas, lib. vii. (in Opp. Ben. tom. ix.). It is interesting to see how *Augustine* seeks to justify *Cyprian*, from whom he differs; the passages are given in *Münscher, von Cölln*, s. 477.—The limitation spoken of was, that the rite of baptism, if performed out of the Catholic Church, might be considered valid, but that so far from proving a blessing to the baptized, it would increase their guilt if they did not afterwards join the Catholic Church. Thus "*the exclusiveness of the Catholic Church, objected to on the one side, was carried to its extreme length on the other,*" *Rothe*, Anfänge der christlichen Kirche, s. 685.—The ceremony of the laying on of hands, as a sign of consecration, was also employed in the case of those who came over to the Church. *Leo the Great* insisted upon this point, Ep. 159, 7; 166, 2; 167, 18 (*Griesbach*, p. 155).

(9) Thus the Donatist, *Petilianus*, maintained that whoever received baptism from an unbeliever, did not receive faith, but guilt. *Augustine* argued against him (Contra Epistol. Parmeniani; see *Neander*, Dg. s. 419). The Donatist doctrine was condemned by the Conc. Arel. 314, Can. 8. *Optatus Mil.* De Schism. Donat. v. c. 3: ... Quid vobis (Donatistis) visum est, non post nos, sed post Trinitatem baptisma geminare? Cujus de sacramento non leve certamen innatum est, et dubitatur, an post Trinitatem in eadem Trinitate hoc iterum liceat facere. Vos dicitis: Licet; nos dicimus: Non licet. Inter Licet vestrum et Non licet nostrum natant et remigant animae populorum.

(10) Concerning the baptism of the Manichæans, on which we have but "*scanty information,*" comp. *Baur*, Manich. Religionssystem, s. 273.

(11) *Socrat.* v. 24, blamed the Eunomians, because ... τὸ βάπτισμα παρεχάραξαν· οὐ γὰρ εἰς τριάδα, ἀλλ' εἰς τὸν τοῦ Χριστοῦ βαπτίζουσι θάνατον. They probably avoided the

use of the common formula, which Eunomius elsewhere adduces as a proof that the Spirit is the third, in order to avoid a possible misunderstanding, in the orthodox sense, among the unlearned. Comp. *Klose*, Eunomius, s. 32. *Rudelbach*, über die Sacramentsworte, s. 25. According to *Sozom.* vi. 26, the Eunomians are said to have rebaptized all who joined their party. *Eunomius* (on anti-Trinitarian grounds) was opposed to the trine immersion in baptism (see *Höfling*, Die Taufe, i. s. 55).

§ 138.

The Lord's Supper.

Marheineke (comp. § 73), p. 32–65. *K. Meyer*, s. 18–38. *Ebrard* (§ 73), s. 278 ff. *Kahnis*, ubi supra. *Rückert*, 350 ff., 403 ff. [*Cardinal Wiseman* attempts (Essays, vol. iii.) to show that Amphilochius, Bishop of Iconium, in the fourth century, taught a real change (on the basis of new accounts of the Constantinople Council of 1166). Syriac Ch. on the Eucharist, by *Prof. Lamy*, of Louvain; see Journal of Sacred Lit., Jan. 1860, p. 374 ff. Philip *Freeman*, Principles of Divine Service, 2 parts, Lond. 1855–1857. Christian Remembrancer, Oct. 1853. *Engelhardt* in Zeitschrift f. d. Luth. theol. 1842. *D. Rock*, Hierurgia; Transubst. and Mass Expounded from Inscriptions in the Catacombs, etc., 2d ed. 1855. *J. Kreusser*, d. heilige Messopfer., Paderborn 1854. *Julius Müller*, Abendmahl, in *Herzog.*] *Steitz* (Jahrbücher f. deutsche Theol. x. 3).

Corresponding to the mysterious union of the two natures of Christ in one and the same person, was the idea of a mystical connection subsisting between the body of Christ and the bread in the Lord's Supper, and between His blood and the wine (1). This idea, which had taken its rise in the preceding period, was now farther carried out by means of the more fully developed terminology of the Church, and by the introduction of liturgical formulas, which substituted mystical ceremonies for the simple apostolical rite (2). The mysterious and often bombastic rhetoric of the Fathers, especially *Gregory* of Nyssa, the two *Cyrils*, and *Chrysostom*, in the Greek Church, and *Hilary* and *Ambrose* in the Latin, makes it exceedingly difficult to decide what dogmatic notions are to be attached to their expressions. By their changing imagery we are sometimes led to think of an ideal, sometimes of a substantial change; now of a subjective change on the part of the recipient, and again of an objective change in the thing received; sometimes it is a wonderful conjunction of the bread and the body of Christ (consubstantiation); sometimes a total change of the elements of the Lord's Supper into this body (transubstantiation, real transformation) (3). Yet still the symbolic view appears, alongside of the metabolic, in some teachers of the Greek Church, as in *Eusebius* of Cæsarea, *Athanasius, Gregory Nazianzen*, and *Theodoret* (4). But it is most unambiguous in the western theologian *Augustine* (5). Although the latter appears to have faith in the wonderful healing virtues of the sacrament (6), yet he decidedly opposed the superstitious reverence of it (7). *Gelasius*, Bishop of Rome, still spoke decidedly against a formal transubstantiation (8). On the other hand, there appears so early as the fifth century, in Bishop *Marutas* of Tagrit, a decided and conscious departure from the symbolical view, in favour of the realistic (9). In respect to the idea of *sacrifice* as connected with it, this was further developed in this period, especially by *Gregory the Great*, in the form that the sacrificial death of Christ was truly repeated in the daily sacrifice of the mass (10).

(1) Comp. *Gieseler*, Dogmengesch. s. 408. The idea which lies at the basis of most of the statements respecting the Lord's Supper may be said to be this—that as the Logos was once united with the flesh, so in the Supper He is now united with the bread and wine; and thus the controversy about the natures of Christ is in some degree repeated in the sacramental sphere. [*Gieseler*, Dogmengesch. 408 ff., argues that the Fathers, with all their strong expressions, could not have meant to teach transubstantiation, for the following chief reasons:—(1) That the change is so often compared with that of water in baptism, and of chrism in consecration. (2) That it is likened to the union of the Logos with the flesh—where there was no transformation of the flesh. (3) The Church

Fathers (many of them) argue against the Monophysites, on the ground that as there was in the Lord's Supper no change, so none in the incarnation. (4) They frequently call the elements τύπος, ἀντίτυπα, figura, signum, etc. *Baur*, Dogmengesch. s. 194, says that the majority of the Fathers of this period often speak of the bread and wine as the body and blood of Christ, in such terms as seem to involve the doctrine of a real change; but yet, comparing these with their other statements, and seeing how fluctuating is the form of their conceptions, we can really find in them only an obscure and exaggerated identification of figure and fact.—*Neander* gives the different modifications of opinions thus:—(1) The sensuous realistic view of *Justin* and *Irenœus*, adopted by *Cyril* of Jerusalem, *Chrysostom*, and *Hilary*, teaching an actual interpenetration of the bread and wine with the body and blood of Christ. (2) A more spiritual view, though with a realistic element at its basis, in *Augustine*. (3) The school of *Origen* (excepting *Gregory* of Nyssa) separated more distinctly the symbol and the divine reality, *e.g.* *Eusebius* of Cæsarea, *Greg. Nazianz.*, etc.]

(2) On such names as λατρεία ἀναίμακτος, θυσία τοῦ ἱλασμοῦ (*Cyril.* Myst. V.), ἱερουργία, μετάληψις τῶν ἁγιασμάτων, ἁγία (μυστικὴ) τράπεζα, μυστικὴ εὐλογία, ἐφόδιον (in reference to the administration of the Lord's Supper to the sick), as well as on the formulas commonly used in connection with the rite of consecration, comp. *Suicer*, Thesaurus, sub vocib.; *Touttée* in Diss. ad Cyr. Hier. 3, p. ccxxxiii. ss. *Marheineke*, l.c. p. 33 ss. *Augusti*, Archäologie, Bd. viii. s. 32 ff. The sacrament is frequently described as a *tremendum* (as φοβερόν, φρικτόν, φρικωδέστατον). It is also characteristic that the fourth petition in the Lord's Prayer is almost uniformly referred, in a mystical way, to the Lord's Supper.

(3) *Gregory* of Nyssa[1] draws a parallel, in a most adventurous

---

[1] The difficulty of describing and classifying the different opinions of the Fathers of this period respecting the Lord's Supper is seen in the contradictory views of the most recent writers in this matter—*Ebrard*, *Kahnis*, *Rückert*. The categories, too, proposed by the latter, viz. *symbolical* and *metabolical*, are not adequate; for the idea of μεταβολή is nowhere definitely settled, and, in the same writer, the metabolical and the symbolical views cross one another. Between the Symbolists and the Metabolists we must place the *Dynamists* (Verticalists), as the transition from the one to the other. *Steitz*, l.c.

style, between the process of physical nutrition and the subsistence of the spiritual body of the believer upon the body and blood of Christ in the Eucharist. Like the earlier Fathers, he sees in this holy food a φάρμακον ἀθανασίας, an antidote to the mortality wrought by sin; comp. Oratio Catech. 37. As by the divine Logos the bread, in the eating thereof, is transformed into the essence of the body united with divinity; so, in the Lord's Supper, the bread and the wine are transformed into the body united with the Logos (τὸ δὲ σῶμα τῇ ἐνοικήσει τοῦ θεοῦ λόγου πρὸς τὴν θεϊκὴν μετεποιήθη); compare the whole passage in *Münscher, von Cölln*, i. 499 ff. *Rupp*, 238 ff. *Rückert* (ubi supra, 403 ff.) investigates this at length, and comes to the conclusion, perhaps too unfavourable: *"Gregory shattered the Supper of the Lord; he cast away all that is glorious in its nature, and in its place left only a magical instrumentality, which, without any influence on the spiritual life, is only (?) designed to nourish the body for immortality."* That Gregory teaches no trans*ubstantiation* (in the Roman sense), but certainly a trans*formation*, see *Steitz*, l.c. s. 444. But according to Steitz this is "the great *significance of Gregory, that he was the first who developed the idea of transformation from the scientific standpoint of his time, and therewith laid the ground for the development of the later Greek doctrine of the Lord's Supper.*" On *Cyril* of Alexandria, see *Rückert*, s. 410 ff.; among other things, he infers from John vi., which he interprets of the Lord's Supper, that those who do not receive this Supper lose salvation (Comm. in Joh. iv. p. 361 A). *Cyril* of Jerusalem so connected (Cat. xxii. § 6) the miracle performed at the marriage of Cana with the μεταβολή of the elements in the Lord's Supper, that it is difficult not to suppose that he believed in a real and total change, the more so as he adds: Εἰ γὰρ καὶ ἡ αἴσθησίς σοι τοῦτο ὑποβάλλει, ἀλλὰ ἡ πίστις σε βεβαιούτω· μὴ ἀπὸ τῆς γεύσεως κρίνῃς τὸ πρᾶγμα, ἀλλ' ἀπὸ τῆς πίστεως πληροφοροῦ ἀνενδοιάστως, σώματος καὶ αἵματος Χριστοῦ καταξιωθείς; and yet he says, § 3: ἐν τύπῳ ἄρτου δίδοταί σοι τὸ αἷμα, etc. Does this mean under the *image*, or under the *form*, of the bread? "*which, however, is no longer bread, but something else*" (as *Rückert* interprets it). But as he spoke (Cat. xxi. 3) of a similar change effected in the oil which was used at the performance of the rite of consecration, without thinking of a real metaphysical change of the substance of the oil into the substance of the Holy Spirit, the interpretation remains a matter of doubt; comp. *Neander, Dg.* s. 426. Here, then, is found "*not indeed a completely developed, but yet a very decided doctrine of transformation, approaching the extreme point,*" *Rückert,* s. 420. But Cyril undoubtedly supposed a real union, spiritual and corporeal, of the communicant with Christ (σύσσωμοι καὶ σύναιμοι Χριστοῦ, χριστόφοροι γινόμεθα), and thought that we participate in the nature of Christ by the assimilation of His body and blood to our members, etc. Cat. xxiii. Comp. *Ebrard,* 278 ; *Rückert,* 415 ff., who cite the passages fully. *Steitz,* s. 417. On *Ephraem Syrus,* see *Steitz,* s. 429 ff.—*Chrysostom* regards the institution of the Lord's Supper as a proof of the highest love of the Redeemer to mankind, inasmuch as He not only gave them an opportunity of seeing Him, but also enabled them to partake of His body, Hom. 45 in Joh. (Opp. t. viii. p. 292).[1] If the wise men from the East saw their Saviour in the manger, we also see Him on the altar and in the hands of the priests (Hom. 83 in Matt.). *Chrys.* also teaches a *real* union with Christ : Ἀναφύρει ἑαυτὸν ἡμῖν, καὶ οὐ τῇ πίστει μόνον, ἀλλ᾽ αὐτῷ τῷ πράγματι σῶμα ἡμᾶς αὐτοῦ κατασκευάζει, Hom. 83 in Matt. (Opp. t. vii. 859); comp. Hom. 24 in Ep. ad Cor. (Opp. t. ix. p. 257), and other passages quoted by *Marheineke,* l.c. p. 44. Chrysostom probably did not have the notion of a descent of the body of Christ from heaven into the bread (*Rückert,* s. 424). On the other hand, he, like all other Church teachers (*e.g. Cyril* of Jerusalem, Cat. xxiii. § 15), supposed that the substance of the bread was not, like other food, again rejected from the body, but consumed, as is the wax in the burning of the light—οὕτως καὶ ὧδε νόμιζε συναναλίσκεσθαι τὰ μυστήρια τῇ τοῦ σώματος οὐσίᾳ, De Pœnit. Hom. 9 (Opera, ii. 350). Yet Chrysostom distinguishes between the spiritual (νοητόν) and the sensuous (αἰσθητόν) in the Lord's Supper. " If we were incorporeal, Christ would nourish us with incorporeal things (ἀσώματα) ; but since the soul is tied to the body, God gives us ἐν αἰσθητοῖς τὰ νοητά." Comp. the passage on Matt. before cited in *Münscher, von Cölln,*

---

[1] He speaks very strongly of a *manducatio oralis,* of an ἐμπῆξαι τοὺς ὀδόντας τῇ σαρκὶ καὶ συμπλακῆναι.

s. 502. *Ebrard*, s. 284 ff. *Steitz*, l.c.—*Hilary*, de Trin. viii. 13, says, in reference to Christ: Naturam carnis suæ ad naturam æternitatis sub sacramento nobis communicandæ carnis admiscuit, that which Irenæus calls ἕνωσις πρὸς ἀφθαρσίαν. *Ambrose* (de Initiandis Mysteriis, c. 8 and 9) regards the Lord's Supper as the living bread which came down from heaven (John vi. 51), and which is none other than Christ Himself. If blessings pronounced by men (viz. the prophets even of the Old Testament) possessed the power of changing the natural elements, how much more must the same be true in reference to the sacrament! Quodsi tantum valuit Sermo Eliæ, ut ignem de cœlo promeret, non valebit Christi sermo ut species mutet elementorum? As the rod of Moses was transformed into a serpent, and the Nile into blood, so this change comes about through the power of grace, which is mightier than the power of nature. All things are created by the Word (Christ); to effect a simple change (mutatio) cannot be too difficult for Him who is the author of creation. *The very body which was miraculously born of the Virgin, is at the same time the sacramental body.* Nevertheless he says (in contradiction to the assumption of a real change): Ante benedictionem verborum cœlestium species nominatur, post consecrationem corpus Christi *significatur*; and in reference to the wine: ante consecrationem aliud dicitur, post consecrationem *sanguis nuncupatur*. (But it ought not to be forgotten that critical doubts have been raised respecting the genuineness of this book.) Against *Ebrard*, s. 306 ff., see *Rückert*, u. s. He calls *Ambrose* "the pillar on which rests the mediæval doctrine of the Lord's Supper," s. 464.

(4) *Eusebius* of Cæsarea, Demonstr. Evangel. i. 10, and Theol. Eccl. iii. 12; *Neander*, Dg. s. 430; *Athanasius*, Ep. iv. ad Serap. (in *Neander*, s. 428); *Voigt*, s. 170. [*Neander* says of *Eusebius*, that "he was partial to such expressions as the following: Christians are admonished to celebrate the remembrance of Christ by the symbols of His body and blood" (Demonstr. Evangel. c. 40). In his interpretation of John vi. (Theol. Eccl. u. s.) he says we are not to believe that Christ spoke of His present body, or enjoined the drinking of His corporeal and sensuous blood; but the words which He spake are spirit and life, so that His words themselves are His flesh and blood.

Eusebius also connected a supernatural, sanctifying power with the outward Supper. Neander says of Athanasius that he represents a spiritual view, with a realistic element at its basis; in commenting on John vi. he says that the eating and drinking of the body and blood of Christ are not to be understood literally; Christ wished to lead His disciples to the conception of a spiritual nourishment. See his Ep. iv. ad Serapionem. *Jacobi* quotes from the Festal Letters of *Athanasius*, translated by Larsow, Letter vii.: "Bread and wine, as symbols of the nourishing divine power of the Logos. Not only here is this bread food for the righteous . . . but also in heaven we eat such food, for the Lord is also the nourishment of the higher spirits and of angels, and is the delight of the whole heavenly host."] *Gregory* of Nazianzus called the bread and wine symbols and types (ἀντίτυπα[1]) of the great mysteries, Orat xvii. 12, p. 325. (*Ullmann*, s. 484.)—Deserving of special note is a fragment of a letter addressed by *Chrysostom* to the monk *Cæsarius*, the authenticity of which is more than questionable.[2] It is here said: Sicut enim antequam sanctificetur panis, panem nominamus, divina autem illum sanctificante gratia, mediante sacerdote, liberatus est quidem ab appellatione panis, dignus autem habitus dominici corporis appellatione, etiamsi natura panis in ipso permansit, et non dua corpora, sed unum corpus filii prædicamus. Comp. *Neander*, Dg. s. 427. Chrysostom's disciple, *Nilus*, made a clear distinction between the symbol and the thing represented by it, comparing (Lib. i. ep. 44, see *Neander*, l.c.) the bread after consecration to a document which, having been confirmed by the emperor, is called a *Sacra*. *Neander*, Kg. (3 Aufl.) i. 2, s. 792, Anm. The distinction made by *Theodoret* between the sign and the thing signified was intimately connected with the similar distinction which he drew between the human and the divine natures of Christ, Dial. ii. (Opp. iv. p. 126): Οὐδὲ γὰρ μετὰ τὸν ἁγιασμὸν τὰ μυστικὰ σύμβολα τῆς οἰκείας ἐξίσταται φύσεως. Μένει γὰρ ἐπὶ τῆς προτέρας οὐσίας, καὶ τοῦ

---

[1] Comp. *Suicer*, Thes. t. i. p. 383 s., and *Ullmann*, l.c., who oppose the interpretation of Elias Cretensis and of John Damascene. According to the one, ἀντίτυπα meant the same as ἰσότυπα; according to the other, *Gregory* only meant that the bread and wine were ἀντίτυπα *before* the consecration.

[2] In *Chrysostom*, Opera, iii. 742. On the history of this fragment, see *Rückert*, s. 129.

σχήματος καὶ τοῦ εἴδους, καὶ ὁρατά ἐστι καὶ ἁπτά, οἷα καὶ πρότερον ἦν. Νοεῖται δὲ ἅπερ ἐγένετο, καὶ πιστεύεται καὶ προσκυνεῖται, ὡς ἐκεῖνα ὄντα ἅπερ πιστεύεται. Παράθες τοίνυν τῷ ἀρχετύπῳ τὴν εἰκόνα καὶ ὄψει τὴν ὁμοιότητα. Χρὴ γὰρ ἐοικέναι τῇ ἀληθείᾳ τὸν τύπον. He also contrasted the μεταβολὴ τῇ χάριτι with the μεταβολὴ τῆς φύσεως, Dial. i. p. 26. (We do not see, then, why *Rückert* puts him among the *metabolists* instead of the *symbolists*.)

(5) *Augustine*, in interpreting the words pronounced by our Lord at the institution of this ordinance, reminds us of their figurative import, Contra Adamant, c. 12. 3. He says, too, that the language of John vi. is highly figurative, Contra Advers. Leg. et Prophetar. ii. c. 9. (The controversy in which he was engaged with the Manichæans led him to defend the figurative style of the Old Testment by adducing similar examples from the New.) He even supposed that the characteristic feature of the sacraments consists in this, that they contain symbols, Ep. 98, 9: Si sacramenta quandam similitudinem earum rerum, quarum sacramenta sunt, non haberent, omnino sacramenta non essent. Ex hac autem similitudine plerumque etiam ipsarum rerum nomina accipiunt. The sacrament in question is the body of Christ secundum quendam modum, but not absolutely; and its participation is a communicatio corporis et sanguinis ipsius (Ep. 54, 1); comp. De Doctr. Chr. iii. 9, 10, 16. In the passage last mentioned he calls the partaking of Christ's body, in the literal (Capernaitic) sense of the word (John vi. 33), facinus vel flagitium, and continues as follows: Figura est ergo, præcipiens passioni Dominicæ communicandum et suaviter atque utiliter recondendum in memoria, quod pro nobis caro ejus crucifixa et vulnerata sit; comp. De Civ. Dei, xxi. c. 25. Respecting the body of Christ he says, Ep. 146: Ego Domini corpus ita in cœlo esse credo, ut erat in terra, quando ascendit in cœlum, comp. *Marheineke*, p. 56 ss. *Neander*, Kg. l.c. 1400; *Ebrard*, s. 309 ff.—On the connection subsisting between the views of Augustine respecting the Lord's Supper and those respecting baptism, comp. *Wiggers*, ii. s. 146; on the connection subsisting between these and his views of the sacraments in general, comp. above, § 137, note 2: "*Augustine certainly did not regard the Lord's Supper as a mere memorial festival, but he certainly brought out, as*

he could hardly help doing, the necessity of the commemoration. As certainly he did not regard the bread and wine as mere signs of the memorial, but he does explain them as signs by which something else, viz. the body and blood of Christ, are figuratively represented," S. L. in *Gelzer's* Monatsbl. xxvii. 5, s. 335; comp. also s. 336 ff.

(6) Comp. Opus. Imperf. contra Julian. iii. 162; see *Gieseler*, Dogmengesch. s. 407. [Augustine here relates that a mother made a plaster of the sacred bread, laid it upon the eyes of her son, born with sealed eyes, and so healed him.] This view of the magical efficacy of the Lord's Supper he held in common with the greatest teachers of the East; thus *Gregory* of Naz., comp. Orat. viii. 17 s. p. 228, and Ep. 240; *Ullmann's* Gregory of Naz. s. 483 ff.—The dread of spilling any of the wine was the same as in the previous period. With this is allied the warning of *Cyril* of Jerusalem, that when a drop of the consecrated wine remains hanging on the lips, the eyes and brow must be wet with it (Cat. xxiii. c. 22); *Gieseler*, ubi supra.—On the *Communion of Children*, which was customary particularly in the Latin Church, see the works on Archæology. [*Gelasius*, Bishop of Rome, writes, about A.D. 495: No one should venture to exclude any child from this sacrament, " without which no one can attain to eternal life." In this prohibition is seen the value attached to infant communion.]

(7) *Augustine*, De Trinit. iii. 10: Possunt habere honorem tanquam religiosa, sed non stuporem tanquam mira. De Doctr. Christ. iii. 9, he calls the New Testament sacraments, in contrast with the Old Testament ceremonies, factu facillima, intellectu augustissima, observatione castissima, which, however, are to be honoured, not carnali servitute, but spiritali libertate. To take the signs for the thing signified, he terms a servilis infirmitas.

(8) *Gelasius* († 496), De duab. Natur. in Christo, in Bibl. Max. PP. t. viii. p. 703, quoted by *Meyer*, s. 34. *Münscher, von Cölln*, s. 504: Certe sacramenta, quæ sumimus, corporis et sanguinis Christi, divina res est, propter quod et per eadem divinæ efficimur participes naturæ *et tamen esse non desinit substantia vel natura panis et vini*. Et certe imago et similitudo corporis et sanguinis Christi in actione mysteriorum

celebrantur. Satis ergo nobis evidenter ostenditur, hoc nobis in ipso Christo Domino sentiendum, quod in ejus imagine profitemur, celebramus et sumimus, ut sicut in hanc, scilicet in divinam transeant, Sancto Spiritu perficiente, substantiam, *permanente tamen in suæ proprietate naturæ*, sic illud ipsum mysterium principale, cujus nobis efficientiam virtutemque veracitur repræsentant.

(9) In his Commentary on the Gospels (*Assemani* Bibl. Orient. i. 179).

(10) After the example of *Cyprian*, the idea of a sacrifice is distinctly set forth by most of the Fathers of this period. Thus by *Gregory* of Nazianzus (Orat. ii. 95, p. 56; *Ullmann*, s. 483) and *Basil the Great* (Ep. 93), though without any more precise definition (*Klose*, s. 72); so, too, by *Leo the Great* (Sermo lxvi. 2, clvi. 5), see *Perthel*, s. 218, Anm. (against *Griesbach*, who interprets it only tropically); against *Perthel*, see *Rückert*, s. 479 ff. On *Ambrose* (who first used the word *missa* directly of the celebration of the Lord's Supper), *Chrysostom*, and *Augustine*, see *Rückert*, and the Histories of Doctrines by *Neander* and *Gieseler*. According to *Steitz*, l.c., "*the germ of the adoration of the host is found in Chrysostom.*" (Compare the passages quoted.) And *Jerome*, too, sees in the feast of the Lord's Supper "a daily offering of unspotted sacrifices for the sins of the bishop and the people who present them" (Comment. in Tit. i. 8; and Ep. 14 ad Heliodor. c. 8). On the other hand, *Augustine* speaks of sacrifice always in the figurative sense. So De Civ. Dei, x. 5: Sacrificium visibile invisibilis sacrificii sacramentum, i.e. sacrum signum est; and further, below: Quod ab hominibus appellatur sacrificium, signum est veri sacrificii. But *Gregory the Great* speaks most distinctly (Moral. Lib. xxii. 26) of a *quotidianum immolationis sacrificium*, and connects it with masses for souls; see *Lau*, s. 484 sq., and the passages he cites. The more ancient idea of the thankoffering (Eucharist) naturally fell into the background more and more, behind this idea of a propitiatory offering, and the communion of the people similarly behind the sacrificial act of the priest.

5. THE DOCTRINE OF THE LAST THINGS.

§ 139.

Millenarianism.—The Kingdom of Christ.

The contest in which Origen had engaged against the advocates of Millenarianism (or Chiliasm), was soon after his death adjusted in his favour. His disciple, *Dionysius* of Alexandria, succeeded more by persuasion than by force in imposing silence on the followers of *Nepos*, an Egyptian bishop, who adhered to the letter of Scripture, and were opposed to all allegorical interpretation, and had the presbyter Coracion for their leader after the death of *Nepos* (1). Millenarianism was from that time supported by but a few of the eastern theologians (2). In the West the chiliastic expectations were advocated by *Lactantius* (3), but combated by *Augustine*, who had himself once entertained similar views (4). Besides, it was very natural that Christianity should confidently expect a longer existence on earth, after it had become the religion of the State, and been permanently established. Thus the period of Christ's second coming, and of the destruction of the world, was inevitably deferred from time to time, and it was only extraordinary events that caused men for a season to look forward to these things as nigh at hand.—The notion of *Marcellus*, that Christ's *heavenly* kingdom itself will at some future period come to an end (founded on 1 Cor. xv. 25), forms a remarkable parallel to Millenarianism (5).

(1) On the treatise of *Nepos* (A.D. 255), entitled ἔλεγχος τῶν ἀλληγοριστῶν, and that of *Dionysius*, περὶ ἐπαγγελιῶν, as well as on the entire controversy, comp. *Euseb.* vii. 24. *Gennadius*, De Dogm. Eccles. c. 55. *Mosheim*, Comment. p. 720–728. *Neander*, Kg. i. 3, s. 1094. *Coracion* retracted his former views in consequence of a disputation brought about by *Dionysius*.

(2) *Methodius*, who was in part an opponent of *Origen*, propounded millenarian notions in his treatise, The Feast of the Ten Virgins (a dialogue on chastity), which was composed in imitation of Plato's Symposium; Orat. ix. § 5 (in *Combefisii* Auctuar. Noviss. Bibl. Pp. Grac. Pars i. p. 109). *Neander*, Kg. i. 3, s. 1233. According to *Epiph.* Hær. 72, p. 1031 (comp. *Hier.* in Jes. lib. xviii.), *Apollinaris*, too, held millenarian notions, and wrote a treatise in two books against the work of Dionysius, which met with great success at the time: Quem non solum (says *Jerome*, l.c.) suæ sectæ homines, sed nostrorum in hac parte duntaxat plurima sequitur multitudo. Although Jerome rejected millenarianism in its full development, he nevertheless expected a time when, after the overthrow of the Roman Empire, the bondage of Israel should cease, and the promise (Rom. xi.) of the admission of the Jews to the privileges of salvation would be fulfilled (Ep. 129 ad Dardan. c. 7). With this he connected the coming of Antichrist. Comp. *Zockler*, s. 443 f. Concerning the millenarian views of *Bar Sudaili*, abbot of Edessa, in Mesopotamia, towards the close of the fifth century, comp. *Neander*, l.c. ii. 3, s. 1181.

(3) Inst. vii. 14-26, c. 14: Sicut Deus sex dies in tantis rebus fabricandis laboravit, ita et religio ejus et veritas in his sex millibus annorum laboret necesse est, malitia prævalente ac dominante. Et rursus, quoniam perfectis operibus requievit die septimo eumque benedixit, necesse est, ut in fine sexti millesimi anni malitia omnis aboleatur e terra et regnet per annos mille justitia, sitque tranquillitas et requies a laboribus, quos mundus jam diu perfert. In the subsequent part of the chapter he gives a full description of the state of the political, the physical, and the religious world antecedent to the millennial kingdom, and appeals both to the Sibylline oracles and to the Hystaspes. Comp. *Corrodi*, ii. s. 410, 423, 441, 455.

(4) Sermo 159 (Opp. t. v. p. 1060), which may be compared with De Civ. Dei, xx. 7 . . . Quæ opinio esset utcunque tolerabilis, si aliquæ deliciæ spiritales in illo sabbato adfuturæ sanctis per Domini præsentiam crederentur. *Nam etiam nos hoc opinati fuimus aliquando.* Sed cum eos, qui tunc resurrexerint, dicant immoderatissimis carnalibus epulis vacaturos, in quibus cibus sit tantus ac potus, ut non solum nullam

modestiam **teneant, sed** modum quoque ipsius incredulitatis excedant: **nullo modo ista possunt** nisi **a carnalibus credi. Hi autem, qui spiritales sunt, istos** ista **credentes** χιλιαστάς appellant græco vocabulo, quos verbum e verbo exprimentes, nos possumus **Milliarios nuncupare.** The first resurrection (Rev. xx. 5) is explained by *Augustine* as the deliverance of the soul from the dominion of sin in this life; as, in general, an orthodoxy which maintains the authority of the Apocalypse, and yet will not allow Millenarianism, **can only escape from** its difficulties by an arbitrary exegesis, like **that of** *Augustine* on this passage.

(5) Comp. the works on *Marcellus*, quoted § 92, note 6; *Klose*, s. 42 ff., and the passages cited by him. *Cyril* of Jerusalem, Cat. xv. 27 (14 *Milles*), combating this opinion, appeals to the words of the angel (Luke i. 33) and of the prophets (Dan. vii. 13, 14, etc.); in reference to 1 Cor. xv. 25, he asserts that the term ἄχρις includes the terminus ad quem.— *Klose*, s. 82, questions whether *Photinus* adopted the views of *Marcellus*. [Comp. *Willenborg*, Die Orthodoxie d. Marcellus von Ancyra, Munster 1859.]

§ 140.

The Resurrection of the Body.

The idea of a twofold resurrection, taken from the Book of Revelation, still held by *Lactantius* (1), afterwards shared the fate of Millenarianism (2). Though *Methodius* combated *Origen's* idealistic doctrine of the resurrection (3), yet several of the eastern theologians adopted it (4), till the zealous anti-Origenist party succeeded in the ensuing controversies in establishing their doctrine, that the body raised from the tomb is in every respect identical with that which formed in this life the organ of the soul. *Jerome* even went so far as to make this assertion in reference to the very hair and teeth (5). *Augustine's* views on this point were, during the earlier part of his life, more in accordance with the Platonic and Alexandrian mode of thinking; but afterwards he gave the preference to more sensuous notions, though he was at much pains **to clear the** doctrine in question as far as possible from all gross **and** carnal additions **(6).** Later definitions have reference rather to unessential points (7).

(1) Inst. vii. 20: Nec tamen universi tunc (*i.e.* at the **commencement of the** millennial reign) a **Deo** judicabuntur, **sed ii tantum qui** sunt in Dei religione versati. Comp. c. 26: ... **Eodem** tempore (*i.e.* at the end of the world after the millennial reign) fiet secunda illa et publica omnium resurrectio, **in qua** excitabuntur injusti ad cruciatus sempiternos.

(2) *Augustine*, De Civ. Dei, xx. 7: De his duabus resurrectionibus Joannes ... eo modo locutus est, ut earum prima a quibusdam nostris **non** intellecta, insuper etiam in quasdam ridiculas fabulas verteretur. Comp. *Epiphan.* Ancor. § 97, p. 99. *Gennad.* lib. i. c. 6, et 25.

(3) Περὶ ἀναστάσεως λόγος. *Phot.* Bibl. Cod. 234. *Fössler*, i. s. 297. Comp. *Epiph.* Haer. 64, 12–62.

(4) *Gregory* of Nazianzus, *Gregory* of Nyssa, and partly also *Basil the Great*, adopted the views of *Origen*. Thus *Gregory* of Nazianzus (Orat. ii. 17, p. 20, and in other places) rested belief in immortality principally on this, that man, considered as a spiritual being, is of divine origin, and consequently has an immortal nature. The body which perishes is transient, but the soul is the breath of the Almighty, and the deliverance from the fetters of the body is the most essential point of future happiness; see *Ullmann*, s. 501, 502. Similar statements are made by *Gregory* of Nyssa, De Anima et Resurrectione (Opp. t. iii. p. 181 [247]), see *Rupp*, s. 187 ff.; *Münscher*, Handbuch, iv. s. 439; *Baur*, Dg. i. 2, s. 434. Both *Gregory* of Nazianzus and *Gregory* of Nyssa compared (in the manner of Origen) the body of man to the coats of skins with which our first parents were clothed after the fall. On the more indefinite views of *Basil* (Hom. viii. in Hexaëmeron, p. 78, and in Famem, p. 72), see *Klose*, s. 77. *Titus* of Bostra (fragm. in *Joh. Damasceni* Parallela Sacra, Opp. t. ii. p. 763) propounded a more refined doctrine of the resurrection. *Chrysostom*, though asserting the identity of the body, Hom. x. in 2 Ep. ad Cor. (Opp. t. ix. p. 603), kept to the Pauline doctrine, and maintained in

particular the difference between the present and the future body: Σὺ δέ μοι σκόπει, πῶς διὰ τῶν ὀνομάτων δείκνυσι (ὁ 'Απ.) τὴν ὑπεροχὴν τῶν μελλόντων πρὸς τὰ παρόντα· εἰπὼν γὰρ ἐπίγειον (2 Cor. v. 1) ἀντέθηκε τὴν οὐρανίαν, κ.τ.λ. *Synesius*, a Christian philosopher of Cyrene, frankly acknowledged that he could not adopt the popular notions on this point (which some interpreted as a complete denial of the doctrine of the resurrection). Comp. *Evagrius*, Hist. Eccl. i. 15, and Ep. 105 ad Euoptium fratrem, in the note of *Valesius* on that passage. [Comp. *Synesius*, Opera Omnia, ed. *Krabinger*, Landshut 1850; and his Homilies traduites pour la première fois, par *E. Kolbe*, Berlin 1850.]

(5) *Epiphanius*, *Theophilus* of Alexandria, and *Jerome*, may be considered as the representatives of this zealous party. The last two had themselves formerly entertained more liberal views, nor did Theophilus even afterwards hesitate to ordain *Synesius* as bishop of Ptolemais; see *Munscher*, Handbuch, iv. s. 442.[1] But they opposed, with especial vehemence, *John* of Jerusalem and *Rufinus*. Jerome was by no means satisfied (Apol. contra Ruf. lib. iv. Op. t. ii. p. 145) with the language of Rufinus, even when he asserted the resurrection *hujus* carnis (in the Expos. Symbol. app.), and still less with the caution of *John*, who distinguished (rightly from the exegetical point of view) between flesh and body. He therefore made the following definite assertions (Adv. Errores Joann. Hier. ad Pammach. Opp. t. ii. p. 118 ss.), which he founds especially on Job xix. 26: Caro est proprie, quæ sanguine, venis, ossibus nervisque constringitur. . . . Certe ubi pellis et caro, ubi ossa et nervi et sanguis et venæ, ibi carnis structura, ibi sexus proprietas. . . . Videbo autem in ista carne, quæ me nunc cruciat, quæ nunc præ dolore distillat. Idcirco Deum in carne conspiciam, quia omnes infirmitates meas sanavit.—And so he goes on to say in reference to the resurrection-bodies: Habent dentes, ventrem, genitalia et tamen nec cibis nec uxoribus indigent. From the stridor dentium of the condemned he infers that we shall have teeth; the passage: Capilli capitis vestri numerati sunt, proves, in his opinion, that not even our hair will be wanting.

---

[1] He accepted the bishopric only on the condition that he might retain his free opinions.

But his principal argument is founded on the identity of the body of believers with that of Christ. In reference to 1 Cor. xv. 50, he lays great stress upon the use of the term *possidere regnum Dei*, which he distinguishes from the *resurrectio*. Comp. *Prudentius* (Apotheos. 1063 ss.)

> Nosco meum in Christo corpus resurgere. Quid me
> Desperare jubes? Veniam, quibus ille revenit
> Calcata de morte viis. Quod credimus, hoc est
> Et totus veniam, nec enim minor aut alius quam
> Nunc sum restituar. Vultus, vigor, et color idem,
> Qui modo vivit, erit. Nec me vel dente vel *ungue*
> Fraudatum revomet patefacti fossa sepulcri.

(6) *Augustine* propounded the more liberal view, De Fide et Symb. c. 10 Tempore immutationis angelicæ non jam caro erit et sanguis, sed tantum corpus—in cœlestibus nulla caro, sed corpora simplicia et lucida, quæ appellat Ap. spiritalia, nonnulli autem vocant ætheria; the opposite view is set forth in his Retractationes, p. 17. The whole doctrine is fully developed in Enchirid. ad Laur. 84–92, and De Civ. Dei, xxii. c. 11–21: Erit ergo spiritui subdita caro spiritalis, sed tamen caro, non spiritus, sicut carni subditus fuit spiritus ipse carnalis, sed tamen spiritus, non caro. In reference to the general aspect of the doctrine, he says, Ad Laur. c. 88 s.: Non perit Deo terrena materies, de qua mortalium creatur caro, sed in quemlibet pulverem cineremve solvatur, in quoslibet halitus aurasque diffugiat, in quamcunque aliorum corporum substantiam vel in ipsa elementa vertatur, in quorumcunque animalium, etiam hominum cedat carnemque mutetur, illi animæ humanæ puncto temporis redit, quæ illam primitus, ut homo fieret, cresceret, viveret, animavit; but this admits of some limitation: Ipsa itaque terrena materies, quæ discedente anima fit cadaver, non ita resurrectione reparabitur, ut ea, quæ dilabuntur et in alias atque alias aliarum rerum species formasque vertuntur (quamvis ad corpus redeant, unde lapsa sunt), ad easdem quoque corporis partes, ubi fuerunt, redire necesse sit (this would be impossible, especially in the case of the hair and nails). . . . Sed quemadmodum, si statua cujuslibet solubilis metalli aut igne liquesceret, aut contereretur in pulverem, aut confunderetur in massam, et eam vellet artifex ex illius materiæ quantitate reparare, nihil interesset

ad ejus integritatem, quae particula materiae cui membro statuae redderetur, dum tamen totum, ex quo constituta fuerat, restituta **resumeret.** Ita Deus mirabiliter atque ineffabiliter artifex de toto, quo caro nostra constiterat, eam mirabili et ineffabili celeritate restituet. Nec aliquid attinebit ad ejus reintegrationem, utrum capilli ad capillos redeant et ungues ad ungues: an quicquid eorum perierat, mutetur in carnem et in partes alias corporis revocetur, curante artificis providentia, ne quid indecens fiat. Nor is it necessary to suppose that the differences of size and stature will continue in the life to come, but everything will be restored in the proportions of the divine image. Cap. 90: Resurgent igitur Sanctorum corpora sine ullo vitio, sine ulla deformitate, sicut sine ulla corruptione, onere, difficultate, etc. All will have the stature of the full-grown man, and, as a general rule, that of thirty years old (the age of Christ), De Civ. Dei, lib. i. c. 12. He gives particular statements respecting children, De Civ. Dei, lib. i. c. 14; the different sexes, c. 17; concerning children born prematurely and lusus naturae, ib. c. 13, and Ad Laur. 85, 87. Moreover: Si quis in eo corporis modo, in quo defunctus est, resurrecturum unumquemque contendit, non est cum illo laboriosa contradictione pugnandum; De Civ. Dei, l. i. c. 16. On the similar views of *Gregory the Great*, see *Lau*, s. 510 ff.

(7) The opinion of *Origen* having been condemned by the decisions of synods (*Mansi*, ix. p. 399 and 516) on the narrow basis of this orthodoxy, there could be but slight modifications. To these belong, *e.g.*, the controversy which arose between *Eutychius*, patriarch of Constantinople, who maintained that the resurrection body was impalpabilis, and *Gregory the Great*, bishop of Rome, who denied it (*Greg. M.* Moral. in Jobum, lib. xiv. c. 29. *Münscher*, Handbuch, iv. s. 449); and the controversy which took place between the monophysitic Philoponites and the Cononites respecting the question, whether the resurrection was to be considered as a new creation of matter, or as a mere transformation of the form? Comp. *Timoth.* De Recept. Haeret. in *Cotelerii* Monum. Eccl. Graecae, t. iii. p. 413 ss. *Walch*, Historie der Ketzereien, Th. viii. s. 762 ff. *Münscher*, Handbuch, iv. s. 450, 451. *Gieseler*, Dogmengesch. s. 427. [The theory of *Philoponus* rested on his Aristotelian principle, that matter and form are inseparable,

and that with the death of the body both matter and form are destroyed; consequently there must be a new creation.—One view condemned as Origenistic was, that the bodies will be raised in the spherical form, that being the most perfect; another, that the bodies will at some future time be annihilated.]

§ 141.

General Judgment.—Conflagration of the World.—Purgatory.

Höpfner, De Origine Dogmatis de Purgatorio, Hal. 1792. *J. F. Cotta*, Historia Succincta Dogmatis de Poenarum Infernalium Duratione, Tübing. 1774. [*Passaglia*, De Æternitate Poenarum, Ratisb. 1854.]

The views concerning the general judgment were still substantially founded on the representations of Scripture, but more fully described and pictorially represented, in the foreground and background, by the imagination of the age (1). The Fathers of the preceding age believed in a general conflagration which was to accompany the general judgment, as well as to destroy the world, and ascribed to it a purifying power (2). The shape given to this by *Augustine* was, that this purifying fire (ignis purgatorius) has its seat in Hades, *i.e.* the place in which the souls of the departed were supposed to remain until the general resurrection (3). This idea, as well as further additions on the part of other theologians, especially *Cæsarius* of Arles (4) and *Gregory the Great* (5), prepared the way for the more definite doctrine of purgatory (6). This doctrine, being brought afterwards into connection with the doctrine of the mass, was made subservient to the purposes of the hierarchy, and contributed to obscure the evangelical doctrine of salvation.

(1) The end of the world will be preceded by signs in the sun, the moon, and the stars; the sun will be changed into blood, the moon will not give her light, etc. Comp. *Basil the Great*, Hom. 6 in Hexaëm. p. 54 (al. 63). *Lactantius*, vii. 19 ss., c. 25 (he refers to the Sibylline oracles). Short descriptions of the general judgment are given by *Gregory* of

Nazianz. Orat. xvi. 9, p. 305 ss., and xix. 15, p. 373.—
According to *Basil*, Moral. Regula, 68, 2, the coming of our
Lord will be sudden, the stars will fall from heaven, etc.; but
we ought not to think of this manifestation as τοπικὴ ἡ
σαρκικὴ, but ἐν δόξῃ τοῦ πατρὸς κατὰ πάσης τῆς οἰκουμένης
ἀθρόως, see *Klose*, s. 74. Comp. Hom. in Ps. xxxiii. p. 184
(al. 193, 194), Ep. 46.—According to *Cyril* of Jerusalem, the
second coming of our Lord will be announced by the appearance of a cross, Cat. 15. 22; comp. the whole description,
19–33.—*Augustine* endeavoured dogmatically to define the
facts which are represented in figurative language,[1] instead of
giving rhetorical descriptions, as the Greek theologians loved
to do; he therefore sought to bring the doctrine of retribution
into agreement with his doctrine of predestination; see De
Civ. Dei, xx. 1: Quod ergo in confessione ac professione tenet
omnis ecclesia Dei veri, Christum de cœlo esse venturum ad
vivos ac mortuos judicandos, hunc divini judicii ultimum diem
dicimus, i.e. novissimum tempus. Nam per quot dies hoc judicium tendatur, incertum est: sed scripturarum more sanctarum
diem poni solere pro tempore, nemo, qui illas litteras quamlibet
negligenter legerit, nescit. Ideo autem cum diem judicii
dicimus, addimus ultimum vel novissimum, quia et nunc
judicat et ab humani generis initio judicavit, dimittens de
paradiso, et a ligno vitæ separans primos homines peccati
magni perpetratores; imo etiam quando angelis peccantibus
non pepercit, quorum princeps homines a se ipso subversus
invidendo subvertit, procul dubio judicavit. Nec sine illius
alto justoque judicio et in hoc aërio cœlo et in terris, et
dæmonum et hominum miserrima vita est erroribus ærumnisque plenissima. Verum etsi nemo peccasset, non sine bono
rectoque judicio universam rationalem creaturam perseverantissime sibi Domino suo hærentem in æterna beatitudine
retineret. Judicat etiam non solum universaliter de genere
dæmonum atque hominum, ut miseri sint propter primorum
meritum peccatorum; sed etiam de singulorum operibus
propriis, quæ gerunt arbitrio voluntatis, etc.—As to the
process of the general judgment itself, see ibid. c. 14.

---

[1] He points out (De Gestis Pel. c. 4, § 11) the variety of figurative expressions used in Scripture in reference to this subject, which can hardly be combined in one representation.

(2) Comp. § 77, note 6. This idea of a purifying fire is very distinctly set forth by *Gregory* of Nazianzus in Orat. xxxix. 19, p. 690 (*Ullmann*, s. 504). Less definitely in Orat. xl. 36, p. 739 (*Ullmann*, s. 505).—Roman Catholic commentators have inferred too much in support of their theory from the general expression πυρὶ καθαιρομένῃ, which *Gregory* of Nyssa makes use of—De iis qui præmature abripiuntur (Opp. iii. p. 322); see *Schröckh*, Kirchengeschichte, xiv. s. 135. *Basil the Great* supposes (Hom. 3 in Hexaëmeron, p. 27 (32)) that the fire which is to destroy the world has existed from the time of the creation, but that its effects are neutralized by a sufficient quantity of water, until the consumption of the latter; see *Klose*, s. 773.

(3) *Augustine* agrees with other theologians in his general views respecting the conflagration of the world, De Civ. Dei, xx. 18; in the same place he endeavours to give a satisfactory reply to the question, Where the righteous will be during the general conflagration? Possumus respondere, futuros eos esse in superioribus partibus, quo ita non adscendet flamma illius incendii, quemadmodum nec unda diluvii. Talia quippe illis inerunt corpora, ut illic sint, ubi esse voluerint. Sed nec igneam conflagrationis illius pertimescent immortales atque incorruptibiles facti: sicut virorum trium corruptibilia corpora atque mortalia in camino ardenti vivere illæsa potuerunt. Like the earlier theologians, Augustine brings the idea of a purification wrought by fire into connection with 1 Cor. iii. 11–15; see Enchirid. ad Laur. § 68. In the next section he continues as follows (in reference to the disposition to cling too much to earthly goods): Tale aliquid *etiam post hanc vitam fieri* incredibile non est, et utrum ita sit, quæri potest. Et aut inveniri aut latere nonnullos fideles *per ignem purgatorium*, quanto magis minusve bona pereuntia dilexerunt, tanto tardius citiusve salvari: non tamen tales, de quibus dictum est, quod regnum Dei non possidebunt, nisi convenienter pœnitentibus eadem crimina remittantur. Comp. De Civ. Dei, lib. i. c. 24, 26; Quæst. ad Dulc. § 13. At the Synod of Diospolis it was objected to *Pelagius*, that he taught that at the last judgment the ungodly and sinners would not be spared, but burn in everlasting fire; to which he replied, that this was according to the gospel, and that whoever taught

otherwise was an Origenist. But Augustine conjectures that Pelagius thereby meant to deny the purifying fire; comp. *Wiggers*, i. 195; *Neander*, Kg. ii. 3, s. 1199, 1225, 1404. [As quoted by *Neander*, the objection reads: " In die judicii iniquis et peccatoribus non esse parcendum, sed æternis eos ignibus esse exurendos;" and *Neander* adds that it is probable that *Pelagius* was combating those who held out the promise of final salvation to a dead church-faith, not connected with a change of heart, etc.,—and that this interpretation "is confirmed by *Augustine's* remark on this passage in his De Gestis Pelagii."] Whether *Prudentius* taught it, see *Schröckh*, Kirchengesch. vii. s. 126. He speaks of different degrees of hell.

(4) Sermo viii. 4 in *August*. Opp. t. v. Append. (the passage is quoted by *Münscher, von Cölln*, i. s. 62). He makes a distinction between capitalia crimina and minuta peccata. None but the latter can be expiated either in this life by painful sufferings, alms, or placability manifested towards enemies, or in the life to come by the purifying fire (longo tempore cruciandi).

(5) *Gregory the Great* may rightly be called (with *Schröckh*) the "*inventor of the doctrine of purgatory*," if on such a subject we may speak of invention. On the one hand (Dial. iv. 39), the doctrine of purgatory, which with Augustine has still the character of a private opinion, he lays down as *an article of faith*, saying: De quibusdam levibus culpis esse ante judicium purgatorius ignis *credendus* est, and rests his opinion on Matt. xii. 31. (He thinks that some sins are not pardoned till after death, but to that class belong only what are called minor sins, such as talkativeness, levity, and dissipated life.[1]) On the other hand, he was the first writer who clearly propounded the idea of a deliverance from purgatory by intercessory prayer, by masses for the dead (sacra oblatio hostiæ salutaris), etc., and adduced instances in support of his view, to which he himself attached credit. Comp. Dial. iv. 25 and 57, Moral. ix. c. 34; *Schröckh*, Kirchengesch. xvii. s. 255 ff.; *Neander*, Kg. iii. s. 271; *Lau*, s. 485 ff., 508 ff. If we compare Gregory's doctrine with the former (more idealistic) notions concerning

---

[1] According to *Gregory*, the passage on which earlier teachers relied, 1 Cor. iii. 13, may be referred to tribulations in hac vita; but he himself prefers the usual interpretation, and understands by the wood, hay, and stubble, mentioned in iii. 12, unimportant and slight *sins!*

the efficacy of the purifying fire, we may adopt the language of *Schmidt* (Kirchengesch. iii. s. 280): "*The belief in an uninterrupted endeavour after a higher degree of perfection, which death itself cannot interrupt*, DEGENERATED INTO A BELIEF IN PURGATORY."

(6) Abuses were already found as to prayers for the dead; and *Aerius*, a presbyter at Sebaste (about A.D. 360), wished to have them abolished, but they still continued. At first they prayed *for* martyrs and saints (*Epiphanius*, 75, § 7). *Augustine*, on the other hand, thought: Injuria est pro martyre orare, cujus *nos* debemus orationibus commendari (Sermo xvii.). It became a more general ecclesiastical observance to introduce into the intercession of the saints a petition for the shortening of the pangs of purgatory.

§ 142.

The State of the Blessed and the Damned.

Gregory of Nazianzus and some other theologians supposed that the souls of the righteous, prior to the resurrection of the body, are at once admitted into the presence of God (passing over the doctrine of Hades); while the majority of the ecclesiastical writers of this period (1) believed that men do not receive their full reward till after the resurrection of the body (2) and the last judgment. According to *Gregory* of Nazianzus, *Gregory* of Nyssa, and other theologians who adopted the views of Origen, the blessedness of heaven consists in more fully developed knowledge, in intercourse with all the saints and righteous, and partly in the deliverance from the fetters of the body; *Augustine* added that the soul then obtained its true liberty. But all writers admitted the difficulty of forming just views on this subject (3). The sufferings of the damned were represented as the opposite of the pleasures of the blessed, and in the descriptions of the punishments of hell greater prominence was given to gross sensuous representations. Many were disposed to regard the fire in question as a material fire; though *Lactantius* depicted it in more refined images, while others painted it in terrible descriptions (4). There were still some theologians who favoured the idea of degrees both of bliss and torment (5). As regarded the duration of the punishments of hell, the opinion was more general that they are eternal (6); but yet *Arnobius* maintained that they would at last cease, but with the annihilation of the individual (7); and even the humane view of Origen, in a few of its representatives, still dared to express a glimmer of hope in favour of the damned (8). *Jerome* at least admitted that those among the damned who have been *orthodox* enjoy a kind of privilege (9). And lastly, it is a remarkable fact, which, however, admits of explanation, that *Augustine* entertained milder views on this point than the legal *Pelagius* (10), who, as well as the practical *Chrysostom* (11), maintained the eternal duration of the punishments of hell, in accordance with his strict doctrine of moral retribution. The doctrine of the restitution of all things shared the fate of Origenism (12), and made its appearance in after ages only in connection with other heretical notions, and especially with the otherwise anti-Origenistic Millenarianism.

(1) Orat. x. p. 173, 174. Comp. *Gennad.* De Dogm. Eccles. c. 46. *Gregory the Great*, Moral. lib. iv. c. 37. *Eusebius*, too, relates (De Vita Constant. iii. 40) that Helena, the mother of the emperor, went immediately to God, and was transformed into an angelic substance (ἀνεστοιχειοῦτο).

(2) Thus *Ambrose*, De Bono Mortis, c. 10; De Cain et Abel, lib. ii. c. 2: Solvitur corpore anima et post finem vitae hujus, adhuc tamen futuri judicii ambiguo suspenditur. Ita finis nullus, ubi finis putatur. *Hilary*, Tract. in Ps. cxx. p. 383. *Augustine*, Enchirid. ad Laur. § 109: Tempus, quod inter hominis mortem et ultimam resurrectionem interpositum est, animas abditis receptaculis continet; sicut unaquaeque digna est vel requie vel aerumna, pro eo, quod sortita est in carne cum viveret; comp. Sermo 48. Even some of the Greek theologians taught that no man receives his full reward before the general judgment. *Chrys.* in Ep. ad Hebr. Hom. xxviii.

(Opp. t. xii. p. 924) et in 1 Ep. ad Corinth. Hom. xxxix. (Opp. xi. p. 436). He there defends the belief in the Christian doctrine of the *resurrection* as distinct from a mere hope in the *continued existence* of the soul after death. *Cyril Alex.* Contra Anthropom. c. 5, 7 ss.

(3) According to *Gregor. Nyss.* Orat. Catech. c. 40, the blessedness of heaven cannot be described by words. *Gregor. Nazianz.* Orat. xvi. 9, p. 306, supposes it to consist in the perfect knowledge of God, and especially of the Trinity (θεωρία τριάδος)—in full accordance with the intellectual and contemplative tendency predominant in the Eastern Church at that time. Gregory, however, does not restrict the enjoyment of eternal happiness to the intuitive vision and knowledge of God; but, inasmuch as this knowledge itself is brought about by a *closer union with God*, the blessedness of the redeemed in heaven will also consist in this inward union with God, in perfect peace both internal and external, in the intercourse with blessed spirits, and in the elevated knowledge of all that is good and beautiful, Orat. viii. 23, p. 232. Rhetorical descriptions are found in Orat. vii. 17, p. 209, vii. 21, p. 213. *Ullmann*, s. 502. *Basil the Great* depicts this blessedness for the most part in a negative way: Homil. in Ps. cxiv. p. 204 (quoted by *Klose*, s. 76). *Augustine* also begins De Civ. Dei, xxii. 29, 30, with the confession: Et illa quidem actio, vel potius quies atque otium, quale futurum sit, *si verum velim dicere, nescio;* non enim hoc unquam per sensus corporis vidi. Si autem mente, i.e. intelligentia vidisse me dicam, quantum est aut quid est nostra intelligentia ad illam excellentiam?—According to Augustine, the happiness of the blessed consists in the enjoyment of heavenly peace which passes knowledge, and the vision of God, which cannot be compared with bodily vision. But while *Gregory* of Nazianzus assigned the first place to *theological* knowledge (insight into the Trinity), *Augustine* founded his theory of the blessed life upon *anthropology*. The blessed obtain true liberty, by which he understood that they *can* no longer sin: nam primum liberum arbitrium, quod homini datum est, quando primum creatus est rectus, potuit non peccare, sed potuit et peccare; hoc autem novissimum eo potentius erit, quo peccare non poterit. Verum hoc quoque Dei munere, non suæ possi-

bilitate naturæ. Aliud est enim, esse Deum, aliud participem Dei. Deus natura peccare non potest; particeps vero Dei ab illo accipit, ut peccare non possit. . . . And as with freedom, so with immortality: Sicut enim prima immortalitas fuit, quam peccando Adam perdidit, posse non mori, novissima erit, non posse mori. Augustine, moreover, thought that the blessed retain the full recollection of the past, even of the sufferings which befell them while on earth, but so that they do not feel what was painful in these. They also know the torments of the damned without being disturbed in their own happiness (similar views were expressed by *Chrysostom*, Hom. x. in 2 Ep. ad Corinth., Opp. t. xi. p. 605). God is the end and object of all desire, and thus the essential substance of the blessedness: Ipse erit finis desideriorum nostrorum, qui sine fine videbitur, sine fastidio amabitur, sine fatigatione laudabitur.— *Cassiodorus*, De Anima, c. 12 (Opp. t. ii. p. 604, 605), gives a summary of what earlier theologians had taught concerning the eternal happiness of the blessed.

(4) *Lactantius*, vii. 21: . . . Quia peccata in corporibus contraxerunt (damnati), rursus carne induentur, ut in corporibus piaculum solvant; et tamen non erit caro illa, quam Deus homini superjecerit, huic terrenæ similis, sed insolubilis ac permanens in æternum, ut sufficere possit cruciatibus et igni sempiterno, cujus natura diversa est ab hoc nostro, quo ad vitæ necessaria utimur, qui, nisi alicujus materiæ fomite alatur, extinguitur. At ille divinus per se ipsum semper vivit ac viget sine ullis alimentis, nec admixtum habet fumum, sed est purus ac liquidus et in aquæ modum fluidus. Non enim vi aliqua sursum versus urgetur, sicut noster, quem labes terreni corporis, quo tenetur, et fumus intermixtus exsilire cogit et ad cœlestem naturam cum trepidatione mobili subvolare. Idem igitur divinus ignis una eademque vi atque potentia et cremabit impios et recreabit, et quantum e corporibus absumet, tantum reponet, ac sibi ipse æternum pabulum subministrabit. Quod poetæ in vulturem Tityi transtulerunt, ita sine ullo revirescentium corporum detrimento aduret tantum ac sensu doloris afficiet.—*Gregory* of Nazianzus supposed the punishment of the damned to consist essentially in their separation from God, and the consciousness of their own vileness (Orat. xvi. 9, p. 306): Τοῖς δὲ μετὰ τῶν ἄλλων

βάσανος, μᾶλλον δὲ πρὸ τῶν ἄλλων τὸ ἀπερρίφθαι θεοῦ, καὶ ἡ ἐν τῷ συνειδότι αἰσχύνη πέρας οὐκ ἔχουσα. *Basil the Great*, on the contrary, gives a more vivid description of that punishment, Homil. in l's. xxiii. (Opp. t. i. p. 151), and elsewhere. Comp. *Klose*, s. 75, 76. *Münscher*, Handbuch, iv. s. 458. *Chrysostom* exhausts his eloquence in depicting the torments of the damned in repulsive pictures; in Theod. Lapsum, i. c. 6 (Opp. t. iv. p. 560, 561). Nevertheless in other places, *e.g.* in his Ep. ad Rom. Hom. xxxi. (Opp. x. p. 396), he justly observes, that it is of more importance to know how to escape hell, than to know where it is, and what is its nature. *Gregor. Nyss.* (Orat. Cat. 40) endeavours to turn the thoughts away from all that is sensuous (the fire of hell is not to be looked upon as a material fire, nor is the worm which never dies an ἐπίγειον θηρίον). *Augustine*, too, sees that first of all separation from God is to be regarded as the death and punishment of the damned (De Morib. Eccles. Cath. c. 11); but he leaves it to his readers to choose between the more sensuous or the more spiritual mode of interpretation; it is at all events better to think of both at once; De Civit. Dei, xxi. 9, 10; comp. *Greg. M.* Moral. xv. c. 17.

(5) *Gregor. Nazianz.* rests his idea of different degrees of blessedness on John xiv. 2, comp. Orat. xxvii. 8, p. 493, xiv. 5, p. 260, xix. 7, p. 367, xxxii. 33, p. 601. *Ullmann*, s. 503. *Basil the Great* sets forth similar views in Eunom. lib. 3, p. 273. *Klose*, s. 77. *Augustine*, too, supposed the existence of such degrees, De Civ. Dei, xxii. 30, 2. He admits that it is impossible to say *in what* they consist, quod tamen futuri sint, non est ambigendum. But in the absence of any feeling of envy whatever, no one's happiness will be the less because he does not enjoy so high a position as others. Sic itaque habebit donum alius alio minus, ut hoc quoque donum habeat, ne velit amplius.—*Jerome* even charged Jovinian with heresy, because he denied the degrees in question; Adv. Jov. lib. ii. (Op. t. ii. p. 58 s.).—According to *Augustine*, there are also degrees of condemnation, De Civ. Dei, xxi. 15: Nequaquam tamen negandum est, etiam ipsum æternum ignem pro diversitate meritorum quamvis malorum aliis leviorem, aliis futurum esse graviorem, sive ipsius vis atque ardor pro pœna digna cujusque varietur (he thus admitted a relative cessation

of damnation) sive ipse æqualiter ardeat, sed non æquali molestia sentiatur. Comp. Enchir. ad Laur. § 113. *Greg. M.* Moral. ix. c. 39, lib. xvi. c. 28. The opinions of the Fathers were most wavering respecting children that die without being baptized. (Comp. § 137, note 5.)

(6) This opinion was principally founded on the use of the word αἰώνιος in Matt. xxv. 41, 46: it must have the same meaning in reference to both life and punishment. Thus *Augustine* says, De Civ. Dei, xxi. 23: Si utrumque æternum, profecto aut utrumque cum fine diuturnum, aut utrumque sine fine perpetuum debet intelligi. Paria enim relata sunt, hinc supplicium æternum, inde vita æterna. Dicere autem in hoc uno eodemque sensu, vita æterna sine fine erit, supplicium æternum finem habebit, multum absurdum est. Unde, quia vita æterna Sanctorum sine fine erit, supplicium quoque æternum quibus erit, finem procul dubio non habebit. Comp. Enchirid. § 112. It is superfluous to quote passages from other Fathers, as they almost all agree.

(7) *Arnobius*, Adv. Gentes, ii. 36 and 61: Res vestra in ancipiti sita est, salus dico animarum vestrarum, et nisi vos adplicatis dei principis notioni, a corporalibus vinculis exsolutos expectat mors sæva, non repentinam adferens extinctionem, sed per tractum temporis cruciabilis pœnæ acerbitate consumens.

(8) Some faint traces of a belief in the final remission of punishments in the world to come, are to be found in those writings of *Didymus* of Alexandria (one of the representatives of this tendency), which are yet extant, especially in his treatise De Trinitate, edited by *Mingarelli*, A.D. 1769; comp. *Neander*, Kg. ii. 3, s. 1407. *Gregory* of Nyssa speaks more distinctly on this point, Orat. Cat. c. 8 and 35, in λόγος περὶ ψυχῆς καὶ ἀναστάσεως, and in his treatise De Infantibus, qui mature abripiuntur (Opp. t. iii. p. 226–229 and 322 ss.), pointing out the corrective design of the punishments inflicted upon the wicked: comp. *Neander*, l.c.; *Münscher*, Handbuch, iv. s. 465. (*Germanus*, patriarch of Constantinople in the ninth century, endeavoured to suppress these passages; see *Münscher*, l.c.) *Rupp*, p. 261. *Greg. Nazianz.* Orat. xl. p. 665 (*Ullmann*, 505), gives but faint hints of a hope of the final remission of the punishments of hell (as φιλανθρωπότερον

καὶ τοῦ κολάζοντος ἐπαξίως). He makes an occasional allusion to the notion of *Origen* concerning an ἀποκατάστασις, *e.g.* Orat. xxx. 6, p. 544.—*Diodorus* of Tarsus and *Theodore* of Mopsuestia inclined to this milder tendency. (The passages may be found in *Assemani* Bibl. Orient. t. iii. pt. i. p. 223, 224. *Phot.* Bibl. Cod. lxxxi. p. 200. *Mar. Mercator*, Opp. p. 346, ed. *Balluzii.*) Comp. *Neander*, l.c. p. 1409. *Augustine* (Enchirid. § 112) and *Jerome*, ad Avit. (Opp. t. ii. p. 103) and ad Pammach. (p. 112), refer to these milder views which to some extent prevailed in the West.

(9) *Jerome* (Comment. in Jes. c. lxvi. at the close): Et sicut diaboli et omnium negatorum et impiorum, qui dixerunt in corde suo: Non est Deus, credimus æterna tormenta, sic peccatorum et impiorum et *tamen* [:] Christianorum, quorum opera in igne probanda sunt atque purganda, moderatum arbitramur et mixtam clementiæ sententiam. "*This impious opinion, according to which all who were not Christians were condemned to everlasting torments, but slothful and immoral Christians were lulled to sleep in the hope of salvation, could not fail to gain friends,*" *Münscher*, Handbuch, iv. s. 473.

(10) *Augustine*, indeed, maintained with all strictness the eternity of punishments as seen above; but when *Pelagius* asserted at the Synod of Diospolis: In die judicii iniquis et peccatoribus non esse parcendum, sed æternis eos ignibus esse exurendos; et si quis aliter credit, Origenista est (comp. § 141, note 3), he urged milder views in opposition to him (De Gestis Pelagii, c. 3, § 9–11), in accordance with the highest principle: Judicium sine misericordia fiet illi, qui non fecit misericordiam. With his supposition, as already intimated, of a gradual diminution of punishment, and of degrees in the same, the gradual vanishing of it was put at a minimum. (Comp. also what is said, note 5.)

(11) It might have been expected that the milder disposition of *Chrysostom* would induce him to adopt opinions more in accordance with those of his master *Diodorus* of Tarsus (Hom. 39 in Ep. 1 ad Cor. Opp. x. p. 372): he alludes, indeed, to the view of those who endeavour to prove that 1 Cor. xv. 28 implies an ἀναίρεσις τῆς κακίας, without refuting it. But his position in the Church, and the general corruption of morals, compelled him to adopt more rigid

views; comp. in Theodor. Lapsum. l.c. in Epist. 1 ad Thessal. Hom. 8 : Μὴ τῇ μελλήσει παραμυθώμεθα ἑαυτούς· ὅταν γὰρ πάντως δέῃ γενέσθαι, οὐδὲν ἡ μέλλησις ὠφελεῖ· πόσος ὁ τρόμος; πόσος ὁ φόβος τότε κ.τ.λ., in Ep. 2, Hom. 3, and other passages. — Comp. Origen's mode of teaching on this point, in § 78, note 6.

(12) Comp. the acts of the Synod of Constantinople (A.D. 544), Can. xii., quoted by *Mansi*, t. ix. p. 399.

THIRD PERIOD.

FROM JOHN DAMASCENE TO THE PERIOD OF THE REFORMATION, A.D. 730–1517.

THE AGE OF SYSTEMATIC THEOLOGY.
(SCHOLASTICISM IN THE WIDEST SENSE OF THE WORD.)

A.—GENERAL HISTORY OF DOCTRINES DURING THE THIRD PERIOD.

§ 143.

Character of this Period.

Engelhardt, Dogmengeschichte, Bd. ii. *Münscher*, Lehrbuch der Dogmengesch., edited by *von Cölln*, Bd. ii. *Ritter*, Gesch. d. Philosophie, Bd. vii. [Christliche Philos. 2 Bde. 1859]. *Gieseler*, Dogmengeschichte, s. 435 ff. [*F. Rehm*, Gesch. des Mittelalters, 2 Thl., Cassel 1831–39. *H. Leo*, Gesch. des M. Alt., Halle 1830. *Hallam*, *Milman*, and other historians of the Middle Ages. *E. Chastel*, Le Christianisme et l'Eglise au moyen âge, Paris 1859. *S. R. Maitland*, Essays on the Dark Ages, 2d ed. 1851. *Capefigue*, L'Eglise au moyen âge, 2 tom., Paris 1852. *K. R. Hagenbach*, Vorlesungen über d. Kirchengeschichte des Mittelalters, 1 Theil, Leipz. 1860. *Dr. J. Langen*, Johannes von Damaskus, eine patrologische Monographie, Gotha 1879.]

A NEW period in the History of Doctrines may be said to commence with the publication of the "Exposition" of the Greek monk *John Damascene* (1), inasmuch as from that time there was manifested a more definite attempt to arrange in a systematic whole, and to prove dialectically, what had been obtained by a series of conflicts (2). The structure of Church doctrine was completed with the exception of a few parts, *e.g.* the doctrine of the sacraments. The main pillars of *Theology* and *Christology* were firmly established by the decisions of councils held during the preceding period; and Augustinianism had given (at least in the West) a definite character to *Anthropology*, to the doctrine of salvation connected with it, and, lastly, to the doctrine of the Church. Consequently all that still remained to be done for the Church doctrine consisted partly in the collection and completion of existing materials, partly in the endeavour to sift them, and partly in the effort made to prove dialectically particular points. Nevertheless the works written in this period deal directly with the substance of theological thought, and are comparatively not wanting in originality and independence of investigation.

(1) The title of this work is: Ἔκδοσις [ἔκθεσις] ἀκριβὴς τῆς ὀρθοδόξου πίστεως (it forms, properly speaking, the third part of a greater work, entitled: πηγὴ γνώσεως). An edition of it was published by *Mich. Le Quien*, Par. 1712, 2 vols. fol.; see also his Dissert. vii. Damascenicæ. Comp. *Schröckh*, Kg. Thl. xx. s. 222 ff. *Rösler*, Bibliothek der Kirchenväter, viii. s. 246-532. *Gieseler*, Dg. s. 437.

(2) We found traces of a systematic treatment during the former two periods in the writings of Origen (περὶ ἀρχῶν) and of Augustine (Enchiridion and De Doctrina Christiana), but they were only beginnings. "*John Damascene is undoubtedly the last of the theologians of the Eastern Church, and remains for later times the highest authority in the doctrinal literature of the Greeks.* HE MAY HIMSELF BE CONSIDERED AS THE STARTING-POINT OF THE SCHOLASTIC SYSTEM OF THE GREEK CHURCH, WHICH IS YET TOO LITTLE KNOWN." *Dorner*, Entwicklungsgeschichte der Christologie, s. 113. (*Tafel*, Supplementa Histor. Eccles. Græcor., sec. XI. XII. 1832, p. 3 ss., 9 ss.) On the importance of John Damascene in relation to the West, see *Dorner*, l.c., and *Baur*, Trin. ii. s. 175. [Cf. also *Dr. J. Langen*, Johannes v. Dam.]

§ 144.

The Relation of the Systematic Tendency to the Apologetic.

The labours of apologists, which had been of less importance even in the preceding period, were naturally limited to a still narrower circle during the present, since Christianity had become almost exclusively the religion of the civilized world. All that remained to combat was Mahometanism and Judaism (1). German and Slavonic paganism appeared, in comparison with Christian civilization, as a sort of barbarism, which was opposed not so much with the weapons of scientific discussion as by the practical efforts of missionaries, and sometimes by physical force (2). But when, especially towards the close of the present period, doubts within Christianity itself were raised by philosophy concerning the truth of revelation, in a more or less open way, apologists were again compelled to enter the lists (3).

(1) The Jews were combated in the ninth century, among others, by *Agobard*, Archbishop of Lyons, in his works: De Insolentia Judæorum — De Judaicis Superstitionibus (compare *Schröckh*, Kirchengesch. xxi. s. 300 ff.); and by *Amulo* (Amularius), Archbishop of Lyons, in his treatise: Contra Judæos (*Schröckh*, l.c. s. 310). In the eleventh and twelfth centuries they were opposed by *Gislebert* of Westminster; he wrote: Disputatio Judæi cum Christiano de fide christiana, in *Anselmi* Cantuar. Opp. p. 512–523, Paris 1721, fol. (*Schröckh*, xxv. s. 358); by *Abélard* in his Dialogus inter Philos. Judæum et Christianum (*Rheinwald*, Anecdota ad Hist. Eccles. pertinentia, Berol. 1835, t. i.); by *Rupert* of Deutz: Annulus seu Dialogus Christiani et Judæi de Fidei Sacramentis (*Schröckh*, l.c. s. 363 ff.); and by *Richard* of St. Victor, who wrote De Emmanuele libri duo (*Schröckh*, l.c. s. 366 ff.). In the thirteenth century they met with an opponent in the person of *Raimund Martini*, who composed the treatises: Pugio Fidei, Capistrum Judæorum (*Schröckh*, l.c. s. 369 ff.), etc. The

Mahometans were combated by *Euthymius Zigabenus* (in the 24th chapter of his work, entitled: πανοπλία, edited by *Beurer* in Frid. Sylburgii Saracenicis, Heidelb. 1595); by *Raimund Martini* in his treatise: Pugio Fidei (*Schröckh*, xxv. s. 27 ff.); by *Peter the Venerable* of Clugny, in his work: Advers. nefandam Sectam Saracenorum (*Martène*, Collect. Ampl. Monum. t. ix. p. 1121; *Schröckh*, l.c. s. 34, and xxvii. s. 245); still later, by *Æneas Sylvius* (Pope Pius II.): Ep. 410, ad Mahom. II. (*Schröckh*, xxxii. s. 291 ff.).

All these apologetic works are, however, in their form rather *polemical*. They are chiefly "*declamations, in which untempered zeal not unfrequently run out into invectives,*" *Baur*, Lehrbuch, s. 172. On the opposition to Islamism in the Middle Ages, see particularly, *Gass*, ubi supra, § 146.

(2) On this point, compare the works on ecclesiastical history (the chapters on the spread of Christianity). The same method was partly adopted with reference to the Jews and Mahometans.

(3) *Savonarola*, Triumphus Crucis de Fidei Veritate, four books; comp. *Rudelbach*, Hieronym. Savonarola, Hamb. 1835, s. 375 ff. [*Meier*, Savonarola, 1836.] *Marsilius Ficinus*, De Rel. Christ. et Fidei Pietate, Opuscul. See *Schröckh*, Kirchengesch. xxxiv. s. 343 ff. [*Villari*, G. Savonarola ed i suoi tempi, Firenze 1859, 1862.]

§ 145.

The Polemics of this Period—Controversies with Heretics.

Engelhardt, Dogmengeschichte, Bd. ii. cap. 3, s. 51 ff.

The heresies which made their appearance during the present period differed from former heretical tendencies in being opposed to the whole ecclesiastical system rather than to any particular doctrines. With regard to doctrinal tenets, they leaned for the most part towards the earlier heresies of Gnosticism and Manichæism, but sometimes demanded a return to the more simple and pure doctrinal notions of the Bible (1). There were some few heresies of a doctrinal character, *e.g.* the

Adoptianist heresy, and the views of Gottschalk and Berengarius, as well as some bolder assertions on the part of scholastic theologians (such as Roscellinus and Abélard—on the Trinity), which gave rise to controversies within the Church, and called forth decisions of synods on points of doctrine (2). It was not until the close of the period that struggles against the existing order of things prepared the way for a change in the general doctrinal views of the age, and thus introduced the period of the Reformation (3).

(1) To the heretical sects belong, in the East, the *Paulicians* (comp. § 85, note 4) and the *Bogomiles* (on their doctrinal tenets, compare *Mich. Psellus*, περὶ ἐνεργείας δαιμόνων διάλ., ed. *Hasenmüller*, Kil. 1688.—*Euthym. Zigabenus*, Panoplia, P. ii. tit. 23. *J. Ch. Wolf*, Hist. Bogomilorum, Diss. III. Vit. 1712, 4to. *Engelhardt*, Kirchenh. Abhandlungen, Erl. 1832, Nr. 2); in the West, the *Cathari* (Leonistae) *Manichaeans* (Paterini, Publicani, Bugri, boni homines), the followers of *Peter of Bruis* and *Henry of Lausanne* (Petrobrusiani, Henriciani); and in later times, the *Waldenses* and *Albigenses*, the *Turlupines*, the *Beghards, Beguines, Fraticelli, Spirituales*, etc. Compare the works on ecclesiastical history, especially *Fusslin*, Kirchen- und Ketzerhistorie der mittlern Zeiten, Frankfurt and Leipzig 1770 ff., 3 vols. (The History of Doctrines can consider these sects only in general.) *Mosheim*, De Beghardis et Beguinabus, Lips. 1790. *Ch. Schmidt*, Histoire et Doctrine de la Secte des Cathares ou Albigeois, Genève 1849. [*Id.* in Niedners Zeitschrift, 1852: Actenstücke zur Gesch. *Hahn's* Gesch. d. Secten, Bd. ii. 1847. *A. W. Dieckhoff*, Die Waldenser, Göttingen 1851. *Herzog*, De Origine . . . Waldensium, 1848 (comp. *Dieckhoff* in Reuters Repertorium, 1850). *Bender*, Gesch. d. Waldenser, Ulm 1850. *Maitland's* Essays on Wald. and Albigenses, 1852. *Herzog*, Die romanischen Waldenser, 1853; *Dieckhoff* in reply, 1858.]

(2) Comp. the sections on Trinity, Christology, Predestination, and the Lord's Supper, in the Special History of Doctrines.

(3) See the works on ecclesiastical history, and *Flathe*, Geschichte der Vorläufer der Reformation, Leipz. 1835, 2 vols. (comp. § 155).

§ 146.

The Greek Church.

Ullmann, Nicolaus von Methone, Euthymius Zigabenus und Nicetas Choniates, oder die dogmatische Entwicklung der griechischen Kirche im 12ten Jahrhundert (Studien und Kritiken, 1833, Heft 3, s. 647 ff.). W. Gass, Gennadius und Pletho, Aristotelismus und Platonismus in der griechischen Kirche, nebst einer Abhandlung über die Bestreitung des Islam im Mittelalter, Bresl. 1844. [J. P. Fallmerayer, Gesch. d. Morea im Mittelalter, Stuttg. 1830. G. Finlay, Hist. of Byzantine and Greek Empires, 6 vols. Lond. J. G. Pitzipios, L'Église Orientale, etc., Rome 1854. Acta et Diplomata Graeca medii Aevi Sacra et Profana, ed. Miklosch et Jos. Müller, tom. i. 1859. Waddington, Hist. of Greek Church, new ed. 1854.]

The appearance of Augustine in the preceding period formed the turning-point in the doctrinal relations of the Greek and Western Churches. The Greek from that time had to surrender its doctrinal precedence. In the present period it receded from the stage of a living development after it had erected its monument in John of Damascus. The learned Photius (who died about 890) shows in his polemic against the Latin Church, and in his theological writings especially, a dogmatic exclusiveness which is not disconcerted by any contradictions (1). The theologians who followed John Damascene, such as *Euthymius Zigabenus* (2), *Nicolas,* Bishop of Methone (3), *Nicetas Choniates* (4), and *Theophylact* (5), the shadows of earlier greatness, are parallel with the scholastic divines of the West.—The principal doctrinal writers among the Chaldean Christians, separated from the orthodox Church (the followers of Nestorius), were *Ebed Jesu* (6); among the Jacobites (Monophysites), *Jacob,* Bishop of Tagritum (7), and *Abuljaradsh* (8). By the contests between the Eastern and Western Churches, which again broke out in the eleventh century, as well as by the attempts at reunion, especially in the fifteenth century, Greek theology was compelled to make new doctrinal efforts, but contributed nothing which entitled it to a place beside the Western Church (9).

(1) In his great Bibliotheca (Μυριόβιβλος) there is much doctrinal material. On his controversy with the Latin Church, see § 169. Comp. on him, *Gass* in *Herzog's Realenc.* xi. s. 628 ff., and the writings there quoted.

(2) He is also called *Zigadenus,* and died about the year 1118, a monk at Constantinople. At the request of the Emperor Alexis Comnenus, he wrote his principal work: Πανοπλία δογματικὴ τῆς ὀρθοδόξου πίστεως ἤτοι ὁπλοθήκη δογμάτων, see *Schröckh,* Kirchg. xxix. s. 332 ff., 373, and *Ullmann,* l.c. s. 19 ff. The original work was only once printed, at Tergovisto (chief town of Wallachia), in the year 1711. Comp. *Fabric.* Bibl. Græca, vol. vii. p. 461 There is a Latin translation of it by *Pet. Franc. Zino* (Venet. 1556, fol.), which was reprinted in Bibl. PP. Maxima, Lugd. t. xix. p. 1 ss.—He also composed exegetical treatises.

(3) Methone was a town in Messenia. Concerning the life of Nicolas little is known. Some maintain that he lived in the eleventh century, others assert with more probability that he lived in the twelfth; comp. *Ullmann,* l.c. s. 57. His principal work is the refutation of *Proclus,* a Platonic philosopher, entitled: Ἀνάπτυξις τῆς θεολογικῆς στοιχειώσεως Πρόκλου Πλατωνικοῦ; it was edited by Director *Vömel,* Frankf. on the Main 1825. To this is to be added: *Nicol. Mth.* Anecdoti, P. i. et ii. 1825, 1826. " *The work of Nicolas of Methone is undoubtedly one of the best writings of that time,*" *Ullmann,* l.c. With regard to the History of Doctrines, his discussions on the atonement are of greatest importance (§ 179).

(4) His family name was *Acominatus.* He was called Choniates, after his native town Chonae (formerly Colosse), in Phrygia: he died after the year 1206.—Of his Θησαυρὸς ὀρθοδοξίας, in twenty-seven books, only the first five (probably the most important) are known in the Latin translation of *Morelli* (Par. 1569), reprinted in Bibl. PP. Max. t. xxv. p. 54 ss. This work was intended to complete the Panoplia of Euthymius. Comp. *Schröckh,* xxix. s. 338 ff. *Ullmann,* s. 30 ff.

(5) Archbishop of the Bulgarians in Achrida; he died in 1107. He is chiefly known as an exegetical writer, and by his polemics against the Latin Church: De iis, in quibus Latini accusantur.

(6) He was Bishop of Nisibis, and died A.D. 1318. On his treatise: Margarita sive de vera fide, comp. *Assemani*. Bibl. Orient. t. iii. P. i. (An account of it is given by *Pfeiffer*, Bd. ii. s. 407.)

(7) He died A.D. 1231. On his work: Liber Thesaurorum, see *Asseman*. l.c. t. ii. p. 237. (*Pfeiffer*, Bd. i. s. 250.)

(8) He occupied the metropolitan see of Edessa, was also called Barhebræus, and died A.D. 1286. On his work: Candelabrum Sanctorum de fundamentis, see *Asseman*. l.c. p. 284.

(9) *Corn. Will*, Acta et scripta, quæ de controversiis ecclesiæ græcæ et latinæ seculo undecimo composita extant, Marb. 1861.

On the Mystics of the Greek Church, see § 153.

§ 147.

The Western Church.

Bossuet, Einleitung in die Allgemeine Geschichte der Welt bis auf Kaiser **Karl den Grossen**, übersetzt und mit einem Anhange historisch-kritischer **Abhandlungen** vermehrt von *J. A. Cramer*, 7 Bde., Lpz. 1757–1786. [Histoire Universelle: numerous editions.]

During the two former periods the Western Church was principally represented by the ecclesiastical writers of Gaul and Italy, and pre-eminently by the theologians of the North African school. When the renown of the latter writers, as well as the glory of the Romano-Byzantine empire, had passed away, a new Christian and theological culture developed itself among the *Germanic* nations. We have here to distinguish three leading periods — I. The *Carolingian*, including the periods before and after Charles the Great, until the commencement of the scholastic period (eighth to eleventh century). II. The age of scholasticism proper (from the eleventh century to the middle of the fifteenth). III. The period of transition to the Reformation (the fifteenth century, and especially the second half of it).

It is of course impossible to draw sharp lines of separation. Thus scholasticism is prefigured in the period mentioned as the first by John Scotus Erigena; the second period merges so gradually into the third, that for some time both tendencies (the scholastic, which was fast disappearing, and that which manifested itself in the writings of Reformers) accompanied each other. Many writers, *e.g. Ritter*, make scholasticism begin as early as the ninth century; but the tenth century breaks the thread in such a way, that what precedes is rather a prelude than the first act of a drama: "*a blossom before its time, which, for that very reason, remained without fruit; two centuries elapsed before the spring-time came*," *Hasse* (in the work cited in the following section, s. 21, comp. s. 32).

§ 148.

The Carolingian Period (with the phenomena immediately preceding and following).

[Staudenmaier, Johann Scotus Erigena und die Wissenschaft seiner Zeit, 1 Thl. Frankfurt am Main 1834. *Kuntsmann*, Hrabanus Magnentius Maurus, Mainz 1841. *Ritter*, Geschichte der Philosophie, Bd. vii. *Hasse*, Anselm von Canterbury, Bd. ii. s. 18-21. [*Rettberg*, Kirchengesch. Deutschlands, Bd. i. Die Franken 1848. *Krafft*, Gesch. d. German. Volker. *A. F. Ozanam*, La Civilisation Chrétienne chez les Francs, Paris 1849. *F. Monnier*, Histoire des Luttes dans les Temps Carlovingiens, Paris 1852. *Th. Christlieb*, Leben und Lehre des Joh. Scotus Erigena: mit Vorwort von Prof. Dr. *Landerer*, Gotha 1860.]

The collection of Sentences composed by *Isidore* of Seville, and others of similar import (1), furnished the rough material, while the schools and scholastic institutions founded by Charles the Great contributed to call forth spiritual activity. The *Venerable Bede* (2) and *Alcuin* (3) were distinguished for the clearness of their views, among the number of those who exerted more or less influence upon the age of the Carolingians. By the former the study of dialectics was introduced into the Anglo-Saxon, and by the latter into the Frankish monastic and cathedral schools. *Claudius*, Bishop of Turin (4), and *Agobard*, Archbishop of Lyons (5), also exerted a greater influence by arousing the minds of the people, and promoting practical reforms, than by investigations of a strictly doctrinal character. It was only the ecclesiastical controversies of the age which called forth in a few a more distinct display of theological ingenuity (6). *John Scotus Erigena*, however, shone as a meteor in the theological sky. Possessed of a high degree of intellectual originality, he endeavoured, in the spirit of Origen, to lay a philosophical foundation for theology, but his speculative tendency led this bold investigator, who first again entered upon the path of speculation, at the same time into the abyss of dangerous errors (7).

(1) Comp., in the previous period, § 82, note 30, and *Ritter*, vii. s. 171 ff. In addition to *Isidore*, the compilers of the seventh century are: *Tajo* of Saragossa, who lived about the year 650, and *Ildefons* of Toledo, A.D. 659–669. Comp. *Münscher, von Cölln*, ii. s. 5.

(2) He was born about the year 672, and died A.D. 735 in England. He is celebrated as a historian, and by his efforts for the promotion of education among the clergy. His commentaries, sermons, and epistles contain much that is of importance in the History of Doctrines. Comp. *Schröckh*, Kg. xx. s. 126 ff. Allgemeine Encykl. viii. s. 308–312. *Herzog's* Realencykl. Bd. i. s. 759 ff. His works were published Paris 1544; 1554; Bas. 1563; Colon. 1612, 1688, 8 vols. fol. [Works, ed. by *J. A. Giles*, with his Life, 12 vols. Lond. 1843 ss. Historia Ecclesiastica, et Opera Hist. Minora, ed. *Stevenson*; another edition by *Hussey*; trans. by *Giles*, 1845 (previous translation by *Stapleton*, 1565, 1723). —On *Bede's* Anthropology, see *Wiggers* in Zeitschrift f. d. hist. Theol. 1857.]

(3) He is also known by the names of *Flaccus Albinus* and *Alchuinus*; he was born in England, in the county of York, became tutor to Charles the Great, and died A.D. 804. His work: De Fide sanctæ et individuæ Trinitatis, in three books, contains a whole system of theology. Comp. *Bossuet*, trans. by *Cramer*, Bd. v. Abth. 2, s. 552–559. With reference to the part which he took in the Adoptianist controversy, etc., see the Special History of Doctrines. Comp. Alcuins Leben

von *F. Lorenz*, Halle 1829 [also translated, London]. *Schröckh*, Kg. xix. s. 77 ff., 419 ff., xx. s. 113 ff., 217 ff., 348, 585 ff. *Neander*, Kg. iii. s. 154, and elsewhere. His works were published by *J. Frobenius*, Ratisb. 1777, 2 vols. (in 4) fol. [*F. Monnier*, Alcuin, and his Religious and Literary Influence among the Franks, Paris 1853.]

(4) He was a native of Spain (perhaps a disciple of Felix of Urgella), adopted the doctrinal tenets of Augustine, was a teacher during the reign of Louis the Pious, and died A.D. 840. His commentaries contain much doctrinal matter. Comp. *Schröckh*, l.c. xxiii. s. 281. *Neander*, l.c. iv. s. 325 ff. **Ch. Schmidt*, Claudius von Turin, in Illgens Hist.-Theol. Zeitschrift, 1843, 2.

(5) He was born A.D. 778, and died A.D. 840. He opposed, like Claudius, many of the superstitions of the age. On his polemical writings against the Jews, see § 144; on his refutation of Felix of Urgella, comp. the special History of Doctrines. Comp. also *Schröckh*, l.c. xxiii. s. 249. *Neander*, l.c. iv. s. 322–324. Comp. *Hundeshagen*, Commentatio de Agobardi Vita et Scriptis, Pars 1. Giessae 1831, and his article in *Herzog's* Realencykl. His works were published Paris 1605, 4to; more complete by Balluze, Paris 1660 (Max. Bibl. Patrum, t. xiv., and Gallandii Bibl. Patr. xiii.).

(6) This was the case with *Rabanus* (Hrabanus) *Magnentius Maurus, Paschasius Radbertus, Ratramnus, Servatus Lupus, Hincmar* of Rheims, *Florus Magister, Fredegis* of Tours, and others in the controversies concerning Predestination, the Lord's Supper, etc. See special History of Doctrines; and on their writings, the works on ecclesiastical history, and *Münscher, von Colln*, ii. s. 6, 7. *Ritter*, Gesch. d. Phil. vii. s. 189 ff. On the position of Fredegis, see *Hasse*, s. 20.

(7) Also called *Scotigena*. He lived at the court of Charles the Bald, and died after the year 877. Comp. *Hjort*, Scotus Erigena oder von dem Ursprung einer christlich. Philosoph., Kopenh. 1823. *Schröckh*, l.c. xxi. s. 208 ff., xxiii. 481–484. *Neander*, iv. s. 388 ff. *Staudenmaier*, l.c., and his essay: Lehre des Joh. Scot. Erig. über das menschl. Erkennen, mit Rücksicht auf einschlägige Theorien früherer und späterer Zeit, in the Freiburger Zeitschr. für Theol. iii. 2. *Frommüller, Die Lehre des Joh. Scot. Erigena vom Wesen des Bösen, in Tüb.

Zeitschr. für Theol. 1830, Heft i. s. 49 ff., iii. s. 74 ff. De Joanne Sc. Erig. Comment. (anonymous), Bonn 1845. [*M. Saint-René Taillandier*, Scot. Erigène et la Phil. Scholastique, Paris 1843. *F. Monnier*, De Gottschalci et J. Scot. Erig. Controversia, Paris 1853. *B. Hauréau*, Un Ouvrage inconnu de *J. S. E.* in Revue de l'Instruction publique, 1859; comp. Hauréau in his Hist. of Scholastic Philos. *F. A. Staudenmaier*, J. Scot. Erig. und die Wissenschaft seiner Zeit, Thl. i. Freib. 1854.] *Theod. Christlieb*, Leben und Lehre des Joh. Scot. Erig. mit Vorr. von *Landerer*, Gotha 1860. †*J. Huber*, Joh. Scotus Erigena, München 1861. His principal writings are: Dialogus de Divisione Naturae, libb. v. (ed. *Th. Gale*, Oxon. 1861. Repub. (Paris 1853) by *Migne*); De Praedestinatione Dei.—Of his edition of pseudo-Dionysius: Opera S. Dionysii latine versa, only the Hierarchia Coelestis is extant in the first volume of the works of *Hugo* of St. Victor. "*In his profound consciousness of the divine omnipresence and universal revelation, and his view of philosophy and religion, as only different manifestations of the same spirit, he stood alone, and so high above the times in which he lived, that he was not condemned by the Church until the thirteenth century*" (*Hase*). Comp. *Ritter*, vii. s. 206–296 [and Christl. Phil. i. 409–467], who says: "*He stands as an enigma among the many riddles which these times present. Among the scientific men of these centuries he is as pre-eminent for the clearness of his thoughts, as was Charles the Great among the princes.*"[1] *Hasse* aptly says of the system of Erigena, that, "if not a revival of Gnosticism, it is at least Origenism upon a higher stage" (ubi supra, s. 21). On his relation to the schoolmen, from whom he is distinguished by his speculation rising above the ecclesiastical tradition, see *Landerer* in *Herzog*, xiii. s. 656.

[1] Between the dawning of Scholasticism in the ninth century, and its proper historical growth from the eleventh to the fifteenth, intervenes the tenth century, famed for its barbarism (see *Baronius*), in which the only man of importance in regard to doctrine is *Gerbert* (Pope Sylvester II.). Comp. on him, *Hock*, Gerbert oder Papst. Sylvester II., und sein Jahrhundert, Wien 1837. *Ritter*, Gesch. d. Phil. vii. s. 300 ff. [and Christliche Philosophie. Also, *Büdinger*, Gerbert's Wissenschaftl. und Polit. Stellung, Abth. I. 1851].

§ 149.

Scholasticism in General.

*Bulæi Historia Universitatis Parisiensis, Paris 1665-1673, 6 vols. fol. *Semler*, Einleitung in die dogmatische Gottesgelehrsamskeit (prefixed to Baumgarten's Evang. Glaubenslehre, Bd. i. s. 16 ff.). *Brucker*, Historia Philosophiæ, tom. iii. *Tennemann, Geschichte der Philosophie, Bd. viii. u. ix. *Hegel, Geschichte der Philosophie, Bd. iii. Thl. ii. *Ritter*, Gesch. d. Phil. Bd. vii. u. viii. *Cramer*, l. c. Bd. v. *Engelhardt*, Dg. s. 14 ff. *Baur*, Lehre von der Versöhnung, s. 142 ff. *The same*, Der Begriff der Christ. Phil. 3 art. in Zellers Jahrb. 1846, 2. [*R. D. Hampden*, The Scholastic Philosophy considered in its relation to Christian Theology, in a course of Lectures delivered at the Bampton Lectures, London 1837.] **Fr. v. Raumer*, Die Philosophie und die Philosophen des 12 u. 13 Jahrh. (Hist. Taschenbuch, 1840). **F. R. Hasse*, Anselm v. Canterbury, 2 Thl. Lpz. 1852. [*F. D. Maurice*, Hist. of Med. Philos., Lond 1857.] The works of *Ueberweg* and *Stöckl*, see § 7. *W. Kaulich*, Geschichte der Scholast. Philosophie, 1 Thl. Prag 1863. *Kohler*, Realismus u. Nominalismus in ihrem Einfluss auf die dogmat. Systeme des Mittelalters, Gotha 1858. *Landerer*, Scholast. Theologie, in *Herzog*, xiii. s. 654. *Erdmann*, Der Entwicklungsgang der Scholastik (Hilgenfeld's Zeitschr. 1865, 2).

The exceedingly bold attempt of Scotus Erigena to effect a union between philosophy and theology remained for some time isolated, but reappeared, though in a less free spirit, in what is properly called *Scholasticism* (1). The scholastic divines had not, like the theologians of the earlier Alexandrian school, to trace out the philosophical ideas that lay at the basis of a new and vigorous form of religion (Christianity), for whose systematic development little had been done; nor yet, like them, to accommodate Christianity to a culture (the ancient, classical) which was already rooted in society. On the contrary, it was their task to lay the foundation of a system of modern Christian philosophy on a system of doctrines which had been handed down from antiquity in a partially corrupt form (2). But in the absence of an independent philosophical system, they again had recourse to ancient philosophy, and formed an alliance with Aristotelianism, quite as unnatural as that which former theologians had formed with Platonism. Their philosophical inquiries had more regard to the form (3) than to the matter, and were of a dialectic rather than of a speculative kind. Hence they were not so much exposed to the danger of letting loose their imagination, and entering upon vague and indefinite discussions (like the Gnostics) (4), as to the adoption of narrow views, and to the wasting their energies upon particulars and minutiæ. Thus a refined and subtle philosophy of the understanding gradually brought about the downfall of scholasticism. On the other hand, the endeavour of theologians to arrive at sharp theological definitions, their scientific statement of the doctrine, and the noble confidence which they displayed in the reasonableness of Christianity (notwithstanding existing prejudices), constituted the bright side and the merit of scholasticism (5). At all events, it is certain that this grand attempt led to the very opposite of that which was intended, that the freedom of thought was followed by the bondage of the letter, the confidence of faith ended in shameful scepticism (6).

(1) On the appellation "Scholasticism," etc., see *Du Fresne*, p. 759. *Giesler*, Dg. s. **446**. The derivation of the term in question, however, is not etymological, but historical. Comp. *Schleiermacher*, Kg. s. 466 ff. On the misleading and confusing character of the name, see *Ritter*, vii. s. **111** ff. Yet it would also be impracticable to give it up.

(2) In the previous period *Cassiodorus* had given a summary of the dialectics of Aristotle, and *Boethius* had translated a part of his Organon. But it was not until the present period that theologians became more generally acquainted with Aristotelianism, see § 151. Platonism, on the other hand, forms as it were the dawn and sunset of the philosophy of the Middle Ages; the one is represented by Scotus Erigena, the other by Marsilius Ficinus and others; even during the first period of Scholasticism several of its adherents were under the influence of Platonism; it was not until the thirteenth century that it was gradually supplanted by Aristotelianism. "*It is only*" (says *Ritter*, vii. s. 70, comp. also s. 80, 90 ff.) "*a fable of old ignorance, when it is said that the Middle Ages were exclusively devoted to the Aristotelian philosophy.*"

(3) "Scholasticism is the progress of the Church towards a school, or, as Hegel expresses it, doubtless in the same sense the Fathers developed the Church, because the mind once developed required a developed doctrine; in after ages there were no more *patres ecclesiæ*, but *doctores*. The Fathers of the primitive Church had to produce the material, or to expound that which was contained in its simplest and most direct form in the Christian dogma; they had further to analyse this material into distinct doctrines and formulas, to present it to the religious consciousness of the Church, and procure its general adoption. Scholasticism, on the contrary, presupposed all this. The material and the contents were given; . . . it became now the task of theologians to effect a reunion between that which had become objective to consciousness (as it were, put outside of itself) and the mind itself, to restore the object to the subject; to mediate between the two in consciousness." Baur, Versöhnungslehre, s. 147, 148 Comp. Baumgarten-Crusius, Lehrb. i. s. 445. Hegel, Gesch. der Philos. Bd. iii. s. 138.

(4) "Those who compare the systems of Christian theologians with those of the Gnostics, for the most part forget that the systems of the latter have not the logical connection of philosophical reason, but only that of imagination." Staudenmaier, Erigena, s. 370.

(5) As early as the time of Semler complaints were made of the unjust treatment which the scholastic divines had to suffer; *Semler* himself says (in the historical introduction to *Baumgarten's* Glaubenslehre, Bd. i.): "*The poor scholastici have been too much despised, and that frequently by people who would not have been worthy to be their transcribers.*" And even Luther, although he contributed much to the downfall of Scholasticism, wrote to Staupitz: Ego scholasticos cum judicio, non clausis oculis lego. . . . *Non rejicio omnia corum*, sed nec omnia probo; see *De Wette*, Briefe, u.s.w. i. s. 102. Comp. also *Möhler's* Schriften und Aufsätze, Bd. i. s. 129 ff. *Ullmann* (Joh. Wessel. 1 Ausgabe, s. 12) calls the scholastic theology, "*in its commencement, a true scientific advance upon the past; in its entire course, a great dialectic preparatory school of Western Christianity; in its completion, like the Gothic cathedrals, a grand and artistically finished production of the human mind.*"

(6) See *Baur*, Lehrbuch der Dogmengesch. s. 11, 154 ff.

§ 150.

The *Principal Scholastic* Systems.

(*a*) *First Period of Scholasticism—to the time* of *Peter Lombard.*

The scholastic spirit was first awakened in the monastic schools founded by Charles the Great and his successors. It was principally cultivated in the monastery of Bec in Normandy, where Lanfranc was a teacher (1). His disciple, Anselm of Canterbury, setting out from faith, and indeed from the positive creed of the Church, sought to rise to philosophical knowledge, as is manifest no less in his theory of satisfaction, than in his proof of the existence of God (2). His views on these points, as well as on the reality of universal ideas, were opposed by *Roscellinus* (3) and *Peter Abélard* (4), the latter of whom rested faith (in opposition to the theory of Anselm) on the evidence of knowledge, while the former defended nominalism in opposition to realism. *Hildebert a Lavardino* (first Bishop of Le Mans, and afterwards Archbishop of Tours) (5) adhered, like Anselm, with whom he was contemporary, to the positive creed of the Church. *Gilbert of Poitiers*, on the contrary, was (like Roscellinus and Abélard) charged with heterodoxy (6).—A peculiar tendency which connected mysticism with scholasticism, manifested itself in the writings of *William of Champeaux* (7), the tutor of Abélard, as well as in those of *Hugo of St. Victor* (8) and *Richard of St. Victor* (9).—After *Robert Pulleyn*, and other theologians besides those already named, had endeavoured to defend the doctrine of the Church philosophically (10), *Peter Lombard* (who lived in the twelfth century) collected the existing materials in his "Sentences," and by his peculiar mode of treatment laid the foundation of that stiff and heavy method which after him was for a long time predominant (11).

(1) He died A.D. 1089. He came into notice principally

by his controversy with *Berengarius*, as will be more fully shown in the Special History of Doctrines. His works were published by *d'Achéry*, Paris 1648, fol. Comp. *Möhler*, Gesammelte Schriften und Aufsätze, Regensburg 1839, i. s. 39. —On the foundation of the monastery of Bec, comp. *Möhler*, l.c. [*A. Charma*, Notice sur Lanfranc, Paris 1851. *Milman's* Latin Christianity, vol. ii.]

(2) He was born at Aosta in Piedmont, about the year 1034, occupied the see of Canterbury from the year 1093 (whence he is called Cantuariensis), and died A.D. 1109. "*He, and nobody else, is the father of scholasticism, for he gave form and language to the philosophical spirit which had been at work in the Church since the time of Isidore, and which had almost come to an expression in Berengarius and Lanfranc; and put it in the way of becoming an element of historical progress.*" *Hasse*, l.c. s. 32. Of his philosophical writings, the most important is the work entitled: Monologium et Proslogium (it contains a proof of the existence of God, and the doctrine of the Trinity): extracts from it are given by *Cramer*, v. 2, s. 341-372. Among his more theological works are: De Casu Diaboli, but especially the treatise: Cur Deus Homo? libb. ii. (which contains a theory of the incarnation and of redemption). In addition to these works he wrote: De Conceptu Virginali et Originali Peccato; de Libero Arbitrio; de Concordia Præscientiæ et Prædestinationis nec non Gratiæ Dei cum Libero Arbitrio, etc.—*Editions of his works:* *Gabr. Gerberon, Par. 1675, fol.; 1721, 2 vols. fol. (Ven. 1744); and *Læmmer*, Berol. 1858. A manual edition of the treatise: Cur Deus Homo? was published by *Heyder*, Erl. 1834. Opuscula philosophica-theologica selecta ed. *C. Haas*, Tüb. 1863 ss. Comp. on himself, *†*Möhler*, Gesammelte Schriften und Aufsätze, Regensb. 1839, i. s. 32 ff.; and on his doctrines, *Möhler*, l.c. s. 129 ff. —*I. G. F. Billroth*, De Anselmi Cantuariensis Proslogio et Monologio, Lips. 1832; *Franck*, Anselm von Canterbury, Tüb. 1842, and *F. R. Hasse*, Anselm von Canterbury, Thl. i. Lpz. 1843; Thl. ii. (Anselm's teaching) 1852. *Ritter*, Gesch. d. Phil. vii. s. 315-354. *Rémusat*, Anselm de Cantorbéry, Paris 1854. *Kling* in *Herzog's* Realencykl. [A translation of the 1st Part of *Hasse's* Anselm, abridged by *Turner*, Lond. 1850. *M. A. Charma*, St. Anselm, Paris 1853. His Meditations and

Prayers to the Holy Trinity, Lond. 1856. Cur Deus Homo, transl. Oxford. Comp. Studien und Krit. 1853 (Kling): Revue des deux Mondes, (Saisset) 1853. Dean R. W. Church, Life of S. Anselm, Lond. and Camb. 1868.]

(3) He is also called Rucelinus or Rüzelin; he was born in Lower Brittany, and was canon at Compiègne in the eleventh century. He is commonly regarded as the founder of the nominalists; see Chladenii Diss. hist. eccles. de Vita et Hæresi Roscellini, Erl. 1756, 4to. On the contrast between nominalism and realism, more fully discussed in works on the history of philosophy, see Baumgarten-Crusius, De vero Scholasticorum Realium et Nominalium Discrimine et Sententia theologica, Jen. 1821, 4to. Engelhardt, Dg. s. 16, 17. Baur, Lehrbuch, s. 165. This conflict was not without some importance for theology, as will be more particularly seen in considering the doctrine of the Trinity. The part which theologians took in the work of reformation (e.g. in the times of Huss) depended, generally speaking, more or less on the views which they adopted with regard to these systems. [Comp. Landerer in Herzog's Realencykl.]

(4) The original form of his name was Abælard. He was born A.D. 1079, at Palais near Nantes, and died 1142. On the history of his eventful life, see Bayle, Dictionnaire; Gervaise, Berington, Schlosser, and others; Neander, Der heilige Bernhard, s. 112 ff. Editions of his works: Opp. Abælardi et Heloisæ, ed. Andr. Quercetanus (Duchesne), Par. 1616, 4to, containing: De Fide S. Trinitatis s. Introductio ad Theologiam in 3 libros divisa.—His Libri V. Theologiæ Christianæ were first edited by Edm. Martène (Thesaur. Anecd. t. v.). On his Dialogus, see § 144, note 1. The unpublished works of Abélard are edited by Cousin in the Collection de Documents inédits sur l'Histoire de France, publiés par ordre du Roi et par les soins du ministre de l'instruction publique. Deuxième série: Ouvrages inédits d'Abeillard, pour servir à l'histoire de la philosophie scolastique en France, Paris 1836, 4to. [Vol. ii. 1859. Comp. Goldhorn in Gersdorf's Repert. Jan. 1860. Victor Cousin, uber die erste Periode der Scholastik; dem wesentlichen historischen Inhalte nach mitgetheilt von I. G. v. Engelhardt. Zeitschrift für die historische Theologie, Jahrg. 1846, i. s. 56-133.] Comp. also: A. E. Lewald

Commentatio de Operibus Petri Abælardi, quae e codicibus manuscriptis Victor Cousin edidit (Heidelb. 1839, 4to). The Sic et Non, edited by *Th. Henke* and *G. S. Lindenkohl*, Marb. 1851. The judgment of *Cousin* respecting Abélard is as follows: "*As St. Bernard represents the conservative spirit and Christian orthodoxy in his faults and the narrowness of his views, as well as by his admirable good sense, his depth without subtlety, and his pathetic eloquence, so Abélard and his school represent in some sense the liberal and innovating spirit of the time, with its frequently deceitful promises, and the unavoidable mixture of good and evil, of reason and extravagance.*"—Comp. also *Frerichs*, Comment. theol. critica de Petri Abæl. Doctrina dogmatica et morali, Jen. 1827, 4to; *Franck*, ein Beitrag zur Würdigung Abälards, in the Tübinger Zeitschrift, 1840, 4to, s. 4. *Rémusat*, Abélard, Paris 1845, 2 vols. *Rettberg* in *Herzog's* Realencykl. *Bohringer*, Die Kirche Christi u. ihre Zeugen, ii. 2. According to *Baur* (Trinitätslehre, II. s. 457), Abélard is more of a dialectic than of a speculative thinker. On the relation in which he stands to Rationalism, comp. the same work, s. 500, 501. *Ritter*, Gesch. der Phil. vii. s. 401 ff. He considers him (s. 161) "*less freethinking than imprudent.*" [*J. H. Goldhorn*, De Summis Princip. Theol. Abælard. Lips. 1836. *Lindenkohl*, De Pet. Abæl. libro Sic et Non, Marb. 1851; also his and Henke's edition of the work, 1851. *C. A. Wilkens*, Petr. Abælard, 1855.]

(5) He was born either A.D. 1055 or 1057, and died A.D. 1134. Though a disciple of Berengarius, he did not adopt all his views. He was Bishop of Le Mans from the year 1097, and raised to the archbishopric of Tours, A.D. 1125. For some time he was thought to be the author of the Tractatus Theol., which modern researches have assigned to *Hugo of St. Victor* (see note 8). Comp. *Liebner* in the Theolog. Studien und Kritiken, 1831, Heft ii. s. 254 ff.— His opinions on the Lord's Supper are also of importance, as will be seen in the Special History of Doctrines.

(6) He was also called *Porretanus* or *Porseta* (de la Porrée), and died A.D. 1154. On his life and works, comp. *Otto Fresing*, De Gestis Friderici, lib. i. c. 46, 50–57. *Cramer*, vi. s. 530–552. His principal opponent was *St. Bernard of Clairvaux*, who had also combated Roscellinus and Abélard.

See *Neander*, Der heilige Bernhard, s. 217 ff. *Ritter*, vii. s. 437 ff. [*J. C. Morison*, Life of S. Bernard, Lond. 1863, 1868.]

(7) *Guilelmus de Campellis;* he died A.D. 1121. He was the founder of the school of *St. Victor*, in one of the suburbs of Paris (A.D. 1109), from which, generally speaking, the *mystical* scholastics came. Respecting him and his dialectics, see *Schlosser*, Abhandlung über den Gang der Studien in Frankreich, vorzüglich von der Schule zu St. Victor, in his Vincenz von Beauvais, Frkf. a. Main 1819, Bd. ii. s. 35, and Abélard's works by *Cousin;* comp. also *Engelhardt* in the work mentioned, note 9, s. 308 ff.

(8) According to Pagi, he died A.D. 1140; according to others, A.D. 1141. He was Count of Blankenburg, canon of St. Victor (alter Augustinus, lingua Augustini, Didascalus), and a friend of St. Bernard. Comp. **A. Liebner*, Hugo von St. Victor und die theologischen Richtungen seiner Zeit, Leipz. 1832.—Opera ex rec. Canonicorum Regularium S. Victoris Paris, Rotomagi 1610, 3 vols. fol. His most important *work* is: De Sacramentis Christianæ Fidei, libri duo, t. iii. p. 487–712. Extracts from it are given in *Cramer*, vi. s. 791–848. Comp. *Ritter*, vii. s. 507 ff.

(9) *Magnus Contemplator!* He was a native of Scotland, and died A.D. 1173. Comp. *Liebner*, Progr. de Richardo a S. Vict., Gött. 1837, 1839. Comp. *Engelhardt, Richard von S. Victor und *Johannes Ruysbroek*, zur Geschichte der myst. Theol., Erl. 1838. *Opera:* Studio Canonicorum S. Victoris, Rotomagi 1650, fol.

(10) He was cardinal, and died between the years 1144 and 1150. *He wrote:* Sententiar. libb. viii., published by *Mathoud*, Par. 1655, fol. Comp. *Cramer*, l.c. vi. s. 442–529. *Ritter*, vii. 547 ff.

(11) Magister Sententiarum. He was born at Novara, raised to the episcopal see of Paris in the year 1159, and died A.D. 1164. His *work:* Sententiarum libri iv., Venet. 1477, edited by *J. Alcaume*, Louvain 1546. *"It was not so much on account of the ingenuity and depth displayed in the work, as in consequence of the position which its author occupied in the Church, of his success in harmonizing antagonisms, and of its general perspicuity, that it became the manual of the twelfth*

century, **and the** model of the subsequent one." *Hase.* A specimen **of** his method is given by *Semler* in his introduction to *Baumgarten's* Glaubenslehre, Bd. ii s. 81 ff. Comp. *Heinrich,* Geschichte der dogmatischen Lehrarten, s. 145 ff. The first **book treats:** De mysterio Trinitatis, s. de Deo uno et trino; **the second :** De rerum corporalium et spiritualium creatione et **formatione** aliisque pluribus eo pertinentibus; the third : De **incarnatione** verbi aliisque ad hoc spectantibus ; and the fourth: De sacramentis et signis sacramentalibus. Comp. *Engelhardt,* Dg. s. 22.—" *The period of systematizing scholasticism and of* **endless** *commenting on the sentences of the Master, commences with* **Peter** *Lombard. This* **period** *is, at the same time, the* **one in** *which there was no end of questioning and answering,* **of** *laying down theses and antitheses, arguments and counter-arguments, of dividing and splitting up the matter of the doctrines ad infinitum." Baur,* l.c. s. 214. *" It was owing to* **him** *that* **the** *scholastic treatment of doctrine assumed that* **more** *steady, well-regulated form* **of** *development in which it* **could be carried out to** *its legitimate consequences, without being* **disturbed by** *opponents." Baur,* Lehrbuch der Dg. s. 159. Comp. *Ritter,* vii. s. 474–501. [*Baur,* Dg. (2te Aufl.) s. 224, says of this first period of scholasticism, **that it** began with **the attempt to** rationalize dogma, **or to** make it dialectically **intelligible; and** that this was unquestionably **first** seen in Anselm of Canterbury, by starting the question of the relation **of faith and knowledge,** which indicates the special **object of scholasticism.**] *Landerer* in *Herzog's* Realencykl. viii. s. 466 ff.

§ 151.

(b) Second Period—to the end of the Thirteenth Century.

The dogmatic works of *Robert of Melun* (1) (Folioth) and *Alanus of Ryssel* (2) (ab Insulis) appeared about the same time, while *Peter of Poitiers* (3), a disciple of Peter Lombard, followed in the steps of his master. But this scholasticism, too, met with opposition, especially on the part of *Walter of St. Victor* (4) and *John of Salisbury* (5). Nevertheless, scholasticism gained ground, partly in consequence of being favoured by circumstances. In the *first* place, the orders of the mendicant friars acquired a greater influence upon the philosophical and theological studies pursued in the universities. And, *secondly*, by means of that more extensive intercourse with the East which followed the Crusades, the Western theologians, from the thirteenth century onwards, became acquainted with a more complete edition of the works of Aristotle, which had been translated and commented upon by the Arabs, and exerted from that time a still more decided influence upon their systems (6). The works called "Summas," the first of which was composed by *Alexander Hales* (7), now took the place of the "Sentences." *Albertus Magnus* wrote the first complete commentary on the works of Aristotle (8). But when scholasticism had reached its height, towards the close of the thirteenth century, a division broke out between the different schools, which continued to exist as long as the system itself. The leader of the one of these schools was the Dominican *Thomas of Aquinum* (9); the leader of the other was his opponent, the Franciscan *John Duns Scotus* (10). The scholastic disputes were connected with the jealousies of the monastic orders (11). But even in the present period the mystical tendency was sometimes united with the scholastic, as in the case of the Franciscan *John of Fidanza* (12) (Bonaventura).

(1) He was Bishop of Hereford from the year 1164, and died A.D. 1195 [1167?]. He composed a Summa Theologiæ (hitherto unpublished); comp. *Buleus*, l.c. t. ii. p. 264, 585 ss., 772 s. *Cramer*, l.c. vi. s. 553-586. [See Art. in Biog. Universelle.]

(2) He was called Doctor universalis, and died A.D. 1203. He belonged to the speculative school of Anselm. *Writings:* Summa quadripartita de fide catholica (a controversial writing, in opposition to the Albigenses, Waldenses, Jews, and Mahometans).—Libri V. de Arte s. Articulis catholicæ Fidei, edited by *Pez*, Thesaur. Anecd. Noviss. t. i. P. ii. p. 475-504 (an abridgment of it is given in *Cramer*, v. 2, s. 445-459), and Regulæ theologicæ.—Comp. *Schleiermacher*, Kg. s. 527 ff. [Comp. *Cave*, Historia Literaria, ii. 229.] *Ritter*, vii. s. 593 ff.

(3) He died A.D. 1205. His Libri V. Sententiarum were edited by *Mathoud*, Paris 1655, fol., together with the sentences of *Pulleyn* (see § 150, note 10). Comp. *Cramer*, vi. s. 754–790.

(4) He flourished about the year 1180, and *wrote:* Libri IV. contra manifestas et damnatas etiam in Conciliis hæreses, quas Sophistæ Abælardus, Lombardus, Petrus Pictavinus et Gilbertus Porretanus, quatuor Labyrinthi Galliæ, uno spiritu Aristotelico efflati, libris sententiarum suarum acuunt, limant, **roborant**. Extracts from this work (hitherto unpublished) are given by *Bulæus*, l.c. t. ii. p. 629–660.

(5) Sarisberiensis; he was Bishop of Chartres from the year 1176, and died A.D. 1182. About the year 1156 he addressed to Thomas Becket: Policraticus, sive de Nugis curialium et Vestigiis philosophorum, libri viii. This work was followed by Metalogici libri iv. (published Lugd. Bat. 1639; Amst. 1664). — Epistolæ cccii. (written from 1155–1180, ed. *Papirius Masson*, Par. 1611, 4to). Comp. Bibl. Patr. Max., Lugd. t. xxiii. *Schleiermacher*, l.c. s. 527. * *Hermann Reuter*, Joh. von Salisbury, zur Geschichte der christlichen Wissenschaft im 12 Jahrhundert, Berl. 1842. *Ritter*, vii. s. 605 ff.

(6) Among the Arabic commentators on Aristotle, *Avicenna*, who died 1036, and *Averrhoes*, who died 1217, deserve particular notice. [Comp. *Ritter*, Ueber unsere Kenntniss der arabischen Philosophie, 4to, Götting. 1844. *Renan*, Averroes et l'Averroisme, Paris 1852, etc. On *Avicebron*, De Materia Universali (probably Jewish, not Arabic), see Theol. Jahrb. (Tübingen) 1856 and 1857, and *Sal. Munk*, Mélanges de Philos. juive et arabe, Paris 1857.] Notwithstanding ecclesiastical prohibitions, the study of Aristotle gradually gained ground. On the historical development of these studies, see *Amad. Jourdain*, Recherches critiques sur l'âge et l'origine des traductions latines d'Aristotle, et sur les commentaires grecs ou arabes, employés par les docteurs scolastiques (Par. 1819), and the works on the History of Philosophy: *Tennemann*, viii. s. 353. *Ritter*, l.c.

(7) *Alexander Alesius;* he was called Doctor irrefragabilis, and died A.D 1246. He was the first theologian who made a thorough use of the Aristotelian philosophy. His *work* entitled: Summa Universæ Theologiæ (divided into Quæs-

§ 141.] SECOND PERIOD OF SCHOLASTICISM. 129

Gones, Membra, and Articuli), was edited after his death by Guilelmus de Melitona about the year 1252, by order of Pope Innocent IV. Other editions are those of Venet. 1576, and of Colon. 1622, 4 vols. fol. Extracts from it are given by Semler, l.c. s. 120 ff. Cramer, vii. s. 161 ff. Heinrich, s. 208 ff. Comp. Schleiermacher, s. 551 f.

(8) Called Simia Aristotelis; the most learned of the scholastics, a native of Suabia, taught at Paris and Cöln, was Bishop of Regensburg (Ratisbon), and died at Cöln 1280. Opera: ed. Petrus Jammy, Ord. Praedic., Lugd. 1651, 21 vols. fol. Among his numerous works we mention his Commentaries on Aristotle and Peter Lombard, as well as his Summa Theol. (ex edit. Basil. 1508, 2 vols. fol.). Ritter, viii. s. 181–256.

(9) The Doctor angelicus; he was born A.D. 1224, in the kingdom of Naples. He was a disciple of Albert, but the strict theological tendency predominated in him more than in his teacher. He taught at Paris, Rome, Bologna, and Pisa, and died A.D. 1274, on his way to the Council of Lyons. He was canonized by Pope John XXII. A.D. 1323. His principal works are: Commentarii in libros iv. Sententiar. Petri Lombardi (c. notis J. Nicolai, Par. 1659, 4 vols. fol.).—Summa Totius Theologiae in 3 partes distributa. (Extracts from these works are given by Semler, l.c. s. 58 ff. Cramer, vii. s. 161 ff. Heinrich, s. 219 ff. Schroekh, xxix. s. 71–196.) Opera Omnia, Romae 1572, 17 vols. fol.; Antverp. 1575; Venet. 1745, 20 vols. fol. For further particulars, see Munscher, von Cölln, ii. s. 19. Comp. C. F. Kling, Descriptio Summae Theologicae Thomae Aquinatis succincta, Bonn. 1846, 4to. H. Hortel, Thomas von Aquino und seine Zeit, nach Touron, Delecluze, und den Quellen, Augsb. 1846. Ritter, viii. s. 257-354. Jourdain, La Philosophie de S. Thomas d'Aquin, Paris 1858. "Thomas, with the finest and sharpest speculation unites the gift of clear exposition to a degree seldom found among the scholastics, and consequently his Summa attained the highest renown in the Catholic Church." Gieseler, Dg. s. 460. [Hampden, Life of Aquinas, 1846. Abbé Malé, La Theol. de St. Thos. 1 vol. Paris 1856. K. Werner, Der heilige St. Thos. von Aquin, Bd. iii. Regensb. 1859. H. E. Plassmann, Die Schule und Lehre des heil. Thos. von Aquin, Bd. v. 1858, 1859.— New edition of his works by Migne, with a full Index, 1860;

also by *Vives*, Paris. *Billuart* edited the Summa, 10 vols. Paris 1839; *Lavergne and Durand*, the De Veritate, Nimes 1854. *Goudin*, Philosophia juxta D. Thomæ dogmata, 4 vols. Paris 1850. Aquinas Catena Aurea, in connection with the Oxford Library of the Fathers, translated, 4 vols.]

(10) *Duns Scotus*, surnamed Doctor subtilis, was born at Dunston in Northumberland, taught theology at Oxford from the year 1301, at Paris from the year 1304, and died at Cöln A.D. 1308. He introduced a number of barbarous technical terms, such as quidditates, hæccitates, incircumscriptibilitates, etc., with these began the degeneracy of scholasticism into hair-splitting subtleties. His *complete works* were edited by *Luc. Wadding*, Lugd. 1639, 12 vols. fol. His *principal work* is: Quodlibeta et Commentaria in libros iv sententiarum, also Quæstiones quodlibeticæ. Comp. *Semler*, l.c. s. 68–73. *Cramer*, vii. s. 295–308. *Heinrich*, s. 226 ff. *Schröckh*, xxix. s. 237 ff. *Baumgarten-Crusius*, De Theologia Scoti, Jena 1826, 4to. *Ritter*, viii. s. 354–472; he calls him "*the most acute and penetrating mind among the philosophers of the Middle Ages.*"

(11) In the formal point of view the systems of Thomas and Scotus differ in this, that the former has regard rather to the scientific, the latter to the practical aspect of religion:[1] *Ritter*, viii. s. 365 f. *Baur*, Lehrb. s. 160 (1st ed.). In the doctrine of ideas (universals) the Thomists were more Aristotelian, the Scotists more Platonic. The former take more profound views of the relation between divine grace and human liberty (Augustinianism); the latter, laying (in the manner of Pelagius) greater stress upon the freedom of the will, advanced notions which commended themselves to common sense and the interests of morality. And, lastly, the same difference respecting the doctrine of the immaculate conception of the Virgin, which caused a bitter enmity between the two orders, also existed between the two schools. ["Thomas and Duns Scotus," says *Baur*, Dg. 226 (2d ed.), "*are the founders of two schools into which the whole of the scholastic philosophy*

---

[1] The same difference is found in the Dominicans and Franciscans; the former were zealous for dogma, and became inquisitors; the latter were zealous for morals, and, in their reformatory zeal, even ran into the danger of becoming heretical.

and theology was divided." Among their differences are these: Thomas makes theology to be essentially theoretical; Scotus, practical; the former makes God to be essentially the one universal, infinite essence; with the latter the *will* is the starting-point, etc.] Compare the Special History of Doctrines.

(12) *John of Fidanza*, surnamed Doctor Seraphicus, and called Eutychius or Eustachius by the Greeks, was (A.D. 1257) Doctor Theol. Parisiensis and Præpositus Generalis of the Franciscan order, died A.D. 1274 as cardinal, and was canonized A.D. 1482 by Pope Sixtus IV.—*Opera:* Romæ 1588–1596, 8 vols. fol. Mogunt. 1609 [in 8vo, by Vivès, Paris].—His *principal works* are: Commentarius in libros iv. Sententiarum; Breviloquium; Centiloquium. He is also said to be the author of the work entitled: Compendium Theologicæ Veritatis (de natura Dei). He wrote several mystical tracts: Speculum Animæ; Itinerarium Mentis in Deum; de Reductione Artium ad Theologiam. Comp. *Semler*, l.c. s. 52–58. *Heinrich*, s. 214 ff. *Gass* in *Herzog's* Realencykl. *W. A. Hollenberg*, Studien zu Bonaventura, Berlin 1862.

• Unique in his way in the history of scholasticism is *Raimundus Lullus*, born at Majorca, 1236, died 1315. *Opera:* Mogunt. 1772, in 10 vols. His chief work is his "Ars Generalis," which, leaving the beaten path of the school, attempted to give a key to the foundations of knowledge. With this is connected his work written in Rome, Necessaria demonstratio articulorum fidei. Comp. *Helfferich* on R. Lullus, Berlin 1858, and *Kling* in *Herzog*, viii. s. 558 ff. Comp. *Ritter*, Christl. Phil. i. s. 662. " It was a leading object with him," says *Neander*, " to prevent the spread of the principles of *Averrhoes* in theology." Kg. (3d ed.) ii. s. 560 f.

§ 152.

(c) *Third Period—the Fall of Scholasticism in the Fourteenth and Fifteenth Centuries.*

During the last period of scholasticism, now approaching its fall, we meet with but few independent thinkers, among whom the most distinguished were *Durandus of St. Pourçain* (1),

Raimund of Sabunde (2), and *William Occam* (3), the nominalistic sceptic. *Gabriel Biel* (4), a disciple of the last mentioned, but less original, was the last of the schoolmen, although the degenerate tendency still lingered to evoke a stronger desire for a complete revolution in theology (5).

(1) *Durandus de Sancto Portiano* (a village in the diocese of Clermont), surnamed Doctor resolutissimus, was from the year 1312 professor of theology in the University of Paris, and afterwards Bishop of Annecy and of Meaux; died in 1333. He wrote: Opus super Sententias Lombardi, Par. 1508; Venet. 1571, fol. (now scarce).—Although a Dominican monk, he ventured to oppose Thomas, on which account he was looked upon as an apostate by the genuine Thomists; see *Cramer*, Bd. vii. s. 801 ff. *Baur*, Dg. 163, 230, 240 (2d ed.). *Ritter*, viii. 547–574. *Gieseler*, Dg. 462: "*He is distinguished for his apt and clear statements of the most difficult positions.*"

(2) He was a teacher at Toulouse about the year 1436, and composed a *work* on natural theology under the title: Liber Creaturarum, seu Theol. Naturalis, Argent. 1496, fol.; Fref. 1635. It was republished in a somewhat altered form by *Amos Comenius* under the title: Oculus Fidei, Amst. 1661. Solisbaci, 1852. Comp. *Montaigne*, Essais, l. ii. c. 12. *F. Holberg*, De theologia naturali Raimundi de Sabunde, Hal. 1843. *Matzke*, Die natürliche Theologie des Raymundus von Sabunde, Bresl. 1846. *Ritter*, viii. s. 658–678.

(3) *Occam* died A.D. 1347. He was called Venerabilis inceptor, Doctor singularis. Though a Franciscan monk, he differed from Duns Scotus, as the Dominican Durandus did from Thomas; in both these cases, therefore, the strict connection between the spirit of the order and the spirit of the school is destroyed. Occam took an independent political position, even in opposition to the Pope (John XXII.), by defending the doctrine of the poverty of Christ; on this point, see the works on ecclesiastical history. As a scholastic divine, he brought nominalism again into repute. Of his *works* the following are doctrinal: Compendium Errorum Joh. XXII. (in *Goldasti* Monarchia, Han. 1612, p. 957).—Quæstiones super iv. libb. Sententiarum.—Quodlibeta vii. Tract. de Sacramento

Altaris.—Centiloquium Theologicum (the last of which, in particular, contains a great many subtleties). See *Cramer*, vii. s. 812 ff. On his ironical scepticism, which he knew how to conceal under the mask of the most rigid orthodoxy, see *Rettberg* in the *Studien* und *Kritiken*, 1839, 1. His works abound with absurd questions (such as those mentioned in note 5). Comp. *Rettberg*, s. 80. *Ritter*, viii. s. 574–604. *Baur*, Trinitätslehre, ii. s. 867 ff. But with philosophical scepticism, he and the later nominalists show only a still more rigid supernaturalism in the theological sphere.

(4) He was born at Spires, was professor of philosophy and theology in the University of Tübingen, and died A.D. 1495. —*He wrote:* Collectorium s. Epitome ex Guilelmo Occam in iv. libros Magistri Sententiarum ed. *Wend. Steinbach*, Tub. 1502, 2 vols. fol. *Wernsdorf*, Diss. Theol. de Gabr. Biel celeberrimo Papista Antipapista, Wittenb. 1749. [*Schröckh*, Kirchengesch. xxx. 425, xxxiii. 534.] Biel was followed by *Antoninus Florentinus* and *Paul Cortesius;* see *Münscher, von Cölln*, s. 30. *Cajetan, Eck*, and others, who lived in the time of Luther, were also thorough scholastics.

(5) Thus it was asked: Num possibilis propositio: Pater Deus odit filium? Num Deus potuerit suppositare mulierem, num diabolum, num asinum, num cucurbitam, num silicem? Tum quemadmodum cucurbita fuerit concionatura, editura miracula, figenda cruci? Et quid consecrasset Petrus, si consecrasset eo tempore, quo corpus Christi pendebat in cruce? . . . "Sunt innumerabiles λεπτολεσχίαι his quoque multo subtiliores, de instantibus, de notionibus, de relationibus, de formalitatibus, de quidditatibus, de ecceitatibus, quas nemo possit oculis assequi, nisi tam Lynceus, ut ea quoque per altissimas tenebras videat, quae nusquam sunt." *Erasmi* Stultitiae Laus, Bas. 1676, p. 141 ss., and in Annotation. in 1 Tim. i. 6, etc. Comp. *Ad Müller*, Erasmus, s. 155, and *Gieseler*, Kg. ii. 4, s. 324. Respecting the decline of scholasticism, *Luther* wrote to John Lange at Erfurt: Aristoteles descendit paulatim, inclinatus ad ruinam prope futuram sempiternam. Mire fastidiuntur lectiones sententiariae, nec est ut quis sibi auditores sperare possit, nisi theologiam hanc, i.e. Bibliam aut S. Augustinum aliumve ecclesiasticae auctoritatis doctorem velit profiteri. The letter in question is

reprinted in *De Wette's* Collection, i. Nr. 34, s. 57. Comp. the sixtieth letter (addressed to Staupitz), s. 102.

[*Baur*, in his Dg. s. 229 (2d ed.) sq., traces the decline of scholasticism back to Duns Scotus. **The more** sharply Duns Scotus distinguished between understanding and will, the **more did he** separate the two, and sever the practical from **the theoretical.** All that remained was to separate thought **from** being, and the dissolution was complete. This was **acco**mplished by the nominalism of Occam, **according** to **which** there was no objective reality corresponding **to** general **ideas.** Between the two stood Durandus, **who** also viewed theology **as** a practical science, and made its object to **be, not** God, but the life of faith. Faith was at last left to rest merely upon authority.—The antagonism of realism and nominalism (s. 233) runs through the whole of the scholastic theology: **it is its** moving principle, and the stages of its development **are** also identical with the different periods of **scholasticism.**—Aristotelianism determined the *form* of scholasticism: but Platonism, through the influence of the **writings of** Dionysius the Areopagite, **went along** with it, **and in the** works of the great scholastics (*e.g.* Aquinas) con**tributed its** substantial elements to scientific **theology.**]

§ 153.

Mysticism.

H. Schmid, Der Mysticismus des Mittelalters in seiner Entstehungsperiode, Jena 1824. * *Charles Schmidt*, Essai sur les mystiques du quatorzième siècle, Strasb. 1836, 4to. *Helfferich*, Die Geschichte der christlichen Mystik in ihrer Entwicklung und in ihren Denkmalen, 2 vols. Hamb. 1843. *Franz Pfeiffer*, Deutsche Mystiker des 14 Jahrhunderts, 1st vol. Leipz. 1845. *Wilh. Wackernagel*, Ueber die Gottesfreunde, s. Beiträge zur vaterländischen Geschichte, Bd. ii. Basel 1843, s. 111 ff. *C. U. Hahn*, Geschichte der Ketzer im Mittelalter, im 11, 12 und 13 Jahr. 3 vols. Stuttg. 1850. *L. Noack*, Die christliche Mystik, nach ihrem geschichtlichen Entwicklungsgange, Theil i. Die christl. Mystik des Mittelalt. *Ullmann*, Reformatoren vor d. Reformation, 2 vols. 1866 [transl. in Clark's Foreign Library, Edinburgh. *Ullmann* in Studien u. Kritiken, 1852. *R. A. Vaughan's* Hours with the Mystics, 2d ed. 2 vols. Lond. 1860. *H. L. J. Heppe*, Geschichte der quietistischen Mystik in der Kathol. Kirche, Berlin 1875.]

The influence of scholasticism was beneficially counterbalanced by *mysticism*, which, in effusions of the heart, rich indeed, although at times indistinct, restored to theology those vital streams of which it had been deprived by the excess of dialectics (1). Theologians, whose tendency was of a positive kind, such as *Bernard of Clairvaux*, had before this insisted upon the importance of religious feeling being connected with the faith of the Church, and of a devout disposition as distinguished from mere speculative tendencies (2). Some of the scholastic divines themselves had endeavoured to reconcile the claims of pious emotion with the demands made by the scientific development of the age, on which account they are commonly called either mystical scholastics or dialectic mystics (3). But about the time of the decline of scholasticism, mysticism made its appearance in a much more vigorous and independent form, though under very different aspects. As had been the case with the scholastics, so some of the mystics adhered more closely to the doctrine of the Church, while others, departing from it, adopted heretical opinions (4). As to the scientific method, one class of mystics manifested a more philosophical culture and preparation than was shown by the other. The doctrines of *Master Eckart* (5) had much in common with the fanatical pantheistic sects, and were consequently condemned by the papal see. Among those who followed more closely (though with various modifications) the doctrine of the Church were *John Tauler* (6), *Henry Suso* (7), *John Ruysbrock* (8), the (anonymous) author of the " Büchlein von der deutschen Theologie" (*i.e.* the little book of German Theology) (9), *Thomas à Kempis* (10), and *John Charlier Gerson* (11); the last also endeavoured to construct a scientific system of mysticism, and to give to it a psychological basis. In the Greek Church, too, mysticism had its representatives (*Nicolas Cabasilas*) (12).

(1) "*Mysticism forms in itself a contrast to scholasticism proper, inasmuch as the prevailing tendency of the latter is a*

dialectical process of the understanding. But mysticism could enter into a union with scholasticism by creating a desire for preserving the very hearth of religion in the inmost depth of the human heart, as its true seat, in order to supply that which **could not** be furnished by purely dialectical thinking," Baur, **Lehrb.** der Dg. s. 167 (1st ed.). On the undoubtedly well-**founded** difference between the psychological (religious) and speculative (theosophic) mysticism, see ibid. p. 168, and his **work** on the Trinity, ii. 880 ff.

(2) He was surnamed Doctor mellifluus, and died A.D. **1153.** His *works* were edited by Mabillon, Par. **(1666-1690) 1719**, 2 vols. fol.; Ven. 1726, 3 vols. fol. He wrote epistles, sermons, and mystical tracts: De consideratione, ad Eugenium III., Papam; Libri v. de Gratia et libero Arbitrio, etc. Comp. *Neander*, Der heilige Bernhard und sein Zeitalter, Berlin **1813.** Ellendorf, Der heilige Bernhard von Clairvaux **und die** Hierarchie seiner Zeit, Essen. 1837. *H. Schmid*, l.c. **s.** 187 **ff.** *D. Wette*, Sittenlehre, ii. 2, s. 208 ff. *Böhringer*, ii. **1.** *J. C. Morrison*, u.s. (Ed. of his works by **Mandernach**, Trier 1864 ff.). Practical activity was also displayed by *Berthold*, a Franciscan, who lived between the years **1247** and 1272; he bordered upon mysticism. See his **sermons, edited** by *Kling*, Berl. 1824, and the review of *Jac.* **Grimm** in the Wiener Jahrbücher, Jahrg. 1825 (Bd. xxxii.), s. **194 ff.** [*Bernard's* Works repub. by *Gaume* and *Migne*, Paris.]

(3) To these belong essentially *William of Champeaux*, and the theologians of the school of St. Victor, as well as *Bonaventura*. Comp. § **150 and 151.** There is also a mystical background in the writings of Anselm of Canterbury, Albertus Magnus, and Thomas Aquinas. And here, too, it cannot but be noticed that the older mysticism shows an internal affinity for realism, while the latter made an alliance with nominalism.

(4) "*The ideas of the Church* mystics rest on the positive foundation of the creed, *and* all the spiritual experience described by them is most intimately connected with the doctrine of the Trinity, the incarnation of Christ, the operation of the Spirit promised by Christ, and the mystery of the Lord's Supper. But the abstract theory of the heretical mystics usually seeks to

fathom **the depths of** the soul, which, according **to** their teaching, is nothing else but God Himself; they teach that Deification is **the work** of man himself, and regard the positive doctrines as at most the symbols of those inward processes on which the attainment of the end of our life depends. IT IS OF SPECIAL IMPORTANCE, IN AN EXPOSITION OF THE HISTORY OF THIS PERIOD, DISTINCTLY TO SEPARATE THESE TWO KINDS OF CHURCHLY AND UNCHURCHLY, OR ORTHODOX **AND** HETERODOX MYSTICS," *Engelhardt*, Richard von St. Victor, s. 2. Comp. s. 97 f.

(5) *Amalrich of Bena* and *David of Dinanto* had previously developed the mystico-pantheistic system of John Scotus Erigena to **a** kind of fanaticism, and given to it that dangerous practical direction which is exhibited by some later sects of the Middle Ages. Comp. *Kronlein*, Amalrich von Bena und David von Dinanto (Studien und Kritiken, 1847, 2¹). *H. Schmid*, l.c. s. 587 ff. *Engelhardt*, Kirchengeschichtliche Abhandlungen, Erlang 1852, s. 251. *Mosheim*, De Beghardis et Beguinabus, p. 211, 255.—Among the mystics of the fourteenth century, *Master Eckart* (Aichard), a native of Saxony, and provincial of the order of Dominicans in Coln, has the same tendency, but in a more systematic form. "*His sense of the nearness of God, and his lofty and ardent love, are overwhelmed by the contemplation of an* abyss *of* lusts and blasphemy" (*Hase*). His doctrines were condemned, A.D. 1329, in **a** bull of Pope John XXII. Comp. *Charles Schmidt*, Essai, p. 51-57, and Studien und Kritiken, 1839, 3. *Mosheim*, l.c. p. 280. Apophthegms of German mystics in *Wackernagels* Lesebuch, i. Sp. 889-892. **H. Martensen*, Meister Eckart; Eine theologische Studie, Hamb. 1842. *Ullmann*, l.c. s. 20.

(6) He was called Doctor sublimis et illuminatus; he was a Dominican, and lived at Coln and Strassburg, and died A.D. 1361. He was a preacher of a high order of intelligence. A Latin edition of his *works by Laur. Surius*, Col. 1548. He wrote among others: Nachfolge des armen Lebens Christi.—Medulla Animæ (a collection of various tracts) is a later compilation; Sermons (3 Bde. Leipz. 1826). Comp.

---

¹ The doctrine of Amalrich is to be distinguished from that of his disciples; so, too, from that of David of Dinanto, whose connection with Scotus Erigena is denied by the author of the above essay.

Wackernagels Altdeutsches Lesebuch, Sp. 857 ff. [*Ch. Schmidt*, **Johannes** Tauler von Strassburg. Beitrag zur Geschichte der Mystik und des religiösen Lebens im **14** Jahrhundert, Hamb. 1841.] *Luther* writes respecting him to **Spalatin** (14th Dec. 1516): Si te delectat puram, solidam, antiquæ simillimam theologiam legere, in germanica lingua effusam, sermones Johannis Tauleri, prædicatoriæ professionis, tibi comparare potes... Neque enim ego vel in latina vel in nostra lingua theologiam vidi salubriorem et cum Evangelio consonantiorem. The letter is given by *De Wette*, Bd. i. Nr. 25, s. 46. *De Wette*, on the contrary, says (Christliche Sittenlehre, ii. 2, s. 220 ff.): "*His mysticism is very profound and fervent, and at the same time very speculative; but it possesses no intrinsic value; inasmuch as it is almost entirely negative, and consists only of a renunciation of all that is earthly and finite. On the contrary, the true, the essential, the divine, is, as it were, an empty space, because it is not brought into any definite relation to the life and heart,*" etc., *Böhringer*, Kirche Christi, ii. 3. [Life and Sermons (25) of John Tauler, by *S. Winkworth*, London 1857.]

(7) *Henry Suso* (Germ. der *Seuse*, sometimes called **Amandus vom Berg**) was born at Constance, and died A.D. 1365. His *works* were translated into Latin by *Laur. Surius*, Col. 1532. *Quétif* et *Echard*, Scriptores Ord. Præd., Par. 1719, t. i. p. 654.—Comp. Heinrich Suso's Leben und Schriften, herausgegeben von *Melch* **Diepenbrock**, mit Einleit. von *Görres*. 1829, 1837,[1] 1840. Geistliche Blüthen von Suso, Bonn 1834. *Wackernagel*, Deutsches Lesebuch, Sp. 871 ff. *Ch. Schmidt* in Stud. u. Kritik. 1843, 1. Suso is more poetical than profound and speculative, his writings are full of allegories and imagery, frequently fantastic, but often full of religious ardour. A romantic, chivalrous, childlike soul! He is not to be confounded with the author of the work "On the Nine Rocks" (Rulman Mersurin); comp. *Ch. Schmidt* in Illgens Zeitschrift, 1839, 2. An important contribution to the history of mysticism is the treatise of *W. Wackernagel*, Ueber die Gottesfreunde in Basel, 1843. *Böhringer*, l.c. *F. Bricker*, Sur la Vie et les Ecrits de H. Suso, Strasb.

---

[1] We quote from the edition of 1837

(8) He was prior of the regular canons of Grünthal in Brabant, and died A.D. 1381. He was surnamed Doctor ecstaticus. His *works* (originally written in the Flemish language) were translated into Latin by *Laur. Surius*, Col. 1552, 1609, 1692; and into German by *Gottfr. Arnold*, Offenbach 1701, 4to. New edition by *Arnswaldt*, with Preface by *Ullmann*, Hamb. 1848. Comp. *Engelhardt* in the work mentioned § 150, note 9.—*Ruysbrock* stands, as it were, on the boundaries between the orthodox and the heterodox mystics; *J. Ch. Gerson*, who wrote against him, numbered him among the latter; but comp. *Engelhardt*, l.c. s. 275: "*The line of demarcation between heterodox and orthodox mysticism, which we find distinctly drawn in the writings of Ruysbrock, was so fine, and might so easily be passed over, that nothing but a firm adherence to that form of belief which was generally adopted and sanctioned by the usage of the Fathers, as well as by the authority of the Church, seemed a sufficient protection against such errors.*"—Comp. *De Wette*, Christliche Sittenlehre, s. 247: "*In the writings of Ruysbrock* (as well as in those of Tauler) *the idea of the absolute, and of the renunciation of all that is finite, of absorption into the one and undivided, is set forth as that to which all is to be referred. Ruysbrock recognized, even more than Tauler, the indwelling of the Divine in man, an admission of much importance. . . . In a moral aspect, the writings of Ruysbrock are of more value than those of Tauler: the former developes more distinctly the nature of a virtuous life, and warns against spiritual sloth . . . ; but he has fallen more frequently than Tauler into the error of mystical sensuousness and extravagance,*" etc. Comp., however, *Ullmann*, i. s. 36 ff.

(9) The full title of this work is: *Deutsche Theologie, oder ein edles Büchlein vom rechten Verstande, was Adam und Christus sei, und wie Adam in uns sterben und Christus in uns leben soll.* It was first published, A.D. 1516, by *Luther* (with a recommendatory Preface); afterwards (also in commendation) by *Joh. Arnd*, 1631; by *Grell*, 1817; by *Detzer*, Erl. 1827; by † *Troxler*, St. Gallen 1837, and by *Pfeiffer*: *Theologia deutsch, die leret gar manchen lieblichen unterscheit gotlicher warheit und seit (sagt) gar hohe und gar schone ding von einem volkommen leben* (neue, nach der einzigen bisjetzt bekannten

Handschrift besorgte Ausg.), Stuttg. 1851, 1853. Comp. Luther's opinion of this work in *De Wette's* collection of Luther's letters, Nr. 60, s. 102: "*This noble little book, though simple and without adornment in words of human wisdom, is much richer and **more** precious in art, and that wisdom which is divine. And, to praise according to my old folly, next to the Bible and St. Augustine, I do not know of any book from which I have learnt or would wish to learn more of what God, Christ, man, and all things are.*" Extract from Luther's Preface. *De Wette* (Christl. Sittenlehre, p. 251) also calls the work "*a sound and marrowy treatise, full of spirit and life, written in a pure and solid style, and worthy of being so strongly recommended by Luther.*" Comp. *Ullmann*, Das Reformatorische und Speculative in der Denkweise des Verf. der deutschen Theologie, in Stud. und Kritiken, 1852, 4, s. 859 ff. [Theologia Germanica, edited by *Dr. Pfeiffer*, transl. by *Susanna Winkworth*, Preface by *C. Kingsley*, Lond.]

'(10) His true name was *Thomas Hamerken* of Kempen; he was sub-prior of the Augustinian monks on St. Agnes' Mount near Zwoll, and died A.D. 1471. "*He was rather a pious, warm-hearted, and edifying preacher, than a mystic properly speaking; at least he possessed scarcely anything of a speculative tendency,*" *De Wette*, l.c. s. 247. He was the author of several pious tracts: Soliloquia Animae, Hortulus Rosarum, Vallis Liliorum, De tribus Tabernaculis, De Solitudine, De Silentio, etc. His most celebrated work (which some, however, have ascribed to other authors, *e.g.* to Abbot Gerson or to John Gerson) is: De Imitatione Christi, libri iv. *Opera:* Norimb. 1494; Par. 1520, fol.; Antw. 1607. [Thomae Kempensis, De Imitatione Christi Libri Quatuor. Textum ex autographo Thomae nunc primum reddidit, etc. *Carolus Hirsche*, Berolini 1874.] Comp. the critical examination of its authorship by †*J. P. Silbert* (who pronounces in favour of Thomas à Kempis), Wien 1828. *Gieseler*, Kg. ii. 4, s. 247 ff. *Ch. Schmidt*, Essai sur Jean Gerson, p. 121. *Ullmann*, Reformatoren, ii. s. 711 ff. *J. Mooren*, Nachrichten uber Thomas à Kempis, Crefeld 1855. [In favour of Gerson as the author: *A. A. Barbier*, Dissertation, Paris 1812, and *J. B. M. Gence*, Paris 1826. In favour of the Abbot Gersen:

G. D. *Gregory*, Memoire revu par Lanjuinais. Paris 1827. *Vot*, Etudes sur l'Imitation, Paris 1836.]

11, *John Charlier Gerson*, surnamed Doctor christianissimus, was chancellor of the University of Paris, and died A.D. 1429. In him "*the mediæval mysticism came to a consciousness of its real character, and succeeded up its really speculative and truly religious principles in a practical form.*" *Meier*, Dg. s. 203. He *wrote* : Considerationes de Theologia Mystica ; De Perfectione ; De Meditatione Cordis, etc. *Works*; Antv. 1706, fol.; Hagæ Comitum, 1728. Comp. *Engelhardt*, De Gersonio Mystico, Erl. 1822. *K. B. Hundeshagen*, Ueber die mystische Theologie des Joh. Charlier Gerson, Leipz 1834 reprinted separately from the fourth volume of the Zeitschr. für hist. Theologie. *A. Liebner*, Ueber Gersons mystische Theologie, in Stud. und Krit. 1835, H. 2, s. 277 ff. *C. Schmidt*, Essai sur Jean Gerson, chancelier de l'université et de l'église de Paris, Strasb. et Paris 1839. *J. B. Schwab*, Johannes Gerson, Würz. 1858. — On the different definitions of the nature of mysticism (Consideratio 28, p. 384) in *Hundeshagen*, s. 49. On his opposition to Ruysbroek, see above, note 8 — Gerson finds "*in the sensuous imagination a powerful foe to pure mystical contemplation, and takes care repeatedly and very strongly to warn against its illusions.*" *Hundeshagen*, s. 81.— On his philosophy, see *Ritter*, viii. s. 626-658. [*Bonnechose*, Gerson, Huss, etc., Paris, 2 vols.]

(12) *W. Gass*, Die Mystik des Nicolaus Cabasilas vom Leben in Christo, Greifswald 1849. Comp. also *Engelhardt* Die Arsenianer und Hesychasten, in Illgens Zeitschr. für hist. Theol. Bd. viii. s. 48 ff. *A. Jahn*, Geschichte byzantinischer Theologie, in Stud. u. Krit. 1843, s. 724.

§ 154.

Scientific Opposition to Scholasticism.

Chr. Meiners, Lebensbeschreibungen berühmter Männer aus den Zeiten der Wiederherstellung der Wissenschaften, Zürich 1795. *A. H. L. Heeren* Geschichte der klassischen Literatur seit dem Wiederaufleben der Wissenschaften, Gött. 1797 1801. *H. A. Erhard*, Geschichte des Wiederaufblühens wissenschaftlicher Bildung, Magdeburg 1827. 1830, 2 vols.

Even as early as the thirteenth century *Roger Bacon* had combated the one-sided speculative tendency of scholasticism, and endeavoured to improve the method of studying theology (1). But the second half of the fifteenth century was distinguished for the restoration of classical studies, by **which the human mind was delivered from that** one-sided theological specula**tion which led** astray both the scholastic and the mystical **divines, and** excited and directed to **a** more harmonious **development** of all the powers of the soul, **to a** more simple **and** natural consideration **of** things, and above all, **to a more jud**icious treatment of all spiritual subjects (2). *Laurentius Valla* (3), *John Reuchlin* (4), and *Desiderius Erasmus* (5) **may**, generally speaking, **be** considered as the restorers of classical (and to some extent of Hebrew) philology. *Marsilius Ficinus* (6) and *John Picus of Mirandola* (7) were the principal advocates **of** the study of **the** Platonic philosophy, and thus, on the one **hand,** limited the excessive authority **of** Aristotle and the dominion of scholasticism, **and, on the** other, showed how **mysticism** might be more closely **reconciled and** united with **speculation.**

(1) *Roger Bacon*, surnamed Doctor mirabilis, **was a Francis**can, **and professor** of theology in **the** University **of** Oxford **from the year 1240.** He *wrote* (A.D. 1267): Opus Majus de **Utilitate** Scientiarum **ad** Clementem **IV., ed.** by *Jebb*, **Lond. 1733. Very** characteristic extracts **from it** are **given by** *Giescler*, **ii. 2, s. 382, Anm.** w. *Brewer*, Rogeri **Baconis opera quædam hactenus inedita, vol. i. (**containing **opus tertium, opus minus, Compendium Philosophiæ), Lond. 1859. Comp.** *Emile Charles*, **Roger Bacon, sa vie, ses ouvrages, ses doctrines, d'après des textes inédits, Paris 1861. Also:** *Gelzers* **Monatsblätter, xxvii. 2, s. 63 : Bacon's opposition to scholasticism is "***fundamental : he* denies the *old system in its premisses and in its conclusions, with its method and its results,* and sub*stitutes for the old principle a new one of his* own, on which he *founds the structure of a new and quite original* doctrine."

(2) " *If we ask what forms the most obvious* contrast with the *scholastic philosophy and theology, as well as with* the tendency

of scholasticism itself, we may say that it is sound common sense, experience (both outward and inward), knowledge of nature, humanity," Hegel, Gesch. der Phil. iii. s. 200.

(3) *Valla* died A.D. 1457. His *works* were published at Basel 1540, 1543. Elegantiarum Lat. Ling. libri vi.: Dialect. libri iii.: Annot. in Nov. Test. (ed. *Erasmus*, Tur. 1505; ed. *Revius*, Amst. 1631): De ementita Constantini Donatione.

(4) *John Reuchlin*, otherwise called Capnio, lived from 1455 to 1522. Comp. *Mayerhoff*, Reuchlin und seine Zeit, Berl. 1830. *Meiners*, l.c. i. s. 44 ff. He especially furthered the study of the Hebrew language as well as that of the Cabbala, and gained a glorious victory over the Viri Obscuri of his age. [*D. F. Strauss* in Ulrich von Hutten, 1858, Bd. i. s. 188–230. Reuchlin's *philosophical works* are: De Verbo Mirifico, 1495; De Arte Cabbalist. 1517. The Epistolæ Obscurorum Virorum, 1515; on the authorship, see *Sir William Hamilton's* Discussions (from Edinburgh Review), p. 202–238.]

(5) *Desiderius Erasmus* (Gerhard) of Rotterdam was born A.D. 1486, and died 1536. *Adolf Muller*, Leben des Erasmus von Rotterdam, Hamb. 1828. *Opera*: Bas. 1540, 8 vols., and Lugd. Bat. 1703–1706, 10 vols. fol. In his Ratio perveniendi ad Veram Theologiam, in the work entitled Laus Stultitiæ, and elsewhere, he severely criticized the extravagances of scholasticism, and pointed the way to a more judicious treatment of theology. His critical edition of the New Testament (edit. princeps, published by *Froben*, Basel 1516[1]) led to a more accurate study of the Bible; in his letters and various essays he endeavoured to spread the light of human civilization. His relation to the Reformation, and to the theology of the Reformers, will come before us in the next period. [His first work, De Contemptu Mundi, 1487. *Lives*: By †*Durand de Laur*, Paris 1872; *Stichart*, Leipz. 1870. *English lives* of Erasmus, by *Knight*, Cambr. 1726; by *Jortin*, 2 vols. 4to, 1758–1760; by *Charles Butler*, Lond. 1825; by *Pennington*, Lond. 1876; by *Drummond*, Lond. 1878.]

(6) Respecting the controversy between the Aristotelians

---

[1] The publication of the Polyglot edition of Cardinal *Ximenes*, just before the rise of the Saxon Reformation, is no less important. [See Introd. to *Tischendorf's* N. T. ed. 8.]

and Platonists, see *Münscher, von Cölln*, ii. s. 27. *Marsilius Ficinus* translated the works of Plato, and *wrote*: De Relig. christ. et Fidei Pietate ad Laur. Med., and De Immortalitate Animæ; his *works* were published at Paris 1641, fol. He died A.D. **1499**. Comp. *Sieveking*, Gesch. d. Platon. Akad. zu Florenz, Gött. 1812. *Ritter*, v. s. 272–291.

(7) *Giovanni Pico della Mirandola* was born A.D. 1463, and died **1494**. He endeavoured to harmonize Plato with Aristotle. His *works* were published at Basel 1601, fol.; he *wrote* among others: In Hexaëmeron, libb. vii. — Quæstiones 900 — De Christi Regno et Vanitate Mundi — In Platonis Convivium, libri iii. — Epistolæ, etc. See *Meiners*, l.c. ii. near the commencement.[1] Comp. *Sigwart*, Ulrich Zwingli, der Charakter seiner Theologie, mit besonderer Rücksicht auf Picus von Mirandula, Stuttg. **1855**, p. 14 sq.

§ 155.

Practical Opposition—Forerunners of the Reformation.

Flathe, Geschichte der Vorläufer der Reformation, 2 vols. Leipz. 1835, 1836. *C. Ullmann*, Reformatoren vor der Reformation, vornehmlich in Deutschland und den Niederlanden, 2 vols. Hamburg 1841, 1842, new ed. 1866 [translated in Clark's For. Theol. Lib., Edin. 2 vols.].

The spirit of the Reformation manifested itself more and more, not only in science, but also directly in the sphere of the practical Christian life. *John Wykliffe* (1), *John Hus* (2), and *Jerome of Prague*, as well as their followers, starting from a purer biblical doctrine, adopted in part the doctrines of the mystics, in part the scholastic forms of thought, although their tendency was on the whole more practical. Some of their followers fell into the errors of former fanatical sects (3). The tendency of *Jerome Savonarola* (4) is quite peculiar; his theology has much of the mystical, with an apocalyptic colouring. *John Wessel* of Groningen, on the contrary, united

---

[1] In the *Greek* Church, *Gemistius Pletho* (in the fifteenth century) followed Plato, while *Gennadius* appears as a representative of Aristotelianism; comp. *Gass*, Gennadius und Plato, Bresl. 1844.

in himself the nobler spirit of mysticism and the true spirit of scientific inquiry, striving to throw off the fetters of scholasticism; he thus became, in a stricter sense, a forerunner of Luther (5).

(1) He was professor of theology at the University of Oxford, and combated from the year 1360 the order of the mendicant friars. Gregory XI. condemned nineteen of his theses (A.D. 1377). His controversy respecting the doctrine of transubstantiation will come under consideration in the Special History of Doctrines.—His principal doctrinal work is: Dialogorum libri v. (Trialogus), Bas. 1525, ed. *L. Th. Wirth*, Francof. et Lips. 1753, 4to. Comp. *R. Vaughan*, Life and Opinions of J. de Wycliffe, Lond. 1829, 1831, 2 vols., new ed. 1853. *Webb le Bas*, Life of Wiclif, Lond. 1832. *Oscar Jäger*, John Wykliffe und seine Bedeutung für die Reformation, Halle 1854. **Böhringer*, Kirchengesch. in Biographien, ii. 4. 1. *Lechler*, Wiclif als Vorläufer der Ref., Lpz. 1858. [*G. V. Lechler*, Johann von Wiclif u. die Vorgeschichte der Reformation, Leipz. 1873, 2 vols. In Eng. slightly abridged, and with add. notes by Dr. *P. Lorimer*, Lond. 1878, 2 vols. *Lechler* has also edited: Trialogus (1869); Tractatus de officio Pastorali (1863). Tracts and Treatises of W. with transl. from his Latin works by *R. Vaughan*, for the Wycliffe Society, 1848. *E. W. Lewald*, Die theol. Doctrin Wycliff's in Zeitschrift f. d. hist. Theol. 1846–47. Fasciculi Zizaniorum Mag. John Wyclif (ascribed to *Thos. Netter*), ed. *W. W. Shirley*, Oxford. *De Reaven Gronemann*, Diatribe in J. W. Vitam, Traj. ad Rhen. 1859. Wycliffe's Bible, Oxf. Univ. Press, 4 vols. 4to, 1850.] Cf. *Landerer* in *Herzog*, xiii. s. 694.

(2) *John Hus of Hussinecz* was, from the year 1402, pastor at Prague, and suffered martyrdom A.D. 1415 at Constance. His opposition to the Church was more of a practical than of a dogmatic nature. The views of Hus on the Lord's Supper differed less from the doctrine of the Church than those of his colleagues *Jerome of Prague* and *Jacobellus of Misa*, as will be shown in the Special History of Doctrines. Comp. *Neander*, Kleine Gelegenheitsschriften, 3d ed. s. 217 ff. †*Helfert*, Hus und Hieronymus, Studie, Prag 1853. [*Böhringer*, Kirche Christi, ii. 4. 2. *F. Palacky*, Gesch. d. Böhmen, Bd. 3.

L. Heller, Hieron. **von** Prag. Tüb. 1835. *A. B. Zurn*, Joh. Hus auf d. Concil zu Costnitz, Leipz. 1836. *Horst*, De Hussi Vita, Amst. 1837. *Bonnechose*, Gerson, Hus, etc., Paris 1853.]

(3) On the history of the Husites (also called Taborites and Calixtines), see the works on ecclesiastical history.—*Lenfant*, Histoire de la Guerre des Hussites, Amst. 1731, 2 vols. 4to. —*John Rokykzana* was one of their most eminent theologians. —*Martin Lokwitz* (Loquis), of Moravia, belonged to the fanatical party among the Husites; see *Schroekh*, xxxiv. s. 687. On their relation to the Waldenses: [*A. Gindely*, Böhmen u. Mähren in Ref., Prag 1858.] *Von Zezschwitz*, Die Katechismen der Waldenser u. böhmischen Brüder als Documente ihres gegenseitigen Lehraustausches, Erlangen 1863.

(4) He was a monk of the order of the Dominicans, born 1452 at Ferrara, lived from the year 1489 in Florence, and suffered martyrdom **A.D.** 1498. — *Picus of Mirandola*, the younger, composed a treatise in his defence [his life], which is reprinted in *Goldast*, Monarchia, t. i. p. 1635. *Burlamacchi*, a monk of his own order, wrote his life.— He *wrote:* Compendio di revelazione, 1495, a Latin translation of which **was** published 1496 [the Latin **was** the earlier]. — De Simplicitate Vitæ Christianæ. — Triumphus Crucis s. de Veritate Fidei, 1497, and various sermons.— Comp. *Rudelbach, Hieronymus Savonarola **und seine** Zeit, Hamburg 1835.—*Karl Meier, Girolamo Savonarola, Berl. 1836. Concerning his *theological* opinions, see *F. W. Ph. Ammon* in Winers und Engelhardts Neues kritisches Journal, Bd. viii. Ht. 3, s. 257–282. *Hase*, Neue Propheten, s. 97 ff. [*Madden*, Life of Savonarola, 2d ed. 2 vols. Lond. 1854. *E. J. Perrens*, Vie de S., 2 vols. Paris 1854, etc. *Pasquale Villari, La Storia di Savon. (from new documents), 2 vols. Firenze 1859, 1862, and in Eng. by *Horner*, London.— Etude sur Jérome Savonarole, par *Bayonne*, Paris 1879]

(5) His family name was *Gansfort;* he was surnamed Lux mundi, magister contradictionum, lived and taught theology at Cöln, Heidelberg, Louvain, and Paris, and died **A.D.** 1489. " *Though himself a scholastic divine, he announced that scholasticism would soon cease to exist, asserted that Scripture is the only foundation of faith, faith the ground of justification with-*

out works, and urged the spiritual nature of the whole **religious life**" (Meier, Dg. s. 238). *Works:* Gron. 1614. — Comp. *Maurling*, De Wesselii cum Vita tum Meritis in præparanda sacrorum Emendatione in Belgio Septentrionali, Traj. ad Rhen. 1831. **C. Ullmann*, Johann Wessel, ein Vorgänger Luthers, Ham. 1834 (2d ed. 1842).

And, lastly, **John Goch** of Mechlin, who died A.D. 1475; *John of Wesel*, professor of theology at Erfurt, and afterwards pastor at Worms (he died A.D. 1482), and others, as well as *Gerhard Groot* and the order of Regular Clerks, must be numbered among this class of men. Comp. *J. G. L. Scholz,* Diss. exhibens Disquisitionem, qua Thomæ a Kempis Sententia de Re Christiana exponitur et cum Gerhardi et Wesselii Gansfortii Sententiis comparatur, Gron. 1840. *Ullmann's* Ref. vor. d. Ref., Bd. i.

§ 156.

The Connection of the History of Doctrines with the History of the Church and the World in the present Period.

The present period illustrates, as much as any other, the intimate connection subsisting between the development of the life of the Church and of mankind in general, and the development of doctrine (1). Thus a parallel may clearly be drawn between the history of scholasticism on the one hand, and that of the papacy and the hierarchy on the other (2). Monasticism and celibacy not only tended to foster the spirit of subtle speculation among the schoolmen, but also awakened the deeper longings of the mystics (3). The splendour and magnificence of the Roman Catholic worship reacted upon the doctrines of the Church (especially on the doctrines of the sacraments and the saints) in proportion as the former itself owed its existence to the latter (4). The dogmatic spirit of the present period was also symbolically expressed in the art of the Middle Ages (5). The advantages which the West derived from the Crusades, the origin of which may be partly ascribed to the religious enthusiasm of the times, were manifold and of various description (6).—The great calamities and plagues of the fourteenth century, also, so impressed the minds **of the** people, as to be at least a partial cause of the religious and mystical phenomena **of** those times (as seen, *e.g.*, in the Flagellants) **(7)**.—After the exclusive use of the Latin language in all ecclesiastical matters had led to the neglect of a searching and critical examination **of the** Bible, and the adoption **of a** barbarous terminology, the spread of Greek literature, since the taking of Constantinople (A.D. 1453), exerted **a** beneficial influence both upon the study of the original languages of the sacred Scriptures and the treatment of theological subjects (8). And, in the last place, although the terrible institution of the Inquisition had for a time succeeded in intimidating the minds of the people, and in preventing the free exchange of ideas (9), yet the invention of printing (about the year 1440) (10), the discovery of America (A.D. 1490), and the entire revolution which took place in the history of nations, prepared the way for a new period, which rendered a new development of religious life necessary, as a consequence of the manifold changes in the modes of thought and life.

(1) Compare the general introduction above.

(2) It was not without significance that scholasticism commenced with the age of Gregory VII. In the dispute respecting episcopal investiture, *Anselm* supported the pretensions of the papal hierarchy, while somewhat later *Arnold of Brescia*, a disciple of Abélard, carried the more liberal doctrinal principles of his master into practical ecclesiastical questions. In a similar manner *Bernard of Clairvaux* united dogmatic orthodoxy with a rigid adherence to the papal institutions of the Church.—Scholasticism reached its highest point of development about the same time that the papacy of the Middle Ages reached its culminating point under Pope Innocent III., and a parallel may be clearly drawn between the disruption of the schools (Thomists and Scotists) and the papal schism which occurred soon afterwards.—As the see of Rome had formerly found a support in the realistic tendency of *Anselm*,

so it now met with open opposition on the part of the nominalist *Occam*.—The history of mysticism may be likewise so traced out, as to show that in one aspect it favoured the pretensions of the Roman see, and opposed them in another. The papacy itself had its roots (according to its real idea) in a mystical view of the world, but by its opposition to that idea, *i.e.* by its externality and worldliness, it called forth opposition on the part of the advocates of that mystical (spiritual) view of the world and its destiny. Comp. *Hagenbach* in the essay, cited § 149.

(3) Certain errors of the scholastics, as well as the mystics, can scarcely be comprehended except from the standpoint of a monastic cell. The earlier scholastic divines were Benedictines or regular canons; in later times the mendicant friars occupied the theological chairs (notwithstanding the long opposition made by the University of Paris), and conferred degrees and preferments. We must also take into consideration the jealousy already alluded to between the different orders, which was in intimate connection with the divisions among the scholastics. [Comp. Count *de Montalembert*, Les Moines d'Occident (from St. Benedict to St. Bernard), 7 vols. (incomplete), Paris 1860–69; English transl. 1861–69.]

(4) Compare the doctrine respecting the saints and the Lord's Supper in the Special History of Doctrines.

(5) Is it altogether accidental that the cities of Strassburg and Cöln, distinguished for their cathedrals, were the favoured seats of the mystical theologians? See *Ch. Schmidt*, Essai, p. 45 and 52. There is also an evident connection between the mystical tendency and romantic poetry (comp. *Liebner*, Hugo von St. Victor, s. 246), as well as, on the one hand, between the old German school of painting and mysticism; and, on the other, between the more cheerful Italian art and the classical tendency mentioned § 154.

(6) See *Heeren*, Entwicklung der Folgen der Kreuzzüge für Europa (Historische Schriften, Göttingen 1808, Bd. ii.).

(7) Comp. *Hecker*, Der schwarze Tod im 14 Jahrhundert, Berlin 1832. *Forstemann*, Die christlichen Geisslergesellschaften, Halle 1828.

(8) Compare § 154.

(9) See *Llorente*, Geschichte der Inquisition, Leipzig 1823.

Neudecker in *Herzog's* Realencyklopädie, vi. 677 ff. [*Hefele* in his Life of Cardinal Ximenes, s. 162.]

(10) " *Religion has undoubtedly gained the powerful, healthy, and clear development of piety, and of Christian piety in particular, by the* invention of printing. The sources of Christian knowledge and education have been multiplied by it ad infinitum, and what was formerly inaccessible has been placed within the **reach** of all classes of society," etc., *Ullmann*, Rede am vierten Säcularfeste der Erfindung der Buchdruckerkunst, Heidelberg 1840, s. 20.

C.—SPECIAL HISTORY OF DOCTRINES DURING THE THIRD PERIOD.

FIRST DIVISION.

APOLOGETICO-DOGMATIC PROLEGOMENA.

TRUTH OF CHRISTIANITY—RELATION OF REASON TO REVELATION—SOURCES OF REVELATION—SCRIPTURE AND TRADITION.

§ 157.

Truth and Divinity of Christianity.

THE point of view assumed by Christian apologists of this period, in opposition to those who were not Christians, was considerably different from that taken during the first period. On the one hand, the Judaism of the Middle Ages was not the same with that which Justin Martyr combated in his Dialogue with Tryphon (1); on the other, the Christianity of the apologists of the Middle Ages differed in many respects from that of the earlier Fathers. Other weapons were also required in the controversy with Islam (Mahometanism) than those which had been used against the ancient polytheism (2). But the scepticism and freethinking, which made their appearance, especially towards the close of the present period, within the Church itself, both in a more open and in a more concealed manner, rendered a philosophical defence of the Christian religion still more necessary than did those historical religions which existed alongside of Christianity (3). Generally speaking, the apologists adopted the earlier methods of argumentation. The arguments derived from miracles and prophecies were retained, as tradition had sanctioned them (4), although some writers attained to the idea that the religion of Christ would recommend itself by its internal excellences, even without miracles (5).

(1) Compare, e.g., the manner in which *Agobard* upbraided the Jews of that time in his treatise, De Insolentia Judæorum, Opp. t. i. p. 59–66 (in *Schroekh*, xxi. s. 302).

(2) Compare the writings mentioned § 144, which were directed against Mahometans, and *Gieseler*, Dg. s. 476 ff.—The heathen (Gentiles), i.e. the heathen philosophers in particular, were combated by *Thomas Aquinas* in his Summa Catholicæ Fidei contra Gentiles, Lugd. 1587, fol., which is not to be confounded with his larger Summa. Extracts from it are given by *Schroekh*, xxix. s. 341 ff. *Munscher, von Colln*, ii. s. 100 ff.

(3) *Anselm* himself held the principle: Fides nostra contra impios ratione defendenda est, non contra eos, qui se Christiani nominis honore gaudere fatentur, Epp. Lib. ii. 41. On the later apologetical writings of Savonarola and Ficinus, see § 154, 155.

(4) *Anselm* endeavoured to define the idea of a miracle by the difference of a threefold *cursus rerum*, viz. the miraculous (mirabilis), the natural (naturalis), and that dependent on the will of the creature (voluntarius). The miraculous cannot be subjected to the conditions and laws of the other two, but rules free; yet it does not do violence to the two others (neque illis facit injuriam), since it is also dependent on the highest will, the will of God. The possibility of miracles, too, is grounded on the fact that creation itself is a miracle, i.e. a product of the divine will. See his De Concept. Virg. et Orig. Peccat. c. 11. *Hasse*, Anselm, ii. s. 457.—A definition of miracle is given by *Thomas Aquinas*, P. I. quæst. 110, art. 4: Dicendum, quod miraculum proprie dicitur, cum aliquid fit præter ordinem naturæ; sed non sufficit ad notionem miraculi, si aliquid fiat præter ordinem naturæ alicujus particularis, quia sic, cum aliquis projicit lapidem sursum, miraculum faceret, cum hoc sit præter ordinem naturæ lapidis. Ex hoc ergo aliquid dicitur esse miraculum, quod fit *præter ordinem totius naturæ creatæ;* hoc autem non potest facere nisi Deus, quia quidquid

facit angelus vel quæcunque alia creatura propria virtute, hoc fit secundum ordinem naturæ, et sic non est miraculum. Unde relinquitur, quod solus Deus miraculum facere possit. From this objective idea of the miracle Thomas distinguishes the subjective one: Sed quia non omnis virtus naturæ creatæ est nota nobis, ideo cum aliquid fit præter ordinem naturæ creatæ nobis notæ per virtutem creatam nobis ignotam, est miraculum quoad nos. From the same point of view he draws a distinction between miraculum and mirum. Comp. *Baur*, Trinitätslehre, ii. s. 749 f. [*Baur*, Dg. 243, says: Aquinas made a step in advance in the doctrinal definition of the miraculous, by referring the question to the doctrine of providence, or the government of the world.] †*Brischar*, Der Wunderbegriff des heiligen Thomas von Aquino, in the Tubing. Quartalschrift, 1845, 3.—*Ritter*, Gesch. d. Phil. viii. s. 266, and the passage there cited from *Aquinas*, Contra Gent. III. 98. Even as late as this period Ficinus and others appealed to the Sibylline oracles in the matter of prophecy. See *Schröckh*, xxxiv. s. 352.

(5) Among their number we may mention, *e.g.*, *Æneas Sylvius*, see *Platina* in Vita Pii II. (towards the end). Comp. also *Dante*, Div. Commed. (Parad. 24. 106-108).

§ 158.

Reason and Revelation—Faith and Knowledge.

Though all Christians were convinced of the truth and divinity of their religion (even where they knew it only through the troubled medium of the doctrine of the Church), yet the problem was raised by the more thoughtful as to the relation between the universally human and the specifically Christian, between revelation and natural reason, between the Christian religion and philosophy. *John Scotus Erigena* was the first who manifested a leaning towards Christian rational- ism, and sought a union between that and supernaturalism, by considering the true religion and true philosophy as one and the same thing, and by looking for the inmost and deepest source of religious knowledge in man himself, *i.e.* in his rational consciousness; although he did not deny the necessity of a positive revelation given from without (1). *Abélard* also **finds** a harmony between philosophy and Christianity in this fact, that the universal truths of reason, and the moral laws **with** which even the heathen were acquainted, are confirmed and enlarged by the higher authority of divine revelation (2). **Although** *Anselm* asserted that it is first **of all** necessary **to** receive by faith, with **the** subjective experience of the **heart,** the truths of revelation sanctioned by the Church, yet he admitted that reason might afterwards examine the grounds of what is believed; but in this he proceeded on the supposition that reason and revelation cannot contradict each other (3). *Thomas Aquinas* endeavoured to prove that the Christian doctrine, on the one hand, may be apprehended by reason, but, **on** the other, transcends reason (4); and *Duns Scotus* pointed out the distinguishing features of revelation in articulated propositions (5). The mystics also admitted (though in a manner different from that **of the** scholastics) the existence **of an** immediate certainty as **to** truth in the mind of man, in a manner allied **to** the **theory of** Anselm. There was, however, this difference among them, that some (viz. those who adhered to ecclesiastical **orthodoxy)** maintained **that the** *internal* revelations were in accordance with the **doctrine of** the Church (6), while others (the fanatical mystics) held that **the new** revelations of the Spirit were not unfrequently **in direct** opposition **to** the **doctrines** historically handed down, and even to the teaching **of Scripture** itself (7).

(1) De divina Præd. (ap. *Mauguin*, t. i. c. 1, § 1, quoted by *Frommüller*, l.c. s. 50): Quid est de philosophia tractare, nisi veræ religionis, qua summa et principalis omnium rerum causa et humiliter colitur et rationabiliter investigatur, regulas exponere? Conficitur inde veram esse philosophiam veram religionem, conversimque veram religionem esse veram philosophiam. (Comp. *Augustine*, De Vera Rel. c. 5.) He held that self-consciousness is the last source of religious knowledge, Div. Nat. v. 31, p. 268: Nulla quippe alia via est

ad principalis **exempli** purissimam contemplationem præter proxime **sibi suæ imaginis** certissimam notitiam. But he does **not on that account** deny the necessity of **an external (positive) revelation.** On the contrary, he says, ii. 31, p. 85: Nisi ipsa lux initium nobis revelaverit, nostræ ratiocinationis studium ad eam revelandam nihil proficiet (comp. § 159 ss.). Thus Scotus Erigena "*may in a certain sense be called the author of rationalism; but his rationalism* **is very** *different from that perverse* (and vulgar?) **form of** *rationalism which exists at the present day; in fact, the rationalism of the Christian philosopher* (at least in one aspect) *is the exact contradiction of this modern rationalism,*" Staudenmaier, Freiburg. Zeitschrift, l.c. s. 241. [Comp. Baur, Trinitätsl. ii. 274.] Ritter, vii. s. 214.

(2) De Theol. Chris. ii. p. 1211 (ed. *Martène*): Hinc quidem facilius evangelica prædicatio a philosophis, quam a Judæis suscepta est, cum sibi eam maxime invenirent ad finem, nec fortasse in aliquo dissonam, nisi forte in his quæ ad incarnationis vel sacramentorum vel resurrectionis mysteria pertinent.[1] Si enim diligenter moralia evangelii præcepta consideremus, nihil ea aliud, quam reformationem legis naturæ inveniemus, quam secutos esse philosophos constat; cum lex magis figuralibus quam moralibus nitatur mandatis, et exteriori potius justitia quam interiori abundet; evangelium vero virtutes ac vitia diligenter examinat, et secundum animi intentionem omnia, sicut et philosophi, pensat. Unde, cum tanta . . . evangelicæ ac philosophicæ doctrinæ concordia pateat, nonnulli Platonicorum . . . in tantam proruperunt blasphemiam, ut Dominum Jesum omnes suas sententias a Platone accepisse dicerent, quasi philosophus ipsam docuisset Sophiam. None but he who obtains a knowledge of the divine by *active* research attains to *firm* belief.[2] After man has done his part, divine love assists his efforts, and grants to him that which he could not acquire by *his own* researches, etc. "*But Abélard was far from imagining that his philosophy could give a full knowledge of divine things which should leave no scope for desire after more.*" *Neander,* Der heilige Bernhard, s. 117 ff. (1st ed.).

---

[1] From this passage it appears that as early as the time of Abélard a distinction was made between articuli puri et mixti. Comp. also what *Thomas Aquinas* said, note 4.

[2] Hence his motto: Qui credit cito, levis est corde (Sir. 19, 4).

Abélard made a distinction between *credere*, *intelligere*, and *cognoscere;* through doubt we come to inquiry, through inquiry to truth (dubitando ad inquisitionem, inquirendo ad veritatem). Abélard uses still stronger language on this point in his Introductio than in his more modified Theologia Christiana; see *Neander*, s. 127, Anm. 4 (comp. *Bahringer*, ubi supra, s. 118 ff.). —*Alanus ab Insulis* also places faith above *opinio*, but below *scientia* (art. 17, quoted by *Pez*, i. p. 482). Comp. the opinion of Clement of Alexandria, § 34, note 6.—The view of *St. Bernard* is in sharpest contrast with that of Abélard. The rationalism of Abélard seems to him to **be in** contradiction not only with faith, but also with reason : Quid enim magis *contra* rationem, quam rationem ratione conari transcendere ? Et quid magis contra fidem, quam credere nolle quicquid non posset ratione attingi ?—On the other hand, *Abélard* (Ep. ad Helois.): Nolo sic esse philosophus ut recalcitrarem Paulo, non sic esse Aristoteles, ut secludar **a** Christo ; non enim aliud nomen est sub **cœlo**, in quo oporteat me salvum fieri; comp. *Neander*, Bernhard, s. 147 ff. *D. J. H. Goldhorn*, De summis principiis theologiæ Abælardeæ, **Lips. 1836.**

(3) Prosl. c. 1 : . . . Desidero aliquatenus intelligere veritatem tuam, quam **credit** et amat **cor meum.** Neque enim quaero **intelligere ut** credam, sed credo **ut** intelligam. **Nam** et hoc **credo, quia, nisi** credidero, non intelligam. De Incarn Verbi, c. 2 : **Nullus quippe** Christianus debet disputare, quod **catholica** Ecclesia corde credit et ore confitetur, quomodo non **sit : sed semper** eandem fidem indubitanter tenendo, amando **et secundum illam vivendo humiliter, quantum potest** quaerere **rationem, quomodo sit. Si** potest intelligere, **Deo gratias** agat : **si non potest, non immittat cornua ad ventilandum,** sed **submittat caput ad venerandum. Citius enim in se potest confidens humana sapientia impingendo cornua sibi evellere, quam innitendo petram hanc evellere** . . . **Palam namque est,** quia **illi non habent fidei firmitatem, qui, quoniam quod** credunt, **intelligere non possunt, disputant contra ejusdem fidei a sanctis patribus confirmatam veritatem, velut si vespertiliones et noctuæ, nonnisi in nocte cœlum videntes, de meridianis solis radiis disceptent contra aquilas, solem ipsum irreverberato visu intuentes. Prius ergo fide mundandum est cor** . . . **prius ea quæ carnis sunt postponentes secundum** spiritum vivamus,

quam profunda fidei dijudicando discutiamus . . . Quanto opulentius nutrimur in Sacra Scriptura, ex his, quæ per obedientiam pascunt, tanto subtilius provehimur ad ea, quæ per intellectum satiant . . . *Nam qui non crediderit, non experietur, et qui expertus non fuerit, non intelliget.* Nam quantum rei auditum superat experientia, tantum vincit audientis cognitionem experientis scientia . . . Nemo ergo se temere mergat in condensa difficillimarum quæstionum, nisi prius in soliditate fidei conquisita morum et sapientiæ gravitate, ne per multiplicia sophismatum diverticula in tanta levitate discurrens, aliqua tenaci illaqueetur falsitate. Comp. De Sacram. Altaris ii. 2 ; Christianæ fidei veritas quasi hoc speciali jure præminet, ut non ipsa per intellectum, sed per eam intellectus quærendus sit . . . Qui ergo nihil credere vult, nisi ratione vel intellectu præcedente, hic rem confundit, et scire omnia volens, nihil credens, fidem, quæ in ipso est, videtur annullare. Epp. Lib. ii. 41 : Christianus per fidem debet ad intellectum proficere, non per intellectum ad fidem accedere, aut si intelligere non valet, a fide recedere. Sed cum ad intellectum valet pertingere, delectatur : cum vero nequit, quod capere non potest, veneratur. Nevertheless, he asserts that the acquisition of knowledge is a duty imperative upon him who has the power of knowing. In Cur Deus Homo, i. c. 2, he represents Boso speaking as follows, without contradicting him : Sicut rectus ordo exigit, ut profunda christianæ fidei credamus, priusquam ea præsumamus ratione discutere, *ita negligentia mihi videtur, si, postquam confirmati sumus in fide, non studemus quod credimus intelligere.* Comp. ibid. c. 10, 25. Nor does Boso declare himself satisfied (respecting the doctrine of satisfaction) until he has recognized the reasons adduced as rationabilia (ii. 19 and 21). *"The scholastic divines did not think it an extravagant notion, that the whole contents of the Old and New Testament should be proved to be in accordance with reason by the way of speculation; but it was always presupposed, that what is matter of faith rests on its own grounds, and needs no proof: thus whatever is added by reason, however valuable in other respects, is nothing but an opus supererogationis,"* Baur, Versöhnungsl. s. 185, Anm. *" The fides præcedens intellectum, which scholasticism assumes as its basis, is not only the faith as it is contained in the Scripture as a doctrine, and faith as a living* principle in the religious experience of individuals, but it is also, and still more distinctly, the formulated faith, the dogma, with all its particular definitions as sanctioned by the Church," *Landerer* (in *Herzog*), s. 660. Thus distinguished from the modern **theory of** *Jacobi* and *Schleiermacher*. Comp. *Mohlers* Schriften, i. s. 137 f. *D. J. H. Goldhorn*, De summis Principiis Theol. Abælardeæ, Lips. 1856. *Hasse's* Anselm, s. 34 ff. Anselm was **followed on this** point by *Albertus Magnus;* comp. the passages in *Ritter*, viii. s. 103.

(4) **Thom.** *Aqu.* Summ. Cath. Fid. contra Gentiles, **l. i. c.** 3 (in *Münscher, von Cölln*, s. 100): Et in his, quæ de **Deo** confitemur, duplex veritatis modus. Quædam **namque vera sunt de** Deo, quæ omnem facultatem humanæ rationis excedunt, **ut:** Deum esse trinum et unum. Quædam vero sunt, ad quæ etiam ratio naturalis pertingere potest: sicut est Deum esse, Deum esse unum, et alia hujusmodi, quæ etiam philosophi demonstrative de **Deo** probaverunt, ducti naturalis lumine rationis. But even these "praeambula fidei" need confirmation by means of revelation; otherwise the knowledge of God would be the privilege of **but a** few (viz. of thinkers and scholars) others whom levity **prevented** during the earlier period of their life from giving heed to these things, would not acquire a knowledge of them until it was too **late.** But even **in the** most favourable case there would be reason for apprehending lest error should be mixed up with truth. [Cap. 5, he proves **that** ea quæ ratione investigari non possunt, convenienter fide tenenda proponuntur.] The truths of revelation, however, though **going** beyond reason, do not contradict it, etc. Comp. *Schröckh*, xxix. s. 342 ff. [*Baur*, Dogmengesch. s. 241–43 (2d ed.): "*The chief idea on which the supernaturalism of Aquinas rests, is the finis superexcedens, viz.* **Man** (Summa Theol. 1, qu. 1. art. 1) *ordinatur ad Deum, sicut ad quendam finem,* **qui** *comprehensionem rationis excedit. Finem oportet esse praecognitum hominibus, qui suas intentiones et actiones debent ordinare in finem.*"]

(5) These elements are: Prænuntiatio prophetica, Scripturarum concordia, auctoritas scribentium, diligentia recipientium, rationabilitas contentorum, irrationabilitas singulorum errorum, ecclesiæ stabilitas and miraculorum claritas; according to *Baur*, Lehrb. s. 174. On the relation of philosophy to theology, see *Ritter*, viii. s. 264 ff.

(6) The series is opened by *Bernard of Clairvaux*, De Consideratione, v. 3: Deus et qui cum eo sunt beati spiritus, tribus modis veluti viis totidem, nostra sunt consideratione vestigandi; opinione, fide, intellectu. Quorum intellectus rationi innititur, fides auctoritati; opinio sola verisimilitudine se tuetur. Habent illa duo certam veritatem, sed fides clausam et involutam, intelligentia nudam et manifestam; ceterum opinio, certi nihil habens, verum per verisimilia quaerit potius, quam apprehendit . . . Verus intellectus certam habet non modo veritatem, sed notitiam veritatis . . . Fides est voluntaria quaedam et certa praelibatio needum prolatae veritatis. Intellectus est rei cujuscunque invisibilis certa et manifesta notitia. Opinio est quasi pro vero habere aliquid, quod falsum esse nescias. Ergo fides ambiguum non habet, aut si habet, fides non est, sed opinio. Quid igitur distat ab intellectu? Nempe quod etsi non habet incertum non magis quam intellectus, habet tamen involucrum, quod non intellectus. Denique quod non intellexisti, non est de eo, quod ultra quaeras; aut si est, non intellexisti. *Nil autem malumus scire, quam quae fide jam scimus.* Nil supererit ad beatitudinem, cum, quae jam certa sunt nobis fide, erunt aequa et nuda. He speaks in the same way of the knowledge of divine things (v. 13): *Non ea disputatio comprehendit, sed sanctitas.* The same view is also espoused by *Hugo of St. Victor* and *Richard of St. Victor.* Comp. *Hugo*, De Sacramentis Fidei, P. iii. l. i. c. 30 (De cognitione divinitatis), quoted by *Liebner*, s. 173 ff., 186: Alia enim sunt *ex ratione*, alia *secundum rationem*, alia *supra rationem*, et praeter haec quae sunt *contra rationem*. Ex ratione sunt necessaria, secundum rationem sunt probabilia, supra rationem mirabilia, contra rationem incredibilia. Et duo quidem extrema omnino *fidem* non capiunt. Quae enim sunt ex ratione, omnino nota sunt et *credi* non possunt, quoniam *sciuntur*. Quae vero contra rationem sunt, nulla similiter ratione credi possunt, quoniam non suscipiunt ullam rationem, nec acquiescit his ratio aliqua. Ergo quae secundum rationem sunt et quae sunt supra rationem, tantummodo suscipiunt fidem. Et in primo quidem genere fides ratione adjuvatur et ratio fide perficitur, quoniam secundum rationem sunt, quae creduntur. Quorum veritatem si ratio non comprehendit, fidei tamen illorum non contradicit. In iis, quae supra rationem sunt, non

adjuvatur fides ratione ulla, quoniam non capit ea ratio, quæ fides credit, et tamen est aliquid, quo ratio admonetur venerari fidem, quam non comprehendit. Quæ dicta sunt ergo secundum rationem, probabilia fuerunt rationi et sponte acquievit eis. Quæ vero supra rationem fuerunt, ex divina revelatione prodita sunt, et non operata est in eis ratio, sed castigata tamen, ne ad illa contenderet.—The theory of *Richard of St. Victor* is somewhat more complicated. According to him, there are six kinds of contemplation. We know—(1) by the imagination (the sensible impressions made by creation); (2) by reason (perception of law and order in creation); (3) *in reason according to imagination* (symbolical knowledge of nature, as a mirror of the spiritual); (4) *in* reason and *according* to reason (the internal referred to the internal, without a sensible image —intellectual intuition?); (5) *above* and not *against* reason (revealed knowledge within the sphere of reason—rational knowledge carried to a higher power by revelation); (6) *above* and (apparently) *against* reason (particularly the mystery of the Trinity). Comp. *Engelhardt*, l.c. s. 60 ff.—*John of Salisbury*, in strict contrast, taught that the endeavours of man after knowledge must be aided by God Himself, Policrat. lib. vii. c. 14 (Bibl. Max. t. xxiii. p. 352): Quisquis ergo viam philosophandi ingreditur, ad ostium gratiæ ejus humiliter pulset, in cujus manu liber omnium sciendorum est, quem solus aperit agnus, qui occisus est, ut ad viam sapientiæ et veræ felicitatis servum reduceret aberrantem. Frustra quis sibi de capacitate ingenii, de memoriæ tenacitate, de assiduitate studii, de linguæ volubilitate blanditur . . . Est autem humilitati conjuncta simplicitas, qua discentium intelligentia plurimum adjuvatur. —The preacher *Berthold* also warned against the pride of speculation (in *Kling*, Grimm's Rec. p. 206): Swer faste in die sunnen sihet, in den brehenden glaft, der wird von ougen sô boese, daz er es niemer mêr gesiht. Zeglicher wise also stêt ez umbe den glouben; wer ze faste in den heiligen cristenglouben sihet, alsô daz in vil gwundert *und ze tiefe darinne rumpelt mit gedenken.*—*Savonarola* appeals to the internal testimony, Triumph. Crucis proœm. (quoted by *Rudelbach*, s. 376): Licet fides ex causis principiisque naturalibus demonstrari non possit, ex manifestis tamen effectibus validissimas rationes adducemus, quas nemo sanæ mentis inficiari poteret.—So, too,

Picus of Mirandola strikingly says: Philosophia veritatem quaerit, theologia invenit, religio possidet (Ep. ad Manut. Opera ed. Basel, p. 243).

(7) Comp. § 161, note 5.

§ 159.

Sources of Knowledge—Bible and Tradition.

[W. J. Irons, The Bible and its Interpreters, Lond. 1865, 1869. *B. F. Westcott,* The Canon, var. ed. u. s.]

Although the Bible was still theoretically reverenced as the highest rule of Christian truth (1), yet it was gradually overshadowed by tradition, which was deemed of equal importance with Scripture (2). Its doctrines were more and more corrupted and supplanted by arbitrary human traditions. Besides the tradition of the Church, the book of nature was also placed beside the written word of God (3). Some of the mystical sects looked upon other writings besides the Bible as coming from heaven (4), and even went so far as to put the imaginations of the natural man on an equality with the word of God (5). On the other hand, the principle of the authority of Scripture, in opposition to a corrupt tradition, made increased progress in the age immediately preceding the Reformation (6).

(1) *Joh. Dam.* De fide orth. i. 1: Πάντα τοίνυν τὰ παραδεδομένα ἡμῖν διά τε νόμου καὶ προφητῶν καὶ ἀποστόλων καὶ εὐαγγελιστῶν δεχόμεθα καὶ γινώσκομεν καὶ σέβομεν, οὐδὲν περαιτέρω τούτων ἐπιζητοῦντες . . . Ταῦτα ἡμεῖς στέρξωμεν καὶ ἐν αὐτοῖς μείνωμεν, μὴ μεταίροντες ὅρια αἰώνια, μηδὲ ὑπερβαίνοντες τὴν θείαν παράδοσιν. Comp. iv. 17.—*Joh. Scot. Erig.* De Div. Nat. i. c. 66, p. 37: Sanctæ siquidem Scripturæ in omnibus sequenda est auctoritas, quum in ea veluti quibusdam suis secretis sedibus veritas; (he makes, however, the following limitation): non tamen ita credendum est, ut ipsa semper propriis verborum seu nominum signis fruatur, divinam nobis naturam insinuans; sed quibusdam similitudini-

bus variisque translatorum verborum seu nominum modis utitur, infirmitati nostrae condescendens nostrosque adhuc rudes infantilesque sensus simplici doctrina erigens. Nor can Scripture contradict reason, c. 68, p. 38: Nulla itaque auctoritas te terreat ab his, quae rectae contemplationis rationabilis suasio edocet. Vera enim auctoritas rectae rationi non obsistit, neque recta ratio verae auctoritati. Ambo siquidem **ex uno** fonte, divina videlicet sapientia, manare dubium non est. Comp. c. 69, p. 39, and *Bahringer*, l. c. s. 134 ff.—*John of Salisbury*, on the contrary, used much more unqualified language, Policrat. l. c. (§ 158, note 5): Serviendum est ergo scripturis, non dominandum; nisi forte quis se ipsum dignum credat, ut angelis debeat dominari. [*Abelard* (Sic et Non, p. 14 of *Henke's* edition) ascribes unconditional authority only to the Scriptures **of** the Old and New Test. *Aquinas* (Summa Theol. P. i. qu. 1, art. 8) defines theology as a science, **in which** the argument is peculiarly derived from authority; and recognizes **only** the canonical Scriptures **as an authority** giving **more than** probabilities. *Baur*, Dg. s. 244, 2d ed.]

(2) *Joh. Damasc.* De fide orth. iv. 12: Αὐτὸν (Χριστὸν) οὖν ἐκδεχόμενοι, ἐπὶ ἀνατολὰς προσκυνοῦμεν ἄγραφος δέ ἐστιν ἡ παράδοσις αὕτη τῶν Ἀποστόλων· πολλὰ γὰρ ἀγράφως ἡμῖν παρέδωκαν; iv. 16: Ὅτι δὲ καὶ πλεῖστα οἱ ἀπόστολοι ἀγράφως παραδεδώκασι, γράφει Παῦλος ὁ τῶν ἐθνῶν ἀπόστολος (2 Thess. ii. 15; 1 Cor. xi. 2). De Imaginibus Orat. i. 23 (Opp. i. p. 318): Οὐ μόνον γράμμασι τὴν ἐκκλησιαστικὴν θεσμοθεσίαν παρέδωκαν (**οἱ** πατέρες), ἀλλὰ καὶ ἀγράφοις, τισὶ **παραδόσεσι** . . . Πόθεν **τὸ** τρὶς βαπτίζειν; πόθεν τὸ κατ ἀνατολὰς εὔχεσθαι; πόθεν ἡ τῶν μυστηρίων παράδοσις; κ.τ.λ. Comp. Orat. ii. 16, p. 338.—*John Scotus Erigena*, **by** drawing **a parallel between Scripture** and reason, seems to subordinate **tradition to both of them** (and especially to reason), **i. c. 71, p. 39**: Omnis autem auctoritas, quae vera ratione non approbatur, infirma videtur esse. Vera autem ratio, quum virtutibus suis rata atque immutabilis munitur, nullius auctoritatis **adstipulatione roborari** indiget. Nil enim aliud videtur mihi **esse vera auctoritas, nisi** rationis virtute cooperta veritas et **a** *sacris patribus* ad posteritatis utilitatem litteris commendata . . . Ideoque *prius* ratione utendum est . . . ac deinde

auctoritate . . . Ibid. iv. 9 : Non sanctorum patrum sententiæ, præsertim si plurimis notæ sunt, introducendæ sunt, nisi ubi summa necessitas roborandæ ratiocinationis exegerit propter eos, qui cum sint rationis uscii, plus auctoritati quam rationi succumbunt.—Erigena, however, was almost alone in these views. Most writers adopted the definitions propounded by Augustine and Vincentius Lirinensis during the preceding period (comp. § 122). Thus Alcuin advised adhesion to the doctrine generally received, and discouraged the invention of new names, etc. (in Ep. ad Felic. Opp. i. p. 783, comp. p. 791 ss.). Porro nos intra terminos apostolicæ doctrinæ et sanctæ Romanæ ecclesiæ firmiter stamus; illorum probatissimam sequentes auctoritatem, et sanctissimis inhærentes doctrinis, nihil novi inferentes, nullaque recipientes, nisi quæ in illorum catholicis inveniuntur scriptis.—Though Abelard, by his work, "Sic et Non," had undermined the authority of the earlier Fathers, and consequently that of tradition, yet the scholastics continued not only to appeal to the older tradition, but also to justify unbiblical doctrines, by saying that the Church had the perpetual right to establish new dogmas, as that of transubstantiation and the immaculate conception of Mary. Even Gerson (in relation to the latter dogma) appealed to this progressive development of doctrines by the Church.—The authority of Aristotle was added in later times to that of the Church (although not formally recognized by the Church, yet practically), till the authority of Scripture was again prominently brought forward as the highest, if not the only authority immediately before the Reformation (thus by Wykliffe, Nicolas de Clémangis, Wessel, etc.).

(3) *John Scotus Erigena* maintains that every creature is a theophany of God, De Div. Nat. iii. 19.—According to the Theol. Naturalis of *Raymund of Sabunde,* God has granted to men *two* books, viz. the book of nature and the book of Scripture; they neither can, nor must, contradict each other; *the latter, however, is not accessible to all, but only to the priests.* All knowledge must commence with the former, which is equally within the reach of the laity; every creature is a letter written by God. But the highest knowledge is the love of God, as being the only thing of his own which man can offer to the Deity. Comp. *Hase,* Kg. § 287. *Tennemann,* viii.

s. 964 ff. *Matzke*, Die Nat. Theol. des Raimund von Sabunde, s. 30 ff.—In a similar manner *St. Bernard* asserted, that what he was able to accomplish in the way of interpreting Scripture, and what he understood of divine things, he acquired by inner contemplation and prayer, especially in the woods and the fields, and that he had no other teachers than beeches and oaks; see *Neander*, Der heilige Bernhard, s. 6. Comp. Brother *Berthold's* Predigten, edited by Kling, s. 113, where the same idea of two books (heaven and earth) occurs.[1]

(4) Thus the Spirituales in particular attached great importance to the Evangelium Æternum (prophecies of *Joachim*, abbot of Floris in Calabria, who died A.D. 1202). On this work, comp. *Engelhardt*, Kirchenhist. Abhandl., Erl. 1832, Nr. 1. Extracts from the Evang. Ætern. are given by *D'Argentré*, Coll. Judiciorum de Novis Error, Paris 1728, t. i. p. 163 ss.

(5) Some went so far as to make the most crazy assertions; thus *David of Dinanto* maintained that God had made communications by Ovid no less than by Augustine (or, by the Bible?); see *Engelhardt*, l.c. s. 255. The Béguines taught, quod homo magis tenetur sequi instinctum interiorem, quam veritatem evangelii, quod quotidie prædicatur; see the Episcopal letter of *John of Strassburg* in *Mosheim*, l.c. p. 258. Comp. § 161.

(6) Thus *Wycliffe* says (Trial. iv. c. 7, p. 199): If there were a hundred popes, and all the monks were to be transformed into cardinals, we ought not to ascribe to their opinion in matters of faith any other value than they have as founded on the Scriptures. Comp. *Schröckh*, xxxiv. s. 504. On the principle of *Hus* respecting the Scriptures, see *Neander*, Züge aus dem Leben des heil. Joh. Hus, in his Kleine Gelegenheitsschriften, s. 217 ff. Thus he demanded that the council should convict him of error from the Scripture.[2] On the whole biblical tendency of the period preceding the Reforma-

---

[1] It is worthy of observation, in this dualism of Scripture and tradition, that one element (Scripture) is much more firmly established, while that of tradition is more variable, and sometimes has something else as a substitute; as, in the above case, nature; or, as with John Scotus Erigena, reason; or with the mystics, the internal revelation.

[2] Accordingly *Helfert* (from the Roman Catholic point of view) calls the principle held by Hus as to Scripture, the Alpha and Omega of his error!

§ 160.

The Canon of the Bible and Biblical Criticism.

The Canon had been closed in the preceding period; and so that in the Latin Church the so-called apocryphal books of the Old Testament were regularly reckoned as a part of it (1). The *Paulicians* in the East rejected (like the Gnostics) the Old Testament and the writings of Peter (2). But as late as the age of the Carolingians doubts were entertained, even within the pale of the Catholic Church itself, respecting the genuineness of particular books of the Old Testament (3).

(1) Comp. the Canon of *Isidore of Seville*, De Eccles. Off. i. c. 12, and the decisions of synods on this point. See also *John Damasc.* iv. 17. (*Münscher*, von Colln, ii. s. 106.) [*John Dam.* says: ἡ δὲ Πανάρετος, τουτέστιν ἡ Σοφία τοῦ Σολομῶντος, καὶ ἡ σοφία τοῦ Ἰησοῦ . . . ἐνάρετοι μὲν καὶ καλαὶ, ἀλλ᾽ οὐκ ἀριθμοῦνται, οὐδὲ ἔκειντο ἐν τῇ κιβωτῷ.] With reference to the apocryphal writings, some Western theologians, such as *Odo of Cluny, Hugo of St. Victor, John of Salisbury, Hugo of St. Caro*, and others, appealed to Jerome, but the Canon of Augustine was more generally adopted. See *Münscher*, l.c. s. 107, and *Liebner*, Hugo von St. Victor, s. 129. The Greek Church allowed that the apocryphal books were useful and edifying, but definitely distinguished these from the canonical: *John Damasc.* De fide orthod. iv. c. 18.

(2) According to *Petrus Siculus*, quoted by *Wetstein*, Nov. Test. ii. p. 681. *De Wette*, Einleitung ins Neue Test. s. 281.

(3) "*The monks of the monastery of St. Gallen ventured to point out what they thought unworthy of God in the Canon of the Sacred Scriptures. Of the Books of Chronicles and Esther, their opinion was:* in eis littera non pro auctoritate, tantum pro memoria tenetur. *So also of the Book of Judith, and of the Maccabees.*" *Joh. von Müller*, Gesch. der schweiz. Eidgen. Bd.

§ 161.

Inspiration.

Generally speaking, the views hitherto entertained respecting inspiration continued to prevail in the Church (1), so that the assertion of *Agobard*, Archbishop of Lyons, that the sacred penmen had not always adhered to the rules of grammar, called forth lively opposition on the part of *Frédégis*, Abbot of Tours, against which, however, *Agobard* defended himself with sound mother wit (2). *Euthymius Zigabenus* met with less opposition on the part of the Greek Church, though he did not hesitate to speak freely of the discrepancies of the evangelists (3). The scholastic divines endeavoured to define inspiration by more exact notes (4), while the mystics confounded more or less the idea of Bible inspiration with that of divine illumination in general (5). On the whole, it is undoubtedly true that the present period, with its imaginative tendencies, continued to believe in the power of divine inspiration (even outside the Canon of the Bible), and was far from restricting for all times the fulness of the manifestations of the Divine Spirit within the limits of a single book, however strictly its divine origin might be maintained (6).

(1) *Joh. Damasc.* De fide orth. iv. c. 17 (Opp. i. p. 282): Διὰ πνεύματος τοίνυν ἁγίου ὅ τε νόμος καὶ οἱ προφῆται, εὐαγγελισταὶ καὶ ἀπόστολοι καὶ ποιμένες ἐλάλησαν καὶ διδάσκαλοι. Πᾶσα τοίνυν γραφὴ θεόπνευστος πάντως καὶ ὠφέλιμος κ.τ.λ. (2 Tim. iii. 16).

(2) *Agobard.* ad Fredegisium Abbatem (Opp. Par. p. 157 ss.). Abbot *Frédégis* wished to extend infallibility even to translators and commentators. Concerning the sacred penmen them-

selves, *Frédégis* **asserted**: **Turpe** est credere Spir. Sanctum, qui omnium gentium linguas mentibus Apostolorum infudit, *rusticitatem* **potius** per eos, quam *nobilitatem* uniuscujusque linguae locutum esse; hence he further maintains: Ut non **solum** sensum praedicationis et modos vel argumenta dictionum Spir. S. eis inspiraverit, sed etiam ipsa *corporalia verba extrinsecus in ore illorum ipse formaverit*. *Agobard* replied as follows: Quodsi ita sentitis, quanta absurditas **sequetur, quis dinumerare poterit?** . . . Restat ergo, ut, sicut **ministerio** angelico vox articulata formata **est in ore asinae, ita dicatis** formari in ore Prophetarum, et tunc **talis etiam absurditas** sequetur, **ut, si tali modo verba et voces verborum acceperunt,** sensum **ignorarent; sed absit** *talia deliramenta* **cogitare.** He quotes several instances from Scripture relative to differences in style, and of confessions on the part of writers themselves, *e.g.* Ex. iv. and 1 Cor. i.—Laus divinae sapientiae (he continues) in sacris mysteriis et in doctrina spiritus invenitur, non in inventionibus verborum. . . . Vos sic laudatis, ut laude **vestra** magis minoretur, quam augeatur (divina majestas), quoniam in his, quae extrinsecus sunt, dicitis nobilitatem linguarum ministrasse Apostolis Spiritum Sanctum, ut confuse et indifferenter cum Apostolis omnes interpretes **et quos-cunque expositores** laudetis **et defendatis.** Near as " *Agobard came to drawing a precise distinction between the divine and* **that** *which is* specifically **human in** the idea of **inspiration**," yet he was far from " *fully developing it.*" Neander, Kg. iv. s. 388. (Thus Agobard supposed, p. 164, that the sacred penmen *could* have written better if they *would* have done so, but that they *accommodated* themselves to human infirmities.) On the other hand, it cannot be inferred from the assertion of *Frédégis* that he would have reason entirely subject to authority. He thought that reason was confirmed and protected by the authority of the Bible. Comp. *Ritter*, vii. s. 189, and the passage there cited, De Nihilo, p. 403.

(3) Comment. in Evang. Matth. c. xii. 8 (t. i. p. 465, ed. *Matthæi*). Comp. *Schröckh*, Kg. xxviii. s. 310. That one evangelist sometimes relates what is omitted by another, etc., he simply attributes to the circumstance that they did not exactly recollect all the facts, because they did not write until a considerable space of time had elapsed.

(4) "However much the scholastic divines have done in the development of the other fundamental ideas which determine the sphere of revelation, and however much we *owe to* them, particularly as regards precise definition of the objective idea of **miracles**, yet their definitions on this point (the doctrine of inspiration) *are* very scanty. This doctrine was assumed as an ἀρχὴ πρώτη which needed no further proof, inasmuch as the **whole** Christian Church moved in this element." Rudelbach, Die **Lehre von** der Inspiration der heiligen Schrift (comp. § 32), **s. 48 f.** We find, however, more precise definitions in the writings **of the** principal scholastic divines, *Thomas Aquinas*, and especially *Duns Scotus*.[1] The former treats of the subject in question **in** his Summa Theolog. Pars i. qu. 1. **art. 9, 10**; the latter in his Prol. Sentent. qu. 2, quoted by *Münscher*, *von Colln*, l.c. s. 103–105; *Gieseler*, Dg. s. 480.

(5) On this point, too, there were different shades of opinion. The more cautious mystics, such **as** the disciples of the school **of St. Victor, adhered closely to** the sacred Scriptures, and **ascribed inspiration to them in a** special sense. Comp. *Liebner*, **Hugo von St. Victor, s. 128 ff.** (where little is **said** respecting **the idea of inspiration itself, but the inspiration of** the Scripture **is everywhere** presupposed). Hugo supposed that in **some instances the sacred** penmen **had drawn** from their own **resources,** *e.g.* **the author of** Ecclesiastes (see *Liebner*, s. 160 ; **but in other places he** distinguished between the **divine** and **that which is peculiarly human.** Thus he observed concerning **Obadiah, that** he combined profound ideas with **a** plain style, **and was sparing in words,** but rich in thoughts (ibid. s. **163).—** *Savonarola*, **whose opinions were** allied to those of the mystics, **also believed that the sacred Scriptures are, in** the strictest **sense, inspired by God; but he proceeded on the** principle (as **Clement of Alexandria and Chrysostom had done before him, comp. § 32, note 8, § 119, note 4) that the gospel was originally written, not on tables of stone or sheets** of paper, **but upon hearts of flesh by means of the finger** and power of

---

[1] Similar definitions were given on Old Testament prophecy by the Rabbins of the Middle Ages, Moses Maimonides and others ; see *Rudelbach*, l.c. s. 50 ff. And how much attention some of the schoolmen must have given to the subject in question, may be seen from the circumstance that Anselm spent *whole nights* in meditating on it ; see *Möhler*, l.c. s. 52.

the Holy Ghost. He admitted at the same time the limitation, that God did not use the sacred writers as instruments which have no will of their own, but suffered women to talk as women, and shepherds as shepherds, etc.; see *Rudelbach*, Savonarola, s. 335 ff. Savonarola, however, did not limit inspiration to the sacred Scriptures, inasmuch as it is well known that he ascribed prophetic gifts to *himself*, though without making any boast of them. [He distinguished between the claim to be a prophet, which he did not put forward, and the reception of revelations, which he asserted.] Concerning this prophetic gift, as well as that claimed by *Joachim* and *Brigitta*, see Rudelbach, l.c. s. 297 ff. [and the works of *Meier*, *Perreus*, and *Villari*]; the views of Savonarola himself on this subject are given, ibid. s. 303 (they are taken from the Compendium Revelationum).—The fanatic mystics, on the contrary, maintained, in opposition to Scripture, that those filled with the Holy Spirit are above the law (see *Mosheim*, De Beguinis, p. 216); or openly taught: multa in Evangeliis esse poëtica quæ non sunt vera, sicut est illud: Venite, benedicti, etc. Item, quod magis homines debent credere humanis conceptibus, qui procedunt ex corde, quam doctrinæ evangelicæ. Item, aliquos ex eis posse meliores libros reparare omnibus libris catholicæ fidei, etc. (quoted by *Mosheim*, l.c. p. 258).—Comp. § 159.

(6) *Thomas Aquinas* says, P. i. qu. 12, art. 13 (the passage refers, properly speaking, to the visions recorded in Scripture, but admits of a more general application): Lumen naturale intellectus confortatur per infusionem luminis gratuiti et interdum etiam phantasmata in imaginatione hominis formantur divinitus, magis exprimentia res divinas, quam ea, quæ naturaliter a sensibilibus accipimus. " *Such an extraordinary and direct inspiration was formerly ascribed to Thomas, Scotus, and other* theologians, when *the accounts of frequent appearances and visits on the part of God, as well as of other blessed and holy beings, were generally believed;*" *Semler*, Introduction to Baumgarten, ii. s. 63.—It was held by the mystics, that higher divine inspiration was still vouchsafed to the pious. *Gerson*, Consid. X.: Intelligentia simplex est vis animæ cognitiva, *suscipiens immediate a Deo* naturalem quandam lucem, in qua et per quam principia prima cognoscuntur esse vera et certis-

sima terminis apprehensis (quoted by *Liebner*, Hugo von St. Victor, s. 340, where further details are given respecting the mystical doctrine of revelation as held by Hugo and Richard of St. Victor). The reader may compare with this opinion the views of *Tauler* (Predigten, i. s. 124), who made a distinction between *active* and *passive* reason. The latter must fructify the former; but it receives its revelations from God. In accordance with earlier notions, inspiration was extended even to worldly subjects, *e.g.* to poetry. Thus it is said, in the Life of St. Elizabeth, of the singers on the Wartburg: "They contended against each other with songs, and wove into their songs pretty mysteries which they borrowed from Holy Writ, without being very learned: *for God had revealed it to them.*" See *Koberstein*, Ueber das Gedicht vom Wartburgkriege, Naumb. 1823, 4to, Anh. § 65. Comp. also Konrads von Wurzburg Trojanerkrieg, in *Wackernagels* Leseb. i. Sp. 706.

§ 162.

Interpretation of Scripture—The Reading of the Bible.

A sound interpretation, resting on a grammatico-historical basis, was scarcely known, in consequence of the neglect of philological studies, and it was not until the close of this period that light began to dawn. Scripture was interpreted, either in close accordance with the dicta of ecclesiastical tradition, or in an arbitrary and allegorical manner, so as to subserve a subtle scholasticism or a refined mysticism (1). *Scotus Erigena* taught an infinite sense of Scripture (2); others, with Origen, a threefold, or, with Augustine, a fourfold sense; while some even went so far as to speak of a sevenfold or eightfold sense (3). Practical and wholesome rules of interpretation, however, were not altogether overlooked (4). The rulers of the Church endeavoured (from fear of heresy) to restrict the perusal of the Bible on the part of the people (5), while private individuals were anxious to recommend it (6). Sound scriptural views and biblical interpretation are found in the writings of *John Wessel,* "*the characteristic feature of whose theology is a biblical tendency*" (7).

(1) See *Liebner*, Hugo von St. Victor, s. 132 f.: "*They* [the **commentators** of the present period] **either** remained satisfied **with** collecting the interpretations of the Fathers according to the **favourite notion** of a threefold sense of Scripture, or they pursued an independent course of exegesis, so as to **dispense** with all investigations of a philosophical **and** antiquarian character, further developing the said notion of a threefold **sense, and** indulging freely in those speculations to which a right or **wrong** apprehension of the Latin version **of the sacred** Scriptures would accidentally give rise. *The* former method was almost exclusively adopted up to the eleventh **century.** But it being found **to be** insufficient, *when from the middle* of that century a **new** spiritual life *began to manifest itself, and* both mysticism and scholasticism were *flourishing, the* other method **was** resorted to. **This** later **kind of** mystico-dialectic exegesis . . . seems to have been principally developed, though not first introduced, and brought into general use by Rupert of Deutz (he died A.D. 1135). A wide and fertile field was thus opened for mystical and subtle investigations. Both the mystics and scholastics, though each in their own way, now brought the **whole mass of their** contemplations and speculations into Scripture, and **carried** this often **to such an** extreme, as to leave scarcely **a trace of the simple** meaning **of** Scripture." Lardner strikingly characterizes (l.c.) the exegesis of the schoolmen as "*not so much an exegesis of Scripture as an exegesis of exegesis.*"

(2) De Div. Nat. iii. 24, p. 132 (134): Infinitus conditor Sacræ Scripturæ in mentibus prophetarum, Spiritus Sanctus, infinitos in ea constituit intellectus, ideoque nullius expositoris sensus sensum alterius aufert, dummodo sanæ fidei catholicæque professioni conveniat, quod quisque dicat, sive aliunde accipiens, sive a se ipso illuminatus, tamen a Deo inveniens. Comp. iii. 26, iv. 5, p. 164. He compares the sacred Scriptures to a peacock's feather, the smallest particle of which glitters in the most various colours. Comp. *Ritter*, vii. s. 213. How anxious he was to penetrate the hidden meaning of Scripture, may be seen from the following passage, v. 37, p. 307: O Domine Jesu, nullum aliud præmium, nullam aliam beati-

tudinem, nullum aliud gaudium a te postulo, nisi ut ad purum absque ullo errore fallacis theoriae verba tua, quae per tuum Sanctum Spiritum inspirata sunt, intelligam.

(3) Thus *Paschasius Radbert* taught a threefold sense of Scripture, viz.: 1. A literal (historical) sense ; 2. A spiritual and mystical (that which refers to the Church); and, 3. A moral (relative to the soul of every individual Christian). *Rabanus Maurus* spoke of a fourfold sense: 1. History; 2. Allegory; 3. Tropology; 4. Anagogy. *Hugo of St. Victor* (see *Liebner*, l.c. s. 153 ff.) and *Savonarola* (see *Rudelbach*, s. 343) did the same. *Angelom*, a monk of Luxeuil, held to a sevenfold sense: 1. The historical; 2. The allegorical; 3. The intermediate sense which lies between the two preceding ones (?); 4. The tropical (that referring to the Trinity); 5. The parabolical; 6. That sense which has regard to the double manifestation of Christ; and, 7. The moral: see *Pez*, Thesaurus, tom. i., and *Schmid*, Mysticismus des Mittelalters, s. 76. Concerning the eightfold sense, see *Morrier* on Odonis Cluniacensis Moralia in Iobum (Bibl. Max. Patr. t. xvii. p. 315): 1. Sensus literalis vel historicus; 2. Allegoricus vel parabolicus; 3. Tropologicus vel etymologicus; 4. Anagogicus vel analogicus; 5. Typicus vel exemplaris; 6. Anaphoricus vel proportionalis; 7. Mysticus vel apocalypticus; 8. Boaracademicus vel primordialis (quo ipsa principia rerum comparantur cum beatitudine æterna et tota dispensatione salutis, veluti loquendo de regno Dei, quod omnia sint ad Deum ipsum, unde manarunt, reditura). The threefold sense of Scripture was itself mystically interpreted, *e.g.* by *St. Bernard* (Sermo 92, De diversis). The bridegroom conducts the bride: 1. Into the garden : the historical sense; 2. Into the different cellars for spices, fruit, and wine: the moral sense; 3. Into the cubiculum : the mystical sense. And *Hildebert* of Le Mans compared the fourfold sense of Scripture to the four legs of the table of the Lord (Sermo ii. in Fest. Assumtionis Mariæ). See *Lentz*, Geschichte der Homiletik, i. s. 275.

(4) Thus *Hugo of St. Victor* cautioned against indulging in allegorical interpretation, and asserted the equally great importance of literal interpretation; Prænott. c. 5, quoted by *Liebner*, s. 142: "Cum igitur mystica intelligentia nonnisi ex his, quae primo loco litera proponit, colligatur: minor qua

fronte quidam allegoriarum se doctores jactitent, qui ipsam adhuc primam literæ significationem ignorant. Nos, inquiunt, scripturam legimus sed non legimus literam. Non curamus de litera, sed allegoriam docemus. Quomodo ergo scripturam legitis, et literam non legitis? *Si enim litera tollitur, scriptura quid est?*"—"Noli itaque de intelligentia scripturarum gloriari, quamdiu literam ignoras."—"Noli igitur in verbo Dei despicere humilitatem, quia per humilitatem illuminaris ad divinitatem. Quasi lutum tibi videtur totum hoc; et ideo fortasse pedibus conculcas. Sed audi: luto isto cæci oculi ad videndum illuminantur." But his own expositions are sometimes fanciful and trifling, as may be seen from the example given by *Lübner*, s. 163. *Thomas Aquinas* laid down the following principle (Summa, P. i. qu. 102, art. 1) : . . . In omnibus, quæ S. Scriptura tradit, pro fundamento tenenda veritas historica, et desuper spirituales expositiones fabricandæ.—According to *Savonarola*, the first condition of a productive system of interpretation is to have the same spirit in which the sacred books are written, *i.e.* the spirit of faith, etc. See *Rudelbach*, s. 339 ff.

(5) This restriction was first imposed in the Greek Church, in the ninth century, in the conflict with the Paulicians; comp. *Petri Siculi* (A.D. 870), Historia Manichæorum, and *Gieseler*, Dg. s. 484. To this came afterwards in the West the prohibitions of Pope Innocent III. (A.D. 1199), of the Concil. Tolosanum (A.D. 1229), Canon the 14th: Prohibemus etiam ne libros Veteris Test. aut Novi laici permittantur habere: nisi forte Psalterium, vel Breviarium pro divinis officiis, aut horas B. Mariæ aliquis ex devotione habere velit. Sed ne præmissos libros habeant in vulgari translatos, auctissime inhibemus. Conc. Tarragonense (A.D. 1234), Can. 2: Item statuimus ne aliquis libros Veteris vel Novi Test. in Romania habeat. Et si aliquis habeat, infra octo dies post publicationem hujusmodi constitutionis a tempore sententiæ tradat eos loci Episcopo *comburendos:* quod nisi fecerit, sive clericus fuerit, sive laicus, tanquam suspectus de hæresi, quousque se purgaverit, habeatur. Then came the prohibitions of the Councils of Béziers, 1223 and 1246 (against the Waldenses), and that of Oxford (1408, against Wykliffe's version of the Bible). Comp. *Gottfr. Hegelmaier*, Geschichte des Bibelverbots, Ulm 1783. See also the works of *Usher, Wharton, Hegelmaier,*

and *Onymus,* which are referred to by *Münscher, von Cölln,* ii. s. 109.

(6) Thus *John Damascene,* iv. 17, recommends the perusal of the sacred Scriptures, though in a rather fanciful manner. He calls it **τὸν** κάλλιστον παράδεισον, τὸν εὐώδη, τὸν γλυκύτατον, τὸν ὡραιότατον, τὸν παντοίοις τῶν νοερῶν θεοφόρων ὀρνέων **κελαδήμασι** περιηχοῦντα **ἡμῶν τὰ** ὦτα κ.τ.λ.—*Anselm* also strongly recommended the reading of the Bible in his Tractatus Asceticus (quoted by *Mohler,* l.c. s. 62). *Bonaventura* (Principium in libros sacros) did the same. Comp. *Lentz,* Gesch. der Homiletik, **i.** s. 290. Respecting the Biblia Pauperum of *Bonaventura,* see ibid. l.c. On the effects produced **by the** perusal of the Scriptures upon the Waldenses, **see the** account given by *Rainerius* in the thirteenth century, in the Bibl. Patr. Lugd. **t.** xxv., quoted by *Neander,* Kleine Gelegenheitsschriften, **s.** 162 ; and on the services of the Brethren of **the** Common Life towards the spread of biblical knowledge among **the** people, see *Neander,* l.c. s. 182, note.—*Gerhard Zerbolt,* **a** priest, who was a member of "the pious association" at Deventer, composed a treatise : **De** Utilitate Lectionis sacrarum Litterarum **in** Lingua vulgari : see *Jacobi Revii* Daventria Illustrata, **p. 41.** Extracts from it are given by *Neander,* l.c.

(7) *Ullmann,* Johann Wessel, **s. 190 ff.**

SECOND DIVISION.

THEOLOGY.

(INCLUDING COSMOLOGY, ANGELOLOGY, DEMONOLOGY, ETC.)

Köstlin, **Geschichtliche** Studien zur Christlichen Lehre von **Gott** (Jahrbb. für deutsche Theol. x. 2, s. 277 ff.).

§ 163.

The Existence of God.

Eberstein, Natürliche Theologie der Scholastiker, Leipz. 1803. *Billroth*, De Anselmi Cant. Proslogio et Monologio, Lips. 1832. *Fricke*, Argumenta pro Dei Existentia exponuntur et judicantur, Lips. **1846**. **F. Fischer*, Der ontologische Beweis für das Dasein Gottes **und seine Geschichte**, Basel 1852, 4to.

THE proofs of the existence of God have their proper foundation in the scholastic philosophy. That which was formerly but the semblance of an argument, now appeared in the form of a valid demonstration. Thus the *cosmological* proof of Diodorus of Tarsus was fully developed by *John Damascene* (1). *Anselm of Canterbury* (2) followed the footsteps of Augustine and Boëthius (see § 123), and endeavoured from the actual idea of God to prove His existence. This was the so-called *ontological* proof, which, however, did not at once obtain the assent of Anselm's contemporaries. *Gaunilo*, a monk, from a more empirical point of view, raised objections of an ingenious character to the proof of Anselm, which were as ingeniously refuted by the latter (3). The fate which this mode of proof encountered was various (4). While *Hugo of St. Victor* attempted a new proof of the existence of God, viz. from *contingency* (5), the theologians of the thirteenth century in general, and *Thomas Aquinas* and *Duns Scotus* in particular, returned to the argument of Anselm, though they modified it in their own way (6). *Raimund of Sabunde* propounded what is called the *moral* proof, according to which the existence of an eternal author of reward and punishment is inferred from the moral freedom and accountability of rational creatures (7). The *historical* proof is found in *Savonarola* (8) and others, who endeavoured to demonstrate the existence of God from the consensus gentium. — There were, however, those who showed the insufficiency of these proofs, or at least abstained from the use of all proofs of this kind, and simply appealed to the immediate revelation of God in the heart of man. *John Duns Scotus* (9) and *William Occam* (10) belonged to the former; *John Wessel* (11), and especially the mystics, belonged to the latter class of theologians (12).

(1) De fide orthod. i. 3. *John Damascene* proceeds from the principle: Ἡ γνῶσις τοῦ εἶναι Θεὸν φυσικῶς ἡμῖν ἐγκατέσπαρται,— but this consciousness of God was impaired by sin. God restored it by His revelation, which was accompanied by miracles. The feeble attempts at proof now take the place of miracles. He enumerates the following proofs: 1. The proof ex rerum mutabilitate (the cosmological); 2. The proof ex earum conversatione et gubernatione; and, 3. Ex rerum ordinato situ (the last two may be comprehended under the designation, physico-theological proof). As for the first, he argues as follows: Πάντα τὰ ὄντα ἢ κτιστά ἐστιν, ἢ ἄκτιστα· εἰ μὲν οὖν κτιστά, πάντως καὶ τρεπτά· ὧν γὰρ τὸ εἶναι ἀπὸ τροπῆς ἤρξατο, ταῦτα τῇ τροπῇ ὑποκείσεται πάντως, ἢ φθειρόμενα, ἢ κατὰ προαίρεσιν ἀλλοιούμενα· εἰ δὲ ἄκτιστα, κατὰ τὸν τῆς ἀκολουθίας λόγον, πάντως καὶ ἄτρεπτα· ὧν γὰρ τὸ εἶναι ἐναντίον, τούτων καὶ ὁ τοῦ πῶς εἶναι λόγος ἐναντίος, ἤγουν αἱ ἰδιότητες. Τίς οὖν οὐ συνθήσεται, πάντα τὰ ὄντα, ὅσα ὑπὸ τὴν ἡμετέραν αἴσθησιν, ἀλλὰ μὴν καὶ ἀγγέλους τρέπεσθαι καὶ ἀλλοιοῦσθαι καὶ πολυτρόπως κινεῖσθαι; ... Τρεπτὰ τοίνυν ὄντα, πάντως καὶ κτιστά· κτιστὰ δὲ ὄντα, πάντως ὑπό τινος ἐδημιουργήθησαν· δεῖ δὲ τὸν δημιουργὸν ἄκτιστον εἶναι. Εἰ γὰρ κἀκεῖνος ἐκτίσθη, πάντως ὑπό τινος

ἐκτίσθη, ἕως ἂν ἔλθωμεν εἴς τι ἄκτιστον. Ἄκτιστος οὖν ὁ δημιουργός, πάντως καὶ ἄτρεπτός ἐστι. Τοῦτο δὲ τί ἂν ἄλλο εἴη ἢ Θεός. Comp. the method adopted by Diodorus of Tarsus, § 123, note 3. In the physico-theological proof (2 and 3) he followed the earlier theologians, especially Athanasius and Gregory of Nazianzus.

(2) The name *ontological* was given only in later times (by Kant?): see *Fischer* in the work above referred to, s. 12. We can here give only the heads of the argument, the thread of reasoning must be seen from the connection. Monol. i.: Cum tam innumerabilia bona sint, quorum tam multam diversitatem et sensibus corporeis experimur et ratione mentis discernimus, estne credendum esse unum aliquid, per quod unum sunt bona, quæcunque bona sunt, aut sunt bona alia per aliud? ... III.: Denique non solum omnia bona per idem aliquid sunt bona et omnia magna per idem aliquid sunt magna, sed quicquid est, per *unum* aliquid videtur esse.... Quoniam ergo cuncta quæ sunt, sunt per ipsum unum: procul dubio et ipsum unum est per se ipsum. Quæcunque igitur alia sunt, sunt per aliud, et ipsum solum per se ipsum. Ac quicquid est per aliud, minus est quam illud, per quod cuncta sunt alia et quod solum est per se: quare illud, quod est per se, maxime omnium est. Est igitur unum aliquid, quod solum maxime et summe omnium est; quod autem maxime omnium est et per quod est quicquid est bonum vel magnum, et omnino quicquid est aliquid est, id necesse est esse summe bonum et summe magnum et summum omnium quæ sunt. Quare est aliquid, quod sive essentia, sive substantia, sive natura dicatur, optimum et maximum est et summum omnium quæ sunt. Comp. Augustine and Boëthius in § 123, note 4. The mode of argument which is found, Proslog. c. ii., is more original (he there proceeds from the reality of the idea): The *fool* may say in his heart, There is no God (Ps. xiv. 1), but he thereby shows himself a fool, because he asserts something which is contradictory in itself. He has the idea of God *in* him, but denies its reality. But if God is given in idea, He must also exist in reality. Otherwise the *real* God, whose existence is conceivable, would be superior to the one who exists only in imagination, and consequently would be superior to the highest conceivable object, which is absurd; hence it

follows, that that beyond which nothing can be conceived to exist really exists (thus idea and reality coincide). Convincitur ergo insipiens, esse vel in intellectu aliquid, quo nihil majus cogitari potest; quia hoc cum audit, intelligit, et quicquid intelligitur, in intellectu est. Et certe id, quo majus cogitari nequit, non potest esse in intellectu solo. Si enim vel in solo intellectu est, potest cogitari esse et in re, quod majus est. Si ergo id, quo majus cogitari non potest, est in solo intellectu: id ipsum, quo majus cogitari non potest, est quo majus cogitari potest: sed certe hoc esse non potest. Existit ergo procul dubio aliquid, quo majus cogitari non valet, et in intellectu et in re. If, therefore, the fool **says**: There is no God; he *says* it indeed, and may, perhaps, even *think* it. But there is a difference between thought **and** thought. To **conceive** a thing when the word is without meaning, *e.g.* that **fire is** water (a mere sound, an absurdity ?), is very different **from** the case **in** which the thought corresponds with the **word.** It is only according to the former mode of thinking **(which** destroys the thought itself) that the fool can say: There **is no** God, but **not according** to the latter.

(3) *Gaunilo* was a monk in the monastery of Marmontier. He *wrote*: Liber pro Insipiente adv. Anselmi in Proslogio Ratiocinationem (in Anselmi Opp. p. 32, Gerb. p. 53).[1] The idea of a thing does not necessarily imply its reality; there are many false ideas. Yea, it is very questionable whether we can have any thought of God at all, since He is above all thought. ... If one, in speaking of an island which he asserted to be more perfect and lovely than all known islands, should infer its existence *from this,* that it could not be the most perfect if it did not exist, we should hardly know which was the greater fool, the man who adduced such an argument, or the one who gave his assent to it. The opposite method should be adopted; we must first prove the existence of the island, and then show that its excellence surpasses that of all others, etc. (comp. *Münscher, von Cölln,* ii. s. 33, 34). "*It is easy to see that Gaunilo argues against Anselm from the empirical, and consequently an essentially different point of view,*"

---

[1] Anselm was probably unacquainted with the author of the treatise in question. It is quoted as the work *incerti auctoris* in the earlier editions of Anselm's works. Comp. *Gerberon,* t. i. p. ii.

Möhler, ubi supra, s. 152.—*Anselm* defended himself against Gaunilo in his treatise: Liber Apologeticus contra Gaunilonem respondentem pro insipiente (it is also called Contra Insipientem, Opp. p. 34, *Gerberon*, p. 37). He returns to the above distinction between thought and thought, and rejects the illustration taken from the island as altogether inappropriate. He observes, that if Gaunilo could *really* imagine an island more perfect than could ever be conceived, he would make him a present of it. "With Anselm the idea *of the most perfect being was a necessary idea of the reason*, between which, and the arbitrary and imaginary notion of a most excellent island, no parallel could be drawn," Möhler, s. 153. (Comp. *Hegel*, Encyklop. der philosoph. Wiss. 2d ed. 1827, s. 61 ff., s. 181: "*Anselm was right in declaring that only that can be perfect which exists not merely subjectively, but also objectively. In vain we affect to despise this proof,* commonly called the ontological, *and this idea of the perfect set* forth by Anselm; it is inherent in the mind of every unprejudiced man, and reappears in every system of philosophy, even *against* knowledge and will, as well as in the principle of direct faith.") On the question whether the proof of Anselm can be properly called a *proof*, see Möhler, l.c. s. 154. On the whole controversy, comp. *W. C. L. Ziegler*, Beitrag zur Geschichte des Glaubens an Gott, Gött. 1792. *Baur*, Trinitatsl. ii. 372 ff. *Fischer*, l.c. *Hasse*, Anselm, ii. s. 233 ff.

(4) The theory of Anselm "*has had a great history. It was not only applied in different ways, and further developed by eminent writers, but, up to the present day, it has been either* opposed or *defended, according* to the respective character of every philosophical school," Möhler, s. 150.

(5) "*Hugo did not perceive the depth of Anselm's idea, being deceived by the superficial, dialectic reasoning of Gaunilo*," *Liebner*, Hugo Von St. Victor, s. 369. The argument from *contingency*, which *Peter of Poitiers* also afterwards adopted, is given in *Hugo's* treatises, De Sacramentis, c. 7–9, De tribus Dieb. c. 17, quoted by *Liebner*, s. 369 f. It is as follows: Reason which, as the creature and image of God, is able to know Him, is essentially distinguished from the body in which it dwells, and from all that is sensuous, being that which is invisible and spiritual. But it is aware that it has

not always been either active or conscious of itself, and that therefore there was a time when it did not exist: for it is impossible to conceive of a faculty of knowledge without knowledge and consciousness. It must therefore have had a beginning. Possessing **a** spiritual nature, it cannot possibly have derived its origin from the sensuous, but must necessarily **have** been created **out** of nothing; hence it follows that it **owes** its existence **to an** external author. But this author **himself** cannot have come into existence, **for** nothing which is created can give existence to another being; otherwise we have the infinite series. We must therefore assume the existence of a self-existent and eternal being as the first cause. (This proof occupies, as **it** were, an intermediate position between the cosmological and the ontological. The cosmological proof has the world for its foundation, the ontological the idea, and the argument of Hugo rests on the basis of the spirit.) Hugo also made use of **the** cosmological and physico-theological proof, which was **at that** time the **most** popular. Nor did even *Peter Lombard* make use of the proof of Anselm; Sententt. i. dist. 3, comp. *Münscher, von* **Colln**, ii. s. 34.

(6) *Thomas Aquinas*, Summa **Theol. P. I.** qu. 2, art. 1, urges against the absolute stringency **of** Anselm's proof: Dato etiam, **quod** quilibet intelligat hoc nomine " Deus " significari hoc quod dicitur, scilicet illud, quo majus cogitari non potest **non tamen** propter hoc sequitur, quod intelligat **id**, quod significatur per nomen, esse in rerum natura, sed in apprehensione **intellectus** tantum. Nec potest argui, quod sit in re, nisi daretur, quod **sit in re** aliquid, quo majus cogitari non **potest**: quod **non est** datum a ponentibus Deum non esse. The argument of Thomas himself (*Münscher, von Colln*, s. 35; *Schröckh*, xxix. s. 77) amounts to this, that the proposition: "*God exists*," may be regarded as evident, if considered in *itself* (quantum in se est), since the predicate is identical with the subject ; but it is not so *in relation to us*. Thomas connected the various modes of proof with each other **on** the principle previously adopted by *Richard of St. Victor*, De Trin. i. c. 6 ss. (comp. *Engelhardt*, Richard von St. Victor, s. 99 ff.). He enumerated altogether five kinds of proof: 1 That derived from the first moving principle (primum movens), which is not itself moved by any other; 2. That derived from

the first great cause (causa efficiens); 3. That derived from what is necessary by itself (per se necessarium—these first three form together the cosmological proof in its dialectic form); 4. That derived from the gradation of things (or the argument from the imperfect to the absolutely perfect— Augustine and Anselm had propounded this proof); 5. That derived from the adaptation of things (the physico-theological or teleological proof). See *Baur*, Trinitätslehre, ii. s. 581 ff. *Duns Scotus* seeks to give more colour (colorari) to the argument of Anselm by different modifications and applications: see his De Primo Rerum Princip. cap. 4, and comp. *Fischer*, l.c. s. 7. Besides this, he appeals to the proofs from experience; see *Münscher*, von *Cölln*, ii. s. 56.

(7) *Abelard* had previously directed attention to this proof, Theol. christ. lib. v. (*Martène*, p. 1349), but not so much as a strictly cogent *proof* (magis honestis, quam necessariis rationibus nitimur); rather in a practical way, as the voice of conscience. Quam honestum vero sit ac salubre, omnia ad unum optimum tam rectorem quam conditorem spectare et cuncta potius ratione quam casu fieri seu regi, nullus est, cui propriæ ratio non suggerat conscientia. Quæ enim sollicitudo bonorum nobis operum inesset, si, quem nec amore nec timore vereremur, Deum penitus ignoraremus? Quæ spes aut malitiam refrænaret potentum, aut ad bona eos alliceret opera, si omnium justissimus ac potentissimus frustra crederetur? Ponamus itaque, ut, dum bonis prodesse ac placere quærimus, obstinatos cogere non possimus, cum ora eorum non necessariis obstruamus argumentis. Ponamus, inquam, hoc si volunt; sed opponamus, quod nolunt, summam eorum impudentiam arguentes, si hoc calumniantur, quod refellere nullo modo possunt, et quod plurima tam honestate quam utilitate commendatur. Inquiramus eos, qua ratione malint eligere, Deum non esse, quam esse, et cum ad neutrum cogi necessario possint, et alterum multis commendetur rationibus, alterum nullis, iniquissimam eorum confundamus impudentiam, qui id, quod optimum esse non dubitent, omnibusque est tam rationibus, quam auctoritatibus consentaneum, sequi respuant et contrarium complectantur. — The argument as used by *Raimund* has more of the logical form of proof; see Theol. Natur. Tit. 83 (quoted by *Münscher*, von *Cölln*, s. 38. *Tenne-*

mann, Gesch. d. Phil. viii. s. 964 ff.). Since man is an accountable being, but can neither reward nor punish himself, it follows that there must be a being superior to him, who rewards and punishes; for if there were no such being, the life of man would be fruitless, a game of chance. As, moreover, the irrational creation is subject to man, and exists for his sake, it would follow, if there were no corresponding higher being above man, that creation itself was without an object. But now we perceive (here comes in the physico-theological as an auxiliary proof) order and harmony in the whole external creation which is subject to man;[1] how can we suppose that the order in the natural world is not repeated in the moral world? As the eye corresponds to things visible, the ear to things audible, the understanding to things comprehensible, so the moral actions of man must have their corresponding judgment and retribution, and consequently a judge and retributive governor. But this judge must necessarily possess a perfect knowledge of human actions, and their moral character; that is to say, he must be omniscient; it is also evident that he must be just, in the highest sense of the word; and, lastly, he must be possessed of unlimited power to execute his judgment,—in other words, he must be almighty. But such a being cannot but be the most perfect of all beings, *i.e.* God. (The similarity between this proof and that of Kant has often been pointed out.)

(8) Comp. Triumph. Crucis, lib. i. c. 6, p. 38 ss., quoted in *Meier's* Savonarola, s. 245.

(9) Sentent. i. dist. 2, qu. 2, art. 1 (quoted by *Münscher*, *von Cölln*, s. 37. *Tiedemann*, Geist der speculativen Philosophie, Bd. iv. s. 632). An objection was especially made to the proof derived from the *necessarium ex se*, inasmuch as Scotus made a distinction between the ideas of possibility and necessity.

(10) Centiloqu. Theol. Concl. 1 (*Tiedemann*, l.c. v. s. 205). He opposed the principal argument of Aristotle derived from the πρῶτον κινοῦν.

---

[1] *Raimund* directs attention to the gradation of beings. Some of them only *exist* (inorganic beings); others *exist* and *live* (plants); others *exist*, *live*, and *feel* (animals); and, lastly, others *exist*, *feel*, and *think* (man). In man, all the earlier stages are repeated. Comp. *Matzke*, l.c. s. 49.

(11) *Wessel* reasoned as follows: The general and most direct means by which man attains to God, is the *original knowledge of God*, inherent in every rational spirit. As no place is so dark as not to receive some degree of light from a sunbeam, so no rational soul is without some sort of indwelling notion (notitia) of God ... (Ps. xix. 6). This knowledge, however, is not the same in all men, but developes itself differently in different persons according to their other capacities, and their whole moral and intellectual condition; just as the universal light of the sun is differently received by different objects according to their susceptibility, position, and distance. Wessel designates this simple and universal knowledge of God as the *name* of God, which dwells, as it were, in every spirit, is expressed in every soul, and may, therefore, in every soul be brought to consciousness; De Orat. lib. v. *Ullmann*, s. 200.

(12) *Tauler*, Pred. Bd. i. s. 58 (on the second Advent): I possess a power in my soul which is altogether susceptible of God; I am as sure as I live that nothing is so near to me as God. *God is nearer to me than I am to myself*, etc. Comp. the following section, note 3.

§ 164.

The Comprehensibility[1] *of God.*

In proportion as men think they can prove the existence of God, will they be more or less assured that they can know His nature. Hence the scholastic divines made the nature of God the special object of their speculation. Nevertheless, they expressly asserted that God cannot be comprehended, and admitted for the most part only a *conditional* knowledge on the part of man (1). The views of *Occam* on this subject bordered on scepticism (2). The mystics, on the contrary, endeavoured, in opposition as well to dogmatism as scepticism, to live a hidden life in God, and *thus* to obtain an immediate vision of God Himself in His light, and of all things *in* Him (3).

---

[1] [This hardly represents the German *Erkennbarkeit*. The nearest word would perhaps be *cognizability*, if it were allowable.]

(1) *John Damascene*, De fide orthod. i. 4, had taught, after the example of some of the earlier Fathers, that God does not come under the category of *things* (οὐδὲν γὰρ τῶν ὄντων ἐστίν), which is equivalent to the modern speculative Deity = Nullity. He is ὑπὲρ γνῶσιν πάντως καὶ ὑπὲρ οὐσίαν, and it is only by way of negation (δι' ἀφαιρέσεως) that we acquire the knowledge of His attributes (comp. Clement of Alexandria, in the first period, § 37, note).—*John Scotus Erigena*, in bolder style, surpassing the limits of what is allowable to man, maintained, De Divis. Nat. ii. 28, p. 78, that God does not know Himself. Deus itaque nescit se, quid est, quia non est quid; incomprehensibilis quippe in aliquo et sibi ipsi et omni intellectui. The whole of theology, according to him, is divided into affirmative and negative (the *cataphatic* and the *apophatic*). But affirmation and negation are abolished in the absolute idea of God, and what to us is contradictory is not so to Him. Comp. *Baur*, Trinitat. ii. s. 276. [Theologia ἀποφατική divinam essentiam seu substantiam esse aliquid eorum, quæ sunt, i.e. quæ dici aut intelligi possunt, negat; altera vero, καταφατική, omnia quæ sunt de ea prædicat, et ideo affirmativa dicitur, non ut confirmet aliquid esse eorum quæ sunt, sed omnia, quæ ab ea sunt, de ea posse prædicari suadeat. Rationabiliter enim per causativa causale potest significari (De Div. Nat. i. 13).]—The more modest *Anselm*, on the contrary, returned to the right path, by confessing in his Monologue that God alone knows His own nature, and that no human wisdom can so much as presume to measure or to comprehend the divine wisdom. For it is certain that what we ascribe to God only relatively, does not express His nature (si quid de summa natura dicitur relative, non est ejus significativum substantiæ). Comp. Monolog. c. 15–17; *Hasse*, ii. s. 129 ff. *Münscher, von Cölln*, s. 44, and *Möhler*, l.c. s. 154 f. Similar language occurs in *Alanus ab Insulis*, De Art. Cathol. Fidei, 16, 17 (quoted by *Pez*, i. p. 482).—*Albertus Magnus* distinguishes between attingere Deum intellectu, and comprehendere. Creatures can only attain to the former. Comp. Summa Theol. i. tr. iv. qu. 18, membr. 3, p. 67 (in *Ritter*, viii. s. 197). Resting on this basis, *Thomas Aquinas* (Summa, P. I. qu. 12, art. 12) proved that man has no cognitio quidditativa of God (*i.e.* no knowledge of God in

Himself), but **only knows habitudo** *ipsius ad creaturas*; while *Scotus* (Sent. i. dist. 3, qu. 1, art. 1 ss.) taught the **opposite doctrine, partly with reference** to the opinions of *Heinrich von Gent* (about 1280), a teacher of the Sorbonne. — The final result of the controversy carried on between the Thomists and Scotists on the question De cognitione Dei quidditativa, was that man has a cognitio quidditatis Dei, but not a cognitio quidditativa, *i.e.* that he may know the *nature* of God (in contrast with a mere *accidental* and superficial notion), but that he cannot know God thoroughly, *i.e.* in such a manner that no part of His nature is concealed from man.[1] Comp. the passages quoted by *Münscher, von Cölln,* s. 44 ff., and *Eberhardstein,* Naturliche Theologie der Scholastiker, s. 52–66. *Baur*, Trin. ii. s. 616 ff. — *Durandus of St. Pourçain* (in Magistri Sentent. i. dist. 3, qu. 1) speaks of a threefold way which leads to the knowledge of God: 1. *Via eminentiæ*, which ascends from the excellences of the creatures to the highest excellence, *i.e.* to the perfection of God. 2. *Via causalitatis*, which ascends from the phenomena of creation to the first cause. 3. *Via remotionis*, which begins with changeable and dependent existence, and ends with necessary and absolute existence (esse de se). — *Alexander of Hales* used similar and still simpler expressions (Summa, P. I. qu. 2, membr. 1, art. 2): Dicendum, quod est cognitio de Deo *per modum positionis et per modum privationis.* Per modum privationis cognoscimus de Deo, quid non est, per modum positionis, quid est. Divina substantia in sua immensitate non est cognoscibilis ab anima rationali cognitione positiva, sed est cognoscibilis cognitione privativa. Comp. *Münscher, von Cölln*, l.c. We must say, *apprehendi* quidem posse Deum, *comprehendi* nequaquam. See *Schröckh,* xxix. s. 15. — On the endeavours of later Greek theologians, *e.g. Nicolas of Methone* (especially after the example of Dionysius the Areopagite), to represent the insufficiency of our knowledge and terminology respecting divine things, see *Ullmann*, l.c. p. 72–74: The Divine is in

---

[1] *Cajetanus*, Summæ P. I. qu. 12, De Arte et Essentia, c. 6, qu. 4: Aliud est cognoscere quidditatem, s. *cognitio quidditatis*: aliud est *cognitio quidditativa*, s. cognoscere quidditative. Cognoscit nempe leonis *quidditatem*, quicunque novit *aliquid* ejus prædicatum essentiale. Cognoscit autem *quidditative* nonnisi ille, qui *omnia* prædicata quidditativa usque ad ultimam differentiam novit. (In *Münscher, von Cölln*, l.c.)

no wise to be co-ordinated and compared with all that exists: on the **whole**, it would be better to express in an exaggerated and exceptional manner (ὑπεροχικῶς καὶ κατεξαίρετον) all that is predicated of the Divine, etc.

(2) *Occam* (**as well** as Alexander of Hales) starts from the **position that there is a positive and** negative knowledge of **God, and** in accordance with this shapes his definitions, which, however, are **different only in form.** Quodlibet Theol. i. **qu. 1:** *e.g.* Deus est aliquid nobilius **et** aliquid melius omni **alio a se**: and, Deus est quo nihil est melius, prius vel perfectius. The former may be used **as an argument for** the *unity*, but not for the existence of God, inasmuch as the latter idea cannot be proved by demonstration. The second **may be** appealed to in support of the doctrine of the *existence*, but **not** of the unity of God, since it may be supposed that such negative perfections belong to several individuals. From this **point of** view he refutes the arguments used by the earlier **scholastics, especially** Duns Scotus. (Centiloq. concl. 2. See *Münscher, von Colln*, **s. 51.**) He combats the arguments **derived from this " first** cause **;"** nor does he give his assent **to the argument derived from "** the uniformity of the world." Thus **he arrives at** the following conclusion: Conclusio, quod **non sunt plures Dei, non tanquam demonstrata, sed** tanquam *probabilior* suo opposito tenenda est: eo quod omnes apparentiae aequaliter apparent, et faciliter **possunt salvari tenendo** unitatem primae causae. Comp. **Sent.** i. dist. 3, qu. **2: Nec divina** essentia, nec divina quidditas, nec aliquid intrinsecum **Deo, nec** aliquid, **quod est** realiter Deus, potest hic cognosci a nobis, ita **quod nihil** aliud a Deo concurrat in ratione objecti .. Deus non potest cognosci a nobis intuitive et puris naturalibus. *Baur*, **Trin.** ii. s. 875.

(3) **Thus** *Gerson* said (Contra vanam Curiositatem, lectio **secunda, t. i. p. 100,** quoted by *Ch. Schmidt*, p. 73): Fides **saluberrima et** omnis metaphysica tradit nobis, quod Deus est simplicissimus **in supremo simplicitatis** gradu, supra quam imaginari sufficimus. **Hoc** dato, quid opus est ipsam unitissimam essentiam **per** formas metaphysices vel quidditates vel **rationes ideales vel alias** mille imaginandi vias secernere, **dividere,** constituere, praescindere ex **parte** rei, ut dicunt, et non **ex intellectus** negotiatione circa **eam ?** Deus sancte, quot

tibi prioritates, quot instantia, quot signa, quot modeitates, quot rationes aliqui ultra Scotum condistinguunt! Jam mille codices talibus impleti sunt, adeo ut longa aetas hominum eos vix sufficiat legere, ne dicam intelligere. — Gerson's theory of the knowledge of God (viz. the knowledge of God through love) was appropriately designated, both by himself and by other theologians, as *Theologia affectiva* (Tract. iii. super Magnificat, t. iv. p. 262). — *Suso* expressed himself as follows in his treatise: Eine Ausrichtung, wo und wie Gott ist (in Diepenbrock, Leben u. Schriften von Heinrich von S. s. 212, c. lv.): "The masters assert that the idea of space cannot be applied to God, but that He is all in all. But now open the inner ears of your soul, and open them wide. The same masters maintain, in the science called Logica, that we may obtain the knowledge of a thing by means of its name. Thus a certain teacher asserts that the name *Being* is the first name of God. Turn now thine eye to Being in all its simplicity, excluding all notion of this or that particular being. Consider Being in itself; look at Being only as such, and as it is unmixed with non-existence;[1] for all that has no existence is contrary to that which has existence; the case is the same with Being as such, for it is contrary to all that has no existence. Anything which either has already existed, or has yet to exist, does not now exist in essential presence. But now mixed existence or non-existence cannot be known but by some mark of that Being which is in all. For if we wish to comprehend anything, reason meets first with existence, viz. that existence [Being] which has made all things. This is not the divided existence of this or that creature; for all divided existence is mixed up with something else, with the possibility of receiving something. Hence it follows that the nameless Divine Being must be in itself the Being which is all in all, and must preserve all compound beings by its omnipresence." Ibidem, s. 214: "Now open your inner eyes, and look, if possible, at Being in its simplicity and purity, and you see at once that it owes its existence to none, has neither a ' before' nor an ' after,' and is susceptible of no change either from within or from without, because it is a simple Being. You will then be convinced that this Being is the *most real*,

---

[1] [Being with not-being: *Wesen* with *Nichtwesen*.]

omnipresent, and *most perfect* **of all** beings, in which there is neither defect **nor** change, because it is **a** single unity in perfect simplicity. And this truth is so manifest to the enlightened **reason** of man, that it cannot conceive of any other; **for the one** proves **and** causes the other. Since this is **a simple Being, it** must necessarily be **the** first of all beings, **owing its being** to none, and existing from eternity; since it **is the first of all** beings **eternal** and simple, it must be omnipresent. It is a necessary quality **of** highest perfection and **simplicity** that nothing can either be added **to or** taken from **it. If** you understand what I have said of **the simple** Godhead, **you** will know something of the incomprehensible light **of the hidden** truth of God. This pure, simple Being **is** the first principle **of** all actual existences; from its peculiar omnipresence it follows that it includes all that has come into **existence in time as** the beginning and the end of all things. **It is at the same time in** all things and out of all things. **Therefore a certain** master says: '*God is a circular ring, the centre of which is everywhere, and the circumference nowhere.*' Compare with these **expressions the** language of *Tauler* (**§ 163, note** 12), of *Ruysbroek*, **quoted by** *Engelhardt*, s. 173 (**God in Himself**), **and** of **the author of the** "Deutsche Theologie," **cap. 1,** where the practical **point of view is most** prominently **brought** forward, viz. the necessity **of leading a divine life in order to know** God.

§ 165.

The Nature of God *in General.*

(*Pantheism and Theism.*)

The ingenious system of **John Scotus** *Erigena*, **which** sought, **for purely scientific purposes, to make a** dialectic mediation **between the antagonism of God and the** world (nature) (1), **was so misunderstood and misused by some of his** imitators, **particularly** *Amalrich of Bena* **and** *David of Dinanto*, **as to give rise to a gross deification of the flesh (2).**[1] **The mystics**

---

[1] [Combated by Albertus Magnus and Thomas Aquinas, and condemned by a Council at Paris (1209), and the fourth Lateran Council (1215).]

also exposed themselves to the charge of pantheism, more or less justified, by asserting that nothing except God has a real existence (3). But the more cautious among them retained, in accordance with the other teachers of the Church, the theistic principle of a difference between God and the creature, though they could not always scientifically prove that to which they practically adhered (4).

(1) In his work, De Divisione Naturarum, *Erigena* divides all nature (which comprehends all being in itself) into four modes of existence: 1. Natura creans, sed non creata = God; 2. Natura creans et creata = the Son of God; 3. Natura creata et non creans = the world; and 4. Natura non creata et non creans = God as the end and object of all things. Inasmuch as Erigena regards God as the principle and cause of all things, he arrives at the conviction that the divine essence, the goodness, the power, and the wisdom, could not be created by another being, because there is no higher being from which it could derive its existence. But since he regards, on the other hand, the Divine Being as the last object at which all things aim, and which is the end of their course, he hence concludes that this nature is neither created nor creating; for as everything which has gone out from it returns to it, and as all existence rests in it, we cannot say that it creates. What could God be supposed to create, since He must be in all things, and can at the same time represent Himself in no other being but in Himself? Therefore he says, i. 74, p. 42: Cum audimus, Deum omnia facere, nihil aliud debemus intelligere, quam *Deum in omnibus esse*, hoc est essentiam omnium subsistere. Ipse enim solus per se vere est, et omne quod vere in his quæ sunt dicitur esse, ipse solus est. The following statements are very beautiful, but easily misunderstood, i. 76, p. 43: Omne quodcunque in creaturis vere bonum vereque pulcrum et amabile intelligitur, ipse est. Sicut enim nullum bonum essentiale est, ita nullum pulcrum seu amabile essentiale præter ipsum solum. Comp. *Tennemann*, Thl. viii. 1, s. 80 ff. *Schmid*, Ueber den Mysticismus des Mittelalters, s. 123 ss. *Frommüller* in the Tüb. Zeitschr. 1830, 1, s. 58 ff. *Staudenmaier*, Freib. Zeitschr. 1840,

iii. 2, s. 272 ff.—That there was also a striving after strict theistic modes of statement, along with the pantheistic tendency of Scotus, is shown by *Ritter* in his Gesch. d. Phil. vii. s. 242, 286.

(2) Comp. § 153, note 5. From the proposition, that he who is in *love* is also in God, they inferred that "*that which is done in love* is no sin*:* therefore stealing, robbing, lasciviousness, etc., would not be sinful, if done in love." Comp. *Ditmars* **Chronik,** edited by *Grautoff* in *Hurter,* Innocenz III., Bd. ii. ·s. 238 ff. Cæsarius of Heisterbach (A.D. 1222), De Miraculis, lib. v. c. 22: Si aliquis est in Spiritu sancto, ajeba**nt, et** faciat fornicationem, aut aliqua alia pollutione polluatur: non est ei peccatum, quia ille Spiritus, qui est Deus omnino separatus a carne, non potest peccare quamdiu ille Spiritus, qui est Deus, est in eo, ille operatur omnia in omnibus. *Engelhardt*, Kirchenhistorische Abhandlungen, s. 255 ff. Compare also § 184. [The doctrine of *David of Dinanto,* says *Baur,* Dogmengesch. s. 248 (2d ed.), note, **was** undoubtedly the same as that of Avicebron, in the newly discovered work, De Materia Universali, or Fons Vitæ, which *Seyerlen* has made known in the Theol. Jahrbucher (Tübing.), 1856. The fundamental idea is that of matter in its unity with form, and the unity of both with God.]

(3) *Master Eckart* approached gross pantheism nearer than any other mystic. He said: "God is nothing, **and** God **is** something. That which is something is also nothing; **what God is, He is altogether."** (Sermon on the Feast of the Conversion **of** St. Paul, fol. 243*b*, quoted by *Schmidt* in **the** Studien und Kritiken, 1839, 3, s. 692.)—" He (God) has the **nature of all creatures *in*** Him; He is an essence, that has all **essences *in* Him."—"** All that is in **the** Godhead is *one,* and **we** cannot speak of it. It is *God* that acts, but **not the** Godhead; it **has not wherewith to work; in** it, then, there is no **work. There is the** same difference **between** God and the **Godhead as there is between working and not** working." (Sermon on the martyrdom of the Baptist, fol. 302*a*, quoted by *Schmidt,* l.c. s. 693.)—In Eckart's opinion, God becomes God through the work of creation. "Before the creatures **existed God was not God, He was what He was;** nor was God **in Himself God, after creatures had been** brought into exist-

ence, but He was only God in them." (Second Sermon on All Saints' Day, fol. 307a, *Schmidt*, l.c. s. 694.)—"*Pantheism is a great and noble phenomenon, deceiving us by a peculiar charm, in the case of those who burn with love, and are, as it were, intoxicated with a sense of God and the contemplation of divine things. But where it is only the result of subtle conclusions and philosophical definitions, or the proud but confused dream of an indefinite religious need, it loses its grand relations and its mysterious poetry, and its faults, which we once felt disposed to overlook, now become manifest, together with all their contradictions.*" *Schmidt,* l.c.

(4) *Suso* showed in a highly characteristic way that a pantheistic disposition was nothing but a transitory excitement of feeling, which must first of all subside (in *Diepenbrock*, s. 189): "I call that state of our mind flourishing, in which the inner man is cleansed from sinful carnality, and delivered from remaining imperfections; in which he cheerfully rises above time and place, since he was formerly bound, and could not make free use of his natural nobility. When he then opens the eyes of his mind, when he tastes other and better pleasures, which consist in the perception of the truth, in the enjoyment of divine happiness, in insight into the present now of eternity, and the like, and when the created mind begins to comprehend a part of the eternal, uncreated mind both in itself and in all things, then he is wonderfully moved. Examining himself and reflecting on what he once *was* and what he now *is*, he finds that he was a poor, ungodly, and wretched man, that he was blind, and lived far from God; but now *it seems to him that he is full of God, that there is nothing which is not God; further, that God and all things are one and the same. He then goes so hastily to work, that he becomes excited in his mind like wine in a state of fermentation, that has not come to itself,*" etc. ... "Such men are like bees which make honey: when they are full grown, and come for the first time out of their hives, they fly about in an irregular manner, not knowing whither to go; some take the wrong direction, and lose themselves, but others come back to the right place. Thus it is with the men before spoken of, when they *see God as all in all, without their reason being regulated,*" etc.—*Gerson* acutely defended the distinction between God and the creature

(however highly endowed) in opposition to Ruysbroek and Eckart, although he was not always consistent with himself. Comp. *Hundeshagen*, s. 62 ff. *Tauler* maintains (Predigten, Bd. i. **s.** 61, that "*nothing* **so** much hinders the soul from knowing God as time and space: time and space are parts, **but** God is one; therefore if the soul will know God, it must **know** Him *above* time and *above* space; for God is neither *this* nor *that*, as those manifold things are, **but** He is One." The assertion of *Wessel*, that "God alone *is*, **and** that all other things are *what* they are through *Him*" (De Orat. iii. 12, p. 76), and some other of his declarations, might lead to the supposition that he too was a pantheist; but compare, **on** the other hand, the appropriate observation of *Ullmann*, s. 230, Anm.

§ 166.

The Attributes of **God.**

(a) God in relation to Time, Space, and Number. (The Omnipresence, Eternity, and Unity of God.)

The writings of *John Damascene* (1), and his successors in the Greek Church (2), contain less ample definitions and classifications of the attributes than the works of the school-men, which **are** very copious on just this point. Though *Anselm* and others insisted upon the importance of **the** proposition laid down by Augustine, that the attributes of God **not only** form **one whole,** but are also identical with the divine **essence itself, and cannot** therefore be regarded as something foreign and manifold, **which is merely** attached to God (3), yet the **speculative and systematizing** tendency of the **scholastics frequently led them to lose sight of this** simple **truth. Among the metaphysical** attributes of God, Anselm **laid most stress upon the** *eternity* and *omnipresence;* the **former showed that there could not be in God** either an *Aliquando* or an *Alicubi* **in the proper sense of** the terms (4). **With reference to the** *omnipresence* **of God, some,** *e.g. Hugo* and *Richard of St. Victor,* defended the substantial omnipresence among the metaphysical attributes of God, in opposition to the merely dynamic view; while others endeavoured to unite the two (5). A difference was also made between the eternity of God and a mere *sempiternitas,* the latter of which may be ascribed even to creatures (e.g. angels and the souls of men) (6). And lastly, it was asserted that the *unity of God,* which many of the schoolmen numbered among His attributes, was not to be regarded as a mere mathematical quantity. The theologians of the Greek Church signified this by extending the idea of a numerical unity to that of a unity which is above all other things (7,).

(1) *John Damasc.* De fide orth. i. 4: Ἄπειρον οὖν τὸ θεῖον καὶ ἀκατάληπτον· καὶ τοῦτο μόνον αὐτοῦ κατάληπτον, ἡ ἀπειρία καὶ ἀκαταληψία· ὅσα δὲ λέγομεν ἐπὶ Θεοῦ καταφατικῶς, οὐ τὴν φύσιν, ἀλλὰ τὰ περὶ τὴν φύσιν δηλοῖ. Κἂν ἀγαθὸν, κἂν δίκαιον, κἂν σοφὸν, κἂν ὅ τι ἂν ἄλλο εἴπῃς, οὐ φύσιν λέγεις Θεοῦ, ἀλλὰ τὰ περὶ τὴν φύσιν. Εἰσὶ δὲ καί τινα καταφατικῶς λεγόμενα ἐπὶ Θεοῦ, δύναμιν ὑπεροχικῆς ἀποφάσεως ἔχοντα· οἷον, σκότος λέγοντες ἐπὶ Θεοῦ, οὐ σκότος νοοῦμεν, ἀλλ' ὅτι οὐκ ἔστι φῶς, ἀλλ' ὑπὲρ τὸ φῶς καὶ φῶς, ὅτι οὐκ ἔστι σκότος. Comp. cap. 9: Τὸ θεῖον ἁπλοῦν ἐστι καὶ ἀσύνθετον· τὸ δὲ ἐκ πολλῶν καὶ διαφόρων συγκείμενον, συνθετόν ἐστιν. Εἰ οὖν τὸ ἄκτιστον καὶ ἄναρχον καὶ ἀσώματον καὶ ἀθάνατον καὶ αἰώνιον καὶ ἀγαθὸν καὶ δημιουργικὸν καὶ τὰ τοιαῦτα οὐσιώδεις διαφορὰς εἴπομεν ἐπὶ Θεοῦ, ἐκ τοσούτων συγκείμενον, οὐχ ἁπλοῦν ἔσται ἀλλὰ σύνθετον· ὅπερ ἐσχάτης ἀσεβείας ἐστίν. Χρὴ τοίνυν ἕκαστον τῶν ἐπὶ Θεοῦ λεγομένων, οὐ τί κατ' οὐσίαν ἐστὶ σημαίνειν οἴεσθαι, ἀλλ' ἢ τί οὐκ ἔστι δηλοῦν, ἢ σχέσιν τινὰ πρός τι τῶν ἀντιδιαστελλομένων, ἢ τι τῶν παρεπομένων τῇ φύσει ἢ ἐνέργειαν. Comp. cap. 19, and what was said § 164, note 1.

(2) Comp. *Ullmann,* Nicolaus von Methone, etc., s. 69 ff., and § 164, note 1.

(3) Monol. c. 14–28. *Hasse,* ii. s. 127 ff. God is not only righteous, but He is righteousness itself, etc., cap. 16: Quid ergo, si illa summa natura tot bona est, eritne composita tot pluribus bonis, an potius non sunt plura bona, sed

unum bonum tam pluribus nominibus significatum? ... Cum igitur illa natura nullo modo composita sit et tamen omni modo tot illa bona sit [sint], necesse est, ut illa omnia non plura, sed **unum** sint. Idem igitur est quodlibet unum **illorum** quod omnia **sunt [sive]** simul, sive singula, ut cum **dicitur vel justitia vel** essentia, idem significet quod alia, vel **omnia simul, vel** singula. Cap. 18: Vita et sapientia et reliqua **non** sunt partes tui, sed omnia sunt unum, et unumquodque horum est totum quod es, et quod sunt reliqua omnia. *Hugo of St. Victor* adopted similar views, see Liebner, s. 371. Comp. also *Abélard*, Theol. Christ. iii. p. 1264: Non itaque sapientia in Deo vel substantialis ei forma vel accidentalis, imo sapientia ejus ipse Deus est. Idem de potentia ejus sentiendum est et de caeteris, quae ex nominum affinitate formae esse videntur in Deo quoque sicut in creaturis, etc. *Alanus* also said, l.c. art. 20 (in *Pez*, i. p. 484): Nomina enim ista: potentia potens, sapientia sapiens, neque formam, neque proprietatem, neque quidquid talium Deo attribuere possunt, cum simplicissimus Deus in sua natura nihil sit talium capax. **Cum ergo ratiocinandi de** Deo causa nomina nominibus copulamus, **nihil quod non** sit ejus essentia praedi**camus, et si** transsumtis **nominibus de** Deo quid credimus, improprie balbutimus. [*Duns Scotus*, Comm. in Sent. i. dist. 8. qu. 4, maintains a real difference in the attributes, *e.g.* in application to the Trinity. Comp. *Baur*, ubi supra, 249.]

(4) See Monolog. c. **18** ff. *Hasse's* Anselm, ii. s. **134** ff. Of God we can say *Est*, and not *Fuit* or *Erat*. Time and space are to Him no bounds. Comp. Proslog. c. **19**. *Hasse*, ii. s. 282 ff. So (in respect to omniscience) God has not His knowledge from the things, but the things have their being from His knowledge. *Hasse*, ii. s. 624.

(5) *Hugo of St. Victor*, De Sacram. c. 17: Deus substantialiter sive essentialiter et proprie et vere est in omni creatura, sive natura sine sui definitione et in omni loco sine circumscriptione et omni tempori sine vicissitudine vel mutatione. Est ergo, ubi est, totum, qui continet totum et penetrat totum; see Liebner, s. 372. From the proposition that God is *potentialiter* in all things, *Richard of St. Victor* drew the inference that He also exists *essentialiter* in them; De Trin. ii. 24. *Engelhardt*, s. 174. He is *above* all heavens, and yet He is at the same

time *in* them; He is in all that is corporeal and spiritual, in all that He has created, and governs according to His will. This notion of an essential presence of God is substantially the same as that of *Peter Lombard*, although he acknowledges that it is above human comprehension; Sent. i. dist. 27, 9. According to *Alexander of Hales*, God is in all things, but He is not *included* in the things; He is without all things, but He is not *excluded* from them. God exists in things in a threefold manner: essentialiter, præsentialiter, potentialiter; these three modes, however, do not differ in themselves, but only in our perception of them. God does not exist in all things in the same manner, *e.g.* in those who are the subjects of grace, in the sacraments, etc. The question was also started: Can God, by His indwelling grace, be in the body of a man prior to its union with the soul, etc.? see *Cramer*, vii. s. 295–297. The definitions of *Thomas Aquinas* are based on the principles of Alexander; Summa, I. qu. 8, art. 1 (quoted by *Munscher, von Cölln*, s. 49): Deus est in omnibus rebus, non quidem sicut pars essentiæ, vel sicut accidens, sed sicut *agens adest ei in quod agit*. Oportet enim omne agens conjungi ei, in quod immediate agit, et *sua virtute* illud contingere ... Art. 2: Deus omnem locum replet, *non sicut corpus* ... immo per hoc replet omnia loca, quod dat esse omnibus locatis, quæ replent omnia loca. Art. 3: Substantia sua adest omnibus ut *causa essendi*, etc. Art. 4: Oportet in omnibus esse Deum, quia nihil potest esse nisi per ipsum.—The dynamic (virtual) scheme of the Thomists was opposed by the ideal view of the Scotists. See *Münscher, von Cölln*, ii. s. 50. —*Bonaventura*, comp. Theol. (ed. Mogunt. 1609, p. 695), said: Ubique Deus est, tamen nusquam est, quia nec abest ulli loco, nec ullo capitur loco (August.). Deus est in mundo non inclusus, extra mundum non exclusus, supra mundum non elatus, infra mundum non depressus. Ex his patet, quod Deus est intra omnia, et hoc quia omnia replet et ubique præsens est. Ita extra omnia est, quia omnia continet, nec usquam valet coarctari. Sed nota, quod hæc propositio, "extra," dicit ibi *non actualem præsentiam ad locum, sed potentialem*, quæ est Dei immensitas, quæ infinitos mundos potest replere, si essent. Idem ipse est supra omnia, quia omnibus præstat nec aliquid ei æquatur. Item infra omnia est, quia omnia sustinet sine ipso nihil subsisteret. Dicimus etiam, quod ubique **est**, non ut indigeat rebus, quod ex eis sit, sed potius res **sui** indigeant, ut per eum subsistant ... Sciendum est ergo, ut aliquid est in loco *circumscriptive et diffinitive*, **ut corpus**; aliquid *diffinitive*, non circumscriptive, ut **angelus**; aliquid nec sic, ut Deus, et hoc ideo, quia non **individuatur** per materiam, ut corpus, neque per suppositum, ut **Angelus**. Aliquid est etiam in loco, partim circumscriptive, partim diffinitive, ut Corpus Christi in sacramento ... Corpus **autem** Christi ... in pluribus tamen locis est ... **sed non ubique**. ... Nota, quod Deus est multipliciter in rebus, scilicet per naturam: et sic est ubique potentialiter, praesentialiter, essentialiter. Item per gratiam; sic est in bonis. ... Item per gloriam; sic est in rationali virtute animae ut veritas, in concupiscibili **ut** bonitas, in irascibili ut potestas. Item per unionem; sic fuit in utero virginis unitus humanae naturae, et in sepulcro unitus carni, et in inferno unitus animae Christi, etc.—They even went so far as to ask, whether and in what manner God was in the devil? and to reply in the *affirmative*, *so far as the devil is composed of nature and spirit!—St. Bernard* said in his Meditations (cap. i. quoted by Bonaventura, l.c.): Deus in creaturis mirabilis, in hominibus amabilis, in angelis desirabilis, in se ipso incomprehensibilis, in reprobis intolerabilis, item in damnatis ut terror et horror.—*Tauler* also made a distinction between the presence of God in things and that in men: "God is also present in a stone and a piece of wood, but they are not conscious of it. If the piece of wood knew God, and felt His nearness, even as the highest angels know Him, the wood would be as happy as the highest angel. And man is for this reason happier than a piece of wood, because he recognizes God, etc. (Predigten, Bd. i. s. 58, 59.)

(6) This was done, *e.g.*, by *Alexander of Hales*, see Cramer, l.c. s. 209 ff. Comp. *Bonaventura*, comp. i. 18. He defined æternitas (after Boëthius) as interminabilis vitæ tota simul et perfecta possessio (interminabilitas).

(7) *John Damasc.* De fide orth. i. 6. *Nicolas of Methone*, Refut. p. 25 (quoted by *Ullmann*, l.c. s. 72), said: "When we call the unity beginning, we do not mean to draw a comparison between it and that which is after the beginning: for the same reason we do not merely use the term 'beginning,'

without further qualifying it, but we say *over*-commencing *beginning*; nor do we restrict ourselves to the term '*unity*' merely, but we call it the *over-all-one*; and instead of the first, and first of all, we say the *over-first*; instead of the great or the greatest, we make use of the term *over-great."* He called God the ὑπερέν, and even used the expression ὑπέρθεος μονὰς καὶ τριάς (Refut. 26). Comp. *Hugo of St. Victor,* quoted by *Liebner,* s. 371; he understood by unity not the numerical unity, but also simplicity (vera unitas) and immutability (summa unitas).

§ 167.

(b) God in relation to Things—Omnipotence and Omniscience.

The application of the divine *knowledge* and *power* to things external to God only too easily gave rise to anthropomorphite notions and absurd subtleties (1), which were best removed by regarding the attributes of omnipotence and omniscience not as separate attributes, but in their connection with the divine essence. Thus *Anselm* (2) and *Abélard* (3) agreed in asserting that God can do everything which may be done without interfering with His infinite perfection; *Peter Lombard, Hugo of St. Victor, Richard of St. Victor,* and others, adopted the same view (4). The *knowledge* of God was further looked upon as immediate and omnipresent, and a distinction was made between the knowledge of God in things (as *habitus*) and the knowledge of Himself (as *actus*) (5). Respecting the divine *omnipotence,* some, *e.g. Abélard,* maintained that God could make nothing else and nothing better than what He actually makes (6); others, *e.g. Hugo of St. Victor,* thought this assertion blasphemous, because thereby limits are assigned to the infinite power of God (7).

(1) *E.g.* whether God could undo that which is done? whether He could change a harlot into a pure virgin? and the like; see the passages quoted § 152, note 5, from *Erasmus.*

(2) Thus Anselm asserted, in reply to the question, whether God could lie, if He would? (Cur Deus Homo, i. 12): Non sequitur, si Deus vult mentiri, justum esse mentiri, sed potius Deum illum non esse. Nam nequaquam potest velle mentiri voluntas, nisi in qua corrupta est veritas, immo quæ deserendo veritatem corrupta est. Cum ergo dicitur Si Deus vult mentiri, non est aliud, quam: Si Deus talis est naturæ, quæ velit mentiri, etc. Comp. ii. 5: Denique Deus nihil facit necessitate, quia nullo modo cogitur aut prohibetur aliquid facere. Et cum dicimus Deum aliquid facere, quasi necessitate vitandi inhonestatem, quam utique non timet, potius intelligendum est, quia hoc facit necessitate servandæ honestatis, quæ scilicet necessitas non est aliud, quam immutabilitas honestatis ejus, quam a se ipso et non ab alio habet; et idcirco improprie dicitur necessitas. Ibid. 18: Quoties namque dicitur Deus non posse, nulla negatur in eo potestas, sed insuperabilis significatur potentia et fortitudo. Non enim aliud intelligitur, nisi quia nulla res potest efficere, ut agat ille, quod negatur posse. Nam multum usitata est hujusmodi locutio, ut dicatur res aliqua posse, non quia in illa, sed quoniam in alia re est potestas; et non posse, non quoniam in illa, sed quia in alia re est impotentia. Dicimus namque: Iste homo potest vinci, pro: Aliquis potest eum vincere, et: Ille non potest vinci, pro: Nullus eum vincere potest. Non enim potestas est, posse vinci, sed impotentia, nec vinci non posse impotentia est, sed potestas. Nec dicimus Deum necessitate facere aliquid, eo quod in illo sit ulla necessitas, sed quoniam est in alio sicut dixi de impotentia, quando dicitur non posse. Omnis quippe necessitas est aut coactio, aut prohibitio, quæ duæ necessitates convertuntur invicem contrarie, sicut necesse et impossibile. Quidquid namque cogitur esse, prohibetur non esse, et quod cogitur non esse, prohibetur esse; quemadmodum quod necesse est esse, impossibile est non esse, et quod necesse est non esse, impossibile est esse, et conversim. Cum autem dicimus aliquid necesse esse aut non esse in Deo, non intelligitur, quod sit in illo necessitas aut cogens aut prohibens, sed significatur, quod in omnibus aliis rebus est necessitas prohibens eas facere, et cogens non facere; contra hoc, quod de Deo dicitur. Nam cum dicimus, quod necesse est Deum semper verum dicere, et necesse est eum nunquam

mentiri, non dicitur aliud, nisi quia tanta est in illo constantia servandi veritatem, ut necesse sit, nullam rem facere posse, ut verum non dicat, aut ut mentiatur.—Comp. Proslog. 7: . . . Inde verius es omnipotens, quia potes nihil per impotentiam et nihil potes contra te. Comp. Hasse, ii. 274. De Concord. Præsc. et Præd. P. i. c. 2 ss. (where the question is discussed, how a necessitas can be asserted of God). Respecting the knowledge of God, Anselm (with Augustine) endeavoured to prove that God does not know things because they are, but that they are because He knows them, ibid. c. 7.

(3) However different the general theories of *Abélard* and *Anselm*, yet in this one point they agree. *Abél.* Theol. Christ. v. p. 1350 (*Martène*): Quærendum itaque primo videtur, quomodo vere dicatur omnipotens, si non possit omnia efficere ; aut quomodo omnia possit, si quædam nos possumus, quæ ipse non possit. Possumus autem quædam, ut ambulare, loqui, sentire, quæ a natura divinitatis penitus aliena sunt, cum necessaria istorum instrumenta nullatenus habere incorporea queat substantia. Quibus quidem objectis id prædicendum arbitror, quod juxta ipsos quoque philosophos et communis sermonis usum numquam potentia cujusque rei accipitur, nisi in his, quæ ad commodum vel dignitatem ipsius rei pertinent. Nemo enim hoc potentiæ hominis deputat, quod ille superari facile potest, immo impotentiæ et debilitati ejus, quod minime suo resistere potest incommodo, et quicquid ad vitium hominis vergit, magisque personam improbat quam commendat, impotentiæ potius quam potentiæ adscribendum est. . . . Nemo itaque Deum impotentem in aliquo dicere præsumat, si non possit peccare sicut nos possumus, quia nec in nobis ipsis hoc potentiæ tribuendum est, sed infirmitati. . . . P. 1351 : . . . Sicut etiam quædam, quæ in aliis rebus potentiæ deputanda sunt, in aliis vero minime. . . . Inde potentem hominem comparatione aliorum hominum diceremus, sed non ita leonem vel elephantem. Sic in homine, quoad ambulare valet, potentiæ est adscribendum, quoniam ejus necessitudini congruit, nec in aliquo ejus minuit dignitatem. In Deo vero, qui sola voluntate omnia complet, hoc omnino superfluum esset, quod in nobis necessarium est, atque ideo non potentiæ, sed vitio penitus tribuendum esset in eo, præsertim cum hoc in multis excellentiæ ipsius derogaret, ut ambulare videlicet posset. . . . Non

absurde tamen et de his omnibus, quæ efficere possumus, Deum potentem prædicabimus, et omnia quæ agimus, ejus potentiæ tribuemus, in quo vivimus, movemur, et sumus. Et qui omnia operatur in omnibus (utitur enim nobis ad efficiendum quæ vult, quasi instrumentis) et id quoque facere dicitur, quæ **nos facere** facit, sicut **dives** aliquis turrem componere per opifices **quos** adhibet, et posse omnia efficere dicitur, qui sive **per se sive** per subjectam creaturam omnia, quæ vult et quomodo vult, operatur, et ut ita fiant, ipse etiam facit. Nam etsi non potest ambulare, tamen potest facere, **ut** ambuletur. . . . *Posse itaque Deus omnia dicitur, non quod omnes suscipere possit actiones, sed quod in omnibus, quæ fieri velit, nihil ejus voluntati resistere queat.*[1] Comp. *Baur*, Trin. ii. s. 487 ff.

(4) *Hugo of St. Victor*, c. 22: Deus omnia potest, et tamen se ipsum destruere non potest. Hoc enim posse, posse non esset, sed non posse. Itaque omnia potest Deus, quæ posse potentia est. Et **ideo vere** omnipotens est, quia impotens esse non potest. Comp. *Liebner*, s. 367.—*Peter Lombard*, Sentent. i. dist. 42 E: Deus **omnino nihil** potest pati, et omnia facere potest præter ea sola, **quibus** dignitas ejus læderetur ejusque excellentiæ derogaretur. In quo tamen non est minus omnipotens: hoc enim posse non est posse, sed non posse. Comp. *Münscher*, **von** *Cölln*, ii. s. 47 f., where other passages are quoted from the writings of *Richard of St. Victor*, De Trin. l. i. c. 21, *Alexander of Hales*, Summa, I. qu. 21, membr. 1, art. 2; *Albertus Magnus*, Summa, P. I. qu. 77, membr. 1; and *Thomas Aquinas*, Summa, P. I. qu. 25, art. 3.

(5) *Hugo of St. Victor*, cap. 9, 14–18 (quoted by *Liebner*, s. 363 f.), expressed himself as follows: " All things which were created by God in time, existed uncreated in Him from eternity, and were known to Him for this very reason, because they existed in Him, and were known to Him in the very manner in which they existed in Him. God knew nothing out of Himself, because He comprehended all things in Himself. They were not in Him, because they should at some future period come into existence; the fact of their being designed to exist in time to come was not the cause of their existence in God, nor were they created in time because they existed in

---

[1] Abélard, speaking of the Trinity, ascribed *omnipotence* principally to the Father, without denying it, however, of the Son or the Spirit. Comp. § 170.

God, as if the eternal could not have existed without the temporal. On the contrary, the former would have existed without the latter; but it would not have stood in any relation to the latter, if this had not existed as something which was to be in the future. There would always have been the knowledge of an existence, viz. of existence in God, though not of a future existence; but the knowledge of the Creator would not therefore have been less comprehensive, because it could only be said that He had no foreknowledge of that which was not future."—In the opinion of *Alexander of* **Hales**, God knows all things *through* Himself and *in* Himself; for if God knew them by means of something else, then the ground of His knowledge would be some perfection existing out of Him, and He could not be the most perfect being if He owed anything to any other being. . . . God knows all things at once; for He sees all things in Himself, and since He knows Himself at once and completely, it is evident that He knows all things in Himself at once and perfectly. The things themselves may be multiplied or lessened, but not the knowledge of God: this is immutable. See *Cramer*, vii. s. 241.—*Bonaventura*, comp. i. 29 : Scit Deus omnia præsentialiter et simul, perfecte quoque et immutabiliter. Præsentialiter dico, hoc est, ita limpide ac si cuncta essent præsentialiter existentia. Simul etiam scit omnia, quia videndo se, qui sibi præsens est, omnia videt. Perfecte quoque, quia cognitio ejus nec potest augeri, nec minui. Scit et immutabiliter, quia noscit omnia per naturam sui intellectus, qui est immutabilis. Dicendum ergo, quod Deus cognoscit temporalia æternaliter, mutabilia immutabiliter, contingentia infallibiliter, creata increate, alia vero a se, in se, et per se. Comp. Brev. i. 8.—*Thomas Aquinas*, Quæst. 14, art. 4 : . . . In Deo intellectus et id, quod intelligitur, et species intelligibilis et ipsum intelligere sunt omnino unum et idem. Unde patet per hoc, quod Deus dicitur intelligens, nulla multiplicitas ponitur in ejus substantia. Comp. art. 13 : Deus autem cognoscit omnia contingentia, non solum prout sunt in suis causis, sed etiam prout unumquodque eorum est actu in se ipso. Et licet contingentia fiant in actu successive, non tamen Deus successive cognoscit contingentia, prout sunt in suo esse, sicut nos, sed simul : quia sua cognitio mensuratur æternitate, sicut etiam suum esse.

Æternitas autem tota simul existens ambit totum tempus. . . . Unde omnia, quæ sunt in tempore, sunt Deo ab æterno præsentia, non solum ea ratione, qua habet rationes rerum apud se præsentes, ut quidam dicunt, sed quia ejus intuitus fertur ab æterno super omnia, prout in sua præsentialitate. Unde manifestum est, quod contingentia et infallibiliter a Deo cognoscuntur, in quantum subduntur divino conspectui secundum suam præsentialitatem, et tamen sunt futura contingentia suis causis comparata. . . . Ea, quæ temporaliter in actum reducuntur, a nobis successive cognoscuntur in tempore, sed a Deo in æternitate, quæ est supra tempus. . Sicut ille, qui vadit per viam, non videt illos, qui post eum veniunt, sed ille, qui ab aliqua altitudine totam viam intuetur, simul videt omnes transeuntes per viam. . . . Sed ea, quæ sunt scita a Deo, oportet esse necessaria secundum modum, quo subsunt divinæ scientiæ, non autem absolute secundum quod in propriis causis considerantur. Comp. *Baur*, Trin. ii. s. 638 ff. — On the relation between knowledge and foreknowledge, see *John of Salisbury*, Policrat. ii. 21. (Bibl. Max. xxiii. p. 268.) An instance of subtle reasoning is given by *Liebner*, l.c. s. 365, Anm.

(6) *Abélard*, Theol. Christ. v. p. 1354: . . . Facit itaque omnia quæ potest Deus, et tantum bene quantum potest. . . . Necesse est, ut omnia quæ vult, ipse velit; sed nec inefficax ejus voluntas esse potest: necesse est ergo, ut quæcunque vult ipse perficiat, cum eam videlicet sumamus voluntatem, quæ ad ipsius pertinet ordinationem. Istis ergo rationibus astruendum videtur, quod plura Deus nullatenus facere possit quam faciat, aut melius facere, aut ab his cessare, sed omnia ita ut facit necessario facere. Sed rursus singulis istis difficillimæ occurrunt objectiones, ut utroque cornu graviter fidem nostram oppugnet complexio. Quis enim negare audeat, quod non possit Deus eum qui damnandus est salvare, aut meliorem illum qui salvandus est facere, quam ipse futurus sit collatione suorum donorum, aut omnino dimisisse, ne eum unquam crearet? Quippe si non potest Deus hunc salvare, utique nec ipse salvari a Deo potest. Necessaria quippe est hæc reciprocationis consecutio, quod, si iste salvatur a Deo, Deus hunc salvat. Unde, si possibile est hunc salvari a Deo, possibile est Deum hunc salvare. Non enim possibile est antecedens,

nisi possibile sit et consequens: alioquin ex possibili impossibile sequeretur, quod omnino falsum est. . . . Comp. the subsequent part of the chapter. And so he comes to the following conclusion: Quicquid itaque facit (Deus), sicut necessario vult, ita et necessario facit.

(7) On the opposition of *Hugo of St. Victor* to the optimism of *Abélard* (by which he was compelled to suppose a higher extent of the divine power than of the divine will), comp. *Liebner*, s. 367 f.

§ 168.

(c) *Moral Attributes.*

The so-called moral attributes of God, viz. His *holiness, wisdom, righteousness,* and *benevolence,* were treated in connection with other doctrines, and sometimes in such a manner as to give the appearance of contradictions (1). As the knowledge of God is one with His being, so likewise is His will, whose final object can be only the absolutely good, that is, God (2). The mystics loved to descend into the abyss of divine *love,* and endeavoured to explain this in their own way (3), while the scholastics proposed wondrous questions respecting even this attribute of God, which least of all admits of being dialectically discussed (4).

(1) This was the case with the righteousness (holiness), omnipotence, and love of God in reference to the theory of satisfaction. Comp. *Anselm,* Cur Deus Homo, i. c. 6–12, and Proslog. c. 8 s.; see the preceding section, note 1. *Hasse,* ii. s. 275 ff.

(2) *Thomas Aquinas,* Summa, P. I. qu. 19, art. 3 : Voluntas divina necessariam habitudinem habet ad bonitatem suam, quae est proprium ejus objectum. The question was raised, whether God has a liberum arbitrium, since in Him everything is necessary. Thomas decided that God is free respecting that which is not an essential determination of His nature, that is, respecting the accidental, finite. But respecting Himself He is determined by His own necessity, comp. art. 10, and *Baur,*

Trin. ii. s. 641.—*Duns Scotus*, on the contrary, asserted the absolute liberty of God; see the passages in *Baur*, l.c.

(3) The language of the author of the *Deutsche Theologie* is worthy of **notice** (c. 50): "God does **not** love Himself as **Himself,** but as the good. For if there were, and if God knew, anything better than God, He would love it, and not Himself. Egoism and selfhood, *i.e.* self-love and self-will, are entirely **foreign to God**; only so much belongs to God as is necessary **to constitute His** personality, or the distinction between the **different persons** of the Trinity."

(4) Thus *Alexander of Hales* asked (the passage is **quoted** by *Cramer*, s. 261) whether His love towards His creatures is quite the same with that which He has towards Himself, **and which** the divine persons have towards each other. He replies **in** the affirmative **in** reference to the principal idea (principale signatum), but **in** the negative respecting the secondary idea (connatum), *i.e.* that love is the same on the part of Him who loves, but not **the** same **with** regard to those who are loved. It is also on that account that God **does** not love all His creatures in the same degree, but the better **more** than the less **good.** He loves **all** creatures **from eternity** (in idea), but He **does not** love them in reality **until they come into** existence. —Another question was: Whom **does God love** most, the angels **or** men? The answer **is: The former, in so far as** Christ is not comprehended among the **latter; but** the love **wherewith** God loves Christ, and consequently men *in Christ*, **surpasses even the love** which He **has** towards the angels.— **We have here a** profound Christian **truth** expressed **in a** scholastic form.

§ 169.

Doctrine of the Trinity.

Doctrine of the Procession **of the Holy Spirit.**

J. G. *Walch*, Historia Controversiæ, etc. *Pfaff*, Historia succincta (comp. § 94). *Hasse*, Anselm, ii. s. 322 ff. [*E. B. Pusey* on the clause "Filioque," u. s.]

Before the doctrine of the Trinity could be more philosophically established and developed, it was necessary to settle the controversy which had arisen between the Eastern and the Western Church respecting the procession of the Holy Ghost from both the Father and the Son. After the tradition of the Greek Church had been received into the orthodox system of the East, through the influence of *John Damascene* (1), the Emperor Charles the Great summoned a Synod at Aachen (Aix-la-Chapelle) in the year 809, which, being influenced especially by the Frankish theologians, *Alcuin* and *Theodulph of Orleans*, confirmed the doctrine of the Western Church, according to which the Holy Ghost proceeds not only from the Father, but also from the Son (2). The Roman Bishop Leo III. approved of the doctrine itself, but disapproved of the uncritical introduction of the clause "filioque" into the creed adopted by the Council of Constantinople. He reckoned the doctrine in question among mysteries difficult to be investigated, and which are of greater importance in a speculative point of view than in the aspect of a living faith (3). But when in later times the controversy between *Photius*, Patriarch of Constantinople, and *Nicolas* I. led to the schism between the two Churches, their difference on this doctrine was again made the subject of discussion. *Photius* defended the doctrine of the procession of the Holy Ghost from the Father alone, and rejected the additional clause "filioque," which the theologians of the Western Church, such as *Æneas*, Bishop of Paris, and *Ratramnus*, a monk of Corvey, wished to retain (4). *Anselm*, Archbishop of Canterbury, likewise defended the doctrine of the Latin Church at the Synod of Bari (in Apulia) in the year 1098, and developed his views more fully in a separate treatise (5). *Anselm*, Bishop of Havelberg, defended it (1135–1145) (6). The attempt made at the Synod of Lyons in the year 1274 to reconcile the two parties did not lead to any satisfactory result. The controversy was resumed in the year 1277; but the formula proposed at the Synod of Florence (A.D. 1439) did not settle the point in question (7). Hence, from that time the two churches have ever differed in this, that according to the Greek Church the Holy Ghost proceeds from the Father alone, but according to the Latin Church, from both the Father and the Son. There were, however, some theologians in the latter who were satisfied with the procession from the Father (8).

(1) De fide orth. i. c. 7. He calls the Holy Ghost (in distinction from a mere breath, or a mere divine power) δύναμιν οὐσιώδη, αὐτὴν ἑαυτῆς ἐν ἰδιαζούσῃ ὑποστάσει θεωρουμένην, καὶ τοῦ πατρὸς προερχομένην; but adds: καὶ ἐν τῷ λόγῳ ἀναπανομένην καὶ αὐτοῦ οὖσαν ἐκφαντικήν, οὔτε χωρισθῆναι τοῦ Θεοῦ ἐν ᾧ ἐστι, καὶ τοῦ λόγου, ᾧ συμπαρομαρτεῖ, δυναμένην, οὔτε πρὸς τὸ ἀνύπαρκτον ἀναχεομένην, ἀλλὰ **καθ'** ὁμοιότητα τοῦ λόγου καθ' ὑπόστασιν οὖσαν, ζῶσαν, προαιρετικήν, αὐτοκίνητον, ἐνεργόν, πάντοτε τὸ ἀγαθὸν θέλουσαν, καὶ πρὸς πᾶσαν πρόθεσιν σύνδρομον ἔχουσαν τῇ βουλήσει τὴν δύναμιν, μήτε ἀρχὴν ἔχουσαν, μήτε τέλος· οὐ γὰρ ἐνέλειψέ ποτε τῷ πατρὶ **λόγος**, οὔτε τῷ λόγῳ πνεῦμα. Comp. *Baur*, Trin. ii. s. 177.

(2) *Alcuinus*, De Processione Spir. S. libellus (Opp. t. i. ed. *Froben.* p. 743).—In support of his views he appealed to Luke vi. 19 (Omnis turba quaerebat eum tangere, quia virtus de illo exibat et sanabat omnes). Comp. John xx. 21; 1 John iii. 23, 24, and the authority of the Fathers. See *Theodulphi* De Spiritu S. liber (in *Theodulphi* Opp. ed. *Sirmond*, Par. 1646; and in *Sirmondii* Opp. t. ii. p. 695); cf. Libb. Carolin. lib. iii. c. 3; Ex patre et filio—omnis universaliter confitetur ecclesia eum procedere. Concerning the historical part, see the works on ecclesiastical history, particularly *Gieseler*.

(3) On the occasion of a controversy between the **Greek and Latin** monks at Jerusalem prior to the Synod of Aachen, the pope had given it as his opinion: Spiritum Sanctum a Patre et Filio æqualiter procedentem.—Respecting the relation in which he stood to the synod itself, see Collatio **cum Papa Romæ a Legatis habita et** Epist. Caroli Imperat. ad Leonem P. III. utraque a Smaragdo Abb. edita (in *Mansi*, t. **xiv.** p. 17 ss.).

(4) See *Photii* Epist. Encyclica, issued A.D. 867 (given by *Montacucius*, Ep. 2, p. 47); the following, among other charges, is there brought forward against the Roman Church: Τὸ πνεῦμα τὸ ἅγιον οὐκ ἐκ τοῦ πατρὸς μόνον, ἀλλά γε ἐκ τοῦ

υἱοῦ ἐκπορεύεσθαι καινολογήσαντες. — The writings of his opponents, *Ratramnus* and *Æneas*, are no longer extant in a complete form, comp. *D'Achéry*, Spicil. ed. 1, t. i. p. 63 ss. *Rösler*, Bibliothek der Kirchenväter, Bd. x. s. 663 ff. [They rested their view upon Gal. iv. 6; Phil. i. 19; Acts ii. 33, xvi. 7; John viii. 42, xx. 22.]—The Greeks considered the Father as the πηγὴ θεότητος, and said that if the Spirit also proceeded from the Son, this would involve a πολυαρχία, which the Latins could not concede, since Father and Son are one. [On *Photius*, see Abbé *Jager*, Histoire de Photius (from original documents), 2d ed. Paris 1853. *J. Hergenrother*, Photii Constantinopol. Liber de Spiriti Sanct. Mystagogia, Regensb. 1857.]

(5) On the synod, see *Eadmer*, Vita Anselmi, p. 21 (quoted by *Walch*, l.c. p. 61).—The work of *Anselm* is entitled: De Processione Spiritus S. contra Græcos (Opp. p. 49, edit. Lugd. p. 115). In chapters 1–3 he shows in a clear and concise manner the points of *agreement* between the two churches (in reference to the doctrine of the Trinity, and that of the Holy Spirit in its general aspects), as well as the points of *difference*. Respecting the doctrine of the Western Church itself, *Anselm* argued from the formula, Deus de Deo, as follows (c. 4): Cum est de Patre Spiritus S., non potest non esse de Filio, si non est Filius de Spiritu Sancto; nulla enim alia ratione potest negari Spiritus S. esse de Filio . . . Quod autem Filius non sit de Spir. S., palam est ex catholica fide; non enim est Deus de Deo, nisi aut nascendo ut Filius, aut procedendo ut Spir. S. Filius autem non nascitur de Spiritu S. Si enim nascitur de Illo, est Filius Spir. Sancti, et Spiritus S. pater ejus, sed alter alterius nec pater nec filius. Non ergo nascitur de Spiritu S. Filius, nec minus apertum est, quia non procedit de Illo. Esset enim Spir. ejusdem Spiritus Sancti, quod aperte negatur, cum Spiritus S. dicitur et creditur Spiritus Filii. Non enim potest esse Spiritus sui Spiritus. Quare non procedit Filius de Spir. Sancto. Nullo ergo modo est de Spir. Sancto Filius. Sequitur itaque inexpugnabili ratione, Spir. Sanctum esse de Filio, sicut est de Patre.—C. 7: Nulla relatio est Patris sine relatione Filii, sicut nihil est Filii relatio, sine Patris relatione. Si ergo alia nihil est sine altera, non potest aliquid de relatione Patris esse sine relatione Filii. Quare sequitur, Spiritum

S. esse de utraque, si est de una. Itaque si est de Patre secundum relationem, erit simul et de Filio secundum eundem sensum ... Non autem magis est Pater Deus quam Filius, sed unus solus verus Deus, Pater et Filius. Quapropter si Spiritus S. est de Patre, quia est de Deo qui Pater est, negari nequit esse quoque de Filio, cum sit de Deo, qui est Filius.— (C. 8–12, he gives the scriptural argument.) In the thirteenth chapter he meets the objection, that the doctrine in question would lower the dignity of the Spirit. ... Qui dicimus Spiritum S. de Filio esse sive procedere, nec minorem, **nec posteriorem cum Filio** fatemur, namque quamvis splendor et calor de sole procedant, nec possint esse nisi sit ille, de quo sunt, nihil tamen prius aut posterius in tribus, in sole et splendore et calore, intelligimus: multo itaque minus, cum hæc in rebus temporalibus ita sint, in æternitate, quæ tempore non clauditur, prædictæ tres personæ in existendo susceptibiles intervalli possunt intelligi.—The concession made by the Greek theologians, viz. Spiritum Sanct. de patre esse *per* filium, does not appear to satisfy Anselm. As a lake is formed as well by the spring as by the river which flows from the spring, so the Spirit proceeds from both the Father and the Son[1] (c. 15 and 16). We must not, however, assume the existence of *two* principles from which the Spirit proceeds, but only *one* divine principle, common to the Father and the Son (c. 17). In chapters 18–20 he considers those scriptures which apparently teach the procession of the Spirit from the Father alone. C. 21, he defends the introduction of the clause "filioque" as a necessary means of preventing any misunderstanding. In chapters 22–27 he repeats and confirms all that he has said before. As Anselm commenced his treatise by invoking the aid of the Holy Spirit Himself, so he concluded it by saying: Si autem aliquid protuli quod aliquatenus corrigendum sit, *mihi* imputetur, non *sensui Latinitatis*. Comp. *Hasse*, l.c. On the progress of the controversy, comp. *Münscher, von Cölln*, ii. s. 113; and on the later definitions of the scholastics, see *Baur*, Trin. ii. s. 705 ff.; especially on Aquinas and Duns Scotus.

---

[1] A similar illustration is adduced by *Abélard*, Theol. Chr. iv. p. 1335: Spir. Sanct. ex Patre proprie procedere dicitur, quasi a summa origine, quæ scilicet aliunde non sit, et ab ipso in Filium quasi in rivum ... et per Filium ad nos tandem quasi in stagnum hujus seculi.

[*Aquinas* argues: The Son is from the Father, as the word from the mind, the Holy Spirit proceeds as love, from the will; but love must also proceed from the word, because we cannot love what we do not conceive; hence the Spirit proceeds from the Son.]

(6) He was, in 1135, the ambassador of Lothair II. in Constantinople, where the controversy was in progress. Pope Eugenius III., in 1145, asked him to put his views in writing. See *Spicker* in Illgens Zeitschrift f. hist. Theol. 1840, 2.

(7) At the Synod of Lyons the Greeks agreed with the council in adopting as Can. 1: Quod Spir. S. æternabiliter ex Patre et Filio, non tanquam ex duobus principiis, sed tanquam ex uno principio, non duabus spirationibus, sed unica spiratione procedit.—But new differences arose, respecting which see the works on ecclesiastical history. Compare *Münscher, von Cölln*, l.c. s. 114.—In the formula of union framed by the Synod of Florence, July 6, A.D. 1439 (given by *Mansi*, t. xxi. p. 1027 ss., and *Gieseler*, ii. 4, s. 541, *Münscher, von Cölln*, s. 115), use was made of the expression, quod Spirit. S. ex Patre et Filio æternaliter est; the phrase: procedere *ex Patre per filium*, was interpreted in accordance with the views of the Latin Church, and the clause *filioque* was retained. But the peace thus established did not last long, and the Patriarchs of Alexandria, Antioch, and Jerusalem issued (A.D. 1443) a synodal letter against the union. Comp. *Leo Allatius*, De Ecclesiæ occidentalis et orientalis perpetua Consensione, p. 939 ss. For the other works, see *Münscher, von Cölln*, and *Gieseler*, l.c.

(8) Thus John *Wessel*, comp. *Ullmann*, Die Reformatoren, etc., i. s. 388, 394.

§ 170.

The Doctrine of the Trinity.

C. Schwartz, De Sancta Trinitate quid senserint Doctores ecclesiastici prima Scholasticæ Theologiæ Periodo, Hal. 1842. [Comp. the works referred to in § 87.]

The doctrine of the Trinity, developed in the preceding period, and to a certain extent summed up by John Damascene (1), challenged the speculative powers and the ingenuity of the scholastics, as well as the imagination of the mystics, to fathom the unsearchable depth of that mystery. But all dialectic attempts were accompanied by the old danger of falling into heresy on the one side or the other. This was especially the case with the first bold and youthful attempts of Western speculation. *John Scotus Erigena* declared that the terms Father and Son are mere names, to which there is no corresponding objective distinction of essence in the Godhead, which strongly savours of pantheism (2). The nominalism of *Roscellinus* exposed him to the charge of Tritheism (3), while that of *Abélard* exposed him to the accusation of Sabellianism (4). The distinction which *Gilbert of Poitiers* drew between the *quo est* and the *quod est* gave to his teaching the semblance of tetratheism (5). *Anselm* (6) and *Peter Lombard* (7) adopted in the main the views held by Augustine; the terminology, however, used by the latter gave rise to misunderstandings. The treatment of the subject by the scholastics of the second period was more strictly systematic and speculative (8). But this very tendency, which more and more lost sight of the practical aspect of the doctrine, led to those subtle distinctions and absurd questions which have for a long time seriously injured the reputation of scholasticism, but which were, in fact, the excesses of an otherwise powerful tendency (9). Among the Greeks, *Nicetas Choniates* contented himself with representing the mystery in question in figurative language (10), while *Nicolas of Methone* manifested a stronger leaning to the dialectic tendency of the Western theologians (11). The mystics followed for the most part *Dionysius the Areopagite*, and wrestled with language in the endeavour either to represent the incomprehensible in itself (12), or to bring it more within the reach of the understanding (in doing which they did not always avoid the appearance of pantheism) (13).—The disciples of the school of St. Victor held, as it were, the medium between sterile dialectics and fantastic mysticism (14). *Savonarola* (15) and *Wessel* (16), instead of indulging in philosophical reasonings from the nature of God, returned to natural and human analogies fitted to men's religious needs, and which might serve to illustrate the mystery, but were not meant to explain it.

(1) *John Damascene* brings forward nothing new. He repeats the earlier propositions, making use of the traditional terms νοῦς and λόγος, and the comparison with the human word and spirit, in the sense of the earlier theologians. God cannot be ἄλογος, but the Logos must have a πνεῦμα. He lays great stress upon the unity *in* the Trinity, so that the Son and the Spirit, though persons, have yet their unity in the Father; what they are, they are through Him. He has therefore been charged with a wavering between Unitarianism and Tritheism, and, at any rate, the dialectic contradictions, from which the logic of the old church could not free itself, is strikingly manifest in his statements. Comp. *Baur*, Trin. ii. s. 176 ff. *Meier*, s. 199 ff.

(2) De Div. Nat. i. 18: Num quid veris ratiocinationibus obsistit, si dicamus, Patrem et Filium ipsius habitudinis, quae dicitur ad aliquid, nomina esse et plus quam habitudinis? Non enim credendum est, eandem esse habitudinem in excellentissimis divinæ essentiæ substantiis, et in his, quæ post eam ab ea condita sunt. Quemadmodum superat omnem essentiam, sapientiam, virtutem, ita etiam habitudinem omnem ineffabiliter supergreditur. According to i. 14, *Scotus* (appealing to earlier theologians and Inquisitores veritatis) calls the Father the *essentia*, the Son the *sapientia*, and the Holy Spirit the *vita Dei*. On the question respecting the relation between the four categories of natura creans, etc. (see § 165), and the three persons of the Trinity, comp. *Baur*, Trin. ii. s. 278 ff. *Meier*, s. 230 ff. *Ritter*, vii. s. 250.

(3) In accordance with his nominalistic notions, *Roscellinus* regarded the appellation *God*, which is common to the three persons, as a mere name, *i.e.* as the abstract idea of a species, under which the *Father, Son,* and *Spirit* are comprehended (as three individuals, as it were). This was at least the meaning which his opponents attached to his language; see Ep. Joannis *Monachi* ad Anselmum (given by *Baluze*, Miscell. l. iv. p. 478): Hanc de tribus Deitatis personis

quæstionem Roscelinus movet: Si tres personæ sunt **una tantum res, et non sunt tres res per se**, sicut tres angeli **aut tres animæ, ita tamen ut voluntate et potentia omnino sint: ergo** Pater et **Spir. S. cum Filio incarnatus est.**—This view was condemned by the Synod of Soissons (A.D. 1093), and combated by **Anselm** in his treatise: De Fide Trinitatis et de Incarnatione Verbi contra Blasphemias Roscelini.—But Anselm doubted the accuracy of the statements made by his opponents, c. 3 : Sed forsitan ipse non dicit : " Sicut sunt tres animæ aut tres angeli ;" he thought it more probable that Roscellinus had expressed himself in general terms : Tres personas esse tres, sine additamento alicujus similitudinis, and that the above illustration was added by his opponent. Nevertheless he was also disposed to attach credit to the statements of his opponents ! comp. c. 2.[1] Comp. *Baur*, Trin. ii. s. 400 ff. *Meier*, s. 243 ff. *Hasse*, ii. s. 287 ff.

(4) On the history of *Abélard's* condemnation at the Synod of Soissons (Concilium Suessionense), A.D. 1121, and at Sens, 1140, comp. the works on ecclesiastical history, and *Neander*, Der heilige Bernhard, s. 121 ff. His teaching is contained principally in his Introductio ad Theologiam, and in his Theologia Christiana. He proceeds from the absolute perfection of God. If God is the absolutely perfect, He must also be the absolutely powerful, wise, and good. Power, wisdom, and love are therefore, in his view, the three persons of the Trinity, and the difference is merely nominal. Theol. Christiana, I. 1, p. 1156 ss.: Summi boni perfectionem, quod Deus est, ipsa Dei sapientia incarnata Christus Dominus describendo tribus *nominibus* diligenter distinxit, cum unicam et singularem individuam penitus ac simplicem substantiam divinam, Patrem et Filium et Spirit. S. tribus de causis appellavit: Patrem quidem secundum illam unicam majestatis suæ potentiam, quæ est omnipotentia, quia scilicet efficere potest, quidquid vult, cum nihil ei resistere queat; Filium autem eandem Divinam substantiam dixit secundum propriæ sapientiæ discretionem,

[1] At a later period *Jerome of Prague* was charged with *tetratheism*, and even with more than that. He is said to have taught: In Deo sive in divina essentia non solum est Trinitas personarum, sed etiam *quaternitas* rerum et *quinternitas*, etc. Istæ res in divinis sunt sic distinctæ, quod una non est alia, et tamen quælibet earum est Deus. Istarum rerum una est aliis perfectior. See *Herrmann von der Hardt*, Acta et Decreta, t. iv. p. viii. ss. p. 645.

quæ videlicet cuncta dijudicare ac discernere potest, et nihil eam latere possit, quo decipiatur; Spiritum S. etiam vocavit ipsam, secundum illam benignitatis suæ gratiam, qua omnia, quæ summa condidit sapientia, summa ordinat bonitate et ad optimum quæque finem accommodat, malo quoque bene semper utens et mirabiliter quantumlibet perverse facta optime disponens, quasi qui utraque manu pro dextra utatur et nesciat nisi dextram. . . . Tale est ergo tres personas, hoc est Patrem et Filium et Spirit. S. in divinitate confiteri, ac si commemoraremus divinam potentiam generantem, divinam sapientiam genitam, divinam benignitatem procedentem. Ut his videlicet tribus commemoratis summi boni perfectio prædicetur, cum videlicet ipse Deus et summe potens, i.e. omnipotens, et summe sapiens et summe benignus ostenditur. Comp. Introd. ad Theol. I. 10, p. 991, and the other passages quoted by *Münscher, von Colln,* s. 53 f.—The relation in which the Father stands to the Son and Spirit, Abélard compares to that in which matter stands to form (materia and materiatum). As a wax figure is composed of wax, but, being a distinctly-shaped figure, differs from the unshapen mass; so the Son, as *materia materiata,* differs from the Father. The latter, however, remains the *materia ipsa;* nor can it be said with the same propriety that the wax owes its origin to the figure, as it can be said that the figure owes its origin to the wax. He also compares the Trinity to a brass seal, and draws a distinction between the substance of which the seal (æs) is composed, the figure carved in the brass (sigillabile) and the seal itself (sigillans), inasmuch as it shows what it is in the act of sealing.—The comparison which Abélard drew (Introd. ii. 12) between the three persons of the Trinity and the three persons in grammar (prima quæ loquitur, secunda ad quam loquitur, tertia de qua loquuntur), was particularly offensive, and might easily be represented as countenancing Tritheism. Comp. *Baur,* l.c. ii. § 503 ff. *Meier,* § 251 ff.

(5) The heretical opinions of *Gilbert* were also connected with the logical controversy between Nominalism and Realism; he started with Realism, but at last arrived at the same results to which Roscellinus had been led by Nominalism. According to the statements made by him in Paris 1147 and in Rheims 1148, in the presence of Eugenius III., he asserted:

Divinam essentiam non esse Deum. The former is the form by which God is God, but it is not God Himself, as humanity is the form of man, but not man himself. The Father, the Son, and the Spirit are *one;* but not in reference to the *quod est*, but only in reference to the *quo est* (*i.e.* the substantial form). We can therefore say: Father, Son, and Spirit *are* one; but not: God *is* Father, Son, and Spirit. Gilbert considered the error of Sabellius to have consisted in this, that he confounded the *quo est* with the *quod est*. He himself was charged with separating the persons in the manner of Arius. There was indeed the semblance of tritheism in his proposition: that that which makes the three persons to be three, are tria singularia quædam, tres res numerabiles. The distinction which he drew between the quod est, the divine essence as such, and the three persons, brought upon him the further charge of believing in a quaternitas.—Gilbert was not formally condemned, but Eugenius III. declared that in theology God and the Godhead could not be separated from one another. Comp. especially *Gaufredi*, Abbatis Clarævallensis, Epistola ad Albinum Card. et Episc. Albanens. (*Mansi*, t. xxi. p. 728 ss.), and his Libellus contra Capitula Gilberti Pictav. Episcopi in *Mabillon's* edition of *Bernard's* works, t. ii. p. 1336 ss. 1342. *Baur*, Trin. ii. s. 508 ff. *Meier*, s. 264 ff.

(6) In *Anselm*, as in Augustine, the Son is the intelligence of God, and the Spirit the love of God; Monol. c. 27 s. In c. 30 he says of the *Son* (the Word): Si mens humana nullam ejus aut sui habere memoriam aut intelligentiam posset, nequaquam se ab irrationabilibus creaturis, et illam ab omni creatura, secum sola tacite disputando, sicut nunc mens mea facit, discerneret. Ergo summus ille spiritus, sicut est æternus, ita æterne sui memor est, et intelligit se ad similitudinem mentis rationalis: immo non ad ullius similitudinem, sed ille principaliter, et mens rationalis ad ejus similitudinem. At si æterne se intelligit, æterne se dicit. Si æterne se dicit, æterne est verbum ejus apud ipsum. Sive igitur ille cogitetur nulla alia existente essentia, sive aliis existentibus, necesse est, verbum illius coæternum illi esse cum ipso ... C. 36: Sicut igitur ille creator est rerum et principium, sic et verbum ejus; nec tamen sunt duo, sed unus creator et unum principium ... C. 37: Quamvis enim necessitas cogat, ut sint duo: nullo

tamen modo exprimi potest, quid duo sint ... C. 38 : Etenim proprium unius est, esse ex altero; et proprium est alterius, alterum esse ex illo. C. 39 : ... Illius est verissimum proprium esse parentem, istius vero veracissimam esse prolem. C. 42 : ... Sicut sunt (pater et filius) *oppositi relationibus*, ut alter nunquam suscipiat proprium alterius : sicut sunt *concordes natura*, ut alter semper teneat essentiam alterius. C. 43 : ... Est autem perfecte summa essentia pater et perfecte summa essentia filius: pariter ergo perfectus pater per se est, et pariter perfectus filius per se est, sicut uterque sapit per se. Non enim idcirco minus perfecta est essentia vel sapientia filius, quia est essentia nata de patris essentia, et sapientia de sapientia : sed tunc minus perfecta essentia vel sapientia esset, si non esset per se, aut non saperet per se. Nequaquam enim repugnat, ut filius per se subsistat, et de patre habeat esse.— Nevertheless he speaks of a priority of the Father, c. 44 : Valde tamen magis congruit filium dici essentiam patris, quam patrem essentiam filii; quoniam namque pater a nullo habet essentiam nisi a se ipso, non satis apte dicitur habere essentiam alicujus nisi suam ; quia vero filius essentiam suam habet a patre, et eandem habet pater, aptissime dici potest, habere essentiam patris.—C. 45 : Veritas quoque patris aptissime dici potest filius, non solum eo sensu, quia est eadem filii veritas, quæ est et patris, sicut jam perspectum est, sed etiam hoc sensu, ut in eo intelligatur non imperfecta quædam imitatio, sed integra veritas paternæ substantiæ, quia non est aliud, quam quod est pater. At si ipsa substantia patris est intelligentia et scientia et sapientia et veritas, consequenter colligitur : quia, sicut filius est intelligentia et scientia et sapientia et veritas paternæ substantiæ, ita est intelligentia intelligentiæ, scientia scientiæ, sapientia sapientiæ, et veritas veritatis. ... C. 47 : Est igitur filius memoria patris et memoria memoriæ, i. e. memoria memor patris, qui est memoria, sicut est sapientia patris et sapientia sapientiæ, i. e. sapientia sapiens patrem sapientiam, et filius quidem memoria nata de memoria, sicut sapientia nata de sapientia, pater vero de nullo nata memoria vel sapientia.—Concerning the *Spirit*, he expresses himself as follows :—C. 48 : l'alam certe est rationem habenti, cum idcirco sui memorem esse aut se intelligere, quia se amat, sed ideo se amare, quia sui meminit et se intelligit: nec cuia se posse amare, si sui non sit memor aut se non intelligit. Nulla enim res amatur sine ejus memoria et intelligentia, et multa tenentur memoria et intelliguntur, quæ non amantur. Patet igitur amorem summi spiritus ex **eo** procedere, quia sui memor **est et se** intelligit. Quodsi in memoria summi spiritus intelligitur pater, in intelligentia filius, manifestum est: quia **a** patre pariter et a filio summi spiritus amor procedit. C. 49: Sed si se amat summus spiritus, procul dubio se amat pater, **amat se filius, et** alter alterum: quia singulus pater summus **est spiritus, et** singulus filius summus spiritus, et ambo simul **unus spiritus.** Et quia uterque pariter sui et alterius **meminit, et** se **et** alterum intelligit, et quoniam omnino id ipsum est quod amat vel amatur in patre et quod **in filio, necesse est, ut** pari amore uterque diligat **se** et alterum.—C. 55. *On the* relation in which the three persons stand to each other, he says: Patrem itaque nullus facit sive creat aut gignit, filium vero **pater solus gignit, sed non** facit; pater autem pariter et **filius non faciunt neque** gignunt, sed quodammodo, si sic dici **potest, spirant suum amorem: quamvis** enim non nostro more **spiret summa incommutabilis essentia,** tamen ipsum amorem **a se** ineffabiliter **procedentem, non discedendo ab** illa, sed **existendo ex illa, forsitan non alio modo** videtur posse dici **aptius ex se emittere quam** spirando. C. 57: Jucundum est **intueri in** patre **et filio et utriusque spiritu, quomodo sint in se invicem tanta æqualitate, ut nullus alium excedat....Totam quippe suam memoriam summus intelligit spiritus**[1] **et amat, et totius** intelligentiæ **meminit et totam amat, et totius amoris meminit et totum intelligit. Intelligitur autem in memoria pater, in intelligentia filius, in amore utriusque spiritus. Tanta igitur pater et filius et utriusque spiritus æqualitate sese complectuntur et sunt in se invicem, ut eorum nullus alium excedere, aut sine eo esse probetur.... C. 60: ... Est enim unusquisque, non minus in aliis quam in se ipso....** (It should be observed that Anselm admitted that this relation can neither be expressed nor explained, c. 62.) Comp. *Baur,* Trin. ii. s. 389 ff. *Meier,* s. 238 ff. *Hasse,* ii. s. 127 ff., 146 ff., 181 ff., 287 ff., 322 ff.

(7) Sentent. lib. i. dist. 5 (quoted by *Münscher, von Cölln,*

---

[1] The word *spiritus* is also used through the whole treatise in reference to God in general.

ii. s. 56 f.), and Dist. 25 K: Alius est in persona vel personaliter pater, i. e. proprietate sua pater alius est quam filius, et filius proprietate sua alius quam pater. Paternali enim proprietate distinguitur hypostasis patris ab hypostasi filii, et hypostasis filii filiali proprietate discernitur a patre, et Spir. S. ab utroque processibili proprietate distinguitur. Comp. *Baur,* Trin. ii. s. 550. *Meier,* s. 268 ff. *Landerer* in *Herzog,* viii. s. 474. *Joachim,* Abbot of Floris, opposed Peter Lombard, and charged him with having taught: Patrem et Filium et Spiritum Sanctum quandam summam esse rem, quae neque sit generans, neque genita, neque procedens. But Peter Lombard had only urged the importance of the distinction often neglected between God (as such) and God the Father (as one of the persons of the Trinity), and had therefore asserted: Non est dicendum, quod divina essentia genuit filium, quia cum filius sit divina essentia, jam esset filius res, a qua generaretur, et ita eadem res se ipsam generaret . . . quod omnino esse non potest. Sed pater solus genuit filium, et a patre et filio procedit Spiritus S. But he thus exposed himself to the appearance of holding to a quaternity. (On the doctrine of Joachim himself, see note 13.)

(8) *Alexander* of *Hales,* Summa, P. I. q. 42, membr. 2 (quoted by *Münscher, von Cölln,* s. 55; *Cramer,* Bd. vii. s. 309 ff.); *Thomas Aquinas,* P. I. qu. 27–43. On the latter and *Duns Scotus,* comp. *Baur,* Trin. ii. s. 685 ff. *Meier,* s. 274 ff.—We meet with a purely speculative apprehension of the Trinity in the work of *Alanus ab Insulis,* i. art. 25 (*Pez,* i. p. 484); he regarded the Father as *matter,* the Son as *form,* and the Holy Spirit as the *union of both.* On *Alexander of Hales,* see *Cramer,* l.c. The generation of the Son is explained by Alexander from the diffusive nature of God; at the same time a distinction is made between *material* generation (from the substance of the Father), *original* generation (as a human son is begotten by his father), and *ordinal* generation (as the morning gives rise to noon); but none of these can be applied to the Divine Being. It is only in so far admissible to speak of the Son being begotten from the substance (essence) of the Father, as such language is not meant to imply anything material, but only intended to teach that the Son in His essence is not distinct from His Father.

(9) Questions such as the following were started: Was it *necessary* that God should beget? or might He have possessed the *power* but not the *will* to beget? Why are there just *three* persons in the Trinity, **no** more and no less? How is it that, in the perfect equality of the persons, the Father is *first named*, and then **the Son and the** Spirit? Is it allowed to **invert** the **order, and why not?** etc. *Anselm* (Monol. c. 40) inquired **into** the reason for calling God *Father*, in reference **to the act of** generation, and not mother. He also demonstrated very seriously that the Son was the fittest of the three persons of the Trinity to become man (Cur Deus **Homo, ii.** 9): Si quaelibet alia persona incarnetur, erunt duo filii in Trinitate, filius scilicet Dei, qui et ante incarnationem filius est, et ille qui per incarnationem filius erit virginis: et erit in personis, quae semper aequales esse debent, inaequalitas secundum dignitatem nativitatum. . . . Item, si Pater fuerit incarnatus, erunt duo **nepotes in** Trinitate, quia Pater erit nepos parentum virginis per **hominem** assumtum, **et** Verbum, cum nihil habeat de homine, **nepos tamen erit virginis,** quia filii ejus erit filius, quae omnia **inconvenientia** sunt, **nec in** incarnatione Verbi contingunt. Est et aliud, cur magis conveniat incarnari filio, quam aliis personis, quia convenientius sonat filium supplicare Patri, quam aliam personam alii.[1] Item, homo, pro quo erat **oraturus, et diabolus, quem erat expugnaturus, ambo** falsam **similitudinem** Dei per propriam **voluntatem** praesumserant. **Unde quasi** specialius adversus **personam Filii peccaverunt, qui vera** Patris similitudo **creditur, etc. (Comp. below, § 179.)**

(10) One of the **illustrations** of *Nicetas* is *e.g.* taken **from a balance (Thesaur. c. 30). The Son** represents the central point of union between the Father and the Holy Spirit, and preserves the most perfect equality between the two; but the whole denotes the pure equilibrium of honour, power, and nature, the internal divine equality and harmony, inasmuch as no one person elevates himself above the other. The double-winged Seraphim also are in his view a figure of the Trinity. But while in the former case the *Son* is made the central point of union, in the latter the Father forms the

---

[1] Why *convenientius*, excepting that in the background the Father always has the priority?

centre, and the extremities represent the Son and the Holy Spirit. Comp. *Ullmann*, l.c. s. 41 f.

(11) "*Many of the earlier theologians asserted the incomprehensibility of God, and at the same* time propounded the *most profound mysteries of the doctrine* of the Trinity with a certainty which would allow of no doubt; *and Nicolas* shows the same inconsistency. In the same sentence he *represents the nature of God as beyond knowledge and expression, beyond the apprehension and investigation even of the highest order of spirits, and gives the most precise and apodictical definitions concerning the relation between the divine essence and the divine persons*" (*e.g.* Refut. p. 23 s.); *Ullmann*, s. 78. Nicolas removed the apparent contradiction of a Trinity in unity by avoiding all analogies with created things. He would not have the terms unity and trinity understood in the sense in which they are used by mathematicians, viz. as *numeric determinations*. But in his opinion the unity of God is only a unity of *essence*, and the trinity a trinity of *persons*. He thought that there was nothing contradictory in the union of *such* a unity with such a trinity; see *Ullmann*, s. 79 f. (He also appealed to Gregory of Nazianzus, Orat. xxix. 2: Μονὰς ἀπ' ἀρχῆς εἰς δυάδα κινηθεῖσα, μέχρι τριάδος ἔστη.) "We adore," said Nicolas (Refut. p. 67, "as the creative principle of all existence, that God who is one as respects His essential nature, but consists of three persons, the Father, the Son, and the Spirit. With regard to these three, we praise the Father as *that which causes* (ὡς αἴτιον), but as to the Son and the Holy Spirit, we confess that they proceeded from the Father as *that which is caused* (ὡς αἰτιατά); not created or brought forth in the common sense of the word, but in a supernatural, superessential manner. Being of the same essence, they are united with the Father (the one by generation, the other by procession) and with each other without being confounded; they are distinct without separation." Regarding the term αἴτιον, he would have it understood that it does not denote a *creative* or formative, but a *hypostatic* causality, which might be called γεννητικόν (*i.e. generating*) in relation to the Son, and προακτικὸν εἴτουν προβλητικόν (*i.e.* the source of *procession*) in reference to the Spirit. Thus he also said (p. 45): ὁ πατὴρ ἓν πνεῦμα προβάλλει. See *Ullmann*, l.c. s. 82.

(12) *Tauler* (Predigten, ii. p. 172) said: "Concerning this most excellent and holy trinity, we cannot find any suitable words in which we might speak of it, and yet we must express this superessential, incomprehensible Trinity in words. If we therefore attempt to speak of it, it is as impossible to do it properly as to reach the sky with one's head. For all that we can say or think of it is a thousand times less in proportion to it than the point of a needle is to heaven and earth, yea a hundred thousand times less beyond all number and proportion. ... We might talk to a wonderful extent, and yet we could neither express nor understand how the superessential unity can co-exist with the distinction of the persons. It is better to meditate on these things than to speak of them; for it is not pleasant either to say much about this matter or to hear of it, especially when words must be introduced (taken from other matters), and because we are altogether unequal to the task. For the whole subject is at an infinite distance from us, and wholly foreign to us, and it is hidden from us, for it even surpasses the understanding of angels. We therefore leave it to great prelates and learned men; they must have something to say in order to defend the faith, but we must simply believe."

(13) In opposition to Peter Lombard, *Joachim*, Abbot of Floris, laid down a theory which was condemned by the fourth Lateran Council (A.D. 1215), although he attributed it to inspiration. He regarded the psaltery of ten strings as the most significant image of the Trinity. Its three corners represent the Trinity, the whole the unity. This unity he compares with the unity of believers in the Church. Concerning the further development of this notion, running out into a crude substantialism, see *Engelhardt*, Kirchenhistorische Abhandlungen, s. 265 ff. *Baur*, Trin. ii. s. 555; *Meier*, s. 272.—The views of Master *Eckart* on the doctrine of the Trinity are given by *Schmidt* in the Studien und Kritiken, l.c. s. 694. In his Sermon on the Trinity, fol. 265a, it is said: "What is the speaking of God? The Father beholding Himself with a simple knowledge, and looking into the simple purity of His nature, sees all creatures there pictured, and speaks within Himself; the Word is a clear knowledge, and that is the Son; therefore the phrase, *God speaks*, is equi-

valent to *God begets.*" For other passages, comp. *Schmidt*, l.c. s. 696.—*II. Suso* taught as follows (c. 55, see *Diepenbrock*, s. 215): "In proportion as any being is simple in itself, it is manifold in its powers and capacities. That which has nothing gives nothing; that which has much can give much. God is in Himself the fulness of all that is perfect, the inflowing and overflowing Good; but, because His goodness is unlimited and higher than all, He will not keep it to Himself, but He delights in sharing it in Himself and *out of* Himself. On this account, the first and highest act of the outpouring of the highest Good must have reference to itself, and that cannot be, except in a presence, inward, substantial, personal, natural, necessary without being compulsory, infinite, and perfect. All other manifestations which are in time or in the creature, are only the reflex of the eternal outpouring of the unfathomable divine goodness. Therefore the masters say, that in the emanation of the creature from the first original there is a *circular return of the end into the beginning:* for as the flowing out of the person from God is a complete image of the origin of the creature, so it is also a type of the re-inflowing of the creature into God. Now observe the difference of the emanation of God. . . . A human father gives to his son in his birth a part of his own nature, but not at once, and not the whole of that which he is; for he himself is a compound good. But as it is evident that the divine emanation is so much more intimate and noble according to the greatness of the good which He Himself is, and as God infinitely surpasses all other goods, it necessarily follows that His emanation is equal to His nature, and that such a pouring out of Himself cannot take place without imparting His nature in personal property. If you can now contemplate with a purified eye, and behold the purest goodness of the highest good, which is in its very nature a present and operative beginning, and loves itself naturally and willingly, then you will see the exceeding supernatural going forth of the Word from the Father, by whose generation and speaking all things are spoken into being and formed, and you will see in the highest good, and in the highest manifestation of it, the necessary origin of the Holy Trinity: Father, Son, and Holy Ghost. And as this highest flowing forth proceeds from the supreme and essential Goodness, there must be in the said Trinity the most supreme and most intimate sameness of essence, the highest equality and selfhood of being which the three persons possess in triumphant process, in the undivided substance and the undivided omnipotence of the three persons in the Deity." (Suso, **however,** acknowledged that none could explain in words **how the** Trinity of the Divine Persons could exist in the **unity of** being. Ibid. s. 217.) Comp. *Schmidt* in Stud. und Kritik. 1840, s. 43.—Similar but more definite views were entertained by *Ruysbroek*, whose opinions concerning the Trinity are given in *Engelhardt's* Monograph, s. 174–177. According to Ruysbroek, there are four *fundamental* **properties** in God. "He flows out from nature through wisdom and love, He draws to Himself by unity and substantiality. The eternal truth is begotten from the Father, the eternal love proceeds from the Father and the Son. These are the two emanating attributes of God. The unity of the divine nature draws the **three persons** within by the bonds of love, and the divine **wisdom comprehends the unity** in a certain repose with a certain **joyful embrace in** essential love. These are the **centripetal attributes of God."**

(14) *Hugo of St. Victor* found in *external nature* an indication of the Trinity. He perceived a still purer impression of it in the *rational* creation, viz. in the *spirit*, which is only assisted by the external world, or the world of bodies; in the **one case** we have a true type, in the other only a sign. How the Trinity manifests itself in the external creation (power, wisdom, and goodness), he showed in his treatise, De tribus Diebus, t. i. fol. 24–33. Comp. De Sacram. P. III. lib. i. c. 28; *Liebner*, s. 375. In his dialectic development, Hugo followed his predecessors, Augustine and Anselm, but employed that fuller and more poetical style which is peculiar to the mystics, especially in his treatise, De tribus Diebus. On the whole, Hugo differed from Anselm "*by remaining at a certain distance, and thus keeping to more general and indefinite expressions, in the use of which he exposed himself to less danger.*" Liebner, s. 381. We may notice as very remarkable, and foreign to the general spirit of mysticism, but truly scholastic, the manner in which Hugo answered the question, *Why* the

Scriptures (?)[1] have ascribed power in particular to the Father, wisdom to the Son, and love to the Holy Spirit, since power, wisdom, and love belong equally and essentially to all the three, and are eternal. He argued as follows: "When men heard of the Father and Son being in God, they might, in accordance with human relations, think of the Father as old and aged, and consequently weaker than the Son, but of the Son as juvenile and inexperienced, and therefore less wise than the Father. To prevent any such mistake, Scripture has with wise prevision ascribed power to the Father and wisdom to the Son. Likewise men, hearing of God the Holy Spirit (Spiritus), might think of Him as a snorting (Germ. *schnaubend*) and restive being, and be terrified at His supposed harshness and cruelty. But then Scripture coming in and calling the Holy Ghost loving and mild, tranquillized them" (De Sacram. c. 26). The passage is cited by *Liebner*, s. 381 f., where further particulars may be compared. Hugo, however, rejected, generally speaking, all subtle questions, and had a clear insight into the figurative language of Scripture.—Nor did *Richard of St. Victor* indulge so much in subtle speculations in his work, De Trinitate, as many other scholastics. It is true, he adopted the same views concerning the trias of power, wisdom, and love, but he laid more stress upon the latter, and ascribed to it the generation of the Son. In the highest good there is the fulness and the perfection of goodness, and consequently the highest love; for there is nothing more perfect than love. But love (amor), in order to be charity (charitas), must have for its object, not itself, but something else. Hence, where there is no plurality of persons, there can be no charity. Love toward creatures is not sufficient, for God can only love what is worthy of the *highest* love. If God loved merely Himself, this would not be the highest love; in order to render it such, it is necessary that it should be manifested towards a person who is God, etc.

[1] It is scarcely necessary to observe that Scripture by no means sanctions such an arbitrary distribution of the divine attributes among the three persons. With equal if not greater propriety, the Son might have been called love, and the Spirit wisdom or power. It was only the tracing of the idea of the Logos to that of the Sophia in the Old Testament, and the predominant speculative tendency (according to which *intelligence* precedes all else,, which led to this inference from the Scripture usage.

But even this is not yet the highest love. Love demands companionship. Both persons (who love each other) wish a third person to be loved as much as *they* love each other, for it would be a proof of weakness not to be willing to allow companionship in love. Therefore the two persons in the Trinity agree in loving a third one. The fulness of love also requires highest perfection, hence the equality of the persons. . . . In **the Trinity** there is neither greater nor less; two are not greater **than** one, three **are** not greater than two. This appears indeed incomprehensible, etc. Compare also the passage, De **Trin**. i. 4 (quoted by *Hase*, Dogmatik, **s**. 637, and comp. *Engelhardt*, l.c. s. 108 ff. *Baur*, Trinit. ii. **s**. 536 ff. *Meier*, s. 292.—The other scholastics who manifested a leaning to mysticism, argued in a similar way. Thus *Bonaventura*, Itinerar. Mentis, c. 6. *Raimund of Sabunde*, c. 49.¹ Compare also *Gerson*, Sermo I. in Festo S. Trin. (quoted by *Ch. Schmidt*, p. 106)

(15) *Savonarola* **showed** in a very ingenious manner (Triumphus Crucis, Lib. iii. c. 3, p. 192-196, quoted by *Rudelbach*, **s**. 366 f.) that a certain *procession* or *emanation* **exists in** all creatures. The more excellent and noble these **creatures are, the more perfect that** procession: the more perfect **it is, the more internal. If you take fire** and bring it **into contact** with wood, **it kindles and** assimilates it. But **this procession is** altogether external, **for the power of** the fire **works only** externally. If you take a plant, **you will find** that **its vital power** works internally, changing the moisture which **it extracts from the** ground into the substance of the plant, and producing the flower which was internal. This procession **is much more internal than** that of fire; but it is not altogether **internal, for it** attracts moisture from without, and produces **the flower externally; and** although the flower is connected **with the tree, yet the** fruit is an external production, and **separates itself from** the tree.—The sentient life is of a higher **order. When I see a picture, a procession and** emanation **comes from the picture which produces an** impression upon

¹ On Raimund's Doctrine of the Trinity, see *Matzke*, s. 54 ff. Among other things, he compares the three persons with the three forms of the verb; the **Father is the active, the Son** the passive, **and the** Holy Spirit **the impersonal verb!** *Matzke*, s. 41.

the eye; the eye presents the object in question to the imagination or to the memory; nevertheless the procession remains internal though it comes from without. Intelligence is of a still higher order; a man having perceived something, forms in his inner mind an image of it, and delights in its contemplation: this gives rise to a certain love which remains in the faculty of thinking. It may indeed be said that even in this case there is something external (the perception). But from this highest and innermost procession we may draw further inferences with regard to God, who unites in Himself all perfection—that the Father, as it were, begets out of Himself an idea, which is His eternal **Word (Logos)**, and that the love, which is the Holy Spirit, proceeds from the Father and the Son. This procession is the most perfect, because it does not come from without, and because it remains in God.[1] Comp. *Meier*, Savonarola, s. 248 ff. [Comp. also *Villari*, l.c.]

(16) *Wessel*, De Magnitudine Passionis, c. 74, p. 606 (quoted by *Ullmann*, s. 206), expressed himself as follows: "In our inner man, which is created after the image and likeness of God, there is a certain trinity: understanding (mens), reason (intelligentia), and will (voluntas). These three are equally sterile, inactive, and unoccupied, when they are alienated from their prototype. Our understanding without wisdom is like the light without the eye, and what else is this wisdom but God the Father?[2] The Word (the Logos) is the law and the clue of our judgments, and teaches us to think of ourselves with humility according to the truth of wisdom. And the Spirit of both, the divine love, is the food of the will (Spiritus amborum, Deus charitas, lac est voluntati)." The practical application follows of course.

The *three persons* in the Trinity were referred in a peculiar way to *the development of the history of the world*. According to *Hugo of St. Victor* (De tribus Diebus, quoted by *Liebner*, s. 383, Anm.), the day of fear commenced

---

[1] But *Savonarola* also pointed out in very appropriate language the insufficiency of our conceptions: "God treats us as a mother treats her child. She does not say to him: Go, and do such and such a thing; but she accommodates herself to the capacity of the child, and makes her wishes known by broken words and by gestures. Thus God accommodates Himself to our ideas." See *Rudelbach*, l.c. s. 369.

[2] Here he calls the *Father*, *Wisdom*; the scholastics applied this term to the *Son*. Comp. above, note 14.

with the promulgation of the law given by the Father (power); the day of truth with the manifestation of the Son (wisdom); and the day of love with the effusion of the Holy Spirit (love). Thus there was a progressive development of the times towards greater and greater light!—Amalrich of Bena and the mystico-pantheistic sects, on the other hand, interpreted these three periods after their own notions, in connection with millenarian hopes. (Comp. the Eschatology.)

Although the doctrine of the Trinity was generally reckoned among the mysteries, which could be made known to us only by revelation (comp. § 158), yet there was still a controversy on the question, whether God could make Himself known to the natural consciousness as triune, and in what way? Comp. on this, *Baur*, Trin. ii. s. 697 ff.

[*Baur*, Dg. s. 252 (2d ed.), says that what the schoolmen called persons, were not persons in the sense of the Church, but relations. To construct the Trinity, they (with the exception of Anselm and Richard) did not get beyond the psychological distinction of *intelligence* and *will*, putting these into a merely co-ordinate relation, instead of endeavouring to grasp the different relations in which God as Spirit stands to Himself, from the point of view of a vital spiritual process in its unity and totality.]

§ 171.

The Doctrine of Creation, Providence, and the Government of the World—Theodicy.

The pantheistic system of *John Scotus Erigena* (1) found no imitators among the orthodox scholastics; they adhered rather to the idea of a creation out of nothing (2). Later writers endeavoured to define this doctrine more precisely, in order to prevent any misunderstanding, as if *nothing* could have been the cause of existence (3).—The Mosaic account of the creation was interpreted literally by some, and allegorically by others (4). The opinion still continued generally to prevail, that the world is a work of divine goodness, and exists principally for the sake of man (5). Though mysticism tended to induce its advocates to regard the independence of the finite creature as a breaking loose from the Creator, and consequently as a revolt, and thus to stamp creation as the work of the devil (after the manner of the Manichæans) (6), yet these pious thinkers were roused by the sight of the works of God to the utterance of beautiful and elevating thoughts, so that they were lost in adoring wonder (7). On the other hand, the schoolmen, fond of vain and subtle investigations, indulged here also in absurd inquiries (8).—Regarding the existence of evil in the world, the scholastics adopted for the most part the views of Augustine. Thus, some (*e.g.* Thomas Aquinas) regarded evil as the absence of good, and as forming a necessary part of the finite world, retaining, however, the difference between physical evil and moral evil (the evil of punishment and the evil of guilt) (9). Others adopted, with Chrysostom, the notion of a twofold divine will (voluntas antecedens et consequens) (10).

(1) Comp. above, § 165, 1, and De Divis. Nat. ii. c. 19 (quoted by *Münscher, von Cölln,* s. 63).

(2) God is not only the former (factor), but the creator and author (creator) of matter. This was taught by *Hugo of St. Victor* (Prolog. c. 1, *Liebner,* s. 355), and the same view was adopted by the other mystics. The advocates of Platonism alone sympathized with the earlier notions of Origen.

(3) *Frédégis of Tours* defended the reality of nothing, as the infinite genus from which all other species of things derive their form; comp. his work, De Nihilo, and *Ritter, Gesch.* der Christl. Phil. vii. s. 189 ff. *Alexander Halesius* (Summa, P. II. quæst. 9, membr. 10) drew a distinction between nihilum privativum and negativum. The one abolishes the act, the other the object of the act. God has not created the world from pre-existent matter, yet not sine causa. See on this point, *Münscher, von Cölln,* s. 61 f.— *Gieseler,* Dg. s. 495. *Thomas Aquinas* (Pars i. qu. 46, art. 2) represented the doctrine of a creation out of nothing as an article of faith (credibile), but not as an object of knowledge and demonstration (non demonstrabile vel scibile), and expressed himself as follows, qu. 45, art. 2: Quicunque facit aliquid ex aliquo, illud, *ex quo* facit, præsupponitur actioni ejus et non producitur per ipsam actionem. . . . Si ergo Deus non ageret, nisi ex aliquo præsupposito, sequeretur, quod illud præsuppositum non esset causatum ab ipso. Ostensum est autem supra, quod nihil potest esse in entibus nisi a Deo, qui est causa universalis totius esse. Unde necesse est dicere,

quod Deus ex nihilo res in esse producit. Comp. *Cramer*, vii. s. **415 ff.** *Baur*, Trin. ii. s. 716: "*The fact that Thomas considered God as the archetypal first cause of all things, plainly shows that in his opinion the creation, which is designated as a **creation out of** nothing, was not a sudden transition from nonexistence to existence.*" Quæst. 44, art. **2**: Dicendum, quod **Deus est** prima causa exemplaris omnium rerum... Ipse **Deus** est primum exemplar omnium.—While *Thomas* and still **more** *Albertus Magnus* draw no clear distinction between the idea of emanation and that of creation (*Baur*, l.c. s. 723 ff.). *Scotus* adheres to the simple notion that **God is the** primum efficiens; nevertheless he distinguishes **between an esse existentiæ and an** esse essentiæ; but both cannot be separated in reality, and the latter presupposes the former; see lib. **ii.** dist. 1, qu. 2, and other passages in *Baur*, l.c. s. 726 ff.

(4) Thus *Hugo of St. Victor* thought that the shaping of formless matter in six days might be literally interpreted. Almighty **God** might have **made** it differently; but He would in this way **show rational beings in a figure** how they are to be transformed from **moral deformity** into moral beauty... In creating the light before **all His** other work, He signified that the works of darkness **above all** things displeased Him. The good and evil angels were separated at the same time that light and darkness were separated. God did not separate light from darkness till He saw the light that it was good. In like manner, we should first of **all** see that our light be **good, and then we** may proceed to a separation, etc. Observing that the phrase, "**and** God **saw** that it was good," is **wanting in reference to the work of the** second day in the **Mosaic account of the** creation, **this mystic** scholastic was led **into further inquiries** respecting the reason of this omission. **He found it in the number two, which is** an inauspicious **number, because it is the departure** from unity. Nor is it **said, with reference to the** waters *above* **the** firmament, as with those *under* **the firmament, that they were** gathered together **unto one place—because the love of God** (the heavenly water) **is shed abroad (poured forth) in our hearts** by the Holy Ghost. **This love must expand itself and rise higher; but** the waters **under the firmament (the lower passions of the soul)** must be **kept together. Fishes and birds are created out of** one and

the same matter, yet different places are assigned to them, which is a type of the elect and the reprobate, from one and the same mass of corrupt nature; comp. *Liebner*, s. 256 f. —Friar *Berthold* saw in the works of the first three days of the creation, faith, hope, and love; see *Kling*, s. 462 f.

(5) *Joh. Dam. De fide orth.* ii. 2 (after Greg. Naz. and Dionys. Areop.): Ἐπεὶ οὖν ὁ ἀγαθὸς καὶ ὑπεράγαθος Θεὸς οὐκ ἠρκέσθη τῇ ἑαυτοῦ θεωρίᾳ, ἀλλ' ὑπερβολῇ ἀγαθότητος εὐδόκησε γενέσθαι τινὰ τὰ εὐεργετηθησόμενα, καὶ μεθέξοντα τῆς αὐτοῦ ἀγαθότητος, ἐκ τοῦ μὴ ὄντος εἰς τὸ εἶναι παράγει καὶ δημιουργεῖ τὰ σύμπαντα, ἀόρατά τε καὶ ὁρατά, καὶ τὸν ἐξ ὁρατοῦ καὶ ἀοράτου συγκείμενον ἄνθρωπον.—*Petr. Lomb. Sentent.* ii. dist. i. C: Dei tanta est bonitas, ut summe bonus beatitudinis suae, qua aeternaliter beatus est, alios velit esse participes, quam videt et communicari posse et minui omnino non posse. Illud ergo bonum, quod ipse erat et quo beatus erat, *sola bonitate, non necessitate* aliis communicari voluit. ... Lit. D: Et quia non valet ejus beatitudinis particeps existere aliquis, nisi per intelligentiam (quae quanto magis intelligitur, tanto plenius habetur), fecit Deus *rationalem creaturam*, quae summum bonum intelligeret et intelligendo amaret et amando possideret ac possidendo frueretur. ... Lit. E: Deus perfectus et summa bonitate plenus, nec augeri potest nec minui. Quod ergo rationalis creatura facta est a Deo, referendum est ad creatoris bonitatem et ad creaturae utilitatem. Comp. *Alan. ab Ins.* ii. 4 (quoted by *Pez*, t. i. p. 487 s.).—*Hugo of St. Victor* also said (quoted by *Liebner*, s. 357 f.): "The creation of the world had man, that of man had *God* for its end. The world should serve man, and man should serve God; but the service of the latter is only for man's own advantage, since in this service he is to find his own happiness. For God, being all-sufficient to Himself, stood in no need of the services of any one, so that man has received both, *i.e.* all, viz. the good under him and the good above him, the former to supply his necessities, the latter to constitute his happiness; the former for his benefit and use, the latter for his enjoyment and possession. Thus man, though created at a later period, was nevertheless the cause of all that was under him, and hence the high dignity of human nature." *Thomas Aquinas* supposes God to have no other object than the communication of His

own being, Summa, P. I. qu. 45, art. 4: Primo agenti, qui est agens tantum, non convenit agere propter acquisitionem alicujus finis: sed intendit solum communicare suam perfectionem, quæ est ejus bonitas. Et unaquæque creatura intendit **consequi suam** perfectionem, quæ est similitudo perfectionis **et bonitatis divinæ.** Sic ergo divina bonitatis est finis rerum omnium. . . . Et ideo ipse solus est maxime liberalis, quia non agit **propter suam utilitatem, sed solum** propter suam bonitatem. Comp. *Cramer*, vii. s. 414 f. *Baur*, Trinit. ii. s. 731 f. *Ritter*, viii. s. 284 ff.

(6) According to the author of the work, *German Theology* (cap. 1, at the beginning), the ideas of creatureliness, egoism, and selfhood are synonymous with love of the world, **love of the creature, self-love, self-will, natural carnal sense, and carnal desire.** The creature must depart, if God is to enter. He thinks it sinful "to esteem created things, and to look upon them as *something*, while they are in reality—*nothing*." Subsequently he admits, however, that those things have their being only in God: "Out of the perfect, or without it, there is no true existence; but all is mere accident, or mere semblance and glitter, which neither is nor has true being, except the fire from which the shining proceeds, like the brightness which proceeds or flows out from fire, or light, or the sun."—Some of the *heretical* sects of the Middle Ages entertained views on these points which bordered upon Manichæism. Thus the Franciscan *Berthold* said in a sermon (quoted by *Kling*, s. 305; *Wackernagel*, Lesebuch, i. Sp. 678): Some heretics believe and maintain that the devil created man, when our Lord created the soul in him. Comp. *Ermengardi* Opusc. contra Hæreticos, qui dicunt et credunt, mundum istum et omnia visibilia non esse a Deo facta, sed a Diabolo, edited by *Gretser* in Bibl. Max. PP. t. xxiv. p. 1602. *Gieseler*, Kg. ii. s. 501.

(7) *Henry Suso* (c. 54, quoted by *Diepenbrock*, s. 208) said: "Now let us remain here for a while and contemplate the high and excellent Master in His works. Look above you and around you, look to the four quarters of the world. How wide and high the beautiful sky is in its rapid course, and how nobly the Master has adorned it with the seven planets, —each of which, with the exception of the moon, is much

larger than the whole earth,—and how it is beautified with the innumerable multitude of the bright stars! Oh, how cloudlessly and cheerfully the beautiful sun rises in the summer season, and how diligently it gives growth and blessings to the soil; how the leaves and the grass come forth; how the beautiful flowers smile; how the forest, and the heath, and the meadows resound with the sweet songs of the nightingale and other small birds; how all the animals which were shut up during the hard winter come forth and enjoy themselves, and go in pairs; how, in humanity, young and old manifest their joy in merry and gladsome utterances! *O tender God! if Thou art so loving in Thy creatures, how fair and lovely must Thou be in Thyself!* Look further, I pray you, and behold the four elements,—earth, water, air, and fire,—and all the wonderful things in them: the variety and diversity of men, beasts, birds, fishes, and the wonders of the deep, all of which cry aloud and proclaim the praise and honour of the boundless and infinite nature of God! O Lord, who preserves all this? Who feeds it? Thou takest care of all, each in its own way, great and small, rich and poor. Thou, God! Thou doest it. Thou, God, art indeed God!"

(8) *John Damasc.* De fide orth. ii. 5 ss., treated of the whole range of natural science (cosmography, astronomy, physics, geology, etc.), so far as it was known to him, in the locus de creatione; and the scholastics followed his example. Comp. *Cramer*, vii. s. 388 ff. But in introducing natural history into the province of dogmatic theology, they thought that they might put limits to physical investigation by the doctrine of the Church. Thus it happened that, *e.g.* in the time of Boniface (Bishop of Mainz), the assertion of Virgilius, a priest, that there are *antipodes*, was considered heretical; see *Schröckh*, xix. s. 219 f.

> An additional point in reference to the work of creation was the question, Whether it is to be assigned to only *one* of the persons of the Trinity? The theologians of the present period adopted the opinion of the earlier Church, that all the three persons participated in it; *Thomas Aquinas*, qu. 45, art. 6. *Cramer*, vii. s. 416. This, however, was scarcely more than a speculative idea. The power of creating was supposed to be more particularly possessed by the Father, for the very reason that *power* was peculiarly ascribed to Him, though various expressions were used in the liturgical services, *e.g.* in the hymn: Veni Creator Spiritus.

(9) *Anselm* himself taught that *this* world is the best (*mundus quod est, recte est*, Dial. de Ver. c. 7); and *Abelard* agreed with what *Plato* asserted (in the Timaeus): Deum nullatenus **mundum** meliorem potuisse facere, quam fecerit (Introd. ad **Theol. iii. c. 5,** quoted by *Münscher, von Cölln,* ii. s. 70). This **assertion, however, met with** opposition on the part of others. **(Comp. § 167, note** 7.) According to *Alexander of Hales*, every **individual** possesses its own perfection, although it may appear imperfect compared with the whole; see *Cramer*, vii. s. 413. —Concerning the nature of evil, *Thomas Aquinas* expressed himself quite in **the** sense of Augustine (qu. 48 and 49,): Evil is not a thing which exists by itself, but **is the absence** and want of good. Evil is, moreover, necessary **to constitute** a *difference of degrees;* the imperfection of individual things belongs even to the perfection of the world (Summa, P. 1. qu. 48, art. 2, quoted by *Münscher, von Cölln,* s. 74. *Cramer,* s. 420 ff.). But Thomas well knew how to make an exception **in the case of moral evil.** The latter is not only a defect, but **the wicked are wanting in** something in *which* they should not *be wanting;* therefore the idea of evil belongs more properly **to the evil of guilt** (malum culpae) than to the evil of punish-**ment (malum poenae).** (Comp. *Tertull.* advers. Marc. ii. 14.) **According to** *Duns Scotus*, all depends on the freedom of the **finite creature; and, accordingly, the goodness of God** revealed **in the perfection of the world is conditioned by that free born.** *Baur, Dg.* s. 254 (2d ed.).

(10) The scholastics commonly **treated of** *Providence* and of the *Theodicy* in connection **with** the attributes, and particularly **with the divine will of God.** *Hugo of St. Victor* **even said that the providence of** God **itself is an** attribute,— **viz. that attribute of God by** which **He takes care of** all the **works of His hands, abandons nothing that belongs to Him, and gives to every one his due and right. Both the actual existence of good and the mode of its existence depend on the** *arrangement* **(dispositio) of God. It is not so with evil. Only the** *mode* **of its existence depends on God, but not its existence itself; for God does not do evil Himself, but when evil is done He overrules it (malum ordinabile est). De Sacram. c. 19–21 (in** *Liebner,* **s. 366.** *Cramer,* **vii. s. 274 ff.). On the** θέλημα προηγούμενον, **etc., comp. § 126, note 5, and** *John*

Damasc. De fide orthod. ii. 29. By the scholastics the θέλημα προηγούμενον (antecedens) was also called **voluntas bene placiti**; the θελ. ἑπόμενον (consequens), voluntas **signi** (sign or expression of one's will). Comp. *Liebner*, Hugo von St. Victor, s. 386. *Peter Lomb.* Lib. i. dist. 45 F. *Alexander of Hales*, Summa, P. I. qu. 36, membr. 1.—*Thomas Aquinas* both denies and admits that evil proceeds from God. So far as evil presupposes a defect, it cannot have its origin in God, for God is the highest perfection. But so far as it consists in the corruption of certain things, and this corruption in its turn belongs to the perfection of the universe, it proceeds indeed from God ex consequenti, and quasi per accidens. The theodicy of Thomas may be comprised in this proposition (Summa theol. P. I. qu. 15, art. 3): Malum cognoscitur a Deo non per propriam rationem, sed per rationem boni. Comp. *Baur*, Trin. ii. s. 734 ff. *Ritter*, viii. s. 285, and the other passages there cited. *Münscher, von Cölln*, s. 72 f. *Cramer*, s. 264 ff.

A peculiar Oriental controversy is that respecting the created and the uncreated light. The *Hesychasts* (Quietists) of Mt. Athos, with *Palamas*, afterwards Archbishop of Thessalonica, at their head, maintained that there is an eternal, uncreated, and yet communicable divine light (the light of the transfiguration on Tabor). The monk *Barlaam* (from Calabria) opposed this assertion, maintaining that the light on Tabor was a created light. A Confession adopted at Constantinople in 1341 was favourable to the Hesychasts. *Acindynus*, Barlaam's coadjutor, resumed the controversy, but lost his case at a second synod at Constantinople. But he almost got the victory at a third synod (after the death of Andronicus, 1341) under the Empress Anna; but a fourth synod (under Cantacuzenus) again declared the doctrine of the Hesychasts to be correct. This dispute was connected with that about the οὐσία and ἐνέργεια of the divine nature. Comp. *Gass* in *Herzog's* Realencykl., under "Hesychasts" (after the report of Nicephorus Gregoras), and the essay of *Engelhardt*, referred to § 153, note 12.

§ 172.

The Angels and the Devil.

John Damascene and others (1) adhered to the classification of the angels given by pseudo-Dionysius (§ 131, note 8). The Lateran Council (A.D. 1215), under Pope Innocent III., pronounced as the doctrine of the Church, that the angels are spiritual beings, and that they were created good (2). But with regard to particular points, such as the nature and the **offices of the** angels, their relation to God, **to** the world, to **man, and to the** work of redemption, **ample** scope was left for **poetical and** fanciful **speculations,** frequently running out into **wilful conceits** (3). The idea **of the devil** penetrated even **deeper than** did the belief **in** angels into **the** popular creed of **the Germanic** nations, sometimes connected in a horrible way **with the** belief in sorcery and witches, so common during the Middle Ages, sometimes treated with levity **and humour,** interwoven with legends and popular tales (4). In the **History of** Doctrines this living and national belief in the devil is **to be** considered as well **as** the theorems and systems of the schools, founded **for the most** part upon traditional definitions (5). From the religious point of view the only matter **of importance is this, that it was held** that the devil cannot **compel any one to commit sin, while he** himself **is** delivered **up to** eternal **condemnation (6). He and the** evil spirits **associated** with **him feel** their **own punishment,** but also **take pleasure in the torments of the damned;** this **is their only compensation, and one worthy of their devilish disposition (7).**

(1) De fide orthod. ii. 3. The scholastics mostly adopted this classification. Thus *Hugo of St. Victor* "*mentioned and explained the orders and names of angels* (according to pseudo-Dionysius) *only very briefly* (De Sacr. i. 5), *a proof of his good sense.*" (*Liebner,* s. 395.) Comp. *Lomb.* Sent. lib. ii. dis. 9 A. *Thom. Aquinas,* Summa, P. I. qu. 108 (quoted by *Münscher, von Cölln,* s. 65).

(2) Conc. Lateran. IV. Can. i. Mansi, t. xxii. p. 982 (*Münscher, von Cölln,* s. 65).

(3) Most of the scholastics adopted the opinion of Augustine, that the angels were created *with* all the other creatures, and only in so far *before* them, as they surpass them in dignity. Thus *Hugo of St. Victor* (quoted by *Liebner,* s. 28 and 29, s. 392), *Alexander of Hales, Thomas Aquinas, Bonaventura,*

etc. (quoted by *Cramer*, vii. s. 426). A fact adverted to about the angels, not unimportant in a religious point of view, is, that the angels are represented only as distinct and isolated creations of God, not forming one whole like the human race; hence, it is said, the fall of individuals did not involve the fall of the whole angelic world. Comp. *e.g.* *Anselm's* Cur Deus Homo, ii. 21: Non enim sic sunt omnes angeli de uno angelo, quemadmodum omnes homines de uno homine. "*There is a human race, but not an angelic race (keine Engelheit)*," *Hasse's* Anselm, ii. s. 391.—According to the statements of the later scholastics, the angels are distinguished from the souls of men—1. Physically (they do not stand in absolute need of a body); 2. Logically (they do not obtain knowledge by inferences); 3. Metaphysically (they do not think by means of images, but by immediate intuition); 4. Theologically (they cannot become better and worse). Alexander of Hales, however, made this last assertion with reserve. As incorporeal creatures, they are not made up of matter and form; yet actus and potentia are not identical with them as with God. Also (according to Thomas) there are no two angels of the same species; but this is denied by Duns Scotus. The question was raised, whether thinking is the essence of an angel? The reply was in the negative. Yet Aquinas says the thinking of an angel is never merely potential, but is at the same time actual. The knowledge of angels is purely *à priori*, and the higher the rank of an angel, so much the more universal are the conceptions by which he knows. Scotus says that the angels have a capacity for obtaining knowledge empirically (intellectum agentem et possibilem); according to others, their knowledge is either matutina (cognitio rerum in verbo), or vespertina (cognitio rerum in se), or, lastly, meridiana (aperta Dei visio). Comp. *Bonaventura*, Compend. ii. c. 15. The knowledge of some angels, however, is more comprehensive than that of others. Some, *e.g.*, foreknew the mystery of the incarnation of Christ, which was unknown to others. The angels also have a language, not, however, born of sense, but intellectual. They have, moreover, a place, *i.e.* they are not omnipresent like God, but move with infinite rapidity from one place to another, and pervade all space more easily than man. It was also asked whether they could work miracles? whether one angel could exert any influence upon the will of another? etc.; see *Cramer*, l.c. (These quotations are for the most part taken from Alexander of Hales and Thomas Aquinas.) See *Baur*, Trinit. ii. s. 751 ff.—*Peter Lombard* and others also retained the idea of *guardian angels*, see Sent. ii. dist. 11 A (in *Münscher, von Cölln*, s. 66). Some entertained the singular notion of a *hatred* on the part of the angels against sinners of the human race, of which *Berthold* speaks in one of his sermons (quoted by Kling, s. 18, 20): "They cry daily at the sight of sinners: Lord, let us kill them! But he appeases and exhorts them to let the tares grow among the wheat." But the more sober scholastics did not enter into any further inquiries of this kind. Thus *Hugo of St. Victor* said: "*We walk among these things timidly, and, as it were, blindfolded, and we grope with the sense of our insignificant knowledge after the incomprehensible*," *Liebner*, s. 393.— *Tauler* expressed himself in similar language, Sermon on Michaelmas Day (Bd. iii. s. 145): "With what words we may and ought to speak of these pure spirits I do not know, for they have neither hands nor feet, neither shape, nor form, nor matter; and what shall we say of a being which has none of these things, and which cannot be apprehended by our senses? *What they are is unknown to us*; nor should this surprise us, for we do not know ourselves, viz. our spirit, by which we are made men, and from which we receive all the good we possess. How then could we know this exceeding great spirit, whose dignity far surpasses all the dignity which the world can possess? *Therefore we speak of the works which they perform towards us, but not of their nature*." Nevertheless Tauler followed the example of his contemporaries in adhering to the hierarchia cœlestis of Dionysius.

(4) "*It is somewhat remarkable that the devil of the Middle Ages seems to have lost* much *of his terror and hideousness, and* to play rather the part of a cunning impostor *and merry fellow* . . . more like a faun, which *excites* laughter *rather than fear*," *Augusti*, Dg. s. 320. Comp. Grimm, Deutsche Mythologie, s. 549 ff. *Hase*, Gnosis, i. s. 263. *Koberstein*, Sage vom Wartburgkriege, s. 67 f. (The trials for witchcraft did not become general until the close of the present period, in the

fifteenth century, from which time faith in the power of the devil became increasingly dismal and portentous.)

(5) *Anselm* composed a separate treatise respecting the fall of the devil (De Casu Diaboli). His leading idea, cap. 4, is: Peccavit volendo aliquod commodum, quod nec habebat, nec tunc velle debuit, quod tamen ad augmentum beatitudinis esse illi poterat . . . Peccavit et volendo quod non debuit, et nolendo quod debuit, et palam est, quia non ideo voluit, quod volendo illam (justitiam) deserunt . . . At cum hoc voluit, quod Deus illum velle nolebat, voluit inordinate similis esse Deo—quia propria voluntate, quae nulli subdita fuit, voluit aliquid. Solus enim Dei esse debet, sic voluntate propria velle aliquid, ut superiorem non sequatur voluntatem. Non solum autem voluit esse aequalis Deo, quia praesumsit habere propriam voluntatem, sed etiam major voluit esse, volendo, quod Deus illum velle nolebat, quoniam voluntatem suam supra voluntatem Dei posuit. Comp. *Hasse*, ii. s. 393 ff. Most theologians still adhered to the opinion that *pride* was the principal cause of the fall of the devil; but *Duns Scotus* finds the word *luxuria* more appropriate (Lib. ii. dist. 3, p. 514; *Baur*, Trin. ii. s. 771 ff.—In accordance with Isa. xiv. 2, Satan was identified with Lucifer, and the latter name was thenceforward constantly applied to the devil.[1] According to *Anselm* (substantially as in *Augustine*, Enchiridion, c. 29), the fall of the devil was the cause of the creation of man, which was to be a kind of compensation, by supplying the deficiency in the number of the elect spirits (Cur Deus Homo, c. 16-18). The same idea was entertained by *Hugo of St. Victor* and *Peter Lombard*, though in a somewhat modified form; see *Liebner*, s. 395. According to *Alexander of Hales*, some fell from among all the different classes of angels, but the number of fallen angels is less than that of those who preserved their innocence. *Duns Scotus* maintains that the fallen angels can even raise themselves up so as to will what is good; but it remains a mere volition, and never

---

[1] *Bonavent.* Compend. ii. 28: Dictus est autem Lucifer quia prae caeteris luxit, suaeque pulchritudinis consideratio eum excaecavit. Among the earlier Fathers of the Church, Eusebius was the only one who applied the appellation Lucifer to the devil (Demonst. Evang. iv. 9). Neither Jerome nor Augustine ever did so. Comp. *Grimm*, l.c. s. 530, Anm.

comes to act (Dist. 7, p. 577; *Baur*, Trinit. ii. s. 786). Neither the evil nor the good angels can perform miracles in the proper sense; the former may, however, exert some power over the corporeal world, though they cannot go so far (as popular superstition would have men believe) as to change men into other beings, *e.g.* wolves or birds (see *Cramer*, s. 44). The scholastics have also contributed their part to free-thinking!

(6) *Thomas Aquinas*, i. qu. 64. The **power of** Satan has **been** especially limited since the appearance of Christ (comp. *Cramer*, s. 447).—*Anselm* declared it impossible that the evil angels should finally be redeemed (as Origen supposed); Cur Deus Homo, ii. **c.** 21: Sicut enim homo non potuit reconciliari nisi per hominem Deum (see below, § 179), qui mori posset . . . ita angeli damnati non possunt salvari nisi per angelum Deum **qui** mori possit. Et sicut homo per alium hominem, qui non esset ejusdem generis, quamvis ejusdem esset naturæ, **non** debuit relevari, ita nullus angelus per alium angelum salvari debet, **quamvis** omnes sint unius naturæ, quoniam non sunt ejusdem generis sicut homines. Non enim sic sunt omnes angeli **de** uno angelo, quemadmodum omnes **homines de** uno homine. Hoc quoque removet eorum restaurationem, quia sicut ceciderunt **nullo** alio suadente ut caderent, **ita nullo ali**o adjuvante resurgere **debent**: quod est illis impossibile.

(7) *Cramer*, l.c. s. 448: "*They may indeed delight in the evil and mischief which they do to man, but this joy is a joy full of bitterness, and prepares them for still more painful punishments.*" According to *John Wessel* (De Magnit. Pass. c. 38, p. 532, quoted by *Ullmann*, s. 236), "Satan (or the dragon) finds his first and greatest misery in his clear knowledge that God is ever blessed in Himself. . . . His second misery is, seeing in his own condition, and in the case of all others, that the Lamb, as the victor, has received from God a name which is above every name. . . . His third misery is, that Satan himself, with the whole host of darkness, has prepared this **crown of victory for the Lamb.**"

THIRD DIVISION.

ANTHROPOLOGY.

§ 173.

General Definitions.

The Greek Church adhered to the opinions of the earlier Fathers, which were collected and more fully developed by *John Damascene* (1). He, as well as most of the Western theologians, adopted the current twofold division into body and soul (dichotomy). While *John Scotus Erigena* regarded the bodily constitution of man, and even his creaturely condition, as a result of sin (2), *John of Damascus* and the disciples of the school of *St. Victor* recognized in the union of the soul with the body a higher purpose of God and a moral lesson for man (3). The theory designated as Creatianism, which had contested the victory with Traducianism during the preceding period, was now more precisely defined (4). The psychological views of the mystics stood in a close relation with their entire system, founded upon subjective experience; and, at all events, it had a greater tendency to lead into the depths of religious self-contemplation than the subtleties of the scholastics, which had rather to do with what is external (5).

(1) On the one hand, cosmology was introduced into the doctrine of creation; on the other, both psychology and physiology were introduced into anthropology. With respect to the last two, theologians founded their notions especially upon the physics of Aristotle. Thus *John Damascene*, De fide

orthod. ii. 12-28, treated of the four temperaments (humoribus, χυμοῖς) of man (as corresponding to the four elements of the world); of the various faculties of the soul, etc. He everywhere retained the principal definitions of earlier theologians respecting human *liberty*, etc. Compare especially, c. 25-28.

(2) **De Divis. Naturæ**, iv. 10 : Non enim homo, si non peccaret, inter partes **mundi** administraretur, sed universitatem **omnino** sibi subditam administraret, nec corporeis his sensibus **mortalis** corporis ad illum regendum uteretur, verum sine ullo **sensibili** motu vel locali vel temporali, sola **rationabili** contuitu naturalium et interiorum ejus causarum facillimo **rectæ** voluntatis usu secundum leges divinas æternaliter ac sine errore gubernaret.

(3) *John Damasc.* l.c. c. 12. According to *Hugo of St. Victor* (quoted by *Liebner*, s. 395), the union of the soul with the body is a type of the mystical union of God with man. *Richard of St. Victor* adopted the same opinion (see *Engelhardt*, s. 181), which was also held by *Peter Lombard* (Sent. lib. i. dist. 3, 9, and lib. ii. dist. 17). *Thomas Aquinas* gave a more fully developed system of psychology; Summa, P. 1. qu. 75-90. (Cramer, vii. s. 473.)

(4) *Anselm* defended creationism *negatively*, by opposing traducianism, De Conceptu Virginali, c. 7 : Quod autem mox ab ipsa conceptione rationalem animam habeat (homo), nullus humanus suscipit sensus. *Hugo of St. Victor* pronounced *positively* in favour of creationism ; De Sacram. P. VII. lib. i. c. 30 : Fides catholica magis credendum **elegit** animas quotidie cor**poribus vivificandis** sociandas de nihilo **fieri**, quam secundum **corporis naturam et carnis** humanæ proprietatem de **traduce** propagari. Comp. *Liebner*, s. 416. *Robert Pulleyn* brought forward some very singular and abstruse arguments against traducianism, see *Cramer*, vi. s. 474. *Peter Lombard* also espoused creationism in decided terms, Sent. lib. ii. dist. 17 C: De aliis (*i.e.* the souls after Adam and Eve), certissime sentiendum est, quod in corpore creentur. Creando enim infundit eas Deus, et infundendo creat.—*Thomas Aquinas*, Summa, P. I. qu. 118, art. 1, made a distinction between the anima sensitiva and anima intellectiva (which was similar to the distinction formerly made between ψυχή and πνεῦμα or νοῦς). The former is propagated in a physical manner, inasmuch as it is

allied to the physical; the latter is created by God. [Comp. *Aquinas*, Contra Gentes, ii. 89: Anima igitur vegetabilis, quae primo inest, cum embryo vivit vita plantae, corrumpitur, et succedit anima perfectior, quae est nutritiva et sensitiva simul; et tunc embryo vivit vita animalis; hac autem corrupta, succedit anima rationalis *ab extrinseco* immissa, licet praecedentes fuerint virtute seminis. Aquinas' chief argument (in Summa Theol. P. I. qu. 118, art. 2) is, that an immaterial substance could be produced only by creation.] More precise definitions were given by *Odo of Cambray* (A.D. 1113), De Peccato Originali, libb. ii. (in Maxima Biblioth. PP. Lugd. t. xxi. p. 230–234. Comp. *Schröckh*, xxviii. s. 436). He designated creatianism as the *orthodox* opinion. — Friar *Berthold* illustrated this theory in a popular way in his sermons (quoted by *Kling*, s. 209; *Grimm*, s. 206): "As life is given to the child in his mother's womb, so the angel pours the soul into him, and Almighty God pours the soul with the angel into him." The pre-existence of the soul had still a defender in *Frédégis of Tours*, in the ninth century; see *Ritter*, Gesch. d. Phil. vii. s. 190 f.

(5) On the mystical psychology of the disciples of the school of St. Victor, see *Liebner*, s. 354 ff. The three fundamental powers by which the soul knows are imaginatio, ratio (rather understanding than reason), and intelligentia. Cogitatio corresponds to the first, meditatio to the second, and contemplatio to the third. The treatise, De Anima, libri iv. (in Opp. *Hugonis*, ed. Rothomag. t. ii. p. 132 ss.), which was used as a compendium by the earlier scholastics no less than by the mystics, is sometimes attributed to Hugo of St. Victor, but has probably *Alcherus*, Abbot of Stella (A.D. 1147), for its author. (See *Liebner*, s. 493 ff., and *Engelhardt*, Dg. ii. s. 119.) — *Bonaventura* and *Gerson* adopted the same psychological notions. According to the former, *spiritual vision* is the principal idea. We see all things in God through the medium of a supernatural light (comp. above, § 161). He, too, distinguished between sensation, imagination, reason (understanding), intellectus, the highest faculty of the mind, and the *synteresis* or conscience. — *Gerson* (De Theol. Myst. consid. x.–xxv.) divided the essence of the soul into two fundamental powers (vis cognitiva et vis affectiva). Starting from its higher

functions, he then divided the former as follows: **intelligentia simplex** (the pure faculty of intellectual vision), **ratio** (understanding), and **sensualitas** (the faculty of perception by the senses). They are related to each other, as **contemplatio, meditatio,** and **cogitatio.** The highest degree of the vis affectiva is the *Synteresis*,[1] the next is the appetitus rationalis, and the lowest is the appetitus animalis; see *Handeshagen*, s. 37 ff.; *Ch. Schmidt*, p. 76 ss.

§ 174.

The Immortality of the Soul.

The assertion of some of the earlier Greek theologians, that the ψυχή, as such, is not immortal, but obtains immortality only from its connection with the πνεῦμα, was repeated in the Greek Church by *Nicolas of Methone* (1). In the West, the schoolmen generally taught the immortality of the soul as a *theological* truth; but the chief leaders of the scholastic sects, *Thomas Aquinas* and *Duns Scotus*, were at issue on the question whether reason furnishes satisfactory proofs of that doctrine (2). *Raimund of Sabunde* rested belief in God, as well as belief in immortality, upon the idea of freedom and the necessity of moral sanctions (3). But the advocates of Platonism, in particular, towards the close of the present period, were at much pains to prove the immortality of the soul, in opposition to the Aristotelians (4). At last, the Lateran Council, held A.D. 1513, under Pope Leo X., pronounced the natural immortality of the soul to be an article of faith, and discarded the distinction between theological and philosophical truths as untenable (5).

(1) *John Damasc.* taught simply, De fide orthod. ii. 12

---

[1] Synteresis est vis animæ appetitiva, suscipiens immediate a Deo naturalem quandam inclinationem ad bonum, per quam trahitur insequi motionem boni ex apprehensione simplicis intelligentiæ præsentati, quoted by *Liebner*, s. 340. Comp. *Bonavent.* Compend. II. 51.

(p. 179, *Le Quien*), that the soul is ἀθάνατος. *Nicolas of Methone*, on the contrary, expressed himself as follows (Refut. p. 207 s., quoted by Ullmann, s. 89 f.): "It is not every soul that neither perishes nor dies, but only the rational, higher spiritual and divine soul, which is made perfect through virtue by participating in the grace of God. For the souls of irrational beings, and still more of plants, may perish with the things which they inhabit, because they cannot be separated from bodies which are made up of parts, and may be dissolved into their elements." Compare with this passage what he said Refut. p. 120: "If any created being is eternal, it is not so by and for itself, nor through itself, but by the goodness of God; for all that is made and created has a beginning, and retains its existence only through the goodness of the Creator."

(2) The scholastics, by closely adhering to *Aristotle*, were naturally led to the inquiry, in what sense their master himself had taught the immortality of the soul, in the definition he gave of its essence, viz. that it is ἐντελέχεια ἡ πρώτη σώματος φυσικοῦ ὀργανικοῦ (De Anim. ii. 1); comp. *Münscher, von Cölln*, ii. s. 90. But Christianity set forth the immortality of the soul in so convincing a manner, that it became necessary either to return to the old distinction made between natural immortality and that immortality which is communicated by grace, which was, however, possible only in connection with the threefold division (viz. body, soul, and spirit), or to admit a collision between theological and philosophical truths. The distinction which *Thomas Aquinas* drew between the anima sensitiva and intellectiva (§ 173, note 4) enabled him to ascribe immortality to the latter alone. Comp. Summa, P. I. qu. 76, art. 6, where he in fact contented himself with saying: Animam humanam, quam dicimus *intellectivum principium*, esse incorruptibilem. But he also held that the intellectus alone is above space and time (hic et nunc), while the sensus moves in these categories, and is restricted in its knowledge to the images (ideas, phantasms) borrowed from this sphere (intelligere cum phantasmate). As Anselm of Canterbury had inferred the existence of God Himself from the idea of God, so *Thomas Aquinas* proved the immortality of the soul, in a similar manner, by an *ontological* argument:

Intellectus apprehendit esse absolute et secundum omne tempus. Unde omne habens intellectum naturaliter desiderat esse semper. Naturale autem desiderium non potest esse inane. Omnis igitur intellectualis substantia est incorruptibilis. Comp. *Engelhardt*, Dg. ii. **s.** 123.—On the other hand, *Scotus*, whose views were more nearly allied to those of the nominalists, maintained: **Non posse** demonstrari, quod **anima** sit immortalis (Comm. in M. Sentent. lib. ii. dist. 17, qu. 1. Comp. lib. **iv.** dist. 43, qu. 2). *Bonaventura*, on the contrary, asserted, De Nat. Div. ii. 55: Animam esse immortalem, auctoritate ostenditur et ratione. On the further attempts of *Moneta of Cremona* (who lived between 1220 and 1250), *William of Auxerre* (Bishop of Paris from 1228 to 1249), and *Raimund Martini* (in his Pugio Fidei adv. Maur. P. 1. c. 4), to prove the immortality of the soul, comp. *Münscher, von Cölln*, s. 94 f.

(3) Theol. Naturalis, tit. 92. Quoniam ex operibus hominis, in quantum **homo** est, nascitur meritum vel culpa, quibus **debetur punitio vel** præmium, et cum homo, quamdiu vivat, **acquirit meritum vel** culpam, **et de illis non** recipit retributiones nec **punitiones dum vivit, et ordo** universi non patitur, **quod aliquid** quantumcumque **modicum** remaneat irremuneratum neque impunitum — ideo necesse **est, quod** remaneat liberum arbitrium, quo fiat radix meritorum **et culparum, ut** recipiat debitum et rectam retributionem sive punitionem: quod fieri non posset, nisi remaneret liberum arbitrium. **Unde cum culpa** vel meritum remanet post mortem, necesse est etiam, quod maneat liberum arbitrium, in quo est culpa vel **meritum, et cui debetur** punitio sive retributio, et **in quo est capacitas præmii vel punitionis.**

(4) *Marsilius Ficinus*, De Immortalitate Animarum Libri xviii. (Opp. Par. 1641, fol.), an extract from which is given by *Buhle* (Gesch. der neuern Phil. Bd. ii. s. 171-341). "This work," says *Gieseler*, Dg. s. 498, "*is the one among all that are extant containing the greatest variety of proofs for the spirituality and immortality of the soul.*"

(5) Acta Concil. Reg. t. xxxiv. (Par. 1644, fol., p. 333 (quoted by *Münscher, von Cölln*, **s. 92 f.**).

§ 175.

Man in the State of Innocence before the Fall.

It was one of the characteristic features of scholasticism to waste the greatest amount of acuteness upon those parts of doctrinal theology which do not belong to the province either of psychological experience or of history, properly so called, and concerning which the sacred Scripture itself gives us only indications rather than instruction. Among such subjects were the doctrine of the angels, and that of the state of our first parents in paradise. Though both scholastics and mystics frequently applied allegorical interpretation to the biblical narrative of the primeval state (1), the former used it in such a manner as to represent the first man (Protoplast) with historical accuracy, and to describe him as he came forth from the hands of his Maker (2). In the opinion of some theologians, the *justitia originalis* was added to the *pura naturalia* as a *donum superadditum*; while others (*e.g. Thomas Aquinas*) distinguished between the purely human, and the divine which is added, only in the abstract, but made them coincide in the concrete. According to the latter notion, man was *at once* created in the full possession of the divine righteousness, and not deprived of it till *after* the fall (3). Most theologians still made a distinction between the *image* of God and *likeness* to God (4), and adventured many conjectures respecting the former, as well as man's state of innocence in general (5).—The definitions concerning the liberty of man were beset with the greatest difficulties. The fall of man would not have been possible without liberty of choice. But (according to Augustine) something more was required to constitute perfect righteousness than this liberty of choice, inasmuch as man continued in the possession of it after his fall, viz. as a liberty to do evil. But if our first parents, on account of their having true freedom, were above the temptations to sin, how could they be seduced and fall? *Anselm* here avails himself of the distinction between *will* in general and a *confirmed* or stedfast will (velle et pervelle) (6). According to *Hugo of St. Victor*, the liberty in question consisted indeed in the possibility of sinning or not sinning, but the disposition to good was stronger than the propensity to evil. Others adopted similar views (7).

(1) *John Damascene* (De fide orthodoxa, ii. c. 10, p. 175) connected the allegorical interpretation with the historical. As man himself consists of body and soul, so his first dwelling-place was αἰσθητός as well as νοητός. According to him, sensual delight in the garden, and spiritual communion with God, are correlative ideas.—*Peter Lombard* theoretically adopted the literal interpretation of the Mosaic narrative, Sent. ii. dist. 17 E, although he also considered it a type of the Church; but many of his practical expositions were allegorical, *e.g.* Dist. 24 H (in *Münscher, von Colln*, s. 94). According to him, the serpent is a type of the sensuality which still suggests sinful thoughts to man. The woman is the lower part of reason, which is first seduced, and afterwards leads man (the higher reason) into temptation. *Thomas Aquinas* also taught, P. I. qu. 102, art. 1: Ea enim, quae de Paradiso in Scriptura dicuntur, per modum narrationis historicæ proponuntur (in accordance with his hermeneutical canons, see above, § 162, note 4). On the other hand, *Scotus Erigena* more boldly raised doubts as to the literal interpretation of the narrative (De Divis. Natur. iv. 15, p. 196), and regarded it as an ideal description of the happiness which would have been the lot of mankind if our first parents had resisted temptation: Fuisse Adam temporaliter in Paradiso, priusquam de costa ejus mulier fabricaretur, dicat quis potest. . . . Nec unquam steterat, nam si saltem vel parvo spatio stetisset, necessario ad aliquam perfectionem perveniret . . . (p. 197): Non enim credibile est, eundem hominem et in contemplatione æternæ pacis stetisse et suadente femina, serpentis veneno corrupta, corruisse. See *Baur*, Versöhnungslehre, s. 127; Trin. ii. s. 306 ff.; and the remarkable interpretation of Luke x. 30, there cited. [Non ait; homo quidam erat in Jerusalem et incidit in latrones. Nam si in Jerusalem, hoc est in paradiso, humana natura permaneret, profecto in latrones, diabolum

scilicet satelitesque ejus, non incurreret. Prius ergo descendebat de paradiso, suae voluntatis irrationabili motu impulsus, et in Jericho praecipitabatur, hoc est, in defectum instabilitatemque rerum temporalium. De Divis. Naturae, iv. 15.]

(2) This led to a multitude of absurd questions respecting the nature and durability of their bodies, *e.g.* why the man had been created before the woman, and why the woman had been taken from the rib of the man; whether, and in what manner, the propagation of the race would have taken place if our first parents had continued in their state of innocence; whether their children would have inherited their original righteousness; whether more males or more females would have been born. "*What dreams! How could men so sedate and grave as monks were, or ought to have been, waste so much time upon the examination, discussion, and defence of such questions? In the Summa of Alexander of Hales this subject fills five pages in folio!*" *Cramer*, vii. s. 493.

(3) The former opinion was adopted by *Scotus Erigena*, Sent. lib. ii. dist. 39; *Bonaventura*, Sent. lib. ii. dist. 29, art. 2, qu. 2; comp. Brev. iii. 25, Cent. ii. § 2; *Hugo of St. Victor*, De Sacram. lib. i. p. 6; *Alexander of Hales*, P. II. qu. 96; comp. *Cramer*, vii. s. 494 ff. *Marheineke*, Symbolik, iii. s. 13 ff. On the contrary, the position of *Thomas Aquinas* P. I. qu. 95, art. 9), that man, *before* the fall, had never been in the condition of the pura naturalia, but, from the moment of his creation, had possessed the donum superadditum, which belonged, therefore, probably to his very nature, was more nearly allied to the view of the later Protestant theologians. See *Cramer* and *Marheineke*, l.c.; and on the other side, *Baur*, Symbolik, s. 54.

(4) *John Damasc.* adhered to the distinction drawn by the Greek Fathers, De fide orthod. ii. c. 12.—*Hugo of St. Victor*, De Sacram. P. VI. lib. i. c. 2, distinguished: . . . Imago secundum *rationem*, similitudo secundum *dilectionem*, imago secundum *cognitionem veritatis*, similitudo secundum *amorem virtutis*; vel imago secundum *scientiam*, similitudo secundum *substantiam*. . . . Imago pertinet ad *figuram*, similitudo ad *naturam*, etc. Hugo, however, restricted the image of God to the soul, and decidedly excluded the body; for the passages, see *Münscher, von Cölln*, s. 94 f.—*Peter Lombard* made a some-

what different distinction (Sent. lib. ii. dist. 16 D), by numbering dilectio among those qualities which form the *image* (memoria, intelligentia, et dilectio); he conceived the likeness to God to consist in the innocentia et justitia, quae in mente rationali naturaliter sunt. He also expressed himself more briefly **thus:** Imago consideratur in cognitione veritatis, similitudo in amore virtutis. In agreement with Hugo, he asserted, Imago pertinet ad formam, similitudo **ad** naturam.[1]

(5) First of all was man's dominion over **the** earth and **over** the animal kingdom: *Thomas Aquinas*, P. I. qu. 96; *Cramer*, vii. s. 499 f. Questions were raised, such **as**, Would Adam have possessed *all* virtues, and in what manner, **if he** had not sinned? In what respect may he be said **to** have possessed, *e.g.*, modesty, since this first entered into the **world** with sin? He did not possess it *actually*, but *habitually* (*i.e.* he possessed the disposition to it). Did man, in his state of innocence, possess affections and passions? Yes, such as **tend** to **good**; they were, however, moderate and harmonious. **Could one man** have ruled over others? No; nevertheless a pre-eminence of wisdom and righteousness might have existed, etc. **The definitions of the earlier** scholastics, such as *Anselm* **of Canterbury (Cur Deus Homo, ii. 1:** Rationalis natura justa **est facta, ut summo bono, i.e. Deo** fruendo beata esset), as well **as of the mystics,** both *before* and *after* **the time of Thomas** Aquinas, were simpler, **or** had at **least regard rather to** what **is** religious and moral. Thus *Hugo* **of** *St. Victor* conceived **the** original excellency of man, in point **of knowledge, to consist:** 1. In a cognitio perfecta omnium visibilium; **2. In a cognitio creatoris per** praesentiam contemplationis **seu per internam inspirationem;** 3. **In the** cognitio sui ipsius, qua **conditionem et ordinem et debitum suum sive** supra **se, sive**

---

[1] The mystics, and those preachers of the Middle Ages who held similar views, endeavoured to point out the image of God in the outward form by the most singular illustrations. God, said *Berthold* (quoted by *Kling*, s. 305, 306; *Wackernagel*, Lesebuch, Sp. 678), has written under the eyes of man that *He* has created him, "with flourishing letters." His eyes correspond to the two letters o in the word homo. The curved eyebrows above, and the nose between the eyes, form the letter m; h is a mere accessory letter. The ear is the letter d, "beautifully circled and flourished;" the nostrils form a Greek ι, "beautifully circled and flourished;" the mouth forms an i, "beautifully circled and flourished." *All together form the phrase* "*homo Dei.*"

in se, sive sub se non ignoraret; see *Liebner*, s. 410, Anm. 61. In reference to the will of man, there existed in his original state two blessings, the one an earthly one, the world; and the other a heavenly one, God. The former was freely given to man, the latter he was to merit. In order that man might retain the earthly blessing, and acquire the heavenly one, the præceptum naturæ was given him for the one, the **præceptum disciplinæ** (*i.e.* the command not to eat of the tree of the knowledge of good and evil) for the other. The former was inspired by nature, the latter given from without. Accordingly, man could guard against negligence (contra **negligentiam**), in respect to the external **command, by reason and foresight**; but God protected him against **violence (contra violentiam)**. Compare *Gerson*, De Meditatione, Cons. 2, p. 449 ss. (quoted by *Hundeshagen*, s. 42): Fuit ab initio bene conditæ rationalis creaturæ talis ordo ordinisque tranquillitas, quod ad nutum et merum imperium sensualitas rationi inferiori et inferior ratio superiori serviebat. Et erat ab inferioribus ad superiora pronus et facilis ascensus, faciente hoc levitate originalis justitia subvehentis sursum corda.—In the writings of *John Wessel* we meet only with occasional and disconnected statements concerning the original state of man; the most important and comprehensive is in De Orat. xi. 3, p. 184 (quoted by *Ullmann*, s. 239): "In the state of innocence there existed a necessity for breathing, eating, and sleeping; and, to counteract the dissolution which threatened man, he was permitted to eat of the fruit of the tree of life;" *i.e.*, though man was subject to certain natural restrictions, he was nevertheless free from pressing wants, from the necessity of suffering, of disease, and death; for the partaking of the fruit of the tree of life secured to him immortality.

(6) The statements of *Anselm* have more direct reference to the nature of the devil, but are also applicable to the will of *created beings* in general (*Hasse*, ii. s. 441), De Casu Diaboli, c. 2–6. *Hasse*, ii. s. 399 ff.

(7) *Hugo of St. Victor* assumed the existence of three or four kinds of liberty: 1. Man, in his *original state*, possessed the power to sin and the power not to sin (posse peccare et posse non peccare); in this is included assistance in good (adjutorium in bono), but weakness towards evil (infirmitas in malo), though

in such a manner as neither to compel him to do good, nor forcibly to restrain him from evil. 2. In the *middle state of man*[1] *after the fall*, the case is as follows:—(*a*) *Before* his restoration (ante reparationem), man lacks the divine grace (assistance) to do good, and the weakness towards evil degenerates into a propensity to evil = posse peccare et non posse non peccare. (Though **the idea of liberty is** not thereby entirely **removed, it is at** least greatly weakened.) (*b*) *After* his restoration (redemption), but *before* he is established in goodness, man possesses grace to do good and infirmity **to** do evil, i.e. posse peccare et posse non peccare (the former **because of** his liberty and infirmity, the latter because of **his liberty and** assisting grace). 3. In the *highest state of perfection*, there is both the possibility of not sinning, and the impossibility of sinning (posse non peccare et non posse peccare), not because the liberty **of** the **will or the** lowliness of nature is abolished, but because man **will never be** deprived of confirming grace, **which** admits no **sin; cap. 16** (see *Liebner*, s. 403). In the **first** state God **shares with** man, in the second man shares **with the** devil, **in the third God receives** all: **cap.** 10, ibid.— In *Raimund of Sabunde*, **too, the abstract notion of** (or destination to) freedom **is distinguished from** its **actual** use (connected **with the** distinction **between the** image **of God** and resemblance to God, comp. **note 4), tit. 239:** Item **quia** homo **debuit ita** formari, ut **posset acquirere aliquid bonum, quod nondum sibi datum fuerat. Quamvis** enim **perfectus esset in natura, tamen nondum** erat totaliter consummatus, quia aliquod **majus adhuc habere** poterat, scilicet confirmationem illius status **in quo erat, quem perdere poterat, sed non nisi voluntarie et non per violentiam . . . Si enim homo fuisset totaliter** completus **et transmutatus et consummatus in gloria, ut amplius** nihil **posset ei dari, jam per ipsum liberum arbitrium non** posset **aliquid lucrari nec mereri sibi. Et sic in natura hominis perfecta duo status sunt considerandi: scilicet status, in quo posset mereri et lucrari per ipsum liberum arbitrium, et status, in quo esset completus et consummatus in gloria;** et sic est *status meriti* et *status præmii*. **. . . Et ideo** convenientissimum **fuit, quod Deus dedit homini occasionem merendi,** nec in

---

[1] We here anticipate (for the sake of the connection, and to give all he says at once) points considered in the following sections, which should be compared.

vanum esset creatus in statu merendi. Et quia nihil est magis efficax ad merendum, quam pura obedientia seu opus factum ex pura obedientia et mera ... convenientissimum fuit, quod Deus daret præceptum homini, in quo pura obedientia appareret et exerceretur. ... Et quia magis apparet obedientia in præcepto negativo, quam affirmativo, ideo debuit esse illud mandatum prohibitivum magis quam affirmativum. ... Et ut homo maxime esset attentus ad servandum obedientiam et fugiendum inobedientiam, et firmiter constaret ei de voluntate Dei mandatis, conveniens fuit, ut Deus apponeret pœnam cum præcepto, et talem pœnam, qua non posset cogitari major, scilicet pœnam mortis. Comp. *Matzke*, Theol. des Raim. von Sabunde, s. 79.—*John Wessel* defined the liberty which man possessed in his original state, so as to ascribe to him the undiminished power of attaining and performing, without the assistance of others, or the influence of education, that which the idea of humanity implies, viz. such a perfection as elevated him to communion with God; see *Ullmann*, s. 240 f.

§ 176.

The Fall of Man, and Sin in general.

One of the chief questions, still debated, was, In what the fall of our first parents consisted, and in what the nature of sin in general consists? Subordinate questions, such as whether Adam's sin or Eve's were the greater? were only occasionally made the subject of discussion (1). Even during the present period there were some, and towards its close *Agrippa of Nettersheim*, in particular, who asserted that the sin of the first man consisted in the awakening of his carnal propensities, and who endeavoured to establish their opinion by the aid of allegorical interpretation (2). But the prevailing view of the Church teachers was, that sin is not to be sought in any particular act, but in the disobedience of man to God, which had its root principally in pride (3). After the example of Augustine, the definitions respecting the nature of sin were for the most part negative (4). *Hugo of St. Victor* endeavoured to explain the nature of sin from the conflict of **two** tendencies in man, the one of which (appetitus justi) **is drawn to God**, the other (appetitus commodi) to the world. The latter propensity is **not** evil in itself, but the abandonment of the right medium is **the** cause of sin (5). The mystics supposed sin generally to consist **in** this, that man, as a creature, wills to exist **for** *himself*; and **the** author of the **work** entitled "Deutsche Theologie," carried this notion so far as to say, that in this respect the fall of man **is like** that of the devil (6). The further enumeration and classification of particular sins, their division into sins mortal and **venial**, belongs rather to the history of ethics than to that of **doctrines** (7).

(1) *Anselm*, De Peccato Orig. c. 9. Although Eve first transgressed **the** divine command, Adam, as the real father **of the human race, is also the** father of sin. Many of the **reasons urged on either side are to be** found **in** the works of *Peter Lombard* (lib. ii. dist. 22) and *Thomas Aquinas* (P. II. qu. 163, art. 4). *Bonaventura* (Brevil. iii. 3, 4) divides the **guilt between the two, but says that** the punishment was **double in the case of the woman.** On the contrary, according to *Agrippa of Nettesheim*, Adam **sinned knowingly,** Eve was **only led astray** (Opp. t. ii. p. 528; in *Meiners'* Biographie, s. 233). According to *Tauler* (Predigten, i. s. 61), **theologians assert that we** should have suffered **no harm** if Eve alone had **eaten the fruit.** On the **further question of the** scholastics, **whether sin would have been communicated to Eve if** Adam **had transgressed the divine command** *before* the creation of **his wife,** comp. *Cramer*, vii. s. 534 ff. On the singular **opinions of** *Pulleyn*, see ibid. Bd. vi. s. 481 ff.

(2) Disputatio de Orig. Pecc. in Opp. t. ii. p. 553 ss. (qu. by *Meiners*, l.c. s. 254, Anm. 3); he regarded the serpent as **the membrum serpens, lubricum.** The opinion, according to **which sin consists in the first instance in** sensuality, **was most decidedly opposed by** *Anselm*, De Pecc. Orig. c. 4: Nec **isti appetitus, quos Ap. carnem vocat (Gal. v.) . . .** justi vel **injusti sunt per se considerandi.** Non enim justum faciunt

vel injustum sentientem, sed injustum tantum voluntate, cum non debet, consentientem. Non eos *sentire, sed* eis *consentire* peccatum est.

(3) *John Damasc.* De fide orth. ii. 30 (in calce): ὅθεν καὶ θεότητος ἐλπίδι ὁ ψεύστης δελεάζει τὸν ἄθλιον, καὶ πρὸς τὸ ἴδιον τῆς ἐπάρσεως ὕψος ἀναγαγών, πρὸς τὸ ὅμοιον καταφέρει τῆς πτώσεως βάραθρον.—According to *Anselm*, every act of self-will of the creature is treason against God; De fide trin. c. 5 (*Hasse*, ii. s. 306): Quicunque propria voluntate utitur, ad similitudinem Dei per rapinam nititur, et Deum propria dignitate et singulari excellentia privare, quantum in ipso est, convincitur.—*Peter Lombard*, lib. ii. dist. 22. *Thomas Aquinas*, P. II. qu. 163. Nevertheless, sensuality (the desire after the forbidden fruit) was also mentioned as a subordinate principle; see *Taulers* Predigten, i. s. 51, 79; *Cramer*, vii. s. 524.

(4) *John Damasc.* lib. ii. c. 30: Ἡ γὰρ κακία οὐδὲν ἕτερόν ἐστιν, εἰ μὴ ἀναχώρησις τοῦ ἀγαθοῦ.—*John Scotus Erigena* looked upon sin from the negative point of view, by comparing it to a leprosy which infects humanity, but which is to be removed by divine grace (De Div. Nat. v. 5, p. 230), and then continues as follows: Magisque dicendum, quod ipsa natura quae ad imaginem Dei facta est, suae pulcritudinis vigorem integritatemque essentiae *inquoquam* perdidit, neque perdere potest. Divina siquidem forma semper incommutabilis permanet, capax tamen corruptibilium poena peccati facta est quibusquid vero naturali corpori ex concretionibus elementorum et animae ex sordibus irrationabilium motuum superadditum est, in fluxu et corruptione semper est. In his opinion, "*Sin is only a vanishing and self-abolishing element, and therefore has not the significance of a moral act;*" *Baur*, Versöhnungsl. s. 135; comp. also *Baur*, Trin. ii. s. 305: "*Sin is to him not something accidental, originating in time, but originating with creation and with human nature.*" (A view allied to pantheism.)—On the other hand, *Abélard* (in his treatise, Scito Teipsum), attaching particular importance to the act as performed with the conscious approval of the person acting, makes sin (formally) depend on the *intention* with which anything is done; see the extracts given by *De Wette*, Sittenlehre, iii. s. 124 ff.—*Anselm's* definitions of sin are also of a negative character; Cur Deus Homo, i. 11: Non est

itaque aliud peccare, quam Deo non reddere debitum; De Conceptu Virginali, c. 26; Justitiæ debitæ nuditas; also in De Causa Diaboli, c. 1 ss. See *Hasse*, ii. s. 394 ff. *Münscher, von Cölln*, i. s. 121 ff.

(5) According to *Hugo of St. Victor* (P. VI. lib. i. c. 1–22, qu. by *Liebner*, s. 412 ff.), the first sin consisted in a twofold disobedience to the **law of** nature and the law of discipline. **Having laid** that basis, he proceeds to a further scientific examination of the nature **of** sin. He supposed it to consist **in a** discord between the appetitus justi **and** the appetitus commodi, both of which are innate in man. **In the fall,** man abandoned the right medium, desiring the higher **good, rising** above himself, and striving, in the presumption and pride **of** his heart, both to be equal to God, and to possess Him before the appointed time. Thus it happened that he also lost the right medium in his **striving** after the lower good; for as the mind **of man, which** held likewise the reins over the flesh, did not **succeed in** its higher **effort,** and fell, as it were, out of the **right medium, he let fall also the** reins over the flesh, and let **it go without** measure **and precaution, in** consequence **of which all** external **evils broke in upon** him (transgressio **superioris et** inferioris appetitus). **The** *former* loss was **accordingly** culpa, the *latter* both culpa **and** pœna; the one **was a loss for the** spirit, the other for the **flesh, since** man **retained** the irregular appetitus commodi without obtaining **the commodum** itself. Abandoning the appetitus **justi,** man **lost at** the **same** time the justitia, which is **not** only insepar**able from it, but also consists in it**; nothing was left to him **but the unsatisfied appetitus** commodi, which is here on earth **a foretaste of hell, a necessitas** concupiscendi, etc., c. **11–22.** *" From what is said above, it follows that evil* does not consist *either in the object desired (for man always desires a good even in the concupiscentia), nor in the act of desiring, in putting the faculty of desire into exercise (for this is a gift of God), but only in not keeping the proper* medium *in our desires,"* Liebner, l.c. **Hugo of St. Victor also endeavoured to give an answer to the question, How the first sin could possibly have been committed by one who was created good? Adam could not have sinned, either nolens or volens. He only** *ceased* **to desire the good (justum velle desiit), c. 12. Conformed to this are his**

negative definitions, c. 16: Et ideo malum nihil est, cum id, quod esse deberet, non est; and P. V. lib. i. c. 26: Peccatum nec substantia est, nec de substantia, sed privatio boni (see *Liebner*, s. 415).—On the views of *Wessel* respecting the nature of sin (want of love), compare Ullmann, l.c. s. 24.

(6) Deutsche Theologie, cap. 2. " The Scriptures, faith, and truth say, that sin is only the turning of the creature from the unchangeable good to the changeable—that is, from the perfect to the imperfect and incomplete, and principally to itself. Now observe: when nature takes to itself anything that is good, or appropriates it as real being (*i.e.* when it imagines that it has its being from itself, and wants to be something, when it is nothing); or as life (*i.e.* when he imagines that he has life in himself); or as knowledge (*i.e.* when it imagines that it knows much and can do much); in short, when it endeavours to obtain all that is called good, imagining that it is the same, or that the same belongs to it, in all such cases it apostatizes. For what else did the devil do, or what was his apostasy or his fall, if not that he thought himself something, and presumed to be something, and pretended that something belonged to him? This presumption to be something, his selfhood [*Ich*] (*i.e.* his self-love), his me [*Mich*] (*i.e.* his self-will), his to me [*Mir*] (*i.e.* his self-esteem), and his mine [*Mein*] (*i.e.* his own good), were, and are still, his apostasy and his fall." Cap. 3: " What else did Adam do than what Lucifer does? They say that Adam fell and was lost because he ate the apple. I say: He fell by accepting, assuming, or appropriating to himself that which belonged to God, viz. by his ego (*i.e.* his self-love), by his me (*i.e.* his self-will), by his mine (*i.e.* because of the good which he had usurped), and by his to me (*i.e.* for his own honour, wisdom, etc.). *Though he had eaten seven apples*, if there had been no appropriation or assumption, he would not have fallen; as soon as he appropriated the apple as his, he fell, *even though he had never bitten it.*"

(7) *De Wette*, Christ. Sittenl. iii. s. 147 ff. (after *Thomas Aquinas*).

§ 177.

Consequences of the First Sin. Original Sin. Freedom of the Will.

The more intimate the supposed connection between the primitive state of **man and the** justitia originalis, the greater was the fall. The theologians of **the Greek** Church contented themselves with believing in a weakening **of the moral** power of man, and retained the earlier **notions concerning** his liberty (1). In the Western Church almost **all the schoolmen** followed Augustine (2), although several of them (consciously or unconsciously) adopted opinions which, in many essential points, differed from his fundamental principles. Thus *Abelard*, **among the** earlier scholastics, understood by the hereditary **character of the** first **sin not** the sin itself, but its punish**ment (3).** Several of the **later** schoolmen also, particularly *Scotus* **and his followers, inclined** towards Semi-Pelagianism, **while the Thomists adhered more** strictly to the definitions **of Augustine (4). The mystics** in general bewailed the unfathomable depravity **of the old Adam, but avoided** indulging **in subtle** definitions (5). And, lastly, **the evangelical theo**logians, previous to the age of the Reformation, such **as** *John Wessel*, also looked upon the unregenerate as children **of wrath,** although they made a distinction between the responsibility for original sin and for actual transgression (6).

(1) *John* **Dam. De** fide orth. ii. c. 12, p. 178 :[1] Ἐποίησε δὲ αὐτὸν φύσει ἀναμάρτητον καὶ θελήσει αὐτεξούσιον· ἀναμάρτητον δέ φημι, οὐχ ὡς μὴ ἐπιδεχόμενον ἁμαρτίαν (μόνον γὰρ τὸ θεῖον ἁμαρτίας ἐστὶν ἀνεπίδεκτον). ἀλλ᾿ οὐχ ὡς ἐν τῇ φύσει τὸ ἁμαρτάνειν ἔχοντα, ἐν τῇ προαιρέσει δὲ μᾶλλον· ἤτοι ἐξουσίαν ἔχοντα μένειν καὶ προκόπτειν ἐν τῷ ἀγαθῷ, τῇ θείᾳ συνεργούμενον χάριτι, ὡσαύτως καὶ τρέπεσθαι ἐκ τοῦ καλοῦ, καὶ ἐν τῷ κακῷ γίνεσθαι, τοῦ Θεοῦ παραχωροῦντος διὰ τὸ

[1] The passage in question refers, in the first instance, to the first man; but, as the context shows, still admits of application to men in general.

αὐτεξούσιον. Οὐκ ἀρετὴ γὰρ τὸ βίᾳ γινόμενον. Comp. c. 22, p. 187 s., c. 24, 27. ... Further, c. 27, p. 194 s. : Εἰ δὲ τοῦτο, ἐξ ἀνάγκης παρυφίσταται τῷ λογικῷ τὸ αὐτεξούσιον· ἢ γὰρ οὐκ ἔσται λογικόν, ἢ λογικὸν ὂν κύριον ἔσται πράξεων καὶ αὐτεξούσιον. Ὅθεν καὶ τὰ ἄλογα οὐκ εἰσιν αὐτεξούσια· ἄγονται γὰρ μᾶλλον ὑπὸ τῆς φύσεως, ἤπερ ἄγουσι· διὸ οὐδὲ ἀντιλέγουσι τῇ φυσικῇ ὀρέξει, ἀλλ᾽ ἅμα ὀρεχθῶσί τινος, ὁρμῶσι πρὸς τὴν πρᾶξιν. Ὁ δὲ ἄνθρωπος, λογικὸς ὤν, ἄγει μᾶλλον τὴν φύσιν ἤπερ ἄγεται· διὸ καὶ ὀρεγόμενος, εἴπερ ἐθέλοι, ἐξουσίαν ἔχει ἀναχαιτίσαι τὴν ὄρεξιν, ἢ ἀκολουθῆσαι αὐτῇ. Ὅθεν τὰ μὲν ἄλογα οὐδὲ ἐπαινεῖται, οὐδὲ ψέγεται· ὁ δὲ ἄνθρωπος καὶ ἐπαινεῖται καὶ ψέγεται. C. 30, p. 198 : ὁ Θεὸς οὐ γὰρ θέλει τὴν κακίαν γίνεσθαι, οὐδὲ βιάζεται τὴν ἀρετήν. — Notice the usage of παρὰ φύσιν and κατὰ φύσιν, ibid. p. 100, and compare it with Augustine's usage of natura. — In his opinion, the effects of the fall consist in this, that man is θανάτῳ ὑπεύθυνος καὶ φθορᾷ καὶ πόνῳ καθυποβληθήσεται καὶ ταλαίπωρον ἕλκων βίον (ibid.). In the moral aspect man is γυμνωθεὶς τῆς χάριτος καὶ τὴν πρὸς Θεὸν παρρησίαν ἀπεκδυσάμενος (lib. iii. c. 1). Comp. iv. 20. — John Damascene was also followed by the rest of the Greek theologians, *Theodore Studita, Theophylact, Euthymius Zigabenus, Nicetas Choniates,* and *Nicolas of Methone.* The views of the latter (according to his Refut.) are given by *Ullmann,* l.c. s. 86 ff. *He* also laid great stress upon the freedom of the will, and held that the divine image was only obscured by the fall.

(2) *Anselm* expressed himself very strongly in favour of the imputation of original sin, to the exclusion of all milder views, De Orig. Pecc. c. 3 : Si vero dicitur originale peccatum non esse absolute dicendum peccatum, sed cum additamento *originale* peccatum, sicut pictus homo non vere homo est, sed vere est homo pictus, profecto sequitur : quia infans, qui nullum habet peccatum nisi originale, mundus est e peccato : nec fuit solus inter homines filius virginis in utero matris et nascens de matre sine peccato : et aut non damnatur infans, qui moritur sine baptismo, nullum habens peccatum præter originale, aut sine peccato damnatur. *Sed nihil horum accipimus.* Quare omne peccatum est injustitia, et originale peccatum est absolute peccatum, unde sequitur, quod est

injustitia. Item si Deus non damnat nisi propter injustitiam, damnat autem aliquem propter originale peccatum: ergo non est aliud originale peccatum, quam injustitia. Quod si ita est, originale peccatum non est aliud quam injustitia, i. e. absentia debitæ justitiæ, etc. — Nevertheless, it is not the sin of Adam as such, but man's *own* sin which is imputed to him, c. 25: Quapropter cum damnatur infans pro peccato originali, damnatur **non pro** peccato Adæ, sed pro **suo**; nam si ipse non haberet suum **peccatum,** non damnaretur. — He opposed the theory of the *material* propagation of sin (by traducianism) in what follows, **c. 7** (compare above, § 173, note 4): Sicut in **Adam** omnes peccavimus, quando ille peccavit: non quia tunc peccavimus ipsi, qui nondum eramus, sed quia de illo futuri eramus, **et** tunc facta est illi necessitas, ut cum essemus, peccaremus (Rom. 5). Simili modo de immundo semine, "in iniquitatibus **et** in peccatis concipi" potest homo intelligi, non quod in semine sit immunditia peccati, aut peccatum sive iniquitas; **sed** quia ab ipso **semine** et ipsa conceptione, ex qua incipit **homo** esse, accipit necessitatem, **ut** cum habebit animam **rationalem,** habeat peccati immunditiam, quæ non est aliud **quam** peccatum et iniquitas. **Nam** etsi ex vitiosa concupi- **scentia** semine generetur infans, non tamen magis est in semine **culpa, quam** est in sputo **vel in** sanguine, **si** quis mala volun- **tate exspuit** aut de sanguine **suo** aliquid **emittit**; non enim sputum **aut** sanguis, sed mala **voluntas arguitur.**[1] — On the question how far we can say that men **have sinned** *in* Adam, compare **chap. i.** and ii., and chap. xxi., xxii. Anselm also **thought that** there **was** a kind **of** mutual **action** between **natural sin and personal sin,** c. 26: Sicut **persona** propter **naturam peccatrix nascitur,** ita natura **propter** personam magis **peccatrix redditur.** Comp. *Hasse*, ii. s. 443 ff.—Concerning *the mode of the propagation of sin,* viz. **whether it** is communicated in **the first instance to the soul or to the body, etc.,** the scholastics

---

[1] Anselm would not have admitted the force of the argument frequently urged in favour of original sin, viz. that certain moral dispositions, which may be called hereditary sins, are propagated like certain physical disorders, inasmuch as he taught, c. 23 (in connection with what has been said above), that *only* the sin of Adam is transmitted to his posterity, but not that of parents to their children. His reasoning was quite logical, because the idea of original sin would otherwise become too relative! On the relation of Anselm's theory to the later Lutheran (Flacian?), see *Möhler*, Kleine Schriften, i. s. 167.

differed in their opinions. Comp. *Münscher, von Cölln*, s. 132 (especially the opinion of *Peter Lombard*, lib. ii. dist. 31): [In concupiscentia et libidine concipitur caro formanda in corpus prolis. Unde caro ipsa quæ concipitur in vitiosa concupiscentia polluitur et corrumpitur: ex cujus contactu anima cum infunditur maculam trahit qua polluitur et fit rea, id est vitium concupiscentiæ, quod est originale peccatum].—Some of the later theologians, following Augustine and Anselm, taught similar views, *e.g. Savonarola*: Quid autem est peccatum originale, nisi privatio justitiæ originalis? Ideo homo, conceptus et natus in hujusmodi peccato, totus obliquus est, totus curvus ... Peccatum itaque originale radix est omnium peccatorum, fomes enim omnium iniquitatum (Medit. in Psalm. p. 17, qu. by *Meier*, Savonarola, s. 260).

(3) Since *Abélard* maintained that the free consent of man was necessary to constitute sin (§ 176, note 4), he could not attribute sin, in the proper sense of the word, to new-born infants; yet he did not feel disposed to deny original sin altogether. He therefore took the word "sin" in a twofold sense, applying it to the punishment as well as to sin itself. Infants have a part only in the former, but not in the latter. Nor did Abélard see how unbelief in Christ could be imputed to infants, or to those to whom the gospel is not announced: Scito te ipsum, c. 14 (qu. by *De Wette*, Sittenlehre, iii. s. 131). He also praised the virtues of the nobler Greeks, especially of the philosophers, in particular of the Platonists; Theol. Christ. ii. p. 1211; compare above, § 158, note 2. *Neander*, Der heil. Bernhard, s. 125.

(4) This difference is connected with the one above alluded to respecting the original state of man (§ 175). As the justitia originalis, according to *Duns Scotus*, was not so intimately united with the nature of man as Thomas Aquinas supposed, the loss of the dona supernaturalia was less great, and might take place without such painful rupture as human nature must undergo, in the strict Augustinian view; see Sentent. lib. ii. dist. 29. On the other hand, *Thomas Aquinas* expressed himself as follows: Summ. P. II. 1, qu. 85, art. 3 (in *Münscher, von Cölln*, s. 134): Per justitiam originalem perfecte ratio continebat inferiores animæ vires, et ipsa ratio perficiebatur a Deo ei subjecta. Hæc autem originalis

justitia subtracta est per peccatum primi parentis . . . et ideo omnes vires animae remanent quodammodo destitutae proprio ordine, quo naturaliter ordinantur ad virtutem, et ipsa destitutio **vulneratio** *naturae* **dicitur.** Comp. *Bonaventura*, Brevil. iii. 6 ss.

(5) Deutsche Theologie, c. **14**: "He who lives a selfish **life, and according to the old man, is, and** may justly be **called, the** child of Adam; **even if he** have sunk so deep as to be the child and brother **of the devil.** . . . All who follow Adam in his disobedience are dead, and can be made alive **only** in Christ, that is, by obedience. **As long as a** man is Adam, and Adam's child, he is his ownself without **God.** . . . Hence it follows, that all the children of Adam are **dead to** God. . . . We shall never repent of sin, nor commence a better life, until we return to obedience. . . . Disobedience **is** sin itself," etc.

(6) *Wessel*, De Magn. Pass. c. 59, and other passages quoted by *Ullmann*, s. 244.—*Savonarola* taught in a similar manner **concerning the posterity** of Adam: Rationem culpae non **habent, reatu non carent.** (Triumph. Cruc. lib. iii. c. 9, p. 280 ss., qu. by *Meier*, s. 261.)

> Besides original sin, there were yet other effects of the fall (death and evil) which had before this been made prominent by the early Church, and to which even a greater importance was attached, on account of their connection with the imputation of sin. Death itself did not actually enter into the world till later, but *mortality* came at the same time with sin. On the question, in how far God may be said to have been the author of death, etc., see *Cramer*, vii. s. 528. According to *Scotus Erigena*, the distinction of the sexes is a consequence of sin; De Div. Nat. ii. 5, p. 49: Reatu suae praevaricationis obrutus, naturae suae divisionem in masculum et feminam est passus et . . . in pecorinam corruptibilemque ex masculo et foemina numerositatem justo judicio redactus est.

§ 178.

Exceptions from Original Sin. The Immaculate Conception of Mary.

Laboulaye, Die Frage der unbefleckten Empfängniss, Berl. 1854. *Jul. Müller* in the Deutsche Zeitschrift f. christl. Wissenschaft, vi. 1. † * *Passaglia*, De Immaculato Deiparae semper Virginis Conceptu, 3 tom. Rom. 1854-55. [J. Perrone, De Immacul. B. V. Mariae Conceptu, Rom. 1848.] *Preuss*, Die römische Lehre von der unbefleckten Empfängniss, Berlin 1865.

The earlier notion, advanced not only by the heretic Pelagius, but also by the orthodox Athanasius, according to which some individuals had remained free from the general corruption, was not likely longer to receive countenance (1). It was only the one personality of the mother of God, who, having long been elevated above the level of humanity by an excessive adoration (the *Hyperdulia*), was to share the privilege with her son Jesus of appearing as sinless in history; although theologians of weight raised their voices against such a doctrine (2). In the course of the twelfth century, the dogma of the immaculate conception of Mary gained great authority, in the first instance in France. But when the canons of Lyons instituted (A.D. 1140) a special festival in honour of that doctrine, by which a new Lady-day was added to those already in existence, *Bernard of Clairvaux*, clearly perceiving that thus the specific difference between our Saviour and the rest of mankind was endangered, strongly opposed both the new doctrine and the festival (3). *Albert the Great, Bonaventura,* **Thomas Aquinas**, and with him the order of the Dominicans in general, were also zealous in opposition (4). On the other hand, the Franciscan monk *Duns Scotus* endeavoured to refute their objections, and to demonstrate, by subtle reasoning, that the greatness of the Redeemer, so far from being lessened, was augmented by supposing that He Himself was the cause of this sinlessness in the nature of Mary; yet even *Scotus* only maintained that the immaculate conception was the more probable among the different possibilities (5). The Church hesitated for a long time without coming to a decision (6). Pope Sixtus IV. at last got out of the difficulty by confirming the festival of the immaculate conception, while he declared that the doctrine itself should not be called heretical, and allowed those who differed to retain their own views (7). Of course the controversy did not come to an end, especially as the tendency of the age was, on the whole, favourable to the dogma (8).

(1) Thus *Anselm*, De Pecc. Orig. c. 16, drew a distinct line between the birth of John the Baptist (which was also relatively miraculous, but did not on that account render him sinless) and the incarnation of the Redeemer (which excluded original sin). Sanctification (*i.e.* the being made holy) in the mother's womb does not **exclude** original sin; and this must be specially noted if **we would** avoid confusion in the matter. So **it** could be, and **was assumed, that** Mary remained free from *actual* sin, without being declared **free** from original sin. See *Gieseler*, Dg. s. 538 f. *Julius Müller*, l.c. **s. 6.**

(2) Concerning the cultus of Mary in general, see § 188 on the worship of saints.—The controversy on the **immaculate** conception was preceded by that carried on between *Paschasius Radbertus* and *Ratramnus* [or Bertram] concerning the virginity of Mary. Comp. § 179 towards the end (Christology). *Radbert* had already maintained that Mary was sanctificata in utero matris (in *W. Echery*, Spic. tom. i. p. 46); **but it** is difficult **to** define precisely what he understood by **that expression** (compare the following note). It was, however, **not only the cultus of the** Virgin as such, which led to **the supposition of her** immaculate conception, but this seemed **a necessary inference from other** doctrinal premisses. Theologians so acute as the scholastics could not but be aware, **that, in order to** explain **the miracle of** Christ's sinlessness **on physical** grounds, **it was not** sufficient **to assert that man** had **no part in** His generation; **for so long as His mother was supposed to be** stained with original **sin, it was impossible to deny that she** had part therein, unless they **had** recourse, **after the manner of the** Docetæ (Valentinians), **to a mere birth** διὰ σωλῆνος **(comp. vol. I. §** 65). *Anselm* endeavoured to **avoid this difficulty by leaving the physical aspect of** original sin **more or less out of the question (comp. the preceding** section), **De Pecc. Orig. c. 8 and c. 11. He also concedes unreservedly, that even a** *sinful* **mother might have conceived the Redeemer without sin. Yet still he considers it was more** fitting (decens **erat) that Mary should be purified from sin** before the Saviour **of the world was conceived in her: De Concep.** Virg. cap. 18, **and Cur Deus Homo, ii. 16 s.** *Boso* **declares** decidedly *against* **the immaculate conception: Virgo tamen ipsa, unde** assumtus **est, est in iniquitatibus concepta, et in peccatis** concepit eam

mater ejus, et cum originali peccato nata est, quoniam et ipsa in Adam peccavit, in quo omnes peccaverunt. To this Anselm replies: Virgo autem illa, de qua ille homo (Christus) assumtus est, fuit de illis, qui ante nativitatem ejus per eum mundati sunt a peccatis, et in ejus ipsa munditia de illa assumtus est. Comp. the conclusion of chap. 16: Quoniam matris munditia, per quam mundus est, non fuit nisi ab illo, *ipse quoque per se ipsum et a se mundus fuit*. And chap. 17: . . . per quam (scil. mortem Jesu Christi) et illa virgo, de qua natus est, et alii multi mundati sunt a peccato. Comp. *Hasse*, ii. 461 and 556. *Müller*, l.c. s. 12 (with reference to the interpretation of the passage by Gabriel Biel, Sent. lib. iii. dist. 3, qu. 1).

(3) *Bernardi* Ep. 174, ad Canonicos Lugdunenses (qu. by *Gieseler*, ii. 2, s. 429; *Münscher*, *von Colln*, s. 136; *Laboulaye*, l.c. s. 16 ff.). *He*, too, admitted that Mary was sanctified in the womb (as Paschasius taught), but he did not from this draw the inference that she was free from original sin: Quatenus adversus originale peccatum haec ipsa sanctificatio valuerit, non temere dixerim—and continues as follows: Etsi quibus vel paucis filiorum hominum datum est cum sanctitate *nasci*, non tamen et *concipi*, ut uni sane servaretur sancti prærogativa conceptus, qui omnes sanctificaret, solusque absque *peccato veniens* purgationem faceret peccatorum, etc. [*Peter Lombard*, Liber Sent. iii. dist. 3 sq., says of the flesh of Mary, which our Lord assumed, that "it was previously obnoxious to sin, like the other flesh of the Virgin, but cleansed by the operation of the Holy Spirit." "The Holy Ghost, coming into Mary, cleansed her from sin." *Alexander of Hales*, Summa, Pars iii. qu. 2, membr. 2, art. 1, 4: "It was necessary that the blessed Virgin in her generation should contract sin from her parents;" "she was sanctified in the womb." *Perrone* attempts to set aside these opinions, and that of Aquinas and others (below), by the position that these mediæval doctors refer to the first or active conception (the marital act), and not to the second conception (the infusion of the soul). But *Aquinas* says that the infusion of grace is "after the infusion of the soul;" and that "before the infusion of the soul the Virgin was not sanctified;" and *Alexander of Hales* and *Bonaventura* have similar statements.]

(4) *Albert Mag.* Sent. lib. iii. dist. 3. *Thomas Aquinas* (Summa, P. III. qu. 27, art. 2) affirms a sanctification in the womb, but only after the infusion of the soul into the embryo. But the lust of sin is not thereby wholly destroyed—secundum essentiam, which was the case **only in** the conception of Christ, yet the concupiscentia is restrained quoad exercitium et operationem. Only later, when Christ was conceived, did the holiness of what she bore **work also** upon the mother, wholly annulling the bias to sin. Comp. *Gieseler*, Dg. s. 560; *Jul. Müller*, l.c. *Bonaventura*, too, with all his enthusiastic veneration for Mary, did not consider her free from original sin: Sent. lib. iii. dist. 3, art. 1, qu. 2: Teneamus **secundum** quod communis opinio tenet, Virginis sanctificationem fuisse post originalis peccati contractionem (*Münscher, von Cölln*, ii. s. 136).

(5) Sent. lib. iii. dist. 3, **qu. 1,** and dist. 18, qu. 1 (qu. by *Gieseler*); see *Schröckh*, Kg. xxxiii. s. 362 ff. *Cramer*, vii. s. 567 ff. *Scotus* takes his departure from different possibilities: Deus *potuit* facere quod ipsa nunquam fuisset in peccato originali; *potuit* etiam fecisse, ut tantum in uno instanti esset in peccato; *potuit* etiam facere ut per tempus aliquod esset in peccato et in ultimo illius temporis purgaretur. And then he finds it *probable* to attribute to her the most excellent of these possibilities, according to the argumentum congruentiæ seu decentiæ. See *Laboulay*, l.c. s. 22. Scotus at any rate expressed himself with reserve, and even the Franciscans did not at first receive the doctrine unconditionally.—*Alvarus Pelagius* (about A.D. 1330) still calls it nova et phantastica. But soon the jealousy of the orders mingled in the controversy, and even visions on both sides were brought to support and refute the dogma. Thus St. Bridget (about A.D. 1370) testified *for* the doctrine; and St. Catharine of Siena, as a member of the order of St. Dominic, had visions *against* it.

(6) The festival spread, although the council of Oxford (A.D. 1222) pronounced against its necessity. In the thirteenth century it was widely observed, but only as the festum *conceptionis* in general, and not as the festum conceptionis *immaculatæ*; see the explanation of it in Durantis Rationale Div. Offic. libr. vii. c. 7 (in *Gieseler*, Dg. s. 559). [*Aquinas* vindicates the festival

as including a reference to the sanctity of Mary, but on the ground that the time of her sanctification could not be accurately assigned; and he opposes the immaculate conception itself, as derogatory to the dignity of Christ.] At the Synod of Paris (1387) the Spanish Dominican *John de Montesono* maintained that it was *against* the faith to assume that original sin did not extend to all men, Mary included. But the university condemned this position, as well as others of this divine. Still more definite than the Paris synod was that of Basel, in favour of the dogma, Sess. xxxvi. (Sept. 17, 1439), in *Harduini* Conce. t. viii. Col. 1266: Nos. ... doctrinam illam dis-erentem gloriosam virginem Dei genitricem Mariam, præveniente et operante divini numinis gratia singulari, nunquam actualiter subjacuisse originali peccato, sed immunem semper fuisse ab omni originali et actuali culpa sanctamque et immaculatam, tamquam piam et consonam cultui ecclesiastico, fidei catholicæ, rectæ rationi, et sacræ scripturæ, ab omnibus catholicis approbandum fore, tenendam et amplectendam diffinimus et declaramus, nullique de cætero licitum esse in contrarium prædicare seu docere. (The festival was fixed on December 8.) The Dominicans, however, adhered to their opposition; and particularly the Dominican *Torquemada* (Turrecremata). The decrees of Basel could not be considered as binding, because this council was held to be schismatical; and it was the very men who guided that council, as *D'Ailly* and *Gerson*, who maintained the new dogma. Even at the Council of Constance, Gerson proposed to introduce also a festival in honour of the immaculate conception of St. Joseph! (*Müller*, l.c. s. 8.)

(7) See the bulls of Pope Sixtus IV., dated February 27, A.D. 1477, and September 4, A.D. 1483 (Grave nimis), in Extravagant. Commun. lib. iii. tit. 12, cap. 1 and 2 (qu. by *Münscher*, *von Cölln*, s. 138 f. Comp. *Gieseler*, ii. 4, s. 338 f.).

(8) Even those who afterwards espoused the cause of the Reformation were *zealous advocates* of the doctrine in question, such as *Manuel*, a poet of Bern, who wrote on the occasion of the scandalous affair of Jetzer; compare his Lied von der reinen unbefleckten Empfängniss, in the work of *Grüneisen*. Nic. Manuel, s. 297 ff., where he also quotes the Fathers as

authorities, even Anselm and Thomas Aquinas,[1] and then proceeds thus:—

Auch miltigklich
und sicherlich
der christen mensch daz
　　glaubet,
daz gott d' herr,
on widersperr,
seyn muter hat bedawet
　　(begabet)
mit heiligkeit,
gnadrich erfreit,
sunst wer sye vndg'legen
sein zorn ins teufels pflegen,
daz nit mocht seyn,
d' lilien reyn,
von dorn behut,
hellischer flut.
In ewigkeit bestandtlich
bistu allein,
christliche ein,
behalten hast gar trewlich.

Die sunn ihr schein
offt leytet eyn
in unflatiges kote,
belibt doch keck
on mass und fleck
in irer schon on note.
Auch gold on luft,
in erdes cluft,
wechst unverseret glantze.
Also beleib auch gantze
Maria hoch
on erbsünd boch (poch — doch)
an sel und leib,
vors teufels streyt
und gottes zorn gefreyet.
Gottlicher gwalt
in ir heym stalt,
und sye vor unfal weyhet.
　　etc.

---

[1] Anselmus mer,
　　in seyner leer,
　　von dir hat schon betrachtet.
　　Er haltet nit
　　liebhabers sitt,
　　der deyn hoch fest verachtet,
　　das dich gantz clor
　　eert preisst fürwor,
　　entpfangen on all sünde,
　　　　　　etc.
Thomas Aquin
halt von dir fin,
du seysst die reinst uff erden,
on schuld und sünd,

fur Adams kind,
gefreyet billich werden,
in der täglich,
auch nicht tödtlich,
keyn erbsünd mocht beliben.
Desgleichen thuud auch scriben
Scotus subtil,
d' lerer vil,
die schul Paris,
mit grossem fliss,
zu Basel ists beschlossen.
Die kristlich kilch,
mit bistumb glich,
halt das gantz unverdross. a.

FOURTH DIVISION.

CHRISTOLOGY AND SOTERIOLOGY.

§ 179.

Christology in the Greek Church. The Adoptianist Controversy in the West. Nihilianism.

*Dorner, Entwicklungsgeschichte der Christologie, s. 106 ff. *Ch. G. F. Walch*, Historia Adoptianorum, Gott. 1755. *Frobenii* Dissertatio Historica de Haeresi Elipandi et Felicis (in his edition of the works of *Alcuin*, t. i. p. 923 ss). [*Huber*, Joh. Scotus Erigena, München 1861.]

AFTER the Monothelite controversy in the East had been brought to a close, no new doubts arose thence respecting the Church doctrine of *two natures and two wills in one person.* But, in the course of the controversy respecting images, the question, whether it was right to represent Christ in a bodily form, gave rise to a renewed discussion concerning the relation of our human nature to the divine. *John Damascene*, in particular, endeavoured to reconcile the duality of natures and wills with the unity of person, by regarding the divine nature as the basis of the personality, and by illustrating the mutual relation in which the two natures stand to each other, through the use of the phrases τρόπος ἀντιδόσεως and περιχώρησις (1). The Greek theologians in general adopted his views (2). The orthodox doctrine was again endangered by the *Adoptianist* interpretation of the Sonship of Christ, advanced by several Spanish bishops, especially *Elipandus of Toledo* and *Felix of Urgella*, whom *Alcuin* and others successfully combated. The Adoptianist theory, by making a distinction between an adopted son and a natural one, leaned towards Nestorianism, though its peculiar modification admitted a milder interpretation (3). *Peter Lombard's* view, that the Son of God *became nothing* by the assumption of human nature (because no change can take place in the divine nature), was branded as the heresy of *Nihilianism*, though he advanced it without any heretical intention, and was falsely interpreted as if he meant that Christ had become *nothing* (4). *Albert the Great* and *Thomas Aquinas* endeavoured to establish the christological doctrines of the Church in a dialectic method (5). But alongside of this dialectic Scholasticism there was constantly found, as its supplement, a mystical and moral tendency of a practical character. Some of this class despised all the subtleties of the schools; while others, partly adopting them, saw in Christ, as it were, the divine representative, the restored prototype of humanity (6), whilst a false mysticism transformed the historical Christ into a mere ideal (7).

(1) *Joh. Dam.* De fide orth. iii. c. 2 s. p. 205. Οὐ γὰρ προϊποστάσῃ καθ᾽ ἑαυτὴν σαρκὶ ἡνώθη ὁ θεῖος λόγος, ἀλλ᾽ ... αὐτὸς ὁ λόγος, γενόμενος τῇ σαρκὶ ὑπόστασις, ὥστε ἅμα σάρξ, ἅμα Θεοῦ λόγου σάρξ, ἅμα σὰρξ ἔμψυχος, λογική τε καὶ νοερά· διὸ οὐκ ἄνθρωπον ἀποθεωθέντα λέγομεν, ἀλλὰ Θεὸν ἐνανθρωπήσαντα. Ὢν γὰρ φύσει τέλειος Θεός, γέγονε φύσει τέλειος ἄνθρωπος ὁ αὐτὸς κ.τ.λ. Concerning the terms τρόπος ἀντιδόσεως (communicatio idiomatum), and περιχώρησις (immeatio), see chap. 3 and 4, p. 210 : Καὶ οὗτός ἐστιν ὁ τρόπος τῆς ἀντιδόσεως, ἑκατέρας φύσεως ἀντιδιδούσης τῇ ἑτέρᾳ τὰ ἴδια διὰ τὴν τῆς ὑποστάσεως ταυτότητα, καὶ τὴν εἰς ἄλληλα αὐτῶν περιχώρησιν. Κατὰ τοῦτο δυνάμεθα εἰπεῖν περὶ Χριστοῦ· οὗτος ὁ Θεὸς ἡμῶν ἐπὶ τῆς γῆς ὤφθη καὶ τοῖς ἀνθρώποις συνανεστράφη· καὶ ὁ ἄνθρωπος οὗτος ἄκτιστός ἐστι καὶ ἀπαθὴς καὶ ἀπερίγραπτος. Compare also the subsequent chapters, and Dorner, s. 106 ff.

(2) *Nicetas Choniates*, Thesaurus, c. 16 (qu. by *Ullmann*, s. 46); *Nicolas of Methone*, Refut. p. 155 (qu. by *Ullmann*, s. 84), in accordance with the communicatio idiomatum, calls the body of Christ σῶμα θεῖον, because by means of the

rational spiritual soul it was united with the God Logos so as to form one person, and was thus deified (θεουργηθέν). Compare Refut. p. 166 (*Ullmann*, l.c.).—Among the Western theologians, *Anselm* adopted these definitions in his Cur Deus Homo, ii. c. 7.

(3) On the history of the Adoptianist controversy, see *Walch*, l.c., Ketzerhist. Bd. ix. s. 667 ff.; *Gieseler*, Kg. ii. 1, s. 83 ff.; *Neander*, Kg. iii. s. 315 ff.; *Hundeshagen* in *Herzog's* Realencykl. i. s. 130.—On the questions, whether Adoptianism had been propounded by earlier theologians; whether the correct reading of *Hilary*, De Trin. ii. 29, is adoptatur or adoratur; and respecting the Liturgia Mozarabica, see *Gieseler*, l.c. On the earlier controversy of Elipandus with the Spanish bishop Megetius, who had a leaning to Sabellianism, see *Baur*, Trin. ii. s. 131. The notion itself is most distinctly set forth in the Epist. Episcop. Hispan. ad Episc. Gallic. (in *Alcuini* Opp. t. ii. p. 568, quoted by *Münscher, von Colln*, s. 81, and *Gieseler*): Nos. . . . confitemur et credimus, Deum Dei filium ante omnia tempora sine initio ex Patre genitum—non adoptione sed genere, neque gratia sed natura—pro salute vero humani generis in fine temporis ex illa intima et ineffabili Patris substantia egrediens, et a Patre non recedens, hujus mundi infima petens, ad publicum humani generis apparens, invisibilis visibile corpus adsumens de virgine, ineffabiliter per integra virginalia matris enixus: secundum traditionem patrum confitemur et credimus, eum factum ex muliere, factum sub lege, *non genere esse filium Dei*,[1] *sed adoptione, neque natura sed gratia*, id ipsum eodem Domino attestante, qui ait: "Pater major me est," etc.—*Felix* (apud *Alcuin.* contra Felic. lib. iv. c. 2): Secundo autem modo *nuncupative* Deus dicitur, etc. "*This union of the human nature, which is mean in itself, with the divine, by the elevation of the former in consequence of a divine judgment, may be called the unio forensis,*

---

[1] No son, says *Felix*, l.c., can have two natural fathers. Christ, now, in His human nature is the son of David as well as the Son of God. Consequently He can be the latter only by adoption, since He is the former by nature.—A subordinate question was this: When did this adoption take place? at His birth, or not until His baptism? According to *Walch* (Hist. der Ketz. ix. s. 574), Felix maintained the latter; see in reply, *Neander*, iii. s. 327, and compare *Baur*, Trinit. ii. s. 139. According to the representation of the latter, the relation of adoption was fully realized only in the resurrection of Christ.

or the juristic union." Dorner, s. 112. On the comparison which may be drawn between this elevation and the υἱοθεσία of the redeemed, see *Baum.-Cruz.* s. 381. Even in Spain the priest *Beatus*, of the province of Libana, and Bishop *Etherius*, of Othma, pronounced against the Adoptianist theory. *Felix* was compelled to retract, first at Regensburg (Ratisbon) (A.D. 792), and afterwards at Rome; the Synod of Frankfurt (A.D. 794) also pronounced against Adoptianism.—Respecting *Alcuini* Libellus adversus Haeresin **Felicis**, ad Abbates et Monachos **Gothiae** missus (t. i. p. 759 ss.), and his Epistola ad Felicem, compare Gieseler, s. 87. *Alcuin's* principal argument was, that the doctrine in question would destroy the *unity* of the Son of God, p. 763: Si igitur Dominus Christus secundum carnem, sicut quidam improba fide garriunt, adoptivus est Filius nequaquam unus est Filius, quia nullatenus proprius Filius, et adoptivus Filius unus esse potest Filius, quia unus verus et alter non verus esse dignoscitur. Quid Dei omnipotentiam sub nostram necessitatem prava temeritate constringere nitimur? Non est nostrae mortalitatis lege ligatus; omnia enim quaecunque vult, Dominus facit in coelo et in terra. Si autem voluit ex virginali utero proprium sibi creare filium, quis ausus est dicere, eum non posse? etc. Comp. p. 813. At the Synod of Aachen (A.D. 799), *Felix* was induced to yield by Alcuin, while *Elipandus* persisted. Felix died A.D. 818, but even he seems before his death to have returned to his former opinions; see *Agobardi* Liber adversus Dogma Felicis Episc. Urgellensis ad Ludov. Pium Imp.; comp. *Baur*, Trin. ii. s. 133 ff. In the twelfth century, *Folmar*, a canon of Traufenstein, was charged (A.D. 1160) with similar Adoptianist (Nestorian?) errors; see *Cramer*, vii. s. 43. And *Duns Scotus* and *Durandus a S. Porciano* admitted the use of the phrase *filius adoptivus* under certain restrictions, whilst *Aquinas* rejected it. *Walch*, l.c. p. 253; *Gieseler*, ii. s. 89; *Baur*, Trin. ii. s. 838.

(4) On the heresy of Nihilianism (*Lombardi* Sent. lib. iii. dist. 5–7, his language is still indefinite), see *Cramer*, Bd. vii. at the commencement; *Dorner*, s. 121 ff.; *Münscher*, von *Colln*, s. 86 f.; *Gieseler*, Dg. s. 506 ff. In compliance with an order issued by Pope Alexander III., the phrase, "Deus non factus est aliquid," was examined by the Synod of Tours (A.D. 1163), and rejected (*Mansi*, t. xxii. p. 239). It was also opposed by

Joh. Cornubiensis, about the year 1175 (*Martène*, Thesaurus, t. v. p. 1658 ss.).[1] But it was principally *Walter of St. Victor* who made it appear that the language of Peter Lombard implied the heretical notion: Deus est nihil secundum quod homo. "The *charge of Nihilianism is at least in so far unjust, as it represents* the denial of existence in a definite individual *form as an* absolute denial of existence. *At all events,* the attacks made upon Peter Lombard were *among the reasons why* theologians were henceforth more anxious to avoid the denial *of* the separate existence of the human nature of Christ. *We meet,* at least, in the writings of almost all the subsequent *scholastics,* with some passage or other, in which they *urge, in opposition* to the phrase '*non aliquid,' used by Peter Lombard, that the* human nature *of Christ is something definite and distinct from all others, but yet subsisting only in the divine person; hence they would not call it either individual* or person." *Dorner,* s. 122 f. Comp. *Baur,* Trin. ii. s. 563 ff. *Landerer* in *Herzog,* viii. s. 474.

(5) *Albertus Magn.* Compend. Theol. lib. iv. De Incarn. Christi, c. 14, and lib. iii. on the Sentences, dist. xiii. (qu. by *Dorner,* s. 124 f.). *Thomas Aquinas,* P. III. qu. 8, 1, etc. (qu. by *Dorner,* s. 126 ff.). Comp. *Cramer,* vii. s. 571 ff. *Baur,* Trin. ii. s. 787 ff. [*Baur*, Dg. s. 259 (2d ed.), says that the christological theory of Aquinas ran out dialectically into the two negative positions, that God became nothing by the incarnation, and that of man as a real subject of the incarnation nothing could be said, because the subject (person) of the union is only the Son of God. The humanity of Christ is only a human nature, and not a human personality; the union kept the nature from becoming a person, otherwise the personality of the human nature must have been annihilated by the union. *Anselm* says "that Christ could have sinned if He had so willed; but this possibility is only hypothetical," Cur Deus Homo, ii. 10. *Abélard,* on Romans, avers "that if Christ be regarded as a mere man, it is doubtful whether we could say of Him *nullo modo peccare posse;* but speaking

---

[1] John of Cornwall appeals, among other things, to the usage of language. When we say, *e.g.,* All men have sinned, Christ is expressly excepted. Or, again, we say, Christ was the most holy, the most blessed of men ; or, we count the twelve apostles and their Master together, and say, there are thirteen persons. All this could not be, if Christ were not aliquis homo. See, further, in *Baur,* l.c.

of Him as God **and** man, only a *non posse peccare* is to be admitted."]

(6) On the mystical mode of interpretation adopted by *John Damascene* **and** others, especially by his supposed disciple *Theodore Abukara*, **comp.** *Dorner*, s. 115 ff. On the connection between the scholastic definitions and the mystical, comp. ibid.—*John Scotus Erigena* considers the historical **Christ as one in** whom the human race is ideally represented; **and at the same time he** always strives to preserve Christ's **specific dignity.** Thus in De Divis. Nat. ii. 13: Humano **intellectui,** quem Christus assumsit, omnes intellectuales essentiæ inseparabiliter adhærent. Nonne plane vides, omnem creaturam, intelligibiles dico sensibilesque mediasque **naturas**, in Christo adunatam? Comp. v. 25, p. 252: Quamquam enim totam humanam naturam, quam totam accepit, totam in se ipso **et** in toto humano genere totam salvavit, quosdam quidem in **pristinum naturæ statum** restituens, quosdam vero per excellentiam ultra naturam **deificans**: in nullo tamen nisi in ipso **solo hum**anitas deitati in unitatem substantiæ adunata est, et in **ipsam d**eitatem mutata **omnia transcendit.** Hoc enim proprium caput Ecclesiæ sibi ipsi reservavit, ut non solum ejus **humanitas** particeps deitatis, **verum** etiam ipsa deitas, postquam ascendit ad Patrem, **fieret: in quam** altitudinem nullus **præter ipsum** ascendit **nec ascensurus est.** [*Erigena* on the *exinanitio* espoused the **view held afterwards by the** Calvinists **in distinction from** the Lutherans, p. 335. He makes the **incarnation to be** necessary, v. 25: Si Dei sapientia in effectus **causarum, quæ in** ea æternaliter vivunt, *non descenderet, causarum ratio periret:* pereuntibus enim causarum effectibus nulla **causa remaneret, etc.** Notwithstanding **Erigena's** strong assertion **about the historical Christ, the drift of** his doctrine is to **give to the incarnation a merely ideal or sy**mbolical character.] **The scholastics in general recognized som**ething universal in **Christ, as the prototype of the race, without,** however, impair**ing His historical individuality; see** *Dorner*, s. 141.—This **was still more the case with the mystics. Some** of them, *e.g. Geroch*, **provost of Reichersberg, protested** against the refining **and hair-splitting tendency which became prevalent** in regard **to Christology (especially in opposition to Folmar);** see *Cramer*, l.c. s. 43–78. **The disciples of the school of St. V**ictor looked

with an indifferent eye upon the subtler development of this dogma (*Dorner*, s. 142, Anm.). All the mystics urged that Christ is quickened *in* us. Thus *Ruysbroek* said, "Christ had His Godhead and manhood by nature; but we have it when we are united to Him in love by grace;" comp. *Engelhardt's* Monogr. s. 179, and the entire section, s. 177–179. *Tauler*, Predigten, Bd. i. s. 55 (on the first Sunday in Advent), expressed himself as follows: "We hold that we are susceptible of blessedness in the same manner in which *He* is susceptible, and that we receive here on earth a foretaste of that eternal blessedness which we shall enjoy hereafter. Since even the meanest powers and bodily senses of our Lord Jesus Christ were so united with the Godhead, that we may say *God saw*, *God* heard, *God* suffered; so we, too, enjoy the advantage, in consequence of our union with Him, that all *our* works may become divine. Further, human nature being united with the divine person and with the angels, all men have more fellowship with Him than other creatures, inasmuch as they are the members of His body, and are influenced by Him as by their head, etc. . . . Not many sons! You may and ought to differ (from each other) according to your natural birth, but in the eternal birth there can be only one Son, since in God there exists only one natural origin, on which account there can be only one natural emanation of the Son, not two. *Therefore, if you would be one son with Christ, you must be an eternal outflowing together with the eternal word.* As truly as God has become man, so truly man has become God by grace; and thus human nature is changed into what it has become, viz. into the divine image, which is consequently an image of the Father," etc. Compare also the sermon on Christmas-day, Bd. i. s. 89, and other passages.—Deutsche Theologie, c. 22: "Where God and man are so united, that we may say in truth, and truth itself must confess, that there is one who is verily perfect God and verily perfect man, and where man is nevertheless so devoted to God that God is there man Himself, and that He acts and suffers entirely without any selfhood, or for self, or for self-having [Germ. ohne alles Ich, Mir und Mein] (*i.e.* without any self-will, self-love, and selfishness): behold, *there is verily Christ, and nowhere else.*" Comp. chap. 24 and 43: "*Where the life of Christ is, there is Christ;*

and where His life is not, there Christ is not."[1]—The language of *Wessel* is simple and dignified, De Causa Incarnat. c. 7, p. 427 (qu. by *Ullmann*, s. 257): "Every noble soul hath something divine in itself, so that it loves to communicate itself. The more noble it is, the more it endeavours to imitate the Divine Being. Accordingly, that holy and divinely beloved soul (*i.e.* Christ), resembling God more than any other creature, gave itself wholly up for the brethren, as it saw that God gave Himself to it." Comp. cap. 16, p. 450, and De Magnit. Passionis, c. 82, p. 627: Qui non ab hoc exemplari trahitur, non est. On the human development of the Redeemer, see ibid. c. 17, p. 486 (qu. by *Ullmann*, s. 259).

(7) Thus the Beghards: Dicunt, se credere, quod quilibet homo perfectus sit Christus per naturam. (*Mosheim*, p. 256, from the letter of the Bishop of Strassburg.) According to *Baur* (Trin. ii. s. 310 f., comp. however, note 6, above), the Church doctrine, as expounded by John Scotus Erigena, was nothing more than that of the immanence of God in the world which appeared in man in the concrete reality of the self-consciousness.

The *partus virgineus* was one of those subjects which greatly occupied the ingenuity of the scholastics. It was at the foundation of the controversy between *Paschasius Radbertus* and *Ratramnus*, about the year 850, on the question whether Mary had given birth to Christ *utero clauso*, to which the former (after Jerome) replied in the affirmative, the latter (as Helvidius had done) in the negative. For further details, see *Münscher*, von Colln, s. 85 f.; and *Ch. G. F. Walch*, Historia Controversiæ sæculi IX. de Partu B. Virginis, Gott. 1758, 4to. *Anselm* sought to prove, in a very ingenious way, that the birth of the Virgin was necessary in the circle of divine possibilities, Cur Deus Homo, ii. 8: Quatuor modis potest Deus facere hominem; videlicet aut de viro et de femina, sicut assiduus usus monstrat; aut nec de viro nec de femina, sicut creavit Adam; aut de viro sine femina, sicut fecit Evam; aut de femina sine viro, quod nondum fecit. Ut igitur hunc quoque modum probet suæ subjacere potestati, et ad hoc ipsum opus dilatum esse, nihil convenientius, quam ut de femina sine viro assumat illum hominem, quem quærimus. Utrum autem de virgine aut de non virgine dignius hoc fiat, non est opus disputare, sed sine omni dubitatione asserendum est, quia de virgine hominem nasci oportet.—In the writings of *Robert Pulleyn* we meet with absurd questions respecting the exact moment at which, and the manner in which, the union of the divine nature of the Son with the human, assumed in the womb of Mary, had taken place (*Cramer*, vi. s. 484 ff.).

---

[1] Lest this passage might be misinterpreted, so as to refer to a mere ideal Christ, comp. what is said, c. 52: "All that is hitherto written, Christ taught by a long life, which lasted for the space of thirty-three years and a half," etc.

The fondness of the scholastics for starting all sorts of questions, led them also to inquire whether the union between the Godhead and manhood of Christ continued to exist after His death (the separation of the body from the soul). *Pulleyn* replied in the affirmative. He supposed that only Christ's body had died, but not the whole man Christ; see *Cramer*, vi. s. 487 f. A controversy was also carried on between the Franciscans and Dominicans respecting the question whether the blood shed on the cross was also separated from the Godhead of Christ. A violent discussion took place in Rome at Christmas 1462. The Dominicans took the affirmative, the Franciscans the negative side of the question. At last Pope Pius II. prohibited the controversy by a bull, issued A.D. 1464; see *Gobbelin*, Comment. Pii II. (Rom. 1584) p. 511. *Fleury*, Hist. ecclesiast. xxiii. p. 107 ss.

§ 180.

Redemption and Atonement.

[Baur, Geschichte der Versöhnungslehre, s. 113 ff. Siehe, Nicolaus Methonensis, Anselmus Cantuariensis, Hugo Grotius, quoad Satisfactionis Doctrinam a singulis excogitatum inter se comparati, Heidelberg 1838. (Thomson's Bampton Lectures; Oxenham, Catholic Doct. of Atonement, u.s.]

The mythical notion, developed in the preceding period, of a legal transaction with the devil, and the deception practised upon him on the part of God and Christ, was also adopted by some theologians of the present period, *e.g. John Damascene* (1). But it soon gave way, or at least became subordinate, to another theological mode of stating the doctrine, viz. that the fact of redemption was deducible with logical necessity from certain divine and human relations. We find the transition to this in the Greek Church made by *Nicolas of Methone* (2), independently of Anselm; whilst, in the Western Church, *Anselm of Canterbury* established his theory with an amount of ingenuity and a completeness of reasoning hitherto unattained (3). It is in substance as follows: In order to restore the honour of which God was deprived by sin, it was necessary that God should become man; that, by voluntary submission to the penalty of death, He might thus, as Godman, cancel the debt which, beside Him, no other being whether a heavenly one or an earthly one, could have paid

And He not only satisfied the requirements of divine justice, but by so doing, **of** His own free-will, He did more than **could** be demanded, and was rewarded by obtaining the deliverance of man from **the** penalty pronounced upon him. Thus **the** apparent contradiction between divine love on the one hand, and divine justice and holiness on the other, was adjusted.

(1) De fide orth. iii. 1: Αὐτὸς γὰρ ὁ δημιουργός τε καὶ **κύριος** τὴν ὑπὲρ τοῦ οἰκείου πλάσματος ἀναδέχεται **πάλην**, καὶ ἔργῳ διδάσκαλος γίνεται. Καὶ ἐπειδὴ θεότητος ἐλπίδι ὁ ἐχθρὸς δελεάζει τὸν ἄνθρωπον, σαρκὸς προβλήματι δελεάζεται καὶ δείκνυται ἅμα τὸ ἀγαθὸν καὶ τὸ σοφὸν, τὸ δίκαιόν τε καὶ τὸ δυνατὸν τοῦ **Θεοῦ**· τὸ μὲν ἀγαθὸν, ὅτι οὐ παρεῖδε τοῦ οἰκείου πλάσματος τὴν ἀσθένειαν, ἀλλ' ἐσπλαγχνίσθη ἐπ' αὐτῷ πεσόντι, καὶ χεῖρα ὤρεξε· τὸ δὲ δίκαιον, ὅτι ἀνθρώπου ἡττηθέντος οὐχ ἕτερον **ποιεῖ** νικῆσαι τὸν τύραννον, οὐδὲ βίᾳ ἐξαρπάζει τοῦ θανάτου τὸν **ἄνθρωπον**, ἀλλ' ὃν πάλαι διὰ τὰς ἁμαρτίας **καταδουλοῦται ὁ θάνατος, τοῦτον** ὁ ἀγαθὸς, **καὶ** δίκαιος νικητὴν **πάλιν** πεποίηκε, **καὶ** τῷ ὁμοίῳ τὸν ὅμοιον ἀνεσώσατο, ὅπερ **ἄπορον ἦν**· τὸ δὲ **σοφὸν, ὅτι** εὗρε τοῦ ἀπόρου λύσιν εὐπρεπεστάτην. He opposed, indeed, the notion (of Gregory of Nyssa) that the devil had received the ransom, iii. 27 Μὴ γὰρ γένοιτο τῷ τυράννῳ τὸ τοῦ δεσπότου προσενεχθῆναι αἷμα, but the following words sound strange enough: Πρόσεισι **τοιγαροῦν ὁ θάνατος καὶ** καταπιὼν **τὸ σώματος δέλεαρ τῷ τῆς θεότητος ἀγκίστρῳ** περιπείρεται, καὶ ἀναμαρτήτου καὶ **ζωοποιοῦ γευσάμενος σώματος** διαφθείρεται καὶ πάντας ἀνάγει, **οὓς πάλαι κατέπιεν**.

(2) Anecd. i. p. 25, ms. fol. 148 b (qu. by Seisen, p. 1); ibid. p. 30 s. fol. 150 b (qu. by Seisen, p. 2): Ἦν γὰρ θανάτῳ ὑπεύθυνον τὸ πᾶν ἡμῶν γένος· πάντες γὰρ ἥμαρτον, κέντρον δὲ τοῦ θανάτου ἐστὶν ἡ ἁμαρτία (1 Cor. xv. 56), δι' ἧς τρώσας ἡμᾶς ὁ θάνατος καταβέβληκε, καὶ ἄλλως οὐκ ἦν τῶν δεσμῶν τῆς δουλείας ἀπαλλαγῆναι τοὺς δόρατι ληφθέντας, ἢ διὰ θανάτου (Rom. v. 14). Τὰ γὰρ λύτρα ἐν τῇ αἱρέσει κεῖται τῶν κατεχόντων. Οὐκ ἦν οὖν ὁ δυνάμενος ὑπελθεῖν τὸ δρᾶμα καὶ ἐξαγοράσαι τὸ γένος, οὐκ ἦν οὐδεὶς τῶν τοῦ γένους ἐλεύθερος· μόγις δὲ τῆς ἰδίας ἐνοχῆς ἐλευθεροῦταί τις, ὃς ἑαυτοῦ ἀποθνή-

σκων οὐ δυνάμενος συνελευθερῶσαι ἵνα γοῦν ἑαυτῷ. Εἰ δὲ οὐδένα, τίς ἦν δυνατὸς, ὅλον κόσμον ἀπαλλάξαι δουλείας ; εἰ γὰρ καὶ ἀξιόχρεως ἦν πρὸς τὴν ἰδίαν ἐλευθερίαν ἕκαστος· ἀλλ' οὖν οὐκ ἦν πρέπον, πάντας ἀποθανεῖν, οὐδὲ ὑπὸ τὴν τοῦ θανάτου ἐξουσίαν καταμεῖναι. Τίνος οὖν ἦν τὸ κατόρθωμα ; δῆλον ὅτι ἀναμαρτήτου τινός. Τίς δὲ τῶν πάντων ἀναμάρτητος ἢ μόνος ὁ Θεός ; ἐπειδὴ τοίνυν καὶ Θεοῦ τὸ ἔργον ἦν καὶ χωρὶς θανάτου καὶ τῶν ἡγησαμένων τοῦ θανάτου παθῶν ἀδύνατον ἦν τελεσθῆναι, ὁ Θεὸς δὲ παθῶν καὶ θανάτου ἐστὶν ἀπαράδεκτος, προσέλαβε φύσιν παθῶν καὶ θανάτου δεκτικὴν, ὁμοουσίαν ἡμῖν ὑπάρχουσαν κατὰ πάντα καὶ ἀπαραλλάκτως ἔχουσαν πρὸς ἡμᾶς, ὅμου λαβὴν διδοὺς τῷ προσπαλαίοντι θανάτῳ κατὰ σάρκα, καὶ δι' αὐτῆς τῆς ὑποκειμένης αὐτῷ φύσεως καταγωνιούμενος αὐτὸν, ἵνα μήτε αὐτὸς χώραν σχοίη λέγειν, οὐχ ὑπὸ ἀνθρώπου, ἀλλ' ὑπὸ Θεοῦ ἡττῆσθαι, μήτε μὴν ἡμεῖς καταμαλακιζοίμεθα πρὸς τοὺς ἀγῶνας· καιροῦ καλοῦντος ἔχοντες παράδειγμα τὴν ὁμοφυῆ καὶ ὁμοούσιον σάρκα, ἐν ᾗ κατεκρίθη ἡ ἁμαρτία, χώραν οὐ δόλως εὑροῦσα ἐν αὐτῇ. . . . Οὐ γὰρ μάτην τι γέγονε τῶν περὶ τὸ τίμιον αὐτοῦ πάθος συμβεβηκότων, ἀλλὰ λόγῳ τινὶ κρείττονι καὶ ἀναγκαίῳ, πᾶσαν λόγων δύναμιν ὑπερβάλλοντι. Comp. Refut. p. 155 ss. (qu. by Seisen, p. 4), and Ullmann, s. 90 ff. " *He agreed* (with Anselm) *principally in endeavouring to demonstrate that the Redeemer must needs have been a God-man, but differed from him in this, that Anselm referred the necessity of the death of Jesus to the divine holiness, while Nicolas brought it into connection with the dominion of Satan over sinful men.*" Ullmann, s. 94.

(3) " *The relation in which Anselm's theory of satisfaction stands to the opinions which had hitherto generally obtained, is chiefly expressed in his decided opposition to the principle on which those views were founded, in relation to the devil;*"[1] *Baur*, Versöhnungsl. s. 155. Cur Deus Homo, i. 7, and ii. 19 : Diabolo nec Deus aliquid debebat nisi pœnam, nec

---

[1] It is worthy of notice that, as the doctrines of the Church were gradually developed in the lapse of ages, the kingdom of Satan was more and more thrust into the background, as the shadows disappear before the light. During the first period up to the complete overthrow of Manichæism, the demons played an important part in the doctrines respecting God and the government of the world, as well as in anthropology, until Augustine (in the second period) showed that the origin of sin is to be found in a profounder view of human nature. And, lastly, in the course of the present period, the connection between the

homo, nisi vicem, ut ab illo victus illum revinceret; sed quidquid ab illo exigebatur, hoc Deo debebat, non diabolo. Comp. Dial. de Verit. c. 8 (in *Hasse*, ii. s. 86): Dominus Jesus, quia solus innocens erat, non debuit mortem pati, quia ipse sapienter et benigne et utiliter voluit eam sufferre. The theory of Anselm is rather established upon the idea of *sin* (comp. § 176, note 4). It is the duty of man to honour God: by sin he has deprived Him of the honour due to Him, and is obliged to make retribution for it in a striking manner. So in i. 11: Hunc honorem debitum qui Deo non reddit, aufert Deo quod suum est, et Deum exhonorat, et hoc est peccare. Quamdiu autem non solvit, quod rapuit, manet in culpa; nec sufficit solummodo reddere, quod ablatum est, *sed pro contumelia illata **plus** debet reddere, quam abstulit*. Comp. also c. 13: Necesse est ergo, ut aut ablatus honor solvatur, aut poena sequatur, alioquin aut sibi ipsi Deus justus non erit, aut ad utrumque impotens erit, quod nefas est vel cogitare. It may be true that God cannot, properly speaking (objectively), be deprived of His honour, but He must insist upon its demands, for the sake of His creatures; the order and harmony of the universe require it; i. e. 14: Deum impossibile est honorem suum perdere. . . . Cap. 15: Dei honori nequit aliquid, quantum ad illum pertinet, addi vel minui. Idem namque ipse sibi honor est incorruptibilis et nullo modo mutabilis. Verum quando unaquaeque creatura suum et quasi sibi praeceptum ordinem sive naturaliter sive rationabiliter servat, Deo obedire et eum dicitur honorare; et hoc maxime rationalis natura, cui datum est intelligere quod debeat. Quae cum vult quod debet, Deum honorat; non quia illi aliquid confert, sed quia sponte se ejus voluntati et dispositioni subdit, et in rerum universitate ordinem suum et ejusdem universitatis pulchritudinem, quantum in ipsa est, servat. Cum vero non vult quod debet, Deum, quantum ad illum pertinet, inhonorat, quoniam non subdit se sponte illius dispositioni, et

doctrines of Christology and Soteriology on the one hand, and the doctrine of demoniacal agency on the other, being dissolved, the latter is pushed back to Eschatology, where the devil finds his proper place in hell. Still further, the relation of the work of redemption to the devil was still so prominent even in the time of Anselm, that Abelard was accused of heresy for contesting the right of the devil to man: see *Bernard*, Epist. exc. 5, in *Mabillon*, tom. i. p. 650 ss. (comp. *Hasse's* Anselm, ii. s. 493).

universitatis ordinem et pulchritudinem, quantum in se est, perturbat, licet potestatem aut dignitatem Dei nullatenus lædat aut decoloret. (With this the idea is connected, that the deficiency in the hierarchia cœlestis, occasioned by the fall of the angels, was made up by the creation of man, c. 16. Comp. above, § 172, note 5.) From the reasons referred to, it would be unworthy of God to pardon the sinner merely by making use of His supreme authority in the way of mercy (i. c. 6), and c. 12: Non decet Deum peccatum sic impunitum dimittere. ... In that case, injustice would be more privileged than justice. (Liberior est injustitia, si sola misericordia dimittitur, quam justitia.) Comp. c. 19. But man cannot make satisfaction, inasmuch as he is corrupted by original sin (i. c. 23: quia peccator peccatorem justificare nequit): nevertheless it was necessary that satisfaction should be given by *a human being*, i. c. 3: Oportebat namque ut sicut per hominis inobedientiam mors in humanum genus intraverat, ita per hominis obedientiam vita restitueretur, et quemadmodum peccatum, quod fuit causa nostræ damnationis, initium habuit a femina, sic nostræ justitiæ et salutis auctor nasceretur de femina, et ut diabolus, qui per gustum ligni, quem persuasit, hominem vicerat, ita per passionem ligni, quam intulit, ab homine vinceretur. But could not God have created a sinless man? Be it so; but then the redeemed would have come under the dominion of Him who had redeemed them, *i.e.* under the dominion of a man, who would himself be nothing but a servant of God, to whom angels would not render obedience (i. c. 5). And, besides, man himself owes obedience to God, i. c. 20: In obedientia vero quid das Deo, quod non debes, cui jubenti totum, quod es et quod habes et quod potes, debes? ... Si me ipsum et quidquid possum, etiam quando non pecco, illi debeo, ne peccem, nihil habeo, quod pro peccato illi reddam. —Nor could any higher being (*e.g.* an angel) take upon him the work of redemption, for so much is sure: Illum, qui de suo poterit Deo dare aliquid, quod superet omne quod sub Deo est, majorem esse necesse est, quam omne quod non est Deus. ... Nihil autem est supra omne quod Deus non est, nisi Deus. ... Non ergo potest hanc satisfactionem facere nisi Deus (ii. c. 6). If, therefore, none can make satisfaction but God Himself, and if it be nevertheless necessary that a man should make it, nothing remains but the God-man. Ibid.: Si ergo, sicut constat, necesse est, ut de hominibus perficiatur illa superna civitas, nec hoc esse valet nisi fiat praedicta satisfactio, quam nec potest facere nisi Deus, nec debet nisi homo: necesse est, ut eam faciat *Deus homo.* It is, moreover, necessary that the God-man should be of the race of Adam, and born of a virgin (c. 8, comp. § 179 at the end); and of the three Persons of the Trinity, it appears most suitable that the Son should assume humanity (ii. c. 9, comp. § 170, note 6). In order to make satisfaction for man, He had to give something to God which He did not owe to Him, but which, at the same time, was of more value than all that is under God. Obedience, however, He owed to God, like every rational creature; but He was not obliged to die (c. 10, 11). Nevertheless He was willing to lay down His life of His own accord, ibid.: Video, hominem illum plane, quem quaerimus, talem esse oportere, qui nec ex necessitate moriatur, quoniam erit omnipotens, nec ex debito, quia nunquam peccator erit, et mori possit ex libera voluntate, quia necessarium erit; for death is the greatest sacrifice which man can offer; ibid.: Nihil asperius, aut difficilius potest homo ad honorem Dei sponte et non ex debito pati, quam mortem; et nullatenus se ipsum potest homo magis dare Deo, quam cum se morti tradit ad honorem illius.[1] But it was because it was voluntary that the act had an infinite value; for His death outweighs all sins, however numerous or great. C. 14: A. Cogita etiam, quia peccata tantum sunt odibilia, quantum sunt mala, et vita ista tantum amabilis est, quantum est bona. Unde sequitur, quia vita ista plus est amabilis, quam sint peccata odibilia. B. Non possum hoc non intelligere. A. Putasne tantum bonum tam amabile posse sufficere ad solvendum, quod debetur pro peccatis totius mundi? B. Imo plus potest in infinitum. (On this account Christ's atonement has also a reacting influence upon our first parents, c. 16, and upon Mary herself, ibid. and c. 17, comp. § 178, note 2.) But the offering, thus voluntarily made, could not but be recompensed. As the

---

[1] Comp. also i. c. 9: Non coëgit Deus Christum mori, in quo nullum fuit peccatum, sed ipse sponte sustinuit mortem, non per obedientiam deserendi vitam, sed propter obedientiam servandi justitiam, in qua tam fortiter perseveravit, ut inde mortem incurreret.

Son, however, already possessed what the Father possesses, the reward due to Him must accrue to the advantage of another, viz. man (ii. 19). Thus the mercy and the justice of God may be reconciled with each other, c. 20: Misericordiam vero Dei, quæ tibi perire videbatur, cum justitiam Dei et peccatum hominis considerabamus, tam magnam tamque concordem justitiæ invenimus, ut nec major nec justior cogitari possit. Nempe quid misericordius intelligi valet, quam cum peccatori tormentis æternis damnato, et unde se redimat non habenti, Deus pater dicit: Accipe Unigenitum meum, et da pro te; et ipse Filius: Tolle me, et redime te? ... Quid etiam justius, quam ut ille, cui datur pretium majus omni debito, si debito datur affectu, dimittat omne debitum? And, lastly, we should not pass by his caution at the close of the treatise (c. 22): Si quid diximus, quod corrigendum sit, non renuo correctionem, si rationabiliter sit. Si autem testimonio veritatis roboratur, quod nos rationabiliter invenisse existimamus, Deo, non nobis attribuere debemus, qui est benedictus in sæcula. Amen.

Notwithstanding all its appearance of logical consequence, the theory of Anselm, as has been remarked, is open to the charge of an internal contradiction. For though Anselm himself admitted that God could not be deprived of His honour essentially, he nevertheless founded his argument upon this fact, and made it necessary that, after all, the love and compassion of God should come in, accept the satisfaction *voluntarily* made by an innocent being, and for *His* sake remit the punishment due to actual transgressors, who on their part could not retrieve their loss. Comp. *Baur*, s. 168 ff. *Schweizer*, too, in his Glaubensl. d. ref. Kirche, ii. s. 391, says that the theory of Anselm wavers between the fœdus operum and the fœdus gratiæ. To this it has been replied, that Anselm clearly distinguishes between the *immanent* and the *declarative* (transeuntem) honour of God, and that his argument starts with this; see *Hasse's* Anselm, ii. s. 576.—But, further, the subjective (ethical) aspect is put too much into the background by the objective (juridical) one; and the rest of the redeeming work of Christ, as seen in His life, almost vanishes out of sight (comp., however, ii. c. 18 b). Nor can it be denied that the reconciliation spoken of is rather one made on the part of God with man, than a reconciliation of man with God; see *Baur*, s. 181. *Ullmann*, Nic. v. Methone, s. 93. We should, however, be careful not to confound the theory of Anselm with its later (Protestant) developments. On the question, whether the satisfaction referred to by Anselm is, properly speaking, *not so much a suffering of punishment, as merely an active rendering of obedience*, inasmuch as he makes a difference between punishment and satisfaction (i. 15, necesse est, ut omne peccatum satisfactio *aut* pœna sequatur), see Baur, s. 189 ff. Nevertheless it is certain that the satisfaction made by Christ, in the view of Anselm, consisted, if not exclusively, at least principally, in submitting to sufferings and death: it cannot therefore be said, with Baur, "*that the idea of a punishment, by which satisfaction is made, and which is suffered in the room of another, does not occur in the scheme of Anselm.*" [But see Thomson and Oxenham, l.c. Anselm says: Nullatenus debet aut potest accipere homo a Deo, quod Deus illi dare proposuit, si non reddit Deo totum, quod illi abstulit, ut sicut per illum Deus perdidit, ita per illum Deus recuperet, Cur Deus Homo, i. 23.] On the other hand, it must be admitted that Anselm rests contented with the idea of the suffering of death: in his writings nothing is said of the Redeemer being under the burden of the *divine wrath*, of His taking upon Him the torments of hell, or what is called the anguish of the soul, etc. The chaste and noble tragical style, too, in which the subject is discussed, forms a striking contrast with the weak and whining, even sensuous "blood theology" of a later time.—On the relation in which Anselm's theory stood to the doctrine of earlier times (whether old or new?), see *Baur*, s. 186 ff. *Neander*, Kg. v. s. 975.

§ 181.

Further Development of the Doctrine.

The contemporaries and immediate successors of Anselm were far from adopting his theory unconditionally (1). On the contrary, *Abélard*, taking in this case, as in other things, the opposite side of the question, attached principal importance to the moral aspect of the doctrine, and declared the love of Christ the redeeming principle, inasmuch as it calls forth love on our part (2). *Bernard of Clairvaux*, on the other hand, insisted upon the mystical idea of the vicarious death of Christ (3). *Hugo of St. Victor* adhered more nearly to the doctrine of Anselm, but modified it so far as to return to the older notion of a legal transaction and struggle with the devil; at the same time he asserted (with Abélard) the moral significance of Christ's death (4); whilst *Robert Pulleyn* and *Peter Lombard* were still more closely allied with Abélard, although the latter combined with it other aspects of the atonement (5). The later scholastics returned to the position of Anselm, and developed it more fully (6). Thus *Thomas Aquinas* brought the high-priestly office of Christ prominently forward, and laid peculiar stress upon the superabounding merit of the death of Jesus (7). *Duns Scotus* went to the other extreme, denying its sufficiency (8); but he supposed a voluntary acceptance (acceptatio) on the part of God. *Wykliffe* and *Wessel* attached importance to the theory of satisfaction in its practical bearing upon evangelical piety, and thus introduced the period of the Reformation (9). The mystics either renounced all claims to doctrinal precision, and, abandoning themselves to the impulses of feeling and imagination, endeavoured to sink into the abyss of the love which died on the cross; or they thought to find the true principle of redemption in the repetition in themselves of the sacrifice once made by Christ, *i.e.* in literally crucifying their own flesh (10). Those of a pantheistic tendency annulled all that was peculiar in the merits of Christ (11). The external and mythical interpretation of the doctrine, as a legal transaction, led to offensive poetical distortions of the truth (12).

(1) "*If we must, on the one hand, acknowledge that Anselm's theory of satisfaction is a brilliant specimen of the dialectical and speculative acuteness of the scholastics, it must appear to us strange, on the other hand, that he stands alone, and does not seem to have convinced any of his successors of the necessity of the standpoint which he assumed,*" *Baur*, Versöhnungsl. s. 189.

(2) *Abelard* opposed, like *Anselm*, but still more decidedly, the introduction of the devil into the plan of redemption: Comment. in Epist. ad Rom. lib. ii. (Opp. p. 550), quoted by *Münscher, von Cölln*, s. 163; *Baur*, s. 191. The real ground of the reconciliation was stated by him as follows, p. 553 (quoted by *Baur*, s. 194): Nobis autem videtur, quod in hoc justificati sumus in sanguine Christi et Deo reconciliati, quod per hanc singularem gratiam nobis exhibitam, quod filius suus nostram susceperit naturam, et in ipso nos tam verbo quam exemplo instituendo usque ad mortem perstitit, nos sibi amplius per amorem astrixit, ut tanto divinae gratiae accensi beneficio, nil jam tolerare propter ipsum vera reformidet caritas. . . . Redemtio itaque nostra est illa summa in nobis per passionem Christi dilectio, quae nos (*lege* non) solum a servitute peccati liberat, sed veram nobis filiorum Dei liber-

tatem acquirit, ut amore ejus potius quam timore cuncta impleamus, qui nobis tantam exhibuit gratiam, qua major inveniri, ipso attestante, non potest. *"Thus the two representatives of scholasticism in its first period, when it developed itself in all its youthful vigour, Anselm and Abélard, were directly opposed to each other with respect to the doctrines of redemption and atonement. The one considered the last ground of it to be the divine justice, requiring an infinite equivalent for the infinite guilt of sin, that is, a necessity founded in the nature of God; the other held it to be the free grace of God, which, by kindling love in the breast of man, blots out sin, and with sin its guilt,"* Baur, Versöhnungsl. s. 195. On the endeavours of Abélard, notwithstanding his other views, to represent redemption in its legal aspect, see ibidem.

(3) *Bernard* opposed Abélard, in the first place, in respect to the point that the devil has no legal claims upon man; see Epist. 190, De Erroribus Abælardi ad Innocentem III. (qu. by *Münscher, von Cölln,* s. 164; *Baur,* Versöhnungsl. s. 202). He made a distinction between jus acquisitum and jus nequiter usurpatum, juste tamen permissum. He ascribed the latter to the devil: Sic itaque homo juste captivus tenebatur: ut tamen nec in homine, nec in diabolo illa esset justitia, sed in Deo. Bernard, moreover, urged especially the fact that Christ, as the Head, had made satisfaction for the members. [Homo siquidem, qui debuit, homo qui salvit. *Nam si unus,* inquit (2 Cor. v. 16) *pro omnibus mortuus est, ergo omnes mortui sunt, ut videlicet satisfactio unius hominis imputetur, sicut omnium peccata unus ille portavit, nec alter jam inveniatur, qui forefecit (i.e. peccavit),* alter, qui satisfecit, quia caput et corpus unus est Christus.]—Satisfecit caput pro membris, Christus pro visceribus suis (see *Baur,* s. 202 f.). Bernard's views were most nearly allied to those of Augustine and Gregory the Great.

(4) In the system of *Hugo,* God appeared as the patronus of man, and the opponent of the devil. But, first of all, it was necessary to conciliate his favour. This idea is largely dwelt upon in his Dialogus de Sacramentis legis naturalis et scriptæ. De Sacram. c. 4: Dedit Deus gratis homini, quod homo ex debito Deo redderet. Dedit igitur homini hominem, quem homo pro homine redderet, qui, ut digna recompensatio

fieret, priori non solum æqualis, sed major esset. Ut ergo pro homine redderetur homo major homine, factus est Deus homo pro homine. Christus ergo nascendo debitum hominis patri solvit et moriendo reatum hominis expiavit, ut, cum ipse pro homine mortem, quam non debebat, sustineret, juste homo propter ipsam mortem, quam debebat, evaderet, et jam locum calumniandi diabolus non inveniret, quia et ipse homini dominari non debuit, et homo liberari dignus fuit. The following is written rather in the spirit of Abélard, c. 10 : ... Ut in Deo humanitas glorificata exemplum esset glorificationis hominibus; ut in eo, qui passus est, videant, quid ei retribuere debeant, in eo autem, qui glorificatus est, considerent, quid ab eo debeant exspectare; ut et ipse sit via in exemplo et veritas in promisso et vita in præmio. (*Liebner*, Hugo von St. Victor, s. 417 ff. *Baur*, Versöhnungsl. s. 206, 208.)

(5) On *Palleyn*, who in other respects was praised by Bernard on account of his orthodoxy, see *Cramer*, Bd. vi. s. 490 ff.; *Baur*, s. 205. [*Palleyn* says, the Redeemer must suffer, in part because this was necessary to our redemption (though we might have been redeemed in some other way), in part as an example to us in the endurance of suffering. But the price of redemption was paid, not to the devil, which is impossible, but to God.] *Peter Lombard*, more than any of the other scholastics, regarded the subject in question from the psychologico-moral point of view (see *Baur*, s. 209), Sent. lib. iii. dist. 19: A. Quomodo a peccatis per ejus mortem soluti sumus? Quia per ejus mortem, ut ait apostolus, commendatur nobis caritas Dei, i. e. apparet eximia et commendabilis caritas Dei erga nos in hoc, quod filium suum tradidit in mortem pro nobis peccatoribus. Exhibita autem tantæ erga nos dilectionis arrha et nos movemur accendimurque ad diligendum Deum, qui pro nobis tanta fecit, et per hoc *justificamur*, i. e. soluti a peccatis justi *efficimur*. Mors ergo Christi nos justificat, dum per eam caritas excitatur in cordibus nostris.—Peter Lombard decidedly opposed the notion that God had, as it were, altered His views in favour of the sinner, by reason of the death of Christ, ibid. F: Reconciliati sumus Deo, ut ait apostolus, per mortem Christi. Quod non sic intelligendum est, quasi nos ei sic reconciliaverit Christus, ut inciperet amare quos oderat, sicut reconciliatur inimicus

inimico, ut deinde sint amici, qui ante se oderant, sed jam nos diligenti Deo reconciliati sumus. Non enim, ex quo ei reconciliati sumus per sanguinem filii, nos cœpit diligere, sed ante mundum, priusquam nos aliquid essemus.—Nevertheless he also admitted the doctrine of substitution, although he expressed himself respecting it in very general terms (as did Bernard of Clairvaux), loc. cit. D. He says: Non enim sufficeret illa pœna, qua pœnitentes ligat ecclesia, nisi pœna Christi coöperaretur, qui pro nobis solvit. (*Baur*, s. 213.) And, lastly, the devil occupied a very strange position in the system of Peter Lombard. (Quid fecit redemptor captivatori nostro? Tetendit ei muscipulam crucem suam: posuit ibi quasi escam sanguinem suum.) *Baur*, s. 211.

(6) *Alanus ab Insulis*, iii. (qu. by *Pez*, t. i. p. 493–498); *Albertus Magnus* (Sent. lib. iii. dist. 20, art. 7); *Alexander of Hales* (Summæ, P. III. qu. 1, membr. 4 ss., see *Cramer*, vii. s. 574 ff.; *Baur*, s. 215, Anm.). *Bonaventura* (Opp. t. v. p. 191 ss., ibid. p. 218 ss.).

(7) Summæ, Pars III. qu. 22 (De Sacerdotio Christi, qu. by *Münscher, von Cölln*, s. 166). His theory of satisfaction will be found ibid. qu. 46–49.[1] (*Baur*, Versöhnungsl. s. 230 ff.) He discussed especially the necessity of suffering, and the question, Whether God could have redeemed man in any other way? and replied to it both in the affirmative and negative, according to the idea formed of necessity. (Art. 2, *Baur*, s. 232.) At all events, the sufferings of Christ were the most proper way, and the one most to the purpose. It was also significant that Christ suffered on the *cross*, which reminds us not only of the tree in Paradise, but also of this, that the cross is a symbol of various virtues, as well as of that breadth, and length, and depth, and height of which the apostle spoke (Eph. iii. 18), of our exaltation into heaven, etc. While Anselm did not go beyond the simple fact of Christ's death, Aquinas endeavoured to demonstrate that Christ endured in His head, hands, and feet *all the sufferings which men* have

---

[1] In *Thomas Aquinas* we also find (as the title indicates) the first hints about the *threefold office* of Christ, since he views Him as legislator, sacerdos and rex. However, he does not use the expression *munus, officium*, and only developes the *sacerdotium*, showing how Christ was at once *sacerdos* and *hostia perfecta*. See *Giesler*, Dg. s. 513.

to endure in their reputation, worldly possessions, body and soul, in head, hands, and feet; accordingly, *the pain of the sufferings of Christ is by far the greatest* which can be endured in the present life (in proof of which he adduced several arguments). Nevertheless *his soul possessed the uninterrupted enjoyment of blessedness*, art. 8 (but Thomas Aquinas himself did not as yet speak of the soul's enduring the torments of hell, or bearing the eternal curse, thus leaving the sufferings incomplete). He further propounded (like Bernard of Clairvaux) the mystical idea, according to which the head suffers for the members (Quaest. 48, art. 1): Christus per suam passionem non solum sibi, sed etiam omnibus membris suis meruit salutem. Passio non est meritoria, inquantum habet principium ab exteriori: sed secundum quod eam aliquis voluntarie sustinet, sic habet principium ab interiori, et hoc modo est meritoria. — Thomas made use of the same mystical idea to refute the objection that one being could not make satisfaction for another; for, inasmuch as two are made one through love, the one may make satisfaction for the other. On the meritum superabundans, qu. 48, art. 2: Christus autem ex charitate et obedientia patiendo majus aliquid Deo exhibuit, quam exigeret recompensatio totius offensae humani generis: primo quidem propter magnitudinem *charitatis*, ex qua patiebatur; secundo propter *dignitatem vitae* suae, quam pro satisfactione ponebat, quae erat vita Dei et hominis; tertio propter *generalitatem passionis et magnitudinem doloris* assumti ... et ideo passio Christi non *solum sufficiens, sed etiam superabundans satisfactio fuit pro peccatis humani generis* (1 John ii. 2). Respecting his further statements, see *Baur*, Versöhnungsl. l.c., and *Münscher, von Cölln*, s. 167.

(8) *Duns Scotus* in Sent. l. iii. dist. 19: ... Quantum vero attinet ad meriti sufficientiam, fuit profecto illud finitum, quia causa ejus finita fuit, videlicet voluntas naturae assumptae, et summa gloria illi collata. Non enim Christus quatenus Deus meruit, sed inquantum homo. Proinde si exquiras, quantum valuerit Christi meritum secundum sufficientiam, valuit procul dubio quantum fuit a Deo acceptatum. Siquidem divina acceptatio est potissima causa et ratio omnis meriti ... Tantum valuit Christi meritum sufficienter, quantum potuit et voluit ipsam Trinitas acceptare, etc. — Thus he destroyed the prin-

cipal argument of Anselm's theory in his Cur Deus Homo; for, since Christ suffered only in His human nature, an angel, or another man, might have suffered quite as well, as Duns Scotus was fully prepared to admit. Comp. *Baur*, s. 256. On this account the sufferings of Christ did not appear to Scotus as something necessary; even less so to him than to Thomas Aquinas. Both their systems are compared by *Baur*, Versöhnungsl. s. 257 ff. *Bonaventura* occupied an intermediate position between the two former, by teaching a *perfectio et plenitudo* meriti Christi (Brev. iv. c. 7, Cent. iii. sec. 30).

(9) *Wykliffe*, Trialogus, iii. c. 25 (De Incarnatione et Morte Christi), qu. by *Baur*, s. 273. Dialog. lib. iii. cap. 25: Salvari enim oportet illum hominem (Adam), cum tam fructuose pœnituit, et Deus non potest negare suam misericordiam taliter pœnitenti. Et cum, juxta suppositionem tertiam, oportet, quod satisfactio pro peccato fiat, ideo oportet, quod idem illud genus hominis tantum satisfaciat, quantum in protoplasto deliquerat, quod nullus homo facere poterat, nisi simul fuerat Deus et homo. . . . Et fuit necessarium, ipsum acceptum fuisse in ligno, ut sicut ex fructu ligni vetito periit homo, sic ex fructu ligni passo salvetur homo. Et sunt aliæ multæ congruentiæ utrobique. He laid, however, quite as much stress upon repentance as upon the theory of satisfaction. — According to *Wessel*, Christ was our Redeemer, even *by representing in Himself the divine life* (an idea which had almost wholly sunk into oblivion since the time of Anselm!). Nevertheless He was also Mediator; yea, He was God, priest, and sacrifice at the same time. We see in Him at once the reconciling and the reconciled God. Comp. De Magnitud. Passionis, c. 17, and Exempla Scalæ Meditationis, Ex. iii. p. 391 (qu. by *Ullmann*, s. 261; *Baur*, s. 277). " *Wessel, too, considered the sufferings of our Lord as being made by a substitute; but going beyond the merely external and legal transaction, he asserted the necessity of living faith, and an appropriation of the Spirit of Christ*," *Ullmann*, s. 264. He attached, therefore (as did Abélard and Peter Lombard), great importance to the principle of love. He who would form a correct estimate of the full measure of the sufferings of Christ, must come to them, above all, with an eye exercised in love;

De Magnit. Passionis, p. 19. Further passages may be seen in the works of *Ullmann* and *Baur* (l.c.).

(10) The sentimental contemplation of the sufferings of Jesus, and expressions such as "*the blood of Jesus, full of love, and red like a rose*" (e.g. in the writings of *Suso*), may indeed be traced to mysticism. But the true mystics did not rest satisfied with this. Thus the author of the "Deutsche Theologie," c. 3, after having proved that God had assumed humanity in order to remove the effects of the fall, continues: "Though God were to take to Himself all men who exist, and to assume their nature, and be incarnated in them, and make them divine in Him, yet if the same did not take place in *me*, my fall and apostasy would never be removed."—With more distinct reference to the design of the atoning *sufferings* of Christ, *Tauler* said (in a sermon on Luke x. 23, qu. by *Wackernagel*, Lesebuch, i. Sp. 868): "Since your great God was thus set at nought, and condemned by His creatures, and was crucified and died, you should, with patient endurance, and with all suffering humility, *behold yourselves in His sufferings, and have your minds thereby impressed.*" Compare also his Sermon, i. s. 289 (on Good Friday).—Bishop Master *Albrecht* said: "Four and twenty hours compose day and night; take one of the hours and divide it into two, and spend it in contemplating the sufferings of our Lord: that is better and more useful to man than if all men, and all the saints, and all the angels of God, and Mary the mother of God, should remember him [i.e. should intercede for him]. As man dies a bodily death, so he dies to all sins by *serious meditation on the sufferings of our Lord Jesus Christ*" (Sprüche deutscher Mystiker, in *Wackernagel's* Lesebuch, Sp. 889).—But not only did the mystics urge the necessity of recalling the sufferings of Christ by inward contemplation, but the same idea was also externally represented by the self-inflicted torments of ascetics, especially of the Flagellantes of the Middle Ages. In the latter case it must, however, be admitted that as the idea of personal merit was set forth, the merits of Christ were thrown into the shade. Thus it is said in one of the hymns of the Flagellantes (A.D. 1349): "Through God *we* shed our blood, which will avail for the expiation of our sins" (*Hoffmann*, Geschichte des deutschen Kirchenliedes, s. 94).

(11) The Beghards taught: Christus non est passus pro nobis, sed pro se ipso. (Mosheim, p. 256.) *Amalrich of Bena* maintained that by all Christians being members of Christ, we are to understand that as such they participated in the sufferings of Christ on the cross. (*Engelhardt*, Abh. s. 253.) Thus he inverted the proposition according to which the head died for the members (that of Bernard of Clairvaux, and Thomas Aquinas).

(12) *Jacob de Theramo*, who lived in the fourteenth century (1382), treated the transaction between Christ and Belial (the devil) in the form of a judicial process; this was translated into German in the fifteenth century, under the title: "Hie hept sich an ein Rechtsbuoch;" comp. *W. Wackernagel*, Die altdeutschen Handschriften der Basler Universitätsbibliothek, 1835, 4to, s. 62 f. *Baur* (relying on *Döderlein's* Diss. Inauguralis, 1774, 1775, in his Opusc. Academ., Jena 1789) calls it "a carnival play;" but it is not so, the subject is intended to be treated in an earnest spirit. Compare a similar drama: Extractio Animarum ab Inferno, in the English Miracle-Plays or Mysteries, by *W. Marriott*, Bas. 1838, p. 161.

§ 182.

Connection of Soteriology with Christology.

Julius Müller in the Deutsche Zeitschrift f. christl. Wissenschaft, Oct. 1850, s. 314 ff.

In the theory of Anselm, so much importance was attached to the incarnation and death of Jesus, as the corner-stones of the work of redemption, that there was danger lest the wonderful life of the Redeemer, which lies between the two, should lose its religious significance. There were, however, those who again directed attention to the life of the God-man, as itself having a redeeming power (1). Some, indeed, made it appear that Christ came into the world only in order to die, and that consequently He would not have been sent at all if there had been no sin to atone. On the other hand, others, *e.g. Wessel*, pointed out in various ways the significance which the manifestation of God in the flesh must have, independently of sin and its effects, as the keystone of creation and crown of humanity (2).

(1) See *Wessel* in the preceding section, note 9.

(2) Comp. above, § 64. "*The question, whether Christ would have assumed the nature of man if there had been no sin, was not discussed till the Middle Ages, being started, as it appears, for the first time by Rupert, Abbot of Deutz, in the twelfth century*" (*Dorner*, s. 134); comp. his work, De Glorificatione Trinitatis et Processione Sp. Sanct. lib. iii. c. 21, iv. 2, and Comm. in Matth. de Gloria et Honore Filii homin. lib. xiii. (Opera, tom. ii. 164 ss.); *Gieseler*, Dg. s. 514. [*Rupert* says that men and angels were created for the sake of the one man, Jesus Christ; He, the head and king of all elect angels and men, did not need sin in order to become incarnate. *Alexander of Hales* adopted the same view: Summa theol. P. III. qu. 2, membr. 13. *Bonaventura* agrees with Aquinas.]—The language of *Thomas Aquinas* sufficiently shows that he too felt disposed to look upon the incarnation of Christ as being in one respect the completion of creation. In his Comment. on the Sentences, lib. iii. dist. 1, art. 3, he said that by the incarnation there was effected not only deliverance from sin, but also humanæ naturæ exaltatio et totius universi consummatio. Comp. Summa, P. III. qu. 1, art. 3 : Ad omnipotentiam divinæ virtutis pertinet, ut opera sua perficiat et se manifestet per aliquem infinitum effectum, cum sit finita per suam essentiam. Nevertheless, he thought it more probable (according to P. III. qu. 1, 3) that Christ would not have become man if there had been no sin. This notion generally obtained, and theologians preferred praising (after the example of Augustine) sin itself as felix culpa (thus *Richard of St. Victor*, De Incarnat. Verbi, c. 8), rather than admit the possibility of the manifestation of the Son of God apart from any connection with sin. *Duns Scotus*, however, felt inclined to adopt the latter view, which was more in accordance with his entire Pelagian tendency;[1] Sent. lib. iii. dist. 7, qu. 3, and dist.

[1] This was done in later times by the Socinians. Nevertheless, the theory in question may be so strained, "*that sin is made light of, and in a kind called,*

19. On the other hand, *Wessel*, whose sentiments were by no means like those of Pelagius, took the same view (De Incarn. c. 7 and c. 11, qu. by *Ullmann*, s. 254). In his opinion, the final cause of the incarnation of the Son of God is not to be found in the human race, but in the Son of God Himself. He became man for His own sake; it was not the entrance of sin into the world which called forth this determination of the divine will; Christ would have assumed humanity even if Adam had never sinned: Si incarnatio facta est principaliter propter peccati expiationem, sequeretur, quod anima Christi facta sit non principali intentione, sed quadam quasi occasione. Sed inconveniens est, nobilissimam creaturam occasionaliter esse introductam (quoted by *Dorner*, s. 140).

rather than the dignity of Christ augmented" (Dorner, s. 137). But whether the notion of a felix culpa, by which sin is so elevated as to appear θεωρίας, might not lead men so far as to worship it on pantheistic grounds, and at the same time to make light of it in the moral point of view, is another question. And, on the other hand, if we, looking at sin in a *serious* light, regard the incarnation of Christ *merely* as something which has become necessary in order to repair the damage, its happy aspect will be lost sight of, and the joy we might experience at Christmas will too soon be changed into the weeping and wailing of the Passion-week. This is the principal defect of Anselm's theory. But with respect to the exaltation of mankind at the expense of the dignity of Christ, the latter, so far from being endangered by the theory of Wessel, is raised by the idea that Christ assumed humanity not on account of man, but *for his own sake*, an idea by which the pride of man is humbled. [This note is omitted in the 5th edition of Hagenbach.]

FIFTH DIVISION.

THE ORDO SALUTIS.

§ 183.

Predestination.

(The Gottschalk Controversy.)

L. Cellot, Historia Gotteschalci, Par. 1655, fol. †*Staudenmaier*, Scotus Erigena, s. 170 f. *Gfrörer* on Pseudo-Isidore in the Tübing. Theol. Zeitschrift, xvii. 2, s. 274 ff. *Wiggers*, Schicksale d. Augustinischen Anthropologie, in Ilgens (Niedners) Zeitschrift f. hist. Theol. 1857, 2. [Archb. *Ussher*, Gottschalcus et Praedest. Controvers. ab eo mota, Dublin 1631, and in *Ussher's* Works, 16 vols. Dublin 1837–40. *F. Monnier*, De Gottschalci et Joan. Scoti Erigenae Controversia, Paris 1853.]

GREAT as was the authority of Augustine in the West, the prevailing notions concerning the doctrine of Predestination contained more or less of the Semi-Pelagian element (1). Accordingly, when, in the course of the ninth century, *Gottschalk*, a monk in the Franconian monastery of Orbais, ventured to revive the rigid Augustinian doctrine, and even went so far as to assert a twofold predestination, not only to salvation, but also to damnation (2), he exposed himself to persecution. He was in the first instance opposed by *Rabanus Maurus* (3), and afterwards condemned by the Synods of Mainz (A.D. 848) and of Chiersey (Cressy, Carisiacum, A.D. 849) (4). *Hincmar*, Archbishop of Rheims, took part in the transactions of the latter synod. Although *Prudentius of Troyes* (5), *Ratramnus* (6), *Servatus Lupus* (7), and several others, pronounced in favour of Gottschalk, though under certain modifications; yet *John Scotus Erigena*, by an ingenious argumentation, contrived to preserve the appearance of Augustinian orthodoxy, by maintaining, on the basis of the position borrowed from Augustine, that evil was something negative, and therefore could not, as such, be predestinated by God (8). The objections advanced by *Prudentius* and *Florus* (*Magister*) were as little heeded as the steps taken by *Remigius*, Archbishop of Lyons, in behalf of Gottschalk (9). On the contrary, the second Synod of Chiersey (Cressy, A.D. 853) laid down four articles, in accordance with the views of Hincmar (10); then several bishops at the Synod of Valence (A.D. 855) drew up six other articles of a contrary tendency, which were confirmed by the Synod of Langres (A.D. 859) (11), but zealously opposed again by Hincmar (12). Gottschalk, the victim of the passions of others, bore his fate with that fortitude and resignation which have at all times characterized those individuals or bodies of men who have adopted the doctrine of Predestination.

(1) The theologians of the *Greek* Church retained the earlier definitions as a matter of course. *Joh. Damasc.* De fide orthod. ii. c. 30 : Χρὴ γινώσκειν, ὡς πάντα μὲν προγινώσκει ὁ Θεὸς, οὐ πάντα δὲ προορίζει· προγινώσκει γὰρ τὰ ἐφ᾽ ἡμῖν, οὐ προορίζει δὲ αὐτά. (Comp. § 177, note 1.)—Respecting the opinions entertained by the theologians of the Western Church, see above, § 114. The venerable *Bede* (Expositio Allegorica in Cantic. Cantic.) and *Alcuin* (de Trin. ii. c. 8) adopted, in the main, the views of Augustine, but rejected the prædestinatio duplex. Comp. *Münscher, von Cölln*, s. 121 f. They were, however, unconscious of the difference between themselves and Augustine; see *Neander*, Kg. iv. s. 412 ff., and *Wiggers*, l.c.

(2) Respecting the history of his life, and the possible connection between it and his doctrine, see *Neander*, l.c. s. 414 ff.; *Staudenmaier*, l.c. s. 175. His own views, as well as those of his opponents, may be gathered from *Guilb. Mauguin*, Vett. Auctorum qui sæc. IX. de Prædestinatione et Gratia scripserunt Opera, Paris 1650, 2 vols. 4to (in t. ii. : Gotteschalcanæ Controversiæ Historica et Chronica Dissertatio). In the

Libellus Fidei, which Gottschalk presented to the Synod of Mainz, he asserted: Sicut electos omnes (Deus) praedestinavit ad vitam per gratuitum solius gratiae suae beneficium ... sic omnino et reprobos quosque ad aeternae mortis praedestinavit supplicium, per justissimum videlicet justitiae suae judicium (after *Hincmar*, De Praed. c. 5). In his confession of faith (given by *Münscher*, *von Cölln*, s. 122) he says: Credo et confiteor, quod gemina est praedestinatio, sive electorum ad requiem, sive reproborum ad mortem. But he referred the praedestinatio duplex not so much to *evil* itself, as to the *wicked*. Compare the passage quoted by *Neander*, s. 418: Credo atque confiteor, praescisse te ante saecula quaecunque erunt futura sive bona sive mala, praedestinasse vero tantummodo bona. On the connection subsisting between his views and those of Augustine, see *Neander*, l.c. s. 417 ff. Comp. *Baur*, Dg. 215.

(3) Epist. synodalis Rabani ad Hincmarum (given in *Mansi*, t. xiv. p. 924, and *Staudenmaier*, s. 179): Notum sit dilectioni vestrae, quod quidem gyrovagus monachus, nomine Gothescalc, qui se asserit sacerdotem in nostra parochia ordinatum, de Italia venit ad nos Moguntiam, novas superstitiones et noxiam doctrinam de praedestinatione Dei introducens et populos in errorem mittens; dicens, quod praedestinatio Dei, sicut in bono, sic ita et in malo, et tales sint in hoc mundo quidam, qui propter praedestinationem Dei, quae eos cogat in mortem ire, non possint ab errore et peccato se corrigere, quasi Deus eos fecisset ab initio incorrigibiles esse, et poenae obnoxios in interitum ire.—As regards the doctrine of *Rabanus Maurus* himself, he made the decree of God respecting the wicked depend on His prescience; see *Neander*, l.c. s. 421.

(4) *Mansi*, t. xiv.—On the outrageous treatment of Gottschalk, see *Neander*, l.c. s. 426.

(5) *Prudentii Trecassini* (of Troyes) Epistola ad Hincmarum Remig. et Pardulum Laudunensem (which was written about the year 849, and first printed in *Lud. Cellotii* Historia Gotteschalci, p. 425, Par. 1655). He asserted a twofold predestination, but made the predestination of the wicked (reprobation) depend on the foreknowledge of God. He further maintained that Christ had died for none but the elect (Matt. xx. 28), and artificially interpreted 1 Tim ii. 4 as meaning: Vel omnes ex omni genere hominum (comp. *Augustine*, Enchirid. c. 103),

vel omnes velle fieri salvos, quia nos facit velle fieri omnes homines salvos. Compare *Neander*, l.c. s. 433.

(6) At the request of the Emperor Charles the Bald, he composed the work, De Prædestinatione Dei libri ii., in which he expressed himself as follows (qu. by *Mauguin*, t. j. p. 94; *Staudenmaier*, s. 182): Verum quemadmodum æterna fuit illorum scelerum scientia, ita et definita in secretis cœlestibus pœnæ sententia; et sicut præscientia veritatis non eos impulit ad nequitiam, ita nec prædestinatio coëgit ad pœnam. Comp. *Neander*, l.c. s. 434.

(7) *Servatus Lupus* was abbot of Ferrières. Respecting his character and the history of his life, see *Siegebertus Gemblac*, De Scriptt. Eccles. c. 94. *Staudenmaier*, s. 188. He was distinguished as a classical scholar, and wrote about the year 850: De Tribus Questionibus (1. de libero arbitrio: 2. de prædestinatione bonorum et malorum; 3. de sanguinis Domini taxatione). See *Mauguin*, t. i. P. ii. p. 9 ss.—*He*, too, interpreted those passages which are favourable to the doctrine of universal redemption, in accordance with the scheme of particularism (*Neander*, l.c. p. 436 ff.); but his milder principles induced him to leave many points undecided, as he was far from claiming infallibility (*Neander*, s. 440).

(8) Probably about the year 851 he addressed a treatise, entitled: Liber de divina Prædestinatione, to Hincmar and Pardulus (see *Mauguin*, t. i. P. i. p. 102 ss.). He, too, did this at the request of the Emperor Charles the Bald.—The idea of a *prædestinatio*, properly speaking, cannot be applied to God, since with Him there is neither a *future* nor a *past*. As, moreover, sin ever carries its own punishment with itself (de Præd. c. 6: Nullum peccatum est, quod non se ipsum puniat, occulte tamen in hac vita, aperte vero in altera), there is no need of a prædestinated punishment. Evil does not exist at all for God; accordingly, the prescience as well as the predestination of evil, on the part of God, is altogether out of question. Comp. *Neander*, s. 441 ff. It is, however, to be noted, that Erigena only denies that the predestination is *twofold*, and the idea that this is *divine*. In harmony with his whole speculative tendency, he could not give up the view that, as God is the ground of all things, so, too, from eternity all is embraced in His purpose; hence he says in De Prædest.

18. 7: Prædestinavit Deus impios ad pœnam vel ad interitum, and in 18, 8, he even speaks of a definite number of the good and evil. Evil itself seems to him to be adopted into God's plan of the world (supralapsarian?); see *Ritter*, Gesch. d. Phil. vii. s. 270 ff. Comp. Erigena's doctrine of sin and the fall, in § 176, note 4, above; and De Divis. Nat. v. 36, p. 283. He says: Prædestinatio essentialiter de Deo prædicari non est dubium. Essentia autem unitas. Prædestinatio igitur unitas. Unitas dupla non est. *Prædestinatio igitur dupla non est, ac per hoc nec gemina* (De Divis. Nat. iii. § 5).

(9) *Prudentii* Epist. Trecassini de Prædestin. contra Joann. Scotum liber (in *Manguin*, t. i. P. i. p. 197 ss.).—*Flori Magistri* et ecclesiæ Lugdunensis Liber adversus Jo. Scoti erroneas Definitiones; ibid. t. i. P. i. p. 585. *Neander*, s. 448–450. On *Remigius* of Lyons, compare *Neander*, l.c. s. 452. *Staudenmaier*, s. 194 ff.

(10) Synodi Carisiacæ Capitula 4 (in *Manguin*, t. i. P. ii. p. 173; *Münscher, von Cölln*, s. 125). Cap. i.: Deus omnipotens hominem sine peccato rectum cum libero arbitrio condidit et in Paradiso posuit, quem in sanctitate justitiæ permanere voluit. Homo libero arbitrio male utens peccavit et cecidit, et factus est massa perditionis totius humani generis. Deus autem bonus et justus elegit ex eadem massa perditionis secundum *præscientiam* suam, quos per gratiam *prædestinavit ad vitam*, et vitam illis prædestinavit æternam. Cæteros autem, quos justitiæ judicio in massa perditionis reliquit, *perituros præscivit, sed non ut perirent prædestinavit; pœnam* autem illis, quia justus est, *prædestinavit æternam*. Ac per hoc *unam Dei prædestinationem tantummodo dicimus*, quæ ad donum pertinet gratiæ aut ad retributionem justitiæ. Cap. ii.: Libertatem arbitrii in primo homine perdidimus, quam per Christum Dominum nostrum recepimus. *Et habemus liberum arbitrium ad bonum*, præventum et adjutum gratia, et habemus *liberum arbitrium ad malum*, desertum gratia. Liberum autem habemus arbitrium, quia gratis liberatum, et gratia de corrupto sanatum. Cap. iii.: *Deus omnipotens omnes homines sine exceptione vult salvos fieri*, licet non omnes salventur. Quod autem quidam salvantur, salvantis est donum: quod autem quidam pereunt, pereuntium est meritum. Cap. iv.: Christus Jesus Dominus noster, sicut nullus homo est, fuit, vel erit, cujus natura in illo

assumta non fuerit: ita nullus est, fuit, vel erit homo, pro quo passus non fuerit; licet non omnes passionis ejus mysterio redimantur. Quod vero omnes passionis ejus mysterio non redimuntur, non respicit ad magnitudinem et pretii copiositatem, sed ad infidelium et ad non credentium ea fide, quæ per dilectionem operatur, respicit partem: quia poculum humanæ salutis, quod confectum est infirmitate nostra et virtute divina, habet quidem in se ut omnibus prosit, sed si non bibitur, non medetur.

(11) Concilii Valentini III. Can. i.-vi. (given by *Mauguin*, l.c. p. 231 ss.). Can. iii.: Fidenter fatemur prædestinationem electorum ad vitam et *prædestinationem impiorum ad mortem:* in electione tamen salvandorum misericordiam Dei præcedere meritum bonum, in damnatione autem periturorum meritum malum præcedere justum Dei judicium. Prædestinatione autem Deum ea tantum statuisse, quæ ipse vel gratuita misericordia vel justo judicio facturus erat ... in malis vero ipsorum malitiam præscisse, quia ex ipsis est, non prædestinasse, quia ex illo non est. Pœnam sane malum meritum eorum sequentem, uti Deum, qui omnia prospicit, præscivisse et prædestinasse, quia justus est ... *Verum aliquos ad malum prædestinatos esse divina potestate, videlicet ut quasi aliud esse non possint, non solum non credimus*, sed etiam si sunt qui tantum mali credere velint, cum omni detestatione sicut Arausica synodus (see § 114), illis Anathema dicimus.—According to Can. iv., Christ shed His blood only for believers.—The general import of the canons was expressed in the following terms: Quatuor capitula, quæ a Concilio fratrum nostrorum minus prospecte suscepta sunt, propter inutilitatem vel etiam noxietatem et errorem contrarium veritati ... a pio auditu fidelium penitus explodimus et ut talia et similia caveantur per omnia auctoritate Spiritus S. interdicimus.—The doctrines of *Scotus Erigena* were also particularly condemned as ineptæ quæstiunculæ et aniles pæne fabulæ (see *Neander*, l.c. s. 457). The six Canones Lingonenses (in *Mauguin*, l.c. p. 235 s.) were merely a repetition of the former four. Attempts at union were made at the Synod of Savonières (apud Saponarias), a suburb of Toul, but it was found impossible to come to an understanding. See *Neander*, s. 458.

(12) He composed (A.D. 859) a defence of the Capitula,

which was addressed to the Emperor Charles the Bald, under the title: De Prædestinatione et libero Arbitrio contra Gothescalcum et cæteros Prædestinatianos (in *Hincmari* Opp. ed. *Sismondi*, t. i. p. 1-110).

§ 184.

Further Development of the Doctrine of Predestination.

[*J. B. Mozley*, Augustinian Doctrine of Predestination, Lond. 1855. Chapters ix. x. p. 250-314, on the Scholastic Theories. *Hampden's* Bampton Lectures, 3d ed. 1848; Lect. iv. p. 153-207.]

Among the scholastics, it was chiefly *Anselm* (1), *Peter Lombard* (2), and *Thomas Aquinas* (3) who endeavoured to retain Augustine's doctrine of an unconditional election, although with many limitations. The entire religious tendency of *Bonaventura* also kept him from restricting the grace of God, even when he maintained, for practical interests, that the ground of His mercy was to be found in the measure of man's susceptibility to that which is good (4). But this idea was also taken up by some who knew how to make use of it in favour of a trivial theory of the meritoriousness of works, and Augustinianism was thus perverted into a new semi-Pelagianism by *Scotus* and his followers (5). Accordingly, *Thomas of Bradwardine*, a second Gottschalk, living in the fourteenth century, found it necessary to commence a new contest in defence of Augustine and his system (6). The forerunners of the Reformation, *Wykliffe*, *Savonarola*, and *Wessel*, were also led by a living conviction of man's dependence on God to return to the more profound fundamental principles of Augustinianism, although the last of these three urged the necessity of a free appropriation of divine grace on the part of man as a conditio sine qua non (7).

(1) *Anselm* composed a separate treatise on this subject, entitled: De Concordia Præscientiæ et Prædestinationis nec non Gratiæ Dei c. libero Arbitrio, in Opp. p. 123-134 (150-

164). He proceeded on the assumption that no difference exists between prescience and predestination. P. ii. c. 10 : Dubitari non debet, quia ejus praedestinatio et praescientia non discordant, sed sicut praescit, ita quoque praedestinat ; he referred, however, the one as well as the other, in the first instance, to that which is good ; c. 9 : Bona specialius praescire et praedestinare dicitur, quia in illis facit, quod sunt et quod bona sunt, in malis autem non nisi quod sunt essentialiter, non quod mala sunt. Comp. P. i. c. 7. But he, too, differed in some points from Augustine. Thus he called the proposition: non esse liberum arbitrium nisi ad mala, an absurdity (ii. c. 8), and endeavoured to hold the doctrine of the freedom of the will, together with that of predestination. But the freedom of the will, in his opinion, does not consist in a mere liberty of choice, for in that case the virtuous would be less free than the vicious. On the contrary, the rational creatures received it, ad servandam acceptam a Deo rectitudinem. Anselm also showed that Scripture is favourable to both systems (that of grace, and that of the freedom of the will), P. iii. c. 11 ; and then continued as follows : Quoniam ergo in sacra Scriptura quaedam invenimus, quae soli gratiae favere *videntur*, et quaedam, quae solum liberum arbitrium statuere sine gratia putantur : fuerunt quidam superbi, qui totam virtutem et efficaciam in sola libertate arbitrii consistere sunt arbitrati, et sunt nostro tempore multi (?), qui liberum arbitrium esse aliquid penitus desperant.—Therefore, cap. 14 : Nemo servat rectitudinem acceptam nisi volendo, velle autem illam aliquis nequit nisi habendo. Habere vero illam nullatenus valet nisi per gratiam. Sicut ergo illam nullus accipit nisi gratia praeveniente, ita nullus eam servat nisi eadem gratia subsequente. Compare also his treatise, De libero Arbitrio, and *Möhler*, Kleine Schriften, i. s. 170 ff.

(2) Sent. lib. i. dist. 40 A : Praedestinatio est gratiae praeparatio, quae sine praescientia esse non potest. *Potest autem sine praedestinatione esse praescientia.* Praedestinatione quippe Deus ea praescivit, quae fuerat ipse facturus, sed praescivit Deus etiam quae non esset ipse facturus, i. e. omnia mala. Praedestinavit eos quos elegit, reliquos vero reprobavit, i. e. ad mortem aeternam praescivit peccaturos. On the election of individuals, see dist. 46 ss.

(3) Summæ, P. i. qu. 23, art. 1 ss. (qu. by *Münscher, von Cölln*, s. 151-154). He there distinguished between electio and dilectio.—God wills that all men should be helped antecedenter, but not consequenter (θέλημα προηγούμενον and ἑπόμενον).—Respecting the causa meritoria, see art. 5.

(4) Comment. in Sent. lib. i. dist. 40, art. 2, qu. 1 (qu. by *Münscher, von Cölln*, s. 154).—The free will, as a causa contingens, is included in the prescience. [*Bonaventura* raises the question, An prædestinatio inferat salutis necessitatem ? and replies : quod prædestinatio non infert necessitatem saluti, nec infert necessitatem libero arbitrio. Quoniam *prædestinatio non est causa salutis, nisi includendo merita*, et ita salvando liberum arbitrium. *Münscher*, l.c.]

(5) *Duns Scotus* in Sent. l. i. dist. 40, in Resol. (qu. by *Münscher, von Cölln*, s. 155): Divina autem voluntas circa ipsas creaturas libere et contingenter se habet. Quocirca contingenter salvandos prædestinat, et posset eosdem non prædestinare. Dist. 17, qu. 1, in Resol.: ... Actus meritorius est in potestate hominis, supposita generali influentia, si habuerit liberi arbitrii usum et gratiam, sed completio in ratione meriti non est in potestate hominis nisi dispositive, sic tamen dispositive, quod ex dispositione divina nobis revelata.

(6) *Thomas of Bradwardine*, surnamed Doctor profundus, was born at Hartfield, in the county of Sussex (about the year 1290), was well read in the works of Plato and Aristotle, was warden of Merton College, confessor of King Edward III., afterwards Archbishop of Canterbury, and died A.D. 1349. In his work entitled " De Causa Dei contra Pelagium et de Virtute Causarum," ad suos Mertonenses, libb. iii. (edited by *Savile*, Lond. 1618, fol.), extracts from which are given by *Schröckh*, Kg. xxxiv. s. 227 ff., he complained that *almost the whole world had fallen into the error of Pelagianism*. In his principles he agreed, on the whole, with Augustine and Anselm, though some of his notions appear more rigid than those of Augustine himself. Among other things, he lowered the free will of man so much, as to represent it as a servant who is following its mistress (*i.e.* the divine will), certainly a mechanical notion. Comp. *Schröckh*, l.c. *Münscher, von Cölln*, s. 156 f. " *That these repulsive (wholly necessitarian) positions were so unnoticed and unopposed, can only be explained by the*

fact that the theologians of the fourteenth century were so absorbed in fruitless subtleties, that they had hardly any interest left in those parts of theology which are of chief practical importance." Gieseler, Dg. s. 524.

(7) *Wykliffe*, Trialog. lib. ii. c. 14 : Videtur mihi probabile ... quod Deus necessitat creaturas singulas activas ad quemlibet actum suum. Et sic sunt aliqui *praedestinati*, h. e. post laborem ordinati ad gloriam, aliqui *praesciti*, h. e. post vitam miseram ad poenam perpetuam ordinati. Compare also what follows, where this idea is more fully discussed in a scholastico-speculative manner. [Comp. on Wiclif the work of *Lechler*, in Eng. by *Lorimer*.] *Wessel* views the atonement, sometimes as general, and again as limited. Christ suffered for all, but His sufferings will avail to any man only as far as he shows susceptibility for them; the susceptibility itself is proportioned to the amount of his inward purity, and to the degree in which his life is conformable to that of Christ: De Magn. Passion. c. 10 (qu. by *Ullmann*, s. 271 f.).—On *Savonarola's* more liberal views on the doctrine of predestination, see *Rudelbach*, s. 361 ff.; *Meier*, s. 269 ff., and *Villari*, vol. ii. ad fin.

§ 185.

Appropriation of Grace.

Rettberg, Scholasticorum Placita de Gratia et Merito, Göttingen 1836.

Although Augustine had demonstrated with logical strictness the natural corruption of mankind, unconditional election by the free grace of God, and the efficacy of that grace, he yet gave no precise statements respecting the appropriation of the grace of God on the part of man, justification, sanctification, etc. (1). It was in consequence of this very deficiency that Semi-Pelagianism again found its way into the Church. *Thomas Aquinas* understood by justification, not only the acquittal of the sinner from punishment, but also the communication of divine life (infusio gratiæ) from the hand of God, which takes place at the same time (2). It was also possible to advance very different definitions of the idea of grace; some regarded it (from the theological point of view) as an attribute, or an act of God, while others looked upon it (in its bearing upon anthropology) as a religious and moral energy, working in man, and belonging to the nature of the regenerate. Hence *Peter Lombard* and *Thomas Aquinas* distinguished between *gratia gratis dans, gratia gratis data,* and *gratia gratum faciens,* the last of which was further divided into *gratia operans* and *gratia co-operans* (præveniens and comitans) (3). Concerning the certainty of divine grace, not only Thomas Aquinas, but also *Tauler,* still entertained doubts (4); while the mystics, generally speaking, attempted to point out more definitely the various steps and degrees of the higher life wrought by the Holy Spirit in the regenerate, and to describe in detail the inward processes of enlightening, awakening, etc. (5). On the other hand, the fanatical sects of the Middle Ages, inclining to pantheism, lost sight of the serious character of sanctification in the fantastic intoxication of feeling (6).

(1) See above, § 114.

(2) *Thomas,* Summ. P. II. 1, qu. 100, art. 12 (qu. by *Münscher, von Cölln,* s. 147): Justificatio primo ac proprie dicitur *factio justitiæ,* secundario vero et quasi improprie potest dici justificatio significatio justitiæ, vel *dispositio ad justitiam.* Sed si loquamur de justificatione proprie dicta, justitia potest accipi prout est in habitu, vel prout est in actu. Et secundum hoc justificatio dupliciter dicitur, uno quidem modo, secundum quod homo fit justus adipiscens *habitum* justitiæ, alio vero modo, secundum quod *opera justitiæ operatur,* ut secundum hoc justificatio nihil aliud sit quam *justitiæ executio.* Justitia autem, sicut et aliæ *virtutes,* potest accipi et *acquisita et infusa.* . . . Acquisita quidem causatur ex operibus, sed infusa causatur ab ipso Deo per ejus gratiam. Comp. qu. 113, art. 1 (qu. by *Münscher, von Cölln,* l.c.).

(3) *Peter Lombard,* Sent. ii. dist. 27 D. He says (ii. d. 26): Operans gratia est, quæ prævenit voluntatem bonam, ea enim liberatur et præparatur hominis voluntas, ut sit bona, bonumque efficaciter velit. Co-operans vero gratia voluntatem jam

bonam sequitur adjuvando. *Thomas Aquinas*, Summa, P. III. qu. 2, art. 10 (qu. by *Münscher, von Cölln*, s. 140 ff.). According to *Aquinas*, God works good in us without our co-operation, but not without our consent: Summa, P. I. qu. 55, art. 4: Virtus infusa causatur in nobis a Deo sine nobis agentibus, non tamen sine nobis consentientibus. Comp. *Ritter*, viii. s. 341. [*Aquinas*, P. II. 1, qu. 109, art. 6: Conversio hominis ad Deum fit quidem per liberum arbitrium, et secundum hoc homini præcipitur quod se ad Deum convertat. Sed liberum arbitrium ad Deum converti non potest, nisi Deo ipsum ad se convertente.] Man's co-operation is much more insisted upon by *Duns Scotus* than by Thomas, Sentent. lib. iii. dist. 34, 5: Deus dedit habitum voluntatis, semper assistit voluntati et habitui ad actus sibi convenientes. We are not to conceive of grace as infused into man, like fire into a piece of wood; and not so that nature is crushed by grace (gratia naturam non tollit, sed perficit); see *Ritter*, l.c. s. 372. *Baur*, Lehrb. s. 189 ff. *Gieseler*, Dg. s. 521 ff.

(4) *Aquinas* supposed (Summa, P. II. 1, qu. 112, art. 5) a threefold way in which man could ascertain whether he was a subject of divine grace or not: 1. By direct revelation on the part of God; 2. By himself (certitudinaliter); 3. By certain indications (conjecturalitur per aliqua signa). But the last two were, in his opinion, uncertain; as for the first, God very seldom makes use of it, and only in particular cases (revelat Deus hoc aliquando aliquibus ex speciali privilegio). *Luther* denounced this notion of the uncertainty of man being in a state of grace (in his Comment. upon Gal. iv. 6) as a dangerous and sophistical doctrine. Nevertheless *Tauler* entertained the same opinion, Predigten, Bd. i. s. 67: No man on earth is either so good, or so blessed, or so well informed in holy doctrine, as to know whether he is in the grace of God or not, unless it be made known to him by a special revelation of God. If a man will but examine himself, it will be evident enough to him that he does not know; thus the desire of knowing proceeds from ignorance, as if a child would know what an emperor has in his heart. Accordingly, as he who is diseased in body is to believe his physician, who knows the nature of his disease better than himself, so man must trust in some modest confessor.

(5) According to *Bonaventura*, the grace of God manifests itself in a threefold way: 1. In habitus virtutum; 2. In habitus donorum; 3. In habitus beatitudinum (Breviloquium, v. 4 ss.; comp. *Richard of St. Victor*, quoted by *Engelhardt*, s. 30 ff.). A lively picture of the mystical doctrine of salvation is given in the work, Büchlein von der Deutschen Theologie, in which it is shown how Adam must die, and Christ live in us. In his opinion, *purification, illumination,* and *union* are the three principal degrees. The last in particular (unio mystica) is to be brought forward as the aim and crown of the whole. According to chap. 25 of this work, it (union) consists in this: "that we are pure, single-minded, and, in the pursuit of truth, are entirely one with the one eternal will of God; or that *we have not any will at all of our own; or that the will of the creature flows into the will of the eternal Creator, and is so blended with it, and annihilated by it, that the eternal will alone wills, acts, and suffers in us.*" Comp. chap. 30: "Behold, man in that state wills or desires nothing but good as such, and for no other reason but because it is good, and not because it is this thing or that, nor because it pleases one or displeases another, nor because it is pleasant or unpleasant, sweet or bitter, etc. . . . for all selfishness, egoism, and man's own interest have ceased, and fallen into oblivion; no longer is it said, I love myself, or I love you, or such and such a thing. And if you would ask Charity, What dost thou love? she would say, I love good. And why? she would say, Because it is good. And because it is good, it is also good, and right, and well done, that it may be right well desired and loved. *And if my own self were better than God, then I ought to love it above God.* On that account God does not love Himself as God, but as the highest good. For if God knew anything better than God, etc. (comp. § 168, note 3). . . . Behold, thus it ought to be, and really is, in a godly person, or in a truly sanctified man, for otherwise he could neither be godly nor sanctified." Chap. 39: "Now, it might be asked, What man is godly or sanctified? The reply is, He who is illuminated and enlightened with the eternal or divine light, and kindled with eternal or divine love, is a godly or sanctified person. . . . *We ought to know that light and knowledge are nothing, and are good for nothing, without charity.*" (He distinguishes, however,

between the true light and the false, between true love and false love, etc.) *Tauler* expressed himself in similar terms (Predigten, i. s. 117): "He who has devoted himself to God, and surrendered himself prisoner to Him for ever, may expect that God, in His turn, will surrender Himself prisoner to him; and, overcoming all obstacles, and opening all prisons, God will lead man to the divine liberty, viz. to Himself. Then man will, in some respects, be rather a divine being than a natural man. And if you touch man, you touch God; he who would see and confess the former, must see and confess him in God. Here all wounds are healed, and all pledges are remitted; here the transition is made from the creature to God, from the natural being, in some respect, to a divine being. This loving reciprocation is above our apprehension, it is above all sensible or perceptible ways, and above natural methods. Those who are within, and are what we have described, are in much the nearest and best way, and in the path to much the greatest blessedness, where they will ever enjoy God in the highest possible degree. It is far better to remain silent on those points than to speak of them; better to perceive, or to feel, than to understand them."—*Suso*,[1] speaking of the unio mystica, in his treatise entitled: Büchlein von der ewigen Weisheit, Buch ii. c. 7, expressed himself poetically as follows (quoted by *Diepenbrock*, s. 275): "O thou gentle and lovely flower of the field, thou beloved bride in the embraces of the soul, loving with a pure love, how happy is he who ever truly felt what it is to possess thee; but how strange is it to hear a man [talk of thee] who does not know thee, and whose heart and mind are yet carnal! O thou precious, thou incomprehensible good, this hour is a happy one, this present time is a sweet one, in which I must open to thee a secret wound which thy sweet love has inflicted upon my heart. Lord, Thou knowest that sharing in love is like water in fire; Thou knowest that true, heartfelt love cannot endure a duality. O Thou! the only Lord of my heart and soul, and therefore my heart desires that Thou shouldst love me with a special love, and that Thy divine eyes would

---

[1] On the further views of Suso as to the method of salvation, and its three degrees (purgatio, illuminatio, perfectio), see *Schmidt*, ubi supra, s. 48. To float in divinity, as the eagle in the air, is the end of his aspirations, s. 50.

take a special delight in me. O Lord! Thou hast so many hearts which love Thee with a heartfelt love, and prevail much with Thee; alas! Thou tender and dear Lord! how is it then with me?" *Ruysbroek* treated very fully of the mystical doctrine of salvation (quoted by *Engelhardt*, s. 190 ff.). In his opinion, man attains unto God by an active, an inward, and a contemplative life. The first has regard rather to the external (exercises of penance). Only when man *loves* do his desires take an opposite direction. When our spirits turn entirely to the light, viz. God, all will be made perfect in us, and be restored to its original state. We are united to the light, and, by the grace of God, are born again, of grace, above nature. The eternal light itself brings forth four lights in us: 1. The natural light of heaven, which we have in common with the animals; 2. The glory of the highest heaven, by which we behold, as it were, with our bodily senses, the glorified body of Christ and the saints; 3. The spiritual light (the natural intelligence of angels and men); 4. The light of the grace of God.—Concerning the three unities in man, the three advents of Christ, the four processions, the three meetings, the gifts of the Spirit, etc., as well as the various degrees of the contemplative life, the degrees of love, see *Engelhardt*, l.c.— *Savonarola* described (in his sermons) the state of grace as a sealing of the heart; Jesus Christ, the crucified One, is the seal with which the sinner is sealed after he has done penance, and received a new heart. The waters of temporal afflictions cannot quench the fire of this love, etc.; nevertheless, grace does not work irresistibly; man may resist, as well as lose it again. Respecting Savonarola's views on the doctrine of the uncertainty of a state of grace, see *Rudelbach*, s. 364, and *Meier*, s. 272.

(6) See the Episcopal letter quoted by Mosheim, p. 256: Item dicunt, quod homo possit sic uniri Deo, quod ipsius sit idem posse ac velle et operari quodcunque, quod est ipsius Dei. Item credunt, se esse Deum per naturam sine distinctione. Item, quod sint in eis omnes perfectiones divinæ, ita quod dicunt, se esse æternos, et in æternitate. Item dicunt, se omnia creasse, et plus creasse, quam Deus. Item, quod nullo indigent nec Deo nec Deitate. Item, quod sunt impeccabiles, unde quemcunque actum peccati faciunt sine peccato (compare

above, § 165, note 2).—The opinions of *Master Eckart* on this question were also pantheistic: Nos transformamur totaliter in Deum et convertimur in eum simili modo, sicut in sacramento convertitur panis in Corpus Christi: sic ego convertor in eum, quod ipse operatur in me suum esse. Unum non simile per viventem Deum verum est, quod nulla ibi est distinctio. (Cf. *Raynald*, Annal. ad a. 1329.) He was opposed by *Gerson* (see *Hundeshagen*, s. 66).

§ 186.

Faith and Works—The Meritoriousness of the Letter.

Though many of the scholastics were inclined to Pelagianism, yet the doctrine of *justification by faith* had to be retained as Pauline. But then the difficult question was, what we are to understand by *faith*. *John of Damascus* had already represented faith as consisting in two things, viz. a belief in the truth of the doctrines, and a firm confidence in the promises of God (1). *Hugo of St. Victor* also defined faith, on the one hand as *cognitio*, and on the other as *affectus* (2). And, lastly, the distinction made by *Peter Lombard* between *credere Deum*, *credere Deo*, and *credere in Deum* (3), shows that he too acknowledged a difference in the usage of the term "faith." Only the last kind of faith was regarded by the scholastics as fides justificans, fides formata (4). The most eminent theologians both perceived and taught that *this* kind of faith must of itself produce good works (5). Nevertheless, the theory of the meritoriousness of good works was developed in connection with ecclesiastical practice. Though the distinction made by *Aquinas* between *meritum ex condigno* and *meritum ex congruo* seemed to limit human claims, yet it only secured the appearance of humility (6). But the evil grew still worse when the notion of supererogatory works, which may be imputed to those who have none of their own, became a dangerous support of the sale of indulgences (7). There were, however, even at that time, some who strenuously opposed such abuses (8).

(1) De fide orth. iv. 10: Ἡ μέντοι πίστις διπλῆ ἐστιν· ἔστι γὰρ πίστις ἐξ ἀκοῆς (Rom. x. 17). Ἀκούοντες γὰρ τῶν θείων γραφῶν, πιστεύομεν τῇ διδασκαλίᾳ τοῦ ἁγίου πνεύματος. Αὔτη δὲ τελειοῦται πᾶσι τοῖς νομοθετηθεῖσιν ὑπὸ τοῦ Χριστοῦ, ἔργῳ πιστεύουσα, εὐσεβοῦσα καὶ τὰς ἐντολὰς πράττουσα τοῦ ἀνακαινίσαντος ἡμᾶς ... Ἔστι δὲ πάλιν πίστις ἐλπιζομένων ὑπόστασις (Heb. xi. 1), πραγμάτων ἔλεγχος οὐ βλεπομένων, ἡ ἀδίστακτος καὶ ἀδιάκριτος ἐλπὶς τῶν τε ὑπὸ Θεοῦ ἡμῖν ἐπηγγελμένων, καὶ τῆς τῶν αἰτήσεων ἡμῶν ἐπιτυχίας. Ἡ μὲν οὖν πρώτη τῆς ἡμετέρας γνώμης ἐστί, ἡ δὲ δευτέρα τῶν χαρισμάτων τοῦ πνεύματος.

(2) On the difference between these two terms, compare *Liebner*, s. 435. [*Hugo of St. Victor*, De Sacramentis, liber 1, part x. cap. 3: Duo sunt, in quibus fides constat: *cognitio et affectus*, i. e. constantia vel firmitas credendi. In altero constat quia ipsa illud est; in altero constat, quia ipsa in illo est. In affectu enim substantia fidei invenitur; in cognitione materia. Aliud enim est fides, qua creditur, et aliud, quod creditur. In affectu invenitur fides, in cognitione id, quod fide creditur.]

(3) Sent. lib. iii. dist. 23 D: Aliud est enim credere in Deum, aliud credere Deo, aliud credere Deum. Credere Deo, est credere vera esse quæ loquitur, quod et mali faciunt. Et nos credimus homini, sed non in hominem. Credere Deum, est credere quod ipse sit Deus, quod etiam mali faciunt (this kind of faith was sometimes called the faith of devils, according to Jas. ii. 9). Credere in Deum est credendo amare, credendo in eum ire, credendo ei adhærere et ejus membris incorporari. Per hanc fidem justificatur impius, ut deinde ipsa fides incipiat per dilectionem operari.—The same holds true of the phrase, credere Christum, etc. Comp. Lit. C.

(4) Generally speaking, the scholastics made a difference between subjective and objective faith, fides *qua* and fides *quæ* creditur (*Peter Lombard*, l.c.). As a subdivision, we find mentioned fides formata, which works by love. Faith without love remains informis, see *Lombard*, l.c.; *Thomas Aquinas*, Summ. P. II. 2, qu. 4, art. 3 (quoted by *Münscher, von Cölln*, s. 175). So, too, a distinction was made between developed and undeveloped faith (fides explicita et implicita); the latter is sufficient, see Summa, II. qu. 1, art. 7; qu. 2, art. 6 and 7.

(5) Thus *Peter Lombard* said, l.c.: Sola bona opera dicenda

sunt, quæ fiunt per dilectionem Dei. Ipsa enim dilectio opus fidei dicitur. — Faith would therefore still be the source of good works; comp. lib. ii. dist. 41 A, where everything which does not proceed from faith (according to Rom. xiv. 23) is represented as sin. — The views of *Thomas Aquinas* were not quite so scriptural; Summ. P. II. 2, qu. 4, art. 7, he spoke of *faith* itself as a *virtue*, though he assigned to it the first and highest place among all virtues. Such notions, however, led more and more to the revival of Pelagian sentiments, till the forerunners of the Reformation returned to the path of the gospel. This was done, *e.g.*, by *Wessel* (see *Ullmann*, s. 272 ff.) and *Savonarola* (see *Rudelbach*, s. 351). On the other hand, even the Waldenses laid much stress upon works of repentance. *Thomas a Kempis* did not start from the central point of the doctrine of justification in *such* a measure and manner as did the above; see *Ullmann*, ubi supra.

(6) *Alanus ab Insulis* also opposed the notion of the meritoriousness of works in decided terms, ii. 18 (quoted by *Pez*, i. p. 492): Bene mereri proprie dicitur, qui sponte alicui benefacit, quod facere non tenetur. Sed nihil Deo facimus, quod non teneamur facere ... Ergo meritum nostrum apud Deum non est *proprie* meritum, sed solutio debiti. Sed non est merces nisi meriti vel debiti præcedentis. Sed non meremur proprie; ergo quod dabitur a Deo, non erit proprie merces, sed gratia.—Some theologians regarded *faith* itself as meritorious (inasmuch as they considered it to be a work, a virtue— obedience to the Church). *Thomas Aq.* P. II. 2, qu. 2, art. 9. —But how externally the doctrine of faith was understood is shown by the scholastics of the later period, who regarded faith as meritorious in proportion to the difficulty of believing in that which has its object. The more incredible a thing, the greater merit in believing it. To compel oneself to faith is accordingly a requirement to be imposed on the will. So *Durandus a Sancto Porciano* and *W. Occam*. Such a forced faith led of necessity to the irony and frivolity of unbelief.— On the distinction made between different kinds of *merita*, see P. II. 1, q. 114, art. 4 (qu. by *Münscher, von Cölln*, s. 145). Men have only a *meritum ex congruo*, but not *ex condigno*. Christ alone possessed the latter.

(7) The development of the doctrine of a thesaurus meritorum, thesaurus supererogationis perfectorum, belongs to *Alexander of Hales* (Summa, Pars iv. quæst. 23, art. 2, membr. 5). To this was added the distinction made by *Thomas Aquinas* between consilium and præceptum, see Summ. P. II. qu. 108, art. 4 (qu. by *Münscher, von Cölln*, s. 177). On the historical development of indulgences, see † (*Eus.*) *Amort*, Historia... de Origine, Progressu, Valore et Fructu Indulgentiarum, Venet. 1738, fol. Comp. *Gieseler*, Kg. ii. 2, s. 452 ff. *Ullmann*, Reformatoren vor d. Ref. i. s. 203 ff. †*Hirscher*, Die Lehre vom Ablass, Tüb. 1844.

(8) Thus the Franciscan monk *Berthold*, in the thirteenth century, zealously opposes the penny-preachers who seduce the souls of men (see *Kling*, s. 149, 150, 235, 289, 384, 398; *Grimm*, s. 210; *Wackernagel*, Deutsch. Lesebuch, i. Sp. 664). On the struggles of *Wykliffe, Hus*, and others, see the works on Church History. Concerning the treatise of Hus: De Indulgentiis, compare *Schröckh*, xxxiv. s. 599 ff. Besides, the actual exercises of penance on the part of the Flagellantes, and those who tormented themselves, formed a practical opposition to the laxity of their principles. See *Gieseler*, l.c. s. 469.

SIXTH DIVISION.

THE DOCTRINE OF THE CHURCH AND THE SACRAMENTS.

§ 187.

The Church.

Even in the preceding period the idea of the Church had become confounded with its historical manifestation, and thus the way was prepared for all the abuses of the hierarchy, and the development of the papal power. The relation in which the ecclesiastical power stands to the secular (or the Church to the State), was often illustrated by the comparison of the two swords, which some supposed to be separated, while others thought them united in the hand o. Peter (1). It belongs, properly speaking, to the province of Canon Law further to develope and define those relations; but, inasmuch as adherence to the decisions of ecclesiastical authorities on such matters was supposed to form a part of orthodoxy, and as every departure from them appeared not only heretical, but as the most dangerous of all heresies, it is obvious that they are not to be passed over with silence in a History of Doctrines. That which exerted the greatest influence upon the doctrinal tendency of the present age was the dogma of the papal power and infallibility, in opposition to the position that the council is superior to the pope (2). The mystical idea of the Church, and the notion of a universal priesthood, which was intimately connected with it, was propounded, with more or less definiteness, by *Hugo of St. Victor*, as well as by the forerunners of the Reformation, *Wykliffe*, *Matthias of Janow*, *Hus*, *John of Wesel*, *Wessel*, and *Savonarola* (3). The anti-hierarchical element referred to, and together with it the anti-ecclesiastical, manifested itself nowhere so strongly as in the fanatical sects of the Middle Ages, whose principles also led them sometimes to oppose not only Christianity, but also the existing political governments (4). On the other hand, the Waldenses and Bohemian brethren endeavoured, in a simple way, and without fanaticism, to return to the foundation laid by the apostles: overlooking, however, the historical development of the Church (5).

(1) This is more fully shown in the work entitled: Vridankes Bescheidenheit,[1] edit. by *Grimm*, Gött. 1834, s. lvii. —*Bernard of Clairvaux* already interpreted the words of Luke xxii. 36–38 in a figurative sense, Epist. ad Eugen. 256 (written A.D. 1146); in agreement with him, *John of Salisbury* (Polic. iv. 3) asserted that both the swords are in the hands of the pope, but yet the pope ought to wield the secular sword by the arm of the emperor. On the other hand, the Emperor Frederick I. referred the *one* of the two swords to the power of the pope, the *other* to that of the emperor (see the letters written A.D. 1157, 1160, 1167, in the work of *Grimm*). The Emperor Otto maintained the same in opposition to Pope Innocent III. Since it was *Peter* (according to John xviii. 10) who drew the sword, the advocates of the papal system inferred that *both* the swords ought to be in *one* hand, and that the pope had only to lend it to the emperor. Such was the reasoning, *e.g.*, of the Franciscan monk *Berthold*. On the contrary, others, as *Freidank*, *Reinmar of Zweter*, and the author of the work entitled: Der Sachsenspiegel, insisted that the power was to be divided; in a note to the Sachsenspiegel it is assumed that Christ gave only one of the two swords

---

[1] The passage in *Vridank* reads (s. 152):
  Zwei swert in einer schei!le
  verderbent lihte beide;
  als der bäbest riches gert,
  so verderbent beidiu swert.

to the Apostle Peter, but the other, the secular one, to the Apostle John. The papal view was defended in the work called: Der Schwabenspiegel. Further particulars are given by *Grimm*, l.c.—There were also not wanting those who advocated the freedom of the Church in opposition to the secular as well as the spiritual domination. Thus *John of Salisbury* maintained the principle: Ecclesiastica debent esse liberrima; see his 95th Epistle, in the collection of *Masson* (in *Ritter*, Gesch. d. Phil. viii. s. 50, Anm.).

(2) Compare, *e.g.*, the bull issued by Pope Boniface VIII. A.D. 1302 (in Extravag. Commun. lib. i. tit. viii. cap. 1), and the decision of the Synod of Basel, Sess. i. July 19, 1431, in which the opposite doctrine was set forth (*Mansi*, t. xxix. Cod. 21: both in *Münscher*, *von Cölln*, p. 316-318).

(3) According to *Hugo of St. Victor* (De Sacram. lib. ii. P. iii. quoted by *Liebner*, s. 445 ff.), Christ is the invisible Head of the Church, and the *multitudo fidelium* is the body. The Church, as a whole, is divided into two halves (walls), the laity and the clergy (the left side and the right side). As much as the spirit is above the body, so much is the ecclesiastical power above the secular. On that account the former has the right not only to institute the latter, but also to judge it when it is corrupt. But since the ecclesiastical power itself is instituted by God, it can be judged only by God when it turns from the right path (1 Cor. vi.). Hugo also acknowledged the pope as the Vicar of Peter. He conceded to him the privilege of being served by all ecclesiastics, and the unlimited power of binding and loosing all things upon earth. —*Wykliffe* made a much more precise distinction between the idea of the Church and the external ecclesiastical power than Hugo (see the extracts from the Trialogus given by *Schröckh*, xxxiv. s. 510 ff., and his other writings of an antihierarchical tendency, ibid. s. 547 ff.). *Neander*, Kg. 3te Aufl. ii. s. 764 ff. *Böhringer*, s. 409. Still more definite was *Matthias of Janow* (De Regulis Vet. et Novi Test.), who says that seeming Christians can no more be regarded as Christians than a painted man can be called a man; comp. *Neander*, l.c. s. 777 ff. *Hus*, in his treatise De Ecclesia, distinguishes between three forms of manifestation of the Church: 1. Ecclesia *triumphans*, i. e. beati in patria quiescentes, qui adversus

Satanam militiam Christi tenentes, finaliter triumpharunt; 2. Ecclesia *dormiens*, i. e. numerus prædestinatorum in purgatorio patiens; 3. Ecclesia *militans*, i. e. ecclesia prædestinatorum, dum hi viant ad patriam. These three Churches are, however, to be one Church on the day of judgment. From this true Church, at present represented in these three forms, he distinguishes again the ecclesia nuncupative dicta (the ecclesia of the *præsciti*); quidam sunt in ecclesia nomine et re, ut *prædestinati*, obedientes Christo catholici; quidam nec re nec nomine, ut præsciti pagani; quidam nomine tantum, ut præsciti hypocritæ; et quidam re, licet videantur nomine esse foris, ut prædestinati Christiani, quos Antichristi satrapæ videntur in facie ecclesiæ condemnare (among whom Hus probably reckoned himself). Comp. further in *Münchmeier*, ubi supra, s. 16 ff. *Hase*, Kirchengeschichte, s. 387, says of him: "*Hus ascended from the idea of the Roman Church to the idea of the true Church, which was in his opinion the community of all who have from eternity been predestinated to blessedness, and whose head can be none but Christ Himself, and not the pope. As Hus, however, retained all the assertions concerning the Church made by Roman Catholics, and applied them to the said community of the elect, who alone can administer the sacraments in an efficient way, his Church must necessarily have assumed the character of an association of separatists.*" On the relation of the views of Hus to those of *Gerson*, see *Münchmeier*, l.c. s. 18, note. Hus' friend, *Nicolas de Clémangis*, also, in agreement with Hus, regarded the vital faith of the individual as the real living principle by which the dead Church was to be revived; hence his declaration: In sola potest muliercula per gratiam manere ecclesia, sicut in sola Virgine tempore passionis mansisse creditur (Disputatio de Concil. Generali). Comp. *Münz*, Nic. Clémanges, sa vie et ses écrits, Stras. 1846, p. 58, 59. *Johann von Wesel* (Disp. adv. Indulgent.), starting from the different definitions of the word ecclesia, shows that we can equally well say, ecclesia universalis non errat and ecclesia universalis errat. Only the Church founded on the rock is to him sancta et immaculata; and he distinguishes from this the Church peccatrix et adultera. *John Wessel* held that the Church consists in the community of saints, to which all who are truly pious belong, viz. those who are united to Christ by *one* faith, *one* hope, and *one* love (he did not exclude the Greek Christians). The external unity of the Church under a pope is in his view merely accidental; nor is the unity spoken of established by the decrees of councils. (Hyperboreans, Indians, and Scythians, who know nothing of the Councils of Constance or Basel?) But he considered love to be still more excellent than the unity of faith. In close adherence to the principle of Augustine (Evangelio non crederem, etc.), which he regarded as a subjective concession, he believed *with* the Church, and *according* to the Church, but not *in* the Church. Respecting the priesthood, he retained the distinction between laity and clergy, but at the same time admitted the doctrine of a universal priesthood, together with the particular priesthood of the clergy. Nor does the Church exist for the sake of the clergy, but, on the contrary, the clergy exist for the sake of the Church. Comp. *Ullmann*, s. 296 ff. (after the various essays, De dignitate et potestate ecclesiastica, De sacramento poenitentiae, De communione Sanctorum et thesauro ecclesiae, collected in the Farrago Rerum Theologicarum), and *Münchmeier*, s. 19.—According to *Savonarola*, the Church is composed of all those who are united in the bonds of love and of Christian truth by the grace of the Holy Spirit; *and the Church is not there, where this grace does not exist*; see the passages collected from his sermons in *Rudelbach*, s. 354 ff., and *Meier*, s. 282 ff. Respecting the mystical interpretation of the ark of the covenant as having regard to the Church, see ibid.

(4) Compare *Mosheim*, p. 257: Dicunt se credere, ecclesiam catholicam sive christianitatem fatuam esse vel fatuitatem. Item, quod homo perfectus sit liber in totum, quod tenetur ad servandum præcepta data ecclesiæ a Deo, sicut est præceptum de honoratione parentum in necessitate. Item, quod ratione hujus libertatis homo non tenetur ad servandum præcepta Prælatorum et statutorum ecclesiæ, et hominem fortem, etsi non religiosum, non obligari ad labores manuales pro necessitatibus suis, sed eum libere posse recipere eleemosynam pauperum. Item dicunt, se credere omnia esse communia, unde dicunt, furtum eis licitum esse.

(5) Comp. *Gieseler*, Kg. ii. 2, s. 506 ff. *Herzog*, Waldenser, s. 194 ff.

§ 188.

The Worship of Saints.

[*Rev. J. B. Morris*, Jesus the Son of Mary; on the Reverence shown by Catholics to His blessed Mother, Lond. 2 vols. 1851. *Newman*, On Development, 173–180.]

The hierarchical system of the papacy, which was reared like a lofty pyramid upon earth, was supposed to correspond to a similar hierarchy in heaven, at the head of which was Mary, the mother of God (1). The objection of the polytheistic tendency of this doctrine, which would naturally suggest itself to reflecting minds, was met by the scholastics of the Greek Church by making a distinction between λατρεία and προσκύνησις; by those of the Latin Church, by distinguishing between *Latria*, *Dulia*, and *Hyperdulia* (2). But such distinctions were by no means safeguards against practical abuses; in consequence of these, the forerunners of the Reformation were induced to oppose with all energy the worship of saints (3).

(1) The adoration of the Virgin (Mariolatry) was advanced by *John Damascene* among the Greeks, and by *Peter Damiani*, *Bernard of Clairvaux*, *Bonaventura*,[1] and other theologians of the Western Church; see Gieseler, Kg. ii. 2, s. 425 (where passages from the songs of the Minnesingers are quoted); *Münscher*, *von Cölln*, s. 180–182; and De Gratiis et Virtutibus beatæ Mariæ Virg., in *Pez*, Thes. Anecd. t. i. p. 509 ss. To these we may add a passage from *Tauler*, Predigt. auf unser lieben Frauen Verkündigung (Predigten, Bd. iii. s. 57). Tauler calls Mary " a daughter of the Father, a mother of the Son, a bride of the Holy Spirit, a queen of heaven, a lady of the world and of all creatures, a mother and intercessor of all those who implore her help, a temple of God, in which God has reposed, like a bridegroom in His chamber, with great pleasure and delight; as in a garden full

---

[1] Comp. the Psalterium beatæ Mariæ Virginis, of the thirteenth century. [Not by Bonaventura.]

of every kind of odoriferous herbs, he found in the Virgin all kinds of virtues and graces. By means of these virtues she has made the heaven of the Holy Trinity pour out honey upon wretched sinners such as we, and has brought to us the Sun of Righteousness, and abolished the curse of Eve, and crushed the head of the hellish serpent. This second Eve has restored, by her child, all that the first Eve lost and marred, and has provided much more grace and riches. She is the star that was to come out of Jacob (of which the Scripture foretold, Num. xxiv. 17), whose lustre imparts light to the whole world: accordingly, in every distress (says Bernard) turn thine eyes to that star, call upon Mary, and thou canst not despair; follow Mary, and thou canst not miss thy way. She will keep thee by the power of her child, lest thou fall in the way; she will protect thee, lest thou despair; she will conduct thee to her child; she is able to perform it, *for Almighty God is her child;* she is willing to do it, for she is merciful. Who could doubt for a moment that the child would not honour His mother, or that she does not overflow with love, in whom perfect love (*i.e.* God Himself) has reposed?"[1]—Besides Mary, it was especially the apostles of Christ, the martyrs, those who had taken an active part in the spread of Christianity, the founders of national churches, the greatest lights in the Church, and ascetics, and lastly, monks and nuns in particular, that were canonized. Imagination itself created some new (mythical) saints, *e.g.* St. Longinus; and, in fine, some of the men and women mentioned in the Old Testament came in for their share in the general adoration. The right of canonizing formerly possessed by the bishops was more and more claimed by the popes; for particulars, see the works on Ecclesiastical History.

(2) In the Greek Church it was, in the first instance, in reference to the adoration of images, that this distinction was made by the second Synod of Nicæa (in *Mansi,* Concil. t. xiii. col. 377), as well as by *Theodore Studita,* Ep. 167, Opp.

---

[1] The mother of Jesus appears as an intercessor before her Son, who is for the most part represented as a severe judge. Thus, in the picture of Rubens in Lyons, Christ is depicted with the thunderbolt; while Mary, with St. Dominic and St. Francis, is interceding at His feet; see *Quandt,* Reise ins mittägliche Frankreich, Leipz. 1846, s. 99.

1521. The λατρεία is due to none but the triune God, the τιμητικὴ προσκύνησις we owe also to images.—In the Latin Church, *Peter Lombard*, Sent. lib. iii. dist. 9 A, ascribed the *Latria* to God alone. He further asserted that there are two species of *Dulia*, the one of which belongs to every creature, while the other is due *only to the human nature of Christ*. *Thomas Aquinas* added (P. II. 1, qu. 103, art. 4) the *Hyperdulia*, which he ascribed to none but Mary. Compare the passages quoted by *Münscher, von Cölln*, s. 182 f.

(3) This was done, *e.g.*, by Hus, in his treatise De Mysterio iniquitatis Antichristi, c. 23. See *Schröckh*, xxxiv. p. 614 f.

<small>The adoration of saints was connected with *the adoration of images* and *the worship of images*. The consideration of the external history of the controversy respecting images belongs to the province of ecclesiastical history. The worship of images was defended upon doctrinal grounds by *John Damascene*, Orationes III pro Imaginibus (Opp. t. i. p. 305 ss.).—The Synod of Constantinople (A.D. 754) decided against the adoration of images, the second Synod of Nicaea (A.D. 787) pronounced in favour of it. A distinction was made between the λατρεία, which is due to God alone, and the προσκύνησις τιμητική (ἀσπασμός), which could be paid as well to the images or pictures of saints, as to the sign of the cross and the holy Gospels.—An intermediate view was at first entertained in the Western Church (imagines non ad adorandum, sed ad memoriam rerum gestarum et parietum venustatem habere permittimus), *e.g.* by the Emperor Charles the Great in the treatise, De impio Imaginum Cultu, libb. iv. (written about the year 790), and the Synod of Frankfurt (A.D. 794); the doctrine of the Synod of Nicaea was defended by Pope Hadrian (he composed a refutation of the books of the Emperor Charles; in *Mansi*, t. xiii. col. 759 ss.), and by Theodulph of Orleans.—*Thomas Aquinas* afterwards asserted (Summ. P. III. qu. 25, art. 3), in reference to the cross of Christ: Cum ergo Christus adoretur adoratione latriæ, consequens est, quod ejus imago sit adoratione latriæ adoranda (here, then, we have real idolatry?). Comp. art. 4, and *John Damascene*, De fide orthod. lib. iv. c. 11.</small>

§ 189.

The Sacraments.

"*The doctrine of the sacraments is the principal point in which the scholastics were productive in the formal aspect, as well as the material*" (1). Not only was the attempt made by several theologians, such as *Hugo of St. Victor* (2), *Peter Lombard* (3), and others, to establish a more precise definition of the term "sacrament," upon the basis laid down by Augustine; but, with regard to the number of sacraments, the sacred number seven was determined upon especially through the influence of Peter Lombard (4). In reference to the latter point, however, nothing had been decided previous to the time of *Bonaventura* and *Thomas Aquinas* (5). But after the number had once been determined, it was a comparatively easy task for theologians, so acute as the scholastics, to find out some profound reasons for it (6). As, moreover, the Greek Church, from the ninth century, manifested a disposition to increase the number of the sacraments (7), when attempts were made at that time to unite the two Churches, the Western computation was confirmed by the Council of Florence (8). Only *Wykliffe*, the Waldenses, and the more rigid among the Husites, either returned to the primitive number two, or dissented more or less from the seven of the Roman Church, and from its idea of the sacrament (9).

(1) *Ullmann*, Wessel, s. 321 f.

(2) *Hugo of St. Victor* was not satisfied with the definition of Augustine: Sacramentum est sacræ rei signum (comp. above, § 136), and called it a mere nominal definition. Letters and pictures, added he, might equally be signs of sacred things. His own definition is given lib. i. P. ix. c. 2: Sacramentum est corporale vel materiale elementum foris sensibiliter propositum, ex similitudine repræsentans, ex institutione significans, et ex sanctificatione continens, aliquam invisibilem et spiritalem gratiam. The definition given in Summ. Tr. ii. c. 1 is shorter: Sacramentum est visibilis forma invisibilis gratiæ in eo collatæ. Comp. De Sacr. lib. ii. P. vi. c. 3 (*Liebner*, s. 426; and *Hahn*, l.c. s. 14).

(3) Sent. l. iv. dist. 13: Sacramentum enim proprie dicitur, quod ita signum est gratiæ Dei et invisibilis gratiæ forma, ut ipsius imaginem gerat et causa existat. The same cannot be said with regard to all signs . . . (omne sacramentum est signum, sed non e converso). Comp. *Bonaventura*, Breviloqu. vi. c. 1 ss. Comp. Dist. 1. Non significandi tantum gratia sacramenta instituta sunt, sed etiam sanctificandi. This idea

was also adopted by *Thomas Aquinas,* Summa, qu. 60, art. 3: Sacramenta sunt quædam sensibilia signa invisibilium rerum, quibus homo sanctificatur. Further definitions by the schoolmen in *Hahn,* s. 21 f. As under the matter of the sacrament might be understood both the material element (water, wine, oil) and also the action used (sprinkling, anointing), some of the schoolmen (Thomas, Scotus, Biel) made a distinction between materia propinqua and materia remota, or even (in the case of penance) remotissima. Compare the passages in *Hahn,* s. 146. On the divine institution of the sacraments, which there was some difficulty in proving, see *Hahn,* s. 154 ff. From the institutio they distinguished the promulgatio, which might be of human origin; or it might be assumed that the Insinuatio institutionis, on the part of God, preceded the actual Institutio, which might then be accomplished by man, that is, by the Church.

(4) As late as the present period the opinions of the theologians on this point were for a considerable time divided. *Rabanus Maurus* and *Paschasius Radbertus* acknowledged only four sacraments, or, more properly speaking, only the two sacraments of baptism and the Lord's Supper; but in connection with baptism they mentioned the Chrisma (confirmation), and divided the sacrament of the Lord's Supper according to its two elements, the body and the blood of Christ. *Rabanus,* De Inst. Cler. i. 24: Sunt autem sacramenta Baptismus et Chrisma, Corpus et Sanguis, quae ob id sacramenta dicuntur, quia sub tegumento corporalium rerum virtus divina secretius salutem eorundem sacramentorum operatur, unde et a secretis virtutibus vel sacris *sacramenta* dicuntur. Comp. *Paschasius,* De Corp. et Sang. Domini, c. 3.—*Berengarius of Tours* expressed himself in similar terms (De S. Cœna, Berolini 1834, p. 155): Duo sunt enim præcipue ecclesiæ sacramenta sibi assentanea, sibi comparabilia, regenerationis fidelium et refectionis (Baptism and the Lord's Supper).—*Gottfried,* Abbot of Vendôme, about 1120, calls the ring and staff with which the bishops were instituted, *sacramenta* ecclesiæ.—*Bernard of Clairvaux* spoke of the washing of the feet as a sacrament (Sermo in Cœnam Domini, § 4, quoted by *Münscher, von Cölln,* s. 188).—*Hugo of St. Victor* (lib. i. P. viii. c. 7) distinguished three classes of sacraments: 1. Those sacraments upon which salvation is

supremely founded, and by the participation of which the highest blessings are imparted (Baptism and the Lord's Supper, together with Confirmation, which is placed, P. vii., between the two others). 2. Those sacraments which promote sanctification, though they are not necessary to salvation, inasmuch as, by their use, the right sentiments of Christians are kept in practice, and a higher degree of grace may be obtained: such are the use of holy water, the sprinkling with ashes, etc. 3. Those sacraments which seemed to be instituted only in order to serve as a kind of preparation for, and sanctification of, the other sacraments; such as holy orders, the consecration of the robes of the clergy, and others.—Besides the said three sacraments of the first class, he made particular mention of the sacraments of matrimony (lib. ii. P. ix.), of penance (P. xiv.), and of extreme unction (P. xv.); "*but he did not state, in reference to any of these sacraments, as he did with regard to baptism and the Lord's Supper, that it was necessary to number it among the sacraments of the first class. It is therefore uncertain whether he has not put some of them among those of the second class.*" Liebner, s. 429. (*Münscher, von Cölln*, s. 188 f.) *Peter Damiani* mentioned as many as twelve sacraments (Opp. t. ii. p. 167–169).—Whether *Otto*, Bishop of Bamberg (who lived between the years 1139 and 1189, and who, according to the Vita Othonis, in *Canisius*, Lectt. Antiq., ed. *Basnage*, t. iii. P. ii. p. 62), introduced the seven sacraments among the Pomeranians whom he had converted to Christianity, is a point which remains to be investigated (see *Engelhardt*, Dg. ii. s. 196. *Münscher, von Cölln*, s. 189 f.).—The views of *Peter Lombard* on the subject in question were more decided; see Sent. lib. iv. dist. 2 A: Jam ad sacramenta novæ legis accedamus, quæ sunt Baptismus, Confirmatio, Panis benedictio, i. e. Eucharistia, Pœnitentia, Unctio extrema, Ordo, Conjugium. Quorum alia remedium contra peccatum præbent, et gratiam adjutricem conferunt, ut Baptismus; alia in remedium tantum sunt, ut Conjugium; alia gratia et virtute nos fulciunt, ut Eucharistia et Ordo. Comp. *G. L. Hahn*, Doctrinæ Romanæ de numero Sacramentorum septenario rationes historicæ, Breslau 1859; and his Lehre von den Sacram. s. 79 ff.

(5) Thus *Alanus ab Insulis*, lib. iv. (quoted by *Pez*, p. 497), enumerated the following sacraments: Baptismus, Eucharistia,

Matrimonium, Pœnitentia, Dedicatio basilicarum, Chrismatis et Olei inunctio, and assigned them their place as means of grace between the *prædicatio* and the *ecclesia*. He spoke only of a plurality of sacraments, but did not state the exact number seven. Comp. iii. 6. Even the third and fourth Lateran Councils (1179 and 1216), as well as Pope Innocent III., do not yet regard the *seven* sacraments as an established dogma of the Church; and even in the year 1229, the Council of Toulouse, held in opposition to the Albigenses, knew only of five sacraments of the Church (penance and matrimony being still excluded from the number). Comp. *Hahn*, s. 109. *Alexander of Hales*, though he adopted the number seven, admitted that baptism and the Lord's Supper alone were instituted by our Lord Himself, and that the other sacraments had been appointed by His apostles and the ministers of the Church. (Summa, P. IV. qu. 8, membr. 2, art. 1, qu. by *Münscher, von Cölln*, s. 196 f.)

(6) According to *Thomas Aquinas*, P. III. qu. 65, art. 1, the first five sacraments serve ad spiritualem uniuscujusque hominis in se ipso perfectionem, but the last two, ad totius ecclesiæ regimen multiplicationemque. He then continues: Per Baptismum spiritualiter renascimur, per Confirmationem augemur in gratia et roboramur in fide; renati autem et roborati nutrimur divina Eucharistiæ alimonia. Quodsi per peccatum ægritudinem incurrimus animæ, per Pœnitentiam spiritualiter sanamur; spiritualiter etiam et corporaliter, prout animæ expedit, per extremam Unctionem. Per Ordinem vero ecclesia gubernatur et multiplicatur spiritualiter; per Matrimonium corporaliter augetur.—*Thomas*, however, agreed with other theologians, Summ. P. III. qu. 62, art. 5, in regarding Baptism and the Lord's Supper as potissima sacramenta.— *Bonaventura* brought (Brevil. vi. Cent. iii. sec. 47, c. 3) the seven sacraments into connection with the seven diseases of man. Original sin is counteracted by baptism, mortal sin by penance, venial sin by extreme unction; ignorance is cured by ordination, malice by the Lord's Supper, infirmity by confirmation, evil concupiscence by matrimony).[1] He also made a corresponding connection between the sacraments and the seven cardinal virtues: baptism leads to faith, confirmation

---

[1] "*Thus the poor laity have no sacrament for ignorance, nor have the poor clergy a sacrament to counteract lusts.*" *Schleiermacher*, Kg. s. 514.

to hope, the Lord's Supper to love, penance to righteousness, extreme unction to perseverance, ordination to wisdom, matrimony to moderation (for further particulars, see ibidem).—Comp. also *Berthold's* Sermons (edited by *Kling*, s. 439 ff.). The "seven sacred things" are, in his opinion, a remedy prepared by Christ, divided into seven parts, etc.[1] See also *Raimund of Sabunde*, tit. 282 H. *Matzke*, s. 90 ff.

(7) *John Damascene* mentioned (De fide orthod. iv. 13) the two mysteries of baptism and the Eucharist, the former in reference to the birth of man, the latter in reference to the support of his new life; these two mysteries were again subdivided by him, viz. baptism into water and Spirit (Chrisma), and the Eucharist into bread and wine.—*Theodore Studita* taught (lib. ii. Ep. 165, Opp. p. 517) six sacraments (after the example of pseudo-Dionysius, see above, § 136, note 3), viz.: 1. Baptism; 2. The Lord's Supper (σύναξις, κοινωνία); 3. The consecration of the holy oil (τελετὴ μύρου); 4. The ordination of priests (ἱερατικαὶ τελειώσεις); 5. The monastic state (μοναχικὴ τελείωσις); and 6. The rites performed for the dead (περὶ τῶν ἱερῶς κεκοιμημένων). See *Schröckh*, Kg. xxxiii. s. 127 f.

(8) *Mansi*, Conc. t. xxxi. col. 1054 ss. The decisions of this Synod had also binding force for the united Armenians.

(9) *Wykliffe* made mention of the ecclesiastical number, lib. iv. c. 1, but in the subsequent chapters critically examined each sacrament separately. Comp. § 190, note 10. Christ was to him "the Sacrament of sacraments" (*Böhringer*, s. 329).—The confession of faith adopted by the Waldenses is given by *Leger*, Histoire Générale des églises évangéliques de Piémont (Leiden 1669), p. 95, quoted by *Schröckh*, Kg. xxix. p. 548. That of the Husites, A.D. 1443, will be found in *Lenfant*, Histoire de la Guerre des Hussites, vol. ii. p. 132 ss. *Schröckh*, Kg. xxxiv. s. 718 ff. Hus himself adopted the doctrine of seven sacraments, though with certain modifications; see *Münscher, von Cölln*, s. 201. The fanatical sects of the Middle Ages, such as the Cathari, the Petrobusiani, the Spirituales, the

---

[1] "The sacraments were also referred by some to the seven kinds of animal sacrifices in the Old Testament, and the sprinkling of their blood." Gieseler, Dg. 531. On the significance generally attributed to the number seven, see *Hahn*, l.c. s. 113.

Fraticelli, either rejected the sacraments entirely, or in the Roman sense, in opposition to which they set up their own (for example, the Manichæan Consolamentum).

§ 190.

The same subject continued.

Many discussions took place among the scholastics as to the antiquity of the sacraments (1), their necessity, design, and significance, as well as respecting their specific virtue and effects (2). In the spirit of the nobler mysticism, *Hugo of St. Victor* traced the design of the sacraments to the inward religious wants of man (3). But *Thomas Aquinas* especially endeavoured both to define the idea of a sacrament still more precisely, and to enlighten himself, as well as others, concerning its effects (4). In consequence of the death of Jesus, the sacraments instituted in the New Testament have obtained what is called a *virtus instrumentalis*, or *effectiva*, which those of the Old Testament did not possess (5). Therefore, by partaking of the sacraments, man acquires a certain *character*, which in the case of some sacraments, such as baptism, confirmation, and the ordination of priests, is *character indelebilis*, and consequently renders impossible the repetition of such sacraments (6). The effects produced by the sacraments arise not only *ex opere operantis*, but also *ex opere operato* (7). Accordingly, they depend upon neither the external nor the internal worth of him who administers the sacrament, nor upon his faith and moral character, but upon his intention to administer the sacrament as such. This intention must at least be *habitual*; but it is not absolutely necessary that it should be *actual* (8).—In opposition to the doctrine of Thomas, which became the ecclesiastically orthodox, *Duns Scotus* denied that the operative power of grace was contained in the sacraments themselves (9). The forerunners of the Reformation, *e.g. Wessel* and *Wycliffe*, combated still more decidedly the doctrine, that the effects of the sacrament are produced *ex opere operato*, while they manifested the highest reverence for the sacraments themselves as divine institutions (10). Thus they preserved the medium between that superstitious and merely external view, by which the sacrament was changed, as it were, into a charm, and the fanatical and subjective theory adopted by the pantheistic sects, who in idealistic pride rejected all visible pledges and seals of invisible blessings (11).

(1) On the question, in what sense the Old Testament may be said to have had sacraments, see *Peter Lombard*, Sent. lib. iv. dist. 1 E: . . . Veteris Testamenti sacramenta promittebant tantum et significabant, hæc autem (Novi Testamenti) *dant* salutem (comp. the opinions of Augustine, ibidem). Inasmuch as the sacraments were made necessary in consequence of sin, but God had instituted *matrimony* in Paradise, *this* sacrament was considered to be the earliest, belonging even to the state of innocence. See *Cramer*, vii. s. 103. Comp. *Thomas Aquinas* (in notes 4 and 5).

(2) "*The common tradition of the Church taught only the notion of a magical efficacy of the sacraments, and thus assigned too great an influence to the mere external dead work. On the contrary, the scholastics clearly perceived that justification and sanctification are something essentially free, internal, and spiritual, and depend upon faith. These two notions being contradictory to each other, it became necessary to reconcile them, which was for the most part done by ingenious reasonings,*" Liebner, Hugo von St. Victor, s. 430.

(3) According to *Hugo of St. Victor*, the design of the sacraments is threefold: 1. Propter humiliationem (submission to the sensuous, in order to attain *by it* to the super-sensuous); 2. Propter eruditionem (the sensuous leads to the super-sensuous. Though a sick person may not see the medicine he is to take, he sees the glass, which gives him an intimation of the healing power it contains, and inspires him with confidence and hope); 3. Propter exercitationem (strengthening of the inner and spiritual life). All the three persons of the Trinity take an active part in the administration of the sacraments. The Father (as the Creator) creates

the elements, the Son (as the Redeemer, God-man) institutes them, and the Holy Ghost sanctifies them (by grace). Man, as the instrument of God, distributes them. God is the physician, man is the patient, the priest is the servant or the messenger of God, *grace* (not the sacrament) is the medicine, and the sacrament is the vessel in which it is contained.— God could have saved man *without* sacraments if He had chosen; but since He has been pleased to institute them, it is the duty of man to submit to His arrangement; nevertheless, God can still save without sacraments. If either time or place prevent one from receiving the sacraments, the res (virtus) sacramenti is sufficient; for the thing itself is of more importance than the sign, faith is more than water, etc. (De Sacram. lib. i. p. ix. c. 3–5. *Liebner*, s. 430 ff.)

(4) *Thomas Aquinas*, Summ. P. III. qu. 60–65. (Extracts from it are given by *Münscher, von Cölln*, s. 192 ff.)

(5) Qu. 62, art. 1: Necesse est dicere sacramenta novae legis per aliquem modum gratiam causare ... Et dicendum est, quod duplex est causa agens, *principalis* et *instrumentalis*. *Principalis* quidem operatur per virtutem suae formae, cui assimilatur effectus, sicut ignis suo calore calefacit. Et hoc modo nihil potest causare gratiam nisi Deus, quia gratia nihil est aliud, quam quaedam participata similitudo divinae naturae. Causa vero *instrumentalis* non agit per virtutem suae formae, sed solum per motum, quo movetur a principali agente. Unde effectus non assimilatur instrumento, sed principali agenti. Et hoc modo sacramenta novae legis gratiam causant. Art. 5: Unde manifestum est, quod sacramenta ecclesiae specialiter habent virtutem ex passione Christi, cujus virtus quodammodo nobis copulatur per susceptionem sacramentorum. Art. 6: Per fidem passionis Christi justificabantur antiqui patres, sicut et nos. Sacramenta autem veteris legis erant quaedam illius fidei protestationes, inquantum significabant passionem Christi et effectus ejus. Sic ergo patet, quod sacramenta veteris legis non habebant in se aliquam virtutem, qua operarentur ad conferendam gratiam justificantem; sed solum significabant fidem per quam justificabantur.[1]

[1] *"The notion that the sacraments of the Old Testament had only prefigured grace, but not communicated it, was rejected by Bonaventura and Scotus, after the opposite doctrine had previously been propounded by the Venerable Bede; it*

(6) *Innocent III.* in Decret. Greg. IX. l. iii. t. 42, c. 3: Et is, qui ficte ad baptismum accedit, *characterem* suscipit christianitatis impressum, *Thomas,* P. III. qu. 63, art. 2: Sacramenta novæ legis *characterem* imprimunt.—The Council of Florence, held under Pope Eugenius IV., laid down the following canon (in *Mansi,* t. xxxi. col. 1054 ss.): Inter hæc Sacramenta tria sunt, Baptismus, Confirmatio, et Ordo, quæ characterem, i. e. spirituale quoddam signum a cæteris distinctivum imprimunt in anima indelebile. *Unde in eadem persona non reiterantur.* Reliqua vero quatuor characterem non imprimunt et reiterationem admittunt.[1]

(7) The distinction between these two terms was most clearly defined by *Gabriel Biel,* in Sent. lib. iv. dist. 1, qu. 3. *Münscher, von Cölln,* s. 199: Sacramentum dicitur conferre gratiam ex opere operato, ita quod ex eo ipso, quod opus illud, puta sacramentum, exhibetur, nisi impediat obex peccati mortalis, gratia confertur utentibus, sic quod præter exhibitionem signi foris exhibiti non requiritur bonus motus interior in suscipiente. Ex opere operante vero dicuntur Sacramenta conferre gratiam per modum *meriti,* quod scilicet sacramentum foris exhibitum non sufficit ad gratiæ collationem, sed ultra hoc requiritur bonus motus seu devotio interior in suscipiente, secundum cujus intentionem confertur gratia, tanquam meriti condigni vel congrui, præcise, et non major

was, however, confirmed by Pope Eugenius IV. at the Council of Florence." *Münscher, von Cölln,* s. 187 (the proofs are given, ibid. s. 198 f.). The doctrine was then established, that the sacraments of the Old Testament produced effects *ex opere operantis,* those of the New Testament *ex opere operato.* Comp. *Engelhardt,* Dg. s. 197 f. Anm.; and *Hahn,* l.c. The whole section 5: Difference of the Sacraments in the different periods of Mankind, s. 41 ff.

[1] Nevertheless, the subject of the character indelebilis remained long undecided. Even the Eucharist was in earlier times considered by some (Hugo of St. Victor and Abélard) to belong to the sacraments, which admitted of no repetition, certainly not in the sense that the same person could not receive the sacrament repeatedly (this was quite necessary), but in the sense that consecration could not be performed more than once on the same host. (Comp. *Hahn,* s. 255.) But even *after* the Council of Florence there was a controversy, on the occasion of the death of Pius II., as to the repetition of extreme unction. Comp. *Platina,* De Vita Pii II., and see below, § 199, note 3. Further, in *Hahn,* s. 261 and 265, note.—The expression *character,* where it was not regarded as indelebilis, was sometimes used interchangeably with the expression *ornatus animæ;* but this was also opposed. See *Hahn,* s. 295; and more fully on the *character indelebilis* in general, s. 298 ff. It follows from this that for a long time this whole subject belonged to the class of "disputable" doctrines.

propter exhibitionem sacramenti. (This latter view was also that of Scotus.) See *Hahn*, s. 396 ff.

(8) *Thomas*, l.c. qu. 64, art. 5: . . . Ministri ecclesiæ possunt sacramenta conferre, etiamsi sint mali. Art. 9: Sicut non requiritur ad perfectionem sacramenti, quod minister sit in charitate, sed possunt etiam peccatores sacramenta conferre; ita non requiritur ad perfectionem sacramenti fides ejus, sed infidelis potest verum sacramentum præbere, dummodo cætera adsint, quæ sunt de necessitate sacramenti. Concerning the *intentio*, compare ibidem and art. 10. *Münscher, von Cölln*, s. 196; *Cramer*, vii. s. 712 f., where the subject of the different kinds of intentio is more closely examined, s. 222 ff.[1]

(9) Compare note 7. There was also a difference of opinion on the question, whether the grace of the sacrament was specifically different from that which was imparted to men in other ways, or whether it was identical with it. The former view was maintained by *Albert the Great* and *Thomas Aquinas*, the latter by *Alexander of Hales, Duns Scotus, Occam, Biel*, and others. See *Hahn*, s. 323 ff., and the passages there adduced. In any case, according to the scholastic view, God Himself remains the causa principalis of grace, while the sacrament is to be regarded as the causa instrumentalis. Thomas Aquinas in *Hahn*, s. 385. According to another view, the sacraments appeared as pledges of grace, as a secondary cause (causa sine qua non), *Hahn*, s. 391.

(10) *Wykliffe* criticized the doctrine of the sacraments very acutely. Trialogus, lib. iv. c. 1 ss. In his opinion, a thousand other things (in their quality of rerum sacrarum signa) might be called sacraments, with quite as much propriety as the seven sacraments. . . . Multa dicta in ista materia habent nimis debile fundamentum, et propter aggregationem ac institutionem in terminis difficile est loquentibus

---

[1] In accordance with this doctrine, the moral condition of the administrant does not come into consideration. "A stable is not less clean when it is cleared out with a rusty iron fork than with a gold one, set with precious stones. A gold ring which a king gives as a present to one of his subjects loses none of its value that it is conveyed to him by a peasant. The rose is no less red in the hand of a dirty woman than in that of an emperor." Thus wrote *Peter Pillichdorf*, in the year 1444, against the Waldenses; qu. by *Hahn*, l.c. Only the sin of Simony is excepted.

habere viam impugnabilem veritatis . . . Non enim video, quin quælibet creatura sensibilis sit realiter sacramentum, quia signum a Deo institutum ut rem sacram insensibilem significet, cujusmodi sunt creator et creatio et gratia creatoris. Comp. c. 25, where he designates the ceremonies which had been added to the sacraments as inventions of Antichrist, by which he had imposed a heavy burden upon the Church. *Wessel* expresses himself in milder terms on this point; he did not altogether disapprove of certain external additions (Chrisma), since out of reverence the Church has surrounded the sacraments with greater solemnity ; but, as regarded their effects, he opposes the doctrine which would represent them as being produced ex opere operato, and makes salvation depend on the disposition of him who receives the sacrament ; De Commun. Sanct. p. 817. *Ullmann*, s. 322 f.

(11) *Mosheim*, l.c. p. 257: Dicunt se credere, quod quilibet Laicus bonus potest conficere corpus Christi, sicut sacerdos peccator. Item, quod sacerdos, postquam exuit se sacris vestibus, est sicut saccus evacuatus frumento. Item, quod corpus Christi æqualiter est in quolibet pane, sicut in pane sacramentali. Item, quod confiteri sacerdoti non est necessarium ad salutem. Item, quod corpus Christi vel sacramentum Eucharistiæ sumere per Laicum, tantum valet pro liberatione animæ defuncti, sicut celebratio Missæ a sacerdote. Item, quod omnis concubitus matrimonialis præter illum, in quo speratur bonum prolis, sit peccatum.—Comp. *Berthold's* Predigten, edited by *Kling*, s. 308 f.

§ 191.

Baptism.

The scholastics exhibited more originality in their definitions respecting the Lord's Supper than in those which had regard to Baptism, where they confined themselves rather to particular points. In adherence to the allegorical system of Cyprian, they adopted the mystical view of the water as the liquid element, but exercised their ingenuity and fondness for subtle distinctions in pedantic definitions concerning the fluids to be used at the administration of the rite of baptism (1). The baptism of blood was as well known during the present period as in preceding ages, with this difference only, that its subjects were those who inflicted tortures upon themselves (Flagellantes), instead of the martyrs (2). The baptism of water could be administered by none but priests, except in cases of necessity (*instanti necessitate*) (3). The doctrine of infant baptism had long been regarded by the Church as a settled point; *Peter of Bruys*, however, and some mystical sects, spoke of it in a disparaging manner (4). As infants, at their baptism, could not enter into any engagement themselves, an engagement was made for them by their godfathers and godmothers, according to the principle of Augustine: Credit in altero, qui peccavit in altero (5).—Infant baptism was supposed to remove original sin, but it did not take away the concupiscentia (lex fomitis), though it lessened it by means of the grace imparted in baptism (6). In the case of grown-up persons who are baptized, baptism not only effects the pardon of sins formerly committed, but it also imparts, according to *Peter Lombard*, assisting grace to perform virtuous actions (7).—The assertion of *Thomas Aquinas*, that children also obtained that grace (8), was confirmed by Pope Clement v. at the Synod of Vienne (A.D. 1311) (9). Baptism forms, besides, the foundation and condition of all other sacraments (10).

(1) Compare *Cramer*, vii. s. 715 ff. *Peter Lombard* taught, Sent. lib. iv. dist. 3 G: Non in alio liquore potest consecrari baptismus nisi in aqua; others, however, thought that the rite of baptism might also be performed with air, sand, or soil. (*J. A. Schmid*, De Baptismo per Arenam, Helmst. 1697, 4to.) Various opinions obtained concerning the question whether beer, broth, fish-sauce, mead or honey water, lye or rose-water, might be used instead of pure water. See *Meiners* and *Spittlers* Neues Götting. histor. Magazin, Bd. iii. St. 2, 1793 (reprinted from *Holderi* dubietatibus

circa Baptismum); *Augusti*, Theologische Blätter, 1 Jahrg. s. 170 ff., and his Archäologie, vii. s. 206 ff. The scholastics carried their absurdities so far as to start the question: Quid faciendum, si puer urinaret (stercorizaret) in fontem? A distinction was also made between aqua artificialis, naturalis, and usualis.—Many other useless and unprofitable contentions took place about the *baptismal formula*; see *Holder*, l.c.—*Sprinkling* also (instead of dipping) gave rise to many discussions. *Thomas Aquinas* preferred the more ancient custom (Summa, P. III. qu. 66, art. 6), because immersion reminded Christians of the *burial* of Christ; but he did not think it absolutely necessary. From the thirteenth century sprinkling came into more general use in the West. The Greek Church, however, and the Church of Milan still retained the practice of immersion; see *Augusti*, Archäologie, vii. s. 229 ff.[1]—On the question whether it was necessary to dip once or thrice, see *Holder*, l.c. (he has collected many more instances of the ingenuity and acuteness of the casuists in reference to all possible difficulties).

(2) *Thomas Aquinas*, qu. 66, art. 11: Præter baptismum aquæ potest aliquis consequi sacramenti effectum ex passione Christi, inquantum quis ei conformatur pro Christo patiendo.—Concerning the Flagellantes, see *Förstemann*, Die christlichen Geisslergesellschaften, Halle 1828.

(3) *Peter Lombard*, Sent. iv. dist. 6 A (after Isidore of Sev.): Constat baptismum solis sacerdotibus esse traditum, ejusque ministerium nec ipsis diaconis implere est licitum absque episcopo vel presbytero, nisi his procul absentibus ultima languoris cogat necessitas: quod etiam laïcis fidelibus permittitur.—Compare *Gratian*. in Decret. de Consecrat. dist. 4, c. 19.—*Thomas Aquinas*, Summ. P. III. qu. 67, art. 1-6, in *Hahn*, s. 174. (The further definitions belong to the province of canon law.)

(4) Comp. *Petr. Ven. Cluniacensis* adv. Petrobrusianos (in Bibl. PP. Max. Lugd. t. xxii. p. 1033).—The Paulicians, Bogo-

---

[1] Various regulations concerning the right performance of baptism may also be found in *Berthold's* Sermons, s. 442 f. Thus it is there said: "Young people ought not to baptize children for fun or mockery; nor ought foolish people to push a Jew into the water against his will. Such doings have no effect."

miles, Cathari, etc., opposed infant baptism; several of these sects (*e.g.* the Cathari) rejected baptism by water altogether. Comp. *Moneta*, Adv. Catharos et Waldenses, lib. v. c. 1, p. 277 ss. *Münscher, von Cölln*, s. 209 f.

(5) Comp. above, § 137, note 6. *Peter Lombard*, Sent. lib. iv. dist. 6 G. *Thomas Aquinas*, qu. 68, art. 9 : Regeneratio spiritualis, quæ fit per baptismum, est quodammodo similis nativitati carnali, quantum ad hoc, quod, sicut pueri in maternis uteris constituti non per se ipsos nutrimentum accipiunt, sed ex nutrimento matris sustentantur, ita etiam pueri nondum habentes usum rationis, quasi in utero matris ecclesiæ constituti, non per se ipsos, sed per actum ecclesiæ salutem suscipiunt.—The regulations concerning the spiritual relationship in which the godfathers and godmothers stand to each other, belong to the canon law. Comp. *Peter Lomb.* lib. iv. dist. 42. *Thomas Aquinas*, P. III. in Supplem. qu. 56, art. 3. Decretalia Greg. IX. lib. iv. t. 11. Sexti Decretal. lib. iv. t. 3.

(6) *Lombard*, lib. ii. dist. 32 A (after Augustine): Licet remaneat concupiscentia post baptismum, non tamen dominatur et regnat sicut ante : imo per gratiam baptismi mitigatur et minuitur, ut post dominari non valeat, nisi quis reddat vires hosti eundo post concupiscentias. Nec post baptismum remanet ad reatum, quia non imputatur in peccatum, sed tantum pœna peccati est; ante baptismum vero pœna est et culpa. Compare what follows. *Thomas Aquinas*, Summ. P. II. qu. 81, art. 3 : Peccatum originale per baptismum aufertur *reatu*, inquantum anima recuperat gratiam quantum ad mentem : remanet tamen peccatum originale *actu*, quantum ad *fomitem*, qui est inordinatio partium inferiorum animæ et ipsius corporis. Comp. P. III. qu. 27, art. 3.

(7) *Lombard*, lib. iv. dist. 4 II : De adultis enim, qui digne recipiunt sacramentum, non ambigitur, quin gratiam operantem et co-operantem perceperint. . . . De parvulis vero, qui nondum ratione utuntur, quæstio est, an in baptismo receperint gratiam, qua ad majorem venientes ætatem possint velle et operari bonum. Videtur, quod non receperint : quia gratia illa charitas est et fides, quæ voluntatem præparat et adjuvat. Sed quis dixerit eos accepisse fidem et charitatem ? Si vero gratiam non receperint, qua bene operari possint cum fuerint adulti, non ergo sufficit eis in hoc statu gratia in baptismo

data, nec per illam possunt modo boni esse, nisi alia addatur: quæ si non additur, non est ex eorum culpa, quia justificati (*al.* non) sunt a peccato. Quidam putant gratiam operantem et co-operantem cunctis parvulis in baptismo dari in munere, non in usu, ut, cum ad majorem venerint ætatem, ex munere sortiantur usum, nisi per liberum arbitrium usum muneris extinguant peccando: et ita ex culpa eorum est, non ex defectu gratiæ, quod mali fiunt.

(8) *Thomas Aquinas,* qu. 69, art. 6: Quia pueri, sicut et adulti, in baptismo efficiuntur membra Christi, unde necesse est, quod a capite recipiant influxum gratiæ et virtutis.

(9) In *Mansi,* t. xxv. col. 441; *Münscher, von Cölln,* s. 203.

(10) Baptismus totius ecclesiastici sacramenti origo est atque primordium (*Petri Damiani,* lib. gratiss. c. 3). Baptismus est janua et fundamentum cæterorum sacramentorum (*Gabr. Biel,* Distinct. 7). This view first receives full recognition after Innocent III., who still ventured to contest it. See *Hahn,* s. 248.

The repetition of the rite of baptism was not in accordance with the nature of that sacrament. But theologians differed in their opinions respecting the question, whether those who are prevented by circumstances from being baptized, may be saved? In opposition to earlier divines (such as *Rabanus Maurus*), later theologians, *e.g. Bernard of Clairvaux, Peter Lombard,* and *Thomas Aquinas,* maintained that in such cases the *will* was sufficient. Compare the passages quoted by *Münscher, von Cölln,* s. 205 f. [*Aquinas,* qu. 68, art. 2: Alio modo potest sacramentum baptismi alicui deesse re, *sed non roto:* sicut cum aliquis baptizari desiderat, sed aliquo casu prævenitur morte, antequam baptismum suscipiat. *Et talis sine baptismo actuali salutem consequi potest propter desiderium baptismi,* quod procedit ex fide per dilectionem operante, per quam Deus interius hominem sanctificat, cujus potentia sacramentis visibilibus non alligatur.]

§ 192.

Confirmation.

Klee, Dogmengeschichte, ii. s. 160-170. J. F. *Bachmann,* Geschichte der Einführung der Confirmation innerhalb d. Evangel. Kirche, Berlin 1852. [*Jo. Dallaus,* De duobus Latinorum ex Unctione Sacramentis, Confirmatione et extrema Unctione, Genev. 1669. In reply, *Natal. Alexander,* Hist. Eccles. Sæc. II. Diss. x. *W. Jackson,* Hist. of Confirmation, Oxford 1878.]

Confirmation (χρίσμα, confirmatio), originally connected with baptism, was, in the course of time, separated from it, as a particular rite, and then came to be viewed as a sacrament, which only the bishop could administer (1). As the first motion to spiritual life is the effect of baptism, so its growth is promoted by the rite of confirmation. Its characteristic is invigoration (2); and so, those who are made members of this spiritual knighthood were smitten on the cheek (3). Moreover, baptism must precede confirmation (4). Nor ought the latter rite to be performed without godfathers and godmothers (5). All these regulations were confirmed by Pope Eugenius IV. (6). But *Wykliffe* and *Hus* declared confirmation to be an abuse (7).

(1) Compare *Augusti*, Archäol. vii. s. 401 ff. *Hahn*, s. 192. On the origin of this sacrament, which was originally connected with the sacrament of baptism, but afterwards came to be regarded as a special sacramental act (§ 136, note 2), and on its false reference to a Synod of Meaux (Concilium Meldense), as alleged by Alexander of Hales, see *Gieseler*, Dg. s. 527. Comp. *Hahn*, s. 89, 147, 161–164. The formula of administration is as follows: Signo te signo crucis, confirmo te chrismate salutis in nomine Patris et Filii et Spir. Sancti, or: in vitam aeternam.

(2) *Melchiades* in Epist. ad Hisp. Episcopos (in *Peter Lombard*, Sent. lib. iv. dist. 7); *Thomas Aquinas*, art. 6 and 7 (quoted by *Münscher, von Cölln*, s. 211 f.). *Bonaventura*, Brevil. P. iv. c. 8 (qu. by *Klee*, Dg. ii. s. 165).

(3) According to *Augusti* (l.c. s. 450 f.), this usage was not known before the thirteenth century; but *Klee* asserts (Dg. ii. s. 165) that it existed soon after the tenth century. At all events, it seems more likely that it had its origin in the customs of the Knights (as *Klee* supposes), than in certain rites which were observed when apprentices had served out their time (according to *Augusti*). But the proper *element* or *matter* of this sacrament was the Chrisma confectum ex oleo olivarum. Compare the authorities cited in notes 2 and 6.

(4) *Thomas Aquinas*, l.c.: Character confirmationis ex necessitate praesupponit characterem baptismalem, etc. Con-

firmation, too, has a character indelebilis; hence it is not to be repeated.

(5) Concerning the godfathers and godmothers, see *Augusti*, l.c. s. 434. *Thomas Aquinas*, art. 10; *Münscher, von Colln*, s. 214. The relation of godfathers and godmothers in confirmation is also a basis of spiritual relationship. [This spiritual relationship is also considered as a hindrance to marriage. Boniface VIII. (1298) *in sexto Decretal*. lib. iv. tit. 3, cap. **1: Ex** confirmatione quoque, **seu** frontis chrismatione spiritualis cognatio eisdem modis (sc. ut ex baptismo) contrahitur, matrimonia similiter impediens contrahenda, et dirimens post contracta.]

(6) Conc. Florent. col. 1055, qu. by *Münscher, von Colln*, s. 215.¹ [The Council of Florence declared the *matter* **of the** sacrament to be Chrisma confectum ex oleo: the bishop to be the *ordinary* administrator. The effect was *robur*. Ideoque in *fronte*, ubi verecundiae sedes est, confirmandus inungitur, ne Christi nomen confiteri erubescat, et praecipue crucem ejus . . . propter quod *signo crucis signatur*.]

(7) Trialog. lib. **iv. c. 14.** *Schröckh*, Kg. xxxiv. s. 508. Wykliffe **doubted** whether confirmation could be proved from Acts viii. **17 (as** was generally supposed), and called it blasphemy to maintain that bishops might again impart the Holy Spirit, which had already been imparted by baptism.—*Hus*, Art. **ii.** apud Trithem. Chron. Hirsaug. **ann. 1402.** *Kbr*, l.c. s. **164.**

¹ **The Greek Church** has the sacrament of confirmation as well as the Latin; **only (in** accordance with the older tradition of the Church) it is performed **immediately** after baptism, and every priest is empowered to do it; see art. "**Greek Church,**" in *Herzog's* Realencyklop. iii. s. 112. In the Greek Church there are added to the olive oil **ninety** different aromatic substances (*Hahn*, l.c. s. 147). [It should be added that, while in the Greek Church the priest **applies the chrism, it is always** consecrated by the bishop.]

§ 193.

The Lord's Supper.

1. *The Controversy* on the Eucharist previous to the Rise of Scholasticism. Paschasius Radbertus and Ratramnus. Berengarius.

Ph. Marheinecke, SS. Patrum de præsentia Christi in Cœna Domini, Heid. 1811, 4to, p. 66 ss. *Ebrard*, **i. s.** 325 ff. *Gfrörer*, Ueber Pseudo-Isidor, in the Freib. Kath. Zeitschrift, 1847, 2, s. 337 ff. *Stotz*, art. " Transsubstantiation," in *Herzog*, xvi. See authorities in § 73, above.

Though at the beginning of this period expressions are sometimes employed which can be interpreted of the Lord's Supper in a symbolical sense (1), yet the usage (2) fixed by the liturgies was constantly shaped more in favour of the doctrine of transubstantiation. The violent controversy between the monks *Paschasius Radbertus* and *Ratramnus* (3), which degenerated into the most unseemly discussions, and gave rise to appellations not less offensive, gave the signal for new contests. The most eminent theologians of the age, such as *Rabanus Maurus* (4) and *Scotus Erigena* (5), took an active part in the dispute. The celebrated *Gerbert* endeavoured to illustrate the doctrine propounded by Paschasius, of a real change of the bread into the body of Christ, by the aid of geometrical diagrams (6). It had been so generally adopted as the orthodox doctrine towards the middle of the eleventh century, that *Berengarius*, a canon of Tours, and afterwards Archdeacon of Angers, who ventured to express doubts concerning its correctness in a letter addressed to *Lanfranc*, was condemned, and obliged by several synods (at Vercelli and Rome, 1050–1079) to retract. He would have suffered still more if the adroitness of Pope Gregory VII. had not at last succeeded in withdrawing him from the rage of his opponents (7). Berengarius, however, was far from rejecting every higher conception which transcended that of a bare sign. Nor did he take

offence at the religious expression, "to partake of the body and
blood of Christ," but he explained it in a more or less ideal
manner (8). On the other hand, Cardinal Humbert was carried
so far by his violent zeal as to interpret the phrase in question
in the grossest Capernaitic manner 9 . It then became
impossible to adopt any moderate view ; and later theologians
found little more to do than to conceal the more objectionable
aspect of the doctrine by an increased subtlety of argumentation, and to weave around the impenetrable mystery, as it
were, a thorny web of syllogisms, as is exemplified in the
scholastic distinction made by Lanfranc between the subject
and the accidents (10).

(1) Thus in the *Venerable Bede* (in Marci Evangel. Opera,
t. v. p. 192, and elsewhere; *Münscher, von Cölln,* s. 223 f.) ;
so, too, in *Walafried Strabo (Ebrard,* s. 366), *Alcuin,* etc. As
early as the times of Charles the Great, however, theologians
seemed agreed that in the bread and the wine of the Lord's
Supper we are not to adore mere signs ; see De impio Imaginum
Cultu, lib. vi. c. 14, p. 491 in *Münscher, von Cölln,* s. 224 f.).
Amalarius of Metz speaks out with special emphasis (about
820) in the Spicileg. t. vii. (see *Ebrard,* s. 368): Ecclesiæ
sacrificium praesens mandendum esse ab humano ore ; credit
namque corpus et sanguinem Domini esse, et hoc morsu
benedictione coelesti impleri animas sumentium. Moreover,
he will not decide, utrum invisibiliter assumatur in coelum an
reservetur in corpore nostro usque in diem sepulturae, an
exhaletur in auras, aut exeat de corpore cum sanguine, an per
poros emittatur.

(2) Compare *Ebrard,* s. 370 ff.

(3) *Paschasius Radbertus* (monachus Corbeiensis) in his
Liber de Corpore et Sanguine Domini (addressed to the Emperor
Charles the Bald, between the years 830 and 832. See
Martène and *Durand,* t. ix. col. 367-470, and extracts from it
in *Rösler,* x. s. 616 ff.). He started from the omnipotence of
God, to whom all things are possible, and consequently maintained, ii. 2 : Sensibilis res intelligibiliter virtute Dei per
verbum Christi in carnem ipsius ac sanguinem divinitus trans-
fertur. He looked upon the elements as no more than a veil

(in a Docetic way) which deceives our senses, and **keeps the body of Christ** concealed from us: Figura videtur esse dum frangitur, **dum in specie visibili** aliud intelligitur quam **quod visu** carnis et **gustu sentitur.** It is the same body which was born of Mary.—At times the true body of Christ has appeared to those who doubted (for encouragement), as well as to those **who** were strong in the faith (as a reward **of** their faith), instead of the bread (for the most part in the form of a lamb), or stains of blood have been perceived, etc.[1]—He was opposed by *Ratramnus* (Bertram), in his treatise, De Corpore et Sanguine Domini ad Carolum **Calvum** (it was written at the request of the king; extracts are given by *Schröckh*, xxiii. s. 445; *Neander*, **iv.** 466 ff., and *Münscher*, **von Colln,** s. 230–235). *Ratramnus* properly distinguished **between the** sign **and the thing represented by** it (figura et veritas), **the internal and** the external, and pointed out the true significance of the *mysteries*, which consists in this, that through their medium the mind of man rises from the visible to the invisible. If it were possible to eat the body of Christ, in **the proper** sense of the word, faith would be no longer required, **and** the mystery, as such, would lose all its significance. The gross reality would destroy the idea, and nothing but a mere materialism would remain. Ratramnus also **supposed a** *conversio* of the bread and wine into the body **of Christ, but only** in the ideal sense of the word, as **the ancient Church held to a** transition from the profane to the sacred (sub velamento corporei panis corporeique **vini** spirituale **corpus Christi spiritualisque** sanguis existit). The mnemonic **character is emphasized; and he also** appealed to **the authority of earlier writers. Respecting the later appellation,** *Stercoranists* (in allusion to Matt. xv. 17), which had its origin in these discussions (*Paschasius*, c. 20. 2), see *Schröckh*, xxiii. s. 493 ff., and *C. M. Pfaff*, Tractatus de Stercoranistis medii ævi, Tub. 1750, 4to.[2]

(4) The treatise of *Rabanus*, addressed to Egilo, Abbot of Prüm, was professedly edited by *Mabillon* (Acta SS. t. vi.);

---

[1] Concerning such miraculous appearances, compare also *Bossuet*, edited by *Cramer*, v. 2, s. 105.

[2] A controversy of quite as unprofitable a nature was carried on between the above-named *Amalarius* (who composed a liturgical work about the year 820) and the priest *Guntrad*, concerning spitting during the celebration of the mass; see

but both *Münscher, von Cölln*, s. 229, and *Neander*, Kg. ii 1, s. 91, deny the genuineness of that edition. The real opinion of Rabanus may be inferred from the following passage (De Inst. Cler. i. c. 31, and iii. 13, qu. by *Gieseler* and *Münscher, von Cölln*, l.c.). Maluit enim Dominus corporis et sanguinis sui sacramenta fidelium ore percipi, et in pastum eorum redigi, ut per visibile opus invisibilis ostenderetur effectus. Sicut enim cibus materialis *forinsecus* nutrit corpus et vegetat, ita etiam **verbum** Dei *intus animum* nutrit et roborat . . . Sacramentum ore percipitur, *virtute* sacramenti interior homo satiatur. Sacramentum in alimentum corporis redigitur, virtute autem sacramenti aeterna vita adipiscitur.

(5) This was at least the common opinion (compare the letter of Berengarius to Lanfranc). It is, however, uncertain **whether** the treatise (De Eucharistia) commonly ascribed to Scotus, which was condemned by the Synod of Vercelli (A.D. 1050), is the same with the treatise ascribed to Ratramnus as *De Marca* says (who ascribes it to Scotus), or whether we have here two distinct treatises; see *Gieseler*, as above. *F. W. Lauf* (Studien und Kritiken, 1828, **4, s. 755** ff.) ascribes the **authorship to Ratramnus, and** denies **it to** Scotus. Compare also *Neander* (s. 471, who thinks it at least probable that **Scotus** gave his opinion on the subject in question, though the **notion of a** lost treatise written **by him may have** arisen from a mistake. To judge from **some** passages contained in his treatise, De Div. Nat. (qu. by *Neander*, l.c.), he would not have given countenance to the doctrine propounded **by Paschasius.** [*Neander* says that *Scotus* taught, like some of the **Greek** Fathers, that the glorified body of Christ, by its union **with the divinity, was** freed from the defects of a sensuous **nature. He impugned** those who said that the body of Christ **after the resurrection** occupied **some** limited space, and held **to its ubiquity. He denied the doctrine** of transubstantiation, **and admitted a spiritual presence at the** Supper: Christ's **presence here is a symbol of His presence everywhere.]**

d'Achery, Spicil. t. iii. in *Schröckh*, Kg. xxiii. s. 496. *Gerbert* (De Corpore et Sanguine Christi) remarks against the Stercoranistic inferences: Et nos saepe vidimus non modo infirmos, sed etiam sanos, quod per se intromittunt, per vomitum dejecisse . . . subtilior tamen succus per membra usque ad ungues diffundebatur. " *That surely was medicinal,*" *Ebrard*, s. 439.

(6) De Corpore et Sanguine Domini, edited by Pez, in Thesaur. Anecdd. Noviss. t. i. P. ii. fol. 133. Schroekh, xxiii. s. 493.¹ *Gerbert* also tried to make clear the relation between Christ, the Supper, and the Church, in a logical way, by the three terms of the syllogism, or the three parts of an arithmetical proportion; see *Ritter*, vii. s. 304; *Ebrard*, s. 348 f.

(7) On the external history of the controversy, see *J. Mabillon*, Dissert. de multiplici Berengarii Damnatione, Fidei Professione, et Relapsu, deque ejus Pœnitentia (in *J. Vogtii* Biblioth. Hæresiolog., Hamb. 1723, t. i. Fasc. i. p. 99 ss. *Schroekh*, xxiii. s. 507 ff.; *Neander*, iv. s. 476 ff.; and *Giesler*, ii. 1, s. 219 ff.).—*Sources from which his opinions may be ascertained* are: the Epistle of his schoolfellow, *Adelmann*, De Veritate Corp. et Sang. Domini, ad Berengarium (which he wrote previous to his nomination as Bishop of Brixen in Tyrol, A.D. 1049), edited by *J. Coster*, Lovan. 1551, in Biblioth. Patrum, t. xviii., and by *Schmidt*, Brunsv. 1770; *Hugonis Lingonensis* (of Langres), Lib. de Corpore et Sanguine Dom. (*d'Achéry* in Opp. Lanfranci, Append. p. 68 ss. Biblioth. Patrum, t. xviii. p. 417 ss.); *Lanfrancus*, De Corp. et Sang. Dom. adv. Berengar. Turonens. (written between the years 1063 and 1070), in Opp. ed. *L. d'Achéry*, Lutet. 1648, fol., and Biblioth. Patrum, t. xviii. p. 763–777. This work also contains the *first* treatise which Berengarius wrote in opposition to Lanfranc, from which we must distinguish his second: Liber de sacra Cœna adv. Lanfrancum (edited by *Staudlin* in 6 programmes, Gött. 1820–1829, 4to).—Comp. *Goth. Ephr. Lessing*, Berengarius Turonensis, Brunsv. 1770, 4to (in the edition of his complete works, publ. Berlin 1825 ff., Bd. xii. s. 143 ff.); *Staudlins* and *Tschirners* Archiv für Kg. Bd. ii. St. 1, s. 1–98. *Berengarii Turonensis* quæ supersunt tam edita quam inedita, typis expressa, moderante *A. Neandro*, t. i. Berol. 1834. (*Berengarii* De Sacra Cœna adv. Lanfrancum, liber posterior, e codice Guelferbytano primum ediderunt *A. F. et F. Th. Vischer*, ibid. 1834.) A more detailed account of the literature is given by *Giesler*, l.c. *Leading historical*

---

¹ Gerbert's method of illustrating such supernatural truths by ocular demonstration, was imitated even by later theologians. Thus Melanchthon informs us that his tutor *Lempus*, at Tübingen, drew a representation of transubstantiation on a board (Ep. de suis studiis, written A.D. 1541. See *Galle*, Melanchthon, s. 6).

facts: **The** first condemnation of Berengarius, A.D. 1050, at Rome under Pope Leo IX., without an opportunity of defence.—The repetition of the sentence passed upon him at Verceli in the same year.—(On the supposed Council of Paris, see *Neander,* l.c. s. 491.)—Council at Tours (A.D. 1054.)—Berengarius' justification with the assistance of Hildebrand.—Another council at Rome (A.D. 1059.)—The violent conduct of Humbert.—The inconstancy manifested by Berengarius in this matter.—Correspondence with Lanfranc.—Other synods at Rome (A.D. 1078 and 1079).—Berengarius again admitted to sign the confession of faith drawn up by his enemies, but retracted afterwards.—The Litteræ Commendatitiæ of Pope Gregory VII.—Berengarius' death on the isle of St. Côme, near Tours, A.D. 1088.

(8) *Berengarius* combated principally the doctrine of an entire *change,* in such a manner as to make the bread cease to be bread, and to have nothing left but the accidents, for then in reality a *portiuncula carnis* was eaten instead of bread. In accordance with the earlier Fathers, he retained the doctrine **of a change** from an inferior to a superior form, and of a **mystical participation** in the body of Christ under the figure of **bread, p. 67** (edit. *Vischer*): **Dum** enim dicitur: panis et vinum sacramenta sunt, minime pani**s** aufertur **et** vinum, et nominibus rerum ita natarum significativis aptatur nomen, quod non nata sunt, ut est sacramentum; simul etiam esse aliud aliquid minime prohibentur, sunt enim, *sicut secundum religionem sacramenta, ita secundum aliud alimenta, sustentamenta.* The subject of which anything is predicated must remain, otherwise that which is predicated would have no meaning. Pag. 71: Dum dicitur: panis in altari consecratur, **vel** panis sanctus, panis sacrosanctus est Christi corpus, omni veritate panis superesse conceditur. Verbi gratia, si enuntias: Socrates justus **est, aliquid eum esse** constituisti, nec potest **justus esse, si contingat,** Socratem **non esse.** Pag. 76: Sicut **enim, qui dicit: Christus est lapis** angularis, non revera **Christum lapidem esse constituit, sed** propter aliquam similitudinem, **quam ad se** invicem gerunt, **tale** nomen ei imponit, **eodem modo,** cum **divina** pagina **corpus** domini panem vocat, **sacrata ac** mystica locutione id agit. Pag. 86: Quando autem **afferuntur ad altare vel** ponuntur in altari, adhuc sunt, ut ait

beatus Augustinus contra Faustum, alimenta refectionis, nondum sacramenta religionis, (h)ac per hoc, nondum **corpus Christi et sanguis** existentia, non tropica, sed propria sunt **locutione** pendenda. Dicens ergo Humbertus ille tuus, panem, qui ponitur in **altari,** post consecrationem esse corpus Christi, **panem** propria locutione, corpus Christi tropica accipiendum esse constituit, et illud quidem recte, quia ex auctoritate scrip**turarum.** Pag. 90 : Dicitur autem in scripturis panis altaris de pane fieri corpus Christi, sicut servus malus dicitur fieri de malo servo bonus filius, non quia amiserit animae propriae naturam aut corporis. Pag. **91** : **Unde** insanissimum **dictu** erat et christianae religioni contumeliosissimum, corpus Christi de pane vel de **quocunque** confici per generationem subjecta... ut pane absumto per corruptionem subjecti corpus **Christi** esse inci**piat per** generationem subjecti, quia nec **pro** parte, nec pro **toto** potest incipere nunc esse corpus Christi. Pag. **95** : **Novit autem revera** secundum carnem Christum, qui Christi **corpus asserit adhuc** esse corruptioni vel generationi obnoxium, **vel** quarumcunque qualitatum vel collineationum, quas prius **non habuerit,** susceptivum. Pag. 98 : Denique verbum caro **factum** assumsit quod non erat, non amittens quod erat, et **panis** consecratus in altari amisit vilitatem, amisit mellicaciam, **non** amisit naturae proprietatem, cui naturae quasi **loco,** quasi fundamento dignitas divinitus augeretur et efficacia. (A comparison is drawn between the change in **question, and the** change at the **conversion of** Saul into Paul, **p. 144.)** Pag. 161 : Est ergo **vera procul dubio panis et vini per consecra**tionem altaris convers**io in corpus Christi et sanguinem, sed** attendendum, quod **dicitur :** per consecrationem, **quia hic est hujus conversionis modus, etc. . . . Pag. 163 : Per consecrationem, inquam, quod nemo interpretari poterit : per subjecti corruptionem.** Pag. **167 : Sed quomodo manducandus est Christus ? Quomodo ipse dicit : Qui manducat carnem meam et bibit sanguinem meum, in me manet et ego in eo ; si in me manet, et ego in illo, tunc manducat, tunc bibit ; qui autem non in me manet, nec ego in illo, etsi accipit sacramentum, adquirit magnum tormentum. Pag. 171 : Apud eruditos enim constat, et eis, qui vecordes non sint, omnino est perceptibile, nulla ratione colorem videri, nisi contingat etiam coloratum videri. Ita enim scribit Lanfrancus, colorem et** qualitates portiunculæ carnis Christi, quam sensualiter esse in altari desipit, videri oculis corporis, ut tamen caro illa, cujus color videtur, omnino sit invisibilis, cum constet, omne quod in subjecto est, sicut, ut sit, ita etiam, ut videatur, non a se habere, sed a subjecto, in quo sit, nec visu vel sensuo aliquo corporeo comprehendi colorem vel qualitatem, nisi comprehenso quali et colorato.[1] Pag. 188: Rerum exteriorum est, panis et vini est, confici, consecrari; hæc incipere possunt esse, quod non erant, corpus Christi et sanguis, sed per consecrationem, non per corruptionem panis et vini et generationem corporis Christi et sanguinis, quæ constat semel potuisse generari. Pag. 191: ... Verissimum est nec ulla tergiversatione dissimulari potest, aliud esse totum corpus Christi, quod ante mille annos sibi fabricavit in utero virginis sapientia Dei, aliud portiunculam carnis, quam tu tibi facis de pane per corruptionem panis ipsius hodie factam in altari per generationem ipsius carnis. — Further passages are quoted by *Gieseler*, l.c.; by *Münscher, von Cölln*, s. 242 ff. Comp. especially his confession made (though with reservation) at the Synod of Rome (A.D. 1078), in Mansi, xix. p. 761, and *Gieseler*, s. 234: Profiteor, panem altaris post consecrationem esse verum corpus Christi, quod natum est de virgine, quod passum est in cruce, quod sedet ad dexteram Patris; et vinum altaris, postquam consecratum est, esse verum sanguinem, qui manavit de latere Christi. Et sicut ore pronuncio, ita me corde habere confirmo. Sic me adjuvet Deus et hæc sacra.

(9) According to the confession of faith imposed by *Humbert* upon *Berengarius* at the Synod of Rome (A.D. 1059), he was to take an oath, in the name of the Holy Trinity, that he believed: Panem et vinum, quæ in altari ponuntur, post consecrationem non solum sacramentum, sed etiam verum corpus et sanguinem Domini nostri Jesu Christi esse, et sensualiter, non solum sacramento, sed in veritate *manibus sacerdotum tractari, frangi, et fidelium dentibus atteri;* he retracted, however, as soon as he had obtained his liberty.

(10) The doctrine of *Lanfranc*, though propounded in less rigid terms than that of Humbert, was nevertheless opposed

---

[1] Only in so far may it be said that the bread of the Lord's Supper is no bread; as Christ says, *My doctrine is not mine, but His who sent me*; or Paul: *I live, yet not I, but Christ liveth in me.* Comp. p. 178.

to the view adopted by Berengarius, and rendered impossible any further attempt to return to a symbolizing and spiritualizing interpretation. He taught (l.c. c. 18, p. 772, quoted by *Münscher, von Cölln*, s. 244): Credimus terrenas substantias, quæ in mensa dominica per sacerdotale ministerium divinitus sanctificantur, ineffabiliter, incomprehensibiliter, mirabiliter, operante superna potentia, converti in essentiam dominici corporis, reservatis ipsarum rerum speciebus et quibusdam aliis qualitatibus, ne percipientes cruda et cruenta horrerent, et ut credentes fidei præmia ampliora perciperent, ipso tamen dominico corpore existente in cœlestibus ad dexteram Patris immortali, inviolato, integro, incontaminato, illæso, ut vere dici possit, et ipsum corpus quod de Virgine sumtum est nos sumere, et tamen non ipsum: ipsum quidem, quantum ad essentiam veræque naturæ proprietatem atque naturam; non ipsum autem, si spectes panis vinique speciem cæteraque superius comprehensa. Hanc fidem tenuit a priscis temporibus et nunc tenet ecclesia, quæ per totum effusa orbem catholica nominatur. (To this last view Berengarius opposed proofs drawn from the writings of Ambrose and Augustine, in the treatise above mentioned. Comp. note 8.)

§ 194.

2. *Scholastic Development of the Doctrine.   Transubstantiation. The Sacrifice of the Mass.*

A name is often of great consequence! *Hildebert of Tours* was the first who made use of the full-sounding term "*transsubstantiatio*" (1), though similar expressions, such as *transitio*, had previously been employed (2). Most of the earlier scholastics (3), and the disciples of Lanfranc in particular, had defended the doctrine of the change of the bread into the body of Christ, and the doctrine of the *accidentia sine subjecto*; these were now solemnly confirmed by being inserted *together with* the term *transsubstantiatio* into the Decretum Gratiani,[1] and were made an unchangeable article of faith by Pope

[1] Composed about A.D. 1150, by *Gratianus*, a Benedictine monk.

Innocent III. (4). Thus nothing was left to the later scholastics but to answer still more subtle questions, such as: In what respect can it be said that the body of Christ is actually broken together with the bread (5)? Do animals partake of the body of Christ when they happen to swallow a consecrated host (6)? Is the bread used in the Lord's Supper changed only into the flesh of our Lord, or also into His blood (what is called the doctrine of *concomitance*) (7)? Is the bread, in the former case, changed only into the flesh of Christ, or also into His body and soul, or into His Godhead, or even into the Holy Trinity (8)? Does the change take place gradually, or suddenly (9)? Is there only one body in the multitude of hosts, so that the same Christ is sacrificed at the same time upon all altars, which constitutes the mystery of the mass (10)?—By the institution of the feast of Corpus Christi by Pope Urban IV. (A.D. 1264), and Pope Clement V. (A.D. 1311) at the Synod of Vienne, the doctrine in question was expressed in a liturgical form, and its popularity secured (11). Henceforth the sacrifice of the mass formed more than ever the centre of Catholic worship (12), and reflected new glory upon the priesthood. Nevertheless, many pious minds found elevation and powerful motives in the idea of a special presence of the Redeemer, and the daily repetition of His sacrifice, as well as in that of the mystical union with Him in the act of communion. Thus here again it became the office of an idealizing mysticism, by the spirit of inward contemplation, to transform into a heavenly thing that which the scholastics had brought down into the sphere of the external and earthly (13).

(1) In Sermo VI. Opp. col. 689; comp. Sermo V. in Coena Domini, Col. 422; and De Sacram. Altaris, col. 1106 (in *Münscher, von Cölln,* s. 249 f.).

(2) Thus by *Hugo of St. Victor,* see *Liebner,* s. 455 ff.

(3) *Anselm,* a disciple of Lanfranc, followed the example of his master in his Tractatus bipartitus de Corpore et Sanguine Domini, sive de Sacramento Altaris. (Disputatio dialectica de

grammatico, P. ii.) P. i.: ... Sicut in mensa nuptiali aqua in vinum mutata solum adfuit vinum, in quod aqua mutata **erat**; sic in mensa altaris solum adest corpus Domini, in quod vere mutata **est vera** panis substantia; nisi, quod de aqua nihil remansit **in** mutatione illa, de pane vero mutato, ad peragendum sacri institutum mysterii, sola remanet species visibilis. (He expressly condemns the heretical doctrine of Berengarius. Yet we ought not to think of the transaction as something magical: Nihil enim falsum factum putandum est in sacrificio veritatis, sicut fit **in** magorum praestigiis, ubi delusione quadam falluntur oculi, ut videatur illis esse, quod non est omnino. Sed vera species visibilis panis, quae fuit in pane, ipsa facta praeter substantiam suam quodammodo **in** aliena peregrinatur, continente eum, qui fecit eam **et** ad suum transferente corpus. Quae tamen translata ad corpus Domini, non **eo** modo se habet ad illud, quomodo accidens **ad** substantiam; quia corpus Domini in substantia sua nec albam efficit albedo illa, nec rotundum rotunditas, sicque de reliquis. Nor ought we to rest satisfied with the mere carnal participation. P. ii. c. 12: Et cum de altari sumimus carnem Jesu, curemus sollicite, ne cogitatione remaneamus in carne, et a spiritu non vivificemur; quodsi non vivificamur a spiritu, caro non prodest quicquam, etc. (comp. note 12. The principles of Lanfranc were also partially adopted by *Durandus* (Abbas Troarnensis; he died A.D. 1088), De Corp. et Sang. Domini, c. Bereng. (in Bibl. PP. Max. t. xviii. p. 419; *Galland,* t. xiv. p. 245), and *Guitmundus* (Archiepisc. Aversanus), De Corporis et Sanguinis Christi Veritate in Eucharistia, libb. iii. (in Bibl. PP. **Max. t.** xviii. **p.** 441). *Eusebius Bruno* (Bishop of Anjou), whom Durandus places among the followers of Berengarius, wished to have a stop put to all discussions concerning this sacrament (see *Münscher, von Cölln,* s. 247 f.). But **in** vain! The theory of Paschasius and Lanfranc gained the victory. — *Hugo of St. Victor* himself called the few advocates of Berengarius' doctrine "perverters of Scripture," **and** distinctly opposed a *merely* symbolical interpretation, though **he** would have retained it together with the real (see *Liebner,* s. **453** ff.). — *Peter Lombard* appealed, Sent. lib. iv. dist. 10 D, to (Pseudo-) Ambrose, De initiand. myster. (see above, § 138, note 3): Ex his (continues **he**) aliisque pluribus constat, verum corpus Christi et sanguinem in altari esse, immo integrum Christum ibi sub utraque specie et substantiam panis in corpus, vinique substantiam in sanguinem converti. But he confesses his inability to explain the mode of that change, dist. xi. A: Si autem quaeritur, qualis sit illa conversio, an formalis, an substantialis, vel alterius generis, definire non sufficio. Formalem tamen non esse cognosco, quia species rerum, quae ante fuerant, remanent, et sapor et pondus. Quibusdam esse videtur substantialis, dicentibus sic substantiam converti in substantiam, ut haec essentialiter sit illa, si sensui praemissae auctoritates consentire videntur. B: Sed **huic** sententiae sic opponitur ab aliis: Si substantia **panis**, inquiunt, vel vini convertitur substantialiter in corpus **vel** sanguinem Christi, quotidie fit aliqua substantia corpus vel sanguis Christi, quae ante non erat corpus, et hodie est aliquod corpus Christi, quod heri non erat, et quotidie augetur corpus Christi atque formatur de materia, de qua in conceptione non fuit factum. Quibus hoc modo responderi potest, quia non ea ratione dicitur corpus Christi confici verbo coelesti, quod ipsum corpus in conceptu virginis formatum deinceps formetur: sed quia substantia panis **vel** vini, quae ante non fuerunt corpus Christi **vel** sanguis, verbo coelesti fit corpus et sanguis. Et ideo *sacerdotes dicuntur conficere* **corpus** *Christi et sanguinem*, quia eorum ministerio substantia panis fit caro, **et** substantia vini fit sanguis Christi, nec tamen aliquid additur corpori vel sanguini, nec augetur corpus Christi vel sanguis. C: Si vero quaeris modum, quo id fieri possit, breviter respondeo Mysterium fidei credi salubriter potest, investigari salubriter non potest. Comp. dist. xii. A: Si autem quaeritur de accidentibus, quae remanent, i. e. de speciebus et sapore et pondere, **in quo** subjecto fundentur, potius mihi videtur fatendum **existere** sine subjecto quam esse in subjecto, quia ibi non est substantia, nisi corporis et sanguinis dominici, quae non allicitur **illis** accidentibus. **Non** enim corpus Christi talem habet in **se formam**, sed qualis **in** judicio apparebit. Remanent ergo **illa accidentia** per se **subsistentia ad** mysterii ritum, ad gustus **fideique** suffragium: quibus corpus Christi, habens formam et **naturam** suam, tegitur.

(4) Conc. Lat. IV. c. i. (qu. by *Münscher, von Cölln,* s. 251): **Una est fidelium** universalis ecclesia, **extra** quam nullus

omnino salvatur. In qua idem ipse sacerdos est sacrificium Jesus Christus, cujus corpus **et** sanguis in sacramento altaris **sub speciebus panis** et vini veraciter continentur, transsubstantiatis pane in corpus **et vino in** sanguinem potestate divina, **ut** ad perficiendum mysterium unitatis accipiamus ipsi de suo, **quod** accepit **ipse de** nostro. Et hoc utique sacramentum nemo potest conficere nisi sacerdos, qui rite fuerit ordinatus secundum claves ecclesiae, quas ipse concessit Apostolis eorumque successoribus Jesus Christus. Pope Innocent III. himself maintained, De Mysteriis Miss., **lib. iv. c. 7**: Non solum accidentales, sed etiam naturales proprietates remanere: *panitatem*, quae satiando famem expellit, et *vinositatem*, **quae satiando** sitim expellit.

(5) *Thomas Aquinas (Summa* **P. III.** qu. **75, art. 6 and 7**; **qu. 76, art.** 5, made the assertion, that the body **is** broken **only secundum** speciem sacramentalem, but is itself incorruptibile **et** impassibile; see the passages in *Münscher, von Colln*, s. **253 f.** [*Baur*, s. **267** (2d ed.), says: Aquinas says, transubstantiation is neither an annihilation nor a continuance of the substance; and **if** the accidents continue without their substance, this is to be taken in the same sense as a miracle **in general, a** working of the first cause without the intervention **of** the secondary causes. The whole Christ was conceived as being in each part of the species; and to explain how this could be, how a body of greater quantity **could be in a** smaller, not locally, not as a *dimensive*, but **as a** *substantial quantity*, the scholastics made distinctions, which at **last run out** into this—that existence in **space does** not belong **to the essence** of things that appear in **space.** *Aquinas*, dist. **76, art. 4.**] The **whole** Christ **remains in every** particle of **the host. In** the same way the consecrated **wine, though other liquids may be added, remains the blood of** Christ as **long as it does not cease to be** wine. **Fortunately,** these **subtle definitions required only** a fides implicita, but not explicita; **see** *Cramer*, **vii. s. 728 f.** The theory **of Thomas** is more fully **developed by** *Engelhardt*, Dg. ii. s. **214, Anm.** *Ebrard*, **i. s. 487.**

(6) *Peter Lombard* started **this question, Sent. lib. iv. dist. 13 A, and** decided: Illud **sane dici potest, quod a brutis animalibus corpus Christi non sumitur, etsi** videatur. Quid **ergo sumit mus vel quid manducat? Deus** novit hoc.—

Alexander of Hales, however, who lived about a century later, pretended to a fuller knowledge respecting this point (Summa P. IV. qu. 45, membr. 1, art. 1 and 2). He took the affirmative side of the question, in support of which he asserted that, if a *sinner* could receive the body of Christ, the same might be supposed, with much more propriety, in the case of an *innocent* animal; on the other hand, he professed to be aware that God abhors only the **sin of** the sinner, but not his human nature, which alone is susceptible of the beneficial effects of the sacrament. Nevertheless, he was compelled to admit, that if a dog or a pig swallowed a whole host, the body of our Lord entered into the belly of the animal.—*Thomas Aquinas* held similar views, P. III. qu. 80, art. 3: Etiamsi mus vel canis hostiam consecratam manducet, substantia corporis Christi non desinit esse sub speciebus, quamdiu species illæ manent, hoc est quamdiu substantia panis maneret; sicut etiam si projiceretur in lutum.—On the other hand, *Bonaventura* expressed himself with more reserve (after he had stated **all that** might be said for and against the doctrine) in Comment. ad Sent. iv. dist. **13, art.** 2, qu. **1**: Quantumcunque hæc opinio muniatur, nunquam tamen ita munitur, *quomquam aures piæ* **hoc** *abhorreant audire*, **quod in** ventre muris vel in cloaca sit corpus Christi, quamdiu species ibi subsistunt. Propter hæc est alia opinio, quod corpus **Christi nullo** modo descendit in ventrem muris. . . . Et hæc opinio **communior est, et** certe honestior et rationabilior. Nevertheless, this more appropriate **and** rational view was determined by the Synod of Paris, A.D. 1300, to be one of those articles, in quibus Magister Sententiarum non tenetur (*Münscher, von Cölln*, s. 255).—Thomas Aquinas, however, **held** that an animal can partake of the body of Christ **only** accidentaliter, but not sacramentaliter; and Pope *Innocent III.* endeavoured **(De Myst.** Missæ, iv. 21) to **get rid of all difficulties by supposing** that the body of our **Lord left the host in the same miraculous** way in which it had entered it (reconversio). Compare *Wilhelm Holder's* **satire: Mus exenteratus, etc., published in the** sixteenth **century, in** *Meiners* **and** *Spittlers* **Neues Götting.** histor. **Magazin, Bd. i. s. 716-734, where** some other curiosities are **collected.**

(7) See the next section.

(8) The elements are, properly speaking, changed only into the body and blood of Christ, but His soul is united to His body, and His divine nature to His soul ; see *Thomas Aquinas*, P. III. qu. 76, art. 1. On the controversy which took place in the kingdom of Valencia, A.D. 1582 (respecting the transubstantiation of the bread into the whole Trinity), see *Baluze, Note* ad Vitas Paparum Avenionensium, t. i. p. 1368 ss. (from an ancient MS.); and *Schröckh*, xxxiii. s. 325.

(9) The transubstantiation takes place in instanti, not successive. Comp. *Alex. Hales.* P. IV. qu. 10, memb. 5, art. 5. *Thom. Aquinas*, P. III. qu. 75, art. 7. *Albertus Magnus*, Sentent. iv. dist. 10, art. 3. (*Klee*, Dg. ii. s. 204.)

(10) Thus *Anselm* said, l.c. P. ii. c. 4 : Sic ergo constat, in diversis locis uno horæ momento esse posse corpus Christi, sed lege creatricis naturæ, non creatæ. The other scholastics adopted the same opinion. Similar views were also entertained by the mystics. Compare *Ruysbroek*, Specul. æternæ Salutis, c. 8, and *Engelhardt's* Monogr. s. 261 : " All the bread which our Lord Himself consecrated for His body (at the institution of the Lord's Supper),[1] as well as the bread which the priests now everywhere consecrate, is, according to its true nature, only one bread (only one bread in its nature). In the act of consecration, all the hosts, by means of the secret intention of the priest, and the enunciation of the words of consecration, are united into one matter and one substance, and what was formerly bread now becomes entirely the body of Christ. . . . Every bit of bread, every drop of wine, contains the whole Christ, who is in heaven, but not confined to any particular place, as the one undivided soul is equally diffused throughout the body. . . . The body of Christ is present in all countries, places, and churches ; hence we may preserve it in various ways, and keep it in various places ; we may have it in the casket, receive it, and give it. But as He exists in heaven, with hands, and feet, and all His members, and is seen by angels and saints in full glory, He does not change His abode,

---

[1] It was thought that Christ Himself partook, by way of accommodation, of His own body at the institution of the sacrament in question ; see *Thomas Aquinas*, l.c. qu. 81 ; *Schröckh*, xxxix. s. 163. On a chalice at Hildesheim is inscribed : Rex sedet in cœna, turba cinctus duodena, se tenet in manibus, et cibat ipse cibus. Comp. *Riemer*, Mittheilungen über Goethe, ii. s. 701.

and remains ever present." In illustration of such things, the instance was adduced of a mirror composed of many pieces, in which a single image is variously reflected; see *Klee*, ii. s. 211.[1]

(11) Respecting the institution of this festival (whether in consequence of a revelation to the nun, Juliana of Liège?), see *Gieseler*, ii. 2, s. 409 ff.

(12) The idea of a sacrifice is intimately connected with the dogma of transubstantiation. *Peter Lombard*, Sent. lib. iv. dist. 12 G: Breviter dici potest, illud quod offertur et consecratur a sacerdote vocari sacrificium et oblationem, quia memoria est et repraesentatio veri sacrificii et sanctae immolationis factae in ara crucis. Et semel Christus mortuus in cruce est ibique immolatus est in semetipso (Heb. vii. 27), quotidie autem immolatur in sacramento, quia in sacramento recordatio fit illius quod factum est semel. *Thomas Aquinas* entered into more lengthened discussions, Summ. P. III. qu. 83, art. 1 ss. (qu. by *Münscher*, *von Cölln*, s. 270 f.). The mystical theory was, that Christ is both priest and sacrifice at the same time; see Conc. Lateran. IV. can. 1, note 4. Concerning the usual canon of the mass, the various kinds of masses (missæ solitariæ), etc., comp. the archæological and liturgical works of *Calixt* (Dissert. de Pontificio Missæ Sacrificio, Francof. 1644; and De Missis Solitariis, Helmst. 1647); *Buddeus* (Dissert. de Origine Missæ Pontificiæ, in Miscell. Sacr., Jen. 1727, t. i. p. 1–63); *Augusti* (Archäologie, Bd. iv. and viii.). On the adoration of the host during the mass, as well as at other times (*e.g.* when it was carried to the sick, etc.), which may be dated from the thirteenth century, see *Cæsarius of Heisterbach*, De Miraculis et Visionibus sui Temporis Dialog. lib. ix. c. 51 (qu. by *Gieseler*, ii. 2, s. 408); and *C. de Lith*, De Adoratione Panis consecrati et Interdictione sacri Calicis in Eucharistia, 1753. Decret. Gregorii IX. lib. iii. tit. 41, c. 10 (qu. by *Münscher*, *von Cölln*, s. 262): Sacerdos vero quilibet frequenter doceat plebem suam, ut, cum

---

[1] Since every host contains the body of Christ, and one priest may raise one host at the same time that another priest lowers another, it follows (according to *W. Occam*) that a body may move at one and the same time in two different directions: Aristotle indeed makes the opposite assertion, but this is because he looked at the matter merely from the natural point of view; see Centiloq. conclus. 27. *Rettberg* in the Studien und Kritiken, 1839, 1, s. 76.

in celebratione missarum **elevatur hostia salutaris, quilibet se reverenter inclinet, idem faciens,** cum eam defert presbyter ad **infirmum.** Hence it evidently resulted that the more **prominent the adoration of the** consecrated host, as such, became, the **more the reception of** the sacrament fell into the background. **So it ordinarily** happened, and attempts were made to justify it **theoretically.** Hence, according to *Thomas Aquinas* and other schoolmen, the highest aspect of **the** Eucharist is **found not** in usu fidelium, but in consecratione **materiæ (*Thom.* Sent. iv.** dist. 8, qu. 2, art. **1.** *Durand.* **Sent. iv. dist. 1, qu. 3, § 8);** nevertheless, the **reception of the sacrament (at least three times, afterwards only once in the year) was made a duty to** the faithful. **Conc. Turon. iii. (A.D. 813), can. 50; and Conc.** Later. **iv. (A.D. 1215), can. 21.**

(13) This is the more cheering aspect of the history of the doctrine in question, which has too often been overlooked in works on the history of doctrines. Thus *Anselm* said, De Sacram. Altaris, P. ii. c. 8 (p. 73): Cum ergo de carne sua amandi se tantam ingerit materiam, magnam et mirificam animabus nostris vitæ alimoniam ministrat, quam tunc avidis faucibus sumimus, cum dulciter recolligimus et in ventre memoriæ recondimus, quæcumque pro nobis fecit et passus est Christus. Hoc est convivium de carne Jesu et sanguine, qui cum communicat, habet vitam in se manentem. Tunc enim communicamus, cum fide ardente, quæ per dilectionem operatur, reposuimus in mensa Domini, qualia ipsi sumsimus, videlicet, ut, sicut ille totum se præbuit pro salute nostra nulla sua necessitate, sic nos totos fidei ejus et charitati exhibeamus necessitate salutis nostræ. In hoc convivio quicunque saginatur, nescit panem suum otiosus comedere, sed sollicite cum muliere ejus ardet de nocte hujus seculi consurgere ad lucernam verbi Dei, ut labores manuum suarum manducet, et bene sit ei. Sique in Christo manet bonus conviva Christi propriæ dilectionis affectu, habetque Christum in se manentem per sanctæ operationis effectum. Quod cum utrumque donum Dei sit, totum accrescit magis ac magis ad cumulum amoris in illum, quem perfecte amare est perfecte bonum esse. Hunc autem cibum plus manducat, qui amplius amat, et plus amando rursus qui plus et plus manducat, et plus et plus amat. Licet hujus amoris in hac vita non nisi pignus quoddam accipiamus,

plenitudinem ejus, in præmium, in futuro seculo expectantes. Et ecce hoc est manducare illam carnem, de qua dicit Jesus (John vi. 56): Qui manducat carnem meam, in me manet et ego in eo.—Similar language was used by *Hugo of St. Victor*, who here again "*combined the dialectic prudence of the scholastics with the warmth and depth of the mystics.*" He expressed himself as follows (lib. i. P. viii. c. 5): "He who eats without being united to Christ, has the sacrament indeed, but he has not the essence of the sacrament. On the contrary, he who eats and is united to our Lord, has the essence of the sacrament, because he has faith and love. Even suppose he could neither take nor eat, yet he would be far more esteemed by our Lord than he who takes and eats, but neither believes nor loves, or than he who believes, but does not love." (*Liebner*, s. 435.) Comp. *Bonaventura*, Sent. iv. dist. 10, P. i. qu. 1, art. 1 (qu. by *Klee*, Dg. ii. s. 190). Breviloq. vi. 9, Centiloq. iii. 50.—*Tauler*, Vier Predigten auf unsers Herrn Frohnleichnamstag (Bd. ii. s. 178 ff.); Zwei Predigten von dem heiligen Sacrament (ibid. s. 294 ff.; comp. s. 333 ff). *Ruysbroek*, l.c.—*Gerson*, **Sermo** de Eucharistia in Festo Corporis Domini; **Opp.** (Haag) P. i. p. 1284-1292. His illustrations are all pervaded by the spirit of mysticism; thus he says, p. **1291:** Est panis angelorum, qui factus fuit et **formatus in** pretioso **ventre Virginis** gloriosæ et decoctus in **fornace** ardente dilectionis, **in arbore crucis, qui** manducari **debet cum** baculo spei, cum **boni exempli** calefactorio, cum **acetosis** lachrymis bonæ patientiæ, **velociter recordando** finem **nostrum, in** una domo per unitatem integre, per veram credulitatem, **tostus per ignem** charitatis, etc.—*Suso* calls the Lord's Supper the sacrament of love, and celebrates in it the mystic union of the soul with God; see his Ewige Weisheit, fol. (in *Schmidt*, l.c. s. 51; *Diepenbrock*, s. 350).—In like manner, *Thomas a Kempis*, De Imit. Christi, lib. iv. 4 [lib. ii. cap. 2, ed. of *Hirsche*]: Ecce, unde dilectio procedit, qualis dignatio illucescit! quam magnæ gratiarum actiones et laudes tibi pro his debentur! O quam salutare et utile consilium tuum, cum istud instituisti! quam suave et jucundum convivium, cum te ipsum in cibum donasti! O quam admirabilis operatio tua, Domine! quam potens virtus tua, quam ineffabilis [infallibilis¹]

¹ [So in ed. of *Hirsche*.]

veritas tua! Dixisti enim, et facta sunt omnia, et hoc factum est, quod ipse jussisti. 5. Mira res et fide digna, ac humanum vincens intellectum, quod tu, Domine Deus meus, verus Deus et homo, sub modica specie panis et vini integer contineris, et sine consumtione a sumente manducaris. Tu Domine universorum, qui nullius habes indigentiam, voluisti per Sacramentum tuum habitare in nobis: conserva cor meum et corpus immaculatum, ut laeta et pura conscientia saepius tua valeam celebrare mysteria, et ad meam perpetuam accipere salutem, quae ad tuum praecipue honorem et memoriale perenne sanxisti et instituisti. 6. Laetare, anima mea, et gratias age Deo pro tam nobili munere et solatio singulari in hac lacrymarum valle tibi relicto. Nam quoties hoc mysterium recolis et Christi corpus accipis, toties tuae redemtionis opus agis, et particeps omnium meritorum Christi efficeris. Charitas enim Christi nunquam minuitur et magnitudo propitiationis ejus nunquam exhauritur. Ideo nova semper mentis renovatione ad hoc disponere te debes, et magnum salutis mysterium attenta consideratione pensare. Ita magnum, novum, et jucundum tibi videri debet, cum celebras aut Missam audis, ac si eodem die Christus primum in uterum Virginis descendens homo factus esset, aut si in cruce pendens pro salute hominum pateretur et moreretur. — Wessel entertained similar views (though he somewhat differed from the ecclesiastical doctrine, see § 196, note 7), comp. De Orat. viii. 6, p. 148; De Sacram. Eucharist. c. 26, p. 699 (qu. by *Ullmann*, s. 329): "The bread set before believers is the purest and most perfect mirror of love, lifted up on the hills, that all may see it, and none hide himself from its warming beams," etc. Compare also the impassioned speech of *Nicolaus of Cus* at the administration of the Holy Communion, in his writings, ed. by *Scharpff*, Freib. 1862, s. 593 ff.

§ 195.

The Withholding of the Cup from the Laity—Concomitance.

*Spittler, Geschichte des Kelches im Abendmahl, Lemgo 1780.

In the Western Church the custom was gradually adopted of administering to the laity only the consecrated host, while the priests alone partook of the cup (1). This practice was justified doctrinally by the doctrine of *concomitance*, developed **about the** same time, according to which the whole Christ is **present in** each of the elements, so that those who receive the consecrated host, partake of His **blood** no less than **of** His **body (2).** *Robert Pulleyn* is said **to** have been the first who **raised the** participation **of the cup** to a prerogative of the priesthood (3). *Alexander of Hales, Bonaventura,* and *Thomas Aquinas* followed him **(4).** But *Albertus* **Magnus**, while conceding that the blood of Christ was also present **in** the body, said that this was only ex unione naturali, and not ex virtute sacramentali (5). In the fifteenth century the cup **was** again violently reclaimed in Bohemia. It was not at first *Hus*, but his colleague, *Jacobellus of Misa*, who demanded, in the absence of the former, that the laity should be readmitted to the participation **of** the Lord's Supper *sub utraque forma;* but **Hus was afterwards unable** to withhold his approval of what **he had done (6).** It is well known that this demand, which was in **opposition to the decisions of** the Synod of Constance (7), **gave rise to the wars of** the Hussites. The consequence was, that the Council of Basel confirmed the doctrine **of** the Church, according to **which it is** sufficient **to** partake of the Lord's Supper sub una forma; **but it permitted exceptions** when the Church deemed it desirable (8).

(1) **Had this** custom its origin in the apprehension that **some portion of the wine** might be spilt? Concerning the dipping of the bread—the introduction of the Fistula (canna) eucharistica, **etc., see** *Spittler*, l.c., **and** the works **on** ecclesiastical history **and** archæology: *Augusti*, Archäologie, viii. s. 392 ff., comp. s. 485. (Comp. § 194, note 12.)

(2) *Peter Lombard* taught, Sent. lib. iv. dist. **10 D** (in calce): Integrum **Christum esse in altari** sub utraque specie, **et substantiam** panis in corpus, **vinique** substantiam in sanguinem converti. *Thomas Aquinas* **was** the first who made **use of** the term *concomitantia*, Summa, P. III. qu. 76, art. 1: **Sciendum, quod aliquid Christi est in** hoc sacramento dupli-

citer: uno modo quasi ex vi sacramenti, alio modo *ex naturali concomitantia.* **Ex vi** quidem sacramenti est sub speciebus hujus sacramenti id, in quod directe convertitur substantia panis et vini præexistens, prout significatur per verba formæ, quæ sunt effectiva in hoc sacramento. . . . Ex naturali autem concomitantia est in hoc sacramento illud, quod realiter est conjunctum ei, in quod prædicta conversio terminatur. Si enim aliqua duo sunt realiter conjuncta, ubicunque est unum realiter, **oportet** et aliud esse. Sola enim operatione animæ discernuntur, quæ realiter sunt conjuncta. (He made use of the same concomitance to explain the union of the soul and the Godhead of Christ with His body. Compare above, § 194, note 8.)

(3) Sent. P. VIII. c. 3 (he spoke of the danger alluded to above). The command of Christ: "*Drink ye all of it*," was applied to the priests (as the successors of the apostles). See *Cramer*, vi. s. 515 f.

(4) *Alexander of Hales*, Summa, P. IV. qu. 53, membr. 1 (qu. by *Münscher, von Cölln*, s. 263). *Bonaventura* in Sent. lib. iv. dist. 11, P. 2, art. 1, qu. 2 (ibidem). *Thomas Aquinas*, see above, note 2. (Alexander of Hales speaks of the withholding of the cup as of something quite common in the Church.)

(5) *Gieseler*, Dg. s. 544.

(6) *Æneæ Sylvii* Historia Bohemica, c. 35. *Hermann von der Hardt*, Acta Conc. Constant. t. iii. p. 338 ss. *Gieseler*, Kg. ii. 4, s. 420 ff. The approbation of *Hus* was given later. Comp. De Sanguine Christi sub Specie vini a Laicis sumendo, quæstio M. Joannis Hus, quam Constantiæ conscripsit priusquam in carcerem conjiceretur, in "Joannis Hus Historia et Monument.," Norimb. 1558, t. i. fol. xlii. ss. *Gieseler*, l.c. s. 413.

(7) Sess. xiii. (A.D. 1415, June 15), see in *Herm. von der Hardt*, tom. iii. col. 646 ss. (qu. by *Gieseler*, l.c. p. 329, note f., and *Münscher, von Cölln*, s. 266): Firmissime credendum et nullatenus dubitandum, integrum corpus Christi et sanguinem tam sub specie panis quam sub specie vini veraciter contineri.

(8) Mansi, t. xxx. col. 695: Sancta vero mater ecclesia, suadentibus causis rationabilibus, facultatem communicandi populum sub utraque specie potest concedere et elargiri.—

Nevertheless, the council adhered to the earlier definition: Nullatenus ambigendum est, quod non sub specie panis caro tantum, nec sub specie vini sanguis tantum, sed sub qualibet specie est integer totus Christus, etc.; comp. also Sess. xxx. (Dec. 23, A.D. 1437), in Mansi, xxix. col. 158. *Gieseler*, l.c. s. 442. *Münscher*, *von Colln*, s. 267 f.

§ 196.

Dissenting Opinions.

After the doctrine of transubstantiation had been thus established, it was only now and then that a few individuals ventured to dissent from it, or at least to modify the commonly received notion. Thus in the twelfth century, *Rupert of Deutz* (Rupertus Tuitiensis), to judge from some passages in his works, supposed that there is a wonderful union of the body of Christ with the bread, but without any disturbance of the sensible elements (1). *John of Paris* (Johannes Pungensasinum) narrowed the notion of Rupert into the scholastic idea of *impanation,* according to which the corporeitas panis (paneitas) forms a union with the corporeitas Christi—an idea which would readily work upon the fancy in a more repulsive way than the more daring doctrine of transubstantiation (2). *William Occam* also inferred the co-existence of Christ's body *with* the accidents from the nominalistic theory about the quantity of things, and thus partly prepared the way for the later Lutheran view (3). Similar opinions were taught by *Durandus de Sancto Porciano* (4). On the other hand, *Wykliffe* combated the doctrine of transubstantiation, as well as that of impanation, with polemical acumen (5). His views were probably adopted by *Jerome of Prague,* while *Hus* expressed himself in accord with the orthodox doctrine of the Church (6). *John Wessel* attached particular importance to spiritual participation in the Lord's Supper, and asserted that none but *believers* can partake of the body of Christ. Though he retained the idea of a sacrifice, allied to the Catholic view, he applied it mystically to the spiritual priesthood (7).

(1) "*With regard to* Rupert of Deutz, *it is difficult to state his opinion in precise terms, inasmuch as he expressed himself at different times in different ways,*" Klee, Dg. ii. s. 202. But compare his Commentar. in Exod. lib. ii. c. 10 : Sicut naturam humanam non destruxit, cum illam operatione sua ex utero Virginis Deus Verbo in unitatem personæ conjunxit, sic substantiam panis et vini, secundum exteriorem speciem quinque sensibus subactam, non mutat aut destruit, cum eidem Verbo in unitatem corporis ejusdem quod in cruce pependit, et sanguinis ejusdem quem de latere suo fudit, ista conjungit. Item quomodo Verbum a summo demissum caro factum est, non mutatum in carnem, sed *assumendo* carnem, sic panis et vinum, utrumque ab imo sublevatum, fit corpus Christi et sanguis, non mutatum in carnis saporem sive in sanguinis horrorem, sed assumendo invisibiliter utriusque, divinæ scilicet et humanæ, quæ in Christo est, immortalis substantiæ veritatem.—De div. Off. ii. 2 : Unus idemque Deus sursum est in carne, hic *in pane*. He called the bread Deifer panis. Panem *cum* sua carne, vinum *cum* suo jungebat sanguine. But he also spoke of the bread and wine being converted and transformed into the body and blood of Christ. Compare the passages quoted by *Klee,* l.c.

(2) He died A.D. 1306. He *wrote:* Determinatio de Modo existendi Corpus Christi in Sacramento Altaris alio quam sit ille quem tenet Ecclesia; this work was published, Lond. 1686. Comp. *Cas. Oudinus,* Dissertatio de Doctrina et Scriptis Jo. Parisiensis, in Comment. de Scriptt. Eccles. t. iii. col. 634 ss. *Schröckh,* Kg. xxviii. s. 70 ff. *Münscher, von Cölln,* s. 256-259.[1]

(3) It is of special importance that he acknowledged the impossibility of proving the doctrine of transubstantiation from Scripture (Quodl. iv. qu. 35). He developed his own

---

[1] As early as the middle of the thirteenth century, several professors in the University of Paris had been charged with holding incorrect opinions concerning the Lord's Supper; see the letter addressed to Pope Clement IV. in *Bulæus,* vol. iii. p. 372, 373 . . . : Esse Parisiis celebrem opinionem tunc temporis de mysterio Eucharistiæ, qua contendebatur, corpus Christi non esse vere in altari, sed sicut signatum sub signis.

views in his Tractatus de Sacramento Altaris, and elsewhere; the passages are collected by *Rettberg*, Occam und Luther (in the Studien und Kritiken, 1839, 1). Though Occam retained the orthodox doctrine of the *accidents* (§ 193, note 6), he could not attach any distinct meaning to the notion that the substance of **the** elements **had** vanished, because he was still obliged to conceive of the **body of** Christ and the bread as being in *one and the same* place. Thus we may " *suppose the real theory of Occam to* **have** *been this, that the body of Christ is contained in the host, in the same manner in which soul and body together occupy one and the same space; and as the soul exists wholly in every member, so the whole Christ exists in every single host,*" *Rettberg,* s. 93. Occam carried out his notion of the ubiquity of the body of Christ with all its paradoxes. The stone thrown into the air is, in its transit, in the same place where the body of Christ is, etc. This ubiquity, however, is not the foundation, but the consequence of his doctrine. See *Rettberg,* **s. 96.**—The systems of Occam and of Luther are compared with each other, ibid. s. 123 ff.

(4) See *Cramer,* vii. s. 804 f., who says, " *none of the scholastics entertained views more nearly allied to those of Luther than Durandus.*" He did not directly oppose transubstantiation; but he conceded that there were other possible ways in which Christ might be present, and particularly this, that the substance **of the bread might remain, and the** substance of the **body of** Christ be united **with it.** The *hoc est* might mean the same as *contentum sub hoc est.* He distinguished between matter and form; the matter of the bread, he says, **exists under** the form of the body of Christ.

(5) Trialogus, lib. iv. c. 2–10, *e.g.* c. 6, p. 197 (alias, p. cix.): Inter omnes hæreses, quæ unquam pullularunt in ecclesia sancta Dei, non fuit nefandior, quam hæresis ponens accidens sine subjecto esse hoc venerabile sacramentum. He also opposed the doctrine of impanation, c. 8 : Sum certus, quod sententia ista impanationis est impossibilis atque hæretica. He could not endure the thought that in that case the *baker* would prepare the body of Christ instead of the priest! According to Wykliffe, Christ is not present in the bread realiter, sed habitudinaliter, secundum similitudinem. In illustration of his views, he also referred to mirrors, in which

the one countenance of Christ is reflected in various ways to the eyes of the devout. The conversio, which takes place, is a change from the inferior to the superior (this was the ancient opinion, which was also adopted by Berengarius). He distinguished (in his confession in presence of the Duke of Lancaster) a triplex modus essendi corpus Christi in hostia consecrata: 1. Modus virtualis, quo benefacit per totum suum dominium secundum bona naturæ vel gratiæ; 2. Modus spiritualis, quo corpus Christi est in eucharistia et sanctis per Spiritum Sanctum; 3. Modus sacramentalis, quo corpus Christi *singulariter* est in hostia consecrata. On the other hand, Christ is only in heaven, substantionaliter, corporaliter, dimensionaliter. Of like import are the following three of the ten Conclusiones Hæreticæ, which were condemned by the London Council of 1382 (*Mansi*, xxvi. p. 691): 1. Quod substantia panis materialis et vini maneat post consecrationem; 2. Quod accidentia non maneant sine subjecto; 3. Quod Christus non sit in sacramento altaris identice, vere, et realiter. Comp. *Ebrard*, i. s. 501, Anm. 51. *Schröckh*, xxxiv. s. 501 ff.

(6) *Jerome of Prague* at least was charged by the Council of Constance with holding such opinions as follow: Quod panis non transubstantiabatur in corpus Christi, nec *est* corpus Christi in sacramento præsentialiter et corporaliter, sed ut signatum in signo. Item, quod in hostia sive sacramento altaris non est vere Christus.—Christus passus est in cruce, sed hostia altaris nunquam est passa neque patitur; ergo hostia in sacramento altaris non est Christus.—Mures non possunt comedere Christum; sed mures possunt hostiam consecratam comedere: ergo hostia in sacramento altaris non est Christus; see *Hermann von der Hardt*, t. iv. P. viii. p. 646. —On the other hand, *Poggi* (Ep. ad Aretin.) gives the following relation: Cum rogaretur, quid sentiret de sacramento, inquit: Antea panem, postea vero Christi corpus, et reliqua secundum fidem. Tum quidam: Ajunt te dixisse, post consecrationem remanere panem. Tum ille: Apud pistorem, inquit, panis remanet; see *Klee*, Dg. ii. s. 205, Anm. 7.—*Hus* did not oppose the doctrine of the Church in decided terms; he only endeavoured to justify himself on the point, that he believed in the real presence of the body of Christ, without entering into any further explanation of the modus; see his

Tractatus de Corpore Christi in the above Histor. et Monum. fol. cxxiii. ss. *Münscher, von Cölln,* s. 260.

(7) See *Ullmann,* s. 328–340 (where extracts are given from *Wessel's* treatises: De Oratione VIII., De Sacram. Eucharistiæ, especially c. 10, 24, 26, 27; Scal. Medit. Exempl. i. ii. iii.). **In his** opinion, the Lord's Supper is the *realization and appropriation of the love of Christ;* but he is not aware of any essential difference between the presence and appropriation of Christ **in** the Lord's Supper, **and that of** which believers are conscious *without* the sacrament. The *spiritual* participation **of the** body of Christ is to him the principal thing, not the *sacramental.* The sacramental act (the sacrifice **of the** mass) **can be** performed by none but the priest; the inward communion with Christ may be renewed by every Christian.

§ 197.

The Greek Church.

Corn. Will, Acta et Scripta de controversiis Ecclesiæ græcæ et latinæ seculo undecimo composita, Marb. 1861.

The use of unleavened bread at the commemoration of Christ's death, which had been introduced into the Latin Church from the ninth century (1), gave rise to a controversy with the Greek Church, in the course of which the latter went so far as to charge the former with a departure from pure Christianity (2). As regards the doctrine of the sacrament itself, the Greek theologians agreed in the main with the divines of the Western Church so far as this, that some of them propounded rather a doctrine of consubstantiation (3), while others taught rather a formal transubstantiation (4), but without sharing in all the consequences which the schoolmen drew from it. The Greek Church also preserved the custom of administering the Lord's Supper to the laity under both forms (5).

(1) On this point, see *Neander,* Kg. iv. s. 637 f. The hosts, properly so called (*i.e.* the consecrated wafers), did not

come into use till later, and, according to some writers, **not till the second half** of the twelfth century. Compare *J. A. Schmidt*, De Oblatis Eucharisticis, quæ Hostiæ vocari solent, ed. 2, Helmst. 1733, 4to. *Augusti*, viii. s. 375 ff.

(2) This was done by *Michael Cerularius*, Patriarch of **Constantinople** (and *Leo of Acrida* with him), in a letter addressed to John, Bishop of Trani in Apulia (in *Baronius*, Annals, ad ann. 1053, Not. 22, and *Canisius*, Lectt., ed. *Basnage*, t. iii. P. i. p. 281). He derived, **strangely** enough, the noun ἄρτος from the verb αἴρω, and appealed, in support of his theory, to Matt. xxvi. 17, 18, 20, 26-28, as well as to Matt. v. 13, and xiii. 33 (the three measures of meal are, in his opinion, an image of the Trinity !).—Division into Azymites and Prozymites (Fermentarii). Vain attempts of the Emperor Constantine Monomachus and the Pope Leo IX. to make peace. —The reply of *Humbert* (prim. ed. *Baronius*, in Append. t. xi.; *Canisius*, l.c. t. iii. P. i. p. 283 ss.) is given by *Gieseler*, l.c. s. 309. After the controversy had been carried on for some time (*e.g.* by Nicetas Pectoratus and others), the Council of Florence at last granted permission to the Greeks to retain their own rite; see *Mansi*, t. xxxi. col. 1029 and 1031; and *Will*, l.c. Comp. *Schroeckh*, xxiv. s. 210 ff. *Neander* and *Gieseler*, l.c.

(3) *John Damascene* quoted (De fide orthodoxa, iv. 13) from the writings of Cyril, Jerome, and Gregory of Nazianzus those passages which appeared to him to carry with them the greatest weight. He decidedly rejected the symbolical interpretation, p. 271: Οὐκ ἐστι τύπος ὁ ἄρτος καὶ ὁ οἶνος τοῦ σώματος καὶ αἵματος τοῦ Χριστοῦ· μὴ γένοιτο· ἀλλ' αὐτὸ τὸ σῶμα τοῦ κυρίου τεθεωμένον, αὐτοῦ τοῦ κυρίου εἰπόντος· Τοῦτό μου ἐστὶν, οὐ τύπος τοῦ σώματος, ἀλλὰ τὸ σῶμα· καὶ οὐ τύπος τοῦ αἵματος, ἀλλὰ τὸ αἷμα. (Compare John vi.) He also used in illustration (applied likewise in Christology) the coal spoken of by Isa. vi. 6: Ἄνθραξ δὲ ξύλον λιτὸν οὐκ ἐστιν, ἀλλ' ἡνωμένον πυρί. Οὕτω καὶ ὁ ἄρτος τῆς κοινωνίας οὐκ ἄρτος λιτός ἐστιν, ἀλλ' ἡνωμένος θεότητι· σῶμα δὲ ἡνωμένον θεότητι, οὐ μία φύσις ἐστιν, ἀλλὰ μία μὲν τοῦ σώματος, τῆς δὲ ἡνωμένης αὐτῷ θεότητος ἑτέρα· ὥστε τὸ συναμφότερον, οὐ μία φύσις, ἀλλὰ δύο. See p. 273, where he shows in what sense the elements may be called ἀντίτυπα (after the example of

Basil). The views which the Greek theologians entertained with respect to the Lord's Supper, were also connected with the part which they took in the controversy concerning images; those who *opposed* the worship of images appealed to the fact that we have an *image* of our Lord in the Holy Supper, which was denied by the advocates of that doctrine. Hence the contradictory decisions of the Council of Constantinople (A.D. 754) and of the second Council of Nicæa (A.D. 787); see *Mansi*, t. iii. col. 261 ss. 265, and *Münscher, von Cölln*, s. 222. In the decrees of the Council of Nicæa it is distinctly denied that either Christ or His apostles had called the elements used at the Lord's Supper *images*. Comp. *Rückert, Das Abendmahl*, s. 441 ff. *Gieseler*, Dg. 533. [According to Constantinople, the elements were the true εἰκών of Christ; according to Nicæa, they were αὐτὸ σῶμα καὶ αὐτὸ αἷμα.]

(4) Thus the expressions μεταποιεῖσθαι and μεταβάλλεσθαι were employed by *Theophylact* in his comment on Matt. xxvi. 28. Compare also what *Euthymius Zigabenus* said on this passage (in *Münscher, von Colln*, s. 223). Nicolas *of Methone* made use of the same expression in his treatise quoted by *Ullmann*, s. 97 (Biblioth. PP. t. ii. Græco-Latin.; Auctuar. Biblioth. Ducæan. Par. 1624, p. 274); he also there speaks of a change of the added water into the blood of Jesus. He entertained, in addition, the scholastic notion, that the bread and wine do not change their external appearance, lest men might be terrified by the sight of the real flesh and blood. The true design of the Lord's Supper he conceived to consist in the μετουσία Χριστοῦ. "*The beginnings of theological speculation may be traced in the theory of Nicolas, but he rested satisfied* (like the Greek theologians of the present period in general) *with mere suggestions, while the scholastics of the Western Church fully exhausted such subjects*" (*Ullmann*).

(5) See *Augusti*, Archäol. viii. s. 398. On the question, whether it was sufficient to administer *only* wine at the communion of children, see ibidem.[1]

---

[1] Concerning the communion of children, which ceased to be practised from the twelfth century, see Zorn, Historia Eucharistiæ Infantium, Berol. 1736 ff. *Gieseler*, Dg. s. 512.

§ 198.

The Sacrament of Penance.

The doctrine of penance, which is, properly speaking, implied in the *ordo salutis*, presupposes the sacrament of baptism. In the scholastic system it found its place among the sacraments (1). Though it is only by a most unnatural interpretation that this sacrament can be proved to possess a visible element, both *Peter Lombard* and *Thomas Aquinas* endeavoured to show that it had the matter as well as the form of a sacrament, and, as far as possible, to distinguish the one from the other (2). The scholastics taught that penance is composed of three parts: *contritio cordis* (in distinction from attritio), *confessio oris*, and *satisfactio operis* (3). Pious minds took offence, not so much at the formal error of regarding penance as a sacrament, as at the lax and merely external theory of penance in general. Thus the Waldenses, while formally adopting the threefold division of penance, rejected the mechanism of the ecclesiastical practice (4). *John Wessel* found fault not only with the threefold division of penance, but also with the definitions of its component parts (5). *Gerson* and others opposed the sale of indulgences (6). *Wykliffe* attacked auricular confession (7). But the discussion of these points belongs more properly to the history of the Church and of ethics, than to that of doctrine (8).

(1) The earlier custom of bringing penance into connection with *baptism* (by making a distinction between sins committed *before* and *after* baptism—by the notion of a baptism of tears—by calling it the second plank after shipwreck, etc.) led the scholastics to enumerate penance among the sacraments. Comp. *Peter Lombard*, Sent. iv. dist. 14 A; *Thomas Aquinas*, P. III. qu. 86, art. 4 (*Klee*, Dg. ii. s. 236 ff.).

(2) *Peter Lombard* observed (dist. 22 C) that some theologians regarded the external performance of the works of

penance, which is perceptible by our bodily senses, as the *signum*. The external works of penance are the signs of *inward* penance, as the bread and wine used in the Lord's Supper are the signs of the body and blood of Christ which are contained in the accidents. *Thomas Aquinas* also conceived (qu. 84, art. 1) the res sacramenti to consist in *internal* penance, of which the *external* is only the sign. (Every outward act might in that sense be called a sacrament?) In the second article he further distinguished between materia and forma. The materia of penance are the sins which are to be removed; the form consists in the words of the priest: Absolvo te. Compare the passages quoted by *Münscher, von Cölln*, s. 276 f. Further in *Hahn*, s. 164 ff.

(3) This distinction was made by *Hildebert of Tours* (who referred it to Chrysostom and Augustine); see his Sermo iv in Quadrag. Opp. col. 324; Sermo xv. col. 733 (in *Münscher, von Cölln*, s. 274,); and *Peter Lombard*, Sent. lib. iv. dist. 16, litt. A: In perfectione autem pœnitentiæ tria observanda sunt, scilicet *compunctio cordis, confessio oris, satisfactio operis* . . . Hæc est fructifera pœnitentia, ut, sicut tribus modis Deum offendimus, scilicet corde, ore, et opere, ita tribus modis satisfaciamus . . . Huic ergo triplici morti triplici remedio occurritur, *contritione, confessione, satisfactione.* Conc. Florent. 1439 (under Pope Eugenius IV. in *Mansi*, xxxi. col. 1057; *Münscher, von Cölln*, s. 284): Quartum Sacramentum est pœnitentiæ, cujus quasi materia sunt actus pœnitentis, qui in tres distinguuntur partes. Quarum prima est cordis contritio, ad quam pertinet ut doleat de peccato commisso cum proposito non peccandi de cætero. Secunda est oris confessio, ad quam pertinet ut peccator omnia peccata, quorum memoriam habet, suo sacerdoti confiteatur integraliter. Tertia est satisfactio pro peccatis secundum arbitrium sacerdotis, quæ quidem præcipue fit per orationem, jejunium, et eleemosynam. Forma hujus sacramenti sunt verba absolutionis, quæ sacerdos profert cum dicit: Ego te absolvo, etc. Minister hujus sacramenti est sacerdos, habens auctoritatem absolvendi vel ordinariam, vel ex commissione superioris. Effectus hujus sacramenti est absolutio a peccatis.—On the difference between contritio and attritio, see *Alexander of Hales*, P. IV. qu. 74, membr. 1: Timor servilis principium est attritionis, timor

initialis (*i.e.* that with which the life of sanctification begins)[1] principium est contritionis ... Item, contritio est a gratia gratum faciente, attritio a gratia gratis data. Comp. *Thom. Aquinas,* qu. 1, art. 2 ; *Bonaventura* in lib. iv. dist. 17, P. i. art. 2, qu. 3.—[*Attritio* proceeds from fear, and not from love to God : *contritio* is the real sorrow for sin, proceeding from love ; attritio is the terminus a quo, contritio is the terminus ad quem. Contritio is necessary to forgiveness.] The necessity of confessio oris (*i.e.* that it was necessary to confess our sins not only to God, but also to the *priest*) was asserted by *Thomas Aquinas,* in Supplem. tertiæ Part. qu. 8, art. 1 ; *Peter Lombard* expressed himself more indefinitely on this point, Sent. iv. dist. 17, litt. B.—The ecclesiastical institution of *auricular confession* was established by the fourth Lateran Council (1216, under Pope Innocent III.), Can. xxi. in Decretis Greg. l. v. tit. 38, c. 12 : Omnis utriusque sexus fidelis, postquam ad annos discretionis pervenerit, omnia sua solus peccata confiteatur fideliter, saltem semel in anno, proprio sacerdoti,[2] et injunctam sibi pœnitentiam studeat pro viribus adimplere, etc. (*Gieseler,* ii. 2, s. 444 ; *Münscher, von Cölln,* s. 282. The satisfactio operis consisted in fastings, prayers, alms, pilgrimages, mortifications, etc. *Thomas Aquinas,* l.c. qu. 15, art. 3 (in *Münscher, von Cölln,* s. 279). The practice of imposing fines, instead of bodily punishments, gave rise to the sale of indulgences.

(4) The Waldenses even attempted to vindicate this threefold division by allegorizing. The spices with which the women went to anoint the body of the Lord on Easter morning, were myrrh, aloes, and balsam. From these three costly spices is prepared that spiritual ointment, which is called penance. See *Herzog,* Die Romanischen Waldenser. But the Waldenses still differed from the Catholic Church in this, that

---

[1] On this account, others (such as *Thomas* and *Bonaventura*) also called the contritio, timor filialis, as opposed to the timor servilis.

[2] In the absence of a priest it was permitted to confess to a layman ; but this led to the question as to how far the sacrament was complete in such a case. See *Thom. Aquinas,* in Suppl. qu. 8, art. 2 ; on the other side, *Bonaventura,* P. iii. ad Expos. text. dub. 1, p. 229. *Duns Scotus,* in lib. iv. dist. 17, qu. 1. —The sects of the Middle Ages, even the Flagellantes, preferred confession to a layman. Comp. *Münscher, von Cölln,* s. 283 f. ; *Gieseler,* ii. 2, s. 277 ; *Klee,* Dg. ii. s. 252 ff.

confession was not necessarily to be made to a priest of that Church, and that they went beyond the external works of penance to the internal penitence of the heart.

(5) De Sacramento Pœnitentiæ, p. 782: Est enim actus *mentis* pœnitentia, sicut peccatum: utrumque enim *voluntatis*. Et sicut peccatum voluntatis tantum est, ita pœnitentia solius est voluntatis. For further particulars, see *Ullmann*, s. 340 ff.

(6) Epistola de Indulgentiis (Opp. t. ii.), c. 3–5, and c. 9.
(7) Trialog. lib. iv. c. 32.
(8) See *Gieseler*, Kg. ii. 1–3.

§ 199.

Extreme Unction.

(Sacramentum Unctionis Extremæ, Unctionis Infirmorum, egredientium, exeuntium, et emeritorum.)

The apostolic injunction respecting the sick, Jas. v. 14 (comp. Mark vi. 13), which probably had **a** symbolical and **religious significance, as well as a** medicinal and therapeutic (1), gave rise **to the** institution **of a new sacrament,** which came into general **use** from the **ninth century, and** could **be** administered **only in the** dying hour **(2). But various** opinions obtained **on** the question, whether **it was proper** to repeat the administration **of the sacrament in the case of a** dying person **who had received it on a former** occasion, **but** who had **recovered, and been restored to life; or, whether** it was sufficient **to have administered it once? The Church** did not ascribe **a character indelebilis to this sacrament (3). Its sign is** the **consecrated oil,** its essence consists in **the** forgiveness of sins, **and partly also in the alleviation of the bodily** sufferings of **the sick (4).**

(1) See the commentators on this passage; *Bede*, Opp. t. v. col. 693; and on Mark vi. 13, ibid. col. 132 (in *Münscher, von Cölln*, s. 297). [*Bede* on Mark vi. 13: Unde patet ab ipsis

Apostolis hunc sanctum Ecclesiæ morem esse traditum, ut energumeni, vel alii quilibet ægroti, unguantur oleo pontificali benedictione consecrato.] *Innocent I.* Ep. 21, ad Decentium Episc. Eugubinum (written about the year 416), cap. 8 (*Münscher*, *von Cölln*, s. 298). [Innocent III.: Quod non est dubium de fidelibus ægrotantibus accipi vel intelligi debere, qui sancto oleo chrismatis perungi possunt : quod ab Episcopo confectum, non solum sacerdotibus, sed omnibus uti Christianis licet in sua aut in suorum necessitate ungendum.]

(2) Concil. Regiaticinum (A.D. 850), Canon 8 (in *Münscher, von Cölln,* s. 298). [Magnum sane ac valde appetendum mysterium, per quod, si fideliter poscitur, et remittuntur (peccata), et consequenter corporalis salus restituitur.]—For earlier indications of the anointing of the sick, as a sacrament, see *Hahn,* l.c. s. 96. As regards the institution, in accordance with the distinction noticed (§ 89, note 3) between insinuatio and institutio, the latter is attributed to James; but the insinuatio to Christ. Comp. *Hahn,* s. 169. — Among the scholastics, *Hugo of St. Victor* was the first who spoke of extreme unction as a sacrament; De Sacram. ii. P. xv.; comp. Summa Sent. Tract. vi. c. 15 (*Liebner,* s. 481). The doctrine of extreme unction formed, in his system, the transition to eschatology.— *Peter Lombard*, Sent. iv. dist. 23, mentioned three different kinds of consecrated oil (χρίσματα): 1. That with which priests and kings are anointed (on the head), or those who are confirmed (upon the forehead). 2. That with which catechumens and newly baptized persons are anointed (upon the chest, and between the shoulders). 3. The unctio infirmorum (which may be performed on various parts of the body. Compare note 4).[1] He also distinguished between the sacramentum and the res sacramenti. B: Sacramentum est ipsa unctio exterior, res sacramenti unctio interior, quæ peccatorum remissione et virtutum ampliatione perficitur. Et si ex contemtu vel negligentia hoc prætermittiur, periculosum est et damnabile.

(3) *Ivo of Chartres* (Ep. 225), Ad Radulfum, and *Geoffrey of Vendome* (who lived about the year 1110), Opusculum de Iteratione Sacramenti (in *Sirmondi* Opp. t. iii.), opposed the

---

[1] On the further significance of consecrated oil, see *Thom. Aquinas*, Supplem. quæst. xxix. art. 4.—*Klee,* ii. s. 263 f.

repetition of extreme unction (comp. *Münscher, von Colln,* s. 299); *Peter Lombard* pronounced in *favour* of it, l.c. lit. C. [*Lombard* here follows Hugo of St. Victor almost verbally: Sacramentum unctionis spiritualis est quædam medicina, corporis et animæ languores mitigans et sanans: nam oleum membra dolentia sanat. Itaque oleum ad utrumque curandum prodest. Si morbus non revertitur, medicina non iteretur; si autem morbus non potest cohiberi, quare deberet medicina prohiberi? . . . Quare ergo negatur quod unctionis sacramentum super infirmum *iterari possit* ad reparandam sæpius sanitatem, et ad impetrandam sæpius peccatorum remissionem.]— On the controversy concerning this point, which arose on the occasion of the death of Pope Pius II., see above, § 190, note 6.—The opinion also obtained during the Middle Ages, that extreme unction does away with all the relations in which man stands to the present life; the person who had received extreme unction immediately renounced all kinds of meat, and the continuance of matrimony. Bishops, however, as well as councils, *e.g.* the Council of Worcester (A.D. 1240), combated this notion. See *Klee,* ii. s. 272.

(4) Comp. the opinion of *Peter Lombard,* note 2, and *Hugo of St. Victor,* De Sacram. Fid. lib. ii. P. xv. c. 2: Duplici ex causa sacramentum hoc institutum; et ad peccatorum scilicet remissionem, et ad corporalis infirmitatis allevationem. Comp. *Thomas Aquinas,* P. III. in Supplem. qu. 30, art. 1.—Decret. *Eugenii IV.* in Conc. Florent. a. 1439 (*Mansi,* t. xxxi. col. 1058): Quintum Sacramentum est extrema unctio. Cujus materia est oleum olivæ per episcopum benedictum. Hoc sacramentum nisi infirmo, de cujus morte timetur, dari non debet. Qui in his locis ungendus est: in oculis propter visum, in auribus propter auditum, in naribus propter odoratum, in ore propter gustum vel locutionem, in manibus propter tactum, in pedibus propter gressum, in renibus propter delectationem ibidem vigentem. Forma hujus sacramenti est hæc: per istam unctionem et suam piissimam misericordiam, quicquid peccasti per visum etc. . . . et similiter in aliis membris. Minister hujus sacramenti est sacerdos. Effectus vero est mentis sanatio, et, in quantum autem expedit, ipsius etiam corporis (he appeals to Jas. v. 14).

§ 200.

The Sacrament of Orders.

(Sacramentum Ordinis.)

This sacrament is intimately connected with the article of the Church, and with the distinction there made between the laity and the clergy. It is that sacrament by which men are fitted to administer the other sacraments (1). Accordingly, its essence lies in the ecclesiastical power which it communicates (2). None but bishops can ordain (3), and only baptized and grown-up males can receive ordination (4). Opinions differed respecting the validity of ordination by heretical bishops (5). Further regulations (concerning ordines majores et minores, etc.) belong to the canon law (6). This sacrament has a character indelebilis (7).

(1) *Thomas Aquinas*, Pars III. Supplem. qu. 34, art. 3: Propter Ordinem fit homo dispensator aliorum sacramentorum, ergo Ordo habet magis rationem, quod sit sacramentum, quam alia.—*Raimund of Sabunde* says that the administrators to the sacraments stand in the same relation to the sacred acts in which parents stand to the act of generation. They dispense the external signs, God effects the inward grace; as parents beget the body, but God creates the soul (the creatianist view); see *Matzke*, Raimund von Sabunde, s. 101.

(2) The statements are very vacillating as to what really constitutes the material (in distinction from the formal) part of ordination. As regards the external sign of ordination, there was a considerable difference of opinion. The earlier Church regarded the laying on of hands (χειροτονία) as having a higher, a magical virtue, while the later theologians attached no great importance to it; comp. *Klee*, ii. s. 280 f. [He says: The ancients, in accordance with the Scriptures, made the laying on of hands to be the matter of ordination; by this is effected the elevation and consecration to the episcopate, the presbyterate, and the diaconate. Anointing is also very early

mentioned in the inauguration of bishops and priests (*Eusebius*, Hist. Eccl. x. 4; *Greg. Naz.* Orat. V.; *Greg. Nyss.* Virg. cap. xxiv.; *Leo*, often); and the laying of the gospels on the head, at the ordination of bishops (*Hippolytus*, De Charism. cap. 1 : *Chrysost.* Homil. quod Veteris Test. Unus Legislator, in *Photii* Cod. cclxxvii.).] The consecrated oil was only occasionally mentioned. *Thomas Aquinas*, l.c. art. 5, candidly avowed, that while the efficacy of the other sacraments consisted in the matter, quod divinam virtutem et significat et continet, it depended, in the present case, on the person who administered the sacrament, and that it was transmitted by him to the person to be ordained. Therefore, in his view, *the act of ordination is the material, and not the symbols*, which are used at its administration. Nevertheless, it is said in the Decret. *Eugenii IV.* in Conc. Florent. a. 1439, l.c. col. 1058: Sextum Sacramentum est Ordinis, cujus materia est illud, per cujus traditionem confertur Ordo, sicut Presbyteratus traditur per calicis cum vino et patenæ cum pane porrectionem, Diaconatus vero per libri Evangeliorum dationem, Subdiaconatus vero per calicis vacui cum patena vacua superposita traditionem, et similiter de aliis per rerum ad ministeria sua pertinentium assignationem. Forma sacerdotii talis est: Accipe potestatem offerendi sacrificium in ecclesia pro vivis et mortuis, in nomine Patris et Filii et Spiritus Sancti. Et sic de aliorum ordinum formis, prout in pontificali Romano late continetur. Compare also *Peter Lombard*, lib. iv. dist. 24. He calls (lit. B) the tonsure (corona) the signaculum, quo signantur in partem sortis ministerii divini . . . Denudatio capitis est revelatio mentis (God grant it!). Clericus enim secretorum Dei non ignarus esse debet. Tondentur etiam capilli usque ad revelationem sensuum, scilicet oculorum et aurium, ut vitia in corde et opere pullulantia doceantur præcidenda, ne ad audiendum et intelligendum verbum Dei præpediatur mens, pro quo servato reddetur in excelsis corona.

(3) Decret. *Eug. IV.* l.c.: Ordinarius minister hujus sacramenti est Episcopus. Comp. *Thom. Aqu.* qu. 38, art. 1.

(4) This is self-evident. Nevertheless, a Benedictio might be conferred upon women (deaconesses) for certain clerical functions; but this was essentially distinct from ordinatio, and had no character indelebilis (comp. *Hahn*, s. 270, and the

passages quoted by him from Thom. Aqu., Scotus, and Biel). Concerning the age at which persons might be ordained, the following regulations were made : Ut Subdiaconus non ordinetur ante quatuordecim annos, nec Diaconus ante viginti quinque, nec Presbyter ante triginta. Deinde, si dignus fuerit, ad episcopatum eligi potest; see *Peter Lombard*, l.c. lit. I. Priests were to be thirty years old, because Christ (according to Luke iii.) commenced His public ministry at the age of thirty years.

(5) The views of *Peter Lombard* on this point were still unsettled, Sent. iv. dist. 25, De ordinatis ab hæreticis. *Thomas Aquinas*, P. III. in Supplem. dist. 38, art. 2, gave it as his final opinion, quod (hæretici) vera sacramenta conferunt, sed cum eis gratiam non dant, non propter inefficaciam sacramentorum, sed propter peccata recipientium ab eis sacramenta contra prohibitionem ecclesiæ. The whole question was analogous to that respecting the baptism of heretics, and had to be decided on the same principles; see *Auxilius*, quoted by *Klee*, ii. s. 282. [Si enim non perdit baptizatus baptismum, etiam eliminatus ab ecclesia, quo pacto perdit sacratus licet excommunicatus sacramentum suæ impositionis posse nisi ad tempus obtemperando priori, ut paulo post absolutus iterum fungatur officio, sicut et baptizatus ecclesiæ ingressum? Est igitur posse, sed non in actu. Libell. super Caus. et Negot. Formosi Papæ.]

(6) *Peter Lombard*, l.c. The seven orders are enumerated in the following succession, commencing with the lowest: Ostiarii, Lectores, Exorcistæ, Acoluthi—Subdiaconi, Diaconi, Presbyteri.

(7) *Thomas Aquinas*, qu. 25, art. 2; qu. 37, art. 5 (in *Münscher, von Cölln*, s. 303). [*Aquinas* says: Quantumcunque homo ad laicatum se transferat, semper tamen manet in eo character. Quod patet ex hoc quod, si ad clericatum revertatur, non iterum Ordinem quem habuerat suscipit.]

§ 201.

The Sacrament of Matrimony.

(Sacramentum matrimonii, conjugii.)

One of the strange contradictions found in the general views of the Catholic Church during the Middle Ages was, that while on the one hand single life was thought to be a special virtue, on the other hand matrimony was raised to the place of a sacrament (1). Much ingenuity was indeed required to show the signs of a sacrament in matrimony in the concrete, as they were specified by the Church itself in the abstract. In the absence of a visible material element, *matrimony itself* was regarded as a type of the union of Christ with the Church (according to Eph. v. 32), and the word μυστήριον translated by *sacramentum*, as the Vulgate has it (2). That it was a divina institutio was more easily shown; in fact, as regards antiquity, matrimony occupied the first place among the sacraments, since it was instituted in Paradise (3). Though it has not a character indelebilis, it is indissoluble as a sacrament, even where bodily separation may have taken place (4). Further regulations concerning conjugal duties, prohibited degrees, dispensations, etc., belong partly to the canon law, partly to ethics (5). According to the laws of the Western Church, the two sacraments of matrimony and of holy orders so exclude each other, that he who receives the one must, as a general rule, renounce the other (6).

(1) *Peter Lombard*, l.c. dist. 26 F. *Thomas Aquinas*, qu. 53, art. 3.—Some scholastics, however, restricted the idea of a sacrament. Thus *Durandus*, Sent. iv. dist. 26, qu. 3, not. 8 (in *Klee*, Dg. ii. s. 302; Cramer, vii. s. 807): Quod matrimonium non est sacramentum stricte et proprie dictum, sicut alia sacramenta novæ legis. On the opinions of *Abélard* and *Peter John Oliva*, see ibidem.—[*Abélard*, Theol. Christ. c. xxxi.: Quod (conjugium) quidem sacramentum est, sed non confert

aliquod donum, sicut cætera faciunt, sed tamen mali remedium est, datur enim propter incontinentiam refrænandam, unde magis ad indulgentiam pertinet.]—That which constitutes the sacrament of matrimony is not the performance of the ceremony by the priest, but the consensus of husband and wife. *Peter Lombard*, dist. 27 C. Respecting particular decrees of popes and councils, see *Klee*, ii. s. 305. [The scholastics generally held that the will of the contracting parties constitutes the marriage; they complete the sacrament; secret marriages, though forbidden, are valid. In none of the ancient rituals is there a sacramental form of marriage to be spoken by the priests.]

(2) *Peter Lombard*, lib. iv. dist. 26 F: Ut enim inter conjuges conjunctio est secundum consensum animorum, et secundum permixtionem corporum: sic Ecclesia Christo copulatur voluntate et natura, qua idem vult cum eo, et ipse formam sumsit de natura hominis. Copulata est ergo sponsa sponso spiritualiter et corporaliter, i. e. charitate ac conformitate naturæ. Hujus utriusque copulæ figura est in conjugio. Consensus enim conjugum copulam spiritualem Christi et Ecclesia, quæ fit per charitatem, significat. Commixtio vero sexuum illam significat, quæ fit per naturæ conformitatem.— *Eugen. IV.* in Conc. Florent. l.c. col. 1058 s.: Septimum est sacramentum Matrimonii, quod est signum conjunctionis Christi et Ecclesiæ secundum Apostolum dicentem (Eph. v. 31): *Sacramentum hoc* etc.

(3) Compare above, § 190, note 1. A distinction, however, should be made, viz. *before* the fall matrimony was instituted ad officium, *after* it, ad remedium (propter illicitum motum devitandum); see *Peter Lombard*, l.c. dist. 16 B. *Thomas Aquinas*, qu. 42, art. 2, conclus. *Albert the Great* and *Thomas* distinguished three different institutions of the sacrament: 1. Before the fall (quoad naturam secundum se); 2. Under the Mosaic law (quoad naturam corruptam); and 3. Under the law of Christ (secundum statum naturæ reparatum per Christum). See the passages in *Hahn*, s. 172. The later schoolmen, as *Scotus* and *Gabriel Biel*, expressed themselves to the effect that pre-Christian marriage was not, in the essential meaning of the word, a sacrament (*Hahn*, l.c.).

(4) *Peter Lombard*, l.c. dist. 31, lit. B: Separatio autem

gemina est, corporalis scilicet et sacramentalis. Corporaliter possunt separari causa fornicationis, vel ex communi consensu causa religionis, sive ad tempus sive usque in finem. Sacramentaliter vero separari non possunt dum vivunt, si legitimæ personæ sint. Manet enim vinculum conjugale inter eos, etiamsi aliis a se discedentes adhæserint. — *Eugen. IV.* in Conc. Florent. l.c.: Quamvis autem ex causa fornicationis liceat tori divisionem facere, non tamen aliud matrimonium contrahere fas est, cum matrimonii vinculum legitime contracti perpetuum sit. — The notions of the Greeks concerning the indissolubility of matrimony were less rigid; the Nestorians alone form an exception; see *Klee,* ii. s. 297 f.

(5) The theologians of the time treated of all those regulations in their works on dogmatic theology. *Peter Lombard* had set them an example. Comp. dist. 24–43. Many definitions of Peter Lombard, Bonaventura, and others, do not at all involve the idea of *sacrament;* such as, that matrimony is conjunctio legitima maris et fœminæ, individuam vitæ consuetudinem retinens, etc. The same may be said with regard to their statements, that the design of matrimony is the propagation of the race, to be a safeguard against sin, etc.

(6) *Thomas Aquinas,* qu. 53, art. 3 : Ordo sacer de sui ratione habet ex quadam congruentia, quod matrimonium impediri debeat, quia in sacris Ordinibus constituti sacra vasa et sacramenta tractant, et ideo deceas est, ut munditiam corporalem per continentiam servent. Sed quod impediat matrimonium, ex constitutione ecclesiæ habet. Tamen aliter apud Latinos, quam apud Græcos. Quia apud Græcos impedit matrimonium contrahendum solum ex vi Ordinis, sed apud Latinos impedit ex vi Ordinis et ulterius ex voto continentiæ, quod est Ordinibus sacris annexum : quod etiamsi quis verbotenus non emittat, ex hoc ipso tamen, quod Ordinem suscipit secundum ritum occidentalis ecclesiæ, intelligitur emisisse. Et ideo apud Græcos et alios Orientales sacer Ordo impedit matrimonium contrahendum, non tamen matrimonii prius contracti usum : possunt enim matrimonio prius contracto uti, quamvis non possunt matrimonium denuo contrahere. Sed apud occidentalem ecclesiam impedit matrimonium et matrimonii usum, nisi forte ignorante aut contradicente uxore vir Ordinem sacrum susceperit, quia ex hoc non potest ei aliquod præjudi-

cium generari. On the one hand, priests are excluded from the sacrament of matrimony, nor are the laity, on the other hand, under any necessity of contracting it. Therefore matrimony is neither a sacramentum necessitatis, as baptism, penance, and the Lord's Supper, nor a sacramentum dignitatis, as holy orders, but a sacramentum consilii. *Alanus ab Insulis* in his Expositio (quoted by *Klee*, ii. s. 304, Anm.).

> Protestant writers on the History of Doctrines cannot be expected to investigate fully the history of each separate sacrament. Nevertheless, some Protestant theologians (like *Hahn*) have done good work in clearing up this difficult and unremunerative matter. But this much appears to be certain, that it is exceedingly difficult, in the case of most of the so-called sacraments, to prove that they are founded upon a definite idea of sacrament, according to the canon established by the Church itself. In the case of some (such as penance, the ordination of priests, and matrimony), we have no visible element, properly speaking, which might be regarded as sacræ rei signum (as bread and wine in the Lord's Supper, or water in baptism, or the χρίσμα), unless we transpose the whole thing, and convert into the symbol that which is properly the res sacramenti. In the case of others, the divina institutio is either altogether wanting (*e.g.* in the case of confirmation), or it can only be demonstrated by that sort of interpretation by which we may prove anything (as in the case of extreme unction). But as these theologians were accustomed to regard the external element in the Lord's Supper as mere accidens, and thus destroyed its originally *symbolical* character, they did not think it necessary to be very precise in the case of other sacraments. And as for the divina institutio, they appealed not only to Scripture, but also to tradition.

SEVENTH DIVISION.

ESCHATOLOGY.

§ 202.

Millenarianism (Chiliasm). The approaching End of the World. Antichrist.

Though Millenarianism (Chiliasm) had been suppressed by the earlier Church, it was nevertheless from time to time revived by heretical sects. Millenarian notions were propounded in the prophecies of *Joachim*, Abbot of Floris, and the *Evangelium aeternum* of the Fratricelli, which was based upon his works (1). The dynasty of the Father and the Son was to be followed by the golden age, viz. the dynasty of the Holy Spirit (2). On the other hand, the almost universal expectation of the approaching end of the world, which was to take place about the year 1000, was founded upon a too literal interpretation of Scripture, rather than upon millenarian enthusiasm. A similar expectation repeatedly manifested itself at other important epochs of the Middle Ages (3). It was connected with the expectation of Antichrist, concerning whom several theologians adventured various suggestions, while many of those who were enemies to the Roman hierarchy thought that he was none other than the pope himself (4). This view was transmitted to the age of the Reformation.

(1) Admiranda Expositio venerabilis Abbatis *Joachimi* in librum Apocalypsis beati Joannis Apostoli et Evangelistæ.—

Liber Concordiæ Novi ac Veteris Testamenti—Psalterium decem Chordarum—Interpretatio in Jeremiam Prophetam. Comp. *Engelhardt*, Kirchenhist. Abhandlungen, s. 1–150. *Lücke*, Einleitung in die Offenb. Johannis, s. 519.—On the Fratricelli, who originally belonged to the order of the Franciscan monks, but were excommunicated in the fourteenth century, comp. *Gieseler*.

(2) Compare *Engelhardt* and *Lücke*, as above. The first status lasts 5000 years (from Adam to Christ), the second lasts 1000 years, from Christ to the commencement of the last age of the world. This last age is the seventh sabbatical period of a thousand years. *Joachim* further divided the ages of the world into forty-two generations (ætates), after the forty-two periods in the genealogy of Christ, etc.

(3) "*It was a prevailing tradition among commentators, that the millennial kingdom, or thousand years' reign, spoken of in* Rev. xx., *commenced with the manifestation, or the passion of Christ, and that the establishment of the Christian Church was to be regarded as the first resurrection, and the first epoch of the kingdom of a thousand years. This interpretation, which had been adopted in the West, especially from the time of Augustine, had the advantage of precluding the fancies of millenarian enthusiasts, and accustoming the minds of Christians to a more spiritual apprehension of the Apocalypse. But the tradition of the Church had not decided whether the computation of the thousand years was to be founded upon the common system of chronology, or whether that number was to be looked upon as an apocalyptical symbol. Inasmuch as the literal interpretation of the numbers was generally adopted by the common mind, notwithstanding all allegorical conceits, the notion began to spread in the Christian world, with the approach of the year* 1000, *that, in accordance with Scripture, the millennial kingdom would come to a close at the completion of the first period of a thousand years after Christ; that, further, Antichrist would then appear, and the end of the world take place,*" *Lücke*, l.c. s. 514 f. On the commotions which happened at that time in the Church, comp. *Trithemii* Chronic. Hirsaug. ad ann. 960. *Glaber Rudulphus*, Hist. sui Temp. lib. iv. c. 6 (in *Duchesne*, Scriptt. Francorum, t. iv. p. 22 ss.). *Schmid*, Geschichte des Mysticismus im Mittelalter, s. 89. *Gieseler*, Kg. ii. 1, s. 213 (229). The Crusades

were also connected with millenarian expectations, see *Corodi*, ii. s. 522 f.; *Schmid*, l.c.—When, in the course of the fourteenth century, the plague, famine, and other divine punishments reminded men of the uncertainty of all that is earthly, and signs were seen in the heavens, it was especially the Flagellantes who announced that the end of the world was nigh at hand; the same was done by *Martin Loquis*, a native of Moravia, and priest of the Taborites; see *Schröckh*, xxxiv. s. 687.

(4) Comp. *John Damascene*, De fide orthod. iv. 26. Elucidarium, c. 68.[1] It was a current opinion during the Middle Ages, that Antichrist would either be brought forth by a virgin, or be the offspring of a bishop and a nun. About the year 950, *Adso*, a monk of western Franconia, wrote a treatise on Antichrist, in which, in opposition to the prevailing expectation, he assigned a later time to his coming, and also to the end of the world (see *Schröckh*, Kirchengesch. xxi. s. 243). He did not distinctly state whom he understood by Antichrist. For a time it was thought that Mahomet was the Antichrist. He was thus designated by Pope Innocent III. (A.D. 1213). The numeral 666 indicated the period of his dominion, which was therefore now about to come to an end.—The anti-Christian prophets spoken of in the Book of Revelation were thought to denote the heresy which spread with increased rapidity from the close of the twelfth century. On the other hand, during the struggles of the Emperors with the Popes, it happened more than once that the former applied the title Antichrist to the latter; we find instances of this as early as the times of the Hohenstaufens. The Emperor Lewis, surnamed the Bavarian, also called Pope John XXII. the *mystical* Antichrist (*Schröckh*, xxxi. s. 108). The fanatical sects of the Middle Ages agreed, for the most part, in giving that name to the popes. Thus *Amalrich of Bena* taught: Quia Papa esset Antichristus et Roma Babylon, et ipse sedet in monte Oliveti, i.e. in pinguedine potestatis (according to *Cæsarius of Heisterbach*), comp. *Engelhardt*, Kirchenhist. Abhandl. s. 256. The same was done by the Spirituales, etc., see *Engelhardt*, l.c. s. 54, 56, 78, 88; *Lücke*, l.c. s. 520 f. Even *Wykliffe* agreed with them

---

[1] Concerning this work (which was formerly ascribed to Anselm), see *Schröckh*, Kg. xxviii. s. 427.

(Trialogus, quoted by *Schröckh*, xxxiv. s. 509), as well as his disciples, *Lewis Cobham* (ibid. s. 557) and *Janow*: Liber de Antichristo et membrorum eius anatomia (in Historia et Monumentis, Joh. Huss. P. i. p. 423–464, quoted by *Schröckh*, l.c. s. 572).—Most of the orthodox Catholic theologians, *e.g. Thomas Aquinas*, were opposed to all literal interpretation of the Apocalypse. On the other hand, there were some, such as *Roger Bacon*, who delighted in apocalyptical interpretations and calculations of the time of Antichrist; see his Opus Majus, ed. *Jebb*, p. 169. *Lücke*, l.c. s. 522.

§ 203.

Influence of Mediæval Tendencies and of Christian Art upon Eschatology.

The tendency of the age manifested itself in the works of Christian art (1), in which those subjects were preferred which had reference to the doctrine of the last things. While the hymn "*Dies Iræ*" (2) sounded the terrors of the judgment into the ears and heart of Christendom, painters were employed in keeping alive a remembrance of the end of all things by their representations of the dance of death, and of the last judgment (3); and *Dante* disclosed in his *Divina Commedia* the worlds of hell, purgatory, and paradise (4). There was an evident action and reaction between these works of imagination on the one hand, and the subtle reasonings and definitions of the scholastics on the other, so that the one may be explained by the other.

(1) Thus most of the magnificent cathedrals on the Continent were built at that very time, when the end of all things was supposed to be nigh at hand; see *Gieseler*, ii. 1, s. 214.

(2) The author of it was *Thomas of Celano*; see *Lisco*, Dies Iræ, Hymnus auf das Weltgericht, Berlin 1840, 4to.

(3) *Grüneisen*, Beiträge zur Geschichte und Beurtheilung der Todtentänze (im Kunstblatt zum Morgenblatt, 1830, Nr. 22–26), and his Nicolas Manuel, s. 73.

(4) *Dante Alighieri* was born A.D. 1265, and died A.D. 1321.

(As a theologian, he belonged to the school of Thomas Aquinas.) There are German translations of his Divina Commedia by *Streckfuss* (Halle 1834, 1840), *Philalethes, Gusck, Kopisch,* and others. [The Vision, or Hell, Purgatory, and Paradise, of *Dante Alighieri.* Translated by the *Rev. H. T. Cary,* Lond. var. edd. *E. Magnier,* Dante et le moyen âge, Paris 1860. Also translations of the Commedia by *C. B. Cayley,* 1854; *J. C. Wright,* 1845; *J. W. Thomas,* 1850. The Inferno was translated by *J. Dayman,* 1843; *C. A. Carlyle,* 1840. The whole poem, by *H. W. Longfellow,* in 3 vols. and in 1 vol. var. edd.] **A. F. Ozanam,* Dante et la phil. cath. au 13me Siècle, Par. 1839.

§ 204.

The Resurrection of the Body.

The resurrection of the human body, with all its parts, remained, from the time of Jerome and Augustine, the prevailing doctrine of the Church. *John Scotus Erigena* adopted the earlier notions of Origen (1), but his views did not meet with approval in the Catholic Church. On the other hand, the Bogomiles, Cathari, and other heretical sects, revived the erroneous notion of the Gnostics, who, looking upon matter as the seat of sin, rejected the resurrection of the body (2). *Moneta,* a Dominican monk, defended the doctrine of the Church in opposition to the Cathari (3). It was then further developed into particulars by the schoolmen (4), especially by *Thomas Aquinas,* with many strange conjectures respecting the nature of the resurrection-body (5). The theologians of the Greek Church held more closely to Scripture and the old faith of the Church (6).

(1) De Div. Nat. iv. 12 s. p. 192: Omne siquidem quod in mundo ex mundo compositum incipit esse, necesse est resolvi et cum mundo interire. Necessarium erat exterius ac materiale corpus solvi in ea elementa, ex quibus assumtum est: non autem necessarium perire, quoniam ex Deo erat, manente

semper interiori illo et incommutabiliter stante in suis rationibus, secundum quas cum anima et in anima et per animam et propter animam constitutum est. Quoniam vero illius corporis materialis atque solubilis manet in anima species, non solum illo vivente, verum etiam post ejus solutionem et in elementa mundi reditum. . . . Est enim exterius et materiale corpus signaculum interioris, in quo forma animae exprimitur, et per hoc forma ejus rationabiliter appellatur. Et ne me existimes duo corpora naturalia in uno homine docere: verum enim est corpus, quo connaturaliter et consubstantialiter animae compacto homo conficitur. Illud siquidem materiale, quod est superadditum, rectius vestimentum quoddam mutabile et corruptibile veri ac naturalis corporis accipitur, quam verum corpus; non enim verum est, quod semper non manet (Aug.). . . . Inde fit, quod semper non simpliciter, sed cum additamento aliquo ponitur corpus mortale vel corruptibile vel terrenum vel animale, ad discretionem ipsius simplicis corporis, quod primitus in homine editum est, et quod futurum est.— Compare ii. 23, p. 71: Semel enim et simul animas nostras et corpora in Paradiso conditor creavit, corpora dico coelestia, *spiritualia, qualia post resurrectionem futura sunt.* Tumida namque corpora, mortalia, corruptibilia, quibus nunc opprimimur, non ex natura, sed ex delicto occasionem ducere, non est dubitandum. Quod ergo naturae ex peccato adolevit, eo profecto renovata in Christo, et in pristinum statum restituta, carebit. Non enim potest naturae esse coaeternum, quod ei adhaeret propter peccatum.

(2) The Beguines are said to have asserted, quod mortuo corpore hominis solus spiritus vel anima hominis redibit ad eum, unde exivit, et cum eo sic reunietur, quod nihil remanebit, nisi quod ab aeterno fuit Deus (qu. by *Mosheim*, p. 257 s., compare below, § 206, note 9).—On the teaching of the Bogomiles, see *Engelhardt*, Kirchenhist. Abhandl. s. 187 f.

(3) Summa adv. Catharos, lib. iv. cap. 7, § 1.

(4) *Peter Lombard*, Sent. lib. iv. dist. 43 ss. (he follows for the most part Augustine's Enchiridion), and *Hugo of St. Victor*, De Sacram. ii. 1, 19. The former still modestly expresses himself as follows: Omnibus quaestionibus, quae de hac re moveri solent, satisfacere non valeo.

(5) These definitions are also for the most part founded

upon Augustine (comp. above, § 140). All men will die before the general resurrection (on account of original sin); the resurrection will probably take place towards evening, for the heavenly bodies which rule over all earthly matter must first cease to move. Sun and moon will then meet again in that point where they were probably created. The resurrection will take place suddenly in relation to the effects produced by the divine power; it will be gradual in relation to the part the angels will have in it. Thomas Aquinas denied that dust and ashes have a natural tendency to reunite themselves to the souls to which they were united in this world (a kind of pre-established harmony), but supposed that no other matter would rise from the grave than what existed at the moment of death. If that substance were to rise again which has been consumed during the present life, it would form a most unshapely mass.—According to qu. 81, those who are raised from the dead will be in the ætas juvenilis, quæ inter decrementum et incrementum constituitur. The difference of sexes will continue to exist, but without sensual appetites. All the organs of sense will still be active, with the exception of the sense of taste. It is, however, possible that even the latter may be rendered more perfect, and fitted for adequate functions and enjoyments. Hair and nails are among the ornaments of man, and therefore must as little be lacking as blood and other fluids. The new bodies will be exceedingly fine, and will be delivered from the corpulence and weight which is now so burdensome to them; nevertheless, they will be tangible, as the body of Christ could be touched after His resurrection. Their size will not increase after the resurrection, nor will they grow either thicker or thinner. To some extent they will still be dependent on space and time; yet the resurrection bodies will move much faster, and more easily, from one place to another, than our present bodies; they will be at liberty to follow the tendencies and impulses of the soul. They are glorified, bright, and shining, and can be perceived with glorified eyes alone. But this is true only in reference to the bodies of the blessed. The bodies of the damned are to be ugly and deformed, incorruptible indeed, but capable of suffering, which is not the case with the bodies of the saints. *Thom. Aquinas*, Summ. P. III. in

Supplem. qu. 75 ss. *Cramer*, vii. s. 777 ff. Comp. also Elucidar. c. 69. On the opinions of *Duns Scotus*, see *Ritter*, Gesch. der Philos. viii. s. 459 ff.

(6) *Joh. Damasc.* iv. 27, p. 303: Ἀλλ' ἐρεῖ τις· Πῶς ἐγείρονται οἱ νεκροί; Ὦ τῆς ἀπιστίας· ὦ τῆς ἀφροσύνης· ὁ χοῦν εἰς σῶμα βουλήσει μόνῃ μεταβαλών, ὁ μικρὰν ῥανίδα τοῦ σπέρματος ἐν τῇ μήτρᾳ αὔξειν προστάξας, καὶ τὸ πολυειδὲς τοῦτο καὶ πολύμορφον ἀποτελεῖν τοῦ σώματος ὄργανον, οὐχὶ μᾶλλον τὸ γεγονὸς καὶ διαρρυὲν ἀναστήσει πάλιν, μόνον βουληθείς; Ποίῳ δὲ σώματι ἔρχονται; Ἄφρον, εἰ τοῖς τοῦ Θεοῦ λόγοις πιστεύειν ἡ πώρωσις οὐ συγχωρεῖ, κἂν τοῖς ἔργοις πίστευε· σὺ γὰρ ὃ σπείρεις, οὐ ζωοποιεῖται, ἐὰν μὴ ἀποθάνῃ κ.τ.λ. (1 Cor. xv.) Θέασαι τοίνυν, ὡς ἐν τάφοις ταῖς αὔλαξι τὰ σπέρματα καταχωννύμενα. Τίς ὁ τούτοις ῥίζας ἐντιθεὶς, καλάμην καὶ φύλλα, καὶ ἀστάχυς καὶ τοὺς λεπτοτάτους ἀνθέρικας; οὐχ ὁ τῶν ὅλων δημιουργός; οὐ τοῦ τὰ πάντα τεκτηναμένου τὸ πρόσταγμα; Οὕτω τοίνυν πίστευε, καὶ τῶν νεκρῶν τὴν ἀνάστασιν ἔσεσθαι θείᾳ βουλήσει, καὶ νεύματι· σύνδρομον γὰρ ἔχει τῇ βουλήσει τὴν δύναμιν.

§ 205.

The Last Judgment.

The second advent of Christ to judgment was, with all its imagery, interpreted as literally as possible. After it has been preceded by those signs of which Scripture speaks, Christ will appear in the same human form which He had when on earth, but glorified and in triumph, accompanied by the heavenly hosts. The wicked, too, will behold His countenance, but with horror (1).—The judgment, it was supposed, would take place in the valley of Jehoshaphat, to which some, however, also attached an allegorical meaning (2). But in proportion as theologians were disposed to give free scope to their imagination, and to represent the proceedings of the judgment in relation to time and sense, the greater was the difficulty of uniting those various images in a connected picture (3). *Thomas Aquinas* therefore reminded them that the judgment would take place *mentaliter*, because the oral trial and defence of each individual would require too much time (4). According to Matt. xix. 28 and 1 Cor. vi. 2, perfect Christians are to sit with Christ in judgment; and inasmuch as monks were supposed to attain the highest degree of piety even in this world, the power which was committed into their hands by the institution of the Inquisition, would easily familiarize men with the idea of being also judged by them in the world to come (5). It was natural that the heretics should beg to be excused from such a judgment; in accordance, too, with their entire idealistic tendency, they preferred resolving the idea of a *last* judgment into the more general notion of the retribution immediately after death (6).

(1) *Thomas Aquinas*, l.c. qu. 73, art. 1 : Christus ... in forma gloriosa apparebit propter auctoritatem, quæ judici debetur. Ad dignitatem autem judiciariæ potestatis pertinet habere aliqua indicia, quæ ad reverentiam et subjectionem inducant, et ideo adventum Christi ad judicium venientis multa signa præcedent, ut corda hominum in subjectionem venturi judicis adducantur et ad judicium præparentur, hujusmodi signis præmoniti. Comp. Elucid. c. 70. *Disc.* Qualiter veniet Dominus ad judicium ? *Mag.* Sicut Imperator ingressurus civitatem, corona ejus et alia insignia præferuntur, per quæ adventus ejus cognoscitur : ita Christus in ea forma, qua ascendit, cum Ordinibus omnibus Angelorum ad judicium veniens. Angeli crucem ejus ferentes præibunt, mortuos tuba et voce in occursum ejus excitabunt. Omnia elementa turbabuntur, tempestate ignis et frigoris mixtim undique furente. (Ps. xcvi., Wisd. v.)—Respecting the damned it is said, c. 75 : Videbunt (Christum), sed ad sui perniciem. Comp. *Thomas Aquinas*, qu. 90, art. 3.

(2) Elucid. l.c. *D.*: Erit judicium in valle Josaphat ? *M.* Vallis Josaphat dicitur vallis judicii. Vallis est semper juxta montem. Vallis est hic mundus, mons est cœlum. In valle ergo fit judicium, i. e. in isto mundo, scilicet in isto aëre, ubi justi ad dexteram Christi ut oves statuentur, impii autem ut hœdi ad sinistram ponentur. Comp. *Thomas Aquinas*, qu. 88, art. 4.

(3) Thus *Thomas Aquinas* was at a loss to account for what is said concerning the sun and the moon being darkened (Matt. xxiv. 29), inasmuch as the coming of Christ will be accompanied by the fullest effusion of light, l.c. qu. 73, art. 2 : Dicendum, quod, si loquamur de sole et luna, quantum ad ipsum momentum adventus Christi, sic non est credibile, quod obscurabuntur sui luminis privatione, quia totus mundus innovabitur Christo veniente.... Si autem loquamur de eis secundum tempus propinquum ante judicium, sic esse poterit, quod sol et luna et alia cœli luminaria, sui luminis privatione obscurabuntur, vel diversis temporibus, vel simul, divina virtute faciente ad hominum terrorem.

(4) Ibid. qu. 88, art. 2, conclusio.

(5) In the work entitled Elucidarium, four classes are distinguished (instead of two as was usual, viz. the blessed and the damned), c. 71 : Unus ordo est *perfectorum, cum Deo judicantium*; alter justorum, qui per judicium salvantur; tertius impiorum sine judicio pereuntium ; quartus malorum, qui per judicium damnantur. . . . *Disc.* Qui sunt qui judicant? *Mag.* Apostoli, Martyres, Confessores, *Monachi*, Virgines. *D.* Quomodo judicabunt justos ? *M.* Monstrabunt eos suam doctrinam et sua exempla fuisse imitatos, et ideo regno dignos. — *Peter Lombard*, lib. iv. dist. 47 B: Non autem solus Christus judicabit, sed ed Sancti cum eo judicabunt nationes. . . . Judicabunt vero non modo coöperatione, sed etiam auctoritate et potestate. Compare *Thomas Aquinas*, qu. 89, where he examines the question, whether the righteous will take part in the judgment of the world merely as having places of honour (assessorie), or in reality. As the former would be too little, we may assume that they will judge in reality, provided they do so in accordance with the divine will, but not propria auctoritate. On the question, whether the angels will also take part in the judgment, see *Peter Lombard*, l.c. litt. C. *Thomas Aquinas*, art. 8.

(6) See *Mosheim*, p. 157 : Dicunt se credere, quod judicium extremum non sit futurum, sed quod tunc est judicium hominis solum, cum moritur.

§ 206.

Purgatory.

From the time of Gregory the Great, the doctrine of a purifying fire, through which souls have to pass after death, came to be more and more generally adopted. The belief in it was strengthened by supposed facts furnished by legends (1). Missionaries carried this notion, already developed and complete, to the nations which were newly converted (2); and the writers of the present age, scholastics as well as poets and orators, gave the fullest description of it. Many believed in the real existence of purgatory as a material fire (3), which, however, in the absence of a body susceptible of physical sufferings, torments the lost souls in an ideal manner (by means of the conception of suffering) (4). Even men who leaned to mysticism, such as *Bonaventura* and *Gerson* (5), maintained the reality of the fire. But that which made the doctrine practically injurious was the belief built upon it, that souls might be relieved from their pains, or even relieved from their state of suffering, sooner than would otherwise have been the case, by means of the intercessory prayers and good works of the living, and particularly by means of masses for the dead (missæ pro requie defunctorum) (6). Inasmuch as these masses and ecclesiastical indulgences were paid for, the question arose, whether the rich were not, in this respect, more privileged than the poor; to which Peter Lombard replied in the affirmative (7). Therefore it is not surprising that the increasing avarice and injustice of the clergy (8) should have induced the Cathari and Waldenses (9), as well as *Wykliffe* (10), to combat the doctrine in question as a most dangerous one. It never met with full acceptance in the Greek Church (11). On the other hand, *John Wessel* endeavoured to divest it of its pernicious consequences, by regarding the fire as a spiritual fire of love, which purifies the soul from its remaining dross, and consists in the longing after union with God. Accordingly, it is not so much a punishment, as the commencement of that blessedness which God alone has the power of bringing to perfection (12).

(1) *Bede*, Hist. Eccles. Gent. Anglor. l. iii. c. 19, v. c. 13. *Schröckh*, xx. s. 185.

(2) *Bonifacius*, Ep. xxi. c. 29, ad Serrar (qu. by *Schröckh*, l.c.). On the doctrine of purgatory as propounded by *St. Patrick*, the Apostle of Ireland (according to the account of Matthew Paris), see *Schröckh*, xvi. s. 229.

(3) The author of the work entitled Elucidarium, expresses himself still more indefinitely, c. 61 : Post mortem vero purgatio erit *aut* nimius calor ignis, *aut* magnus rigor frigoris, *aut* aliud quodlibet genus pœnarum, de quibus tamen minimum majus est, quam maximum, quod in hac vita excogitari potest. —*Hugo of St. Victor*, De Sacram. l. ii. P. xvi. c. 4 : Est autem alia pœna post mortem, quæ purgatoria dicitur. In qua qui ab hac vita cum quibusdam culpis, justi tamen et ad vitam prædestinati exierunt, ad tempus cruciantur, ut purgentur. The language of *Thomas Aquinas* is more decided, qu. 70, art. 3, concl.: Respondeo : Dicendum, quod ignis inferni[1] non sit metaphorice dictus, nec ignis imaginarius, sed verus ignis corporeus, etc. He thought, however, that all men do not go to purgatory, but only those who require it. The decidedly pious go at once to heaven, the decidedly wicked go at once to hell; see qu. 69, art. 2.

(4) Compare *Thomas Aquinas*, l.c.: Alii dixerunt, quod, quamvis ignis corporeus non possit animam exurere, tamen anima apprehendit ipsum ut nocivum sibi, et ad talem apprehensionem afficitur timore et dolore. But this notion did not satisfy him fully. Comp. *Cramer*, vii. p. 773–775.

(5) *Bonav.* Comp. Theol. Verit. vii. 2 (qu. by *Klee*, ii. s. 333) ; comp. *Schröckh*, xxix. s. 219.—Concerning the views of *Gerson* (according to Sermo ii. De Defunctis, t. iii. p. 1558), see *Schröckh*, xxxiv. s. 293.

(6) Elucidar. c. 61 : Dum ibi sunt positi, apparent eis Angeli vel alii Sancti, in quorum honore aliquid egerunt in hac vita, et aut auram aut suavem odorem aut aliquod solamen

[1] By which we are to understand the fire of purgatory, as the context shows.

eis impendunt, usque dum liberati introibunt in illam aulam, quæ non recipit ullam maculam. *Peter Lombard*, lib. iv. dist. 45 B. *Thomas Aquinas*, 71, art. 1. In his opinion, intercessory prayers (opera suffragii) do not avail per viam meriti, but per viam orationis.—He expressed himself very cautiously, art. 2, concl.: Respondeo: Dicendum, quod charitas, quæ est vinculum ecclesiæ membra uniens, non solum ad vivos se extendit, sed etiam ad mortuos, qui in charitate decedunt.... Similiter etiam mortui in memoriis hominum viventium vivunt, et ideo intentio viventium ad eos dirigi potest, et sic suffragia vivorum mortuis dupliciter prosunt, sicut et vivis, et propter charitatis unionem, et propter intentionem in eos directam: non tamen sic eis valere credenda sunt vivorum suffragia, ut status eorum mutetur de miseria ad felicitatem vel e converso; sed valent ad *diminutionem pœnæ* vel aliquid hujusmodi, *quod statum mortui non transmutat*. Comp. art. 6: Respondeo: Dicendum, quod pœna purgatorii est in supplementum satisfactionis, quæ non fuerat plene in corpore consummata, et ideo, quia opera unius possunt valere alteri ad satisfactionem, sive vivus sive mortuus fuerit, non est dubium, quin suffragia per vivos facta existentibus in purgatorio prosint. Compare art. 10 concerning Indulgences. They are useful to the souls in purgatory indirectly, but not directly.—Respecting the festival founded on this doctrine, which was first instituted at Clugny, A.D. 993, and was afterwards adopted by the whole Western Church (All-Souls' Day, Nov. 2), see *Sigibert. Gemblacens.* ad ann. 998. *Gieseler*, ii. 1, s. 252.

(7) Lib. iv. dist. 45 D: Solet moveri quæstio de duobus, uno divite, altero paupere, pariter sed mediocriter bonis, qui prædictis suffragiis indigent et meruerunt pariter post mortem juvari: pro altero vero, i. e. pro divite, speciales et communes fiunt orationes, multæque eleemosynarum largitiones; pro paupere vero non fiunt nisi communes largitiones et orationes. Quæritur ergo, an tantum juvetur pauper paucioribus subsidiis, quantum dives amplioribus? Si non pariter juvatur, non ei redditur secundum merita. Meruit enim pariter juvari, quia pariter boni extiterunt. Si vero tantum suffragii consequitur pauper, quantum dives: quid contulerunt diviti illa specialiter pro eo facta? Sane dici potest, non ei magis valuisse gene-

ralia et specialia, quam pauperi sola generalia suffragia. Et tamen profuerunt diviti specialia, non quidem ad aliud vel majus aliquid, sed ad idem, ad quod generalia, ut ex pluribus et diversis causis unum perciperetur emolumentum. *Potest tamen dici aliter, illa plura subsidia contulisse diviti celeriorem absolutionem, non pleniorem.*

(8) See the works on ecclesiastical history. *This* superstition was also combated by the friar *Berthold*. (See *Kling*, s. 396.)

(9) *Moneta*, l. iv. c. 9, § 2 : Dicit ecclesia purgatorium esse post hanc vitam animabus, quae de hoc mundo migraverunt *inchoata condigna poenitentia, sed nondum perfecta*. Omnes autem haeretici, tam Cathari, quam Pauperes Lugdunenses, a quodam qui dicebatur Valdisius derivati, hoc negant. The Beguines also denied, quod non est infernus, nec purgatorium (see *Mosheim*, p. 257). On the rejection of purgatory by the Waldenses, see *Dieckhoff*, Waldenser, s. 295. According to *Stephen de Borbone*, they said : Non esse poenam purgatorii nisi in praesenti.

(10) *Schröckh*, Kircheng. Bd. xxxiv. s. 444. The Husites (Bohemian Brethren) also questioned the reality of purgatory ; ibid. s. 753 f.

(11) Nevertheless, the Greek Church was compelled, by the Council of Florence (A.D. 1439), to make some concessions. (See *Mansi*, t. xxxi. col. 1029. *Münscher, von Cölln*, s. 313 f.) [The Synod declared: Ἐὰν οἱ ἀληθῶς μετανοήσαντες ἀποθάνωσιν ἐν τῇ τοῦ Θεοῦ ἀγάπῃ, πρὶν τοῖς ἀξίοις τῆς μετανοίας καρποῖς ἱκανοποιῆσαι περὶ τῶν ἡμαρτημένων ὁμοῦ καὶ ἡμελημένων (in the Latin copy: de commissis et omissis), τὰς τούτων ψυχὰς καθαρτικαῖς τιμωρίαις καθαίρεσθαι (poenis purgatoriis purgari) μετὰ θάνατον.] Therefore *Leo Allatius* asserted that the Eastern and Western Churches agreed in this point, De Ecclesiae Occidentalis et Orientalis perpetua in Dogmate de Purgatorio Concessione, Rom. 1655, 4to.

(12) De Purgatorio, quis et qualis sit ignis purgatorius in the edition of Gröningen, s. 826 ff. (qu. by *Ullmann*, Joh. Wessel, s. 363 ff.).

On the locality of purgatory, see § 203.

§ 207.

The Sleep of the Soul.

The original idea of purgatory had its origin in the necessity which men felt of supposing the existence of a place where the soul, separated from the body, might dwell until its reunion with the body. The assumption of the possibility of the soul's deliverance from this intermediate state before this reunion, gave rise to new difficulties, so that it became necessary to fill up the interval between those two moments of time. This led to a revival of the earlier notion of a death of the soul (which had been propounded by the false teachers of Arabia whom Origen combated), though under the milder form of a sleep of the soul (Psychopannychy) (1). It is, however, uncertain whether Pope John XXII., as is asserted, really adopted this opinion (2). At all events, his views were opposed by the professors of the University of Paris (3), and disapproved of by Pope Benedict XII. (4).

(1) On the Thnetopsychites, see above, § 76, note 8. Respecting the notion of a sleep of the soul (which was rejected by Tertullian), see ibid.

(2) The idea of a sleep of the soul was by no means distinctly expressed in those words of his which were thought objectionable (they occur in a sermon preached on the first Sunday in Advent 1331); on the contrary, all that is there said is, quod animæ decedentium in gratia non videant Deum per essentiam, nec sint perfecte beatæ, nisi post resumptionem corporis.—This opinion perfectly agreed with the views of earlier theologians. Comp. § 77. But from the fifth century onwards, it was abandoned and condemned, A.D. 1240, by the University of Paris. (*D'Argentré*, Collectio Judiciorum de novis Erroribus, i. 186.) *Gieseler*, Kg. (4th ed.) ii. s. 59 ff.

(3) See *d'Argentré*, Collectio Judic. t. i. p. 316 ss. *Bulæus*, t. iv. p. 235. *Gieseler*, l.c. *Münscher*, *von Cölln*, s. 312.

(4) Jan. 29, A.D. 1366. See *Raynald*, ad hunc annum,

Not. 3.—*Gieseler* and *Münscher, von Cölln,* l.c. On the pretended recantation of Pope John XXII., see *Gieseler,* l.c.—On a picture representing the state of the departed, see *Quandt, Reise ins mittägliche Frankreich,* s. 149 ff.

§ 208.

The Localities of the Future World.

(Heaven, Hell, and Intermediate State.)

The Schoolmen endeavoured to draw into the sphere of their researches, not only the bright regions of heaven, but also the dark abodes of hell. Thus heaven was divided into three parts: viz. the *visible* heavens (the firmament), the *spiritual* heaven, where saints and angels dwell, and the *intellectual* heaven, where the blessed enjoy the immediate vision of the triune God (1). Different departments (receptacula) were also ascribed to hell (2). These were: 1. Hell properly so called, where the devils dwell, the abode of the damned (3). 2. Those subterranean regions which may be regarded as the intermediate states between heaven and hell, and which are again subdivided into: (*a*) Purgatory, which lies nearest to hell (4); (*b*) The Limbus Infantum (puerorum), where those children remain who die unbaptized (5); (*c*) The Limbus Patrum, the abode of the Old Testament saints, the place to which Christ went to preach redemption to the souls in prison. The Limbus last mentioned was also called Abraham's bosom: different opinions obtained concerning its relation of proximity to heaven and hell (6). These positions were rejected by the mystics, who were inclined to more spiritual views, and assigned to subjective states what the scholastics fixed in external localities (7).

(1) Elucidarium, c. 3. Paradise was also supposed to be there. Comp. c. 50, and note 7.

(2) *Peter Lombard*, lib. iv. dist. 45 A. *Thomas Aquinas*, qu. 69, art. 1 ss. *Cramer*, vii. s. 771–773.

(3) Elucidar. c. 62 D. Quid est infernus? vel ubi? *M.* Duo sunt inferni, superior et inferior. Superior infima pars hujus mundi, quæ plena est pœnis, nam hic exundat nimius æstus, magnum frigus, etc. Inferior vero est locus spiritualis, ubi ignis inextinguibilis . . . qui sub terra dicitur esse, ut, sicut corpora peccantium terra cooperiuntur, ita animæ peccantium sub terra in inferno sepeliantur.[1]

(4) See above, § 206.

(5) According to *Thomas Aquinas*, qu. 69, art. 6, the limbus puerorum is distinguished from the limbus patrum, secundum qualitatem præmii vel pœnæ, because children who die without baptism have no hope of eternal salvation, such as the fathers had before the coming of Christ. As regards the site (situs), it is probable that the limbus puerorum lies nearer to hell than the limbus patrum. Others, however, identified the one with the other. Thus friar *Berthold* says (quoted by *Kling*, s. 443): "If your children die without baptism, or are baptized improperly, they can never enter into the heavenly joys. They go, together with the Jewish and Gentile children, who are still without belief, to the limbus to which those of old went. There they do not suffer any pain, except this, that they do not go to heaven." Comp. s. 210. Those children who are baptized ride in the little carriage (the constellation of the Little Bear) straight to heaven (paradise). But if the child happened to be baptized irregularly, one of the wheels breaks, and the child is lost. See ibid. s. 169 f.

(6) *Thomas Aquinas* treated of this point very fully, l.c. art. 4. He made a distinction between the state *before* and that *after* the coming of Christ. Quia ante Christi adventum Sanctorum requies habebat defectum requiei adjunctum, dice-

---

[1] The term "Hölle" (hell) had, in German, primarily the more comprehensive signification of the under world (whence the phrase in the Apostles' Creed, "He descended into hell"). It was not till later (from the thirteenth century) that the word was used to denote the place of torment. Comp. *Grimms* Deutsche Mythologie, s. 462.—"*The Christians substituted, in place of the heathenish notion of a pale and gloomy hell, that of a pool filled with flames and brimstone, pitch dark, and yet at the same time bright like fire, in which the souls of the damned are always burning.*" Grimm, l.c. s. 464. On the mixture of Christian with heathen notions, ibid. s. 465.

batur idem infernus et sinus Abrahæ, unde ibi non videbatur Deus. Sed quia post Christi adventum Sanctorum requies est completa, cum Deum videant, talis requies dicitur sinus Abrahæ, et nullo modo infernus. Et ad hunc sinum Abrahae ecclesia orat fideles perduci. Comp. Elucidar. 64 : *D.* In quo inferno erant justi ante adventum Christi ? *M.* In superiori, in quodam loco juncto inferiori, in quo poterant alterutrum conspicere. Qui erant ibi, quamvis carerent supplicio, videbatur eis esse in inferno, cum essent separati a regno. Illis autem, qui erant in inferiori inferno, videbatur, quod illi, qui erant in illo inferno juncto inferiori, erant in refrigerio paradisi, unde et dives rogabat a Lazaro, guttam super se stillari. *D.* Quam pœnam habebant illi, qui erant in illo inferno juncto inferiori ? *M.* Quasdam tenebras tantum, unde dicitur: " *Habitantibus in regione umbræ mortis, lux orta est eis.*" Quidam ex eis erant in quibusdam pœnis. Venit ergo Dominus ad infernum superiorem nascendo, ut redimeret captivos a tyranno, ut dicitur: " *Dices his, qui vincti sunt: Exite! et his qui in tenebris sunt: Redeamini.*" Vinctos vocat, qui erant in pœnis, alios vero in tenebris, quos omnes absolvit et in gloriam duxit rex gloriæ. Comp. *Dante*, Inferno, 4 ; comp. 31 ss.

(7) The author of the work entitled Elucidarium, expressed himself as follows, c. 59: Paradisus non est locus corporalis, quia spiritus non habitant in locis; sed est spiritualis mansio beatorum, quam æterna sapientia perfecit in initio, et est intellectuali cœlo (comp. note 1), ubi ipsa divinitas, qualis est, ab eis facie ad faciem contuetur. The language of *Tauler*, in his Sermon on Good Friday (Predigten, i. s. 291 f.), was still more spiritualizing: . . . Christ granted to the thief on the cross " to behold Himself, His divine countenance and nature, which is the true and living paradise of all joy. . . . To behold the glory of God, that is paradise."[1]

[1] On the relation between the Christian notions of paradise commonly entertained, and the earlier ideas of heathen nations (the Walhalla), see *Grimm*, Deutsche Mythologie, s. 475.

§ 209.

Future State of the Blessed and the Damned.

Both the spirit of the age and its degree of culture were reflected in the representations and descriptions of heaven and hell. According to *John Scotus Erigena*, the personal spirit of man is resolved into God, a notion which he thought reconcilable with the idea of self-conscious continuance (1). The pantheistic sects of the Middle Ages went so far as to destroy all individuality, and to deny the future life (2). The scholastics, whose principal happiness even in this world consisted in making the most subtle distinctions, supposed that the greater acuteness of the intellectual powers would constitute the especial blessedness of heaven; *Duns Scotus* started such questions as, whether the blessed would perceive the quiddities of things, etc. (3). The paradisaical enjoyments of refined sense were not quite excluded, although it was admitted that the highest and most real pleasures would consist principally in communion with God and the mutual communion of the saints (4). *Thomas Aquinas* supposed different gifts (dotes) of blessedness. In addition to the corona aurea, which is given to all the blessed, there are particular *aureolæ* for martyrs and saints, for monks and nuns (5). The mystics also represented the world to come in bright colours (6). But the age was especially inventive in devising all sorts of ingenious punishments which the wicked would have to suffer in hell, after the refined cruelty of the criminal processes of the Inquisition (7). According to *Thomas Aquinas*, the torments of the damned consist in useless repentance (8). They can change neither for the better nor for the worse (9). They hate God, and curse the state of the blessed (10). But the latter are not disturbed in the enjoyment of their happiness by any feeling of compassion (11). The views of *John Scotus Erigena* differed from the popular notion in making the consciousness of sin itself, and of its impotence, to constitute the principal misery of the damned (12). *Master Eckart* declared it to be a spiritual nonentity (13), an expression from which the Beghards drew the hasty inference that hell had no existence (14).

(1) De Div. Nat. v. 8, p. 232: Prima igitur humanæ naturæ reversio est, quando corpus solvitur, et in quatuor elementa sensibilis mundi, ex quibus compositum est, revocatur. Secunda in resurrectione implebitur, quando unusquisque suum proprium corpus ex communione quatuor elementorum recipiet. Tertia, quando corpus in spiritum mutabitur. Quarta, quando spiritus et, ut apertius dicam, tota hominis natura in primordiales causas revertetur, quæ sunt semper et incommutabiliter in Deo. Quinta, quando ipsa natura cum suis causis movebitur in Deum, sicut aër movetur in lucem. Erit enim Deus omnia in omnibus: quando nihil erit nisi solus Deus.... Mutatio itaque humanæ naturæ in Deum, non in substantiæ interitu æstimanda est, sed in pristinum statum, quem prævaricando perdiderat, mirabilis atque ineffabilis reversio. Pag. 234: ... Inferiora vero a superioribus naturaliter attrahuntur et absorbentur, non ut non sint, sed ut in eis plus salventur et subsistant et unum sint. Nam neque aër suam perdit substantiam, cum totus in solare lumen convertitur: in tantum, ut nihil in eo appareat nisi lux, cum aliud sit lux, aliud aër; lux tamen prævalet in aëre, ut sola videatur esse. Ferrum aut aliud aliquod metallum in igne liquefactum, in ignem converti videtur, ut ignis purus videatur esse, salva metalli substantia permanente. Eadem ratione existimo corporalem substantiam in animam esse transiturum: non ut pereat quod sit, sed ut in meliori essentia salva sit. Similiter de ipsa anima intelligendum, quod ita in intellectum movebitur, ut in eo pulchrior Deoque similior conservetur. Nec aliter dixerim de transitu, ut non adhuc dicam omnium, sed rationabilium substantiarum in Deum, in quo cuncta finem positura sunt, et unum erunt. — As the many separate lights (*e.g.* in a church) flow together into *one sea of light*, though every single light may be removed, as a part may be taken from the whole; and as many voices form together *one chorus*, without losing their individuality in one confused mass of sounds, — so, thinks Scotus, are souls related to God. Comp. cap. 12 and 13, p. 236.

(2) Thus *Amalrich of Bena* taught: He who possesses the knowledge of God has paradise *within* himself; but he who commits a mortal sin has hell in his own heart, as a man has a bad tooth in his mouth. (Compare *Engelhardt*, s. 255.) Of his followers it is said: Item semetipsos jam resuscitatos asserebant, fidem et spem ab eorum cordibus excludebant, se soli scientiæ mentientes subjacere (ibid. p. 259). Comp. p. 260: Dixit etiam (Amalricus), quod Deus ideo dicitur finis omnium, quia omnia reversura sunt in ipsum, ut in Deo immutabiliter quiescant, et unum individuum atque incommutabile in eo permanebunt; et sicut alterius naturæ non est Abraham, alterius Isaac, sed unius atque ejusdem, sic dixit omnia esse unum et omnia esse Deum. The Beguines taught the same. Comp. § 204, note 2.

(3) *John Scotus Erigena*, v. c. 31 ss. — *Peter Lombard*, lib. iv. dist. 49 A: Habere ergo vitam, est *videre* vitam, *cognoscere* Deum in specie (according to John xvii.). — Elucid. c. 79: His (beatis) Salomonis sapientia esset magna insipientia. Porro ipsi omni sapientia affluunt, omnem scientiam de ipso fonte sapientiæ Dei hauriunt. Omnia quippe præterita, præsentia, et si qua futura sunt, perfecte sciunt. Omnium omnino hominum, sive in cœlo, sive in inferno, nomina, genera, opera bona vel mala unquam ab eis gesta norunt, et nihil est quod eos lateat, cum in sole justitiæ pariter videant omnia. — *Thom. Aquin.* qu. 92, art. 1, 2, 3. — *Duns Scotus*, quoted by *Cramer*, vii. s. 786 f.

(4) Elucid. 77: Salomonis deliciæ essent eis miseriæ. O qualis est justorum voluptas, quibus ipse Deus fons omnium bonorum est insatiabilis satians satietas. Duæ sunt beatitudines, una minor Paradisi, altera major cœlestis regni. (We have no idea of it, and can infer the notion of happiness only in a negative way from that of unhappiness.) ... Sicut ferrum alicujus capiti si esset infixum et sic candens per omnia membra transiret, sicut ille dolorem haberet, ita ipsi per contrarium modum in omnibus membris suis interius et exterius voluptatem habent. ... O qualem voluptatem visus ipsi habebunt, qui ita clausis sicut apertis oculis videbunt. ... O qualis voluptas auditus illorum, quibus incessanter sonent harmoniæ cœlorum et concentus Angelorum, dulcisona organa omnium Sanctorum. Olfactio qualis, ubi suavissimum odorem de ipso

suavitatis fonte haurient, et odorem de Angelis et omnibus Sanctis percipient. Eia qualis voluptas gustus, ubi epulantur et exultant in conspectu Dei, et, cum apparuerit gloria Dei, saturabuntur et ab ubertate domus ejus inebriabuntur (Ps. lxxvi., xvi., xxxv.). Voluptas tactus qualis, ubi omnia aspera et dura aberunt, et omnia blanda et suavia arridebunt.—Nor will the recollection of sins formerly committed, but now expiated, disturb the enjoyment of heavenly bliss. Cap. 79. Concerning the blessedness arising from the fellowship of the saints, see ibidem: Nihil plus cupient, quam habebunt, et nihil plus potest adjici gaudio eorum. Quod enim quisque in se non habuerit, in altero habebit, ut. v. g. Petrus in Joanne, gloriam habebit virginitatis, Joannes in Petro gloriam passionis. Et ita gloria uniuscujusque erit omnium, et gloria omnium uniuscujusque erit.... O Deus, quale gaudium habebunt, qui Patrem in Filio, et Verbum in Patre, et Spiritus Sancti charitatem in utroque, sicuti est, facie ad faciem semper videbunt. Gaudium habebunt de consortio Angelorum, gaudium de contubernio omnium Sanctorum.

(5) According to *Thomas Aquinas*, qu. 95, art. 2, the following distinction may be made between *beatitudo* and *dos:* Dos datur sine meritis, sed beatitudo non datur, sed redditur pro meritis. Præterea: beatitudo est una tantum, dotes vero sunt plures. Præterea: beatitudo inest homini secundum id quod est potissimum in eo, sed dos etiam in corpore ponitur. According to art. 5, there are three dotes: visio, quæ fidei, comprehensio, quæ spei, fruitio, quæ charitati respondet.—On the relation in which the particular aureolæ stand to the corona (aurea), see qu. 96, art. 1: Præmium essentiale hominis, quod est ejus beatitudo, consistit in perfecta conjunctione animæ ad Deum, in quantum eo perfecte fruitur, ut viso et amato perfecte: hoc autem præmium metaphorice corona dicitur vel aurea; tum ex parte meriti, quod cum quadam pugna agitur, tum etiam ex parte præmii, per quod homo efficitur quodammodo divinitatis particeps, et per consequens regiæ potestatis.... Significat etiam corona perfectionem quandam ratione figuræ circularis, ut ex hoc etiam competat perfectioni beatorum. Sed quia nihil potest superaddi essentiali, quin sit eo minus: ideo superadditum præmium aureola nominatur. Huic autem essentiali præmio, quod aurea dicitur, aliquid superadditur

dupliciter : uno modo ex conditione naturæ ejus, qui præmiatur, sicut supra beatitudinem animæ gloria corporis adjungitur, unde et ipsa gloria corporis interdum aureola nominatur . . .; alio modo ex ratione operis meritorii, etc. In art. 2, aureola is further distinguished from fructus : Fructus consistit in gaudio **habito de** dispositione **ipsius** operantis, aureola in gaudio per**fectionis operum (the one is the** subjective reward, the other **is the objective one).** Compare the subsequent notes.

(6) *Suso*, Von der unmässigen **Freude** des Himmelreichs (quoted by *Diepenbrock*, s. 293 ff. ; *Wackernagels* Lesebuch, i. Spalte 881 ff.): " Now arise with me, **I will lead thee** to contemplation, and cause thee to cast a **look at a rough** parable. Behold ! above the ninth heaven, which is far **more than a** hundred thousand times larger than our whole globe, **there is** yet another heaven, which is called cœlum empyreum, and has its name, not from its being a fiery substance, but from the intense shining brightness which it possesses by nature. It is immoveable and unchangeable, **and is** the glorious court **where the heavenly hosts dwell, and where** the evening star **and all the** children **of** God sing unceasing praise and adora**tion. There are the eternal** thrones, surrounded by the in**comprehensible light, from which** the evil spirits were cast **out, and which are now occupied by** the **elect.** Behold the **wonderful** city shining **with pure gold, glittering** with precious pearls, **inlaid with precious jewels, transparent** like a crystal, **resplendent with red roses, white lilies, and all sorts of living** flowers. **Now cast** thine own **eyes upon the beautiful heavenly fields. Ay ! here** is the whole charm **of summer,** here the **meadows of the bright** May, **the true valley of joy ;** here are **happy moments spent in** mutual **love, harps, viols,** singing, **springing, dancing, and** pleasures without **end ;** here the ful**filment of every desire, and love without sorrow, in** everlasting **security. And behold, round about thee, the** innumerable **multitude of the redeemed, drinking of the fountain of** living **water after their hearts' desire, and looking in the** pure and **clear mirror of the unveiled Deity, in which all** things are **made manifest to them. Proceed farther, and** behold the **sweet queen of the heavenly country, whom thou** lovest with **such intensity, occupying her throne with dignity** and joy, **elevated above all the** heavenly **hosts, surrounded by the** flowers

of roses and lilies of the valley. Behold her charming beauty imparting joy, and delight, and admiration to all the heavenly hosts, etc. . . . behold the bright cherubim and their company, receiving a bright emanation of my eternal, incomprehensible light, and the heavenly principalities and powers enjoying sweet repose in me, and I in them . . . behold my elect disciples and my dearest friends, occupying the venerable thrones of judgment in great peace and honour; behold how the martyrs appear in their robes red like roses, the confessors shining in their splendid beauty, the tender virgins gleaming in angelic purity, and all the heavenly host enjoying divine sweetness! Ah, what a company, and what a happy country!"—But Suso regards all this as a mere image. In his opinion, true happiness, "the essential recompense," as distinct from that which is "accidental," consists in union with God. P. 296: "Essential reward consists in the union of the soul with the pure Deity in the beatific vision. For never more can the soul be in repose until it is elevated above all its powers and possibilities, and brought into the very essence of the persons, into the natural simplicity of the essence. And in this union and reaction it finds its satisfaction and eternal blessedness; the more entire and simple the outgoing, the freer is the upgoing, the surer is the entrance into the wild waste and the deep abyss of essential deity, into which it is absorbed, whelmed, and united; so that it wills nothing but what God wills, and becomes the same that God is; it becomes blessed by grace, as He is blessed by nature." Much, however, as Suso exalts this "swallowing up" of the human spirit in the divine, he yet insists upon the perpetuity of the individual consciousness. "In this absorption of the spirit in the Deity it vanishes, *but not wholly;* it gains some property of divinity, but it does not become essential God; all that happens to it comes through grace, for the soul is an existence created from nothing, eternally loved and favoured." *Schmidt,* l.c. s. 50 (*Diepenbrock,* s. 227). Compare the dialogues, there cited, of Suso "with the wild one," which show that Eckart's disciples were divided into two classes, the one of which adopted the pantheistic consequences of his system, and the other not; Suso belonged to the latter class.

(7) Elucidarium, c. 80: Ecce, sicut isti amici Dei decore

maximo illustrantur, ita illi maximo horrore deturpantur. Sicut isti summa agilitate sunt alleviati, ita illi summa pigritia prægravati. Sicut isti præcipuo robore solidati, ita illi sunt præcipua invaletudine debilitati. Sicut isti augusta libertate potiuntur, ita illi anxia servitute deprimuntur. Sicut isti immensa voluptate deliciantur, ita illi immensa miseria amaricantur. Sicut isti egregia sanitate vigent, ita illi infinita infirmitate deficient. Sicut isti de beata immortalitate triumphantes lætantur, ita illi de dolenda sua diuturnitate lamentantur. Sicut isti politi sunt splendore sapientiæ, ita illi obscurati sunt horrore insipientiæ. Si quid enim sciunt, ad augmentum doloris sciunt. Sicut istos dulcis amicitia copulat, ita illos amara inimicitia excruciat. Sicut isti concordem concordiam cum omni creatura habentes, ab omni creatura glorificantur, ita illi, cum omni creatura discordiam habentes, ab omni creatura execrantur. Sicut isti summa potentia sublimantur, ita illi summa impotentia angustiantur. ... Sicut isti ineffabili gaudio jubilantes, ita illi mœrore sine fine ejulantes, etc. ... According to *Thomas Aquinas*, qu. 97, art. 4, outer darkness reigns in hell, and only so much light is admitted as is sufficient to see that which is to torment the souls. The fire is (according to art. 5 and 6) a real, material fire, differing only in a few points (but not specifically) from terrestrial fire. It is under the surface of the earth, etc. — *Guibert of Nogent*, however, denied that the fire was material (he died A.D. 1124). See *Gieseler*, Dg. s. 564. A full description of the torments of hell is given by *Dante*. [Dante's descriptions are chiefly derived from Aquinas.]

(8) *Thomas Aquinas*, qu. 98, art. 2 : Pœnitere de peccato contingit dupliciter : uno modo per se, alio modo per accidens. Per se quidem de peccato pœnitet, qui peccatum, in quantum est peccatum, abominatur. Per accidens vero, qui illud odit, ratione alicujus adjuncti, utpote pœnæ vel alicujus hujusmodi. Mali igitur non pœnitebunt, per se loquendo, de peccatis, quia voluntas malitiæ peccati in eis remanet : pœnitebunt autem per accidens, in quantum affligentur de pœna, quam pro peccato sustinent. (He seems to speak of an attritio sine contritione.)

(9) L.c. art. 6 : Post diem judicii erit ultima consummatio bonorum et malorum, ita quod nihil erit addendum ulterius

de bono vel de malo. Comp. *Peter Lombard*, lib. iv. dist. 50 A.

(10) Elucidar. c. 80 : Odium enim Dei habent . . . odium habent Angelorum . . . odium habent omnium Sanctorum . . . odium a novo cœlo et a nova terra et ab omni creatura habent. Comp. *Thomas Aquinas*, l.c. art. 4 : Tanta erit invidia in damnatis, quod etiam propinquorum gloriæ invidebunt, cum ipsi sint in summa miseria . . . Sed tamen minus invident propinquis quam aliis, et major esset eorum pœna, si omnes propinqui damnarentur et alii salvarentur, quam si aliqui de suis propinquis salvarentur. (He then quotes the instance of Lazarus.)—As regards the hatred which the lost feel towards God, comp. art. 5. God as such cannot be hated, but ratione effectuum.

(11) *Peter Lombard*, lib. iv. dist. 50 G. *Thomas Aquinas*, qu. 94, art. 2, 3. They witness the sufferings of the damned, without being seen by the latter. *Peter Lombard*, l.c. litt. E. *Thomas Aquinas*, qu. 98, art. 9.

(12) De Div. Nat. v. 29, p. 265 : Diversas suppliciorum formas non localiter in quadam parte, veluti toto hujus visibilis creaturæ, et ut simpliciter dicam, neque intra diversitatem totius naturæ a Deo conditæ futuras esse credimus, et neque nunc esse, et nusquam et nunquam, sed in malarum voluntatum corruptarumque conscientiarum perversis motibus, tardaque pœnitentia et infructuosa, inque perversæ potestatis omnimoda subversione, sive humana sive angelica creatura. Comp. c. 36, p. 288, c. 37, p. 294, and some other passages. *Frommüller* (Tübinger Zeitschrift, 1830, 1, s. 84 ff.).[1] *Guibert of Nogent* entertained similar views, De Pignoribus Sanctorum (in Opp. ed. *d'Achéry*, Par. 1651, fol.), lib. iv. c. 14, p. 363 (*Münscher, von Cölln*, s. 96 ff.).

(13) The question has been raised, what it is that burns in hell. The masters generally say, it is self-will. But I say, in truth, it is *not having* (*Nicht*) which constitutes the burning of hell. Learn this from a parable. If you were to take a burning coal, and put it on my hand, and I were to assert that the coal is burning my hand, I should be wrong.

---

[1] In other passages, however, *Erigena* speaks of material fire, and illustrates the possibility of its perpetuity by the asbestos and the salamander ; De Præd. xvii. 7, xix. 1, 4. *Ritter*, Gesch. der Philosophie, vii. s. 282.

But if I be asked what it is that burns me, I say it is the not having, *i.e.* the coal has something which my hand has not. You perceive, then, that it is the not having which burns me. But if my hand had all that which the coal has, it would possess the nature of fire. In that case you might take all the fire that burns, and put it on my hand without tormenting me. In the same manner I say, if God, and those who stand before His face, enjoy that perfect happiness which those who are separated from Him possess not, it is the "*not having*" which torments the souls in hell more than self-will or fire. (Predigt auf den ersten Sonnt. nach Trin. in *Schmidt*, Studien und Kritiken, 1839, s. 722.)

(14) *Schmidt*, however, thinks it probable (l.c.) that the assertion of the Bishop of Strassburg (quoted by *Mosheim*, p. 257), that the Beghards taught, quod non est infernus, nec purgatorium (comp. § 206, note 9), was founded upon a mistake. They are further said to have maintained: quod nullus damnabitur nec Judaeus nec Sarazenus, quia mortuo corpore spiritus redibit ad Dominum.

§ 210.

Eternity of the Punishments of Hell. Restitution of all Things.

John Scotus Erigena, on the basis of the universality of redemption, ventured to intimate a revival of the Origenistic notion of the restitution of all things, without denying the eternity of the punishments of hell (1). This idea met with approbation among the mystical sects (2). The Catholic Church, however, simply abode by the doctrine of the eternity of the punishments of hell (3), as is shown in the concise superscription to the hell of *Dante* (4). The imagination of the orthodox mystics, inflamed by the vision of infinite woe, dwelt with painful elaboration upon this for ever and ever (5).

(1) *Erigena* maintained, with Augustine, the eternity of the punishments of hell, De Div. Nat. v. 31, p. 270. Nevertheless, he said, p. 72: Aliud est omnem malitiam generaliter

in omni humana natura penitus aboleri, aliud phantasias ejus, malitiæ dico, in propria conscientia eorum, quos in hac vita vitiaverat, semper servari, eoque modo semper puniri. Comp. v. 26, p. 255 s., v. 27, p. 260: Divina siquidem bonitas consumet malitiam, æterna vita absorbet mortem, beatitudo miseriam . . . nisi forte adhuc ambigis dominum Jesum humanæ naturæ acceptorem et salvatorem non totam ipsam, sed quantulamcunque partem ejus accepisse et salvasse. *Frommüller*, l.c. s. 86 f.

(2) Comp. § 209, note 14, and § 202 (on millenarianism).

(3) *Thomas Aquinas*, qu. 99.

(4) Canto iii. v. 9 : " *Ye who enter here, leave all hope behind.*" (Lasciate ogni speranza, voi che entrate.)

(5) *Suso* (Büchlein von der Weisheit, cap. xi. Von immerwährendem Weh der Hölle, quoted by *Diepenbrock*, s. 289 ..; by *Wackernagel*, Sp. 879) expressed himself as follows :—
" Alas ! misery and pain, they must last for ever. O! eternity, what art thou ? O! end without all end ! O! death which is above every death, to die every hour and yet not to be able ever to die ! O! father and mother and all whom we love ! May God be merciful to you for evermore ; for we shall see you no more to love you ; we must be separated for ever ! O! separation, everlasting separation, how painful art thou ! O! the wringing of hands ! O! sobbing, sighing, and weeping, unceasing howling and lamenting, and yet never to be heard !
. . . Give us a millstone, say the damned, as broad as the whole earth, and so large as to touch the sky all around, and let a little bird come once in a hundred thousand years, and pick off a small particle of the stone, not larger than the tenth part of a grain of millet, and after another hundred thousand years let him come again, so that in ten hundred thousand years he would pick off as much as a grain of millet, we wretched sinners would ask nothing but that when this stone has an end, our pains might also cease ; yet even that cannot be ! "

FOURTH PERIOD.

FROM THE REFORMATION TO THE RISE OF THE PHILOSOPHY OF LEIBNITZ AND WOLF IN GERMANY: FROM THE YEAR 1517 TO ABOUT 1720.

THE AGE OF POLEMICO-ECCLESIASTICAL SYMBOLISM.
(THE CONFLICT OF CONFESSIONS OF FAITH.)

A.—GENERAL HISTORY OF DOCTRINES DURING THE FOURTH PERIOD.

§ 211.

Introduction.

On the sources, and the works on the history of the Reformation, compare *Hase*, Kirchengeschichte, § 315 ff. *Gieseler*, iii. 1, s. 1 ff. *Hagenbach's* Encyklopädie; also the two works containing material for the History of Doctrine: " Leben und ausgewählte Schriften der Väter u. Begründer der reformirten," and " der Lutherischen Kirche " (Elberfeld 1857 ff., 1861 ff.).

THE Reformation of the sixteenth century was neither a mere scientific correction of doctrine, nor a revolution which affected only the external relations of life (Church constitution and worship), without touching doctrinal questions. It was rather *a comprehensive reformation of the Church on the basis of the newly awakened evangelical faith, as it manifested itself in its practical and moral aspects.* As primitive Christianity did not present a complete scheme of systematic theology to its adherents, so those who restored a pure and scriptural religion did not make it their first object to establish a perfected and final system of doctrines. The heart and the action of the heart preceded, and then gradually scientific forms of statement followed. Thus the publication of the ninety-five theses (31st Oct. A.D. 1517), in which Luther came out against Tetzel on high moral grounds, and the zeal which Zwingli displayed about the same time, in combating the prevailing abuses of the Church and the corruptions of his age, became the signal for further contests. The attack upon the theory of indulgences shook the scholastic doctrinal system to its very foundations; starting from this, the opposition to all that was unscriptural in the constitution of the Church, as well as in its doctrines, soon spread farther, though its success was not everywhere the same.

"*Questions concerning ultimate philosophical principles were, on the whole, not in the spirit and thoughts of that age;*" Baumgarten-Crusius, Compend. Dg. i. s. 326. "*It was neither the vulgar jealousy of the monastic orders against each other, nor yet any mere theoretical interest, however noble this might have been, which led Luther in the path of reform. Luther became a reformer because he had learned at the confessional the spiritual wants of the people. . . . It was from a heartfelt sympathy with the simple and honest souls, whom he saw abandoned to the arbitrary will of the priesthood, and deceived in respect to the highest good of life;*" Der deutsche Protestantismus, seine Vergangenheit und seine heutige Lebensfragen, Frankf. 1847, s. 15. See also *Gass*, Gesch. d. Protest. Dogmatik, i. s. 7 ff.; and *Neander*, Katholicismus u. Protestantismus, s. 18 ff., and his judgment on *Baur*.

§ 212.

The Principles of Protestantism.

M. Göbel, Die religiöse Eigenthümlichkeit der lutherischen und der reformirten Kirche, Bonn 1837. *Dorner*, Das Princip unsrer Kirche nach dem inneren Verhältniss seiner zwei Seiten betrachtet, Kiel 1842. *D. Schenkel*, Das Wesen des Protestantismus aus den Quellen des Reformationszeitalters dargestellt, Schaffh. 1846-52, 3 vols. *The same:* Das Princip des Protestantismus mit besonderer Berücksichtigung der neuesten hierüber geführten Verhandlungen, Schaffh. 1852. *J. H. Merle d'Aubigne*, Luther und Calvin, oder die luth. u. reform. Kirche in ihrer Verschiedenheit und wesentlich. Einheit (Deutsch von *P. E. Gottheil*, Baireuth 1849). [English translation, London 1846 ff.] *F. Baur*, Kritische Studien über d. Wesen des Protestantismus (in Zeller's Jahrb. 1847, s. 506 ff.). *II. Heppe*, Dogmatik des deutschen Protestantism. im 16 Jahrh., 3 vols. Gotha 1857-59. *The same:* Geschichte des deutschen Protestantismus in den Jahren 1555-1581, Marburg 1852-1857, 3 vols. *The same:* Entstehung u. Fortbildung des Lutherthums, Kassel 1863. See the works referred to in the following sections. *F. A. Holzhausen*, Der Protestantismus nach seiner geschichtlichen Entstehung, Begründung, u. Fortbildung, Lpz. 1859, 3 vols. *K. F. A. Kahnis*, Über die Principien des Protestantismus, Lpz. 1865. [†*Möhler's* Symbolik var. edd., and *Baur's* reply.]

The common principle on which the Reformers planted themselves, was nothing else than the principle of Christianity itself, as revealed in the canonical Scriptures. The only difference was in the mode in which they respectively attained and enforced this principle, which was determined by their personal characteristics and by external circumstances. Luther, by the deep experience of his own heart and life, was led to the *material* principle of Protestantism, viz. justification by faith, which is the central point for the right understanding of the development of the whole Protestant system of theology. With this is connected the breaking away from the authority of the Church, and the subjection to the authority of *Scripture*, or the *formal* principle of the Reformation. The two principles hang together (1). Though there is a relative truth in the remark that the Reformation, as aroused and guided by Luther in Germany, laid chief stress on the *material* principle, and that the Zwinglian (later, the Calvinistic or Reformed) movement in Switzerland laid greatest stress upon the *formal* principle (2), yet the difference of these two main tendencies, which sprung up within the bosom of Protestantism, is not adequately explained by their difference on this point (3).

(1) Compare *A. Schweizer*, Glaubenslehre der evang.-ref. Kirche, Zürich 1844, Bd. i. s. 3. *Baur*, Lehrbuch, s. 198 ff. [s. 272-278, 2d ed. *Baur* says, that the most general difference between Catholicism and Protestantism is found in the different relation in which the external and the internal in religion are placed to one another. As Catholicism is external, so Protestantism is internal. . . . In opposition to the externality of Catholicism, the fundamental idea of Protestantism is that

of the absolute value of the religious sentiment, in distinction from all that is merely external. All that is external has a value only in relation to this internal experience and conviction. In this aspect the principle of subjectivity is the principle of Protestantism; but this is only one side of its nature. The other, equally essential, is the objective element, viz. that in all that concerns his salvation, man is entirely dependent on God and divine grace.]

(2) *M. Goebel*, l.c. Compare *Ullmann* in the Studien und Kritiken, 1843, s. 756 ff.

(3) *Schweizer*, Glaubenslehre, i. s. 35, 38, 40. *Schenkel*, Wesen des Protest. i. s. 11. *Ebrard*, Abendmahlslehre, ii. s. 25 ff. The difference of the two has also been thus stated: the one (the Lutheran) was chiefly devoted to opposing the Judaism, and the other (the Reformed) to opposing the heathenism of the old Church; comp. *Herzog* in Tholuck's lit. Anzeiger, 1838, Nr. 54 f.; *Schweizer*, l.c. s. 15. But even this cannot be carried out without qualifications. *Schweizer* says (l.c.), that the peculiarity of the Reformed (Calvinistic) theology consisted in holding fast to the absolute idea of God in opposition to all idolatry of the creature, while the centre of gravity of the Lutheran system is to be sought in the sphere of anthropology. *Ebrard's* position (l.c. s. 27) is, that the material principle of justification by faith is common to both, and that the difference consists in this, that Luther emphasized this justification (subjectively) in opposition to works, while Zwingli insisted upon it (objectively) in contrast with human mediation and reconciliation.—*Neander* apprehends the opposition differently (l.c. s. 64 ff.), when he sees in Lutheranism rather a repetition of *Alexandrian* supernaturalism, and in Zwinglianism a repetition of the naturalistic tendencies of the *Antiochene* school; or when (in other words) he sees in Zwingli's reformation rather an extensively negative tendency of mind, and in Luther's an intensively positive. But this opposition must not be stretched so far as to make it appear, as many do, that Luther represented an extreme supernaturalism, while Zwingli was a forerunner of rationalism. So much seems to be certain, that no fundamental difference can be said to exist between the principles of the Lutheran and Zwinglian reformation, but a difference simply in the mode of combining the external and

internal conditions, under which the common principles were established and modified. Comp. below, § 219, note 3. [See also *Baur*, Dg. ubi supra, who says that the real Protestant antagonism to Catholicism is found in Calvinism, and there too in the very doctrine which was at first common to all the Reformers, but which attained its systematic development only in Calvinism, that is, the absolute decree. Against the Catholic absolutism of the external Church was placed the Calvinistic absolutism of the divine purpose—it is immanent in God. The Melanchthonian type of theology, with its principle of moral freedom, is here, on the Protestant side, the antagonism to Calvinism. Strict Lutheranism is merely intermediate between these two, historical rather than ideal or material.]

§ 213.

Relation of the History of Doctrines of the Present Period to that of the Former Period. (Symbolism.)

Compare above, § 4, 13, 16 (note 9).

The important events which occurred during the present age, the introduction of new relations affecting the whole development of the Church, the division of Christendom into the two great sections of *Protestantism* and *Roman Catholicism*,—the separation between the *Lutherans* and the *Reformed* Church (*Calvinists*), which took place at an early period,—and the abiding schism between the Roman Catholic and the Greek orthodox Churches, render it necessary to adopt another method in the treatment of the History of Doctrines. We shall have to consider the dogmatic development of each of these great sections of the Church separately, as well as the relation in which they stand to each other. Nor must we pass over those religious parties, which made their appearance in that time of commotion, without joining any of the larger bodies, but which rather set themselves in opposition to each and all of them, and were looked upon by all of them as heretical. And here, too, is found the determining element, which gives a new shape to the History of Doctrines, so that in its flow it is expanded into the form of symbolism.

I. THE LUTHERAN CHURCH.

§ 214.

Luther and Melanchthon.

J. G. Planck, Gesch. d. Entstehung, Veränderung, u. Bildung des Prot. Lehrbegriffs bis zur Concordienformel, Lpz. 1791-1800, 7 vols. *Ph. Marheineke,* Gesch. d. deutschen Reformation bis 1555, Berlin 1831, 4 vols. *L. Ranke,* Deutsche Gesch. im. Zeitalter d. Reform., Berl. 1839-1843, 5 vols. [English version, by *Sarah Austin.*] *Dieckhoff*, Luther's evang. Lehrgedanken, in Deutsche Zeitschrift, Berl. Mai 1852. Lives of Luther, by *Spieker, Jürgens, Pfizer, Gelzer, Meurer, Audin, Döllinger, Michelet, Worsley,* etc. See lit. in *Hase, Gieseler,* and *Schürers* Literaturzeitung, 1876 ff. [*Hare's* Mission of the Comforter, Appendix on Luther's views, against Sir Wm. Hamilton, 1855; also published separately, as *Hare's* Vindication of Luther.] *D. Schenkel*, Die Reformatoren und die Reformation, im Zusammenhange mit den der evangelischen Kirche durch die Reformation gestellten Aufgaben, Wiesbaden 1856. *J. Köstlin*, Die Theologie Luthers, Stuttg. 1863; and his art. "Luther," in *Herzog*, viii. s. 568 ff. *Harnack*, Luthers Theologie mit besonderer Beziehung auf seine Versöhnungs und Erlösungslehre, Erlangen 1862 ff. **F. Galle*, Versuch einer Charakteristik Melanchthons als Theologen, und einer Entwicklung seines Lehrbegriffs, Halle 1840.

While it may be said, on the one hand, that *Dr. Martin Luther* became the reformer of the German Church κατ' ἐξοχήν, and thus the reformer of a great part of the universal Church, by his grand personal character and heroic career (1), by the publication of his theses (2), by sermons and expositions of Scripture (3), by disputations and bold controversial writings (4), by numerous letters and circular epistles, by memorials and judgments on controverted points (5), by intercourse with persons of all classes of society, by pointed maxims and hymns (6), but especially by his translation of the Sacred Scriptures into the German language (7); on the other hand, it was the work of the calmer and more learned *Master Philip Melanchthon* to conduct the mighty stream of the newly-awakened life of faith into a scientifically-defined channel. In addition to many other valuable theological works, he composed the first compendium of the doctrines of the Protestant Church (Loci Communes sive Theologici), which formed the basis of other treatises (8).

(1) He was born at Eisleben, Nov. 10, A.D. 1483.—In the year 1507 he enters the monastery of the Augustinian monks at Erfurt; removes in the following year to Wittenberg, where he teaches first philosophy, and afterwards theology; makes a journey to Rome, 1510; and takes his degree of doctor of theology, 1512.—Posting of the theses, Oct. 31, 1517.—Luther is summoned before the pope; has an interview with Cajetan in Augsburg, Oct. 1518.—Interview with Miltitz; Controversy with Eck, Wimpina, and others.—Dispute of Leipzig, June 1519.—Excommunication of Luther, 1520.—He burns the bull and the papal decrees, Dec. 1520.—Diet of Worms under the Emperor Charles V.; Luther's defence on that occasion, April 1521.—He is outlawed, and constrained to take up his abode in the Wartburg (from May 1521 to March 1522).—He leaves his place of concealment to oppose the prophets of Zwickau.—Further spread of the Reformation in Germany, commencing at Wittenberg.—The peasants' war, controversy concerning the sacraments, Luther's marriage (1524–1525).—Visitation of the churches, 1527.—Diet of Augsburg, 1530.—Luther's residence at Coburg—a period of manifold sufferings and vexations.—His death, Feb. 18, 1546. —*Complete editions of his works are:* that of Wittenberg, twelve volumes in German (1539–1559), and seven volumes in Latin (1545–1558); that of Jena, eight volumes in German (1555–1558), and four in Latin (1556–1558), in addition to which two supplementary volumes were published by *Aurifaber*, Eisleben 1564, 1565; that of Altenburg, in ten volumes in German (1661–1664); that of Leipzig, in twenty-two volumes (1729–1740); and that of Halle, edited by *Walch*, in twenty-four volumes (1740–1750). See *Giesler*, iii. 1, s. 3; and *H. V. Rotermund*, Verzeichniss der verschiedenen Ausgaben der sämmtlichen Schriften Luthers, Bremen 1813. [Luther's Sämmtliche (Deutsche) Werke, herausg. v. *J. G. Plochmann* u. *J. K. Irmischer*, 67 Bde. Erlangen 1826–1857; L.'s Exegetica Opera Latina, cur. *Elsperger S. Schmid* et *Irmischer*,

vols. 1–23 and 28–30, 1839–1861.]—Luther did not compose a system of doctrinal theology, but others have compiled it from his writings. This was done, *e.g.*, by *Heinrich Majus*, professor at Giessen, who wrote: Lutheri Theologia pura et sincera, ex Viri divini Scriptis universis, maxime tamen Latinis, per omnes fidei Articulos digesta et concinnata, Francof. ad M. 1709 (with a supplement). Similar works were composed by *Timoth. Kirchner*, *Andr. Musculus*, *Theodos. Fabricius*, *Michael Neander* (Theologia Megalandri Lutheri, Eisl. 1587), *Elias Veiel*. See *Semler*, Einleitung zu *Baumgartens* Glaubenslehre, Bd. ii. s. 146; *Heinrich*, Geschichte der Lehrarten, s. 248; and the writings of *Dieckhoff*, *Köstlin*, *Hornack*, etc., referred to above.

(2) They are given in *Löschers* Reformationsacten, i. s. 438, and *Herm. von der Hardt*, Historia Reformat. Litt. P. iv. p. 16. Compare also *Gieseler*, Kg. iii. s. 24, where the most important theses may be found. "*The whole life of believers on earth is to be one of unceasing repentance; this is the sum and kernel of these theses, and of evangelical Protestantism in general*," *Schenkel*, Die Reformatoren, s. 24.

(3) For an account of the different collections of sermons, homilies, etc. (Kirchen- und Hauspostille, etc.), see *Lentz*, Geschichte der christlichen Homiletik, ii. s. 22 f.—His exegetical works (*e.g.* his Commentary on the Epistle to the Galatians, 1535–1538) furnish contributions to the History of Doctrines.

(4) The several controversial writings which he composed, in opposition both to the advocates of the old system and to the real or supposed corrupters of the new doctrines, as well as the reports of public disputations, will be specified in their proper connections in the Special History of Doctrines.

(5) Briefe, Sendschreiben, und Bedenken, edited by *de Wette*, five volumes, Berlin 1825–1828; vol. vi. ed. *Seidemann*, 1856. (Comp. the chronological table of de Wette, prefixed to these Epistles, with that in note 1 above.) Briefwechsel, unter vorzüglicher Berücksichtigung der de Wetteschen Ausgabe, herausgegeben von *C. A. Burkhardt*, Lpz. 1866.

(6) *Gebauer*, Luther als Kirchenliederdichter, Leipz. 1828. The latest edition appeared under the care of *Winterfeld*, 1840. Luther's maxims are for the most part collected in the "Tischreden" (Table-talk), published by *Aurifaber*. An

edition of the Tischreden, by *Förstemann* and *Bindseil*, 1844–1848. [A translation, with Life, by *A. Chalmers*, in *Bohn's Standard Library*.]

(7) The translation of the Bible was commenced during his residence in the Wartburg, and that of the New Testament was completed 1522. The first German translation of the whole Bible was published by Hans Lufft, in Wittenberg, A.D. 1534 (compare the editions of 1541 and 1545). Further particulars will be found in *G. W. Panzer*, Entwurf einer vollständ. Geschichte der Bibelübersetzung Dr. M. Luthers, Nürnb. 1783; and the other works on this subject written by *Marheinecke, Weidemann, Lücke, Schott, Grotefend, Mann* (Stuttgart, 1835), *Hopf* (1847), and others.

(8) His original name was *Schwarzerd*. He was born at Bretten, in the Palatinate, Feb. 16, 1497, and delivered lectures in the University of Wittenberg. He was surnamed *Præceptor Germaniæ*. His lectures on Paul's Epistle to the Romans gave rise to his celebrated work: Loci Communes Rerum Theologicarum seu Hypotyposes Theologicæ,[1] 1521, 4to. In the same year it was also published in 8vo; it has passed through upwards of a hundred editions, more than sixty of which appeared during his lifetime. The Loci were several times revised (particularly in 1535 and 1543), and from the year 1550 published under the title: Loci Præcipui Theologici. Comp. *Herm. von der Hardt*, Hist. Reform. Liter. P. iv. p. 30 ss. One of the best of the late editions is that of *Augusti*, Lips. 1821. *H. Balthasar*, Historia Locorum Phil. Melanc., Gryphisw. 1761.—*Luther* (De Servo Arbitrio) called the work: "invictum libellum, non solum immortalitate, sed canone etiam ecclesiastico dignum." Compare the passage quoted from his "Tischreden" by *Galle*, s. 20. *Strobel*, Literargeschichte von Phil. Melanchthons Locis Theologicis, Altdorf und Nürnberg 1776. Concerning other doctrinal and polemical writings of Melanchthon, see *Heinrich*, l.c. s. 268 ff. in

---

[1] On the signification of the word Locus, see *Heppe*, Dogmatik des deutschen Protestant. s. 6. By the *Loci* are meant the proper δόγματα, the sedes doctrinæ. [The classical sense of τόπος, locus, is a principle: Cicero speaks of *loci*, "quasi sedes, e quibus argumenta promuntur." The Loci Communes are the fundamental ideas or truths of theology. Melanchthon says that his Hypotyposes are wholly different from the Sententiæ of Peter Lombard; they are not a system, but rather an introduction to the study of the Scriptures. *Heppe*, u.s.]

Galle, Melanchthons Characteristik, l.c. *Schwarz*, Melanchthons Loci nach ihrer weiteren Entwicklung (Stud. u. Kritik. 1857, s. 297; cf. ibid. 1855, 1. *Gass*, Gesch. d. Prot. Dogmatik, § 23. *Heppe*, Dogmatik des deutschen Protest. s. 9 ff. *Bretschneider, Corpus Reformat. xxi. (a critical collection of the different editions by Bindseil). [The edition of *Melanchthon's* works, projected by *Bretschneider* in his Corpus Reformat., was brought to its completion in 1860, by the publication of the 28th vol., edited by *H. E. Bindseil*. An edition of the *Loci*, after that of 1559, Berlin 1856; a reprint of the edition of 1521, edited by *J. E. Volbeding*, Leipz. 1860.] Compare also **C. Schmidt*, Phil. Melanchthons Leben und ausgewählte Schriften, Elberfeld 1861.

§ 215.

The Symbolical Books of the Lutheran Church.

On the literature, compare above, § 13 and 16. [*H. Heppe*, Die Bekenntnissschriften der altprotestantischen Kirche Deutschlands, Kassel 1855.]

Melanchthon was chosen by the newly-formed Protestant Church to draw up a confession of faith in a form concise and clear, and as pacific as possible, on the basis of those doctrines which he, with Luther and other divines, agreed in receiving. From its solemn presentation at the diet of Augsburg (A.D. 1530), it received the name of the *Confession of Augsburg* (Confessio Augustana) (1). The *Confutatio*, published by the Roman Catholics, in opposition to the Confession of Augsburg (2), gave rise, soon after, to a new symbolical book of the Lutheran Church, the *Apology of the Confession*, of which Melanchthon was the sole author (3). The *Articles of Schmalkalden*, composed by Luther, in much bolder terms, followed somewhat later (A.D. 1536, 1537) (4). These completed the series of official documents and apologies which bore upon the external relations of the new Church (5). But in order to establish the internal relations of the Protestant Church on a definite doctrinal basis, the two *Catechisms of Luther* were added to the collection of symbolical books as normal compendiums (6). And lastly, in consequence of many and violent controversies respecting the fundamental principles of Protestantism which arose within the Lutheran Church itself (7), it was found necessary, after various but unsuccessful attempts to restore peace, to draw up the *Formula Concordiæ* (*Germ.* Concordienformel, A.D. 1577), in which the disputed points were considered, and, as far as possible, determined (8). All these books were now collected into a symbolical canon (A.D. 1580), called the *Liber Concordiæ* (*Germ.* Concordienbuch). In the course of time this canon acquired such high authority, that the clergy had to subscribe it as solemnly as the Scripture itself (9).

(1) Confessio Augustana, on the basis of the seventeen articles of Torgau (Schwabach), composed by order of the Electoral Prince of Saxony, by Luther, Jonas, Bugenhagen, and Melanchthon. The original edition was published in German and Latin, A.D. 1530, by *G. Rhaw* (in modern times it has been edited by *Winer*, 1825; *Tittmann*, 1830; *Twesten*, 1840, 1850; *Francke*, 1846), new edition by *Heppe*, Kassel 1855. It consists of twenty-eight articles; in the first twenty-one the principal doctrines (Articuli fidei præcipui) are discussed with reference to the Roman Catholic doctrines, but in moderate terms; the last seven treat of the abusus mutatos. Further particulars (of its literary history) are given by *Winer*, Comparative Darstellung, s. 13 (older ed.); *Gieseler*, l.c. s. 243 ff. Many details respecting its origin, and the elevation of mind of its confessors, will be found in the work of *Rotermund*, Geschichte des Reichstages in Augsburg, Hannover 1829. On the critical part, see *Weber*, Geschichte der Augsburgischen Confession, Frankf. 1783, 1784, 2 vols. *Förstemann*, Urkundenbuch, Halle 1833, 1835. *A. G. Rudelbach*, Historisch-kritische Einleit. in die Augsb. Conf., Dresden 1841. On *Luther's* share in the confession, see the writings of *Rückert* (1854), *Calinich* (1862), *Knaake* (1863). On the relation of the *Variata* edition of 1540, considered as the more complete and enriched (locupletirte) edition, to the *incariata*, see *Heppe*, Die confessionelle Entwicklung der

altprotestantischen Kirche Deutschlands, Marb. 1854, s. 110 ff. [English translation of the Augsb. Confession in *P. Hall*, Harmony of Confessions, Lond. 1842.]

(2) It was composed by a commission of Roman Catholic theologians (among whom were *Eck* and *Faber*), and read aloud (in German) in the Diet, Aug. 3, 1530, but no copy of it was communicated to the Protestant Estates. It was only afterwards that Melanchthon obtained a copy. It is reprinted in *Hase*, Libri Symbolici, p. 55 ss. (5th ed.), p. lxxvi. ss. (older ed.).

(3) The first sketch of the Apology was composed from the remembrance of what was contained in the *Confutatio*, as the author had no copy of the writing of his opponents, and presented to the Emperor Charles v., Sept. 22, 1530. It was afterwards revised, after Melanchthon had seen the Confutatio, and published 1531, both in Latin and in German, together with the Confession of Augsburg. The same arrangement is adopted in the Apology as in the Confession, but the number of articles is reduced to sixteen. "*With regard to the importance of its contents, this work, no doubt, occupies the first place among the symbols of the Lutheran Church,*" *Winer*, s. 15. Even *Ernesti* called it "*a masterpiece in the argument ex dictis Scripturæ, ex natura rerum, and consensu patrum,*" etc. See *Ernesti*, Neue theologische Bibliothek, Bd. ii. s. 413. It was edited by *Lücke* in Latin and German, Berl. 1818.

(4) These were drawn up in German, in order to be presented at the council summoned by Pope Paul III. (A.D. 1536), and signed by the Assembly of Schmalkalden (Feb. 1537). Hence the name. The first German edition appeared at Wittenberg 1538. They were republished from a MS. in the Library of Heidelberg by Dr. *Phil. Marheinecke*, Berl. 1817, 4to.—The work falls into three divisions : 1. De summis articulis divinæ majestatis ; 2. De summis articulis, qui officium et opus Jesu Christi s. redemtionem nostram concernunt ; 3. Articuli, de quibus agere potuerimus cum doctis et prudentibus viris vel etiam inter nos ipsos. (An appendix was afterwards added of Melanchthon's treatise, De potestate et primatu Papæ.)—The relation of the polemical element to the eirenical is here different from what it is in the Augsburg Confession. Here the polemical preponderates. On the ques-

tion whether those articles had from the first symbolical authority, see *Heppe*, Dogmatik des deutschen Protestantismus, s. 106. *G. L. Plitt*, De auctoritate articulorum Smalcaldicorum Symbolica, Erlang. 1862.

(5) On the distinction between those symbolical writings which have regard to *external* relations, and those which refer to *internal* relations, see *Schleiermacher*, Ueber den eigenthümlichen Werth und das Ansehen symbolischer Bücher, in the Reform. Almanach, 2 Jahrg. 1819, s. 235 ff. [For the Confessio Saxonica, Confessio Würtembergica, the Frankfurt Recess, and the Naumburg Repetition of the Augsburg Confession, see *Heppe*, ubi supra.]

(6) In the year 1529, Luther wrote both the Catechismus major (for the use of the clergy and schoolmasters) and the Catechismus minor (for the use of the people and children), not in order to force a system of doctrines upon the Church, but to supply a practical deficiency. Both were divided into the five so-called leading parts. On the different editions, appendices, etc., see Winer, l.c. s. 16. *Augusti*, Einleitung in die beiden Hauptkatechismen der evangelischen Kirche, Elberfeld 1824. *C. F. Illgen*, Memoria utriusque Catech. Lutheri, Lips. 1828–1830, 4 Programmes 4to.

(7) The most important of these controversies are the following:—

    (*a*) The *Antinomian Controversy*; it originated with *Johann Agricola* of Eisleben (from the year 1536 he was professor in the University of Wittenberg) during Luther's lifetime. Comp. *Elwert*, De Antinomia J. Agricolæ Islebii, Tur. 1836.

    (*b*) The *Adiaphoristic Controversy*, which had its origin in the Interim of Leipsic (from the year 1548), and gave rise to a lasting difference between the moderate views of Philip Melanchthon (philippistisch) and the more rigid doctrines of the orthodox Lutherans. The former view was represented by the University of Wittenberg, the latter by that of Jena. This difference manifested itself especially in

    (*c*) The *Controversy* between *Georg Major* and *Nicolas Amsdorf*, on the question whether good works are necessary to salvation, or whether they rather possess a dangerous tendency (about the year 1559 ff.). This controversy was connected with the two following, viz. :—

(d) The *Synergistic Controversy*, on the relation of human liberty to divine grace; it was called forth (A.D. 1555) by the treatise of *John Pfeffinger* (of Leipzig): De libero Arbitrio, which was combated by *Amsdorf*.

(e) The *Controversy* respecting the nature of original sin, between *Victorin Strigel* (at Jena) and *Matthias Flacius*. It commenced A.D. 1560, and led to the disputation of Weimar, A.D. 1561. *Twesten*, Matthias Flacius Illyricus, Berlin 1844. About the same time was carried on in Prussia

(f) The *Controversy* between *Andreas Osiander* (in Königsberg) and *Joachim Mörlin, Franz Stancarus*, etc.; it bore upon the relation in which justification stands to sanctification, and to the main point in the work of redemption. Comp. *Tholuck*, Literarischer Anzeiger, 1833, Nr. 54 ff.

(g) The *(Cryptocalvinistic) Controversy* concerning the Lord's Supper: *First*, In the Palatinate between *W. Klebitz* and *Tilemann Hesshus*[1] (A.D. 1559). In consequence of it, not only were both these pastors dismissed, but Frederick III., Electoral Prince of the Palatinate, also went over to the Reformed Church. *Secondly*, The controversy which took place in Bremen between *Albrecht Hardenberg* and the said *Hesshus* (A.D. 1561), together with its consequences. *Thirdly*, The controversy carried on in Saxony itself. There *Caspar Peucer*, the son-in-law of Melanchthon, succeeded in gaining over the Prince Elector Augustus, as well as Crell and others, to the Calvinistic doctrine (Consensus Dresdensis), until the former, having obtained a better knowledge of the real state of things by the Exegesis perspicua Controversiae de Coena Domini, in which the views of Peucer's party were more distinctly set forth, commenced a bloody persecution of the Crypto-

---

[1] On Hesshus, see *C. A. Wilkens: Tilemann Hesshusius, ein Streittheolog der Lutherkirche*, Leipz. 1860.

calvinists, and adopted measures for the restoration of Lutheran orthodoxy. Comp. *E. L. Th. Henke*, Caspar Peucer u. Nic. Crell, Marb. 1865.

On all these controversies, compare the works on ecclesiastical history, and the history of the Reformation, as well as the well-known works of *Walch*, *Planck*, etc. They will be considered in the Special History of Doctrines. *Gass*, Gesch. d. prot. Dogmatik, i. s. 56 ff.

(8) The Formula Concordiæ was based upon the articles drawn up (1576) in Torgau (Torgisches Buch), and composed in the monastery of Bergen near Magdeburg (1577), by *Jacob Andreä* (Schmidlin), chancellor of Würtemberg, on the one hand, and the Saxon theologians, *Martin Chemnitz, Nicolaus Selnekker, David Chytraeus, Andreas Musculus*, and *Christoph Körner*, on the other. It was called the "Bergisches Buch," and acquired symbolical authority, not only in Saxony, but also in other towns and countries; while it met with opposition in Hessen, Anhalt, Pomerania, and several of the free cities. In Brandenburg and the Upper Palatinate it was first adopted, but afterwards lost its reputation.—The Formula consists of two parts: 1. The (shorter) Epitome; 2. The (more complete) Solida Declaratio. It was originally published in German, and translated into Latin by *L. Osiander*. Comp. *Nic. Anton*, Geschichte der Concordienformel, Lpz. 1779, 2 vols. *Planck*, vi. *Heppe*, Gesch. d. Concordienformel, Marb. 1857. *F. K. Göschel*, Die Concordienformel nach ihrer Geschichte, Lehre und Kirchl. Bedeutung, Lpz. 1858. *F. H. R. Frank*, Die Theologie der Concordienformel historisch-dogmatisch entwickelt u. beleuchtet, Erlangen 1858-1861. †*J. G. Martens*, De Formula Concordiæ, Münster 1860.

(9) The German title of it is: "Concordia, christliche, wiederholte, einmüthige Bekenntniss nachgenannter Churfürsten, Fürsten, und Stände Augsburgischer Confession und derselben zu Ende des Buchs unterschriebenen Theologen Lehre und Glaubens, mit angehefter, in Gottes Wort, als der einigen Richtschnur, wohlgegründeter Erklärung etlicher Artikel, bei welchen nach Dr. Martin Luthers seligem Absterben Disputation und Streit vorgefallen. Aus einhelliger Vergleichung und Befehl obgedachter Churfürsten, Fürsten, und Stände derselben Landen, Kirchen, Schulen und Nach-

kommen zum Unterricht und Warnung in Druck verfertigt," Dresden 1580, fol.

§ 216.

The Systematic Theology of the Lutheran Church.

Buddei Isagoge (Lips. 1727), i. p. 387 ss. *Walchii* Bibliotheca Theologica selecta, i. p. 33 ss. *Semler*, Einleitung in die dogmatische Gottesgelehrsamkeit (the introduction to *Baumgarten's* Glaubenslehre, Bd. ii. iii.). *Heinrich*, Geschichte der Lehrarten der protestantischen Kirche, s. 271 ff. *De Wette*, Dogmatik der protestantischen Kirche (ed. 3), s. 17 ff. *Hase*, Hutterus Redivivus, oder Dogmatik der evangel. lutherischen Kirche (9th ed.), 1862. *A. Tholuck*, Der Geist der lutherischen Theologen Wittenbergs im Verlaufe des 17 Jahrhunderts, Hamb. 1852. *W. Gass*, Gesch. d. protest. Dogmatik, 2 Bde. Berl. 1854-1857. *G. Frank*, Geschichte der prot. Theologie, 1 Thl. Lpz. 1862. (Comp. § 212.)

Many works on systematic theology were published by different writers; some of whom, such as *Martin Chemnitz* (1), *Victorin Strigel* (2), and *Nicolaus Selnecker* (3), followed Melanchthon; while others, *e.g. Leonhard Hutter* (4), *Johann Gerhard* (5), *Jakob Heerbrand* (6), *Matthias Haffenreffer* (7), and others, adopted the strict Lutheran view, and closely adhered to the Formula Concordiæ. These works were, for the most part, called *Loci Theologici*, and arranged after the synthetic method (8). But after *Georg Calixt* (9) had separated ethics from systematic theology, and applied the analytic method of investigation to the latter (10), *Johann Hülsemann* (11), *Joh. Conrad Dannhauer* (12), *Abraham Calov* (13), *Johann Fr. König* (14), *Johann Andreas Quenstedt* (15), *Johann Wilhelm Baier* (16), and others, followed more or less the course which he had adopted. These theologians may, in many respects, be compared to the scholastics of the preceding period; though in either case we may show a variety of modifications and transitions (17).

(1) *Chemnitz*, born at Treuenbriezen, Nov. 9, A.D. 1522, was the most learned of the disciples of Melanchthon, on whose Loci he delivered lectures in the University of Wittenberg.

He took part in the composition of the Formula Concordiæ (comp. § 213), as well as in the Reformation at Brunswick. He died 1586.—*He wrote:* Loci Theologici, editi Op. et Stud. *Polycarpi Lyseri* (Leyser.), Francof. 1591, 4to, 1599, 1604, 3 vols. 8vo; Viteberg. 1615, 1623, 1690, fol.—" *These commentaries are written with much learning. . . . Accuracy and clearness in the definition of doctrines, mature judgment, prudent choice of matter and proofs, and order in the arrangement, are everywhere apparent,*" *Heinrich*, s. 274. Comp. *Gass*, s. 51 ff., 70 ff. *Heppe*, s. 119 ff.—Examen Concilii Tridentini, Francof. 1615 (1578?), 1707. Concerning the other dogmatic works of Chemnitz, see *Heinrich*, s. 276.

(2) *Strigel* was born at Kaufbeuren, A.D. 1524, and obtained a professorship of divinity in the University of Jena, A.D. 1548. (On the controversy between him and Flacius, see the preceding section.) He died A.D. 1569, as an exile at Heidelberg. His Loci Theologici were edited, Lab. et Studio *Christ. Pezelii*, Neap. Nemet. (Neustadt on the Hardt), 1582–1585, 2 vols. 4to. " *In many points he is so profound and edifying, that I am not sure whether any other theologian of that period has surpassed him,*" *Semler*, in his edition of *Baumgarten's* Glaubenslehre, ii. s. 158.—The book is scarce. Comp. *Otto*, De Victorino Strigelio, liberioris mentis in Eccl. Luth. Vindice, Jena 1843.

(3) *Schnekker* was born A.D. 1530, at Hersbruck in Franconia, studied theology in the University of Wittenberg, was chaplain to the Electoral Prince of Saxony, professor of divinity in the Universities of Jena and Leipzig, superintendent at Wolfenbüttel, etc., and died A.D. 1592. He also took part in the composition of the Formula Concordiæ. *He wrote:* Institutiones Christianæ Religionis, Partes III. Francof. 1573, 1579. This work was the first system of dogmatic theology in the Lutheran Church which contained the so-called Prolegomena (on the Scriptures, revelation, etc.). Comp. *Gass*, s. 51. *Heppe*, s. 96 ff.

(4) *Hutter* was born A.D. 1563, at Nellingen, in the district of Ulm. He was surnamed Lutherus redivivus, and defended the Formula Concordiæ (Concordia Concors, Viteb. 1614, fol.) in opposition to Hospinian (Concordia Discors, Tig. 1607, fol.). By order of Christian II., Elector of Saxony, *he wrote:* Compendium Locorum Theol. ex Sacra Script. et Libro Concord. collat., Viteb. 1610; new edition by *Twesten*, Berol. (1855)

1863.—Loci Communes Theol. ex Sacris Litteris diligenter eruti, Veterum Patrum Testimoniis passim roborati, et conformati ad meth. locc. Mel., Viteb. 1619, 1653, 1661, fol. While he speaks of Melanchthon with high regard, he still charges him with "defectio a puritate doctrinæ cœlestis." Comp. *Gass*, s. 251 ff. *Heppe*, s. 133 ff.

(5) *Gerhard* was born A.D. 1582, at Quedlinburg, occupied a chair of divinity in the University of Jena, and died Aug. 17, 1637. *He wrote:* Loci Theolog. cum pro adstruenda veritate, tum pro destruenda quorumvis contradicentium falsitate, per theses nervose, solide, et copiose explicati, Jenæ 1610–1625, 9 vols. 4to. Denuo edid. variique gen. obss. adjec. *J. Fr. Cotta*, t. i.–xx. Tüb. 1762–1789, 4to.—Exegesis s. uberior Explicatio Articulorum de Scriptura S. de Deo et de Persona Christi in Tomo I. Locorum (*Cotta*, t. ii. iii.).—*J. E. Gerhard*, Isagoge Loc. Theol. in qua ea, quæ in ix. tomis uberius sunt exposita, in Compendium redacta, Jen. 1658.— Comp. *Heinrich*, s. 314 ff. *Semler*, s. 72 ff. *Gass*, s. 259 ff.

(6) *Heerbrand* was chancellor in Tübingen, died 1600. His Comp. Theol., Tüb. 1573 (ed. by *Crus.*, Wittenb. 1582), had almost symbolical authority in Würtemberg. See *Gass*, s. 77 ff. *Heppe*, s. 124 ff.

(7) *Haffenreffer* was born 1561, and died 1619, as Provost, in Stuttgard. His Loci Theologici (Tübingen 1601, frequently republished) "*obtained at once the widest currency in Upper and Lower Germany, because they gave in the most precise and intelligible manner the doctrinal points of the Formula Concordiæ, which was what they wanted to hear exclusively in the Lutheran lecture rooms,*" *Heppe*, i. s. 129. Comp. *Gass*, s. 78 ff. Besides these divines may also be named *Nicolaus Hemming, Abdias Prätorius, Johann Wigand;* and later (in the seventeenth century), *Erasmus Brochmand* (Universæ Theologiæ Systema, etc., Hafniæ 1633, 2 tom. 4to), *Bircherod, Friedlieb*, etc. See *Semler*, s. 71, 80. *Heinrich*, s. 283, 328. *Gass* and *Heppe*, l.c.—On the relation of this aftergrowth ('Ἐπίγονοι) to Melanchthon, see *Heinrich*, as above, s. 310 ff. *Gass*, s. 80.

(8) The synthetic method starts from the highest principle, God, and proceeds to man, to Christ, to redemption, till it comes down to the end of all things.

(9) Of his writings the following are of a doctrinal charac-

ter: Apparatus in Theol. Stud., ed. *F. U. Calixt.*, Helmst. 1656, 1661. Epitome Theol., Gosl. 1619, ed. *Gerh. Titius*, 1666. Epit. Theol. Mor., Helmst. 1634. For further particulars, see below, § 218. On his analytic method, compare *Heinrich*, s. 330 f. *Gass*, s. 303 ff.[1]

(10) The analytic method begins with the end or final cause (the "final method") of all theology, blessedness, and hence takes the opposite course from the synthetic. On other complicated methods, see *Hase*, Hutterus Redivivus, p. 41 ss. *Gass*, s. 47.

(11) *Hülsemann* was born A.D. 1602, at Esens in East Friesland; held several situations in Saxony, was superintendent at Meissen, and died A.D. 1661. *He wrote:* Breviarium Theologicum, Viteb. 1640. Extensio Breviarii Theol., Lips. 1648, 1655.—(*Valent. Alberti* Brev. Theol. Hülsemanni encl. et auct., Lips. 1687, 4to.) His opponents called his style: stilum barbarum, scholasticum, holcoticum, scoticum, ac tenebrosum. See *Scherzeri*, Prolegomena, quoted by *Heinrich*, s. 333. *Tholuck*, Theolog. Wittenb. s. 164 ff. *Gass*, s. 316.

(12) *Dannhauer*, born A.D. 1603 at Köndringen (in the county of Baden-Hochberg), was professor of theology in the University of Strassburg, instructed Spener, and died A.D. 1666. "*He had considerable influence, chiefly from his profound exegetical lectures, delivered in a popular style.*" *Hossbach* (Spener, i. s. 17). *He wrote:* Hodosophia Christiana s. Theol. Posit. in Methodum redacta, Argent. 1649, 1666, 8vo; Lips. 1713, 4to. Spener arranged this work in the form of tables, Franc. 1690, 4to. On the so-called phenomenal method which Dannhauer adopted (*i.e.* the symbolico-allegorical representation of man under the figure of a pilgrim, etc.), see *Hossbach*, l.c. s. 23. *Semler*, s. 85. *Heinrich*, s. 334. *Gass*, s. 318.—In addition to the above work, he composed: Christosophia, 1638, and Mysteriosophia, 1646.

(13) *Calov* was born A.D. 1612 at Morungen, filled the office of superintendent at Wittenberg, and died A.D. 1686. He used daily to offer this prayer: Imple me, Deus, odio hæreticorum! *He wrote:* Systema Locorum Theol. e Sacra potissimum Script. et Antiquitate, nec non Adversariorum Confessione Doctrinam, Praxin et Controversarium Fidei cum veterum tum

---

[1] Under the influence of *Calixt* were the divines *Joachim Hildebrand* and *Johann Henich* (died 1671); see *Gass*, s. 311 ff.

imprimis recentiorum Pertractationem luculentam exhibens, Viteb. 1655–1677, 12 vols. 4to. Theol. Positiva per Definitiones, Causas, Adfectiones, et Distinctiones Locos Theol. universos ... proponens, ceu Compendium System. Theol., Viteb. 1682. See *Tholuck*, l.c. s. 185, and particularly *Gass*, s. 332 ff.

(14) *König* was born A.D. 1619, at Dresden, and died A.D. 1664, at Rostock, where he was professor of theology. He wrote: Theologia Positiva Acroamatica synoptice tractata, Rost. 1664. An improved edition of it appeared in *J. Casp. Haferungi* Colleg. Thet., Viteb. 1737. According to *Buddeus* (Isagoge, p. 399), it is a mere skeleton of a system of doctrinal theology, without sap or force. But compare *Gass*, s. 321, who reckons him among the "dogmatic virtuosi."

(15) *Quenstedt*, born at Quedlinburg, A.D. 1617, was professor of theology in the University of Wittenberg, and died A.D. 1688. He wrote: Theologia Didactico-polemica s. Systema Theol. in duas sectiones ... divisum, Viteb. 1685 and 1696, Lips. 1702, 1715, fol. Comp. *Semler*, s. 103 ff. *Tholuck*, l.c. s. 214 ff. *Gass*, s. 357.

(16) *Baier* was born A.D. 1647, at Nürnberg, and died A.D. 1695, at Weimar, where he was superintendent. He composed a Compendium Theol. Positivæ, Jen. 1686, 1691, etc., which has been widely used. An improved edition of it was edited by *Reusch*, 1757. A new manual edition after that of 1694, by *E. Preuss*, Berol. 1864. It was founded upon the "Einleitung in die Glaubenslehre," and some shorter doctrinal treatises, composed by *Johann Musæus* (who died 1681, at Jena).—Concerning the analytic method adopted by its author, see *Heinrich*, s. 548 ff. *Gass*, s. 353.

(17) As, e.g., the theologians of the school of St. Victor manifested a leaning towards mysticism, so *Johann Gerhard*, *Dannhauer*, and others, endeavoured to combine strict science with practical piety. On the scholasticism of the Lutheran divines in the seventeenth century, see *Tholuck*, Der Geist d. lutherischen Theologen, s. 246. On the necessary limitation of the notion of "Protestant Scholasticism," ibid. s. 55 ff. On the grandeur of the Protestant dogmatic system, see *Gass*, Gesch. d. prot. Dogmatik, s. 6 ff., who says that it was "*more profound than the theology of the Fathers of the Church, more*

true and consistent than that of the scholastics, and more scientifically developed and honestly outspoken than the theories of the Roman Church."

§ 217.

Lutheran Mysticism, Theosophy, and Asceticism.

Baur, Zur Geschichte der Protest. Mystik (in Zellers Jahrbücher, 1848, 4, 1849, 1). *Noack*, Die christliche Mystik seit dem Reformationszeitalter (see § 153). *Hamberger*, Stimmen aus dem Heiligthum d. christlichen Mystik und Theosophie, Stuttg. 1857. [*R. A. Vaughan*, Hours with the Mystics, 2d ed. 2 vols. 1860. *Heppe*, u.s.]

As the scholasticism of the Middle Ages had been counterbalanced by mysticism, so the new scholastic tendency of the Lutheran Church, during the present period, was accompanied by a mystical tendency, representing the deeper interests of practical religion. And further, as we had there to distinguish between the mysticism of the sects and orthodox mysticism (though its advocates spiritualized, and sometimes idealized, the doctrines of the Church, by internal interpretation), so here again we must distinctly separate these two tendencies as far as possible from each other. Even in the lifetime of Luther, *Andreas Carlstadt* (1), *Sebastian Frank* (2), and *Johann Caspar Schwenkfeld* (3), endeavoured, in a manner similar to that adopted by the prophets of Zwickau, and the Anabaptists (4), to break up the rigid adherence to the letter of Scripture, opposing to it a fantastic idealism, and a spiritualizing theology running over into pantheism. In later times, the mystico-theosophic writings of *Theophrastus Paracelsus* (5), *Valentin Weigel* (6), and *Jakob Böhm* (7), on the one hand, exerted a quickening influence; yet, on the other, they perplexed the minds of the people, and endangered the unity of the Church. On the contrary, the more considerate *Johann Arnd* (8), and his followers (9), sought to introduce "*True Christianity*" into all the relations of life, and to revive, by means of godly sentiments and pious exercises, the spirit of true religion, which had been buried under a load of scholastic definitions. *J. Gottfried Arnold* was induced, by his preference for mysticism, to undertake the defence of the heretical sects against the sentence which the orthodox passed upon them (10).

(1) On *Carlstadt*, see *Göbel*, Andreas Bodenstein von Carlstadt nach seinem Charakter und Verhältniss zu Luther (Studien und Kritiken, 1841, s. 88 ff.). *Erbkam*, Geschichte der Protestantischen Secten im Zeitalter der Reformation, Hamb. 1848, s. 174 ff. *C. F. Jäger*, Andreas Bodenstein von Carlstadt, Stuttg. 1856. *Baur* in Zellers Jahrb. 1848, s. 481 ff. (Carlstadt belongs to this class only in part, for he held more strictly than the rest of the mystics to the letter of Scripture.)

(2) *Sebastian Frank* was born at Donauwörth in the beginning of the sixteenth century; died in 1545. *His chief works are:* Weltbuch — Zeitbuch — Encomium Moriæ — Sprüchwörter—Paradoxa. Compare *Wackernagel*, Proben deutscher Prosa, i. s. 319 ff. *K. Hagen*, Geist der Reformation und seiner Gegensätze, ii. s. 314 ff. *Schenkel*, Wesen des Protest. i. s. 136 ff. *Erbkam*, l.c. s. 286 ff. *Baur*, l.c. s. 490 ff. "*It is only in the most recent times that the originality of Sebastian Frank has been particularly recognized, and that a place has been assigned him among those men, in whose varying tendencies are found the elements that determine the character of the period of the Reformation.*"

(3) *Schwenkfeld* was born A.D. 1490, at Ossigk, in Silesia, and died 1561. (Luther called him Stenkfeld.) Concerning Schwenkfeld and his friend *Valentin Krautwalt*, see *Planck*, v. 1, s. 89 ff., and compare Special History of Doctrines. See also *G. L. Hahn*, Schwenkfeldii Sententia de Christi Persona et Opere Exposita, Vratislav. 1847. *Erbkam*, s. 357 ff., and in *Herzog's* Realenc. xiv. s. 130. *Baur*, s. 502 ff. "*With Schwenkfeld we come first into the real sphere of Protestant mysticism; he, if any one of the earlier time, is the representative of the Protestant, and especially of the Protestant-Lutheran, mysticism.*"

(4) See below, § 233. *Erbkam*, l.c. 479 ff.

(5) His proper name was *Philippus Aureolus Theophrastus Bombastus Paracelsus von Hohenheim;* he was a native of

Switzerland, and died A.D. 1541. His *works* were published at Basel, 1589 ff., 11 vols. 4to. Compare *H. A. Preu*, Die Theologie des Theophrastus Paracelsus, Berlin 1839. *M. Carrière*, Philosophische Weltanschauung der Reformationszeit, Stuttg. 1847.

(6) *Weigel* was born A.D. 1533, at Hayn, in Misnia, and died 1588, at Tschopau, where he was pastor. His *writings* were not published till after his death; viz. Güldener Griff, d. i. alle Dinge ohne Irrthum zu erkennen, 1616. Erkenne dich selbst, 1618. Kirchen- und Hauspostill, 1618.—Comp. *Arnolds* Kirchen- und Ketzerhistorie, Thl. ii. Bd. 17, c. 17. *Walch*, Einleitung in Die Religions-Streitigkeiten, iv. s. 1024–1065. *Planck*, Geschichte der protestantischen Theologie, s. 72 ff. *Hagenbach*, Vorlesungen über die Reformation, iii. s. 337 ff. *H. Schmidt* in *Herzog's* Realenc. xvii. s. 577.

(7) *Böhm* was born A.D. 1575, at Altseidenburg, in Upper Lausatia, and lived at Görlitz, where he was a shoemaker; died 1620. His *writings* were edited by *Gichtel* (Amst. 1682, 1730, 6 vols.); *Schiebler*, Leipz. 1831, 6 vols., and Stuttg. 1835 ff., 4 vols.; in the Amst. edition, his life by *Albert von Franckenberg*. Comp. *Wullen, Böhme's Leben und Lehre, Stuttg. 1836. By the *same*: Blüthen aus J. Böhme's Mystik, Stuttg. 1838. *A. E. Umbreit*, Jacob Böhme, Heidelberg 1835. *Baur*, Gnosis, s. 558 ff. *Hagenbach*, Vorlesung. über die Reform. l.c. s. 345 ff. *Baur* in Zellers Jahrb. 1850, i. s. 85 ff. *Hamberger*, Die Lehre des deutschen Philosophen J. Böhme, München 1844. *Carrière*, l.c. s. 609 ff. *Tholuck* in Zeitschrift f. Christl. Wissenschaft u. Christ. Leben, 1852, Nr. 25 ff. *Auberlen* in *Herzog's* Realenc. ii. s. 265 ff.

(8) *Arnd* was born A.D. 1555, at Ballenstädt, in the duchy of Anhalt, suffered much from persecution, filled the office of superintendent in Celle, and died 1621. *He wrote*: Vier Bücher vom wahren Christenthum, 1605, often reprinted (criticized unfavourably by Lucas Osiander)—Paradiesgärtlein voll christlicher Tugenden — Evangelienpostille, and other works. Comp. *Freheri* Theatr. Viror. Eruditione Claror. p. 409. *Tschirners* Memorabilien, iii. 1, Leipz. 1812. *Hagenbach*, Vorlesungen, l.c. s. 371 ff. *M. Göbel*, Gesch. des christl. Lebens in der rheinisch-westphäl. evang. Kirche, Coblenz 1852, ii. s. 464 ff. *H. L. Pertz*, De Johanne Arndio,

Hanov. 1852, 4to. *Tholuck* in *Herzog's* Realenc. j. s. 536; and Lebenszeugen der lutherischen Kirche, Berlin 1859, s. 261 ff.

(9) *Joach. Lütkemann, Heinr. Müller, Christian Scriver*, and others. The better class of preachers, and especially the authors of spiritual songs, exerted also a living influence upon the belief of the people. Comp. *Hagenbach*, Vorlesungen, s. 163 ff.

(10) *Arnold* was born A.D. 1665, at Annaberg, and died 1714, at Perleberg, where he was a pastor.—*He wrote:* Unparteiische Kirchen- und Ketzerhistorie, Frankf. 1699, fol.; Schaffh. 1740 ff., 3 Thle. fol.—Wahre Abbildung des inwendigen Christenthums—Erste Liebe—Geistliche Erfahrungslehre, and several other treatises. See *Gobel*, l.c. s. 698 ff.

Lutheran mysticism degenerated especially in the case of *Quirinus Kuhlmann* (1651-1689), *Joh. Georg Gichtel* (1638-1710), and his fellow-labourers. *Breckling, Ueberfeldt*, etc. Compare *Hagenbach*, Vorlesungen, iv. s. 325 ff. These enthusiasts are of only negative value for the History of Doctrines.

§ 218.

Reforming Tendencies. Johann Valentin Andreä, Calist, Spener, Thomasius.

Not, however, mysticism alone, but also the sound common sense (*bon sens*) of mankind, threw off the fetters of the theology of the schools, and united with those of a more pious tendency for the purpose of regenerating the Church. *Johann Valentin Andreä* combated with the weapons of satire, and yet with the deepest earnestness, the corruptions both of the schools and of the mysticism of his age (1). *Georg Calist*, guided by a spirit of Christian moderation, endeavoured to reduce the doctrines necessary to salvation to the contents of the Apostles' Creed, and thus by degrees to effect a union of the divided confessions, but exposed himself, in consequence, to the charge of *Syncretism* (2). The influence which he exerted upon his age was less positive than that of *Philipp Jakob Spener*, whose sermons, writings, and life were in this respect of great importance (3). Proceeding from the central point of Christian experience, and resting on the basis of scriptural truth which he had practically studied, he equally avoided scholastic subtlety and theosophic fancifulness, and was animated by the pure and glowing mysticism of the heart alone. He, as well as his followers (the Pietists), were at first attacked with rage and scorn, but nevertheless imparted a most beneficial impulse to their age. He was upheld by the jurist *Christian Thomasius*, who assisted in preparing the more enlightened culture of a new century, rather, however, by his scientific and political attainments, than by profound and original views in theology (4).

(1) *Valentin Andreä* was the nephew of Jakob Andreä (who was one of the authors of the Formula Concordiæ). He died A.D. 1654. On his life, as well as on the sect of the Rosicrucians, who stand in close connection with the history of mysticism, see *Hossbach*, Val. Andreä und sein Zeitalter, Berlin 1819 ; also Vita ab ipso conscripta, Berol. 1849 [ed. *F. H. Rheinwald*].

(2) *Calixt* was born A.D. 1586, in the duchy of Holstein, and was professor of theology in the University of Helmstädt. His *works* are mentioned § 216, note 9. Compare **Henke*, Calixts Briefe, Halle 1832. By the *same*, Die Univ. Helmstädt im 16 Jahrh., Halle 1833. *Planck*, Geschichte der protestantischen Theologie, s. 90 ff. *G. W. Gass*, Georg Calixt und der Synkretismus, Breslau 1846. *Hainr. Schmid*, Geschichte der synkretistischen Streitigkeiten in der Zeit des Georg Calixt, Erlang. 1846. *Gass* says, " *Calixt, to a certain extent, wished to maintain a Lutheran Protestantism, but not a Protestant Lutheranism; he sought Protestantism in Lutheranism, but not the converse,*" Gesch. d. Prot. Dogmatik, s. 308.

(3) *Spener* was born A.D. 1635, at Rappoldsweiler, in Alsatia. Strassburg, Frankfurt, Dresden, and Berlin were successively the scenes of his labours. He was prebendary of Coln on the Spree, and died 1705. *He wrote :* Das geistliche Priesterthum, Frankfurt 1677, and other editions. — Pia Desideria, Francof. 1678.—Theol. Bedenken, Halle 1700 ff., 4 vols.—Consilia et Judicia Theol., Francof. 1709, 3 vols. 4to.

—Letzte Theol. Bedenken, Halle 1721, 3 vols. 4to. Comp. *Hossbach*, Spener u. seine Zeit, Berlin 1827, 2 vols. (3d ed. 1853). *Aug. Herm. Francke* co-operated with Spener, exerting an influence rather on Christian life than on doctrine. Nevertheless, the pietistic tendency is of importance in the History of Doctrines, formally, because it was indifferent to all scholastic definitions; materially, because it laid great stress upon the doctrines concerning sin, repentance, etc.; and lastly, on account of the peculiar colouring which it gave to the theology of the evangelical Church. The diligent study of the Bible, which was insisted on, could not but produce good fruit. See *C. F. Illgen*, Historia Collegii philobiblici, Lips. 1836–1840, 3 Progr.

(4) He died A.D. 1728. Comp. *Luden*, Thomasius nach seinen Schicksalen und Schriften, Berlin 1805. *Tholuck* in *Herzog's* Realenc. xvi. s. 88 ff.

II. THE REFORMED CHURCH.

§ 219.

Zwingli and Calvin.

Handeshagen, Die Conflicte des Zwinglianismus, Lutheranismus, und Calvinismus in der Bernischen Landeskirche, Bern 1842. *Al. Schweizer*, Die Glaubenslehre der Reform. Kirche dargestellt und aus den Quellen belegt, Zürich 1844–1847, 2 vols. *The same*, Nachwort zur Glaubenslehre (in Zellers Jahrb. 1848, 1 ff.). *Baur*, Ueber Princip und Charakter des Lehrbegriffs der Ref. Kirche (in Zellers Jahrb. 1847, 3, s. 309 ff.). *Schneckenburger*, Die Reform. Dogmatik mit Rücksicht auf Schweizers Glaubensl. (in die Stud. und Kritiken, 1848, 1 and 3 Heft). *The same*, Die neueren Verhandlungen, betreffend das Princip des Ref. Lehrbegriffs (in Zellers Jahrb. 1848, 1). *Ebrard*, Vindiciæ Theol. Reform., Erlangen 1848. *Al. Schweizer*, Die Synthese des Determinismus und der Freiheit in der Reform. Dogmatik (against Ebrard; in Zellers Jahrb. 1849, 2). *Ebrard*, Das Verhältniss der Ref. Dogmatik zum Determinismus, Zürich 1849. *Zeller*, Das Theologische System Zwingli's (Tubing. Jahrb. 1853, 1). *Ch. Sigwart*, Ulrich Zwingli, Stuttg. 1855. *Spörri*, Zwingli-Studien, Lpz. 1866; *Sam. Cramer*, Zwinglii Leer van het gottsdienstig geloof, Middelburg 1866. *J. C. Scholten*, Die Lehre der ref. Kirche nach ihren Grundsatzen aus den Quellen dargestellt, 3 Aufl. Lpz. 1855. (Comp. § 223.)

In the Swiss cities of Glarus and Einsiedeln first, and then permanently in Zürich, *Ulrich Zwingli* preached the pure evangelical doctrine, and combated the abuses of the papacy, independently of Luther (1). In consequence of a difference of opinion respecting the doctrine of the Lord's Supper (2), which manifested itself as soon as Luther's views became known in Switzerland, Zwingli and the other Swiss Reformers were compelled to take their own course; and a Church was formed, alongside of the Lutheran, based on peculiarities of its own, in respect to doctrinal matters, as well as in its constitution and mode of worship (3), called, by way of distinction the Reformed Church, although it did not receive this appellation until a later period (4). Zwingli himself propounded the principles of pure evangelical faith in several writings, which formed the beginning of a systematic theology of the Reformed Church (5). But it was reserved for the French Reformer, *John Calvin* (6), after the death of Zwingli, to compose the work entitled *Institutio Religionis Christianæ*, in which those principles were set forth in a system more comprehensive, connected, and orderly than the Loci of Melanchthon (7).

(1) He was born Jan. 1, A.D. 1484, at Wildhaus, in Toggenburg. On his life, compare the biographies composed by *Oswald Myconius, Nüscheler, Hess, Schuler, Hottinger, Röder*, and *Christoffel, Huldreich Zwingli's Leben und ausgewählte Schriften, Elberfeld 1857 [transl. by *John Cochrane*, Edin. 1858. *Hess's* Life, transl. by *Lucy Aikin*, Lond. 1812]. His *works* were edited by *Gualther*, Tig. 1545 ss., 1581, 4 vols. fol., and by *Schuler and *Schulthess*, Zwingli's Werke, vols. i. and ii. in German, vols. iii. to vii. in Latin.—*Leading historical points in the Swiss Reformation during its first period:* 1. Disputation at Zürich (Jan. 29, A.D. 1523).—Zwingli's interpretation of the articles, and his reasons.—2. Disputation (Oct. 26–28). Zwingli's treatise entitled Christenliche Ynleitung. —Decree of the magistracy respecting images, the mass, etc. —Final establishment of the Reformation at Zürich. Disputation at Baden (1526), at Bern (1528).—The Reformation of Bern (*Bernard Haller, Sebastian Meier*, and others).— The Reformation of Basel (1529, *Oecolampadius*). The war of Kappel.—The death of Zwingli, Oct. 11, 1531.—For further

particulars, see *Bullinger*, Reformationsgeschichte herausgeg. von Hottinger and Vögeli, Frauenf. 1838, 3 vols. *J. J. Hottinger*, Evangelische Kirchengeschichte, Zürich 1708 ff., 4 vols. (A new edition by *Wirz-Kirchofer* was published, Zürich 1813–1819.) *Johannes von Müller*, Geschichte der schweizerischen Eidgenossenschaft, fortgesetzt von *J. J. Hottinger*, vols. vi. and vii. Comp. *Gieseler*, iii. 1, s. 5–7. The more recent writings on this period, by *Göbel, Lange, Gaupp, Herzog, Meyer*, reviewed by *Ullmann* in the Studien und Kritiken, 1843, s. 759 ff. The special characteristics of *Spörri* (see lit.) consist in clear observations and studies; but his work, on the whole, is too largely influenced by speculative assumptions.

(2) See the Special History of Doctrines (on the Lord's Supper).

(3) Theologians are still divided on the question as to what constitutes the peculiarity of the Reformed Church; see § 212, note 3, and the works there referred to. According to *Schweizer*, the principle of the Reformed theology, running through all its doctrinal statements, is to be sought in the attempt to derive all salvation, and all that leads to it, absolutely from God alone (not from anything created); with which, too, is connected the stronger emphasis laid on Holy Scripture, and the closer relation in which the law is made to stand to the gospel (opposition to all heathenizing, see above, § 212). *Baur* sought for this peculiarity in the absoluteness of God. *Schneckenburger* especially urges the Christological element, as the Reformed theology makes the historical side more prominent, and the Lutheran the speculative aspect of Christology (see his Christologie, s. 189, note). However it may be with these statements, it is at least certain that the differences, which it is the office of dogmatic science to search out, are entirely subordinate in comparison with the essential and thoroughgoing opposition between Catholicism and Protestantism; and it would only impede the healthful growth of Protestantism, if the undeniable difference should be so exaggerated as to make out an irreconcilable antagonism among Protestants themselves.—While formerly the exact distinction between the Lutheran and Reformed systems was hardly stated, dogmatic acumen is

now in danger of degenerating into subtle refinements. The times recommend holding to that in which there is agreement. On the shaping of the Reformed theology in distinction from the Lutheran, see *Gass*, s. 82 ff.

(4) Luther and the Lutherans called them Sacramentarians, enthusiasts, etc. (afterwards Calvinists). It was in France that the name " religion prétendue reformée " took its rise.

(5) In addition to the polemical writings, sermons, letters, etc., of *Zwingli*, we may mention as bearing upon systematic theology: Commentarius de Vera et Falsa Religione (it was addressed to Francis I.), Tigur. 1525.—Fidei Ratio, ad Carol. Imp., Tig. 1530, 4to.—Christianae Fidei brevis et clara Expositio, ad Regem christ. (ed. *Bullinger*), Tig. 1536. On Zwingli's importance as a systematic theologian, see the works of *Zeller, Sigwart, Spörri, Cramer*, referred to, also *Gass*, s. 91. It should not be forgotten, as *Spörri* remarks (s. 22), that Zwingli "*was taken away at a time when his thoughts were far from being thoroughly matured and developed in depth and width. . . . Zwingli had first lighted up only those portions* (of the building) *in which old illusions lay immediately in the way of practical needs; along with the clear consequences of his fundamental principles there appear also, here and there, the windings of the old doctrinal system.* The characteristic of the man, however, is without question to be sought where real individual laborious thought is to be recognized."

(6) He was born at Noyon, in Picardy, July 10, A.D. 1509, and died at Geneva, May 27, 1564. Concerning his life, see *Henry, Leben Calvins, Hamb. 1835–1844, 3 vols., translated by *Stebbing*. The same, An abridgment. *Bungener*, Vie de Calvin, var. edd. French and English. *Bretschneider*, Bildung und Geist Calvins und der Genfer Kirche (Reformations-Almanack, 1821). *Ernst Stähelin, Joh. Calvin, Leben u. ausgewählte Schriften, Elberfeld 1863, 2 vols. O. F. *Fritzsche*, Gedächtnissrede auf J. Calvin, Zürich 1864. †*Audin*, var. edd. French and English.

(7) Christianae Religionis Institutio, totam fere pietatis summam, et quicquid est in doctrina salutis cognitu necessarium, complectens; omnibus pietatis studiosis lectu dignissimum opus (with a preface to Francis I.). It was composed at Basel, A.D. 1535. Only the edition of 1536 (published in

Basel by Thomas Plater) is undoubtedly the first; the theory of an earlier edition in 1535, written in French (see *Henry*, i. s. 102 ff.), having been proved untenable.—The edition of Basel was followed by those of Strassburg slightly altered (published by *Rihelius*), 1539 (some copies under the name *Alcuinus*), 1543, 1545, and Geneva, 1550, 1553, 1554.—An entirely new edition appeared, 1559, at Geneva (published by *Robert Stephanus*), from which the following editions were reprinted:—A Latin manual edition by *Tholuck*, ed. 2, Berol. 1846. A German translation by *Krummacher*, Elberf. 1823. A complete critical edition of the Institutio, followed by the other works of Calvin, is that of the Strassburg professors, *Baum*, *Cunitz*, and *Reuss:* *Corpus Reformatorum*, vols. i.–xiv. and xxix.–xlii., Brunsv. 1863–1877. Of the Institutio there are the following edd.: (1) Editio Princeps, 1536; (2) Editiones annorum, 1539–1554; (3) Editio postrema, 1559; (4) Institution de la religion chrétienne, nouvelle edition critique, 1865. Comp. Henry, l.c. s. 286 ff., and the opinions of *Bretschneider* and *Krummacher*, which he cites. The German translation of *Bretschneider* appeared 1823, at Elberfeld.—In addition to his Institutio, Calvin composed many other doctrinal and exegetical works, which will be mentioned in the Special History of Doctrines.—The complete works of Calvin were published, Geneva 1617, 12 vols. fol., Amst. 1671 (1677), 9 vols. fol. Comp. also the Anecdota edited by *Bretschneider*, Lips. 1835 (from the library of Gotha). See *Gass*, i. s. 99 ff. [English translations published by the Calvin Translation Society.] On the characteristics of the theology of Calvin, see *Stähelin*, l.c., Bd. ii. s. 414 ff. If Zwingli's system remained imperfect, Calvin had, on the other hand, closed his principal doctrinal points very early. "*This is shown by his steady but early development, and his logical, systematic acuteness, which proceeded without wavering from the foundation which he had laid. We conclude that Calvin was as one born late, who could more easily reduce to unity the elements provided by the Reformation, and who needed only (?) the work of completion and arrangement*" (*Fritzsche*, l.c. s. 8).

§ 220.

The Symbolical Books of the Reformed Church.

Compare the collections mentioned vol. i. § 13. [The collections of *Augusti*, 1828; *Moss*, 1839; *Niemeyer*, 1840; Sylloge Confess., Oxon. 1827; *G. B. Winer*, Comparative Darstellung, ed. by *Preuss*, Berlin. Eng. trans. in For. Theol. Lib., Edinr.]

The different mode of development of the Reformed Church on the one side, and of the Lutheran Reformation in Germany on the other (1), accounts for the difference in the character of their symbolical writings. In the case of the Reformed Church they were less complete in themselves, being at first restricted to confessions of faith drawn up by individuals, or in separate localities, and only by degrees coming into general use as representations of the doctrines held by the Church. Nor should we overlook the evident difference between the characters of Zwingli and Calvin (2). Hence, in forming a more precise estimate of the doctrines, it is important to make a distinction between those symbolical writings which were composed *before*, and those *after*, the influence of Calvin was felt (3). From what has already been said, it follows that we are not to expect a definitely limited number of Calvinistic symbolical writings, inasmuch as only some of them acquired general authority in the Reformed Church, though not all in the same degree; while the importance of others was limited to certain localities (4), or to individuals (5), or to certain periods, at the expiration of which they lost their significance (6).

(1) Compare *Hagenbach*, Ueber Wesen und Geschichte der Reformation, 17 Vorles. *Schweizer*, l.c. i. s. 7 ff.

(2) As regards his personal character, Zwingli probably had far more of Luther in him than Calvin, while the latter is rather to be compared with Melanchthon (at least as regards his scientific attainments and writings). Yet we must not exaggerate the doctrinal differences between Calvin and Zwingli (see the Special History of Doctrines). They touch in essential points.

(3) Compare *Winer*, s. 18 and 19.

(4) *E.g.* the First Confession of Basel. Nor were the Confessions of different countries (such as the Gallicana, Anglicana, Scotica, Belgica, Marchica, etc.), in the first instance, adopted by any but the Protestants of the respective countries, though the principles contained in them were tacitly recognised in other Protestant countries, and sometimes signed by their representatives.

(5) This was the case with the Fidei Ratio of Zwingli mentioned above, as well as with his Clara et Brevis Expositio; comp. *Winer*, s. 18. On the other hand, the private confession of *Bullinger* obtained such authority as to become the second Confessio Helvetica; the private confession of *Guido de Bres* stood in the same relation to the Confessio Belgica. See § 222, notes 4 and 9.

(6) Thus the Confessio Tetrapolitana, which fell into oblivion, the second Confessio of Basel (the first Confessio Helvetica, 1536), the Formula Consensus, and several others; see the subsequent sections.

§ 221.

(a) *Symbolical Writings prior to the Time of Calvin.*

* *Escher* in the Encyklop. of Ersch and Gruber, 2d Sect. Bd. v. s. 223 ff.

As early as the Diet of Augsburg, the four cities of *Strassburg, Constance, Memmingen,* and *Lindau,* in Upper Germany, which were favourably disposed to the doctrines of Zwingli, presented a separate confession of faith, which is on that account called *Confessio Tetrapolitana* (or sometimes Conf. Argentinensis, Suevica) (1); and Zwingli also presented a statement of his faith to the Emperor Charles v. The Church of Basel gave (A.D. 1534) the first public testimony of its evangelical faith by the publication of a creed, which was also adopted in Mühlhausen (Confessio Basileensis I., Mülhusana) (2). The continuance of the sacramentarian controversy, and the efforts made by Bucer and others to restore peace, gave rise to the *Second Confession of Basel*, or the *First Helvetic Confession*, which was drawn up A.D. 1536, signed by various Swiss cities, and transmitted to the Lutheran theologians then assembled at Schmalkalden (3).

(1) It was drawn up by *M. Bucer*, and published A.D. 1531, 4to, both in German and in Latin. German editions of it also appeared, Neustadt on the Hardt 1580, and Zweibrücken (Deux Ponts) 1604, 4to. It consists of twenty-three articles. The 18th article, concerning the Lord's Supper, differs *but little* from the Confessio Augustana (see the Special History of Doctrines). *Planck*, iii. 1, s. 83 ff. — The Latin text is given in the Corpus et Synt. i. p. (215 ss.) 173 ss., and by *Augusti*, p. 327. Comp. *Winer*, l.c., and *Wernsdorf*, Historia Confess. Tetrapol. Viteb. 1721, 4to. The four cities afterwards (1532), at the Schweinfurt Convention, subscribed the Augsburg Confession. See *Heppe*, Confessionelle Entwicklung, s. 72.

(2) "Bekanntnuss vnsres heyligen Christenlichen Gloubens wie es die kylch zu Basel haldt" (with the motto: Corde creditur ad justitiam, ore autem fit confessio ad salutem, Rom. x.), in twelve articles; it was founded upon a sketch drawn up by Oecolampadius (see *Hagenbach*, Geschichte der Basler Confession, Basel 1827, Appendix A); the German copy of it is given, ibid. s. 37 ff., the Latin in Corpus et Synt. i. (93), 72 ss. *Augusti*, p. 103 ss.

(3) It was composed at a synod in Basel, 1536, by theologians deputed by the cities Zürich, Bern, Basel, Schaffhausen, St. Gallen, Mühlhausen, and Biel (drawn up by H. Bullinger, Oswald Myconius, Simon Grynæus, Leo Judæ, and Caspar Grosmann), with the assistance of Bucer and Capito, the delegates from Strassburg. — On the occasion and origin of this confession, see *Kirchofer, Oswald Myconius, Zürich 1813, s. 271–316. *Hess*, Lebensgeschichte M. Heinrich Bullingers, Bd. i. s. 199 ff., 217 ff. *Escher*, l.c. On the relation in which it stood to the First Confession of Basel, see *Hagenbach*, Geschichte der Basler Confession, s. 67.

§ 222.

(b) Symbolical Writings under the Influence of Calvin.

The Church of Geneva having been at first founded upon the basis of the Calvinistic doctrine, independently of the Church of Zürich, was brought into closer connection with it (A.D. 1549) by means of the *Consensus Tigurinus* (which had reference to the doctrine of the Lord's Supper) (1); while the doctrine of predestination, more fully developed by Calvin, was established in the *Consensus Genevensis* (A.D. 1552) (2). But it was not until Frederick III., Prince Elector of the Palatinate, had joined the Reformed Church, that symbols were adopted which bound the Churches more closely together. These were, on the one hand, the *Catechism of Heidelberg* (A.D. 1562), drawn up by *Caspar Olevianus* and *Zacharias Ursinus* (3); on the other, the *Second Helvetic Confession*, composed by Bullinger, and published at the request of the Prince Elector, A.D. 1566 (4). The principles contained in them are also set forth more or less distinctly in the other Reformed creeds, *e.g.* in the *Confessio Gallicana* (5), *Anglicana* (6), *Scoticana* (7), *Hungarica* (Czengerina) (8), *Belgica* (9), the *Confessio Sigismundi* (Brandenburgica, Marchica) (10), the *Catechismus Genevensis* (11), the *Declaratio Thoruncnsis* (12), etc. And lastly, the controversies carried on between the different sections of the Reformed Church (especially concerning the doctrine of predestination) (13), showed the necessity of symbolical definitions similar to those contained in the *Formula Concordiæ* of the Lutheran Church. Such were the *Decrees of the Synod of Dordrecht (Dort*, A.D. 1618) (14), and the *Formula Consensus*, drawn up in Switzerland (15).

(1) Consensio Mutua in Re Sacramentaria Ministror. Tigur. et J. Calvini, consisting of thirty-six articles, in *Calcini* Opp. viii. p. 648 ss., and in his Tract. Theolog. (Geneva 1611, Amst. 1667, fol.). It was separately printed, 1554, by R. Stephanus

(Etienne). *Winer*, s. 19. Comp. *Hess*, Leben Bullingers, ii. s. 15–20. *Henry*, Leben Calvins, ii. 473, note and appendix 18. "*Calvin's spirit showed itself in such a way in relation to the first Swiss type of theology, and to the German-Lutheran form, that he was able to develope the former, freeing it from what was rude and immature, without merging it in the latter,*" *Gass*, Gesch. d. Prot. Dogmatik, i. s. 126. *C. *Pestalozzi*, Heinrich Bullinger, Elberfeld 1858, s. 373 ff. - *Stähelin*, Calvin, ii. s. 112 ff.

(2) De æterna Dei Prædestinatione, qua in salutem alios ex hominibus elegit, alios suo exitio reliquit, it. de providentia, qua res humanas gubernat, Consensus pastorum Genevensis ecclesiæ, a J. Calvino expositus, Genev. 1552 (in Opp. vii. 688 ss., and in vol. viii. of the Dutch edition, p. 593 ss.; Tract. Theol. p. 688). On the (erroneous) statement of *Planck* and *Marheinecke*, that this Consensus had also been adopted by the citizens of Zürich, see *Escher*, l.c. *Hagenbach*, Geschichte der Basler Confess. s. 83. *Winer*, s. 19. *Henry*, ii. 1, s. 42.

(3) Its German title is: Christlicher Underricht, wie der in Kirchen und Schulen der churf. Pfalz getrieben wirdt (*i.e.* Christian instruction, as imparted in the churches and schools of the Palatinate). It was also called Catech. Palatinus, the Palatine Catechism. *Josua Lagus* and *Lambert Ludolph Pithopæus* translated it into Latin. An edition, which contained both the Latin and the German, appeared, Heidelberg 1563. In later times it was translated into almost all modern languages, and very frequently commented upon: *e.g.* by *Heinr. Alting*; see the edition of *E. A. Lewald*, Heidelb. 1841. It consists of three principal parts: 1. Of the misery of man resulting from sin; 2. Of redemption from that state; and 3. Of man's gratitude for that redemption. It is divided into 129 questions. (The 80th question concerning the Mass was omitted in many editions.) Comp. *Simon von Alpen*, Geschichte und Literatur des Heidelberg Katechismus, Frankf. a. M. 1810. *Rienäcker* (in the Allgem. Encykl. 2d sect. 4 Thl.). *Beckhaus* in Illgens Historische Zeitschrift, viii. 2, s. 39, and *Augusti* (see above, § 215). *Scisen*, Gesch. der Reformation in Heidelb., Heid. 1846. *Zyro*, Handbuch zum Heid. Kat., Bern 1848. *Sudhoff*, Der Heidelb. Kat., Creuznach 1851. *The same*, Fester Grund christ. Lehre, ein Hülfs-

buch zum Heidelb. Kat. (drawn up from the German writings of Caspar Olevianus, with dissertations by the author), Frankf. a. M. 1854. [*Niemeyer* gives both the German and the Latin form, s. 390–461. The Catechism was introduced in various parts of Switzerland (St. Gall, Zürich); in Hungary and Poland; in most of the German Reformed Churches; in the Netherlands, by the Synod of Wesel, 1688, of Dort, 1574 and 1618; in the Dutch Reformed and German Reformed Churches of America—of the latter it is the only symbolical book.] On *Olevianus* and *Ursinus*, see *Sudhoff*, C. Olevianus u. Z. Ursinus, Elberfeld 1857. *O. Thelemann*, Geschichte des Heid. Kat. u. seiner Verfasser, Erlangen 1863.

(4) Confessio Helvetica Posterior (it was also called: Confessio et Expositio brevis et simplex sincerae Religionis Christianae). At the request of Frederick III., Prince Elector of the Palatinate (1564), it was edited by *Bullinger*, first in Latin (1566), and afterwards in a German translation made by the author himself. It has been often republished: by *Kindler*, 1825, and by **O. F. Fritzsche*, Tur. 1839 (with Prolegomena). **Ed. Böhl*, Vindob. 1866. Compare *Escher*, l.c. It has thirty chapters. It was sanctioned not only in Switzerland,[1] but also in Germany (in the Palatinate) and Scotland, as well as by the Polish, Hungarian, and French Reformed Churches. It was translated into French by *Theodore Beza*, Geneva 1566, and by *Cellérier*, ibid. 1819.

(5) It consisted of forty articles. It was set forth and sanctioned, under the influence of the preacher *Chandieu*,[2] by the Synod of Paris, A.D. 1559; presented first to Francis II., A.D. 1560, and afterwards to Charles IX., at Poissy, by Beza, A.D. 1561; and confirmed by Henry IV. and his mother at the Synod of Rochelle, 1571. A Latin translation of it appeared, 1566 and 1581. (Comp. Corp. et Synt. i. p. (99) 77 ss.; *Augusti*, p. 110 ss.) A shorter confession in eighteen articles was handed in to Henry IV.; see *Henry*, Leben Calvins, iii. 1, s. 469, note. It is a different work from that which was published at Heidelberg, 1566, under the title: Confession

---

[1] Only in Basel it was not received until a later period; this delay was occasioned by the Crypto-Lutheran movements of *Sulzer*; see *Hagenbach* Gesch. d. Confess.

[2] He was not its author. See *Herzog* (Supp.), "Chandieu."

und Kurze Bekanntnuss des Glaubens der reformirten Kirchen in Frankreich (*i.e.* a Creed and short Confession of Faith adopted by the French Reformed Churches), which was intended to be given to Maximilian II., and the Estates of the German Empire on the day of election at Frankfurt. For further particulars, see Winer, s. 19.

(6) Commonly called the XXXIX. (at first XLII.) Articles, drawn up by *Cranmer* and *Ridley* in the reign of King Edward VI. (A.D. 1551), revised in the reign of Queen Elizabeth, and confirmed 1562 by a synod at London. They were originally published under the title: Articuli, de quibus convenit inter Archiepiscopos et Episcopos utriusque Provinciæ et Clerum universum in Synodo Londini anno 1562, secundum computationem Ecclesiæ Anglicanæ, ad tollendam opinionum dissensionem et consensum in vera rel. firmandum; editi auctoritate serenissimæ Reginæ, 1571: often reprinted. The English edition is given in the *Book of Common Prayer*, the Latin in Corp. et Synt. i. p. (125) 99 ss. *Augusti*, p. 126 ss. A *Church Catechism* was composed by *John Poinet* (1553), in four sections, by order of King Edward VI. Comp. *Winer*, s. 22. Bp. *H. Marsh*, Comparative View of the Churches of England and Rome, 1814, 1841. Germ. transl. by *F. Eichel*, Grimma 1848. [*Ch. Hardwick*, Hist. of Articles of Religion (documents from 1536 to 1615), new ed. 1859. *Burnet, Beveridge, Browne,* and *Forbes* on the XXXIX. Articles. *Strype's* Annals. *E. Cardwell*, Hist. of Conferences on Book of Prayer (1558–1690), var. edd. *The same*, Documentary Annals of Church of England, 1546–1716, 2 vols.; Formularies of Faith, put forth in the reign of Henry VIII., and Three Primers, put forth in the same reign; Collection of Articles, etc. Dean *Nowell's* Catechism, 1572, new ed. by *W. Jacobson*. *Wheatley*, Rational Illustration of Book of Common Prayer, 1720, 1846. *Thos. Lathbury*, Hist. of Book of Common Prayer. *The same*, History of Convocation. *Procter*, Book of Common Prayer, 1857 ff. *H. J. Blunt*, Annotated Book of Common Prayer. **E. Daniel*, Book of Common Prayer. — The Homilies of the Church of England, 1st Book, 1547; 2d Book, 1563; edited by Prof. *Corrie*, Camb. 1850. — *Gibson*, Codex Juris Ecclesiastici Anglicani, 2 vols. fol. 1761. — First Prayer Book, 1549; revised, 1552; XLII. Articles,

1552, 1553, by Cranmer, not adopted by Convocation—several of the articles from Augsb. Confession; XXXIX. Articles, 1552, by Abp. Parker, making use of Würtemberg Confession; altered to XXXVIII. in 1563; in 1571 restored to XXXIX., and made binding. The XXXIX. Articles were ratified by the Protestant Episcopal Church in the United States; the Book of Common Prayer, revised under direction of the First General Convocation, Phila. 1786 (omitting Nicene and Athanasian Creeds, absolution, baptismal regeneration, etc.), but nearly all restored (excepting the Athanasian Creed and absolution in visitation of the sick), in consequence of the objections of the English bishops. The Nic. Creed still omitted in Com. Service, when that follows Morning Prayer; but may be used instead of Ap. Creed in Morning Prayer.]

(7) It was published A.D. 1560, and consisted of twenty-five articles. Its principal author was the Scotch Reformer *John Knox* (his views on the doctrine of predestination were less Calvinistic than those on the Lord's Supper). Corpus et Syntagma, i. p. (137) 109 ss. *Augusti*, p. 143 ss. Another confession from the year 1581 is appended. Different is the Westminster Confession of Faith of 1643 (Cantabr. 1659; in English, Edinb. 1671). Comp. *Gemberg*, Schottische Nationalkirche, s. 11. *Winer*, l.c. See note below.

(8) It was drawn up at a Synod of the Hungarian Reformed Churches, A.D. 1557 or 1558, and consisted of eleven articles. *Schröckh*, Kirchengeschichte nach der Reformation, ii. s. 737. Corp. et Synt. i. p. (186) 148 ss., after the Debreczin edition, 1570. *Winer*, s. 20. *Augusti*, p. 241 ss.

(9) It was originally a private confession of *Guido de Bres*, and was first published A.D. 1562, in the Walloon language (it consisted of thirty-seven articles). It was soon after translated into Dutch, approved by the Dutch Churches, and even signed by several princes. It was solemnly confirmed by the Synod of Dort. It was edited by *Festus Hommius*, Lugd. Bat. 1618, 4to, and several times subsequently. See *Augusti*, p. 170 ss. Comp. *Bartels*, Die Prädestinationslehre in der ref. Kirche von Ostfriesland bis zur Dordrechter Synode (Jahrb. für deutsche Theol. 1860, 2).

(10) Its original title was: Des hochgebornen Fürsten Joh.

Siegmund, etc., Bekänndniss von jetzigen unter den Evangelischen schwebenden und in Streit gezogenen Punkten, etc. (*i.e.* the Confession of the illustrious Prince John Sigismund, etc., concerning those points respecting which Protestants are now at issue). It consisted of sixteen articles. It is not to be confounded with the confession of faith adopted by the Reformed Evangelical Churches of Germany, which was published at Frankfurt on the Oder, 1614, by order of the same prince. For further particulars, see *Winer*, s. 21. It is reprinted by *Augusti*, p. 369 ss.

(11) It was composed by *Calvin*, and appeared 1541 in a French edition, and 1545 in a Latin one. It consists of four principal parts (Faith, Law, Prayer, and Sacraments). *Calvini* Opera t. viii. (Dutch ed.) p. 11 ss. *Winer*, s. 22. *Augusti*, p. 460 ss. *Stähelin*, Calvin, i. s. 124 ff., and chap. v. of *Sudhoff's* Ursinus u. Olevianus. [*Calvin* drew up a Catechism in 1536, published in Latin 1538.]

(12) Adopted by a General Synod in Poland, convened for pacification, under Vladislas IV., in Thorn 1645, it came to be very generally received in a considerable portion of the Reformed Church of Eastern Europe.

(13) See the Special History of Doctrines (on predestination).

(14) It lasted from Nov. 13, A.D. 1618, to May 9, A.D. 1619, and held 145 sessions. Its decrees, etc., were published in the Acta Synodi Nationalis, etc., Dordr. 1620, 4to. [In *Niemeyer*, p. 690–728. In English, in Appendix to Constitution of the Reformed Dutch Church, p. 60–75. Acts of the Synod of Dort, Lond. 1620, fol.]

(15) It was directed, in the first instance, against the theory of the universality of grace, advocated in the Academy of Saumur (comp. § 225, note 3), and was instigated chiefly by *Heinrich Heidegger* of Zürich, *Francis Turretin* of Geneva, and *Lucas Geraler* of Basel. The draft was drawn up by *Heidegger* under the title: Formula Consensus Ecclesiarum Helveticarum Reformatarum circa doctrinam de gratia universali, et connexa, aliaque nonnulla capita. It consists of twenty-six articles. As to its history, and the controversies to which it gave rise, as well as concerning its final abolition (by the intervention of Prussia and England, A.D. 1723), see *C. M.*

Pfaff, Schediasma de Form. Consens. Helvet., Tub. 1723, 4to. J. J. *Hottinger*, Succincta ac Genuina Formulæ Consensus Helv. Historia (in the Bibl. Brem. vii. p. 669 ss. It was separately published, Zur. 1723). Mémoires pour servir à l'histoire des troubles arrivées en Suisse à l'occasion du Consensus, Amst. 1726 (by *Barnaud*, pastor at La Tour, near Vevay). *Leonh. Meister*, Helvet. Scenen der neuern Schwärmeri und Intoleranz, Zürich 1785, s. 3 ff. *Escher* in the Allgem. Encykl. l.c. s. 243 ff. *Alex. Schweizer*, Die theologisch-ethischen Zustände (§ 223, note 21), s. 35 ff. The form of subscription stood thus : "Sic sentio, sic profiteor, sic docebo, et contrarium non docebo."

<small>Among the symbols of the Reformed Church are further enumerated : the Confessiones *Polonicæ*.—1. Consensus Sendomiriensis, 1570. 2. Thoruniensis Synodi generalis, A.D. 1595, d. 21. Aug. celebratæ canones. Confessio *Bohemica*, 1535 (1558). Colloquium Lipsiacum, 1631. Declaratio Thoruniensis, 1645. (They are all reprinted in the works of *Augusti* and *Niemeyer*, who also give all necessary historical information.)—On the symbols of the Puritans, see *G. A. Niemeyer*, Collectionis Confessionum in Ecclesiis Reformatis publicatarum, Appendix, Lips. 1840. Conf. Westmonasteriensis (1659, 1660, 1664), and the two Catechisms (1648). Hallische Literatur Zeitung, Jan. 1841.

[The *Westminster Assembly*, convened by order of Parliament, 1643, consisting of 151 members. The Confession was presented to the Commons, Dec. 11, 1646 ; Shorter Catechism, Nov. 5, 1647 ; Larger Catechism, April 5, 1648. The General Assembly of Scotland ratified the Confession, Aug. 27, 1647, and the Catechism, July 1648. The Synod of Cambridge, New England, adopted the Confession in 1648. The *Savoy Confession*, drawn up by the Independents, 1658, is, in its doctrinal parts, nearly identical with the Westminster ; a Boston Synod, 1680, adopted this Confession ; in 1708 it was adopted at Saybrook, for the Connecticut Churches.]</small>

§ 223.

The Systematic Theology of the Reformed Church.

<small>On the literature, compare § 216 and 219. *Al. Schweizer*, Reformirte Glaubenslehre (Introduction), and his *Protestant. Centraldogmen, Zürich 1854–1856. *Ebrard*, Dogmatik, i. s. 62 ff. *Gass*, ubi supra. *Heppe*, Dogmatik des Deutschen Protest. Bd. i. s. 139–204, Entstehung und Ausbildung der deutsch-reformirt Dogmatik. *Hagenbach's* Leben und ausgewählte Schriften der Väter und Begründer der reformirt Kirche, IX. Bande.</small>

Systematic theology was on the whole less cultivated in the Reformed Church than exegesis, though it was not kept in the background. In addition to the labours of Zwingli and Calvin (§ 219), many of their followers,[1] such as *Heinr. Bullinger* (1), *Andr. Gerh. Hyperius* (2), *Wolfgang Musculus* (3), *Ben. Aretius* (4), *Wilh. Bucanus* (5), *Theodore Beza* (6), *Petrus Ramus* (7), *Daniel Chamier* (8), and others, wrote compendiums of dogmatic theology. The scholastic method, too, soon found its way into the Reformed Church, as the representatives of which we may mention *Bartholomäus Keckermann* (9), *Amandus Polanus a Polansdorf* (10), *J. H. Alsted* (11), *John Sharp* (12), *Johann Wollebius* (13), *Heinrich Alting* (14), *Johann Maccovius* (15), *Gisbert Voëtius* (16), *Marcus Friedrich Wendelin* (17), *Johann Hoornbeek* (18), *Samuel Maresius* (19), *Andreas Rivetus* (20), and, pre-eminently, *Johann Heinrich Heidegger* (21). A peculiar theological system, in the so-called federal method, was inaugurated by *J. Coccius* (22), and more fully developed by his followers, the most eminent of whom were *Franz Burrmann* (23), *Abraham Heidanus* (24), *Hermann Witsius* (25). *Melchior Leydecker*, on the other hand, treated the whole system of theology in the order of the three persons of the Trinity (26). Others, again, adopted other methods (27).

(1) *Bullinger* was born A.D. 1504, and died 1575. See *Hess*, Lebensgeschichte Heinrich Bullingers, 2 vols. 1828, 1829.—*He wrote:* Compend. Rel. Christ. e puro Dei Verbo depromtum, Basil. 1556. Concerning the part which he took in the composition of various confessions of faith, see the preceding section. [See *Schenkel* in Herzog's Realencyklop. s.v. *Bullinger*.] Leben, by *C. Pestalozzi*, Elberfeld 1858 (5th Part of the "Väter u. Begründer ref. Kirche"), where see also

---

[1] [*Peter Martyr Vermilius, Bucer, Capito, Oecolampadius, Pictet*, and *Myconius* also deserve mention as helping to give shape to the Reformed system. *Peter Martyr*, an Italian, taught in Strassburg, Oxford, and Zürich; died 1562. His Loci Communes were published (ed. *Gualter*), Zürich 1580, 1626; Heidelb. 1622. *Bucer* (Butzer, Mart.), born 1491, taught in Strassburg, in England 1549, died 1551. No complete edition of his works. See *Schenkel* in *Herzog's* Encykl. —*Capito* (Köpfel), born 1478, also in Strassburg, died 1541. See *Hagenbach* in *Herzog's* Encykl. —Of *Oecolampadius* and *Myconius, Hagenbach* has written the lives in his Leben d. Väter d. reform. Kirche.]

his Dogmatisches Handbuch in outline, s. 505 ff. Comp. s. 386 and 469.

(2) *Hyperius* was born A.D. 1511, at Ypres, and died 1564, as professor of theology in the University of Marburg. His theological works are: Methodi Theologiæ sive præcipuorum Christ. Rel. Locorum Communium, libb. iii. Basil. 1568. Varia Opuscula Theol. ibid. 1570, 1571. Comp. *Semler's* Einleitung zu *Baumgarten's* Glaubenslehre, s. 46 ff. *Heinrich*, s. 293 ff. *Heppe*, s. 144 ff. *Gass*, s. 131.

(3) His proper name was Müslin, or Mösel. He was born A.D. 1497, in Lotharingia (Lorraine, Lothringen), and died 1563, as professor of theology in the University of Bern. He is the *author* of: Loci Communes Theol., Bern. 1573. (Opp. Basil. 9 vols. fol.) *Semler*, l.c. s. 56, note 28. *Gass*, s. 131.

(4) *Aretius* died A.D. 1574, as professor of theology in the University of Bern; was previously professor in Marburg. *He wrote:* Theologica Problemata sive Loci Communes, Bern. 1604. See *Semler*, l.c. s. 54, note 26. *Heinrich*, s. 296. *Gass*, s. 132.

(5) *Bucanus* was professor of theology in the University of Lausanne towards the commencement of the seventeenth century, and *wrote:* Institutt. Theol., etc., Brem. 1604, Genev. 1612.

(6) *Beza* was born A.D. 1519, at Vécelay, and died 1605. (Compare his biography by *Schlosser*, Heidelb. 1809; *Baum*, 1843, 1852, and *Heppe*, 1861.) *He wrote:* Quæstionum et Responsionum Christ. Libellus, in his Tractt. Theol. vol. i. p. 654.

(7) *Peter Ramus* (*de la Ramée*) was born at Cuth, in Picardy, and died a martyr, St. Bartholomew's night, Aug. 25, 1572. *He wrote:* Commentariorum de Religione Christ., libb. iv. Francof. 1576. (De Fide, de Lege, de Precatione, de Sacramentis.)

(8) *Chamier* was born in Dauphiné; died Oct. 16, 1621, as professor at Montauban, during the siege of that city. *He wrote:* Panstratia Catholica, s. Corpus Controversiarum adversus Pontificios, Genev. 1696, 5 vols. fol. Corpus Theologicum, s. Loci Communes Theologici, ib. 1653, fol. (opus posthumum).

(9) *Keckermann*, born at Danzig, was professor in the University of Heidelberg, and died Aug. 25, 1609 (*Adami* Vitæ Philos. p. 232 ss. *Bayle*, Dict.: "*His works abound in plagiarisms, and have themselves been well plagiarized*"). He wrote: Systema Theol. tribus libris adornat., Hanoviæ 1607. (Opp. Genev. 1614, 4to.) *Gass*, s. 408.

(10) *Polanus* was born at Troppau, in Silesia, A.D. 1561, delivered lectures in the University of Basel, and died 1610 (comp. Athenæ Raur. p. 37). *He composed* a Syntagma Theol. Christ., Han. 1610. See *Gass*, s. 396.

(11) *Alsted* was born A.D. 1588, at Herborn, and died at Weissenburg, A.D. 1638, where he was professor of theology. *His works* are very numerous: Theologia Naturalis, Francof. 1615, 1622, 4to. — Theologia Catechetica, ib. 1622, 4to, Han. 1722, 4to.—Theologia Scholastica, ib. 1618, 4to.— Theol. Didactica, ib. 1627, 4to.—Theologia Polemica, ib.— Theologia Prophetica, ib. 1622, 4to.—Theol. Casuum., Hanov. 1630, 4to.—Comp. *Gass*, s. 411.

(12) *J. Sharp* (Scoto-Britannus) was professor at Die on the Drome, in Dauphiné. *He wrote:* Cursus Theologicus, in quo Controversiæ omnes de Fidei Dogmatibus inter nos et Pontificios pertractantur, et ad Bellarmini Argumenta respondetur. Ed. 2, Genev. 1620. See *Schweizer*, s. xxi.

(13) *Johann Wollebs* was born 1586, died 1629, professor of theology at Basel. *He wrote:* Compendium Christ. Theolog., Basel 1626; translated into English, under the title: Abridgment of Christ. Divinitie [by *Ross*, with the Anatomy of the whole Body of Divinitie, 1650]. He is distinguished for simplicity. *Ebrard* (Dogmatik) calls him "*one of the greatest theologians that ever lived.*" Comp. *Gass*, s. 397 [and *Schweizer*, ii. s. 26, who contests this judgment].

(14) *Johann H. Alting*, born at Emden, was professor at Heidelberg from 1613, died 1644, professor in Groningen. *Works:* Problemata tum theoretica, tum practica, Amst. 1662, 4to.—Theologia Elenchtica, Bas. 1679, Amst. 1664.— Method. Theol. Didact., Amst. 1650, Tiguri 1673. His son, *Jakob Alting*, was also distinguished in theology and polemics; Methodus Theol. in his Opera, Amst. 1687. See *Gass*, s. 434.

(15) His proper name was *Makowsky;* he was born at Lobzenik, in Poland, A.D. 1508, professor of theology in

Franecker, and died A.D. 1644. He adopted the Aristotelian method of investigation, and *composed:* Loci Communes Theol., Fran. 1639, ed. auct. *Nic. Arnold,* 1650, 4to. An improved and enlarged edition of this work appeared 1658. In addition, *he wrote:* Quæstiones Theolog., Fran. 1626. Distinctiones et Regulæ Theolog., Amst. 1656. See *Heinrich,* s. 355. *Gass,* s. 441.

(16) *Voëtius* was born A.D. 1589, at Heusden, in South Holland, held a professorship of theology in the University of Utrecht, and died 1676. (He opposed Descartes.) *Works:* Theol. Naturalis Reformata, Lond. 1656, 4to. Institutiones Theol., Traj. 1642, 4to.—Disputationes Selectæ, ibid. 1648, Amst. 1669, 5 vols. 4to.—See *Buddeus,* i. p. 417 (375). *Heinrich,* s. 355 f. *Gass,* s. 460.

(17) *Wendelin* was born A.D. 1584, at Sandhagen, near Heidelberg, and died 1652, at Zerbst, where he was Rector of the Gymnasium. *He wrote:* Christ. Theol. Libri ii. methodice dispositi, Han. 1634, 1641, Amst. 1646; Christ. Theol. Systema Majus., Cassell. 1656, 4to. See *Buddeus,* p. 416. *Heinrich,* s. 356. *Gass,* s. 416.

(18) *Hornbeck* was born A.D. 1617, at Haarlem, and died 1666, as a professor in the University of Leyden. *He composed:* Institutt. Theol., Ultraj. 1653, Lugd. Bat. 1658. See *Buddeus,* p. 417. *Heinrich,* s. 357.

(19) His proper name was *Des Marets;* he was born A.D. 1598, at Oisemont, in the province of Picardy, and died 1673, at Groningen. *Works:* Collegium Theologicum sive Systema Universale, Gron. 1658, 4to.—Theologiæ Elenchticæ nova Synopsis sive Index Controversiarum, etc., ibid. 1648, 2 vols. 4to, and several others. *Gass,* s. 442.

(20) *Rivetus* was born A.D. 1573, and died 1651. Most of his *works* were exegetical. The following is of a Polemico-dogmatic character: Catholicus Orthodoxus sive Summa Controversiarum inter Orthodoxos et Pontificios, Lugd. Bat. 1630, 2 vols. 4to. He also composed several controversial writings, and other treatises. Opp. Roterod. 1651, 1660, 3 vols. fol.

(21) *Heidegger* was born in 1633; died, professor of theology, in Zürich in 1698. He was the author of the Formula Consensus (see § 222). He also *wrote:* Medulla

Theologiæ Christian., Tur. 1696, 1702, 1713; Corpus Theol. Christ. s. Theol. didacticæ, moralis et historicæ Systema, 2 vols. fol., Tur. 1700, 1732. Medulla Medullæ, ibid. 1701. Also several dissertations. See *Alex. Schweizer*, Die theologisch-ethischen Zustände der 2. Hälfte des 17. Jahrh. in d. Zürchisch. Kirche, Zürich 1857, s. 12 ff.

(22) *Cocceius'* original name was *Koch*. He was born at Bremen, 1603, and died 1669. His doctrinal system was founded upon the idea of a covenant between God and man. He distinguished between (1) the covenant *before* the fall (the covenant of works), and (2) the covenant *after* the fall (the covenant of grace). The latter covenant embraces a threefold economy: 1. The economy prior to the law. 2. The economy under the law. 3. The economy under the gospel. His principles are developed in his Summa Doctrinæ de Fœdere et Testamentis Dei, 1648. See *Buddeus*, p. 417. *Heinrich*, s. 358 ff. *Heppe*, s. 201 ff.: "*The fruit of his influence on the Reformed systematic theology was to lead theologians back to the freedom of the word of God, delivering it from the bondage of a traditional scholasticism, and of a mode of handling the topics which subserved the interests of the culture of the schools.*" Compare on his method, *Diestel*, Studien zur Föderaltheologie (Jahrb. für deutsche Theol. 1865, 2, s. 1 ff.).

(23) *Burmann* was born at Leyden, 1628, professor of theology at Utrecht from 1662, died 1679. *He wrote:* Synopsis Theologiæ et Oeconomiæ Fœderum Dei, Amst. 1671, 1691, 2 vols.

(24) *Heidanus*, born at Frankenthal, in the Palatinate, 1648, professor of theology at Leyden; deposed on account of the controversies about the Cartesian Philosophy; died 1678. *Wrote:* Corpus Theol. Christ., 2 vols. 1687.

(25) *Witsius* was born in West Friesland, 1626, professor of theology at Franecker, Utrecht, and Leyden; died 1708. *Works:* Miscellanea Sacra, 2 vols. Amst. 1692. Oeconomia Fœderum, Traj. 1694. Meletemata Leidensia, Lugd. 1703. *Collected works:* Herborn 1712–1717, 6 vols; Basel 1739, 4to. [Economy of the Covenants, transl. by *Crookshank*, 2 vols. Edinb. 1803.]—On other disciples of Cocceius, *Wilhelm Moma* [died 1677; wrote De Varia Conditione et Statu Ecclesiæ Dei sub triplici Oeconomia Fœderum Dei, etc.,

Utrecht 1671], *Joh. Braun* [died 1709; Doctrina Fœderum, sive Syst. Theol., Amst. 1688], and *Nic. Gürtler*, see *Walch*, p. 222 ss. *Heinrich*, s. 362 ff.

(26) *Leydecker* was born A.D. 1642, at Middelburg, in the Dutch province of Zeeland, and died 1721, as professor of theology in the University of Utrecht. (His views were opposed to those of Cocceius.) *He wrote:* De Oeconomia trium Personarum in Negotio Salutis Humanæ, libri vi. Traj. 1682.

(27) So *Heinrich Hulsius, Le Blanc, Markius, Turretin.* Comp. *Walch*, p. 225 ss. *Heinrich*, s. 373 ff.

[NOTE.—The American editor has here introduced a whole section, § 223*a*, on the German Reformed Theology, more particularly as represented by the Heidelberg Catechism. We give a single quotation from one of the notes: "*Dr. Heppe* makes the peculiarities of this theology to consist in three points: (1) Making the central idea to be that of the covenant (fœdus Dei), particularly as seen in the kingdom of Christ; (2) The idea of an essential union with Christ (insitio in Christum); (3) Deduced from these two, the doctrine of the perseverance of the saints."

We have resolved not to reproduce this section for two reasons. Dr. Hagenbach, the author, had it before him in preparing his fifth edition, and he did not find it necessary to make any use of it, in order to give completeness to his work. When we remember that the addition has reference to Germany, this may be regarded as conclusive. Additions respecting English theology will be carefully considered, and whatever is of value will be retained or adapted. A second reason for the omission is found in the contents of the section. A mere list of names, and these for the most part utterly undistinguished, together with the dates belonging to them, would simply encumber our pages, already sufficiently full in this respect.

The explanation now given will, it is hoped, tend to assure those who may miss anything which has appeared in the American edition, that nothing of value has been omitted.]

§ 224.

Mysticism in the Reformed Church.

M. Göbel, Geschichte des christlichen Lebens in der Rheinisch-westphälischen evangel. Kirche, Coblenz 1852, 2d ed. 1862, 2 vols. *Hamberger*, Stimmen aus dem Heiligthum, Stuttg. 1857. *Noack*, Mystik. See § 217.

Mysticism was transplanted from the Roman Catholic Church into the Reformed Church, first by *John Labadie* and his followers (1), and afterwards by *Peter Poiret* (2), a disciple of *Antoinette Bourignon* (3). In England, *Joanna* (Jane) *Leade* (4) was followed by *John Pordage* (5), *Thomas Bromley*, and others. But this kind of mysticism, which was partly fantastic, partly indifferent to all systematic forms, has exerted little or no influence upon the development of dogma (6).

(1) *Labadie* was born A.D. 1610, at Bourg, in the province of Guienne, joined the Reformed Church without accepting its fundamental principles, and died 1674, at Altona. In many points he agreed with the Anabaptists.—Among his admirers were *Anna Maria von Schürmann*, *Peter Yvon*, *Peter du Lignon*, *Henry* and *Peter Schluter*. Comp. *Arnold*, Kirchen- und Ketzergeschichte, Thl. ii. Bd. 17, s. 680. *Hagenbach*, Vorlesungen über die Geschichte der Reformation, iv. s. 307. *Göbel*, ii. s. 181; and on Anna Schürmann, ibid. s. 273 ff. The judgments of Reformed orthodoxy on these phenomena were often very severe; comp. *J. C. Schweizer*, as quoted by *Al. Schweizer*, l.c. s. 19.

(2) *Poiret* was born A.D. 1646, at Metz, and died 1719, at Rheinsberg. His writings are of greater importance for the History of Doctrines than those of the other mystics (though only in a negative aspect). Concerning his life and his works, see *Arnold*, l.c. iii. s. 163; Biographie universelle, s. voce; and *Hagenbach*, Vorlesungen, iv. s. 325.

(3) *Antoinette Bourignon* was born A.D. 1616, at Lisle, in French Flanders, and died 1680, at Franecker. A memoir of her life was published, Amst. 1683. See Evangelische Kirchenzeitung, March 1837. *Hagenbach*, Vorlesungen, iv. s. 312 ff. *Amos Comenius*, *Swamerdam*, and others, adopted her opinions.

(4) *Jane Leade* was born A.D. 1633, and died 1714 [1704?]; she was an enthusiast. Comp. *Corrodi*, Geschichte des Chiliasmus, iii. s. 403 ff. *Arnold*, Kirchen- und Ketzergesch. s. 199–298 ff. *Hagenbach*, Vorlesungen, iv. s. 345.

(5) *Corrodi*, l.c. [Pordage died 1688.]

(6) The mysticism of the *Lutheran* Church was of greater speculative importance than that of the Reformed. The former also exerted a greater influence upon the life of the German nation (family worship, etc.) than the latter, which was more confined to private individuals and separatists.

§ 225.

Influence of the Cartesian Philosophy. More Liberal Tendencies.

Mysticism exerted less influence upon the gradual transformation of the doctrinal views of the Reformed Church than did the philosophical system of Descartes, especially in the Netherlands (1). *Balthasar Bekker*, who, in combating the "Enchanted World," also shook the orthodox doctrines of the Church, belonged to this school (2). But, apart from the influence of any definite system of philosophy, a more liberal tendency, which endeavoured to shake off the yoke of symbolical writings, manifested itself in different quarters. Such was the case in the University of Saumur (3), where this tendency was connected with Arminian views, and among the Latitudinarians of England (4). Among the Swiss theologians, *John Alph. Turretin* (5), *Ben. Pictet* (6), and *Samuel Werenfels* (7) were distinguished for moderate views, though they remained orthodox; thus they formed, by their principles, as well as the period in which they lived, the transition to the eighteenth century.

(1) *Renatus Cartesius* (René Descartes) was born A.D. 1596, and died 1650, at Stockholm. His maxim: "Cogito, ergo sum," is well known. His philosophy gave rise to commotions in Holland. *Gisbert Voëtius*, the principal opponent of

Descartes, charged him, A.D. 1639, with atheism. The philosophy of Descartes was condemned, A.D. 1647 (and again 1676), by the senate of the University of Leyden, as well as, 1657, by the Synod of Delft. Several of the mystics just mentioned belonged originally to the school of Descartes. But some orthodox divines also espoused the system. See *Tholuck*, Das akademische Leben des 17 Jahrb., 2te. Abth. 1854, and in *Herzog's* Realencykl. ii. s. 591. *Gass*, s. 454. [*Cousin*, Leçons; *Dugald Stewart's* Dissertations; *Morell's* Hist. of Philos.; *Ritter's* Gesch. d. Phil. Comp. also the works of *Maurice, Ueberweg*, and *Stöckl*, u.s.]

(2) *Bekker* was born A.D. 1634, in West Friesland, adopted the principles of Descartes, was dismissed from office on account of his opinions, and died 1698. (Compare the chapter on demonology in the Special History of Doctrines.) His principal work, "*Die bezauberte Welt*" (Franecker 1692, 4to; in German, Amst. 1693), contains the germs of the rationalism of later times.

(3) Representatives of the more liberal tendency were, among others, *Moses Amyraldus* (Amyraut), *Josua de la Place* (Placæus), *Louis Capellus*, etc. It was especially in opposition to their views that the Formula Consensus was drawn up. On *Amyraut*, see *Schweizer* in Zellers Jahrb. 1852, 1, 2; and *Edmond Saigey*, Strassb. 1849. *Herzog's* Realencykl. s.v. Amyraut. On the doctrine of *Pajon*, see *Schweizer* in Zellers Theol. Jahrb. 1853, Heft 1.

(4) Among them were *William Chillingworth* (1602-1644), *Ralph Cudworth* (he died 1688), *Tillotson, Stillingfleet*, and others.

(5) *Alphonse Turretin* was the son of the strictly orthodox Francis Turretin, born 1671, and died at Geneva A.D. 1737. *He wrote*: Opuscula, Brunsv. 1726, 2 vols.—Dilucidationes phil., theol., et dogmatico-morales, quibus præcipua Capita Theologiæ et naturalis et revelatæ demonstrantur, Lugd. Bat. 1748, 3 vols. 4to, and several other works. *Thomas* in *Herzog's* Realencykl. xvi. s. 516.

(6) *Pictet* was born A.D. 1655, and died A.D. 1724, at Geneva. He *composed* a Theologia christiana, Gen. 1696, 2 vols.—Medulla Theologiæ, ibid. 1711, 1712, and several other works. [Theol., transl., London 1847.]

(7) *Werenfels* was born 1657, and died 1740. (Athenæ rauricæ, p. 57, *R. Hanhart* in the Wissenschaftliche Zeitschrift, Basel 1824, part 1, s. 22 ; part 2, s. 53 ff.) *He wrote:* Opuscula Theologica, Basil. 1782, 3 vols.

§ 225a.[1]

[*The French School of Saumur.*]

[*A. Schweizer*, Centraldogmen, ii. 225-430, 564-663 ; and article *Amyraut* in *Herzog's* Encykl. *Ebrard*, Dogmatik, i. § 43.]

[Under the influence of *John Cameron* (1), who succeeded Gomarus at Saumur in 1618, a modification of the Calvinistic system was introduced into the French Reformed theology, represented by the names of *Amyraut* (2), *Placæus* (3), and *Pajon* (4). Cameron himself taught, after Piscator, the imputation of Christ's passive obedience alone ; and advocated the theory of the hypothetic universalism of divine grace, which was more fully developed by Amyraut (5). One of the most eminent members of this school was *Dallæus* (Jean Daillé) (6).]

(1) [*John Cameron* was born in Glasgow about 1580, prof. at Sédan, pastor at Bordeaux 1608-1618, prof. at Saumur 1618-1624, died at Montauban 1625. His Amica Collatio cum Tileno, 1621, is against Arminianism ; also his Defensio de Gratia et libero Arbitrio. See *Schweizer* in *Herzog's* Realencykl. *Gass*, s. 331.]

(2) [*Moses Amyraldus* (Amyraut) was born at Bourgueil, in Touraine, 1596, succeeded Daillé at Saumur 1626, became prof. there in 1631. His views were first published in a treatise on Predestination, 1634, and opposed by Du Moulin and Andr. Rivetus. He was acquitted by the French Synod of 1637, and at Charenton 1644 ; the charge renewed at Loudun 1659, but not carried through. He died 1664. See *Schweizer*, l.c. *Gass*, ii. s. 328.]

(3) [*Josua de la Place* (Placæus), born 1596, prof. at

[1] [Abridged from Dr. H. B. Smith.]

Saumur 1632, died 1655. His theory of original sin, as consisting only in native corruption, was condemned by the French Synod of 1645, although Placæus himself was not named. He accepted the statement of the Synod, by distinguishing between immediate and mediate imputation. Comp. *A. Schweizer* in *Herzog's* Realencykl., and in Centraldogmen, ii. s. 319. *Gass*, ii. s. 347.]

(4) [*Claude Pajon*, born 1626, studied in Saumur; prof. of theology there, after Amyraut's death, 1666; died 1685. He denied the immediate concursus in providence, and the immediate influence of the Holy Spirit in conversion. See *Schweizer*, ubi supra, ii. 564–663. *Gass*, ii. 359 sq.]

(5) [*Schweizer*, in *Herzog*, says the difference between Arminianism and Amyraldism is " an essential one. The Arminian has a *gratia universalis sub conditione fidei*, in *opposition* to the Reformed doctrine of a *gratia particularis absoluta*; the Amyraldian, on the contrary, assumes a *gratia universalis hypothetica* (i.e. *sub conditione fidei*), in order the better to defend the rigid particularism of election according to the Reformed view."]

(6) [*Jean Daillé* (Dallæus), born 1594, from 1626 to 1670 preached in Paris. De Usu Patrum, 1656, and often; Eng. version by Thos. Smith, 1651. Answered by Prof. *Blunt* of Cambridge. See *Schweizer*, ii. s. 387–439. *Gass*, ii. s. 345.]

§ 225*b*.[1]

[*Theology in England and Scotland*.]

[The Anglican theology, like its polity, was gradually shaped, and occupied an intermediate position between the Roman Catholic and the Reformed systems. Doctrinal controversies were subordinated to ecclesiastical questions. The earlier Reformers (1), *Cranmer, Latimer, Hooper, Ridley*, opposed chiefly the practical abuses of the papacy. The exiles under Mary returned (1559) from Frankfurt, Zürich, and Geneva,

[1] [With slight alteration from Dr. H. B. Smith.]

imbued with the principles of the Reformed (Calvinistic) system. But the polity and faith of England, as shaped under Elizabeth, contained conflicting elements, represented respectively by the Book of Common Prayer and the Thirty-nine Articles (which latter were thought to be of a Calvinistic tendency) (2). An intermediate position was occupied by *Jewel* (3), *Grindal*, *Pilkington*, and Abp. *Parker* (4). Puritan principles were advocated by *Hooper* (5) and *Thos. Cartwright* (6). As late as 1578, Calvin's Catechism was ordered to be used in the University of Cambridge. The Lambeth Articles of 1595 (7) taught the strictest scheme of predestination. Ireland was represented by the learning and orthodoxy of Archbishop *Ussher* (8). Scotland, with the Presbyterian system, also received from *John Knox* the principles of the school of Geneva, advocated by *Andrew Melville*, *Henderson*, and others (9). At the end of the sixteenth century and beginning of the seventeenth, the Anglican system was represented by *Richard Hooker* (10) and others; the Episcopal system was defended by *Donne*, *Field*, *Andrewes*, and *Jackson* (11). Abp. *Laud* (12) put forth High Church and sacramentarian views, in conjunction with a modified Arminianism, opposed in vain by the moderate Puritans (13), *Davenant*, Bp. *Reynolds*, Bp. *Hall*, and others. The conflict of the systems resulted in the temporary triumph of Presbyterianism and Calvinism in the *Westminster Assembly*, followed by the reaction under the Restoration (Charles II.). The Anglican system was subsequently developed and expounded in a prolific and learned theological literature, which had for its ideal the theology of the Church of the first four or five centuries (Bp. *Bull* (14), *Jeremy Taylor* (15), *Isaac Barrow* (16), Bp. *Cosin* (17), Abp. *Bramhall* (18), *Stillingfleet*, *Waterland*, *Sherlock*, Abps. *King* and *Wake*, and was ably defended in its main doctrinal position by the nonjurors, *Hickes*, *Leslie*, *Kettlewell*, *Johnson*, *Brett*, and others) (19). It reached the term of its development about the close of this period (1720). It was exhibited in its most systematic form in the works of

Beveridge (20), *Pearson* (21), and *Burnet* (22). Yet there were not wanting those in the Established Church who still advocated the main principles of the Reformed theology (Abp. *Leighton* (23), *Ez. Hopkins*, *Manton*, *Barlow*, and others). The more distinctive Puritan theology was advocated chiefly by the Nonconformists in doctrinal treatises and practical works by *Charnock*, *Thomas Watson*, *W. Bates*, by *Flavel* and *Bunyan* (24), by *Thos. Goodwin*, and many others; and in a stricter and more comprehensive method by *Richard Baxter* (25), *John Owen* (26), *John Howe* (27), *Theophilus Gale* (28), *Thomas Ridgeley*, *Matthew Henry* (29), and *Calamy*. The Antinomian tendency was represented by *Crisp*. The Scotch divines and the New England colonists from Great Britain remained faithful to the strict Calvinistic tradition.]

[There were also other phases of theological opinion of a less permanent influence. A Platonizing tendency was represented by *Cudworth* (30), *More* (31), and *Norris* (32), *John Smith* (33) of Cambridge, *Gale*, *Culverwell*, and others. Under Latitudinarianism was included a somewhat undefined class, as *John Milton* (34), *Chillingworth* (35), Archbishop *Tillotson* (36), *Samuel Clarke* (37), and others. (The most important doctrinal controversy was the Trinitarian, in which *Bull*, *Waterland*, *Samuel Clarke*, *Whiston*, *Sherlock*, *Watts*, *South*, *Stillingfleet*, and *Allix* bore a part. See § 234, 262.)]

(1) [The works of the early English Reformers are published most completely by the Parker Society, 1840–1855, in 55 vols. *Thomas Cranmer* was born 1489, Abp. Canterb. 1532, burnt at the stake, Oxford, Mar. 25, 1556. He had chief part in drawing up the Prayer Books (1549, 1552), the Catechism of 1548, and the XLII. Articles of 1553. In the Homilies he wrote that on Justification, 1547. *Cranmer's Bible*, 1539. *Works:* Miscel. Writings and Letters, ed. *J. E. Cox* for Parker Soc., 2 vols. 1844. Defence of Sacrament, 1550; and Answer to Stephen Gardiner on Eucharist, 1580, 4to. Works by *Jenkyns*, 4 vols. 8vo, 1834. Life, by *Strype*, *Le Bas*, *H. J. Todd*, and others. — *Hugh Latimer*, born 1490,

Bp. of Worcester 1535, burnt at Oxford 1555. Works by *G. E. Corrie* for Parker Soc., 2 vols. 1845 (with Life by *Watkins*, 2 vols. 1824). — *Nicholas Ridley*, born 1500, Bp. of Rochester 1548, of London 1550, burnt 1555. Works for Parker Soc. by *H. Christmas*, 1841.]

(2) [See above, § 222, note 6. In the Arian controversy, Dr. *Waterland*, in his "Case of Arian Subscription," took the ground against Clarke, that an Arian could not subscribe, to which *Sykes* replied that an Arian might, as well as an Arminian, since the Articles were Calvinistic. See Dr. *Richard Lawrence*, Reg. Prof. in Oxf., the Bampton Lect. 1844: An Attempt to illustrate those Articles of the Church of England, improperly considered Calvinistic; var. edd. Bp. Tomline (*Prettyman*), Refutation of Calvinism, 1811; and also *Ed. Williams* (born 1730, died 1813), Defence of Modern Calvinism against Bp. Tomline, 1812.]

(3) [*John Jewel*, born 1522, Bp. of Salisbury 1560, died 1571. "The Church of England may be best studied in the writings of Jewel."—*Warburton*. "It may be said of his surname, *nomen omen*."—*Fuller*. His Apologia Eccles. Anglic. 1522 (Eng. transl. by *Russell*, Oxf. 1840, and many others), and Defence of the same against *Hardinge*, 1567, have been often reprinted. Works, 1609, 1611, etc.; ed. by *Jelf*, 8 vols. 1847, 1848, and for Parker Soc. by *Ayre*, 4 vols. 1845–1850. Life by *Le Bas*, 1835.]

(4) [*Matthew Parker*, born 1504, Master of Corp. C. Camb. 1544, Abp. of Canterb. 1559, died 1575. Revised Bishops' Bible, 1568. See *Hook's* Lives of the Archbishops.]

(5) [*John Hooper*, born 1495, Bp. of Worcester and Gloucester 1550, martyr 1554. Works for Parker Soc. by *Carr* and *Nevinson*, 2 vols. 1843–1852. "The first Puritan."]

(6) [*Thos. Cartwright*, born 1535, prof. Cambr. 1570, 1571, died 1602. Contest with Whitgift on the Admonition to Parliament, 1588, involving the questions of episcopacy and the liturgy. — *John Whitgift*, born 1530, prof. Div. Camb. 1563, Abp. Cant. 1583, died 1604. Works by Parker Soc., ed. *John Ayre*, 3 vols. Camb. 1851–1854. Life, by *Strype*.]

(7) [The *Nine Lambeth Articles* were occasioned by *Peter Baro* (French), prof. in Cambridge, and *Barret*, of Caius College, teaching universal redemption; they inculcated pre-

destination and reprobation. They had no formal Church sanction in England, but were adopted by the Dublin Convocation in Ireland, 1615. "*The Reformation in England ended* (?) *by showing itself a decidedly Calvinistic movement*" (Christ. Remembr. 1845). The theological professors at Cambridge and Oxford were Calvinistic for fifty years from Elizabeth's accession. Bucer and Peter Martyr were called by Cranmer to the chairs of divinity in Cambridge and Oxford during the reign of Edward. Cranmer, too, in 1552, invited Calvin, Bullinger, and Melanchthon to England, to aid in drawing up a Confession of Faith for the Protestant Churches. Calvin's Consensus Genevensis (on Predestination) also had influence upon the framers of the Articles; see Zürich Letters (by Parker Soc.), vol. iii. p. 325, where a letter by Traheren, Dean of Chichester, to Bullinger is given, in which he says: "The greater number among us, of whom I own myself to be one, embrace the opinion of John Calvin, as being perspicuous and agreeable to Holy Scripture."]

(8) [*James Ussher*, born 1580, Bp. of Meath 1620, Abp. of Armagh 1624, died 1656. Whole works by *Elrington*, 16 vols. Dubl. 1847. He proposed a modified episcopacy.]

(9) [*John Knox*, born at Gifford, East Lothian, 1505, prisoner in France 1547–1549, chaplain to Edward VI. 1552, Geneva 1552–1555, died 1572. Conf. of Faith, 1560. Book of Discipline, 1560. Hist. of Ref. 1584, 1732. Works, by *Laing*, 4 vols. 1846 ff. Life, by *Thos. M‘Crie*, Edinb. 1840, etc.—*Andrew Melville*, born 1545, principal of St. Mary's College, St. Andrews, 1580, prof. at Sédan, where he died 1622. Life, by *M‘Crie*, 2 vols. 1824, etc.—*Robert Baillie*, born 1602, principal of Univ. of Glasgow, died 1662. Letters and Journals (2 vols. 1775), 3 vols., by *Laing*, 1841, 1842. See *Carlyle's* Essays. — *Samuel Rutherford*, born 1600 (?), prof. St. Andrews 1639, died 1662.]

(10) [*Richard Hooker*, born 1554, Master of Temple 1585, prebendary of Salisbury 1591, died 1600. His Ecclesiastical Polity, more than any single work, has given shape to the Anglican divinity: first four books, 1594, fol.; fifth, 1597; three last posthumous; seventh, 1617; sixth and eighth, 1648, 4to, interpolated (?). Works, fol. 1723. *Keble's* ed. 1836, 4 vols., repr. 3 vols. 1841. An edition by *B. Hanbury*,

1830, 3 vols. (with Life of *Cartwright*), from the Puritan side. Life, by *Isaak Walton*, 1665, and often. "There is no learning which this man hath not searched into; nothing too hard for his understanding."—*Stapleton*. "The adamantine and imperishable worth of Hooker in his Eccl. Pol."—*Dr. Parr*. The work was in reply to Mr. *Travers* of the Temple, who followed the views of *Cartwright*, whose lectures were prohibited by Abp. Whitgift; *Travers* published a Memorial, to which Hooker replied.—*Martin Marprelate Tracts*, 1580 ff.]

(11) [*John Donne*, born 1573, brought up as a Rom. Cath., ordained at the age of 42, died 1631, an eloquent preacher and poet; Dryden calls him "the greatest wit of our nation." Works, fol. 1640, 1644, 1660; new ed. 6 vols. 8vo, by *Alford*, Camb. 1839.—*Rd. Field*, Dean of Gloucester, born 1561, died 1616. Of the Church, five books, 1606, 3d ed. 1635; for Eccl. Hist. Soc., 4 vols. 1847–1852.—*Lancelot Andrewes*, born 1565, Bp. of Winchester 1618, died 1626. Ninety-six Sermons, 5 vols. Oxf. Lib. 1841–1843; Tortura Torti, ibid. 1851; Responsio ad Apolog. Card. Bellarmini, ibid. 1852.—*Thos. Jackson*, Dean of Peterborough, born 1579, died 1640; originally a Calvinist, became an Arminian. Works, 3 vols. fol. 1673; new ed. Oxf. 12 vols. 1844; twelve books on the Apost. Creed.—*Thos. Fuller*, born 1608, Prebend. Sarum, died 1661. Church Hist. Britain, *Nichols*' ed. 3 vols. 1837. Life, by *A. T. Russell*. Essay, by *H. Rogers*. Worthies of England, Holy War, Holy State, etc.]

(12) [*William Laud*, born 1573, Bp. of Bath and Wells 1628, London same year, Chanc. of Univ. of Oxf. 1630, Abp. of Canterb. 1633, beheaded 1645. Remains, by *Henry Wharton*, 2 vols. fol. 1695–1700. Works, in Lib. Angl. Cath. Theol., Oxf. 5 vols. 1847 sq. Life, by *C. Webb Le Bas*, 1836; also by *Heylin*, 1668. Comp. *Mozley's* Essays, vol. i. 1878.]

(13) *Joseph Hall*, born 1574, at Synod of Dort, Bp. of Exeter 1627, of Norwich 1641, died 1656. Meditations and Contemplations, principal work. Known as the "English Seneca." New ed. of works by *Pratt*, 1808, 10 vols.; by *Peter Hall*, 12 vols. 1837–1839.—*Ed. Reynolds*, born 1599, Bp. of Norwich 1660, died 1676. Works, fol. 1658, 1679; 6 vols. 1826, by *Birday*.]

(14) [*George Bull*, born 1634, Bp. of St. David's 1705,

died 1709. Harmonia Apostol. (Paul and James on Justification) 1670, transl. by *Wilkinson* 1801, Oxf. 1842. Defensio Fidei Nicenæ, 1685; new transl. Oxf. 2 vols. 1851, 1852. Judicium Eccles. Cathol. . . . de necessitate credendi quod. . . . Jesus Christus sit verus Deus, transl., York 1825 (for which *Bossuet* transmitted " the congratulations of the whole clergy of France "). Latin works, ed. *Grabe*, 1703. Works, ed. *Burton*, 8 vols. 1846. Latin works, transl. in Angl. Cath. Lib.]

(15) [*Jeremy Taylor*, born 1613, sequestered 1642, Bp. of Down and Connor 1660, died 1667. Works collected by *Heber*, 15 vols., 3d ed. 1839; by *Eden*, 10 vols.: Liberty of Prophesying, Holy Living and Holy Dying, Life of Christ, Deus justificatus—on Original Sin, Real Presence, Dissuasive from Popery, Rule of Conscience, etc. " Most eloquent of divines."—*Coleridge*. Biography, by *R. A. Wilmott*, 1847.]

(16) [*Isaac Barrow*, born 1630, Master of Trinity Coll. Cambr. 1672, died 1677. Theol. works by *Tillotson*, 3 vols. fol. 1683, vol. iv. 1687; in 8 vols., Camb. 1830.]

(17) [*John Cosin*, born 1594, Bp. of Durham 1663, died 1672. Works in Lib. Angl. Cath. Theol., Oxf. 5 vols. 1843–1853.]

(18) [*John Bramhall*, born 1593, Abp. of Armagh 1662, died 1663. Works, 5 vols., in Lib. Angl. Cath. Theol., Oxf. 1842–1845.]

(19) [*Edward Stillingfleet*, born 1635, Dean of St. Paul's 1678, Bp. of Worcester 1689, died 1699. Works, 6 vols. fol., Lond. 1710. Origines Sacræ (1701, 1837). Orig. Britan., repr. 1842.—*Daniel Waterland*, born 1683, Archd. of Middlesex 1730, died 1740. Works, 11 vols. in 12, Oxf. 1823–1828, 6 vols. 1843; Life, by Bp. *Van Mildert*. Vindication of Christ's Divinity in reply to Clarke—History of Athanasian Creed—Importance of Doctrine of Trinity—Regeneration—Eucharist, etc.—Abp. *King*, born 1650, Bp. of Derry 1691, Abp. of Dublin 1702, died 1729. De Origine Mali, 1702; Origin of Evil, ed. by *Edm. Law*, 4th ed. 1758. —*Peter Heylin*, born 1600, Prebend. of Westminst. 1631, died 1662. Theologia Veterum, on Apostles' Creed, fol. Lond. 1673. Hist. of Ref. of Ch. of Eng. 1674, 2 vols. 1849, by *Robertson*, for Eccl. Hist. Soc., etc.—*George Hickes*, born 1642, Dean of Worcester, afterwards Nonjuring Bp. of Thetford

1694, died 1715. On Christ. Priesthood, 4th ed. 2 vols. Lib. Angl. Cath. Theol., Oxf. 1847. Order of Lord's Supper. His most learned work is his Thesaurus Grammatico-Criticus et Archæologicus Linguarum veterum Septentrionalium. — *Ch. Leslie* (Nonjuror), died 1772. Theol. Works, 2 vols. fol. 1721, 7 vols. Oxf. 1832. — *John Johnson*, vicar of Cranbrook, born 1662, died 1725 (a Nonjuror). The Unbloody Sacrifice, 2 vols., in Oxf. Lib. 1847. Collect. of Eccl. Laws, 2 vols. 1720, Oxf. 1850, 1851; Discourses, etc. — *William Wake*, born 1657, Bp. of Lincoln 1705, Abp. of Canterb. 1716, died 1737. Expos. of Doct. of Church of England, and Defence, 1686. Authority of Christian Princes, and Appeal, 1697, 1698. Comm. on Catechism. On Convocation, 1703 (most important of the works on this topic). Transl. of the Epistles of the Fathers. Sermons and Disc.]

(20) [*William Beveridge*, born 1638, Bp. of St. Asaph 1704, died 1708. Works by *T. H. Horne*, 9 vols. 1824. Eng. Theol. Works, 10 vols. Oxf. 1844–1848 (vol. vii. contains the lost MS. Exposition of Art. 31–39, discovered by Routh). On Thirty-nine Articles, Church Catechism, Codex Canonum, 2 vols. Oxf. 1848. Synodicon: Pandectæ Canonum ab Eccles. Græc. recept., 2 vols. fol., Oxf. 1672–1682; Vindication of same, 1679.]

(21) [*John Pearson*, born 1612, Margaret Prof. Camb. 1661, Bp. of Chester 1673, died 1686. Exposition of the Creed, 3 ed. (last corrected by the author) fol. 1669; *Burton's* ed. 1847; *Chevallier's*, 1849. Minor Theol. Works, ed. *Churton*, 2 vols. Oxf. 1844. Vind. Epist. S. Ignat. in *Cotelerius*, and in 2 vols. ed. *Churton*, Lib. Angl. Cath. Theol., Oxf. 1852.]

(22) [*Gilbert Burnet*, born 1643, prof. in Glasgow 1669, Bp. of Salisbury 1689, died 1715. Expos. of XXXIX. Articles, 1699, fol. Hist. Ref. Ch. Engl., vol. i. 1679, vol. ii. 1681, vol. iii. 1715 (the only work for which the English Parliament voted public thanks, with a request for its continuation. *Bossuet* was employed upon a reply); 7 vols. Oxf. 1829; by *Pocock*, 4 vols. Oxf. (with annotations). Hist. of his own Times, posthumous, 1724–1734.]

(23) [*Robert Leighton*, born 1613, principal of Univ. Edinburgh, Abp. of Glasgow 1670–1674, died 1684. Exposition

of Creed. Theolog. Lectures (Prælect. Theol., Lond. 1808). "Comm. on 1st Peter. Works, by *Pearson*, 4 vols. 1830; by *Webb*, London, 7 vols. *Coleridge* spoke of the writings of Leighton "as the vibration of that tone (of Holy Scripture) yet lingering in the air."]

(24) [*John Bunyan*, born 1628, died 1688. He wrote as many works as he lived years (60). *Pilgrim's Progress* ("the best Summa Theol. Evangelicæ ever produced by a writer not miraculously inspired."—*Coleridge*. No book but the Bible, and the Imitation of Christ, has been translated into so many languages), original ed. repr. by *Offor*, 1849. Works, 2 vols. 1692, and often; 6 vols. by *Mason*, 1684; best ed. by *Offor*, 3 vols. 1853. (Doctrines of Law and Grace. Defence of Justif. by Faith. Life, by *Southey*, *Offor*, *Philip*, 1839, etc.)]

(25) [*Richard Baxter*, born 1615, minister at Kidderminster 1640, died 1691. He published 168 treatises. Practical Works, 4 vols. fol. 1707, 23 vols. 1830. Life, by *Orme*. Christian Ethics, Ecclesiastics, and Politics. Gildas Salvianus, the Reformed Pastor. Reformed Liturgy. Saints' Rest. Call to the Unconverted. Dying Thoughts.—His theological system has been termed Baxterian, intermediate between Calvinism and Arminianism.]

(26) [*John Owen*, the most eminent of the Independent divines, born 1616, died 1683. Works, by *Russell*, 21 vols. 1826, and Comm. on Heb., 7 vols.; new ed. by *Goold*, Edinb. 24 vols. Life, by *Orme*. Disc. concerning Holy Spirit. Display of Arminianism. Saints' Perseverance. Vindiciæ Evangelicæ (agst. Socinians). Justification by Faith.]

(27) [*John Howe*, born 1630, minister in London, died 1705. Works, 2 vols. fol. 1724, with Life, by Calamy; 3 vols. 1848, ed. by *Hewlett;* by Hunt, 8 vols. (including posthumous works) 1810–1820. New ed. in 6 vols., by R. T. S. Life, by *Rogers* (new ed.), 1864. Living Temple ("a masterpiece of profound argumentation."—*Williams*. Part 2 contains Animadversions on Spinoza). Blessedness of Righteous. Work of Holy Spirit. Possibility of a Trinity in God. God's Prescience ("the most profound, most philosophical, and most valuable of his writings."—*Robert Hall*). The Redeemer's Dominion over the Invisible World.]

(28) [*Theophilus Gale*, born 1628, died 1678. The Court

of the Gentiles, 1672 (the original of human literature from the Scriptures); Bk. 2 is on Divine Predetermination, a vindication of Calvinism.]

(29) [*Matthew Henry*, born 1662, minister at Chester and Hackney, died 1714. Exposition of Old and New Test. (from Romans to the end by other hands). Miscel. Works, with an Appendix on what Christ is made to Believers, by *P. Henry*, Lond. 1830.]

(30) [*Ralph Cudworth*, born 1617, educated at Cambridge, prof. Hebrew 1645, Preby. of Gloucester 1678, died 1688. The True Intellectual System of the Universe, fol. 1678; 2 vols. 4to, 1742; and Life by *Birch*, 1830; 3 vols. 1845, with transl. of Mosheim's notes; True Notion of Lord's Supper, 1670, and often. Systema Intellectuale, ed. Mosheim, 2 vols. fol., Jen. 1733; 2 vols. 4to, Lugd. Bat. 1773. "The Latin transl. is greatly to be preferred."—*Warburton*. *Paul Janet*, Essai sur le médiateur plastique de Cudworth, Paris 1860.]

(31) [*Henry More*, born 1614, died 1687. Theological Works, fol., Lond. 1708. (Mystery of Godliness. Mystery of Iniquity. Grounds of Certainty of Faith. Antidote against Idolatry.) Collection of Philosoph. Writings, 2 vols. fol., Lond. 1712. (On Atheism, Enthusiasm, Immortality, Epistol. ad R. Descartes, Conjectura Cabbalistica.) Discourses, Lond. 1692. Enchiridion Ethicum, Amst. 1695. Divine Dialogues, Glasg. 1743. Opera, 3 vols. fol., Lond. 1675–1679.]

(32) [*John Norris* of Bemerton, born 1657, died 1711; a Cambridge Platonist. Miscellanies, 2 ed. Lond. 1690. Theory and Regulation of Love, 1680. Disc. on Beatitudes, 4 vols. 1699 ff. Reason and Faith, 1697. Theory of Ideal World, 2 vols. 1701–1704 (his chief work on Basis of Malebranche).]

(33) [*John Smith* of Cambridge, born 1618, died 1652. Select Discourses, 4to, 1660, often republished.—The Disc. on Prophecy was transl. by Le Clerc for his Commentary on the Prophets. The other Discourses are on True Way of attaining Divine Knowledge, Superstition, Atheism, Immortality, Existence and Nature of God, Legal and Evang. Righteousness, Excellence and Nobleness of True Religion, etc.—*Benjamin Whichcote*, born 1610, prof. Div. King's College, died 1683. Discourses, 4 vols.—*Nathanael Culverwall* (Culverel), died 1650 or 1651. An elegant and learned

Discourse of the Light of Nature (written in 1646). The Light of Nature, ed. by *J. Brown*, with Essay by *Cairns*, Edinb. 1857. This remarkable work anticipated *Cumberland's* theory (1672) of independent morality; it is not noticed by Stewart, or Mackintosh, or Hallam.]

(34) [*John Milton*, born 1608, Latin Secretary to Cromwell 1649, pub. Par. Lost, 1667, died 1674. Prose Works, by *Toland*, 3 vols. fol., Amst. 1697–1698; whole works, 8 vols. 1851, Lond. De Doctrina Christ. curav. *C. R. Sumner*, 1825, also translated. Life, by *Keightley*, 1855; *D. Masson*, Camb. 6 vols. 1859 ff.]

(35) [*William Chillingworth*, born 1602, became a Rom. Cath. through the influence of John Fisher, *alias* John Perse, but was brought back by Laud 1631, died 1644. Religion of Protestants, 1638; 6th ed., with other works, 1704; 10th, fol., with memoir by *Birch*, 1742, frequently reprinted. Life, by *M. Des Maizeaux*, Lond. 1725. His Religion of Protestants was written in reply to Edward Knott's (real name Matthias Wilson, a Jesuit) Charity Mistaken. Tillotson calls C. "the glory of the age and nation." His great work also takes a position in contrast with Hooker's theory of the rightful authority of the national Church.]

(36) [*John Tillotson*, born 1630, Dean of St. Paul's 1689, Abp. of Canterb. 1691, died 1694. Works (254 Discourses), 3 vols. fol. 1752; 12 vols. 1757 (Life, by *Birch*, publ. 1753).]

(37) [*Samuel Clarke*, born 1675, rector of St. James', Westminster, 1709, died 1729. He aided in displacing the Cartesian by the Newtonian system (ed. *Rohault's* Physics). Boyle Lectures, Demonstr. of Being and Attrib. of God, and Obligations of Nat. Rel., 2 vols. 1705, 1706. Script. Doctrine of Trinity, 1712 (provoked a long controversy: Waterland, Whitby, Nelson, Jackson, etc.). Collect. of Papers bet. C. and Leibnitz, 1717; on Collins on Liberty, 1717 (in French by *Des Maizeaux*, 1720). Letter to Dodwell on Immortality, etc. Sermons. Works: Life, by *Hoadley*, 4 vols. fol. 1738.]

END OF VOLUME II.

T. and T. Clark's Publications.

In Three Volumes, 8vo, price 31s. 6d.,

(*Volume I. now ready.   Volume II. shortly.*)

THE LIFE OF CHRIST.

BY DR. BERNHARD WEISS,
PROFESSOR OF THEOLOGY, BERLIN.

'The authority of John's Gospel is vindicated with great fulness and success. Altogether the book seems destined to hold a very distinguished, if not absolutely unique, place in the criticism of the New Testament. Its fearless search after truth, its independence of spirit, its extent of research, its thoughtful and discriminating tone, must secure for it a very high reputation.'—*Congregationalist.*

'If the work in its completeness fulfil the promise of this instalment, it will be an exposition of the divine character and mission of our Lord more thorough and penetrating and conclusive than any that we yet possess.'—*British Quarterly Review.*

'Able and learned volumes. . . . A careful perusal of these books will amply repay the reader. They are replete with original matter, and are evidently the result of painstaking conscientiousness on the part of the author.'—*Rock.*

'A valuable treatise. . . . A thoroughly exhaustive work; a work in which learning of the most severe type, combined with a perfect knowledge of the languages drawn upon for the elucidation of his purpose, is apparent in every page.'—*Bell's Weekly Messenger.*

'From the thoroughness of the discussion and clearness of the writer, we anticipate a very valuable addition to the Great Biography.'—*Freeman.*

By the same Author.

In Two Volumes, 8vo, price 21s.,

BIBLICAL THEOLOGY OF THE NEW TESTAMENT.

'We can bear grateful testimony to the vigour, freshness, and richly suggestive power.'—*Baptist Magazine.*

'Further references to this work, so far from diminishing the high estimate we have previously expressed, have induced us to value it still more. The issue of the second and concluding volume gives aid to this enhanced appreciation.'—*Theological Quarterly.*

'Written throughout with freshness, vigour, and perfect command of the material. . . . This is a field which Weiss has made his own. His work far excels the numerous works of his predecessors in thoroughness and completeness.'—*Methodist Recorder.*

'The work which this volume completes is one of no ordinary strength and acumen. It is an exposition of the books of the New Testament arranged scientifically, that is, according to the authorship and development. It is the ripe fruit of many years of New Testament exegesis and theological study. . . . The book is in every way a notable one.'—*British Quarterly Review.*

'A work so thorough as this, and which so fully recognises the historical character of the science of Biblical Theology, was well worth translating.'—*Academy.*

'Able contributions to theological literature.'—*Scotsman.*

T. and T. Clark's Publications.

In Twenty Handsome 8vo Volumes, SUBSCRIPTION PRICE £5, 5s.,

MEYER'S
Commentary on the New Testament.

'Meyer has been long and well known to scholars as one of the very ablest of the German expositors of the New Testament. We are not sure whether we ought not to say that he is unrivalled as an interpreter of the grammatical and historical meaning of the sacred writers. The Publishers have now rendered another seasonable and important service to English students in producing this translation.'—*Guardian.*

Each Volume will be sold separately at 10s. 6d. to Non-Subscribers.

CRITICAL AND EXEGETICAL
COMMENTARY ON THE NEW TESTAMENT.

BY DR. H. A. W. MEYER,
OBERCONSISTORIALRATH, HANNOVER.

The portion contributed by Dr. MEYER has been placed under the editorial care of Rev. Dr. DICKSON, Professor of Divinity in the University of Glasgow; Rev. Dr. CROMBIE, Professor of Biblical Criticism, St. Mary's College, St. Andrews; and Rev. Dr. STEWART, Professor of Biblical Criticism, University of Glasgow.

- **1st Year**—Romans, Two Volumes.
  Galatians, One Volume.
  St. John's Gospel, Vol. I.
- **2d Year**—St. John's Gospel, Vol. II.
  Philippians and Colossians, One Volume.
  Acts of the Apostles, Vol. I.
  Corinthians, Vol. I.
- **3d Year**—Acts of the Apostles, Vol. II.
  St. Matthew's Gospel, Two Volumes.
  Corinthians, Vol. II.
- **4th Year**—Mark and Luke, Two Volumes.
  Ephesians and Philemon, One Volume.
  Thessalonians. (*Dr. Lünemann.*)
- **5th Year**—Timothy and Titus. (*Dr. Huther.*)
  Peter and Jude. (*Dr Huther.*)
  Hebrews. (*Dr. Lünemann.*)
  James and John. (*Dr. Huther.*)

The series, as written by Meyer himself, is completed by the publication of Ephesians with Philemon in one volume. But to this the Publishers have thought it right to add Thessalonians and Hebrews, by Dr. Lünemann, and the Pastoral and Catholic Epistles, by Dr. Huther. So few, however, of the Subscribers have expressed a desire to have Dr. Düsterdieck's Commentary on Revelation included, that it has been resolved in the meantime not to undertake it.

'I need hardly add that the last edition of the accurate, perspicuous, and learned commentary of Dr. Meyer has been most carefully consulted throughout; and I must again, as in the preface to the Galatians, avow my great obligations to the acumen and scholarship of the learned editor.'—BISHOP ELLICOTT *in Preface to his* 'Commentary on Ephesians.'

'The ablest grammatical exegete of the age.'—PHILIP SCHAFF, D.D.

'In accuracy of scholarship and freedom from prejudice, he is equalled by few.'—*Literary Churchman.*

'We have only to repeat that it remains, of its own kind, the very best Commentary of the New Testament which we possess.'—*Church Bells.*

'No exegetical work is on the whole more valuable, or stands in higher public esteem. As a critic he is candid and cautious; exact to minuteness in philology; a master of the grammatical and historical method of interpretation.'—*Princeton Review.*

T. and T. Clark's Publications.

In Three Volumes, Imperial 8vo, Price 24s. each,

VOLUME II. Just Published,

ENCYCLOPÆDIA

OR

DICTIONARY

OF

BIBLICAL, HISTORICAL, DOCTRINAL, AND PRACTICAL THEOLOGY.

BASED ON THE REAL-ENCYKLOPÄDIE OF HERZOG, PLITT, AND HAUCK.

EDITED BY

PHILIP SCHAFF, D.D., LL.D.,

PROFESSOR IN THE UNION THEOLOGICAL SEMINARY, NEW YORK.

'As a comprehensive work of reference, within a moderate compass, we know nothing at all equal to it in the large department which it deals with.'—*Church Bells.*

'The work will remain as a wonderful monument of industry, learning, and skill. It will be indispensable to the student of specifically Protestant theology; nor, indeed, do we think that any scholar, whatever be his especial line of thought or study, would find it superfluous on his shelves.'—*Literary Churchman.*

'We commend this work with a touch of enthusiasm, for we have often wanted such ourselves. It embraces in its range of writers all the leading authors of Europe on ecclesiastical questions. A student may deny himself many other volumes to secure this, for it is certain to take a prominent and permanent place in our literature.'—*Evangelical Magazine.*

'Dr. Schaff's name is a guarantee for valuable and thorough work. His new Encyclopædia (based on Herzog) will be one of the most useful works of the day. It will prove a standard authority on all religious knowledge. No man in the country is so well fitted to perfect such a work as this distinguished and exact scholar.'—HOWARD CROSBY, D.D., LL.D., *ex-Chancellor of the University, New York.*

'This work will prove of great service to many; it supplies a distinct want in our theological literature, and it is sure to meet with welcome from readers who wish a popular book of reference on points of historical, biographical, and theological interest. Many of the articles give facts which may be sought far and wide, and in vain in our encyclopædias.'—*Scotsman.*

'Those who possess the latest edition of Herzog will still find this work by no means superfluous. . . . Strange to say, the condensing process seems to have improved the original articles. . . . We hope that no minister's library will long remain without a copy of this work.'—*Daily Review.*

'For fulness, comprehensiveness, and accuracy, it will take the first place among Biblical Encyclopædias.'—WM. M. TAYLOR, D.D.

NEW SERIES

OF THE

FOREIGN THEOLOGICAL LIBRARY.

The Issue for 1883 *will comprise—*

WEISS ON THE LIFE OF CHRIST. Vols. I. and II.
WEISS ON BIBLICAL THEOLOGY OF NEW TESTAMENT. Vol. II. (completion).
GOEBEL ON THE PARABLES. One Vol.

1880.—**GODET'S COMMENTARY ON THE EPISTLE OF ST. PAUL TO THE ROMANS. Vol. I.**
    HAGENBACH'S HISTORY OF DOCTRINES. Vols. I. and II.
    DORNER'S SYSTEM OF CHRISTIAN DOCTRINE. Vol. I.

1881.—**GODET'S COMMENTARY ON THE EPISTLE OF ST. PAUL TO THE ROMANS. Vol. II.**
    DORNER'S SYSTEM OF CHRISTIAN DOCTRINE. Vol. II.
    MARTENSEN'S CHRISTIAN ETHICS. (Individual Ethics.)
    HAGENBACH'S HISTORY OF DOCTRINES. Vol. III. (completion).

1882.—**DORNER'S SYSTEM OF CHRISTIAN DOCTRINE. Vols. III. and IV. (completion).**
    WEISS'S BIBLICAL THEOLOGY OF THE NEW TESTAMENT. Vol. I.
    MARTENSEN'S CHRISTIAN ETHICS. (Social Ethics.)

The FOREIGN THEOLOGICAL LIBRARY was commenced in 1846, and from that time to this Four Volumes yearly (or 156 in all) have appeared with the utmost regularity.

The Publishers decided to begin a NEW SERIES with 1880, and so give an opportunity to many to subscribe who are possibly deterred by the extent of the former Series.

The Publishers are sanguine enough to believe that a Series containing the works of writers so eminent, upon the most important subjects, cannot fail to secure support.

The Binding of the Series is modernized, so as to distinguish it from the former Series.

The Subscription Price will remain as formerly, 21s. annually for Four Volumes, payable in advance.

A SELECTION OF TWENTY VOLUMES
FOR FIVE GUINEAS
(OR MORE AT SAME RATIO)

May be had from the Volumes issued previously to New Series, viz.:—
Works mentioned on pages 3, 4, 5.

[*See pages* 3, 4, 5.

FOREIGN THEOLOGICAL LIBRARY.

ANNUAL SUBSCRIPTION: One Guinea for Four Volumes, Demy 8vo.

N.B.—Any *two* Years in this Series can be had at Subscription Price. *A single Year's Books* (except in the case of the current Year) *cannot be supplied separately.* Non-subscribers, price 10s. 6d. each volume, with exceptions marked.

1864—Lange on the Acts of the Apostles. Two Volumes.
Keil and Delitzsch on the Pentateuch. Vols. I. and II.

1865—Keil and Delitzsch on the Pentateuch. Vol. III.
Hengstenberg on the Gospel of John. Two Volumes.
Keil and Delitzsch on Joshua, Judges, and Ruth. One Volume.

1866—Keil and Delitzsch on Samuel. One Volume.
Keil and Delitzsch on Job. Two Volumes.
Martensen's System of Christian Doctrine. One Volume.

1867—Delitzsch on Isaiah. Two Volumes.
Delitzsch on Biblical Psychology. (12s.) One Volume.
Auberlen on Divine Revelation. One Volume.

1868—Keil's Commentary on the Minor Prophets. Two Volumes.
Delitzsch's Commentary on Epistle to the Hebrews. Vol. I.
Harless' System of Christian Ethics. One Volume.

1869—Hengstenberg on Ezekiel. One Volume.
Stier on the Words of the Apostles. One Volume.
Keil's Introduction to the Old Testament. Vol. I.
Bleek's Introduction to the New Testament. Vol. I.

1870—Keil's Introduction to the Old Testament. Vol. II.
Bleek's Introduction to the New Testament. Vol. II.
Schmid's New Testament Theology. One Volume.
Delitzsch's Commentary on Epistle to the Hebrews. Vol. II.

1871—Delitzsch's Commentary on the Psalms. Three Volumes.
Hengstenberg's Kingdom of God under the Old Testament. Vol. I.

1872—Keil's Commentary on the Books of Kings. One Volume.
Keil's Commentary on the Book of Daniel. One Volume.
Keil's Commentary on the Books of Chronicles. One Volume.
Hengstenberg's History of the Kingdom of God. Vol. II.

1873—Keil's Commentary on Ezra, Nehemiah, and Esther. One Volume.
Winer's Collection of the Confessions of Christendom. One Volume.
Keil's Commentary on Jeremiah. Vol. I.
Martensen on Christian Ethics.

1874—Christlieb's Modern Doubt and Christian Belief. One Vol.
Keil's Commentary on Jeremiah. Vol. II.
Delitzsch's Commentary on Proverbs. Vol. I.
Oehler's Biblical Theology of the Old Testament. Vol. I.

1875—Godet's Commentary on St. Luke's Gospel. Two Volumes.
Oehler's Biblical Theology of the Old Testament. Vol. II.
Delitzsch's Commentary on Proverbs. Vol. II.

1876—Keil's Commentary on Ezekiel. Two Volumes.
Luthardt's Commentary on St. John's Gospel. Vol. I.
Godet's Commentary on St. John's Gospel. Vol. I.

1877—Delitzsch's Commentary on Song of Solomon and Ecclesiastes.
Godet's Commentary on St. John's Gospel. Vols. II. and III.
Luthardt's Commentary on St. John's Gospel. Vol. II.

1878—Gebhardt's Doctrine of the Apocalypse.
Luthardt's Commentary on St. John's Gospel. Vol. III.
Philippi's Commentary on the Romans. Vol. I.
Hagenbach's History of the Reformation. Vol. I.

1879—Philippi's Commentary on the Romans. Vol. II.
Hagenbach's History of the Reformation. Vol. II.
Steinmeyer's History of the Passion and Resurrection of our Lord.
Haupt's Commentary on the First Epistle of St. John. One Volume.

. *For New Series commencing with* 1880, *see page* 2.

MESSRS. CLARK allow a SELECTION of TWENTY VOLUMES (*or more at the same ratio*) from the Volumes issued previously to New Series (*see below*).

At the Subscription Price of Five Guineas.

NON-SUBSCRIPTION PRICES WITHIN BRACKETS.

Dr. Hengstenberg.—Commentary on the Psalms. By E. W. HENGSTENBERG, D.D., Professor of Theology in Berlin. In Three Vols, 8vo. (33s.)

Dr. Gieseler.—Compendium of Ecclesiastical History. By J. C. L. GIESELER, D.D., Professor of Theology in Göttingen. Five Vols. 8vo. (£2, 12s. 6d.)

Dr. Olshausen.—Biblical Commentary on the Gospels and Acts. Adapted especially for Preachers and Students. By HERMANN OLSHAUSEN, D.D., Professor of Theology in the University of Erlangen. In Four Vols. 8vo. (£2, 2s.)—Commentary on the Romans. In One Vol. 8vo. (10s. 6d.)—Commentary on St. Paul's First and Second Epistles to the Corinthians. In One Vol. 8vo. (9s.)—Commentary on St. Paul's Epistles to the Philippians, to Titus, and the First to Timothy. In continuation of the Work of Olshausen. By Lic. AUGUST WIESINGER. In One Vol. 8vo. (10s. 6d.)

Dr. Neander.—General History of the Christian Religion and Church. By AUGUSTUS NEANDER, D.D. Nine Vols. 8vo. (£3, 7s. 6d.)

Prof. H. A. Ch. Hävernick.—General Introduction to the Old Testament. By Professor HÄVERNICK. One Vol. 8vo. (10s. 6d.)

Dr. Müller.—The Christian Doctrine of Sin. By Dr. JULIUS MÜLLER. Two Vols. 8vo. (21s.) New Edition.

Dr. Hengstenberg.—Christology of the Old Testament, and a Commentary on the Messianic Predictions. By E. W. HENGSTENBERG, D.D. Four Vols. (£2, 2s.)

Dr. M. Baumgarten.—The Acts of the Apostles; or, The History of the Church in the Apostolic Age. By M. BAUMGARTEN, Ph.D. Three Vols. (£1, 7s.)

Dr. Stier.—The Words of the Lord Jesus. By RUDOLPH STIER, D.D., Chief Pastor and Superintendent of Schkeuditz. In Eight Vols. 8vo. (£4, 4s.)

Dr. Carl Ullmann.—Reformers before the Reformation, principally in Germany and the Netherlands. Two Vols. 8vo. (£1, 1s.)

Professor Kurtz.—History of the Old Covenant; or, Old Testament Dispensation. By Professor KURTZ of Dorpat. In Three Vols. (£1, 11s. 6d.)

Dr. Stier.—The Words of the Risen Saviour, and Commentary on the Epistle of St. James. By RUDOLPH STIER, D.D. One Vol. (10s. 6d.)

Professor Tholuck.—Commentary on the Gospel of St. John. One Vol. (9s.)

Professor Tholuck.—Commentary on the Sermon on the Mount. One Vol. (10s. 6d.)

Dr. Hengstenberg.—On the Book of Ecclesiastes. To which are appended: Treatises on the Song of Solomon; the Book of Job; the Prophet Isaiah; the Sacrifices of Holy Scripture; and on the Jews and the Christian Church. In One Vol. 8vo. (9s.)

Dr. Ebrard.—Commentary on the Epistles of St. John. By Dr. JOHN H. A. EBRARD, Professor of Theology. In One Vol. (10s. 6d.)

Dr. Lange.—Theological and Homiletical Commentary on the Gospels of St. Matthew and Mark. By J. P. LANGE, D.D. Three Vols. (10s. 6d. each.)

Dr. Dorner.—History of the Development of the Doctrine of the Person of Christ. By Dr. I. A. DORNER, Professor of Theology in the University of Berlin. Five Vols. (£2, 12s. 6d.)

Lange and Dr. J. J. Van Oosterzee.—Theological and Homiletical Commentary on the Gospel of St. Luke. Two Vols. (18s.)

Dr. Ebrard.—The Gospel History: A Compendium of Critical Investigations in support of the Historical Character of the Four Gospels. One Vol. (10s. 6d.)

Lange, Lechler, and Gerok.—Theological and Homiletical Commentary on the Acts of the Apostles. Edited by Dr. LANGE. Two Vols. (21s.)

Dr. Hengstenberg.—Commentary on the Gospel of St. John. Two Vols. (21s.)

Professor Keil.—Biblical Commentary on the Pentateuch. Three Vols. (31s. 6d.)

T. and T. Clark's Publications.

CLARK'S FOREIGN THEOLOGICAL LIBRARY—Continued.

Professor Keil.—Commentary on Joshua, Judges, and Ruth. One Vol. (10s. 6d.)
Professor Delitzsch.—A System of Biblical Psychology. One Vol. (12s.)
Dr. C. A. Auberlen.—The Divine Revelation. 8vo. (10s. 6d.)
Professor Delitzsch.—Commentary on the Prophecies of Isaiah. Two Vols. (21s.)
Professor Keil.—Commentary on the Books of Samuel. One Vol. (10s. 6d.)
Professor Delitzsch.—Commentary on the Book of Job. Two Vols. (21s.)
Bishop Martensen.—Christian Dogmatics. A Compendium of the Doctrines of Christianity. One Vol. (10s. 6d.)
Dr. J. P. Lange.—Commentary on the Gospel of St. John. Two Vols. (21s.)
Professor Keil.—Commentary on the Minor Prophets. Two Vols. (21s.)
Professor Delitzsch.—Commentary on Epistle to the Hebrews. Two Vols. (21s.)
Dr. Harless.—A System of Christian Ethics. One Vol. (10s. 6d.)
Dr. Hengstenberg.—Commentary on Ezekiel. One Vol. (10s. 6d.)
Dr. Stier.—The Words of the Apostles Expounded. One Vol. (10s. 6d.)
Professor Keil.—Introduction to the Old Testament. Two Vols. (21s.)
Professor Bleek.—Introduction to the New Testament. Two Vols. (21s.)
Professor Schmid.—New Testament Theology. One Vol. (10s. 6d.)
Professor Delitzsch.—Commentary on the Psalms. Three Vols. (31s. 6d.)
Dr. Hengstenberg.—The Kingdom of God under the Old Covenant. Two Vols. (21s.)
Professor Keil.—Commentary on the Books of Kings. One Volume. (10s. 6d.)
Professor Keil.—Commentary on the Book of Daniel. One Volume. (10s. 6d.)
Professor Keil.—Commentary on the Books of Chronicles. One Volume. (10s. 6d.)
Professor Keil.—Commentary on Ezra, Nehemiah, and Esther. One Vol. (10s. 6d.)
Professor Keil.—Commentary on Jeremiah. Two Vols. (21s.)
Winer (Dr. G. B.)—Collection of the Confessions of Christendom. One Vol. (10s. 6d.)
Bishop Martensen.—Christian Ethics. One Volume. (10s. 6d.)
Professor Delitzsch.—Commentary on the Proverbs of Solomon. Two Vols. (21s.)
Professor Oehler.—Biblical Theology of the Old Testament. Two Vols. (21s.)
Professor Christlieb.—Modern Doubt and Christian Belief. One Vol. (10s. 6d.)
Professor Godet.—Commentary on St. Luke's Gospel. Two Vols. (21s.)
Professor Luthardt.—Commentary on St. John's Gospel. Three Vols. (31s. 6d.)
Professor Godet.—Commentary on St. John's Gospel. Three Vols. (31s. 6d.)
Professor Keil.—Commentary on Ezekiel. Two Vols. (21s.)
Professor Delitzsch.—Commentary on Song of Solomon and Ecclesiastes. One Vol. (10s. 6d.)
Gebhardt (H.)—Doctrine of the Apocalypse. One Vol. (10s. 6d.)
Steinmeyer (Dr. F. L.)—History of the Passion and Resurrection of our Lord. One Vol. (10s. 6d.)
Haupt (E.)—Commentary on the First Epistle of St. John. One Vol. (10s. 6d.)
Hagenbach (Dr. K. R.)—History of the Reformation. Two Vols. (21s.)
Philippi (Dr. F. A.)—Commentary on Romans. Two Vols. (21s.)

And, in connection with the Series—

Murphy's Commentary on the Book of Psalms. To count as Two Volumes. (12s.)
Alexander's Commentary on Isaiah. Two Volumes. (17s.)
Ritter's (Carl) Comparative Geography of Palestine. Four Volumes. (32s.)
Shedd's History of Christian Doctrine. Two Volumes. (21s.)
Macdonald's Introduction to the Pentateuch. Two Volumes. (21s.)
Gerlach's Commentary on the Pentateuch. 8vo. (10s. 6d.)
Dr. Hengstenberg.—Dissertations on the Genuineness of Daniel, etc. One Vol. (12s.)

The series, in 163 Volumes (including 1883), price £42, 15s. 9d., forms an *Apparatus* without which it may be truly said *no Theological Library can be complete;* and the Publishers take the liberty of suggesting that no more appropriate gift could be presented to a Clergyman than the Series, in whole or in part.

*** No DUPLICATES can *be included in the Selection of Twenty Volumes; and it will save trouble and correspondence if it be distinctly understood that* NO LESS *number than Twenty can be supplied, unless at non-subscription price.*

Subscribers' Names received by all Retail Booksellers.

LONDON: (*For Works at Non-subscription price only*) HAMILTON, ADAMS, & Co.

In Twenty Handsome 8vo Volumes, SUBSCRIPTION PRICE £5, 5s.,

MEYER'S
Commentary on the New Testament.

'Meyer has been long and well known to scholars as one of the very ablest of the German expositors of the New Testament. We are not sure whether we ought not to say that he is unrivalled as an interpreter of the grammatical and historical meaning of the sacred writers. The Publishers have now rendered another seasonable and important service to English students in producing this translation.'—*Guardian.*

Each Volume will be sold separately at 10s. 6d. to Non-Subscribers.

CRITICAL AND EXEGETICAL
COMMENTARY ON THE NEW TESTAMENT.
By Dr. H. A. W. MEYER,
OBERCONSISTORIALRATH, HANNOVER.

The portion contributed by Dr. MEYER has been placed under the editorial care of Rev. Dr. DICKSON, Professor of Divinity in the University of Glasgow; Rev. Dr. CROMBIE, Professor of Biblical Criticism, St. Mary's College, St. Andrews; and Rev. Dr. STEWART, Professor of Biblical Criticism, University of Glasgow.

1st Year—Romans, Two Volumes.
Galatians, One Volume.
St. John's Gospel, Vol. I.

2d Year—St. John's Gospel, Vol. II.
Philippians and Colossians, One Volume.
Acts of the Apostles, Vol. I.
Corinthians, Vol. I.

3d Year—Acts of the Apostles, Vol. II.
St. Matthew's Gospel, Two Volumes.
Corinthians, Vol. II.

4th Year—Mark and Luke, Two Volumes.
Ephesians and Philemon, One Volume.
Thessalonians. (Dr. *Lünemann.*)

5th Year—Timothy and Titus. (Dr. *Huther.*)
Peter and Jude. (Dr. *Huther.*)
Hebrews. (Dr. *Lünemann.*)
James and John. (Dr. *Huther.*)

The series, as written by Meyer himself, is completed by the publication of Ephesians with Philemon in one volume. But to this the Publishers have thought it right to add Thessalonians and Hebrews, by Dr. Lünemann, and the Pastoral and Catholic Epistles, by Dr. Huther. So few, however, of the Subscribers have expressed a desire to have Dr. Düsterdieck's Commentary on Revelation included, that it has been resolved in the meantime not to undertake it.

'I need hardly add that the last edition of the accurate, perspicuous, and learned commentary of Dr. Meyer has been most carefully consulted throughout; and I must again, as in the preface to the Galatians, avow my great obligations to the acumen and scholarship of the learned editor.'—BISHOP ELLICOTT *in Preface to his* '*Commentary on Ephesians.*'

'The ablest grammatical exegete of the age.'—PHILIP SCHAFF, D.D.

'In accuracy of scholarship and freedom from prejudice, he is equalled by few.'—*Literary Churchman.*

'We have only to repeat that it remains, of its own kind, the very best Commentary of the New Testament which we possess.'—*Church Bells.*

'No exegetical work is on the whole more valuable, or stands in higher public esteem. As a critic he is candid and cautious; exact to minuteness in philology; a master of the grammatical and historical method of interpretation.'—*Princeton Review.*

LANGE'S COMMENTARIES.

(*Subscription price, nett*), 15s. each.

THEOLOGICAL AND HOMILETICAL COMMENTARY ON THE OLD AND NEW TESTAMENTS. Specially designed and adapted for the use of Ministers and Students. By Prof. JOHN PETER LANGE, D.D., in connection with a number of eminent European Divines. Translated, enlarged, and revised under the general editorship of Rev. Dr. PHILIP SCHAFF, assisted by leading Divines of the various Evangelical Denominations.

OLD TESTAMENT—14 VOLUMES.

I. GENESIS. With a General Introduction to the Old Testament. By Prof. J. P. LANGE, D.D. Translated from the German, with Additions, by Prof. TAYLER LEWIS, LL.D., and A. GOSMAN, D.D.

II. EXODUS. By J. P. LANGE, D.D. LEVITICUS. By J. P. LANGE, D.D. With GENERAL INTRODUCTION by Rev. Dr. OSGOOD.

III. NUMBERS AND DEUTERONOMY. NUMBERS. By Prof. J. P. LANGE, D.D. DEUTERONOMY. By W. J. SCHROEDER.

IV. JOSHUA. By Rev. F. R. FAY. JUDGES and RUTH. By Prof. PAULUS CASSELL, D.D.

V. SAMUEL, I. and II. By Professor ERDMANN, D.D.

VI. KINGS. By KARL CHR. W. F. BAHR, D.D.

VII. CHRONICLES, I. and II. By OTTO ZÖCKLER. EZRA. By FR. W. SCHULTZ. NEHEMIAH. By Rev. HOWARD CROSBY, D.D., LL.D. ESTHER. By FR. W. SCHULTZ.

VIII. JOB. With an Introduction and Annotations by Prof. TAYLER LEWIS, LL.D. A Commentary by Dr. OTTO ZÖCKLER, together with an Introductory Essay on Hebrew Poetry by Prof. PHILIP SCHAFF, D.D.

IX. THE PSALMS. By CARL BERNHARDT MOLL, D.D. With a new Metrical Version of the Psalms, and Philological Notes, by T. J. CONANT, D.D.

X. PROVERBS. By Prof. OTTO ZÖCKLER, D.D. ECCLESIASTES. By Prof. O. ZÖCKLER, D.D. With Additions, and a new Metrical Version, by Prof. TAYLER LEWIS, D.D. THE SONG OF SOLOMON. By Prof. O. ZÖCKLER, D.D.

XI. ISAIAH. By C. W. E. NAEGELSBACH.

XII. JEREMIAH. By C. W. E. NAEGELSBACH, D.D. LAMENTATIONS. By C. W. E. NAEGELSBACH, D.D.

XIII. EZEKIEL. By F. W. SCHRÖDER, D.D. DANIEL. By Professor ZÖCKLER D.D.

XIV. THE MINOR PROPHETS. HOSEA. JOEL, and AMOS. By OTTO SCHMOLLER, Ph.D. OBADIAH and MICAH. By Rev. PAUL KLEINERT. JONAH, NAHUM, HABAKKUK, and ZEPHANIAH. By Rev. PAUL KLEINERT. HAGGAI. By Rev. JAMES E. M'CURDY. ZECHARIAH. By T. W. CHAMBERS, D.D. MALACHI. By JOSEPH PACKARD, D.D.

THE APOCRYPHA. By E. C. BISSELL, D.D. One Volume.

NEW TESTAMENT—10 VOLUMES.

I. MATTHEW. With a General Introduction to the New Testament. By J. P. LANGE, D.D. Translated, with Additions, by PHILIP SCHAFF, D.D.

II. MARK. By J. P. LANGE, D.D. LUKE. By J. J. VAN OOSTERZEE.

III. JOHN. By J. P. LANGE, D.D.

IV. ACTS. By G. V. LECHLER, D.D., and Rev CHARLES GEROK.

V. ROMANS. By J. P. LANGE, D.D., and Rev. F. R. FAY.

VI. CORINTHIANS. By CHRISTIAN F. KLING.

VII. GALATIANS. By OTTO SCHMOLLER, Ph.D. EPHESIANS and COLOSSIANS. By KARL BRAUNE, D.D. PHILIPPIANS. By KARL BRAUNE, D.D.

VIII. THESSALONIANS. By Drs. AUBERLIN and RIGGENBACH. TIMOTHY. By J. J. VAN OOSTERZEE, D.D. TITUS. By J. J. VAN OOSTERZEE, D.D. PHILEMON. By J. VAN OOSTERZEE, D.D. HEBREWS. By KARL B. MOLL, D.D.

IX. JAMES. By J. P. LANGE, D.D., and J. J. VAN OOSTERZEE, D.D. PETER and JUDE. By G. F. C. FRONMÜLLER, Ph.D. JOHN. By KARL BRAUNE, D.D.

X. THE REVELATION OF JOHN. By Dr. J. P. LANGE. Together with double Alphabetical Index to all the Ten Volumes on the New Testament, by JOHN H. WOODS.

In Twenty-four Handsome 8vo Volumes, Subscription Price £6, 6s. 0d.,

Ante-Nicene Christian Library.

A COLLECTION OF ALL THE WORKS OF THE FATHERS OF THE CHRISTIAN CHURCH PRIOR TO THE COUNCIL OF NICÆA.

EDITED BY THE

REV. ALEXANDER ROBERTS, D.D., AND JAMES DONALDSON, LL.D.

MESSRS. CLARK are now happy to announce the completion of this Series. It has been received with marked approval by all sections of the Christian Church in this country and in the United States, as supplying what has long been felt to be a want, and also on account of the impartiality, learning, and care with which Editors and Translators have executed a very difficult task.

The Publishers do not bind themselves to *continue* to supply the Series at the Subscription price.

The Works are arranged as follow:—

FIRST YEAR.

APOSTOLIC FATHERS, comprising Clement's Epistles to the Corinthians; Polycarp to the Ephesians; Martyrdom of Polycarp; Epistle of Barnabas; Epistles of Ignatius (longer and shorter, and also the Syriac version); Martyrdom of Ignatius; Epistle to Diognetus; Pastor of Hermas; Papias; Spurious Epistles of Ignatius. In One Volume.

JUSTIN MARTYR; ATHENAGORAS. In One Volume.

TATIAN; THEOPHILUS; THE CLEmentine Recognitions. In One Volume.

CLEMENT OF ALEXANDRIA, Volume First, comprising Exhortation to Heathen; The Instructor; and a portion of the Miscellanies.

SECOND YEAR.

HIPPOLYTUS, Volume First; Refutation of all Heresies, and Fragments from his Commentaries.

IRENÆUS, Volume First.

TERTULLIAN AGAINST MARCION.

CYPRIAN, Volume First; the Epistles, and some of the Treatises.

THIRD YEAR.

IRENÆUS (completion); HIPPOLYTUS (completion); Fragments of Third Century. In One Volume.

ORIGEN: De Principiis; Letters; and portion of Treatise against Celsus.

CLEMENT OF ALEXANDRIA, Volume Second; Completion of Miscellanies.

TERTULLIAN, Volume First; To the Martyrs; Apology; To the Nations, etc.

FOURTH YEAR.

CYPRIAN, Volume Second (completion); Novatian; Minucius Felix; Fragments.

METHODIUS; ALEXANDER OF LYcopolis; Peter of Alexandria; Anatolius; Clement on Virginity; and Fragments.

TERTULLIAN, Volume Second.

APOCRYPHAL GOSPELS, ACTS, AND Revelations; comprising all the very curious Apocryphal Writings of the first three Centuries.

FIFTH YEAR.

TERTULLIAN, Volume Third (completion).

CLEMENTINE HOMILIES; APOSTOlical Constitutions. In One Volume.

ARNOBIUS.

DIONYSIUS; GREGORY THAUMAturgus; Syrian Fragments. In One Volume.

SIXTH YEAR.

LACTANTIUS; Two Volumes.

ORIGEN, Volume Second (completion). 12s. to Non-Subscribers.

EARLY LITURGIES & REMAINING Fragments. 9s. to Non-Subscribers.

Single Years cannot be had separately, unless to complete sets; but any Volume may be had separately, price 10s. 6d.,—with the exception of ORIGEN, Vol. II., 12s.; and the EARLY LITURGIES, 9s.

In Fifteen Volumes, demy 8vo, Subscription Price £3, 19s.
(*Yearly issues of Four Volumes, 21s.*)

The Works of St. Augustine.

EDITED BY MARCUS DODS, D.D.

SUBSCRIPTION:

Four Volumes for a Guinea, *payable in advance* (24s. when not paid in advance).

FIRST YEAR.

THE 'CITY OF GOD.' Two Volumes.

WRITINGS IN CONNECTION WITH the Donatist Controversy. In One Volume.

THE ANTI-PELAGIAN WORKS OF St. Augustine. Vol. I.

SECOND YEAR.

'LETTERS.' Vol. I.

TREATISES AGAINST FAUSTUS the Manichæan. One Volume.

THE HARMONY OF THE EVANgelists, and the Sermon on the Mount. One Volume.

ON THE TRINITY. One Volume.

THIRD YEAR.

COMMENTARY ON JOHN. Two Volumes.

ON CHRISTIAN DOCTRINE, ENCHIRIDION, ON CATECHIZING, and ON FAITH AND THE CREED. One Volume.

THE ANTI-PELAGIAN WORKS OF St. Augustine. Vol. II.

FOURTH YEAR.

'LETTERS.' Vol. II.

'CONFESSIONS.' With Copious Notes by Rev. J. G. PILKINGTON.

ANTI-PELAGIAN WRITINGS. Vol. III.

Messrs. CLARK believe this will prove not the least valuable of their various Series. Every care has been taken to secure not only accuracy, but elegance.

It is understood that Subscribers are bound to take at least the issues for two years. Each volume is sold separately at 10s. 6d.

'For the reproduction of the "City of God" in an admirable English garb we are greatly indebted to the well-directed enterprise and energy of Messrs. Clark, and to the accuracy and scholarship of those who have undertaken the laborious task of translation.'—*Christian Observer.*

'The present translation reads smoothly and pleasantly, and we have every reason to be satisfied both with the erudition and the fair and sound judgment displayed by the translators and the editor.'—*John Bull.*

SELECTION FROM
ANTE-NICENE LIBRARY
AND
ST. AUGUSTINE'S WORKS.

THE Ante-Nicene Library being now completed in 24 volumes, and the St. Augustine Series being also complete (*with the exception of the* 'LIFE') in 15 volumes, Messrs. CLARK will, as in the case of the Foreign Theological Library, give a Selection of 20 Volumes from both of those series at the *Subscription Price* of FIVE GUINEAS (or a larger number at same proportion).

CHEAP RE-ISSUE OF
STIER'S WORDS OF THE LORD JESUS.

To meet a very general desire that this now well-known Work should be brought more within the reach of all classes, both Clergy and Laity, Messrs. CLARK are now issuing, for a limited period, the *Eight* Volumes, handsomely bound in *Four*, at the *Subscription Price* of

TWO GUINEAS.

As the allowance to the Trade must necessarily be small, orders sent either direct or through Booksellers must *in every case* be accompanied with a Post Office Order for the above amount.

'The whole work is a treasury of thoughtful exposition. Its measure of practical and spiritual application, with exegetical criticism, commends it to the use of those whose duty it is to preach as well as to understand the Gospel of Christ.'—*Guardian*.

New and Cheap Edition, in Four Vols., demy 8vo, *Subscription Price* 28s.,

THE LIFE OF THE LORD JESUS CHRIST:

A Complete Critical Examination of the Origin, Contents, and Connection of the Gospels. Translated from the German of J. P. LANGE, D.D., Professor of Divinity in the University of Bonn. Edited, with additional Notes, by MARCUS DODS, D.D.

'We have arrived at a most favourable conclusion regarding the importance and ability of this work—the former depending upon the present condition of theological criticism, the latter on the wide range of the work itself; the singularly dispassionate judgment of the Author, as well as his pious, reverential, and erudite treatment of a subject inexpressibly holy. . . . We have great pleasure in recommending this work to our readers. We are convinced of its value and enormous range.'—*Irish Ecclesiastical Gazette.*

BENGEL'S GNOMON—CHEAP EDITION.
GNOMON OF THE NEW TESTAMENT.

By JOHN ALBERT BENGEL. Now first translated into English. With Original Notes, Explanatory and Illustrative. Edited by the Rev. ANDREW R. FAUSSET, M.A. The Original Translation was in Five Large Volumes, demy 8vo, averaging more than 550 pages each, and the very great demand for this Edition has induced the Publishers to issue the *Five* Volumes bound in *Three*, at the *Subscription Price* of

TWENTY-FOUR SHILLINGS.

They trust by this still further to increase its usefulness.

'It is a work which manifests the most intimate and profound knowledge of Scripture, and which, if we examine it with care, will often be found to condense more matter into a line than can be extracted from many pages of other writers.'—Archdeacon HARE.

'In respect both of its contents and its tone, Bengel's Gnomon stands alone. Even among laymen there has arisen a healthy and vigorous desire for scriptural knowledge, and Bengel has done more than any other man to aid such inquirers. There is perhaps no book every word of which has been so well weighed, or in which a single technical term contains so often far-reaching and suggestive views. . . . The theoretical and practical are as intimately connected as light and heat in the sun's ray.'—*Life of Perthes.*

HISTORY OF THE CHRISTIAN CHURCH.

By PHILIP SCHAFF, D.D., LL.D.

Just published, in Two Volumes, ex. demy 8vo, price 21s.,

SECTION FIRST—APOSTOLIC CHRISTIANITY, A.D. 1-100.

A New Edition, thoroughly Revised and Enlarged.

CONTENTS.—General Introduction.—I. Preparation for Christianity. II. Jesus Christ. III. The Apostolic Age. IV. St. Peter and the Conversion of the Jews. V. St. Paul and the Conversion of the Gentiles. VI. The Great Tribulation. VII. St. John and the Last Stadium of the Apostolic Period—The Consolidation of Jewish and Gentile Christianity. VIII. Christian Life in the Apostolic Church. IX. Worship in the Apostolic Age. X. Organization of the Apostolic Church. XI. Theology of the Apostolic Age. XII. The New Testament. Alphabetical Index.

'No student and, indeed, no critic can with fairness overlook a work like the present, written with such evident candour, and, at the same time, with so thorough a knowledge of the sources of early Christian history.'—*Scotsman.*

'I trust that this very instructive volume will find its way to the library table of every minister who cares to investigate thoroughly the foundations of Christianity. I cannot refrain from congratulating you on having carried through the press this noble contribution to historical literature. I think that there is no other work which equals it in many important excellences.'—Rev. Prof. FISHER, D.D.

'In no other work of its kind with which I am acquainted will students and general readers find so much to instruct and interest them.'—Rev. Prof. HITCHCOCK, D.D.

Just published, in demy 4to, Third Edition, price 25s.,

BIBLICO-THEOLOGICAL LEXICON OF NEW TESTAMENT GREEK.

By HERMANN CREMER, D.D.,
PROFESSOR OF THEOLOGY IN THE UNIVERSITY OF GREIFSWALD.

TRANSLATED FROM THE GERMAN OF THE SECOND EDITION

(WITH ADDITIONAL MATTER AND CORRECTIONS BY THE AUTHOR)

By WILLIAM URWICK, M.A.

'Dr. Cremer's work is highly and deservedly esteemed in Germany. It gives with care and thoroughness a complete history, as far as it goes, of each word and phrase that it deals with. ... Dr. Cremer's explanations are most lucidly set out.'—*Guardian.*

'It is hardly possible to exaggerate the value of this work to the student of the Greek Testament. ... The translation is accurate and idiomatic, and the additions to the later edition are considerable and important.'—*Church Bells.*

'We cannot find an important word in our Greek New Testament which is not discussed with a fulness and discrimination which leaves nothing to be desired.'—*Nonconformist.*

'This noble edition in quarto of Cremer's Biblico-Theological Lexicon quite supersedes the translation of the first edition of the work. Many of the most important articles have been re-written and re-arranged.'—*British Quarterly Review.*

'A majestic volume, admirably printed and faultlessly edited, and will win gratitude as well as renown for its learned and Christian Author, and prove a precious boon to students and preachers who covet exact and exhaustive acquaintance with the literal and theological teaching of the New Testament.'—*Dickinson's Theological Quarterly.*

Just published, **Second Edition**, *in One Volume, 8vo, price* 12s.,

FINAL CAUSES.

By PAUL JANET, Member of the Institute, Paris.

Translated from the latest French Edition by William Affleck, B.D.

CONTENTS.—PRELIMINARY CHAPTER—The Problem. BOOK I.—The Law of Finality. BOOK II.—The First Cause of Finality. APPENDIX.

'This very learned, accurate, and, within its prescribed limits, exhaustive work. . . . The book as a whole abounds in matter of the highest interest, and is a model of learning and judicious treatment.'—*Guardian.*

'Illustrated and defended with an ability and learning which must command the reader's admiration.'—*Dublin Review.*

'A great contribution to the literature of this subject. M. Janet has mastered the conditions of the problem, is at home in the literature of science and philosophy, and has that faculty of felicitous expression which makes French books of the highest class such delightful reading; . . . in clearness, vigour, and depth it has been seldom equalled, and more seldom excelled, in philosophical literature.'—*Spectator.*

'A wealth of scientific knowledge and a logical acumen which will win the admiration of every reader.'—*Church Quarterly Review.*

Just published, in demy 8vo, price 10s. 6d.,

THE BIBLE DOCTRINE OF MAN

(Seventh Series of Cunningham Lectures.)

By JOHN LAIDLAW, D.D.,
Professor of Systematic Theology, New College, Edinburgh.

'An important and valuable contribution to the discussion of the anthropology of the sacred writings, perhaps the most considerable that has appeared in our own language.'—*Literary Churchman.*

'The work is a thoughtful contribution to a subject which must always have deep interest for the devout student of the Bible.'—*British Quarterly Review.*

'Dr. Laidlaw's work is scholarly, able, interesting, and valuable. . . . Thoughtful and devout minds will find much to stimulate, and not a little to assist, their meditations in this learned and, let us add, charmingly printed volume.'—*Record.*

'On the whole, we take this to be the most sensible and reasonable statement of the Biblical psychology of man we have met.'—*Expositor.*

'The book will give ample material for thought to the reflective reader; and it holds a position, as far as we know, which is unique.'—*Church Bells.*

'The Notes to the Lectures, which occupy not less than 130 pages, are exceedingly valuable. The style of the lecturer is clear and animated; the critical and analytical judgment predominates.'—*English Independent.*

Just published, Second Edition, demy 8vo, 10s. 6d.,

THE HUMILIATION OF CHRIST,

IN ITS PHYSICAL, ETHICAL, AND OFFICIAL ASPECTS.

By A. B. BRUCE, D.D.,

PROFESSOR OF DIVINITY, FREE CHURCH COLLEGE, GLASGOW.

'Dr. Bruce's style is uniformly clear and vigorous, and this book of his, as a whole, has the rare advantage of being at once stimulating and satisfying to the mind in a high degree.'—*British and Foreign Evangelical Review.*

'This work stands forth at once as an original, thoughtful, thorough piece of work in the branch of scientific theology, such as we do not often meet in our language. . . . It is really a work of exceptional value; and no one can read it without perceptible gain in theological knowledge.'—*English Churchman.*

'We have not for a long time met with a work so fresh and suggestive as this of Professor Bruce. . . . We do not know where to look at our English Universities for a treatise so calm, logical, and scholarly.'—*English Independent.*

By the same Author.

Just published, Third Edition, demy 8vo, 10s. 6d.,

THE TRAINING OF THE TWELVE;

OR,

Exposition of Passages in the Gospels exhibiting the Twelve Disciples of Jesus under Discipline for the Apostleship.

'Here we have a really great book on an important, large, and attractive subject—a book full of loving, wholesome, profound thoughts about the fundamentals of Christian faith and practice.'—*British and Foreign Evangelical Review.*

'It is some five or six years since this work first made its appearance, and now that a second edition has been called for, the Author has taken the opportunity to make some alterations which are likely to render it still more acceptable. Substantially, however, the book remains the same, and the hearty commendation with which we noted its first issue applies to it at least as much now.'—*Rock.*

'The value, the beauty of this volume is that it is a unique contribution to, because a loving and cultured study of, the life of Christ, in the relation of the Master of the Twelve.'—*Edinburgh Daily Review.*

HANDBOOKS FOR BIBLE CLASSES.

'These volumes are models of the multum in parvo style. We have long desired to meet with a Series of this kind—Little Books on Great Subjects.'—*Literary World.*

THE EPISTLE OF ST. PAUL TO THE GALATIANS.
With Introduction and Notes
By the Rev. Professor JAMES MACGREGOR, D.D. [Price 1s. 6d.

THE POST-EXILIAN PROPHETS—
HAGGAI, ZECHARIAH, MALACHI.
With Introduction and Notes
By MARCUS DODS, D.D. [Price 2s.

THE LIFE OF CHRIST.
By Rev. JAMES STALKER, M.A. [Price 1s. 6d.

THE CHRISTIAN SACRAMENTS.
By Professor JAMES S. CANDLISH, D.D. [Price 1s. 6d.

THE BOOKS OF CHRONICLES.
By Rev. Professor MURPHY, Belfast. [Price 1s. 6d.

THE WESTMINSTER CONFESSION OF FAITH.
With Introduction and Notes
By Rev. JOHN MACPHERSON, M.A. [Price 2s.

THE BOOK OF JUDGES.
By Rev. Principal DOUGLAS, D.D. [Price 1s. 3d.

THE BOOK OF JOSHUA.
By Rev. Principal DOUGLAS, D.D. [Price 1s. 6d.

THE EPISTLE TO THE HEBREWS.
By Rev. Professor A. B. DAVIDSON. [Price 2s. 6d.

SCOTTISH CHURCH HISTORY.
By Rev. NORMAN L. WALKER, M.A. [Price 1s. 6d.

THE CHURCH.
By Rev. Professor WM. BINNIE, D.D. [Price 1s. 6d.

THE EPISTLE TO THE ROMANS.
By Rev. Principal BROWN, D.D. [Price 2s.

THE BOOK OF GENESIS.
By MARCUS DODS, D.D. [Price 2s.

THE REFORMATION.
By Rev. Professor LINDSAY, D.D. [Price 2s.

PRESBYTERIANISM.
By Rev. JOHN MACPHERSON, M.A. [Price 1s. 6d.

LESSONS ON THE LIFE OF CHRIST.
By Rev. WM. SCRYMGEOUR, M.A.

www.ingramcontent.com/pod-product-compliance
Lightning Source LLC
Chambersburg PA
CBHW051232300426
44114CB00011B/707